THE MEDAL YEARBOOK

2024

Edited by
Philip Mussell & Carol Hartman
and
the Editorial Team of MEDAL NEWS

ISBN: 978-1-908828-66-8
Deluxe edition ISBN: 978-1-908828-67-5

Published by
TOKEN PUBLISHING LIMITED
8 Oaktree Place, Manaton Close,
Matford Business Park,
Exeter EX2 8WA

Telephone: 01404 46972
email: info@tokenpublishing.com   Website: www.tokenpublishing.com

Front cover illustration: The new portrait of His Majesty the King by Jack McDermott

Printed in Great Britain by Short Run Press, Exeter

5

CONTENTS

Index to advertisers

FOREWORD

THIS year's MEDAL YEARBOOK, the 30th we have published here at Token Publishing Ltd, is a little different. First and foremost it is the first since the passing of Token's Group Managing Editor John Mussell, the man behind the decision to start publishing a YEARBOOK in the first place. His death, at 81, following a short illness, was well documented in MEDAL NEWS magazine and little needs be said here apart from a nod to the fact that without John this book simply would not exist.

Secondly, you may have noticed, depending on which version you're holding, that the emphasis has changed a little. The softback now concentrates exclusively on official British Medals, whilst the deluxe hardback holds everything—that includes the index, absent from the standard version but available separately online at www.tokenpublishing.com. The reasons for this change are twofold—first is, inevitably, cost. The price of paper, of postage, of everything has skyrocketed and it was a straightforward choice: we keep the book as it is and charge even more for it or we make changes. The second is that in the past few years many readers have expressed their desire for a basic price guide and handbook for British Medals without all the "add-ons" that they are neither interested in nor have in their collections. Now, of course to completely discard those medals, the unofficial ones that appear in groups these days (even if they shouldn't) the Life Saving awards, etc., would be unfair to those people who do want to know about them and so the decision has been made to include them but only in the deluxe edition—that way we make the book lighter and easier to use for some whilst still producing a full, comprehensive guide to medals for others! We hope you'll approve of us going "back to basics" but if you don't then please do let us know as only through feedback can we get it right. This is the decision for this year, but that doesn't mean it's set in stone. This time next year we may have changed our minds but for now we think this is the way forward.

Lastly, there have, of course, been a number of medallic changes this year because of the accession to the throne of His Majesty King Charles III; in addition to the inevitable new portrait(s) there have been a number of brand-new medals not to mention name changes for many others. Where new medals have been introduced they will have their own entry, however, where a name has changed (Queen's Police Medal to King's Police Medal for example) the entry will remain as was with an acknowledgment of any changes. At this stage we don't have any values for the new raft of medals as of course, some, like the Humanitarian Service Medal, have yet to be issued and others, like the Nuclear Test Medal or King's Volunteer Reserves Medal, will still be in the hands of the recipients who are unlikely to part with them just yet. We anticipate that the Coronation Medal of the new King is likely to be the first that appears on the open market but they haven't done so to date. We'll be keeping an eye on the auctions and dealers' lists and will introduce values when a reasonable number have appeared for sale—the first ones to be offered always attract a premium and a true representation of value will only come in time.

In addition to the new medals (Coronation Medal, Nuclear Test Medal and Humanitarian Service Medal) the big news this year has to be the new obverses, of which there are actually six (seven if you include the Martin Jennings designed conjoined busts on the Coronation Medal). Admittedly the left-facing bust in uniform (Admiral of the Fleet, Field Marshal, Marshal of the Royal Air Force) only appears on the Long Service & Good Conduct Medals of the respective service and the right-facing crowned bust with coronation robes only features on the oval medals, the Volunteer Reserves Service Medal and Efficiency Medal, but they are still official obverses and, alongside the right-facing crowned effigy that appears on 32 medals and the uncrowned portrait that appears on a further 12, they represent the largest obverse issue we have seen to date. Every one of the new portraits, apart from that on the aforementioned Coronation Medal, has been designed by Jack McDermott (his middle name is Stanley and JSM appears on the designs) and the level of detail that has gone into the uniformed busts in particular is quite astonishing, they are reminiscent of the best obverses of George V and before. Where

9

possible we have made a note of which bust is being used for which medal but as new medals are issued this will not be exhaustive. One thing we did discover, both on His Majesty's coins and his medals, is that he did not opt for the Latin version of his name as his grandfather, great grandfather and great-great grandfather had done. Charles stayed Charles and did not become Carolvs as some had suspected he might. There had also been comment that he didn't "change direction" on his medals like he did on the coins. On our new coinage he is facing left, the opposite way to his mother, and when the Coronation Medal was released, there was speculation that he was to face left on his medals too but, with the exception of the LS&GC medals, he is most decidedly facing right, the same as Queen Elizabeth II did. In fact there is no hard and fast rule with medals, and even in coinage it is only tradition not a rule as such. If you look at the effigies of Victoria, Edward (with one exception) and both King Georges they all face left, it was actually Her Majesty Queen Elizabeth II that broke with that tradition. King Charles is simply following his mother. The reason for the left-facing bust on the LS&GCs is, apparently, to be able to better show the details of the uniform and medals being worn, something it does well.

Of course, whilst we may not have values for the King's medals yet the medal market itself continues to grow and prices are, in the main, holding steady, with some increasing quite considerably. As ever we are indebted to everyone who has helped us check the pricing in particular Richard Black, Charles Brooks, Chris Dixon, Colin Hole, Michael Kaplan, John Millensted, Michael O'Brien, Charles Riley, Allan Stanistreet, John Wilson, and, of course, many members of the online British Medal Forum. We are also especially indebted to Phil McDermott and his team at Worcestershire Medal Services for their invaluable help with the new issue of medals following the King Charles' accession.

Happy reading!

We dedicate this edition of the MEDAL YEARBOOK to our Group Managing Editor, John Mussell, who sadly passed away on September 7, 2023.

PORTRAITS OF A KING

With the passing of Queen Elizabeth II and the accession of King Charles III on September 8, 2022 there was, as one might expect, much that needed changing. Everything that bore the late Queen's image or cypher will, in time, be updated as necessary—every time a post box is replaced, for example, it will now bear CIIIR rather than EIIR. The coinage and notes will all change (the coins are being released now, the notes sometime next year) and any organisation that uses the Royal Cypher or name of the current monarch will need to update too—this was especially evident with British Army regiments, with some cap badges changing radically. In the medal world a number of medals have changed name (our cover star this year has gone from Queen's to King's Volunteer Reserves Medal for example) and there have been a raft of new obverses. Seven in total to date. The conjoined busts on the Coronation Medal were designed by Martin Jennings (the sculptor who designed the new coinage effigy of His Majesty) but the other six obverses, which will be used on medals as laid out below, have all been designed by Jack Stanley McDermott and the initials JSM appear below the busts. We were particularly taken by the level of detail on the LS&GC Medals with His Majesty facing left on these in order for his full regalia and medals to be on display.

Conjoined busts of King Charles III
and Queen Camilla.

*King Charles III
Coronation Medal (MYB 318D)*

Crowned with
Coronation robes.

*Volunteer Reserves Service
Medal (MYB 242A)
Efficiency Medals (MYB 237)*

In Admiral of the Fleet uniform.

*Royal Naval Long Service
& Good Conduct Medal
(MYB 218)*

In Field Marshal uniform.

*Army Long Service &
Good Conduct Medal
(MYB 229)*

In Air Chief Marshal uniform.

*Royal Air Force Long Service
& Good Conduct Medal
(MYB 268)*

Uncrowned head to be used on:
Associate Royal Red Cross (MYB 31)
Coastguard Long Service Medal (MYB 227)
Jersey Honorary Police Long Service Medal (MYB 281)
King's Merchant Navy Medal for Meritorious Service (MYB 242K)
Meritorious Service Medal (MYB 208–210)
Overseas Territories Special Constabulary Long Service Medal (MYB 275)
Polar Medal (MYB 322)
Royal Household Long & Faithful Service Medal (MYB 217)
Royal Red Cross (MYB 31)
Royal Victorian Medal (MYB 13)
Sea Gallantry Medal (MYB 67)
Special Constabulary Long Service Medal (MYB 272)

Crowned head (Tudor crown) to be used on:
Accumulated Campaign Service Medal (MYB 198B and 198C)
Ambulance Long Service Medal (MYB 264A)
Badge of Honour (MYB 328)
Cadet Forces Medal (MYB 262)
Civil Defence Long Service Medal (MYB 264)
Fire and Rescue Service Long Service & Good Conduct Medal (MYB 286)
General Service Medal 2008 (MYB 198D)
George Medal (MYB 45)
Humanitarian Medal (MYB 397)
Imperial Service Medal (MYB 29)
King's Gallantry Medal (MYB 63)
King's Ambulance Medal (MYB 48B)
King's Fire Service Medal (MYB 48)
King's Medal for Champion Shots in the Military (MYB 334)
King's Medal for Champion Shots in the Royal Air Force (MYB 336)
King's Medal for Champion Shots in the Royal Navy
*   and Royal Marines (MYB 335)*
King's Police Medal (MYB 46)
King's Volunteer Reserve Medal (MYB 48A)
National Crime Agency Long Service Medal (MYB 291CC)
Northern Ireland Home Service Medal (MYB 261B)
Northern Ireland Prison Service Medal (MYB 288A)
Nuclear Test Medal (MYB 396)
Operational Service Medal (MYB 198A)
Overseas Territories Fire Brigade Long Service Medal (MYB 287)
Overseas Territories Police Medal (MYB 61)
Overseas Territories Police Long Service Medal (MYB 274)
Overseas Territories Prison Service Medal (MYB 289)
Police Long Service & Good Conduct Medal (MYB 271)
Police Service of Northern Ireland Service Medal (MYB 273A)
Prison Services Long Service & Good Conduct Medal (MYB 288B)
Realms—Governor General's Medal of Honour (MYB 329A)
Royal Fleet Auxiliary Service Medal (MYB 264C)

(Pictures courtesy of www.gov.uk)

Guide To
PRICES PAID
When buying at auction

Buying at auction can be confusing to those not used to it—it isn't like buying from a dealer's list nor, crucially, like buying from an Internet auction. With a dealer the price you see is the price you pay (unless you can do some haggling that is) and with eBay and the like you bid up to the price you want and the price the auction ends at is how much the item will cost. "Real" auctions are a little different and you have to remember that when the hammer falls the final price might not be what you think.

Auctioneers make their money through buyers' premiums (and sellers' premiums' but that's another matter), i.e. a "fee" on top of the hammer price that goes directly to them, not the vendor. On top of that premium is VAT—which currently stands at 20% in the UK. VAT is only really relevant to those in the EU—buyers from outside are exempt although they may be liable for their own import duties and other taxes so it's always worth checking.

These "extras", often referred to by seasoned auction goers as the "bits", can add a significant sum to your purchase. For example, if you bid on an item up to £100 and that's where the hammer falls, it isn't £100 you pay—you will have to find that £100 plus the premium (this varies from auction house to auction house) plus VAT on that premium (not on the £100, just the premium)—that can add up to £24 to the original hammer price—not something to be ignored! It can all get rather confusing and can come as a shock to those new to the game or only used to buying at on-line auctions (it's worth noting that even if you bid on-line at a "real" auction you are still liable for the "bits": there have been those who believe that on-line bidding exempts them from the fees as they treat it like eBay!). Some buyers ignore the "bits" and concentrate on the hammer price, worrying about the extras only when they've secured their purchase. But as premiums rise most of us have to factor them in at the start—so remember, if you have a strict budget you may well have to stop bidding quite a bit before that figure is reached in order to come in on target. Of course, when you just have to have something, what do budgets matter…?

Below is an indication of what you will have to pay on certain hammer prices depending on the Premium (we've given you 10%, 15% 20% and 22.5% options—the actual premium varies so check with the auctioneer before bidding). These figures assume VAT at 20%. Happy bidding!

10%			15%		
Hammer	Plus premium	Plus premium and VAT	Hammer	Plus premium	Plus premium and VAT
£75	£82.5	£84	£75	£86.25	£88
£175	£192.50	£196	£175	201.25	£206.50
£500	£550	£560	£500	£575	£590
£1500	£1650	£1680	£1500	£1725	£1770
£2500	£2750	£2800	£2500	£2875	£2950

20%			24%		
Hammer	Plus premium	Plus premium and VAT	Hammer	Plus premium	Plus premium and VAT
£75	£90	£93	£75	£93	£96.60
£175	£210	£217	£175	£217	£225.40
£500	£600	£620	£500	£620	£644
£1500	£1800	£1860	£1500	£1860	£1932
£2500	£3000	£3100	£2500	£3100	£3220

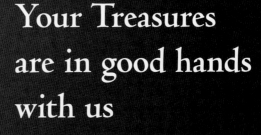

BANKNOTES
BOARD OF COMMISSIONERS OF CURRENCY
SINGAPORE REPLACEMENT $10000
SOLD IN MARCH 2023 **HAMMER PRICE: S$100,000**

COINS
EAST INDIA COMPANY BOMBAY PRESIDENCY ENGLISH
DESIGN, GOLD HALF-MOHUR, 1765
SOLD IN FEBRUARY 2023 **HAMMER PRICE: £95,000**

JEWELLERY
A LATE 19TH CENTURY BURMESE RUBY FIVE STONE RING
SOLD IN MARCH 2023 **HAMMER PRICE: £36,000**

MEDALS & MILITARIA
A PARTICULARLY FINE 'OPERATION HERRICK IX -
AFGHANISTAN' C.G.C. GROUP OF FOUR AWARDED
TO CORPORAL BRADLEY 'BUGSY' MALONE
SOLD IN JULY 2023 **HAMMER PRICE: £160,000**

ALL ENQUIRIES PLEASE CALL 020 7016 1700 **OR EMAIL** MEDALS@NOONANS.CO.UK

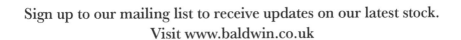

WEARING
Awards

The wearing of Orders, Decorations and Medals is a complex subject too complicated to cover in a publication such as this. However, there are a number of questions that collectors frequently ask, so we have attempted to deal with these as fully as possible.

Full-size Awards Mounted for Wear

Orders, decorations and medals are worn on the left breast in a line suspended from a single brooch mount or a rectangular frame (court mounted), the latter gives a firmer grip which occasions less damage than medals hanging more loosely from a brooch. The brooch/frame is covered by the medal ribbons. The most senior medal (see the following Order of Precedence) is furthest from the left shoulder. The obverse of the medals should show (this will usually be the sovereign's head, coat of arms, cypher, etc.).

If more than five medals are worn (three for the Navy), they should not be suspended side by side, but overlapped, the senior medal and ribbon is the one to be positioned so it can be seen completely. Medals should be lined up straight by the bottom rim/point, the length of ribbon should be one and a quarter inches (33mm) from the top of the mount to the first clasp or the suspension, which ever is appropriate (one and three quarters (45mm) for the Navy). Where the awards differ in size then a ribbon adjustment will be necessary to ensure a straight line.

Emblems for Mentions-in-Despatches or King's and Queen's Commendations for personnel and civilians should be worn on the relevant campaign medal, for example on the Victory Medal for the First World War and the War Medal 1939–45 for the Second World War. Where a recipient has no relevant campaign medal, the MID or commendation emblem is worn directly on the coat after any medal ribbons, or, if no ribbons then in the position of a single ribbon.,

There are a number of awards for which the sovereign has granted permission that they be worn on the right breast, including:

Royal Humane Society Medals
Stanhope Gold Medal
Royal National Lifeboat Institution Medals
Order of St John of Jerusalem Life Saving Medal.

Foreign Orders, Decorations and Medals

The British sovereign's subjects are not permitted to accept and wear the orders, decorations and medals of a foreign country of which the sovereign is not head of state. Application can be made for wear and permission is of two types: (a) restricted, that is instructions are given as to the exact occasions on which the award(s) may be worn; (b) unrestricted which allows the item(s) to be worn on all occasions according to the Order of Precedence, that is, generally speaking, arranged after British awards by date—first orders, then decorations, followed by medals (there are exceptions for the members of the armed services serving in an overseas force and receive that country's awards).

Awards are worn on a variety of State, evening or other occasions and the rules governing the wearing of orders according to dress are quite detailed. The subject is covered fully in *Medals Will Be Worn* by Lieutenant Colonel Ashley R. Tinson (Token Publishing Ltd., 1999) and in Spink's *Guide to the Wearing of Orders, Decorations and Medals* (Spink, 1990). The wearing of awards in civilian clothes is also fully detailed in *Wearing Your Medals in Civilian Clothes* by Lieutenant Colonel Ashley R. Tinson (Token Publishing Ltd., 2003).

ELM™
EST. 1968

Celebrating the art of Precision and Excellence.

With over half a century of medal-making history, exquisite craftsmanship and dedicated customer care are hallmarks of every ELM product.
To learn more, contact us at info@elm.com.sg or visit us at www.elm.com.sg

ELM is fully supported by:

- A proprietary 46,000 sq ft state-of-the-art production facility
- A proficient design and production team
- An experienced and dedicated team that provides highly personalised services
- Serving clients in Europe, Middle East, Oceania and Asia Pacific

Eng Leong Medallic Industries Pte Ltd
Medal House, 57 Yishun Industrial Park A, Singapore 768730
Tel: +65 6487 7777   **Fax:** +65 6756 0366

SCAN ME

THE ORDER
of Wear

The following list shows the order in which Orders, Decorations and Medals should be worn in the United Kingdom, certain countries of the Commonwealth and in Overseas Territories, as announced by the Central Chancery of the Orders of Knighthood (*London Gazette* Supplement No. 1, January 10, 2019). However, since the passing of Her Majesty Queen Elizabeth II there will inevitably be changes to the name of some medals, which will be recorded in the next edition of the Yearbook.

Victoria Cross
George Cross
Most Noble Order of the Garter
Most Ancient and Most Noble Order of the Thistle
Most Illustrious Order of St Patrick (obsolete since the death of the Duke of Gloucester, the last holder)
Knights Grand Cross, The Most Honourable Order of the Bath
Order of Merit
Baronet's Badge
Knight Grand Commander, The Most Exalted Order of the Star of India
Knights Grand Cross, The Most Distinguished Order of St Michael and St. George
Knight Grand Commander, The Most Eminent Order of the Indian Empire
The Order of the Crown of India
Knights Grand Cross, The Royal Victorian Order
Knights Grand Cross, The Most Excellent Order of the British Empire
Order of the Companions of Honour
Knight Commander, The Most Honourable Order of the Bath
Knight Commander, The Most Exalted Order of the Star of India
Knight Commander, The Most Distinguished Order of St Michael and St. George
Knight Commander, The Most Eminent Order of the Indian Empire
Knight Commander, The Royal Victorian Order
Knight Commander, The Most Excellent Order of the British Empire
Knight Bachelor's Badge
Companion, The Most Honourable Order of the Bath
Companion, The Most Exalted Order of the Star of India
Companion, The Most Distinguished Order of St Michael and St George
Companion, The Most Eminent Order of the Indian Empire
Commander, The Royal Victorian Order
Commander, The Most Excellent Order of the British Empire
Distinguished Service Order
Lieutenant, The Royal Victorian Order
Officer, The Most Excellent Order of the British Empire
Imperial Service Order
Member, The Royal Victorian Order
Member, The Most Excellent Order of the British Empire
Indian Order of Merit—Military

DECORATIONS, MEDALS FOR GALLANTRY AND DISTINGUISHED CONDUCT

Conspicuous Gallantry Cross
Distinguished Conduct Medal
Conspicuous Gallantry Medal
Conspicuous Gallantry Medal (Flying)
George Medal
Royal West African Field Force Distinguished Conduct Medal
Queen's Police Medal for Gallantry
Queen's Fire Service Medal for Gallantry
Royal Red Cross, Class 1
Distinguished Service Cross
Military Cross
Distinguished Flying Cross
Air Force Cross
Royal Red Cross, Class II
Order of British India
Kaisar-I-Hind Medal
Order of St John
Union of South Africa Queen's Medal for Bravery in gold
King's African Rifles Distinguished Conduct Medal
Indian Distinguished Service Medal
Union of South Africa Queen's Medal for Bravery in silver
Distinguished Service Medal
Military Medal
Distinguished Flying Medal
Air Force Medal
Constabulary Medal (Ireland)
Medal for Saving Life at Sea
Indian Order of Merit (Civil)
Indian Police Medal for Gallantry
Ceylon Police Medal for Gallantry
Sierra Leone Police Medal for Gallantry
Sierra Leone Fire Brigades Medal for Gallantry
Colonial Police Medal for Gallantry
Overseas Territories Police Medal for Gallantry
Queen's Gallantry Medal
Royal Victorian Medal (gold, silver and bronze)
British Empire Medal
Queen's Police Medal for Distinguished Service
Queen's Fire Service Medal for Distinguished Service
Queen's Ambulance Service Medal
Queen's Volunteer Reserves Medal
Queen's Medal for Chiefs

BADGE OF HONOUR

CAMPAIGN MEDALS AND STARS
Campaign Medals and Stars, including authorised UN, EU, EC and NATO medals in order of date of participation in the campaign for which awarded, as well as GSMs and OSMs.

POLAR MEDALS — in order of date of award

MEDALS FOR VALUABLE SERVICE
Imperial Service Medal
Indian Police Medal for Meritorious Service
Ceylon Police Medal for Merit
Sierra Leone Police Medal for Meritorious Service
Sierra Leone Fire Brigades Medal for Meritorious Service
Colonial Police Medal for Meritorious Service
Oversea Territories Police Medal for Meritorious Service

JUBILEE, CORONATION, DURBAR MEDALS
Queen Victoria's Jubilee Medal 1887 (gold, silver and bronze)
Queen Victoria's Police Jubilee Medal 1887
Queen Victoria's Jubilee Medal 1897 (gold, silver and bronze)
Queen Victoria's Police Jubilee Medal 1897
Queen Victoria's Commemoration Medal 1900 (Ireland)
King Edward VII's Coronation 1902
King Edward VII's Police Coronation 1902
King Edward VII's Durbar 1903 (gold, silver and bronze)
King Edward VII's Police Medal 1903 (Scotland)
King's Visit Commemoration Medal 1903 (Ireland)
King George V's Coronation Medal 1911
King George V's Police Coronation Medal 1911
King George V's Visit Police Commemoration Medal 1911 (Ireland)
King George V's Durbar Medal 1911 (gold, silver and bronze)
King George V's Silver Jubilee Medal 1935
King George VI's Coronation Medal 1937
Queen Elizabeth II's Coronation Medal 1953
Queen Elizabeth II's Silver Jubilee Medal 1977
Queen Elizabeth II's Golden Jubilee Medal 2002
Queen Elizabeth II's Diamond Jubilee Medal 2012
Queen Elizabeth II's Platinum Jubilee Medal 2022
Royal Household Long and Faithful Service Medal

EFFICIENCY AND LONG SERVICE DECORATIONS AND MEDALS
Meritorious Service Medal
Accumulated Campaign Service Medal
Accumulated Campaign Service Medal 2011
Army Long Service and Good Conduct Medal
Naval Long Service and Good Conduct Medal
Medal for Meritorious Service (Royal Navy 1918–28)
Indian Long Service and Good Conduct Medal (for Europeans of Indian Army)
Indian Meritorious Service Medal (for Europeans of Indian Army)
Royal Marines Meritorious Service Medal (1849–1947)
Royal Air Force Meritorious Service Medal 1918–28
Royal Air Force Long Service and Good Conduct Medal
Ulster Defence Regiment Long Service and Good Conduct Medal

Indian Long Service and Good Conduct Medal (Indian Army)
Royal West African Frontier Force Long Service and Good Conduct Medal
Royal Sierra Leone Military Forces Long Service and Good Conduct Medal
King's African Rifles Long Service and Good Conduct Medal
Indian Meritorious Service Medal (for Indian Army)
Police Long Service and Good Conduct Medal
Fire Brigade Long Service and Good Conduct Medal
African Police Medal for Meritorious Service
Royal Canadian Mounted Police Long Service Medal
Ceylon Police Long Service Medal
Ceylon Fire Services Long Service Medal
Sierra Leone Police Long Service Medal
Sierra Leone Fire Brigade Long Service Medal
Colonial Police Long Service Medal
Overseas Territories Police Long Service Medal
Mauritius Police Long Service and Good Conduct Medal
Mauritius Fire Service Long Service and Good Conduct Medal
Mauritius Prisons Service Long Service and Good Conduct Medal
Colonial Fire Brigades Long Service Medal
Overseas Territories Fire Brigades Long Service Medal
Colonial Prison Service Medal
Overseas Territories Prison Service Medal
Hong Kong Disciplined Services Medal
Army Emergency Reserve Decoration
Volunteer Officers' Decoration
Volunteer Long Service Medal
Volunteer Officers' Decoration (for India and the Colonies)
Volunteer Long Service Medal (for India and the Colonies)
Colonial Auxiliary Forces Officers' Decoration
Colonial Auxiliary Forces Long Service Medal
Medal for Good Shooting (Naval)
Militia Long Service Medal
Imperial Yeomanry Long Service Medal
Territorial Decoration
Ceylon Armed Service Long Service Medal
Efficiency Decoration
Territorial Efficiency Medal
Efficiency Medal
Special Reserve Long Service and Good Conduct Medal
Decoration for Officers of the Royal Naval Reserve
Decoration for Officers of the Royal Naval Volunteer Reserve
Royal Naval Reserve Long Service Medal
Royal Naval Volunteer Reserve Long Service Medal
Royal Naval Auxiliary Sick Berth Reserve Long Service Medal
Royal Fleet Reserve Long Service and Good Conduct Medal
Royal Naval Wireless Auxiliary Reserve Long Service Medal
Royal Naval Auxiliary Service Medal
Air Efficiency Award
Volunteer Reserves Service Medal
Ulster Defence Regiment Medal
Northern Ireland Home Service Medal
Queen's Medal (for Champion Shots of the Royal Navy and Royal Marines)
Queen's Medal (for Champion Shots of the New Zealand Naval Forces)

Queen's Medal (for Champion Shots in the Military Forces)
Queen's Medal (for Champion Shots of the Air Forces)
Cadet Forces Medal
Coastguard Auxiliary Service Long Service Medal
Special Constabulary Long Service Medal
Canadian Forces Decoration
Royal Observer Corps Medal
Civil Defence Long Service Medal
Ambulance Service IEmergency Dutioes) Long Service
    and Good Conduct Medal
Royal Fleet Auxiliary Service Medal
Prison Service (Operational Service) Long Service and
    Good Conduct Medal
Jersey Honorary Police Long Service and Good
    Conduct Medal
Merchant Navy Medal for Meritorious Service
Ebola Medal for Service in West Africa
National Crime Agency Long Service and Good
    Conduct Medal
Rhodesia Medal 1980
Royal Ulster Constabulary Service Medal
Northern Ireland Prison Service Medal
Union of South Africa Commemoration Medal
Indian Independence Medal
Pakistan Independence Medal

Ceylon Armed Services Inauguration Medal
Ceylon Police Independence Medal (1948)
Sierra Leone Independence Medal
Jamaica Independence Medal
Uganda Independence Medal
Malawi Independence Medal
Guyana Independence Medal.....
Fiji Independence Medal
Papua New Guinea Independence Medal
Solomon Islands Independence Medal
Service Medal of the Order of St. John
Badge of the Order of the League of Mercy
Voluntary Medical Service Medal
Women's Voluntary Service Medal
South African Medal for War Services
Colonial Special Constabulary Medal
Honorary Membership of Commonwealth Orders
    (instituted by the Sovereign, in order of date of award)
Other Commonwealth Members, Orders, Decorations
    and Medals (instituted since 1949 otherwise
    than by the Sovereign, and awards by States of
    Malaysia and Brunei in order of date of award)
Foreign Orders in order of date of award
Foreign Decorations in order of date of award
Foreign Medals in order of date of award

THE ORDER IN WHICH CAMPAIGN STARS AND MEDALS AWARDED FOR SERVICE DURING WORLD WAR I AND II AND KOREA WAR ARE WORN

1914 Star with dated "Mons" clasp "
    15th AUGUST–22nd NOVEMBER 1914"
1914 Star
1914/15 Star
British War Medal
Mercantile Marine War Medal
Victory Medal
Territorial Force War Medal
1939/45 Star
Atlantic Star
Arctic Star
Air Crew Europe Star
Africa Star

Pacific Star
Burma Star
Italy Star
France and Germany Star
Defence Medal
Canadian/Newfoundland Volunteer Service Medal
1939/45 War Medal
1939/45 Africa Service Medal of the Union of South Africa
India Service Medal
New Zealand War Service Medal
Southern Rhodesia Service Medal
Australian Service Medal
Korea Medal
United Nations Service Medal with bar KOREA

POST-NOMINAL LETTERS (as published in the London Gazette)
Recipients of some awards are entitled to use post-nominal letters including the following:

AE	Air Efficiency Award (officers)		CMG	Companion, The Most Distinguished Order of St Michael and St George
AFC	Air Force Cross			
AFM	Air Force Medal		CPM	Overseas Territories Police Medal
AM	Albert Medal		CSI	Companion, The Most Exalted Order of the Star of India
ARRC	Royal Red Cross, Second Class			
BEM	British Empire Medal		CVO	Commander, The Royal Victorian Order
BGM	Burma Gallantry Medal		DBE	Dame Commander, The Most Excellent Order of the British Empire
Bt or Bart	Baronet			
CBE	Commander, The Most Excellent Order of the British Empire		DCB	Dame Commander, The Most Honourable Order of the Bath
CB	Companion, The Most Honourable Order of the Bath		DCMG	Dame Commander, The Most Distinguished Order of St Michael and St George
CD	Canadian (Forces) Decoration			
CGC	Conspicuous Gallantry Cross		DCM	Distinguished Conduct Medal (King's African Rifles)
CGM	Conspicuous Gallantry Medal			
CH	Order of the Companion of Honour		DCM	Distinguished Conduct Medal (West Africa Frontier Force)
CIE	Companion, The Most Eminent Order of the Indian Empire		DCM	Distinguished Conduct Medal
CI	The Order of the Crown of India (women only)		DCVO	Dame Commander, The Royal Victorian Order
CM/MduC	Canada Medal		DFC	Distinguished Flying Cross

DFM	Distinguished Flying Medal	KG	Knight, Most Noble Order of the Garter
DSC	Distinguished Service Cross	KP	Knight, Most Illustrious Order of St
DSM	Distinguished Service Medal		Patrick
DSO	Distinguished Service Order	KPFSM	King's Police and Fire Service Medal
ED	Efficiency Decoration	KPM	King's Police Medal
EGM	Empire Gallantry Medal	KT	Knight, Most Ancient and Most Noble
EM	Edward Medal		Order of the Thistle
ERD	Army Emergency Reserve Decoration	LVO	Lieutenant, The Royal Victorian Order
GBE	Knight Grand Cross, The Most Excellent	MBE	Member, The Most Excellent Order of the
	Order of the British Empire		British Empire
GCB	Knight Grand Cross, The Most	MC	Military Cross
	Honourable Order of the Bath	MM	Military Medal
GCIE	Knight Grand Commander. The Most	MSM	Meritorious Service Medal (Navy, awards
	Eminent Order of the Indian Empire		up to 20.7.28)
GCMG	Knight Grand Cross—The Most	MVO	Member, The Royal Victorian Order
	Distinguished Order of St Michael and	OBE	Officer, The Most Excellent Order of the
	St George		British Empire
GCSI	Knight Grand Commander, The Most	OBI	Order of British India
	Exalted Order of the Star of India	OB	Order of Burma (distinguished service)
GCVO	Knight Grand Cross, The Royal	OB	Order of Burma (gallantry)
	Victorian Order	QASM	Queens Ambulance Service Medal
GC	George Cross	OM	Order of Merit
GM	George Medal	QAM	Queen's Ambulance Medal
IDSM	Indian Distinguished Service Medal	QFSM	Queen's Fire Service Medal
IOM	Indian Order of Merit (civil)	QGM	Queen's Gallantry Medal
IOM	Indian Order of Merit (military)	QPM	Queen's Police Medal
ISO	Imperial Service Order	QVRM	Queen's Volunteer Reserves Medal
KBE	Knight Commander, The Most Excellent	RD	Royal Naval Reserve Decoration
	Order of the British Empire	RRC	Royal Red Cross First Class
KCB	Knight Commander, The Most	RVM	Royal Victorian Medal
	Honourable Order of the Bath	SGM	Sea Gallantry Medals
KCIE	Knight Commander, The Most Eminent	TD	Territorial Decoration
	Order of the Indian Empire	UD	Ulster Defence Regiment Medal (officers)
KCMG	Knight Commander, The Most Distin-	VC	Victoria Cross
	guished Order of St Michael and St	VD	Volunteer Officers' Decoration
	George	VR	Volunteer Reserve
KCSI	Knight Commander, The Most Exalted	VRD	Royal Naval Volunteer Reserve
	Order of the Star of India		Decoration
KCVO	Knight Commander, The Royal Victorian		
	Order		

Only honours, decorations and medals which an individual has been authorised to wear by the Sovereign may be worn in uniform. As a general rule this also applies when wearing civilian clothes. Medals should not be worn on the right hand side, with the following exceptions: Royal Humane Society Medals, Stanhope Gold Medal, RNLI Medals, Order of St John of Jerusalem Life Saving Medal. Occasionally one may witness medals worn on the right hand side at church parades, Remembrance Day, etc. In this case the medals will be have been awarded to the wearer's next of kin, and the wearer will not be the recipient.

NB By Royal Warrant dated June 14, 2012, medals titled "Colonial . . ." are to be renamed "Overseas Territories . . .".

BRITANNIA
MEDAL FAIR
2024

Europe's Largest Independent Medal Bourse

•

SUNDAY 12 MAY & SUNDAY 17 NOVEMBER
9:30 AM–2 PM

CARISBROOKE HALL, THE VICTORY SERVICES CLUB
63/79 SEYMOUR STREET, LONDON W2 2HF

FREE ENTRY

•

We are pleased to announce that there continues
to be no charge for visitors or trade stands

Specialist Collectors, Dealers and Auctioneers
from across the UK and beyond will be in attendance.

The event is hosted by Noonans on a not-for-profit basis
as a service to the medal collecting community.

The popular Britannia curry will be available from the canteen!

NOONANS MAYFAIR
ALL ENQUIRIES PLEASE CALL 020 7016 1700 OR EMAIL EVENTS@NOONANS.CO.UK
WWW.NOONANS.CO.UK

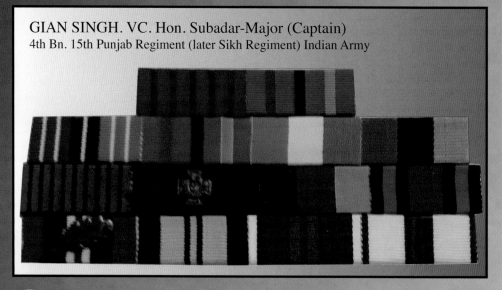

COLLECTING
Medal Ribbons

There is nothing new or old about collecting medal ribbons, in fact the founders of the present Orders and Medals Research Society originally set out as medal ribbon collectors. The ribbon has, ever since the early 18th century, been an important complement to the medal or badge of an order and its importance has grown over the years. Since those early orders of chivalry when it was deemed necessary to identify the various religious or secular orders one belonged to by the colour of its ribbon, the emphasis has been on the ribbon to identify the order or medal. This practice has continued down through the centuries, even to today when the avid enthusiast can recognise a warrior's medals simply by identifying his ribbons.

However, times are changing. The practice of wearing medals is on the decline, reserved only for ceremonial occasions, whilst the wearing of ribbon bars and the awarding of a single campaign or service medal with different ribbons to denote specific operations is on the increase. Our very own Operational Service Medal (OSM), the NATO medal and of course the plethora of United Nations medals are all classic examples of today's expansion of the medal ribbon. There is of course the growing cost of collecting medals and decorations compared to that of medal ribbons. There is also the down side to all of this—the opportunity to acquire medal ribbons has become a challenge to many, as sources such as tailors' shops, small ribbon manufacturers and numerous regimental or quartermasters stores have all gone into decline, if not altogether vanished.

Before one can collect ribbons properly one must first be able to identify them. It is therefore important to have a reasonable reference library—nothing elaborate or expansive is needed. It is probably wise to start collecting ribbons of the United Kingdom before branching out into those of other countries. There are several good books on the subject and most ribbons can be obtained quite easily.

The more one handles ribbons the quicker one starts to get a feel for the subject and gets to know which colours are used by certain countries or organisations; whether they always use silk or fine cottons; prefer moiré (watered) or corded ribbons; whether they use wide or narrow ribbons—all are

skills one picks up along the way. However, today this can sometimes prove difficult as the quality of many modern manufactured ribbons is really quite poor compared to the silk watered ribbons of bygone days.

Once over the initial teething problems of deciding how to store ribbons and ultimately mount or display them, the desire to expand and even specialise creeps in. Do you collect ribbons from just one country, state or organisation such as the Red Cross or the United Nations? Campaign medals and their numerous emblems? Famous chests? Regimental battle streamers? Religious or chivalric orders past and present? British or foreign orders and their various rosettes? The choice can be endless. Whatever the path you choose, you will almost certainly have to do a little research to obtain the reason for the award and the colours adopted for the ribbon. In reality, a true ribbon collector will know just as much about the medal or decoration as they will about the ribbon. Depending on the amount of time you have, research can lead you to museums, reading rooms or even portrait galleries, as well as societies such as the Ribbon Branch of the Orders and Medals Research Society (see their advertisement opposite). But whatever path is chosen you will be in awe of the sacrifices made by mankind down the centuries.

The Orders and Medals Research Society

MINIATURE MEDALS BRANCH

If you have an interest in miniature medals, you should join the only organisation dedicated to their collection and study – the Miniature Medals Branch of the OMRS.

This friendly group was founded in 1986 and now boasts an enthusiastic world-wide membership. The quarterly branch journal – *Miniature Medals World* – is illustrated in colour and remains the only publication specifically about this absorbing subject.

Whatever your interest – single medals or groups, from Victorian to current – there will be something to attract, delight and inform you.

There are five meetings a year in central London, with a mix of speakers, members' displays, auctions and members' own sessions.

Contact the Branch Secretary or visit the Branch table at the OMRS Convention to learn how you can tap into the broad experience and unrivalled expertise that has been accumulated.

Mark Furniss-Roe, Branch Secretary,
The Miniature Medals Branch, OMRS
miniaturemedalsbranch@gmail.com

MINIATURE
Medals & Decorations

There was a time when you had to ask a dealer if they had any miniature medals. A box was normally produced from under the counter and you were told to get stuck in, picking up pieces for pennies. Those days are long gone with this side of the hobby now being taken more seriously. When someone does start to collect miniature medals they are guaranteed one thing and that's variety.

Collecting miniatures can provide the same amount of excitement that full-size medals bring, only they take up less space and can be a fraction of the price. Most people start collecting full-size medals only to reach a point where the mind says buy it but the bank says no. Wanting to continue with the hobby, miniature medals are the next best thing, but what to collect? Orders, decorations, campaign medals, long service, military, civilian . . .? The list is endless. Most collectors keep to a theme while others will buy absolutely everything they see.

The next question is where can you find them? The answer is at auctions, medal fairs, medal dealerships, online catalogues or online auction sites. The first three would be preferable, with the all-important opportunity to handle the piece before parting with your hard earned cash. Occasionally miniature medals are sold with their full-size counterpart. A polite conversation can sometimes convince the vendor to let them go their separate ways, but make sure you get the details of the recipient from the full-size, as this will save a lot of time later.

There are other avenues to take in your quest and they can sometimes prove to be very productive if prepared to get up early and maybe drive a few miles. These are antique, flea and collectors' fairs, markets, bric-a-brac shops, emporiums and car boot sales.

Deciding what to do with your new find has always raised eyebrows. Should it be cleaned or left like it is? New ribbon or keep the old one on? Pin on, pin off? Only you the collector can make this decision. Taking a group to pieces for the sake of gaining one medal should certainly be discouraged as once this is done it is a little bit of history lost.

There are many ways of storing miniatures. Many collectors use albums, but be careful as some plastic envelopes can degrade a medal. Occasionally taking them out and giving them a wipe over is recommended. Mounting in frames is a nice way to show off your collection, but just make sure they are out of sight from windows and prying eyes. Display cases with the medals laid out in trays is another way to keep them, but ensure you don't use a cheap felt lining as this can also degrade the metal over a long period of time.

There are plenty of books on miniatures available and it is useful to start building up your own library. You can't have enough books on the subject. A good start has already been made in buying this Yearbook. The same publishers also produce the magazine MEDAL NEWS which has a regular feature, "Talking Miniatures", where particular topics are covered. The internet obviously has made researching medals so much easier in recent years with many of the auction houses having an archive section available to all on-line.

If you're happy to continue collecting on your own that is fine but sometimes help, advice and guidance is crucial if you don't want to end up with an album full of worthless items. Societies and clubs exist throughout the country (such as the Miniature Medals Branch of the Orders and Medals Research Society) and are certainly worth joining, as are social media groups. They will contain many learned individuals who will steer you in the right direction when it comes to identifying and researching miniature medals.

Note that the prices given in this publication are for contemporary medals unless otherwise stated.

ORDERS
of Knighthood

The most colourful and romantic of all awards are those connected with the orders of chivalry. Many of them have their origins in the Middle Ages, when knights in armour formed the elite fighting force in every European country. From the idea of a select band of knights, pledged to the support of a king or an ideal (usually religious), sprang the orders of chivalry.

Many of the orders of chivalry existed in the Middle Ages but most of them died out as feudalism went into decline. In some cases they survived; in others they disappeared for centuries, only to be resurrected at a later date. Still others were devised and instituted in relatively modern times, and indeed, continue to evolve. For example, Canada instituted the Order of Canada in 1967 and both Australia and New Zealand introduced their own orders in 1975.

In their original form membership of the orders of chivalry were just as highly coveted as they are today, but the insignia was usually simple or even non-existent. The complicated system of insignia which now surrounds these orders is fairly modern, dating from the 16th century or later. Nowadays most orders also exist in several classes, with the insignia becoming increasingly elaborate with each higher class.

Britain's senior order is the Garter, and although it consists of one class only it provides a good example of the pomp and ceremony which often surrounds these awards. It was founded by King Edward III and is said to derive its name from the fact that the King was attending a dance one day, when a lady's garter slipped from her leg and fell to the floor. To save her the embarrassment of retrieving her garter—and thus letting everyone know it was hers—the King himself picked it up and tied it round his own leg. Lest anyone should doubt that it was his garter he said, in court French, "Let evil be to him who evil thinks". From this curious incident came the idea of a very exclusive order of knighthood, consisting of the sovereign and 26 knights.

The insignia of this order consists of a Garter, a mantle of blue velvet lined with taffeta with the star of the Order embroidered on the left breast, a hood of crimson velvet, a surcoat of crimson velvet lined with white taffeta, a hat of black velvet lined with white taffeta, with a plume of white ostrich and black heron feathers fastened by a band of diamonds, a collar of gold composed of buckled garters and lovers' knots with red roses, the George (an enamelled figure of St George slaying the dragon) suspended from the collar, the Lesser George or badge, worn from a broad blue sash passing over the left shoulder to the right hip, and the star, a silver eight-pointed decoration bearing the red cross of St George surrounded by the garter and motto.

The insignia is exceptionally elaborate, the other orders of chivalry varying considerably in their complexity according to the class of the order. The full insignia is only worn on special occasions. In the case of the Garter usually the Lesser George and the breast star are worn on their own.

On the death of a Knight of the Garter the insignia should be returned to the Central Chancery of Orders of Knighthood, and therefore few examples of the Garter ever come on to the market. Those that do are usually examples from the 17th and 18th centuries when regulations regarding the return of insignia were not so strict. In the case of the lesser orders, insignia is returnable on promotion to a higher class. All collar chains are returnable, although that of the Order of St Michael and St George could be retained prior to 1948.

British orders are manufactured by firms holding contracts from the Central Chancery of Orders of Knighthood, and the values quoted in this Yearbook are for the official issues. It should be noted, however, that holders of orders frequently have replicas of breast stars made for use on different uniforms and it is sometimes difficult to tell these replicas from the originals as in many cases the replicas were made by the court jewellers responsible for making the originals. In addition, many jewellers in such European capitals as Vienna, Berlin and Paris have a long tradition of manufacturing the insignia of orders for sale to collectors.

The badges and breast stars of orders of chivalry are very seldom named to the recipient and therefore often lack the personal interest of campaign medals and many gallantry awards. For this reason they do not command the same interest or respect of collectors. Nevertheless, in cases where the insignia of orders can be definitely proved to have belonged to some famous person, the interest and value are enhanced. In any case, these orders are invariably very attractive examples of the jeweller's art, and they often possess titles and stories as colourful and romantic as their appearance.

1. THE MOST NOBLE ORDER OF THE GARTER

KG Star
(a Victorian example)

Instituted: 1348.

Ribbon: 102mm plain dark blue. Not worn in undress uniform.

Garter: Dark blue velvet. Two versions may be encountered, with embroidered lettering and other details, or with gold lettering, buckle and tab. Worn on the left leg by gentlemen and on the left forearm by ladies.

Collar Chain: Gold composed of alternate buckled garters, each encircling a red enamelled rose, and lovers' knots in gold although sometimes enamelled white.

Collar badge: An enamelled figure of St George fighting the dragon.

Star: Originally always embroidered in metal thread, a style which continues in the mantle to this day. Prior to 1858 knights often purchased metal stars in addition and since that date metal stars have been officially issued. These consist of a silver eight-pointed radiate star bearing in its centre and red cross of St George on a white ground, surrounded by the garter and motto HONI SOIT QUI MAL Y PENSE (Evil be to he who evil thinks).

Sash Badge: The Lesser George, similar to the collar badge but encircled by an oval garter bearing the motto.

Comments: *Membership of the Order of the Garter is confined to the reigning sovereign, the Prince of Wales and 25 other Knights, and is the personal gift of the monarch. In addition to the 25 Knights there have, from time to time, been extra Knights, occasionally non-Christians such as the Sultans of Turkey or the Emperor of Japan. The Emperor Hirohito, incidentally had the dubious distinction of being the only person awarded the Garter twice: in 1922 and again in 1971, having forfeited the original award as a result of the Japanese entry into the Second World War in 1941. Sir Winston Churchill was invested with the insignia originally presented in 1702 to his illustrious ancestor, the Duke of Marlborough. All official insignia should be returned to the Central Chancery of Knighthood on the death of the holder. Ladies (other than royalty) are now eligible for the Order.*

Lesser George
(this early example has the garter enamelled in blue)

VALUE:

Collar chain	Rare
Collar badge (the George)	From £50,000*
Star (in metal)	From £6500
Star (embroidered)	£1000–2000
Mantle star	£1000–2000
Sash badge (Lesser George)	From £20,000
Garter (embroidered)	£800–1000
Garter (gold lettering and buckle)	£4000–8000
Miniature	
Star (metal)	£500–650
Collar badge	£875–1000
Sash badge	£450–550

This price is for privately made examples, many of which are jewelled and enamelled.

2. THE MOST ANCIENT AND MOST NOBLE ORDER OF THE THISTLE

KT Star

Examples of Sash Badges

Instituted: 1687.

Ribbon: 102mm plain dark green. Not worn in undress uniform.

Collar Chain: Gold of alternate thistles and sprigs of rue enamelled in proper colours.

Collar Badge: The jewel is a gold and enamelled figure of St Andrew in a green gown and purple surcoat, bearing before him a white saltire cross, the whole surrounded by rays of gold.

Star: Silver, consisting of a St Andrew's cross, with other rays issuing between the points of the cross and, in the centre, on a gold background, a thistle enamelled in proper colours surrounded by a green circle bearing the Latin motto NEMO ME IMPUNE LACESSIT (No-one assails me with impunity).

Sash Badge: The medal of the Order is a gold figure of St Andrew bearing before him a saltire cross, surrounded by an oval collar bearing the motto, surmounted by a gold cord fitted with a ring for suspension. Examples are found in plain gold, or with enamelling and/or set with jewels.

Comments: *This order is said to have been founded in AD 787, alluding to barefoot enemy soldiers who cried out when they trod on thistles and thus alerted the Scots of an imminent attack. The order had long been defunct when it was revived by King James VII and II and re-established in December 1703 by Queen Anne. It now consists of the sovereign and 16 Knights, making it the most exclusive of the orders of chivalry. At death, the official insignia is returned to the Central Chancery. Ladies (other than royalty) are now eligible for the Order.*

VALUE:

Collar chain	Rare
Collar badge	Rare
Star (metal)	From £6000
Star (embroidered)	From £1000
Mantle star	From £850
Sash badge	From £10,000
Miniature	
Star (metal)	£500–550
Collar badge	£550–600
Sash badge	From £450

3. THE MOST ILLUSTRIOUS ORDER OF ST PATRICK

KP Star

Sash badge

Instituted: February 5, 1783.

Ribbon: 100mm sky-blue. Not worn in undress uniform.

Collar Chain: Gold, composed of five roses and six harps alternating, each tied together with a gold knot. The roses are enamelled alternately white petals within red and red within white.

Collar Badge: An imperial crown enamelled in proper colours from which is suspended by two rings a gold harp and from this a circular badge with a white enamelled centre embellished with the red saltire cross on which is surmounted a green three-petalled shamrock its leaves decorated with gold crowns, the whole surrounded by a gold collar bearing the Latin motto QUIS SEPARABIT (Who shall separate us?) with the date of foundation in roman numerals round the foot MDCCLXXXIII.

Star: A silver eight-pointed star, having in its centre, on a white field, the saltire cross of St Patrick in red enamel charged with a green trefoil bearing a gold crown on each leaf.

Sash Badge: The saltire cross in red enamel surmounted by a green shamrock with gold crowns as above, surrounded by an oval collar of pale blue with the Latin motto round the top and the date of foundation round the foot, the whole enclosed by a gold and white enamel surround charged with 32 shamrocks.

Comments: *Founded by King George III to reward the loyalty of Irish peers during the American War of Independence, it originally comprised the monarch and 15 Knights. In 1833 it was extended to include the Lord-Lieutenant of Ireland and 22 Knights, with certain extra and honorary knights. Appointments of non-royal Knights to the Order ceased with the partition of Ireland in 1922, although three of the sons of King George V were appointed after that date—the Prince of Wales (1927), the Duke of York (1936) and the Duke of Gloucester (1934). It became obsolete in 1974 with the death of the last holder. All items of official insignia were returned at death. Unlike the other two great orders, the sash for this Order is worn in the manner of the lesser orders, over the right shoulder.*

VALUE:

Collar chain	Rare
Collar badge	From £15,000
Star (metal)	From £5500
Star (embroidered)	£850–1000
Mantle star	£850–1200
Sash badge	From £5000
Miniature	
Star (metal)	£400–500
Collar/Sash badge	£650–750

4. THE MOST HONOURABLE ORDER OF THE BATH

GCB Star (Military)

Instituted: 1725.
Ribbon: GCB 102mm (58mm for ladies); KCB/DCB 44mm; CB 38mm, deep red.
Collar Chain: Gold composed of nine crowns and eight devices, each consisting of a rose, a thistle and a shamrock issuing from a sceptre all enamelled in their proper colours. The crowns and devices are joined by gold, white-enamelled knots.
Collar Badge: A skeletal gold badge with an oval collar inscribed TRIA JUNCTA IN UNO (Three joined in one) in white enamelled letters, enclosing a thistle, rose and shamrock issuing from a sceptre, with a crown above the sceptre and two crowns below, at the sides.
Star: A silver flaming star surmounted by a circular gold band enamelled red bearing the motto round the top and having a laurel spray round the foot, enclosing three gold crowns enamelled in red.
Sash Badge: As the Collar Badge but smaller and without white enamelling.
Comments: *Established by King George I, this was a single-class Order comprising the monarch, a prince of the blood royal, a Great Master and 35 Knights of Companions. It was re-organised at the conclusion of the Napoleonic Wars (see below). Ladies (other than royalty) are now eligible for the Order. Promotion to a different division permits the wearing of both types of insignia.*

VALUE:

Collar chain	Rare
Collar badge	£3000–4000
Star (metal)	From £5500
Star (embroidered)	£500–1000
Sash badge	£2000–3000

KNIGHTS/DAMES GRAND CROSS (GCB)

The Order was re-organised in 1815 in two divisions, Military and Civil. The Military Division had three classes: Knight Grand Cross (GCB), Knight Commander (KCB) and Companion (CB), while the Civil Division continued with the single class of Knight Grand Cross. In 1847 the Civil Division came into line with the Military, and divided into three classes.
Metal: Gold (1815–87), silver-gilt (1887–1901), silver gilt with gold centre (1902 on).
Collar Badge: The Military Badge is a gold Maltese cross of eight points, each point tipped with a small gold ball, and in each angle between the arms of the cross is a gold lion. In the centre of the cross is a device comprising a rose, thistle and shamrock issuing from a sceptre, and three imperial crowns . This device is surrounded by a red enamelled circle on which appears the Latin motto TRIA JUNCTA IN UNO (three joined in one) in gold lettering. The circle is surrounded by two branches of laurel, enamelled green, and below is a blue enamelled scroll with the German motto ICH DIEN (I serve) in gold.
   The Civil Badge is of gold filigree work, and oval in shape. It consists of a bandlet bearing the motto, and in the centre is the usual device of the rose, thistle and shamrock issuing from a sceptre, together with the three crowns.
Star: A gold Maltese cross of the same pattern as the Military Badge, mounted on a silver flaming star (Military); or a silver eight-pointed star with a central device of three crowns on a silver ground, encircled by the motto on a red enamelled ribbon (Civil).
Sash Badges: Similar to the Collar Badges, they were originally made in gold but since 1887 silver-gilt has been substituted. They may now be worn at the neck when sashes are not worn.

VALUE:

	Military	Civil
Collar chain (gold)	Rare	Rare
Collar chain (silver-gilt)	£8000–10,000	£8000–10,000
Collar badge (gold)	£4500–5500	£1250–1750
Star (metal)	£3500–4000	£1250–1750
Star (embroidered)	£350–500	£250–350
Mantle star	£750–1000	£650–850
Sash badge (gold)	£5500–7500	£2500–3500
Sash badge (silver-gilt)	£1500–2000	£800–1200

4. THE MOST HONOURABLE ORDER OF THE BATH *continued*

KCB Star (Civil)

GCB Sash badge (Civil)

Emblem worn in
civilian dress

KCB Neck badge (Military)

KNIGHTS/DAMES COMMANDERS (KCB/DCB); COMPANIONS (CB)

Holders of the KCB (DCB) wear a neck badge suspended by a ribbon as well as a breast star. Prior to 1917 Companions wore a breast badge, the same way as a medal: but in that year it was converted into a neck badge.

Star (KCB/DCB): (Military) a star with the gold Maltese cross omitted, and in the shape of a cross pattée, the three crowns and motto in the centre surrounded by a green enamelled laurel wreath. (Civil) similar but omitting the laurel wreath.

Breast Badge (CB): Similar to the Star but smaller.

Neck Badge (KCB/DCB): Similar to the Collar badges of the GCB but smaller, in Military and Civil versions as above.

Neck Badge (CB): Similar to the above, but smaller.

VALUE:	Military	Miniature	Civil	Miniature
Knight Commander				
Star (metal)	£1250–1500		£750–850	
Star (embroidered)	£550–650		£450–550	
Neck badge (gold)	£4500–5500		£1200–1500	
Neck badge (gilt)	£1200–1500		£650–750	
Companion				
Breast badge (gold)	£3500–4500	£175–250	£850–1000	£150–200
Breast badge (gilt)	£1000–1200	£75–100	£350–450	£75–100
Neck badge (gilt)	£800–950		£300–375	

43

5. THE ROYAL GUELPHIC ORDER

Instituted: 1815.
Ribbon: 44mm light blue watered silk.

KNIGHTS GRAND CROSS (GCH)

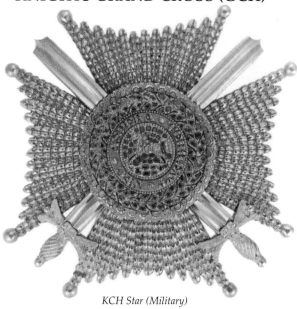

KCH Star (Military)

Collar Chain: Gold, with lions and crowns alternating, linked by scrolled royal cyphers.

Collar Badge: An eight-pointed Maltese cross with balls on each point and a lion passant gardant in each angle. (Obverse) in the centre, on a ground of red enamel, is a white horse of Hanover surrounded by a circle of light blue enamel with the motto in gold lettering NEC ASPERA TERRENT (Difficulties do not terrify). Surrounding this circle is a green enamelled laurel wreath. (Reverse) the monogram GR in gold letters on a red ground, surmounted by the British crown and surrounded by a gold circle with the date of the institution MDCCCXV. In the Military version two crossed swords are mounted above the cross and below a Hanoverian crown. In the Civil version the swords are omited, and the wreath is of oak-leaves instead of laurel.

Star: A radiate star with rays grouped into eight points, the centre being similar to the Collar Badge. Behind the laurel wreathed centre are two crossed swords (Military); in the Civil version the swords are omitted and the wreath is of oak leaves.

Sash Badge: Similar to the Collar Badge but smaller.

Comments: *Founded by HRH the Prince Regent (later King George IV), it took its name from the family surname of the British sovereigns from George I onwards and was awarded by the crown of Hanover to both British and Hanoverian subjects for distinguished services to Hanover. Under Salic Law, a woman could not succeed to the Hanoverian throne, so on the death of King William IV in 1837 Hanover passed to Prince Augustus, Duke of Cumberland, and thereafter the Guelphic Order became a purely Hanoverian award.*

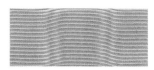

VALUE:

	Military	Civil
Collar chain (gold)	From £25,000	From £20,000
Collar chain (silver gilt)	£10,000–12,000	£8000–10,000
Collar Chain (copper gilt)	£5000–6000	£3500–4500
Collar badge	£6000–8000	£2500–3500
Star	£5000–7000	£3000–4000
Sash badge	£8000–10,000	£6000–8000

KNIGHTS COMMANDERS (KCH) AND KNIGHTS (KH)

Knights Commanders wore a neck badge suspended by a ribbon, and a breast star, while Knights wore a breast badge only.

Star: As above, but smaller.
Neck Badge: Similar to the Collar Badge but smaller.
Breast Badge: Two versions, in gold and enamel or silver and enamel.

VALUE:

	Military	Miniature	Civil	Miniature
Star	£2500–3000		£1500–2000	
Neck badge	£3500–4000		£2000–2500	
Breast badge (gold)	£2500–3000	£450–550	£1200–1500	£500–600
Breast badge (silver)	£1000–1200			

KH Breast Badge (Military)

6. THE MOST DISTINGUISHED ORDER OF ST MICHAEL AND ST GEORGE

Instituted: 1818.
Ribbon: 102mm, 58mm for ladies (GCMG), 50mm (KCMG), 44mm (DCMG), 38mm (CMG) three equal bands of Saxon blue, scarlet and Saxon blue.

GCMG Star

KNIGHTS GRAND CROSS (GCMG)

Knights Grand Cross wear a mantle of Saxon blue lined with scarlet silk tied with cords of blue and scarlet silk and gold, and having on the left side the star of the Order. The chapeau or hat is of blue satin, lined with scarlet and surmounted by black and white ostrich feathers. The collar, mantle and chapeau are only worn on special occasions or when commanded by the sovereign, but in ordinary full dress the badge is worn on the left hip from a broad ribbon passing over the right shoulder and the star on the left breast.

Collar Chain: Silver gilt formed alternately of lions of England, Maltese crosses enamelled in white, and the cyphers SM and SG with, in the centre, two winged lions of St Mark each holding a book and seven arrows.

Star: A silver star of seven groups of rays, with a gold ray between each group, surmounted overall by the cross of St George in red enamel. In the centre is a representation of St Michael encountering Satan within a blue circular riband bearing the motto AUSPICIUM MELIORIS AEVI (A token of a better age).

Sash Badge: A gold seven-pointed star with V-shaped extremities, enamelled white and edged with gold, surmounted by an imperial crown. In the centre on one side is a representation in enamel of St Michael encountering Satan and on the other St George on horseback fighting the dragon. This device is surrounded by a circle of blue enamel bearing the Latin motto in gold lettering. Silver-gilt was substituted for gold in 1887.

Comments: *Founded by HRH the Prince Regent and awarded originally to citizens of Malta and the Ionian Islands in the Adriatic Sea, both of which had been ceded to Britain during the Napoleonic Wars. The Ionian Islands were transferred to Greece in 1859. Towards the end of the 19th century, however, the Order was awarded to those who had performed distinguished service in the colonies and protectorates of the British Empire and in more recent times it has been widely used as an award to ambassadors and senior diplomats as well as colonial governors. Ladies are now eligible for this Order. In recent operations a number of awards have been made to military officers, presumably for "diplomatic" work.*

VALUE:

Collar chain	£5000–6500
Star	£2500–3000
Sash badge (gold)	£5000–6000
Sash badge (gilt)	£2000–3000

6. THE MOST DISTINGUISHED ORDER OF ST MICHAEL AND ST GEORGE *continued*

KCMG Star   CMG Neck badge

KNIGHTS COMMANDERS (KCMG) AND COMPANIONS (CMG)

Knights Commanders wear the badge suspended round the neck from a narrower ribbon of the same colours, and a breast star; Companions wear a neck badge. In undress uniform Knights Grand Cross and Knights Commanders wear the ribbon of Companions of the Order. Prior to 1917 Companions wore a breast badge, worn the same way as a medal, but this was then changed to a neck badge.

Star: A silver eight-pointed star charged with the red St George's cross and having the same central device as the GCMG Star. This was introduced in 1859.

Neck Badge: Similar to the sash badge of the GCMG but smaller. Those worn by Knight Commanders were of gold and enamel until 1887 but silver-gilt and enamel thereafter. The CMG neck badges are invariably of enamel and silver-gilt.

Breast Badge: Similar to the star of the KCMG but smaller and made of gold and enamel till 1887, and silver gilt and enamel from then till 1917.

VALUE:		*Miniature*
Knight Commander		
Star	£1200–1500	
Neck badge (gold)	£2500–3500	
Neck badge (gilt)	£1000–1500	
Companion		
Breast badge (gold)	£2000–2500	£150–200
Breast badge (gilt)	£800–1000	£85–125
Neck badge (gilt)	£550–600	

A NOTE ON IMAGERY

In the wake of the Black Lives Matter protests in the summer of 2020, there were calls in some quarters for a redesign of the breast star of the Order of St Michael and St George as, it was claimed, the central image of St Michael with his foot on Satan's neck had racist undertones as Lucifer is depicted with a much darker skin tone than the saint. Whilst few believed that the image was originally designed with any racist intent, it seems that the issue has arisen before and the Cabinet Office were quick to point out that the image was actually redrawn in 2011. Now the two figures have a similar skin tone. They went on to say that anyone wishing to change their insignia for the newer version was welcome to do so.

7. THE MOST EXALTED ORDER OF THE STAR OF INDIA

Instituted: 1861.
Ribbon: Light blue with white edges (50mm GCSI, KCSI; 38mm CSI).

KNIGHTS GRAND COMMANDERS (GCSI)

KCSI Neck badge

The insignia consisted of a gold collar and badge, a mantle of light blue satin with a representation of the star on the left side and tied with a white silk cord with blue and silver tassels. The collar and mantle were only worn on special occasions and in ordinary full dress uniform a GCSI wore the star on the left breast and the badge on the left hip from a broad sash of light blue edged in white.

Collar Chain: Gold formed of lotus flowers, palm branches and united red and white roses. Later chains are silver-gilt.

Badge: An onyx cameo bearing the left-facing bust of Queen Victoria wearing an imperial crown, set in a gold ornamental oval containing the motto of the Order HEAVEN'S LIGHT OUR GUIDE in diamonds, on a pale blue ground surmounted by a five-pointed star in chased silver.

Star: A five-pointed star in diamonds resting on a circular riband of light blue enamel bearing the motto in diamonds, the whole set on a circular star of golden rays.

Comments: *Founded by Queen Victoria a few years after the British Crown took over the administration of India from the Honourable East India Company, it was intended primarily as an award to loyal Indian princes. The highest class was designated Knight Grand Commander, rather than Cross, because the majority of recipients were not Christians (either Hindus or Muslims). The Order at first consisted of the sovereign, a Grand Master (the Viceroy of India), 36 Knights Grand Commanders (18 British and 18 Indian), 85 Knights Commanders and 170 Companions. The GCSI was the most lavish of all British orders. It lapsed in 1947 when the sub-continent attained independence. Until then all insignia of this Order was returnable on the death of recipients. After 1947, however, recipients or their heirs were allowed in certain cases to purchase the star and badges of any of the three applicable classes, but not the collar chain of the Knight Grand Commander.*

VALUE:

Collar chain	—
Star and badge	From £40,000

KNIGHTS COMMANDERS (KCSI) AND COMPANIONS (CSI)

Knights Commanders wore a badge round the neck and a star on the left breast, while Companions originally had a breast badge which was transmuted into a neck badge from 1917 onwards.

Star: Similar to that of the GCSI but in silver.
Neck Badge: Similar to the collar badge of the GCSI but smaller and less ornate.
Breast Badge: Similar to the above but smaller and less ornate and fitted with a straight bar suspender. Subtle differences in the ornament at the foot of the blue border and the external ornament at the sides and foot of the oval.
Comments: *The second and third classes of the Order were awarded to Indian and British subjects of the armed forces and Indian Civil Service for distinguished service of not less than 30 years' duration.*

VALUE:

		Miniature
Star and Neck badge (KCSI)	From £15,000	
Breast badge (CSI)	£6500–7500	£350–500 (gold), £200–250 (silver gilt)
Neck badge (CSI)	£6000–9000	

8. THE MOST EMINENT ORDER OF THE INDIAN EMPIRE

Instituted: 1878.
Ribbon: Deep indigo blue.

KNIGHTS GRAND COMMANDERS (GCIE)

KCIE Neck badge

The insignia consisted of a collar, badge and mantle of imperial purple or dark blue satin lined with white silk and fastened with a white silk cord with gold tassels, and having on the left side a representation of the Star of the Order. On ordinary full-dress occasions, however, Knights Grand Commanders wore the badge on the left hip from a broad sash, and a star on the left breast.

Collar Chain: Silver-gilt, composed of elephants, lotus flowers, peacocks in their pride and Indian roses with, in the centre, the imperial crown, the whole linked together by chains.

Badge: A gold five-petalled rose, enamelled crimson and with a green barb between each petal. In the centre is an effigy of Queen Victoria on a gold ground, surrounded by a purple riband originally inscribed VICTORIA IMPERATRIX but from 1901 onwards inscribed IMPERATRICIS AUSPICIIS (Under the auspices of the Empress). The letters I N D I A are inscribed on the petals in the first version, but omitted in the second.

Star: Composed of fine silver rays with smaller gold rays between them, the whole alternately plain and scaled. In the centre, within a purple circle bearing the motto and surmounted by the imperial crown in gold, is the effigy of Queen Victoria on a gold ground.

Comments: *Founded by Queen Victoria after assuming the title of Empress of India, it was originally confined to Companions only, together with the Sovereign and Grand Master. Members of the Council of the Governor-General were admitted ex officio as Companions. It was intended for award in respect of meritorious services in India but from the outset it was regarded as a junior alternative to the Star of India. In 1886 the Order was expanded to two classes by the addition of Knights Commanders up to a maximum of 50 in number. In 1887, however, it was again re-organised into three classes: up to 25 Knights Grand Commanders (GCIE), up to 50 Knights Commanders (KCIE) and an unlimited number of Companions (CIE). The Order has been in abeyance since 1947.*

VALUE:

Collar chain	From £20,000
Star and badge	£7000–9000

KNIGHTS COMMANDERS (KCIE) AND COMPANIONS (CIE)

The insignia of Knights Commanders consisted of a neck badge and a breast star, while that of Companions was originally a breast badge, converted to a neck badge in 1917.

Star: Similar to that of the GCIE but fashioned entirely in silver.

Neck badge: Similar to the collar or sash badge of the GCIE but in correspondingly smaller sizes and differing in minor details.

Breast badge: Similar to the sash badge of the GCIE but differing in minor details, notably the spacing ornament at the foot of the blue circle. Two versions exist, with or without INDIA on the petals of the lotus flower.

VALUE:		*Miniature*
Knights Commanders		
Star and Neck badge	£5000–7000	
Companions		
Breast badge (INDIA)	£2000–3000	£450–500 (gold)
Breast badge (smaller, without INDIA)	£1000–1250	£300–400 (gold)
Neck badge	£900–1000	£175–250 (gilt)

9. THE ROYAL FAMILY ORDER

QEII (reduced)

Edward VII

George V

George VI

Elizabeth II

Instituted: 1820.

Ribbon: 50mm sky blue moiré (1820); 38mm dark blue bordered by narrow stripes of yellow and broader stripes of crimson with narrow black edges (1902); 50mm pale blue moire (1911); 50mm pink moire (1937); 50mm pale yellow silk moire (1953). These ribbons are tied in a bow and worn on the left shoulder.

Descriptions: An upright oval heavily bordered by diamonds and surmounted by a crown, also embellished in diamonds. The oval contains a miniature portrait of the sovereign in enamels.

Comments: *Awarded to female relatives of the reigning monarch. It was instituted by King George IV who conferred such orders on his sister, Princess Charlotte Augusta, wife of Frederick William, King of Wurttemberg, and his niece Princess Augusta Caroline, who married the Grand Duke of Mecklenburg-Strelitz. Queen Victoria instituted a separate Order (see next entry), but this Order was revived by King Edward VII in 1902 and continued by successive sovereigns ever since. The insignia of these Family Orders very seldom appear on the market and on account of their immense rarity they are unpriced here. Special badges are given to ladies-in-waiting.*

VALUE:

George IV	—
Edward VII	—
George V	—
George VI	—
Elizabeth II	—
Ladies-in-waiting badges	From £1000

10. THE ROYAL ORDER OF VICTORIA AND ALBERT

Instituted: 1862.

Ribbon: 38mm white moiré, in the form of a bow worn on the left shoulder.

Description: An upright oval onyx cameo bearing conjoined profiles of HRH Prince Albert, the Prince Consort and Queen Victoria. The badges of the First and Second Classes are set in diamonds and surmounted by an imperial crown similarly embellished, the badge of the Second Class being rather smaller. The badge of the Third Class is set in pearls, while that of the Fourth Class takes the form of a monogram "V & A" set with pearls and surmounted by an imperial crown.

Comments: *Personally awarded to female members of the Royal Family by Queen Victoria. This order became obsolete in 1981 with the death of Princess Alice, Countess of Athlone, the last surviving grandchild of Queen Victoria.*

VALUE:

First Class	From £35,000
Second Class	£25,000–30,000
Third Class	£15,000–18,000
Fourth Class	£8000–10,000

49

11. THE IMPERIAL ORDER OF THE CROWN OF INDIA

Instituted: January 1, 1878.

Ribbon: 38mm light blue watered silk with narrow white stripes towards the edges, formed in a bow worn on the left shoulder.

Description: A badge consisting of the royal and imperial monogram VRI in diamonds, turquoises and pearls, surrounded by an oval frame and surmounted by a jewelled imperial crown.

Comments: *Awarded by Queen Victoria to the princesses of the royal and imperial house, the wives or other female relatives of Indian princes and other Indian ladies, and of the wives or other female relatives of any of the persons who had held or were holding the offices of Viceroy and Governor-General of India, Governors of Madras or Bombay, or of Principal Secretary of State for India, as the sovereign might think fit to appoint. Her late Majesty Queen Elizabeth II was the last surviving member of the Order.*

VALUE:

From £15,000	*Miniature* £500–600

IMPORTANT NOTICE

The prices quoted in this publication are average figures for medals and decorations as individual items. Combinations with other decorations and campaign medals will produce a value usually well in excess of the aggregate of the individual items. Value will depend to a large extent on the personal factors and circumstances of the award, but where general factors are involved (e.g. the design of the medal, the period of issue or the campaign concerned, or in some cases the branch of the services) these are itemised separately. "−" indicates that either no examples have come on to the market or no examples have been issued. The figure in brackets (where available) is the approximate number awarded. In the lists which follow, it should be assumed that decorations were instituted by Royal Warrant, unless otherwise stated

12. THE ROYAL VICTORIAN ORDER

Instituted: April 1896.
Ribbon: Dark blue with borders of narrow red, white and red stripes on either side, 95mm (GCVO), 44mm (KCVO, DCVO and CVO), or 32mm (LVO, MVO and RVM, also all classes on uniform when insignia not worn).

KNIGHTS GRAND CROSS/DAMES GRAND CROSS (GCVO)

The insignia consists of a mantle of dark blue silk, edged with red satin, lined with white silk, and fastened by a cordon of dark blue silk and gold; a gold collar and a badge, worn only on special occasions. Knights wear the badge on the left hip from a broad ribbon worn over the right shoulder, with a star on the left breast, while Dames wear a somewhat narrower ribbon over the right shoulder with the badge, and a star similar to that of the Knights. Dames' insignia are smaller than those of the Knights.

GCVO star

Collar: Silver gilt composed of octagonal pieces and oblong perforated and ornamental frames alternately linked together with gold. The pieces are edged and ornamented with gold, and each contains on a blue-enamelled ground a gold rose jewelled with a carbuncle. The frames are gold and each contains a portion of inscription VICTORIA BRITT. FID. DEF. IND. IMP. in letters of white enamel. In the centre of the collar, within a perforated and ornamental frame of gold, is an octagonal piece enamelled blue, edged with red, and charged with a white saltire, superimposed by a gold medallion of Queen Victoria's effigy from which is suspended the badge.

Badge: A white-enamelled Maltese cross of eight points, in the centre of which is an oval of crimson enamel bearing the cypher VRI in gold letters. Encircling this is a blue enamel riband with the name VICTORIA in gold letters, and above this is the imperial crown enamelled in proper colours.

Star: Of chipped silver of eight points on which is mounted a white-enamelled Maltese cross with VRI in an oval at the centre.

Comments: *Awarded for extraordinary, important or personal services to the Sovereign or the Royal Family. Ladies became eligible for the Order in 1936. Most of the badges of the Royal Victorian Order are numbered on the reverse and are returnable on promotion. The early (QV) awards are unnumbered.*

VALUE:	Knights	Dames	*Miniature*
Collar			
gold	From £15,000	From £15,000	
silver gilt	From £6000	From £8000	
Star and Badge (GCVO)	From £3000	From £3000	£300–400

KNIGHTS COMMANDERS (KCVO), DAMES COMMANDERS (DCVO), COMMANDERS (CVO), LIEUTENANTS (LVO) AND MEMBERS (MVO)

The insignia of the Second, Third, Fourth and Fifth Classes follows the usual pattern. Knights wear a neck badge and a breast star, Dames a breast star and a badge on the left shoulder from a ribbon tied in a bow, Commanders the same neck badge (men) or shoulder badge (women), Lieutenants a somewhat smaller breast badge worn in line with other medals and decorations (men) or a shoulder badge (women) and Members breast or shoulder badges in frosted silver instead of white enamel. The two lowest classes of the Order were originally designated member Fourth Class or member Fifth Class (MVO), but in 1984 the Fourth Class was renamed Lieutenant (LVO) and the Fifth Class simply Member (MVO).

VALUE:	Gentlemen	*Miniature*	Ladies
Neck badge and breast star (KCVO)	£2000–3500	£200–250	£1400–1800
Neck badge (CVO)	£500–600	£40–60	£450–500
Breast or shoulder badge (LVO)	£400–500	£40–60	£370–400
Breast or shoulder badge (MVO)	£350–450	£35–50	£300–350

13. ROYAL VICTORIAN MEDAL

Instituted: April 1896.

Ribbon: As for the Royal Victorian Order (above); foreign Associates, however, wear a ribbon with a central white stripe added.

Metal: Silver-gilt, silver or bronze.

Size: 30mm.

Description: (Obverse) the effigy of the reigning sovereign; (reverse) the royal cypher on an ornamental shield within a laurel wreath with ROYAL VICTORIAN MEDAL below.

Comments: *Awarded to those below the rank of officers who perform personal services to the sovereign or to members of the Royal Family. Originally awarded in silver or bronze, a higher class, in silver-gilt, was instituted by King George V. Only two medals (both silver) were issued in the brief reign of King Edward VIII (1936) and only four bronze medals were issued in the reign of King George VI. Any person in possession of the bronze medal to whom a silver medal is awarded, can wear both, and the silver-gilt medal in addition if such be conferred upon him or her. Clasps are awarded for further services to each class of the medal, while the medals may be worn in addition to the insignia of the Order if the latter is subsequently conferred. To distinguish between British and foreign recipients, King George VI decreed in 1951 that the ribbon worn by the latter should have an additional stripe, these recipients to be designated Associates. In 1983 the order for wearing this medal was altered and it was no longer to be worn after campaign medals but took precedence over them. The medal is issued unnamed. A lapel badge or emblem for members of the Order to wear on everyday clothing was introduced in 2011.*

Ribbon for foreign Associates.

Emblem worn by members when in civilian dress.

VALUE:

	Silver-gilt	Miniature	Silver	Miniature	Bronze	Miniature
Victoria	—	£85–120	£350–400	£100–150	£200–250	£85–100
Edward VII	—	—	£325–375	£85–100	£200–250	£55–80
George V	£400–450	—	£275–350	£50–85	£250–300	£25–50
Edward VIII	—	—	Rare	—	—	—
George VI	£450–500	—	£275–350	£35–50	Rare	£20–30
Elizabeth II	£400–450	—	£275–350	£35–50	£400–450	£20–30

14. THE ROYAL VICTORIAN CHAIN

Instituted: 1902.

Ribbon: None.

Metal: Silver gilt

Description: A chain consisting of three Tudor roses, two thistles, two shamrocks and two lotus flowers (the heraldic flowers of England, Scotland, Ireland and India respectively), connected by a slender double trace of gold chain. At the bottom of the front loop is a centre piece consisting of the royal cypher in enamel surrounded by a wreath and surmounted by a crown. From this centrepiece hangs a replica of the badge of a Knight Grand Cross of the Royal Victorian Order. Ladies wear the insignia in the form of a shoulder badge suspended from a miniature chain with links leading to a rose, thistle, shamrock and lotus. An even more elaborate collar, with diamonds encrusting the crown and cypher, was adopted in 1921 and there is a ladies' version of this as well.

Comments: *Sometimes regarded as the highest grade of the Royal Victorian Order, it is actually a quite separate Order and was introduced by King Edward VII for conferment as a special mark of the sovereign's favour, and then only very rarely, upon Royalty, or other especially distinguished personages, both foreign and British.*

VALUE

	Gentlemen	Ladies
Chain	From £20,000	From £20,000
Chain with diamonds	Rare	Rare

15. ORDER OF MERIT

Order of Merit obverse

Order of Merit reverse

Instituted: 1902.
Ribbon: 50mm half blue, half crimson.
Metal: Gold.
Size: Height 80mm overall; max. width 53mm.
Description: A pattée convexed cross, enamelled red, edged blue. (Obverse) FOR MERIT in the centre surrounded by a white band and a laurel wreath enamelled in proper colours. (Reverse) the royal cypher in gold on a blue ground with a white surround and a laurel wreath as above. The cross is surmounted by a crown (changed from a Tudor crown to St Edward crown in 1990) to which is attached a ring for suspension. Naval and military recipients have crossed swords in the angles of the cross.
Comments: *This highly prestigious Order consists of the sovereign and a maximum of 24 members in one class only. There is, however, no limit on the number of foreign honorary members, although only 11 have so far been admitted to the Order. It is intended to honour exceptionally meritorious service in the Crown Services or towards the advancement of the Arts, Learning, Literature and Science or other exceptional service. To date 185 awards have been made, including only nine ladies, from Florence Nightingale (1907) to Baroness Boothroyd (2005). The insignia of those appointed since 1991 have to be returned on the death of the recipient. The insignia of members appointed prior to that date is retained, but understandably few items have come on to the market.*

VALUE:

	Military	Civil
Edward VII	From £25,000	From £15,000
George V	From £25,000	From £15,000
George VI	Very Rare	From £15,000
Elizabeth II	Rare	From £10,000
Miniature	£250–300	

16. THE MOST EXCELLENT ORDER OF THE BRITISH EMPIRE

Instituted: June 1917.

Ribbon: Originally purple, with a narrow central scarlet stripe for the Military Division; since 1936 rose-pink edged with pearl grey, with a narrow central stripe of pearl-grey for the Military Division. A silver crossed oakleaf emblem for gallantry was instituted in 1957. 100mm with 6mm edge stripes (57mm with 4mm edge stripes for ladies) (GBE); 44mm with 2.5mm edge stripes (KBE/DBE/CBE); 38mm with 2.5mm edge stripes (OBE/MBE); 32mm with 1.6mm edge stripes (BEM).

Comments: *Founded by King George V during the First World War for services to the Empire at home, in India and in the overseas dominions and colonies, other than those rendered by the Navy and Army, although it could be conferred upon officers of the armed forces for services of a non-combatant character. A Military Division was created in December 1918 and awards made to commissioned officers and warrant officers in respect of distinguished service in action. The insignia of the Civil and Military Divisions is identical, distinguished only by the respective ribbons. A promotion in a different division permits the wear of both types of insignia and in the case of gallantry awards a third type may be worn. A lapel emblem for wear on ordinary clothing was introduced in December 2006.*

GBE Star (2nd type)

Emblem worn by Members of the Order in civilian dress.

KNIGHTS/DAMES GRAND CROSS (GBE)

The insignia includes a mantle of rose-pink satin lined with pearl-grey silk, tied by a cord of pearl-grey silk, with two rose-pink and silver tassels attached. On the left side of the mantle is a representation of the star of the First Class of the Order. The mantle, collar and collar badge are only worn on special occasions. In dress uniform, however, the badge is worn over the left hip from a broad (96mm) riband passing over the right shoulder, while Dames wear the badge from a narrower (57mm) ribbon in a bow on the left shoulder; both with the breast star of the Order.

Collar: Silver-gilt with medallions of the royal arms and of the royal and imperial cypher of King George V alternately linked together with cables. In the centre is the imperial crown between two sea lions. The collar for Dames is somewhat narrower than that for Knights.

Star: An eight-pointed star of silver chips on which is superimposed the enamelled medallion as for the badge (Britannia or George V and Queen Mary). The star worn by Dames is smaller.

Badge: A cross patonce in silver-gilt, the arms enamelled pearl-grey. In the centre, within a circle enamelled crimson, the figure of Britannia, replaced since 1936 by the conjoined left-facing crowned busts of King George V and Queen Mary, surrounded by a circle inscribed FOR GOD AND THE EMPIRE.

CBE Badge (2nd type)

VALUE:	1st type Britannia	2nd type King & Queen
Knights Grand Cross		
Collar	Rare	Rare
Badge and star	£3000–4000	£3000–4000
Dames Grand Cross		
Collar	From £6000	From £6000
Badge and star	£3000–4000	£3000–4000
Miniature stars	£300–350	£300–350

KBE Star

KNIGHTS COMMANDERS (KBE), DAMES COMMANDERS (DBE), COMMANDERS (CBE), OFFICERS (OBE) AND MEMBERS (MBE)

The insignia of these five Classes follows the same pattern as other Orders. Both Britannia and King and Queen medallion types have been issued.

Star: A star of four large points and four minor points in chipped silver, with the enamelled medallion superimposed. The star worn by Dames is smaller.

Neck Badge: Similar to the badge of the GBE but smaller and worn from a 44mm ribbon round the neck (men) or from a shoulder bow (ladies). Worn by KBE, DBE and CBE.

Breast Badge: As above, but in silver-gilt (OBE) or frosted silver (MBE), with shoulder versions for ladies, worn with a 38mm ribbon.

Gallantry Award: An emblem of silver crossed oak leaves was added to the ribbon of the CBE, OBE and MBE (1957–74).

*Oak leaf emblem for gallantry
(smaller when ribbon only worn).*

VALUE:	1st type Britannia	Miniature	2nd type King&Queen	Miniature
Badge and Star (KBE)	£1500–2000	£250–300	£1200–1500	£285–345
Badge and Star (DBE)	£1500–2000		£1200–1500	
Neck badge (CBE)	£350–400	£35–50	£350–400	£40–55
Shoulder badge (CBE)	£350–400		£350–400	
Breast badge (OBE)	£200–250	£15–25	£180–200	£20–40
Shoulder badge (OBE)	£200–250		£180–200	
Breast badge (MBE)	£200–250	£15–25	£180–200	£20–40
Shoulder badge (MBE)	£200–250		£180–200	

Ribbons: (top to bottom) OBE (Military) 1st type, OBE (Military) 2nd type, OBE (Civil) 1st type, OBE (Civil) 2nd type.

OBE badge (silver-gilt) and reverse of the MBE badge (frosted silver).

17. MEDAL OF THE ORDER OF THE BRITISH EMPIRE

Instituted: June 1917.
Ribbon: 32mm plain purple (Civil), with a narrow scarlet central stripe (Military).
Medal: Silver.
Size: 30mm.
Description: (Obverse) a seated figure of Britannia facing right, her left arm extended and her right holding a trident, with the inscription FOR GOD AND THE EMPIRE round the upper part of the circumference; (reverse) the royal and imperial cypher GRI surmounted by a Tudor crown, the whole enclosed in a cable circle. Fitted with a plain ring for suspension.
Comments: *Instituted as a lower award connected with the Order, it consisted originally of a Civil Division, but a Military Division, distinguishable solely by the ribbon, was added in December 1918. This medal was issued unnamed but many were subsequently engraved or impressed on the rim privately. Fewer than 2000 medals were awarded before they were discontinued in 1922.*

Civil ribbon

Military ribbon

VALUE:		Miniature
Medal unnamed as issued	£375–450	£85–125
Attributable medal	£550–850	

18. EMPIRE GALLANTRY MEDAL

Instituted: December 29, 1922.
Ribbon: Originally plain purple (Civil), with a thin scarlet central stripe (Military); from July 1937 rose-pink with pearl-grey edges (Civil) and a central pearl-grey stripe (Military). A silver laurel branch was added to the ribbon (1933), with a smaller version for wear on the ribbon alone.
Metal: Silver.
Size: 36mm.
Description: (Obverse) the seated figure of Britannia, her left hand resting on a shield and her right holding a trident, with a blazing sun upper right. The words FOR GOD AND THE EMPIRE inscribed round the upper part of the circumference, with FOR in the wave lower left above the exergue which bears the word GALLANTRY. (Reverse) 1st type has six lions passant gardant, with the Royal cypher in the centre surmounted by an imperial crown. The George VI issue has four lions, two either side and round the foot, in two concentric arcs, the words INSTITUTED BY KING GEORGE V. It is suspended from a straight bar ornamented with laurel leaves. Named in seriffed capitals engraved round the rim.
Comments: *This medal, officially known as the Medal of the Order of the British Empire for Gallantry, replaced the Medal of the Order of the British Empire and was awarded for specific acts of gallantry. It was abolished on the institution of the George Cross in September 1940, while it was announced in the London Gazette of April 22, 1941 that a recipient still living on September 24, 1940 but including posthumous awards after September 3, 1939 should return it to the Central Chancery of the Orders of Knighthood and become a holder of the George Cross instead. Not all EGMs, however, were exchanged or returned. Only 130 medals were issued, 64 being civil, 62 military and four honorary.*

1st type rev.

VALUE:		Miniature
George V	£5000–7000	£170–230
George VI	£5000–7000	£170–230

Civil 1922

Military 1922

Civil 1937

Military 1937
(emblem smaller when ribbon only worn).

19. BRITISH EMPIRE MEDAL

Civil 1922

Military 1922

Civil 1937

Military 1937

BEM Gallantry Emblem

Instituted: December 1922.

Ribbon: As MYB 18, but without the silver laurel branch.

Metal: Silver.

Size: 36mm. Specimens are known up to 37.5mm.

Description: As MYB 18 above, but with the words MERITORIOUS SERVICE in the exergue. Suspended from a straight bar ornamented with oak leaves. A silver bar decorated with oak leaves was introduced in March 1941 for further acts, and is denoted by a silver rosette on the ribbon worn on its own. An emblem of crossed silver oak leaves was introduced in December 1957 to denote a gallantry award, a smaller version being worn on the ribbon alone. Named in engraved capitals round the rim.

Comments: *Formally entitled the Medal of the Order of the British Empire for Meritorious Service, it is generally known simply as the British Empire Medal. It is awarded for meritorious service by both civil and military personnel although for some years it was issued as a third grade bravery award, particularly for air raid deeds not considered to be of the level of the GC or GM. The medal may be worn even if the recipient is promoted to a higher grade of the Order. The gallantry awards, instituted in December 1957, ceased in 1974 on the introduction of the Queen's Gallantry Medal. No British awards were made for the BEM between 1995 and 2012 although Commonwealth awards were still being made, however, the medal was resurrected for Her Majesty the late Queen's Diamond Jubilee Honours List for civilians only with over 250 awards announced. The Order of the British Empire emblem for gallantry instituted in December 2006 (qv) may also be worn by holders of the BEM.*

VALUE:

	Military	Civil	Miniature
George V	£450–550	£300–400	£25–40
George VI GRI cypher	£350–450	£150–200	£20–35
George VI GVIR cypher	£350–450	£150–200	£20–35
Elizabeth II	£350–450	£150–200	£20–35
Elizabeth II with gallantry emblem	£850–1000	£750–850	—

20. THE ORDER OF THE COMPANIONS OF HONOUR

Instituted: June 1917.

Ribbon: 38mm carmine with borders of gold thread.

Metal: Silver gilt.

Size: Height 48mm; max. width 29mm.

Description: An oval badge consisting of a medallion with an oak tree, a shield bearing the royal arms hanging from one branch, and on the left a knight armed and in armour, mounted on a horse. The badge has a blue border with the motto IN ACTION FAITHFUL AND IN HONOUR CLEAR in gold letters. The oval is surmounted by an imperial crown. Gentlemen wear the badge round their necks, while ladies wear it from a bow at the left shoulder.

Comments: *Instituted at the same time as the Order of the British Empire, it carries no title or precedence although the post-nominal letters CH are used. The Order consists of the sovereign and one class of members. Not more than 50 men or women who have rendered conspicuous service of national importance were admitted, but in 1943 this was increased to 65. The Order is awarded in Britain and the Commonwealth on a quota basis: UK (45), Australia (7), New Zealand (2), other countries (11). It is awarded for outstanding achievements in the arts, literature, music, science, politics, industry and religion.*

VALUE

Gentlemen	£3000–3500		
Ladies	£3000–3500		
Miniature	Uniface £200–250		Monogrammed reverse £300–400

21. THE BARONET'S BADGE

Baronet's badge—United Kingdom

(Nova Scotia)

(other Baronets)

Instituted: 1629.

Ribbon: 30mm orange watered silk (Nova Scotia); 44mm orange bordered with narrow blue edges (other Baronets).

Metal: Gold or silver-gilt.

Size: Height 55mm; max. width 41mm(Nova Scotia) or 44mm (later badges).

Description: An upright oval badge with a plain ring suspension. The badge of the Baronets of Nova Scotia was originally skeletal, with a shield bearing the lion rampant of Scotland, decorated with pearls and enamels, surmounted by a Scottish crown and surrounded by a blue border inscribed in gold FAX MENTIS HONESTAE GLORIA. The remaining badges (authorised in 1929) have a solid ground and a central shield with the red hand of Ulster surmounted by a crown and a border of gold and blue enamel decorated with roses (England), shamrocks (Ireland), roses and thistles combined (Great Britain) or roses, thistles and shamrocks combined (United Kingdom). Often engraved on the reverse with the recipient's title and date of creation.

Comments: *By Letter Patent of 1611 James I created Baronets whose knighthood became hereditary. In 1624, to raise money independently of Parliament, James I sold grants of land in Nova Scotia (New Scotland) to Scotsmen. In 1625 Charles I conferred on the holders of this land the title and dignity of Baronets of Nova Scotia with the title of Sir, and decreed that they should wear round their necks "an orange tawny ribbon whereon shall be pendent an escutcheon". After the Union with England (1707) English and Scottish baronetcies ceased to be created, being replaced by baronetcies of Great Britain. Irish baronetcies continued to be created until 1801 after which all new creations were of the United Kingdom.*

VALUE:

	Gold	Silver-gilt
Nova Scotia, 18th–early 19th centuries	£3500–4500	£850–1000
Nova Scotia, late 19th and 20th centuries	£2000–2500	£850–1000
England (rose surround)	£1000–1500	£800–1000
Ireland (shamrock surround)	£1000–1500	£800–1000
Great Britain (roses and thistles)	£1000–1500	£800–1000
United Kingdom (roses, thistles and shamrocks)	£1000–1500	£800–1000

22. THE KNIGHT BACHELOR'S BADGE

Instituted: April 21, 1926.
Ribbon: 38mm scarlet with broad yellow borders.
Metal: Silver-gilt and enamels. Some pre-war breast badges are in base metal.
Size: Height 76.50mm; max. width 56.50mm. Reduced in 1933 to 63.25mm and in 1973 to 54mm.
Description: An upright oval medallion enclosed by a scroll, bearing a cross-hilted sword, belted and sheathed, pommel upwards, between two spurs, rowels upwards, the whole set about with the sword-belt.
Comments: *The title Knight Bachelor (KB) was introduced by King Henry III to signify a battelier (one who fought in battle). The badge was authorised by King George V in response to a request from the Imperial Society of Knights Bachelors who wished to have a distinctive badge denoting their rank. The original badge was of the dimensions given above and affixed to the breast by means of a pin on the reverse. This badge was reduced in size in 1933 and again in 1973 when it was fitted with a ring for suspension by a ribbon round the neck. On 4 December 1998 Her late Majesty Queen Elizabeth II signed an amending warrant permitting recipients of this honour to wear both a neck badge and breast badge.*

Emblem worn in civilian dress.

VALUE:

		Miniature
First type breast badge (1926–32)	£550–650	£55–75
Smaller type breast badge (1933–72)	£450–550	(Skeletal type
Neck badge (1973–)	£450–550	£40–55)

23. THE ORDER OF ST JOHN

Neck badge

Emblem worn in civilian dress

Shoulder badge

Instituted: May 14, 1888 and at various dates in other countries.

Ribbon: Plain black watered silk. Sash ribbons for Bailiffs, 102mm; Dames Grand Cross, 57mm. Ribbons for Knights, 51mm; Ribbons for Dames were formerly in a 32mm bow and ribbons for Commanders, officers and Serving Brothers 38mm and 32mm for ladies, but under new regulations (October 2001) all ribbons below Grand Cross are now standardised at 38mm. In 1947, for all grades of the Order, when the ribbon only is worn, a small Maltese Cross in silver is carried on the ribbon to distinguish it against a dark background.

Metal: Gold, silver-gilt and silver, or base metal.

Sash badge: An eight-pointed gold Maltese cross in white enamel with two lions and two unicorns in the angles (*other countries have different beasts in the angles*). Confined to Bailiffs and Dames Grand Cross.

Neck badge: Hitherto in the grades Knight/Dame, Commander and Officer badges worn by women were smaller than those worn by men, but in 2001 this distinction was abolished. The badges worn by Knights of Justice and Chaplains are in gold, while those worn by Knights of Grace and Commanders are in silver.

Star: The eight-pointed Maltese cross in white enamel without the lions and unicorns (Grand Cross and Justice) or with lions and unicorns (Grace and Sub-Prelate). A sub-Prelate is an Order Chaplain (so his badge is included above) who held high rank in the Church as distinct from the Order. The order ceased appointing Sub-Prelates in 1999, and as a result the Sub-Prelate's star (gilt with beasts) is now obsolescent.

Shoulder badge: Worn by Dames of Justice in gold and Dames of Grace, Commanders, Serving Sisters and Officers (Sisters) in silver. It is now mounted on a ribbon with "tails" as in other British orders.

Breast badges: (Officers) The Order badge with beasts (UK lion and unicorn) in angles, from 1926 until 1936 in silver, from 1936 to date the arms of the cross have been enamelled in white.

(Serving Brothers/Sisters, from 2012 known as Members) originally in silver and enamel, in white metal or rhodium subsequently. Those worn by Serving Brothers/Members have undergone six main phases:

1892–1939: a circular badge with white enamel cross and silver beasts raised above the surface of the black enamel medal in a silver rim (two types of suspender) (type 1 & 2).

1939–1949: circular skeletal badge with ring suspension and the cross set in a silver rim, no black background (type 3).

1949–1974: the first badge resumed but with different ring suspender (type 4).

1974–1984: a badge of the same design but with the cross and beasts flush with their background (type 5).

1984–1991: the cross and beasts in white metal alone with no background or rim, slightly smaller than the Officer (Brother) cross and the whole convex on the obverse (type 6).

Since 1991: cross and beasts thicker, with each arm raised and shaped on both sides of a central channel, the whole in rhodium (type 7).

A woman Officer or Serving Sister (from 2012 known as a Member) in uniform was originally invested with her breast badge on a bow but since 1999 a straight ribbon has been used.

Donats' badges: Gold, silver or bronze, consisting of the badge of the Order with the upper arm of the cross replaced by an ornamental piece of metal for suspension.

Comments: *The Most Venerable Order of the Hospital of St John of Jerusalem was incorporated by Royal Charter of Queen Victoria and granted the epithet Venerable in 1926 and Most in 1955; despite its title, it has no connection*

Serving Brothers/Sisters breast badge.

1st type (1892–early 1930s).   2nd type (late 1930s).   3rd type (Wartime issue up to 1947).   4th type (1948– c. 1973).

5th type (1974–84).   6th type (1984–91).   7th type (1991–).

with the Knights Hospitallers of Jerusalem, who were subsequently based at Rhodes and Malta and now have their headquarters in Rome. In 1926 the Order was reorganised into five Classes like certain other Orders. A sixth class was added later. Both men and women are eligible for membership. His Majesty the King is the Sovereign Head of the Order. Next in authority is the Grand Prior, followed by Bailiffs and Dames Grand Cross, Chaplains, Knights and Dames of Justice, Knights and Dames of Grace, Commanders, Officers, Serving Brothers and Sisters and Esquires. Associates were people who were not citizens of the United Kingdom, the British Commonwealth or the Republic of Ireland, or are non-Christians, who have rendered conspicuous service to the Order and may be attached to any grade of the Order. They wear the insignia of that grade, at one time distinguished only by a central narrow white stripe on the ribbon, but now all ribbons are identical. Donats are people who have made generous contributions to the funds of the Order. They are not enrolled as members of the Order but receive badges in gold, silver or bronze. The Statutes and Regulations were revised in 2004. The grade of Chaplain (gold badge) was abolished, but existing Chaplains could retain their insignia or be regarded as Commanders. Before 1999 a Chaplain could be appointed a Sub-Prelate if he held high office in the Church. A sub-Prelate wore the badge of a Chaplain and also a star with gilt lions and unicorns. Those few remaining have now been renamed Honorary Sub-Prelates, a term revived to designate the senior ecclesiastical officer of a Priory. This appointment carries no distinctive insignia.

VALUE:	Gold	Silver/Gilt	Bronze	Miniature
Bailiff badge and star	£2500–3000	£600–1000	—	
Dame Grand Cross	£2500–3000	£600–750	—	
Knight of Justice neck badge and star	£1000–1500	£500–650	£200–300	
Dame of Justice shoulder badge and star	£1000–1500	£500–650	£200–300	
Knight of Grace neck badge and star	—	£350–450	£175–275	
Dame of Grace shoulder badge and star	—	£350–450	£175–275	£25–40
Sub-Prelate neck badge		£200–250	£75–100	
Commander (Brother) neck badge	—	£200–250	£75–100	
Commander (Sister) shoulder badge	—	£50–75	£35–50	
Officer				
1926–36 Silver	—	£85–100	—	
From 1936 Silver with white enamelling	—	£100–150	—	
Serving Brother/Sister (since 2012, this grade was replaced by "Member") breast badge				
1st or 2nd type	—	£65–85	—	£50–70
3rd type	—	£50–75	—	£50–70
4th or 5th type	—	£50–75	—	£30–40
6th or 7th type	—	£50–75	—	£20–30
Donat's badge	£250–300	£55–85	£45–55	£35–50

DECORATIONS

The award of decorations for distinguished military service is an ancient institution. In his Antiquities of the Jews, the historian Josephus relates that, in the second century BC, King Alexander was so pleased with Jonathan the High Priest that he sent him a gold button as a mark of favour for his skill in leading the Jews in battle. Subsequently Jonathan was presented with a second gold button for his gallant conduct in the field, making these incidents among the earliest recorded for which specific military awards were granted. The award of jewels, gold buttons and badges for valour was carried on in most European countries on a sporadic basis but the present system of decorations is essentially a modern one dating back no farther than the middle of the seventeenth century. Earlier medals were quasi-commemorative and include the famous Armada Medal of 1588. A few medals in silver or gold were awarded to officers for distinguished service during the English Civil War, although the first "official" rewards in Britain were probably those issued by Parliament to naval officers following their victories over the Dutch fleet in 1653.

Decorations may be divided into those awarded for individual acts of heroism and those conferred in recognition of distinguished military, political or social service. In general terms collectors prefer a decoration awarded for bravery in the field rather than a political honour given automatically to a civil servant, just because he happens to have been in a particular grade for a certain number of years. The debasement of civil awards, such as the OBE and MBE, is reflected in the relative lack of interest shown by collectors.

It is generally true to say that military decorations are more desirable, but it is important to note that one decoration may be more highly prized than another, while the same decoration may well be more valuable to collectors when issued in one period rather than in another. At one extreme is the greatly coveted Victoria Cross, few of which (including three bars) have been awarded since its inception. VCs won during the Crimean War (111 awarded) are usually less highly regarded than Crosses awarded during the First World War, where, although numerically greater (633) they were far more dearly won. Second World War Crosses are correspondingly more expensive as only 182 were awarded and even now comparatively few of them have ever come on to the market. Today, while pre-1914 Crosses would rate at least £100,000 and those from the First World War slightly more, Second World War Crosses start around £150,000 but have been known to fetch several times as much, depending on the precise circumstances and the branch of the services.

At the other extreme is the Military Medal, of which no fewer than 115,589 were awarded during the First World War alone. For this reason a MM from this period can still be picked up for under £600, whereas one from the Second World War would usually fetch about four times as much, and awards made during the minor campaigns of the 1930s or the Korean War often rate at least ten times as much.

The value of a decoration, where its provenance can be unquestionably established, depends largely on the decoration itself, whether awarded to an officer or an enlisted man, the individual circumstances of the award, the campaign or action concerned, the regiment, unit or ship involved, and the often very personal details of the act or acts of bravery. These factors are extraordinarily difficult to quantify, hence the frequent large discrepancies in the prices fetched by decorations at auction.

The addition of even relatively common decorations, such as the Military Cross or the Military Medal to the average First World War campaign medal group, invariably enhances its value very considerably while the addition of bars for subsequent awards likewise rates a good premium. Decorations awarded to officers tend to fetch more than those awarded to other ranks, mainly because they are proportionately rarer but also because it is usually easier to trace the career details of an officer.

Sometimes the rank of the recipient may have a bearing on the demand for a particular decoration: e.g. Military Crosses awarded to warrant officers are scarcer than those awarded to subalterns and captains. The branch of the armed services may also have some bearing. Thus a Military Medal awarded to a member of the RAF rates far higher than one awarded to a soldier, while a medal awarded to a seaman in one of the naval battalions which fought on the Western Front is also equally desirable.

Initially the Distinguished Service Order could be won by commissioned officers of any rank but after 1914, when the Military Cross was instituted, it was usually restricted to officers of field rank. DSOs awarded to lieutenants and captains in the Army in both World Wars are therefore comparatively rare and invariably expensive, usually as they were awarded for acts of heroism which in earlier campaigns might have merited the VC. As part of the 1993 review of awards, the Conspicuous Gallantry Coss (CGC) replaced the DCM and CGM to remove the distinction between officers and other ranks.

The opportunity for individual acts of bravery varied from service to service, and in different conflicts. Thus sailors in the Second World War generally had less scope than air crew. Consequently specifically naval awards, such as the Conspicuous Gallantry Medal and the Distinguished Service Cross, are much more scarce than the corresponding RAF awards for Conspicuous Gallantry and the Distinguished Flying Cross.

The addition of bars to gallantry decorations greatly enhances the scarcity and value of such medals. The VC, for example, has been won by only three men on two occasions; none of these VC and bar combinations has ever come on the market, but should one come up for sale, it is certain that the price would be spectacular. The average First World War MM is today worth around £500, but with a bar for second award its value immediately jumps to about three times as much, while MMs with two or more bars are very much more expensive.

It is important to note that in some cases (the DSO for example) decorations were issued unnamed; for this reason the citation or any other supporting documents relevant to the award should be kept with the decoration wherever possible to confirm its attribution.

Engraving of Gallantry Decorations

After the special investiture for the South Atlantic campaign held on February 8, 1983, the question as to why certain awards were engraved with the date only was raised within the Ministry of Defence. A joint service working party considered the matter and recommended that procedures for all decorations and medals for gallantry in the face of the enemy and for the Air Force Cross when awarded for a specific act of gallantry should be brought into line. A submission was accordingly made to the late Queen by the Committee on the Grant of Honours, Decorations and Medals and in April 1984 Her Majesty approved the following:

(i) That the Distinguished Service Cross, Military Cross, Distinguished Flying Cross and Air Force Cross when awarded for gallantry should be engraved with the personal details of the recipient with effect from January 1, 1984.

(ii) That there should be no retrospection;

(iii) That the badge of a Companion of the Distinguished Service Order should not be engraved (in common with the badges of other orders); and

(iv) That the Royal Red Cross (RRC and ARRC) and the Air Force Cross when awarded for meritorious service should not be engraved.

Condition

The same terms are applied to describe the condition of medals and decorations as apply to coins, although the wear to which they are put is caused by other factors. In modern times, when the number of occasions on which medals are worn are relatively few and far between, the condition of most items will be found to be Very Fine (VF) to Extremely Fine (EF). Indeed, in many cases, the medals may never have been worn at all. A good proportion of Second World War medals and decorations are found in almost mint condition as they were not issued till long after the war, by which time their recipients had been demobilised. In some cases they even turn up still in the original cardboard box in which they were posted to the recipients or their next-of-kin.

Before the First World War, however, the wearing of medals was customary on all but the most informal occasions and when actually serving on active duty. Thus medals could be, and often were, subject to a great deal of wear. Medals worn by cavalrymen are often found in poor condition, with scratches and edge knocks occasioned by the constant jangling of one medal against another while on horseback. Often the medals in a group have an abrasive effect on each other. For this reason the Queen's Medal for Egypt (1882) for example, is comparatively rare in excellent condition, as it was usually worn in juxtaposition to the bronze Khedive's Star whose points were capable of doing considerable damage to its silver companion.

Apart from these factors it should also be remembered that part of the ritual of "spit and polish" involved cleaning one's medals and they were therefore submitted to vigorous cleaning with metal polish over long periods of service.

For these reasons medals are often sold by dealers "as worn"—a euphemism which conceals a lifetime of hardy service on the chest of some grizzled veteran. Because of the strong personal element involved in medal-collecting, however, genuine wear does not affect the value of a medal to the same degree that it would in other branches of numismatics. There is a school of thought which considers that such signs enhance the interest and value of a medal or group.

This line of thinking also explains the controversy over medal ribbons. Some military outfitters still carry extensive stocks of medal ribbons covering every campaign from Waterloo onwards, so that it is a very easy matter to obtain a fresh length of ribbon for any medal requiring it, and there is no doubt that the appearance of a piece is greatly improved by a clean, bright new ribbon. On the other hand, that ribbon was not the one actually worn by Corporal Bloggs on parade and, to the purist, it would spoil the total effect of the medal. Some collectors therefore retain the original ribbon, even though it may be faded and frayed. As ribbons are things which one cannot authenticate, however, there seems to be little material benefit to be gained from clinging rigidly to a tattered strip of silk when an identical piece can be obtained relatively cheaply. In reality, most collectors compromise by obtaining new ribbons while preserving the old lengths out of sentiment.

The prices quoted in this publication are average figures for medals and decorations as individual items. Combinations with other decorations and campaign medals will produce a value usually well in excess of the aggregate of the individual items. Value will depend to a large extent on the personal factors and circumstances of the award, but where general factors are involved (e.g. the design of the medal, the period of issue or the campaign concerned, or in some cases the branch of the services) these are itemised separately. "—" indicates that either no examples have come onto the market or no examples have been issued. The figure in brackets (where available) is the approximate number awarded. In the lists which follow, it should be assumed that decorations were instituted by Royal Warrant, unless otherwise stated.

SELLING YOUR MEDALS?

Warwick and Warwick have an expanding requirement for medal collections, medal groups and related documentation and individual medals of value. Our customer base is increasing dramatically and we need an ever larger supply of quality material to keep pace with demand. The market has never been stronger and if you are considering the sale of your medals, now is the time to act.

FREE VALUATIONS
We will provide a free, professional and without obligation valuation of your collection. Either we will make you a fair, binding private treaty offer, or we will recommend inclusion of your property in our next specialist public auction.

FREE TRANSPORTATION
We can arrange insured transportation of your collection to our Warwick offices completely free of charge. If you decline our offer, we ask you to cover the return carriage costs only.

FREE VISITS
Visits by our valuers are possible anywhere in the country, usually within 48 hours, in order to value larger collections. Please telephone for details.

EXCELLENT PRICES
Because of the strength of our customer base we are in a position to offer prices that we feel sure will exceed your expectations.

ACT NOW
Telephone or email Richard Beale today with details of your property.

ONLINE BIDDING
Available via www.easyliveauction.com.

24. THE VICTORIA CROSS

Naval ribbon pre-1918.

Naval, Army and RAF ribbon since 1918.

Instituted: January 1856.

Ribbon: Crimson. Originally naval crosses used a dark blue ribbon, but since 1918 the crimson (Army) ribbon has been used for all awards. A miniature cross emblem is worn on the ribbon alone in undress uniform.

Metal: Bronze, originally from Russian guns captured in the Crimea. Modern research, however, reveals that guns captured in other conflicts, e.g. China, have also been used at various periods.

Size: Height 41mm; max. width 36mm.

Description: A cross pattée. (Obverse) a lion statant gardant on the royal crown, with the words FOR VALOUR on a semi-circular scroll. (Reverse) a circular panel on which is engraved the date of the act for which the decoration was awarded. The Cross is suspended by a ring from a seriffed "V" attached to a suspension bar decorated with laurel leaves. The reverse of the suspension bar is engraved with the name, rank and ship, regiment or squadron of the recipient.

Comments: *Introduced as the premier award for gallantry, available for all ranks, to cover all actions since the outbreak of the Crimean War in 1854, it was allegedly created on the suggestion of Prince Albert, the Prince Consort. Of the 1,358 awards since 1856, 836 have gone to the Army, 107 to the Navy, 31 to the RAF, ten to the Royal Marines and four to civilians. Second award bars have been awarded three times. The facility for posthumous awards, made retrospective to 1856, began in 1902 and was confirmed in 1907, while the early practice of forfeitures (eight between 1863 and 1908) was discontinued after the First World War. Two posthumous awards were made in the Falklands War, 1982. In 2005 Private Johnson Beharry was awarded the VC for valour in Iraq, and since then two posthumous awards have been made for Afghanistan: Corporal Bryan Budd in 2006 and Lance Corporal James Ashworth in 2012. The latest award is to L/Cpl Joshua Leakey of the Parachute Regiment (LG February 26, 2015) also for Afghanistan. In 2015 the Government increased the annuity paid to £10,000, tax free.*

VALUE:

	Royal Navy/Army	RFC/RAF	Miniature
1856–1914 (522)	From £150,000	—	£50–80
1914–18 (633)	From £175,000	From £200,000	£20–35
1920–45 (187)	From £200,000	From £250,000	£20–35
post-1945 (15)	From £250,000	—	£10–20

NB: These prices can only be construed as a general guide. Quite a few awards would exceed these price ranges, particularly Commonwealth examples or those appertaining to well known actions. A new world-record price for a VC sold at auction was achieved by Noonans auctioneers in September 2022 when a "civilian" VC awarded to Thomas Kavanagh secured £750,000 (£930,000 total).

25. NEW ZEALAND CROSS

Instituted: 10 March 1869 (by an Order in Council, Wellington).

Ribbon: 38mm crimson. A silver miniature cross emblem is worn on the ribbon alone.

Metal: Silver with gold appliqué.

Size: Height 52mm; max. width 38mm.

Description: A silver cross pattée with a six-pointed gold star on each limb. In the centre are the words NEW ZEALAND within a gold laurel wreath. The cross is surmounted by a gold Tudor crown which is attached by a ring and a seriffed "V" to a silver bar ornamented with gold laurel leaves, through which the ribbon passes. The recipient's name and details are engraved on the reverse.

Comments: *The rarest of all gallantry awards, it was conferred for bravery during the second series of Maori Wars (1860-72). Only 23 Crosses were awarded, the last being authorised in 1910. This medal was called into being solely because local volunteer forces were not eligible for the VC. Today the Cross, with slight amendments to the design, is New Zealand's premier civilian award for bravery (see NZ2).*

VALUE:	From £75,000	
	Official Specimen	£3000–4000
	Modern copy	£650–750
	Miniature	
	Contemporary	£750–1000
	Modern copy	£20–25

26. GEORGE CROSS

Instituted: 24 September 1940.

Ribbon: 38mm dark blue (originally 32mm). A silver miniature cross emblem is worn on the ribbon alone.

Metal: Silver.

Size: Height 49.75mm; max. width 45.85mm.

Description: A plain bordered cross with a circular medallion in the centre depicting the effigy of St George and the Dragon after Benedetto Pistrucci, surrounded by the words FOR GALLANTRY. In the angle of each limb is the Royal cypher GVI. The plain reverse bears in the centre the name of the recipient and date of the award. In the case of exchange awards, the date of the deed is given. The Cross hangs by a ring from a bar adorned with laurel leaves.

Comments: *The highest gallantry award for civilians, as well as for members of the armed forces in actions for which purely military honours would not normally be granted. It superseded the Empire Gallantry Medal whose holders were then required to return it and receive the GC in exchange. By Warrant of December 1971 surviving recipients of the Albert and Edward Medals were also invited to exchange their awards for the GC. Perhaps the most famous Cross was that conferred on the island of Malta in recognition of its gallantry during the Second World War. To date no second award bars have been awarded. Since its inception in 1940 the George Cross has been awarded 165 times, including four women (85 of these have been posthumous). In addition, 112 Empire Gallantry medallists, 69 Albert medallists and 70 Edward medallists who were eligible to exchange their awards for the GC have increased the total to 416. This also includes the collective award to the Royal Ulster Constabulary, presented by Her late Majesty Queen Elizabeth II at Hillsborough Castle on April 12, 2000. On July 5, 2021, the 73rd anniversary of its founding, the National Health Service was awarded a collective GC in recognition of its service to the country, particularly during the Covid pandemic. Arthur Bywater (who died in April 2005) was the only civilian to win both the GC and the GM but seven servicemen have won both. In 2015 the Government increased the annuity to £10,000.*

VALUE:

Service awards 1940 to date	From £30,000	*Miniature* **£15–20** (*in silver add £10*)
Civilian awards 1940 to date	From £25,000	
Service exchange pre-1940	From £12,000	
Civilian exchange pre-1940	From £12,000	

27. DISTINGUISHED SERVICE ORDER

Instituted: 1886.

Ribbon: 29mm crimson with dark blue edges.

Metal: Originally gold; silver-gilt with 18 carat gold centre since 1889.

Size: Height 44mm; max. width 41.5mm.

Description: A cross with curved ends, overlaid with white enamel. (Obverse) a green enamel laurel wreath enclosing an imperial crown on a red enamel background; (reverse) the royal monogram within a similar wreath. The ribbon is hung from a top laureated bar and the cross is suspended from the ribbon by a swivel ring and another straight laureated bar. Additional awards are denoted by bars ornamented by a crown. Silver rosettes on the ribbon alone are worn in undress uniform. Since its inception, the DSO has been issued unnamed, but since 1938 the year of award has been engraved on the reverse of the lower suspension bar as well as the reverse of the bars for second or subsequent awards.

Second ward bar

Comments: *Intended to reward commissioned officers below field rank for distinguished service in time of war, and for which the VC would not be appropriate. Previously the CB had sometimes been awarded to junior officers, although intended mainly for those of field rank. It was also available to officers in both the other armed services. In September 1942 the regulations were amended to permit award of the DSO to officers of the Merchant Navy who performed acts of gallantry in the presence of the enemy. As a result of the 1993 Review of gallantry awards and resultant changes to the operational gallantry award system, the DSO is now awarded for "Leadership"— theoretically to all ranks (it is not awarded posthumously). The Conspicuous Gallantry Cross is now the equivalent reward for specific acts of gallantry.*

VALUE:

	Unnamed single	Attributable group	*Miniature*
Victoria, gold (153)	£4500–6000	From £8500	£100–150
Victoria, silver-gilt (18ct gold centre) (1170)	£1500–2000	From £3500	£60–80
Edward VII (78)	£2000–2500	From £5500	£85–150 (gold)
George V (9900)	£1000–1500	From £2000	£45 (gilt), £120 (gold)
George VI 1st type 1938–48 (4880)	£1500–2000	From £3500	£45–65 (gilt)
George VI 2nd type 1948–52 (63)	£2000–2500	From £5500	£45–65 (gilt)
Elizabeth II	£3000–3500	From £6500	£65–75 (gilt)

28. IMPERIAL SERVICE ORDER

Instituted: August 1902.

Ribbon: 38mm, three equal sections of crimson, blue and crimson.

Metal: Silver with gold overlay.

Size: Height 61mm; max. width 55mm.

Description: The badge consists of a circular gold plaque bearing the royal cypher and surrounded by the words FOR FAITHFUL SERVICE. This plaque is then superimposed on a seven-pointed silver star surmounted by a crown and ring for suspension. The badge of the ISO awarded to women is similar but has a laurel wreath instead of the star-shaped base.

Comments: *Instituted by King Edward VII as a means of rewarding long and faithful service in the Administrative and Clerical grades of the Civil Service at home and overseas. Women were admitted to the order in 1908. The order was awarded after at least 25 years service at home, 20 years and 6 months (India) and 16 years in the tropics, but in exceptional cases awards were made for "eminently meritorious service" irrespective of qualifying period. No UK awards have been made since 1995 but some Commonwealth awards continue to this day. The George VI issue comes in two types: the early ones with GRI cypher and the later GVIR.*

VALUE:

			Miniature
Edward VII	Gentleman (489)	£350–450	£25–30
	Lady (4)	£2500–3000	£200–300
George V	Gentleman (909)	£350–400	£20–25
	Lady (2)	£2500–3000	£200–300
George VI (608 Gentleman and 8 Lady)			
1st type	Gentleman	£350–450	£15–20
	Lady	£1500–2000	£200–300
2nd type	Gentleman	£350–450	£15–20
	Lady	£1500–2000	£200–300
Elizabeth II	Gentleman (2,153)*	£300–350	£10–15
	Lady (114)*	£1000–1500	£150–200

29. IMPERIAL SERVICE MEDAL

Instituted: August 1902.
Ribbon: 38mm, three equal sections of crimson, blue and crimson
Metal: Silver and bronze.
Size: 32mm
Description: Originally similar to the ISO but with a silver plaque and bronze star or wreath. In 1920 the ISM was transformed into a circular medal of silver with the sovereign's effigy on the obverse and a reverse depicting a naked man resting from his labours, with FOR FAITHFUL SERVICE in the exergue.
Comments: *Instituted at the same time as the ISO but intended for junior grades of the Civil Service.*

VALUE:		Miniature
Edward VII, 1903–10 (c. 4,500)		
Star (Gentleman)	£85–150	£15–20
Wreath (Lady)	£500–600	£200–300
George V, 1911-20 (c. 6,000)		
Star (Gentleman)	£85–1505	£12–15
Wreath (Lady)	£500–600	£200–300
George V Circular type		
Coinage profile, 1920–31 (c. 20,000)	£35–45	£10–15
Crowned bust, 1931–37 (c. 16,000)	£35–45	£10–15
George VI		
Crowned bust INDIAE:IMP, 1938–48 (c. 36,000)	£35–45	£10–15
Crowned bust FID:DEF, 1949–52 (c. 16,000)	£35–45	£10–15
Elizabeth II		
Tudor crown BRITT:OMN, 1953–54 (c. 9,000)	£30–35	£15–20
Tudor crown DEI:GRATIA, 1955– (c. 150,000)	£25–35	£15–20

30. INDIAN ORDER OF MERIT

Military

Civil

Instituted: 1837 (by the Honourable East India Company).
Ribbon: Dark blue with crimson edges (military) or crimson with dark blue edges (civil).
Metal: Silver and gold.
Size: Height 41mm; max. width 40mm.
Description: An eight-pointed star with a circular centre surrounded by a laurel wreath and containing crossed sabres and the relevant inscription. The star is suspended by a curvilinear suspension bar. The different classes were denoted by the composition of the star, noted below.
Comments: *The oldest gallantry award of the British Empire, it was founded in 1837 by the Honourable East India Company. Twenty years later it became an official British award when the administration of India passed to the Crown after the Sepoy Mutiny. Originally known simply as the Order of Merit, it was renamed in 1902 following the introduction of the prestigious British order of that name. There were three classes of the order, promotion from one class to the next being the reward for further acts of bravery. A civil division (also in three classes) was introduced in 1902. Ten years later the military division was reduced to two classes, when troops of the Indian Army became eligible for the VC. The civil division became a single class in 1939 and the military in 1945. Both divisions came to an end with the British Raj in 1947.*

VALUE:
Military Division
1837–1912 Reward of Valour

1st class in gold (42)	£6500–8500
2nd class in silver and gold (130)	£3500–4500
3rd class in silver (2740)	£1250–1750

1912–39 Reward of Valour

1st class in silver and gold (26)	£5000–6500
2nd class in silver (1215)	£500–750

continued

30. INDIAN ORDER OF MERIT continued

Reverse

1939-44 Reward of Gallantry		
1st class in silver and gold (2)		Rare
2nd class in silver (332)		£1000–1500
1945-47 Reward of Gallantry (44mm diameter)		£1850–2750
Civil Division		
1902-39 For Bravery (35mm diameter)		
1st class in gold (0)		—
2nd class in silver and gold (0)		—
3rd class in silver (39)		£1500–1850
1939-47 For Bravery (26mm diameter)		
Single class (10)		£3500–4500
Miniature		£150–250

NB *These prices represent unattributable pieces. Values can climb rapidly when in company with related campaign medals, particularly for the Victorian era.*

30A. CONSPICUOUS GALLANTRY CROSS

Instituted: October 1993.
Ribbon: White with blue edges and a red central stripe.
Metal: Silver.
Size: Max. width 44.3mm.
Description: A cross pattée imposed on a wreath of laurel, with the royal crown in a circular panel in the centre. Suspended by a ring from a plain suspension bar.
Comments: *As part of the decision to remove distinctions of rank in awards for bravery, this decoration replaced the DSO for specific acts of gallantry as well as the Conspicuous Gallantry Medal and the Distinguished Conduct Medal. It was first awarded in 1995 to Corporal Wayne Mills of the Duke of Wellington's Regiment and in 1996 to Colour Sergeant Peter Humphreys of the Royal Welch Fusiliers, both for gallantry in action during service with the UN Peacekeeping Forces in Bosnia. Two awards were made in respect of gallantry by members of the SAS and SBS in Sierra Leone in May–June 2000. A further two awards were made to members of the SAS and two awards to members of the SBS in Afghanistan in October 2001–March 2002, while awards to Justin Thomas, RM, and Lance Corporal Michael Flynn, Blues and Royals, both for gallantry in Iraq, were gazetted in October 2003, and that to Sqdn Ldr I. J. McKechnie, Royal Air Force, was gazetted on 9 September 2005, making a total of 11 in the first decade. Since then other awards have been made, including a collective award to the Royal Irish Regiment (retroactively to one of its forebears the Ulster Defence Regiment), which appeared in the LG Supplement, December 18, 2006, and three posthumous awards.*

VALUE: From £65,000   *Miniature* £20–25

31. ROYAL RED CROSS

First Class obverse

Second award bar

Instituted: 27 April 1883.

Ribbon: 25mm dark blue edged with crimson, in a bow.

Metal: Gold (later silver-gilt) and silver.

Size: Height 41mm; max. width 35mm.

Description: (Obverse) The *1st class* badge was originally a gold cross pattée, enamelled red with gold edges, but from 1889 silver-gilt was substituted for gold. At the centre was a crowned and veiled portrait, with the words FAITH, HOPE and CHARITY inscribed on three arms, and the date 1883 on the lower arm. Subsequently the effigy of the reigning monarch was substituted for the allegorical profile; (reverse) crowned royal cypher. *2nd Class:* in silver, design as the 1st class but the inscriptions on the arms appear on the reverse. Awards from 1938 have the year of issue engraved on the reverse of the lower arm.

Comments: *This decoration had the distinction of being confined to females until 1976. It is conferred on members of the nursing services regardless of rank. A second class award was introduced in November 1915. Bars for the first class were introduced in 1917. Holders of the second class are promoted to the first class on second awards. Holders of the first class decoration are known as Members (RRC) while recipients of the second class are Associates (ARRC). The second type GVI award is surprisingly scarce as only 50 first class and 100 second class were awarded.*

VALUE:

	First class (RRC)	Miniature	Second class (ARRC)	Miniature
Victoria, gold	£1250–1850	£100–150	—	—
Victoria, silver-gilt	£500–600	£60–70	—	—
Edward VII	£800–1000	£100–120	—	—
George V	£300–350	£25–35	£150–175	£12–25
George V, with bar	£450–550	£50–60	—	
George VI GRI	£300–350	£25–35	£220–250	£12–25
George VI GVIR	£350–450	£25–35	£250–300	£12–25
Elizabeth II	£300–350	£25–35	£200–250	£35–45

32. DISTINGUISHED SERVICE CROSS

Second award bar

Instituted: June 1901.

Ribbon: 36mm three equal parts of dark blue, white and dark blue.

Metal: Silver.

Size: Height 43mm; max. width 43mm.

Description: A plain cross with rounded ends. (Obverse) crowned royal cypher in the centre, suspended by a ring; (reverse) plain apart from the hallmark. From 1940 onwards the year of issue was engraved on the reverse of the lower limb.

Comments: *Known as the Conspicuous Service Cross when instituted, it was awarded to warrant and subordinate officers of the Royal Navy who were ineligible for the DSO. Only 8 EVII issued. In October 1914 it was renamed the Distinguished Service Cross and thrown open to all naval officers below the rank of lieutenant-commander. Bars for subsequent awards were authorised in 1916 and in 1931 eligibility for the award was enlarged to include officers of the Merchant Navy. In 1940 Army and RAF officers serving aboard naval vessels also became eligible for the award. Since 1945 fewer than 100 DSCs have been awarded. As a result of the 1993 Review of gallantry awards and resultant changes to the operational gallantry award system, this award is now available to both officers and other ranks, the DSM having been discontinued. Since 1 January 1984 the award has been issued named.*

VALUE:

	Unnamed single	Attributable group	Miniature
Edward VII	—	From £25,000	£200–250
George V	£1000–1500	From £2500	£25–35
George VI GRI	£1000–1500	From £2000	£15–25
George VI GVIR	—	From £3000	£25–35
Elizabeth II	—	From £7500	£15–25

33. MILITARY CROSS

Instituted: 31 December 1914.

Ribbon: 34mm three equal stripes of white, deep purple and white.

Metal: Silver.

Size: Height 46mm; max. width 44mm.

Description: An ornamental cross with straight arms terminating in broad finials decorated with imperial crowns. The royal cypher appears at the centre and the cross is suspended from a plain silver suspension bar.

Comments: *There was no gallantry award, lesser than the VC and DSO, for junior Army officers and warrant officers until shortly after the outbreak of the First World War when the MC was instituted. Originally awarded to captains, lieutenants and warrant officers of the Army (including RFC), it was subsequently extended to include equivalent ranks of the RAF when performing acts of bravery on the ground and there was even provision for the Royal Naval Division and the Royal Marines during the First World War. Awards were extended to majors by an amending warrant of 1931. Bars for second and subsequent awards have a crown at the centre. The MC is always issued unnamed, although since 1937 the reverse of the cross or bar is officially dated with the year of issue. As a result of the 1993 Review of gallantry awards and resultant changes to the operational gallantry award system, this award is now available to both officers and other ranks, the Military Medal having been discontinued. Since 1 January 1984 the award has been issued named.*

Second award bar

VALUE:	Unnamed single	Attributable group	*Miniature*
George V 1914–20 (37,000)	£600–750	From £1000	£25–30
one bar (3000)	—	From £1500	
two bars (170)	—	From £3500	
three bars (4)	—	From £8500	
George V 1921–36 (350)	—	From £2000	
one bar (31)	—	From £3000	
George VI GRI 1937–46 (11,000)	£700–750	From £1500	£25–30
one bar (500)	£1000–2000	From £3500	
George VI GVIR (158)	—	From £3500	£30–35
Elizabeth II	£850–1000	From £8000	£20–25

34. DISTINGUISHED FLYING CROSS

Instituted: June 1918.

Ribbon: 30mm originally horizontal but since June 1919 diagonal alternate stripes of white and deep purple.

Metal: Silver.

Size: Height 60mm; max. width 54mm.

Description: (Obverse) a cross flory terminating with a rose, surmounted by another cross made of propeller blades charged in the centre with a roundel within a laurel wreath. The horizontal arms bear wings and the crowned RAF monogram at the centre; (reverse) the royal cypher above the date 1918. The cross is suspended from a bar decorated with a sprig of laurel.

Comments: *Established for officers and warrant officers of the RAF in respect of acts of valour while flying in active operations against the enemy. The DFC is issued unnamed, but Second World War crosses usually have the year of issue engraved on the reverse of the lower limb. After WWII it was expanded to include aviation officers of other services. As a result of the 1993 Review of gallantry awards and resultant changes to the operational gallantry award system, this award is now available to both officers and other ranks, the Distinguished Flying Medal having been discontinued. Since 1 January 1984 the award has been issued named.*

Second award bar

Original ribbon.

Post-1919 ribbon.

VALUE:	Unnamed single	Attributable group	*Miniature*
George V 1918–20 (1100)	£2000–2500	From £3500	£25–35
one bar (70)	£2000–3000	From £6500	
two bars (3)	—	—	
George V 1920–36 (130)	—	—	
one bar (20)	—	—	
two bars (4)	—	—	
George VI GRI 1939–45 (20,000)	£2000–2500	From £4000	£25–35
one bar (1550)	£2500–3500	From £5000	
two bars (42)	—	—	
George VI GVIR 1948–52 (65)	—	—	£30–45
Elizabeth II	£2000–2500	From £6500	£20–25

(in silver add £5)

35. AIR FORCE CROSS

Instituted: June 1918.

Ribbon: 30mm originally horizontal but since June 1919 diagonal alternate stripes of white and crimson.

Metal: Silver.

Size: Height 60mm; max. width 54mm.

Description: (Obverse) the cross consists of a thunderbolt, the arms conjoined by wings, base bar terminating in a bomb, surmounted by another cross of aeroplane propellers, the finials inscribed with the royal cypher. A central roundel depicts Hermes mounted on a hawk bestowing a wreath; (reverse) the royal cypher and the date 1918.

Comments: *This decoration, awarded to officers and warrant officers of the RAF was instituted in June 1918 for gallantry on non-operational missions and for meritorious service on flying duties. After WWII it was expanded to include aviation officers of other services. Since the 1993 Review of gallantry awards it is now available to all ranks for non-operational gallantry in the air only (no longer for meritorious service also). Since 1 January 1984 the award has been issued named.*

Second award bar

Original ribbon.

Post-1919 ribbon.

VALUE:

	Unnamed single	Attributable group	Miniature
George V 1918-20 (678)	£1000–1250	From £2500	£25–35
one bar (12)	—	—	
two bars (3)	—	—	
George V 1920-36 (111)	£1500–2000	From £2500	
George VI GRI (2605)	£1250–2000	From £2500	£25–35
one bar (36)	£2000–2500	From £3500	
two bars (1)	—	—	
George VI GVIR (411)	£1000–1250	From £2000	£35–45
Elizabeth II	£1500–1750	From £2500	£20–25

(in silver add £5)

36. ORDER OF BRITISH INDIA

Instituted: 1837 by the Honourable East India Company.

Ribbon: Worn around the neck, the base colour of the ribbon was originally sky blue but this was altered to crimson in 1838, allegedly because the hair oil favoured by Indians of all classes would soon have soiled a light ribbon. From 1939 onwards the first class ribbon had two thin vertical lines of light blue at the centre, while the second class ribbon had a single vertical line. Originally these distinctive ribbons were only worn in undress uniform (without the insignia itself), but from 1945 they replaced the plain crimson ribbons when worn with the decoration.

Metal: Gold.

Size: Height 42mm; max. width 38mm.

Description: The first class badge consists of a gold star with a crown between the upper two points and a blue enamelled centre bearing a lion surrounded by the words ORDER OF BRITISH INDIA enclosed in a laurel wreath. The second class badge is smaller, with dark blue enamel in the centre and with no crown.

Comments: *Intended for long and faithful service by native officers of the Indian Army, it was thrown open in 1939 to officers of the armed forces, frontier guards, military police and officers of the Indian native states. There were two classes, promotion to the first being made from the second. Recipients of both classes were entitled to the letters OBI after their names, but holders of the first class had the rank of Sardar Bahadur, while those of the second were merely Bahadur. A few awards were made by Pakistan to British officers seconded to the Pakistani forces at the time of independence.*

Original ribbon.

1838 ribbon.

1st class, post-1939 ribbon.

2nd class, post-1939 ribbon.

VALUE:

		Miniature
1st class, light blue centre and dark blue surround	£1750–2000	£200–250
1st class, sky blue centre and surround (1939)	£1450–1750	£200–250
2nd class	£1250–1450	£200–250

NB The prices quoted are for unattributable awards.

37. ORDER OF BURMA

Instituted 1940.
Ribbon: 38mm dark green with light blue edges.
Metal: Gold.
Size: Height 52mm; max. width 38mm.
Description: The badge consists of a gold-rayed circle with a central roundel charged with a peacock in his pride azure, surmounted by an imperial crown.
Comments: *Instituted by King George VI, three years after Burma became independent of British India. Only 24 awards were made, to Governor's Commissioned Officers for long, faithful and honourable service in the army, frontier force and military police of Burma. By an amendment of 1945 the order could also be awarded for individual acts of heroism or particularly meritorious service. It was abolished in 1947.*

VALUE: £4500–5500   *Not known in miniature*

38. KAISAR-I-HIND MEDAL

Victoria obv.   *Victoria rev.*

Instituted: May 1900.
Ribbon: 37mm bluish green.
Metal: Gold, silver or bronze.
Size: Height 61mm; max. width 34mm.
Description: An oval badge surmounted by the imperial crown. (Obverse) the royal cypher set within a wreath; (reverse) FOR PUBLIC SERVICE IN INDIA round the edge and KAISAR-I-HIND (Emperor of India) on a scroll across the centre against a floral background.
Comments: *Queen Victoria founded this medal for award to those, regardless of colour, creed or sex, who had performed public service in India. Originally in two classes George V introduced a 3rd Class in bronze. The medals were originally large and hollow but were changed to smaller in diameter and solid during the reign of George V.*

Second award bar

VALUE:	1st class (gold)	Miniature	2nd class (silver)	Miniature	3rd class (bronze)	Miniature
Victoria	£2000–2500	£175–250	£450–500	£85–100	—	
Edward VII	£2000–2500	£175–250	£350–475	£85–100	—	
George V 1st	£1850–2250	£125–175	£350–475	£35–50	—	
George V 2nd	£1500–2000	£100–150	£300–450	£35–50	£150–175	£25–30
George VI	£1500–2000	£150–200	£350–475	£50–80	£150–175	£25–30

39. ALBERT MEDAL

2nd class land service medal.

2nd class land and sea service ribbons (until 1904).

1st class land service ribbon.

2nd class land service ribbon.
See also ribbon chart

Instituted: 7 March 1866.

Ribbons:

Gold (1st Class) Sea	*Gold (1st Class) Land*
16mm blue with two white stripes (1866)	35mm red with four white stripes (1877–1949)
35mm blue with four white stripes (1867–1949)	
Bronze (2nd Class) Sea	*Bronze (2nd Class) Land*
16mm blue with two white stripes (1867–1904)	16mm red with two white stripes (1877–1904)
35mm blue with two white stripes (1904–71)	35mm red with two white stripes (1904–71)

Metal: Gold (early issues gold and bronze); bronze.

Size: Height 57mm; max. width 30mm.

Description: The badge consists of an oval enclosing the entwined initials V and A. The sea medals have, in addition, an anchor. The oval is enclosed by a bronze garter with the words FOR GALLANTRY IN SAVING LIFE, with AT SEA or ON LAND as appropriate, and enamelled in blue or crimson respectively. The whole is surmounted by a crown pierced by a ring for suspension. The first class medal was originally worked in gold and bronze and later in gold alone, the second class in bronze alone.

Comments: *Named in memory of the Prince Consort who died in 1861, this series of medals was instituted for gallantry in saving life at sea. An amendment of 1867 created two classes of medal and ten years later awards were extended to gallantry in saving life on land. In 1917 the title of the awards was altered, the first class becoming the Albert Medal in Gold and the second class merely the Albert Medal. It was last awarded in gold to a living recipient in April 1943, the last posthumous award being in May 1945. The last bronze medal awarded to a living recipient was in January 1949, and posthumous in August 1970. In 1949 the Medal in Gold was abolished and replaced by the George Cross and henceforward the Albert Medal (second class) was only awarded posthumously. In 1971 the award of the medal ceased and holders were invited to exchange their medals for the George Cross. Of the 69 eligible to exchange, 49 did so. In recent months (2019) the prices for the AM have softened a little as a large private collection came on to the market.*

VALUE:

	Civilian	Service	Miniature
Gold Sea (25)	From £12,000	From £15,000	£75–100*
Bronze Sea (211)	From £8,000	From £10,000	£50–75
Gold Land (45)	From £12,000	From £15,000	£75–100*
Bronze Land (290)	From £8,000	From £10,000	£50–75

*assumed gilt

40. UNION OF SOUTH AFRICA KING'S/ QUEEN'S MEDAL FOR BRAVERY (WOLTEMADE MEDAL)

Instituted: 1939 by the Government of the Union of South Africa.

Ribbon: Royal blue with narrow orange edges.

Metal: Gold or silver.

Size: 37mm.

Description: (Obverse) an effigy of the reigning sovereign; (reverse) a celebrated act of heroism by Wolraad Woltemade who rescued sailors from the wreck of the East Indiaman *De Jong Thomas* which ran aground in Table Bay on 17 June 1773. Seven times Woltemade rode into the raging surf to save fourteen seamen from drowning, but on the eighth attempt both rider and horse perished.

Comments: *This medal was awarded to citizens of the Union of South Africa and dependent territories who endangered their lives in saving the lives of others. It was awarded very sparingly, in gold or silver.*

VALUE:

		Miniature
George VI Gold (1)	—	£250–300
George VI Silver (34)	£2000–3000	£150–200
Elizabeth II Silver (1)	—	£150–200

41. DISTINGUISHED CONDUCT MEDAL

1st type obv.

Instituted: 1854.
Ribbon: 32mm crimson with a dark blue central stripe.
Metal: Silver.
Size: 36mm.
Description: (Obverse) originally a trophy of arms but, since 1902, the effigy of the reigning sovereign; (reverse) a four-line inscription across the field FOR DISTINGUISHED CONDUCT IN THE FIELD.
Comments: *The need for a gallantry medal for other ranks was first recognised during the Crimean War, although previously the Meritorious Service Medal (qv) had very occasionally been awarded for gallantry in the field. The medals have always been issued named, and carry the number, rank and name of the recipient on the rim, together with the date of the act of gallantry from 1881 until about 1901. Bars are given for subsequent awards and these too were dated from the first issued in 1881 until 1916 when the more usual laurelled bars were adopted. Since 1916 it has ranked as a superior decoration to the Military Medal. As a result of the 1993 Review of gallantry awards and resultant changes to the operational gallantry award system, the decoration has been replaced by the Conspicuous Gallantry Cross.*

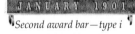

Second award bar—type i

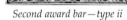

Second award bar—type ii

VALUE*:

Crimea (800)	From £3500
Indian Mutiny (17)	From £7000
India general service 1854–95	From £4000
Abyssinia 1867–68 (7)	From £6500
Ashantee 1873–64 (33)	From £5500
Zulu War 1877–79 (16)	From £10,000
Afghanistan 1878–80 (61)	From £4500
First Boer War 1880–81 (20)	From £9000
Egypt & Sudan 1882–89 (134)	From £5000
India 1895–1901	From £5000
Sudan 1896–97	From £4500
Second Boer War 1899–1902 (2090)	From £1500
Boxer Rebellion 1900	From £8000
Edward VII	Many rarities
George V 1st type (25,000)	From £1000
ditto, unnamed (as issued to foreign recipients)	From £350
George V 2nd type 1930–37 (14)	From £6000
George VI, IND IMP 1937–47	From £4000
ditto, unnamed (as issued to foreign recipients)	From £500
George VI, 2nd type 1948–52 (25)	From £12,000
Elizabeth II, BR: OMN:	From £10,000
Elizabeth II, DEI GRATIA	From £20,000

Miniature (in silver add £5)

Victoria	£75–85
Edward VII	£50–75
George V	Type I £35–45, II £70–100
George VI	Type I £15–20, II £25–40
Elizabeth II	£15–20

*Awards for some specific actions such as the Charge of the Light Brigade command a much higher premium than the figures quoted.

42. DISTINGUISHED CONDUCT MEDAL (DOMINION & COLONIAL)

Instituted: 31 May 1895.
Ribbon: 32mm crimson with a dark blue central stripe.
Metal: Silver.
Size: 36mm.
Description: As above, but the reverse bears the name of the issuing country or colony round the top.
Comments: *A separate DCM for warrant officers, NCOs and men of the colonial forces. Medals were struck for the Cape of Good Hope, New Zealand, New South Wales, Queensland, Tasmania, Natal and Canada, but only the last two actually issued them and the others are known only as specimens.*

VALUE:

Victoria Canada (1)	Rare
Victoria Natal (1)	Rare
Edward VII Natal (9)	Rare

43. DISTINGUISHED CONDUCT MEDAL (KAR & WAFF)

Instituted: early 1900s.
Ribbon: Dark blue with a central green stripe flanked by crimson stripes.
Metal: Silver.
Size: 36mm
Description: As no. 42, with either King's African Rifles or West Africa Frontier Force around the top of the reverse.
Comments: *Separate awards for gallantry were instituted in respect of the King's African Rifles (East Africa) and the West Africa Frontier Force (Nigeria, Sierra Leone, Gambia and the Gold Coast). These were issued until 1942 when they were superseded by the British DCM. An unnamed version of a George VI KAR DCM is known.*

VALUE:	Attributable groups
Edward VII KAR (2)	Rare
Edward VII WAFF (55)	£3500–4500
George V KAR (190)	£2250–2500
George V WAFF (165)	£2250–2500

44. CONSPICUOUS GALLANTRY MEDAL

Second award bar.

RN first type ribbon

Instituted: 1855.
Ribbon: 31mm white (RN) or sky blue (RAF) with dark blue edges. The Royal Navy ribbon was originally dark blue with white central stripe.
Metal: Silver.
Size: 36mm.
Description: (Obverse) the effigy of the reigning monarch; (reverse) the words FOR CONSPICUOUS GALLANTRY in three lines within a crowned laurel wreath.
Comments: *Conceived as the naval counterpart to the DCM, it was instituted for award to petty officers and seamen of the Royal Navy and to NCOs and other ranks of the Royal Marines. Originally awarded only for gallantry during the Crimean War, it was revived in 1874 to recognise heroism during the Ashantee War and has since been awarded, albeit sparingly, for other wars and campaigns. The Crimean issue utilised the dies of the Meritorious Service Medal which had the date 1848 below the truncation of the Queen's neck on the obverse. The raised relief inscription MERITORIOUS SERVICE on the reverse was erased and the words CONSPICUOUS GALLANTRY engraved in their place. When the decoration was revived in 1874 a new obverse was designed without a date while a new die, with the entire inscription in raised relief, was employed for the reverse. In 1943 the CGM was extended to NCOs and other ranks of the RAF. Both naval and RAF medals are identical, but the naval medal has a white ribbon with dark blue edges, whereas the RAF award has a pale blue ribbon with dark blue edges. It ranks as one of the rarest decorations: the only three medals issued in the reign of Queen Elizabeth II were awarded to Cpl. J. D. Coughlan, RAAF, for gallantry in Vietnam (1968), to Staff-Sergeant James Prescott, RE, during the South Atlantic War (1982) (posthumous) and to CPO Diver Philip Hammond, RN, during the Gulf War (1991). As a result of the 1993 Review and resultant changes to the operational gallantry award system, the decoration has been replaced by the Conspicuous Gallantry Cross.*

RN

RAF

VALUE:		Attributable groups
Victoria 1st type (11)		From £10,000
Victoria 2nd type (50)		From £10,000
Edward VII (2)		—
George V (110)		From £8000
George VI Navy/RM (80)		From £12,000
George VI RAF (103)	Immediate	From £12,000
	Non-immediate	From £7500
Elizabeth II (3)		—
Miniature		
Victoria		£50–80
Edward VII		£50–80
George V		£25–35
George VI		£15–20
Elizabeth II		£15–20

45. GEORGE MEDAL

Second award bar.

Instituted: 1940.
Ribbon: 32mm crimson with five narrow blue stripes.
Metal: Silver.
Size: 36mm.
Description: (Obverse) the effigy of the reigning monarch; (reverse) St George and the Dragon, modelled by George Kruger Gray, after the bookplate by Stephen Gooden for the Royal Library, Windsor.
Comments: *Awarded for acts of bravery where the services were not so outstanding as to merit the George Cross. Though primarily a civilian award, it has also been given to service personnel for heroism not in the face of the enemy. Of the approximately 2,000 medals awarded, just over half have been to civilians. 27 second award bars have been issued.*

VALUE:

	Civilian	Service
George VI 1st type 1940–47	From £3500	From £4000
George VI 2nd type 1948–52	From £3500	From £4500
Elizabeth II 1st type 1953	From £3000	From £4500
Elizabeth II 2nd type	From £3000	From £4500

Miniature	
George VI, 1st type	£20–25
2nd type	£25–30
Elizabeth II, 1st type	£15–25
2nd type	£15–25
	Silver add £5

46. KING'S POLICE MEDAL

Second award bar.

Instituted: 7 July 1909.
Ribbons: 36mm. Originally deep blue with silver edges, but in 1916 a central silver stripe was added. Gallantry awards have thin crimson stripes superimposed on the silver stripes.
Metal: Silver.
Size: 36mm.
Description: (Obverse) the monarch's effigy; (reverse) a standing figure with sword and shield inscribed TO GUARD MY PEOPLE. The first issue had a laurel spray in the exergue, but in 1933 two separate reverses were introduced and the words FOR GALLANTRY or FOR DISTINGUISHED SERVICE were placed in the exergue.
Comments: *Instituted to reward "courage and devotion to duty" in the police and fire services of the UK and overseas dominions. Recognising the bravery of the firemen during the Blitz, the medal was retitled the King's Police and Fire Services Medal in 1940, but no change was made in the design of the medal itself. From 1950, the gallantry medals were only awarded posthumously and all medals were discontinued in 1954 when separate awards were established for the two services (see numbers MYB47 and 48).*

VALUE:

		Miniature
Edward VII (100)	£850–1000	£25–30
George V 1st type coinage head (1900)	£600–850	£20–25
George V 2nd type crowned head	£600–850	£40–50
George V for Gallantry (350)	£1000–1500	£15–20
George V for Distinguished Service	£550–600	£15–20
George VI 1st type for Gallantry (440)	£850–1250	£15–20
George VI 2nd type for Gallantry (50)	£1500–2000	£15–20
George VI 1st type for Distinguished Service	£500–550	£15–20
George VI 2nd type for Distinguished Service	£500–550	£15–20

KPM

KPM (Gallantry)

47. QUEEN'S / KING'S POLICE MEDAL

Instituted: 19 May 1954.
Ribbon: Three silver stripes and two broad dark blue stripes. Gallantry awards have thin crimson stripes superimposed on the silver stripes.
Metal: Silver.
Size: 36mm.
Description: (Obverse) effigy of the reigning monarch; (reverse) a standing figure (as on the KPM) but the laurel spray has been restored to the exergue and the words FOR GALLANTRY or FOR DISTINGUISHED POLICE SERVICE are inscribed round the circumference.
Comments: *The QPM <u>for Gallantry</u> has been effectively redundant since November 1977 when it was made possible to award the George Medal posthumously. Prior to this the QPM was the posthumous equivalent of the GM for police officers. Issued in New Zealand under Regulations dated November 18, 1959 by the Minister in Charge of Police.*

VALUE:		*Miniature*
Elizabeth II for Gallantry (23)	£1750–2500	£30–40
Elizabeth II for Distinguished Service	£550–750	£15–25
Charles III	—	—

Gallantry

48. QUEEN'S / KING'S FIRE SERVICE MEDAL

Instituted: 19 May 1954.
Ribbon: Red with three yellow stripes (distinguished service) or similar, with thin dark blue stripes bisecting the yellow stripes (gallantry).
Metal: Silver.
Size: 36mm
Description: (Obverse) effigy of the reigning monarch; (reverse) standing figure with sword and shield (as on KPM), laurel spray in the exergue, and inscription round the circumference FOR GALLANTRY or FOR DISTINGUISHED FIRE SERVICE.
Comments: *To date no award of this medal, which can be awarded posthumously, has been made for gallantry.*

VALUE:		*Miniature*
Elizabeth II for Gallantry	—	£30–40
Elizabeth II for Distinguished Service	£600–750	£15–30
Charles III	—	—

Gallantry

48A. QUEEN'S / KING'S VOLUNTEER RESERVES MEDAL

Instituted: 1999.
Ribbon: Dark green with three narrow gold stripes.
Metal: Silver.
Size: 36mm.
Description: (Obverse) effigy of reigning monarch; (reverse) five ribbons containing the words THE QUEEN'S / KING'S VOLUNTEER RESERVES MEDAL. The medal is fitted with a large ring for suspension.
Comments: *Awarded to men and women of any rank in the volunteer reserves of all three services in recognition of outstanding service which formerly would have merited an award within the Order of the British Empire. Holders are entitled to the post-nominal letters QVRM / KVRM.*

VALUE: £350–500   *Miniature*   £10–15

48B. QUEEN'S / KING'S AMBULANCE SERVICE MEDAL FOR DISTINGUISHED SERVICE

Instituted: July 2012.
Branch of Service: Members of the NHS Ambulance Service.
Ribbon: Dark green with central silver stripe and silver edges.
Metal: Silver.
Size: 36mm.
Description: (Obverse) effigy of reigning monarch; (reverse) the inscription FOR DISTINGUISHED AMBULANCE SERVICE around the ambulance service emblem.
Comments: *Issued to recognise exceptional duty and outstanding service of NHS ambulance personnel. The medals are named around the edge and recipients can use the post-nominals QAM / KAM.*

VALUE: £200–250   *Miniature*   £15–20

49. KING'S POLICE MEDAL (SOUTH AFRICA)

Instituted: 24 September 1937.
Ribbon: Silver with two broad dark blue stripes. Red stripes are added for gallantry awards.
Metal: Silver.
Size: 36mm.
Description: (Obverse) effigy of George VI and title including the words ET IMPERATOR (1937-49), George VI minus ET IMPERATOR (1950-52) and Queen Elizabeth II (1953-60). (Reverse) as UK (no. 47 above) but inscribed in English and Afrikaans. Inscribed FOR BRAVERY VIR DAPPERHEID or FOR DISTINGUISHED SERVICE VIR VOORTREFLIKE DIENS.
Comments: *Awarded to members of the South Africa Police for courage and devotion to duty. In 1938 it was extended to cover the constabulary of South West Africa.*

VALUE:
George VI 1st type 1937-49
    for Gallantry (10)   —
    for Distinguished Service (13)   —
George VI 2nd type 1950-52
    for Distinguished Service (13)   —
Elizabeth II 1953-60
    for Gallantry (20)   —
Elizabeth II 1953-69
    for Distinguished Service (3)   —
Not seen in Miniature

50. EDWARD MEDAL (MINES)

Instituted: July 1907.
Ribbon: Dark blue edged with yellow.
Metal: Silver or bronze.
Size: 33mm.
Description: (Obverse) the monarch's effigy; (reverse) a miner rescuing a stricken comrade, with the caption FOR COURAGE across the top (designed by W. Reynolds-Stephens).
Comments: *Awarded for life-saving in mines and quarries, in two grades: first class (silver) and second class (bronze). Interestingly, the cost of these medals was borne not by the State but from a fund created by a group of philanthropic individuals led by A. Hewlett, a leading mine-owner. Medals were engraved with the names of the recipient from the outset, but since the 1930s the date and sometimes the place of the action have also been inscribed. Since 1949 the medal was only granted posthumously and in 1971 living recipients were invited to exchange their medals for the GC, under Royal Warrant of 1971. Two silver and eight bronze medallists elected not to do so. This is one of the rarest gallantry awards, only 77 silver and 318 bronze medals having been granted since its inception. Only two second award bars have been awarded—both for mine rescues.*

VALUE:	Silver	Bronze
Edward VII	£2500–3500	£2000–2500
George V 1st type	£2500–3500	£1500–2000
George V 2nd type	£4000–6000	£2500–3000
George VI 1st type	£3500–5000	£3500–4500
George VI 2nd type	—	£4000–5000
Elizabeth II	Not issued	£4000–6000
Miniature		
Edward VII	£80–90	£70–80
George V	£70–80	£60–70
George VI	£70–80	£60–70

51. EDWARD MEDAL (INDUSTRY)

1st type rev.

2nd type rev.

Instituted: December 1909.
Ribbon: As above.
Metal: Silver or bronze.
Size: 33mm.
Description: (Obverse) effigy of the reigning monarch; (reverse) originally a worker helping an injured workmate with a factory in the background and the words FOR COURAGE inscribed diagonally across the top. A second reverse, depicting a standing female figure with a laurel branch and a factory skyline in the background, was introduced in 1912.
Comments: *Awarded for acts of bravery in factory accidents and disasters. Like the Mines medal it was also available in two classes, but no first class medals were awarded since 1948. Since 1949 the medal was only granted posthumously and in 1971 living recipients were invited to exchange their medals for the GC, under Royal Warrant of 1971. Two Silver and three Bronze recipients declined to exchange. A total of 25 silver and 163 bronze awards have been issued. Two awards were made to women, the rarest gallantry award to a lady.*

VALUE:	Silver	Bronze
Edward VII	From £5000	£2500–3500
George V 1st Obv, 1st Rev	Unique	£4500–5000
George V 1st Obv, 2nd Rev	From £5000	£1500–2000
George V 2nd Obv, 2nd Rev	From £5000	£2500–3500
George VI 1st type	Unique	£2500–3500
George VI 2nd type	Not issued	£5000–6000
Elizabeth II 1st type	Not issued	£5000–6000
Elizabeth II 2nd type	Not issued	£5000–6000
Miniature		
George V	£150–200	£100–150
George VI	£70–80	
George VI Modern example	£15–20	

52. INDIAN DISTINGUISHED SERVICE MEDAL

Second award bar.

Instituted: 25 June 1907.
Ribbon: Crimson with broad dark blue edges.
Metal: Silver.
Size: 36mm.
Description: (Obverse) the sovereign's effigy. (Reverse) the words FOR
   DISTINGUISHED SERVICE in a laurel wreath.
Comments: *Awarded for distinguished service in the field by Indian
   commissioned and non-commissioned officers and men of the Indian Army,
   the reserve forces, border militia and levies, military police and troops
   employed by the Indian Government. An amendment of 1917 extended
   the award to Indian non-combatants engaged on field service, bars for
   subsequent awards being authorised at the same time. It was formally
   extended to the Royal Indian Marine in 1929 and members of the Indian Air
   Force in 1940. Finally it was extended in 1944 to include non-European
   personnel of the Hong Kong and Singapore Royal Artillery although it
   became obsolete in 1947.*

VALUE:		*Miniature*
Edward VII (140)	£1000–1500	£80–90
George V KAISAR-I-HIND (3800)	£800–1200	£50–60
George V 2nd type (140)	£1250–1750	£50–60
George VI (1190)	£1000–1500	£40–50

53. BURMA GALLANTRY MEDAL

Second award bar.

Instituted: 10 May 1940.
Ribbon: Jungle green with a broad crimson stripe in the centre.
Metal: Silver.
Size: 36mm.
Description: (Obverse) the effigy of King George VI; (reverse) the
   words BURMA at the top and FOR GALLANTRY in a laurel wreath.
Comments: *As Burma ceased to be part of the Indian Empire in April
   1937 a separate gallantry award was required for its armed services. The
   Burma Gallantry Medal was awarded by the Governor to officers and
   men of the Burma Army, frontier forces, military police, Burma RNVR
   and Burma AAF, although by an amendment of 1945 subsequent awards
   were restricted to NCOs and men. The medal became obsolete in 1947
   when Burma became an independent republic and left the Commonwealth.
   Just over 200 medals and three bars were awarded, mainly for heroism in
   operations behind the Japanese lines.*

VALUE:	*Miniature*
£4000–5000	£20–25 for late example, contemporary example unknown

54. DISTINGUISHED SERVICE MEDAL

Instituted: 14 October 1914.

Ribbon: Dark blue with two white stripes towards the centre.

Metal: Silver.

Size: 36mm.

Description: (Obverse) the sovereign's effigy; (reverse) a crowned wreath inscribed FOR DISTINGUISHED SERVICE.

Comments: *Awarded to petty officers and ratings of the Royal Navy, NCOs and other ranks of the Royal Marines and all other persons holding corresponding ranks or positions in the naval forces, for acts of bravery in face of the enemy not sufficiently meritorious to make them eligible for the CGM. It was later extended to cover the Merchant Navy and Army, the WRNS and RAF personnel serving aboard ships in the Second World War. Of particular interest and desirability are medals awarded for outstanding actions, e.g. Jutland, Q-Ships, the Murmansk convoys, the Yangtze incident and the Falklands War. First World War bars for subsequent awards are dated on the reverse, but Second World War bars are undated. As a result of the 1993 Review of gallantry awards and resultant changes to the operational gallantry award system, this award has been replaced by the DSC which is now available both to officers and other ranks.*

Second award bar.

VALUE:

		Miniature
George V uncrowned head 1914-30 (4100)	£1000–2000	£20–25
George VI IND IMP 1938-49 (7100)	£1000–2000	£15–20
George VI 2nd type 1949-53	£3500–4500	£30–40
Elizabeth II BR OMN 1953-7	£5000–8000	£10–15
Elizabeth II 2nd type	£5500–8500	£10–15
		(in silver add £5)

55. MILITARY MEDAL

Instituted: 25 March 1916.

Ribbon: Broad dark blue edges flanking a central section of three narrow white and two narrow crimson stripes.

Metal: Silver.

Size: 36mm.

Description: (Obverse) the sovereign's effigy—six types; (reverse) the crowned royal cypher above the inscription FOR BRAVERY IN THE FIELD, enclosed in a wreath.

Comments: *Awarded to NCOs and men of the Army (including RFC and RND) for individual or associated acts of bravery not of sufficient heroism as to merit the DCM. In June 1916 it was extended to women, two of the earliest awards being to civilian ladies for their conduct during the Easter Rising in Dublin that year. Some 115,600 medals were awarded during the First World War alone, together with 5796 first bars, 180 second bars and 1 third bar. Over 16,000 medals were conferred during the Second World War, with 181 first bars and 2 second bar. About 300 medals and 4 first bars were awarded for bravery in minor campaigns between the two world wars, whilst some 932 medals and 8 first bars have been conferred since 1947. As a result of the 1993 Review of gallantry awards and resultant changes to the operational gallantry award system, this award has been replaced by the MC which is now available both to officers and other ranks.*

Second award bar.

VALUE:

		Miniature
George V uncrowned head 1916–30		
Corps/RA—single	£250–450	£15–20
in group	£400–550*	
Regiment—single	£400–550	
in group	£650–1000*	
named to a woman	£5500–6500	
unnamed as awarded to foreign recipients†	£300–400	
George V crowned head 1930–38	£4000–5000	£70–100
George VI IND IMP 1938–48		
Corps	£1000–1800	£15–20
Regiment	£1500–2500	
unnamed as awarded to foreign recipients†	£400–500	
George VI 2nd type 1948-53	£2500–5000	£25–40
Elizabeth II BR: OMN 1953-8	£3500–6000	£15–20
Elizabeth II 2nd type	£5000–8000	£15–20
		(in silver add £5)

*Groups to RFC, RAF and RND will be considerably higher and obviously, medals with second (or more) award bars are also worth much more.

†*Note: Some MMs to foreign recipients are found named.*

56. DISTINGUISHED FLYING MEDAL

Instituted: 1918.

Ribbon: Originally purple and white horizontal stripes but since July 1919 thirteen narrow diagonal stripes alternating white and purple.

Metal: Silver.

Size: 42mm tall; 34mm wide.

Description: An oval medal, (obverse) the sovereign's effigy; (reverse) Athena Nike seated on an aeroplane, with a hawk rising from her hand. Originally undated, but the date 1918 was added to the reverse with the advent of the George VI obverse. The medal is suspended by a pair of wings from a straight bar.

Comments: *Introduced at the same time as the DFC, it was awarded to NCOs and men of the RAF for courage or devotion to duty while flying on active operations against the enemy. During the Second World War it was extended to the equivalent ranks of the Army and Fleet Air Arm personnel engaged in similar operations. First World War medals have the names of recipients impressed in large seriffed lettering, whereas Second World War medals are rather coarsely engraved. Approximately 150 medals have been awarded since 1945. After WWII it was expanded to include aviation officers of other services. As a result of the 1993 Review of gallantry awards and resultant changes to the operational gallantry award system, this award has been replaced by the DFC which is now available both to officers and other ranks.*

Second award bar

Pre-1919

Post-1919

VALUE:	Attributable group	Miniature
George V uncrowned head 1918–30 (105)	From £5000	£18–20
George V crowned head 1930–38	From £8000	£70–100
George VI IND IMP 1938–49 (6500)	From £3000	£10–12
George VI 2nd type 1949–53	From £5000	£25–40
Elizabeth II	From £6000	£10–12

(in silver add £5)

͟H.STUBBINGTON.H   *Example of WWI impressed naming*

SGT. W.H.HITCHCOCK·R.A.   *WWII engraved naming.*

57. AIR FORCE MEDAL

Instituted: 1918.

Ribbon: Originally horizontal narrow stripes of white and crimson but since July 1919 diagonal narrow stripes of the same colours.

Metal: Silver.

Size: 42mm tall; 32mm wide.

Description: An oval medal with a laurel border. (Obverse) the sovereign's effigy; (reverse) Hermes mounted on a hawk bestowing a laurel wreath. The medal is suspended by a pair of wings from a straight bar, like the DFM.

Comments: *Instituted at the same time as the AFC, it was awarded to NCOs and men of the RAF for courage or devotion to duty while flying, but not on active operations against the enemy. About 100 medals and 2 first bars were awarded during the First World War, 106 medals and 3 bars between the wars and 259 medals during the Second World War. After WWII it was expanded to include aviation officers of other services. After the 1993 Review of gallantry awards the AFM was discontinued; the AFC is now available both to officers and other ranks.*

Second award bar

Pre-1919

Post-1919

VALUE:	Attributable group	Miniature
George V uncrowned head 1918–30	From £2500	£25–30
George V crowned head 1930–38	From £5000	£80–100
George VI IND IMP 1939–49	From £3000	£15–20
George VI 2nd type 1949–53	From £3000	£30–40
Elizabeth II	From £3000	£15–20

(in silver add £5)

58. CONSTABULARY MEDAL (IRELAND)

1st type obv.

2nd type obv.

Instituted: 1842.

Ribbon: Originally light blue, but changed to green in 1872.

Metal: Silver.

Size: 36mm.

Description: (Obverse) a crowned harp within a wreath of oak leaves and shamrocks, with REWARD OF MERIT round the top and IRISH CONSTABULARY round the foot. In the first version the front of the harp took the form of a female figure but later variants had a plain harp and the shape of the crown and details of the wreath were also altered. These changes theoretically came in 1867 when the Constabulary acquired the epithet Royal, which was then added to the inscription round the top, although some medals issued as late as 1921 had the pre-1867 title. (Reverse) a wreath of laurel and shamrock, within which are engraved the recipient's name, rank, number, date and sometimes the location of the action.

Comments: *Originally awarded for gallantry and meritorious service by members of the Irish Constabulary. From 1872, however, it was awarded only for gallantry. It was first conferred in 1848 and became obsolete in 1922 when the Irish Free State was established. Bars for second awards were authorised in 1920. About 315 medals and 7 bars were awarded (or, in some cases, second medals—the records are inconclusive), mostly for actions in connection with the Easter Rising of 1916 (23) or the subsequent Anglo-Irish War of 1920 (180) and 1921 (55).*

VALUE:		Miniature
First type	£5000–8000	—
Second type	£5000–8000	£200–250

Original ribbon

Post-1872 ribbon

59. INDIAN POLICE MEDAL

1st type

2nd type (after 1944)

Instituted: 23 February 1932.

Ribbon: Crimson flanked by stripes of dark blue and silver grey. From 1942 onwards additional narrow silver stripes appeared in the centre of the blue stripe intended for the gallantry medal.

Metal: Bronze.

Size: 36mm.

Description: (Obverse) the King Emperor; (reverse) a crowned wreath inscribed INDIAN POLICE, with the words FOR DISTINGUISHED CONDUCT across the centre. In December 1944 the reverse was re-designed in two types, with the words FOR GALLANTRY or FOR MERITORIOUS SERVICE in place of the previous legend.

Comments: *Intended for members of the Indian police forces and fire brigades as a reward for gallantry or meritorious service. The medal became obsolete in 1948 when India became a republic.*

VALUE:

		Miniature
George V	£500–650	£35–45
George VI Distinguished Conduct	£500–650	£35–45
George VI for Gallantry	£850–1000	£45–55
George VI for Meritorious Service	£500–650	£35–45

From 1942 for gallantry

Second award bar.

60. BURMA POLICE MEDAL

Instituted: 14 December 1937.
Ribbon: A wide central blue stripe flanked by broad black stripes and white edges.
Metal: Bronze.
Size: 36mm.
Description: (Obverse) the effigy of George VI; (reverse) similar to the Indian medal (first type)and inscribed FOR DISTINGUISHED CONDUCT, irrespective of whether awarded for gallantry or distinguished service.
Comments: *Introduced following the separation of Burma from India, it was abolished in 1948. All ranks of the police, frontier force and fire brigades, both European and Burmese, were eligible.*

VALUE:

For Gallantry (53)	£1950–2500	*Miniature*	£60–75
For Meritorious Service (80)	£1200–1700		

61. COLONIAL POLICE MEDAL

Instituted: 10 May 1938.
Ribbon: Blue with green edges and a thin silver stripe separating the colours, but the gallantry award had an additional thin red line through the centre of each green edge stripe.
Metal: Silver.
Size: 36mm.
Description: (Obverse) the sovereign's effigy; (reverse) a policeman's truncheon superimposed on a laurel wreath. The left side of the circumference is inscribed COLONIAL POLICE FORCES and the right either FOR GALLANTRY or FOR MERITORIOUS SERVICE.
Comments: *Intended to reward all ranks of the police throughout the Empire for acts of conspicuous bravery or for meritorious service. The number to be issued was limited to 150 in any one year. Only 450 were awarded for gallantry (with nine second award bars), whilst almost 3000 were issued for meritorious service. As from June 14, 2012 this medal was renamed the Overseas Territories Police Medal.*

Second award bar.

Ribbon for gallantry award

VALUE:

		Miniature
George VI GRI for Gallantry	£850–1250	£40–50
George VI GRI for Meritorious Service	£400–500	£30–40
George VI GVIR for Gallantry	£850–1250	£40–50
George VI GVIR for Meritorious Service	£400–500	£30–40
Elizabeth II 1st type for Gallantry	£850–1250	£40–50
Elizabeth II 1st type for Meritorious Service	£400–500	£30–40
Elizabeth II 2nd type for Gallantry	£850–1250	£40–50
Elizabeth II 2nd type for Meritorious Service	£400–500	£30–40

62. COLONIAL FIRE BRIGADE MEDAL

Instituted: 10 May 1938.
Ribbon: As above.
Metal: Silver.
Size: 36mm.
Description: (Obverse) the effigy of the reigning sovereign; (reverse) a fireman's helmet and axe, with the inscription COLONIAL FIRE BRIGADES FOR GALLANTRY or FOR MERITORIOUS SERVICE.
Comments: *This medal was intended to reward all ranks of the Colonial fire brigades for gallantry or meritorious service but very few were awarded for gallantry. As from June 14, 2012 this medal was renamed the Overseas Territories Fire Brigade Medal.*

VALUE:

		Miniature
George VI GRI for Gallantry	Rare	£40–50
George VI GRI for Meritorious Service	Rare	£30–40
George VI GVIR for Gallantry	Rare	£40–50
George VI GVIR for Meritorious Service	£350–500	£30–40
Elizabeth II 1st type for Gallantry	From £750	£40–50
Elizabeth II 1st type for Meritorious Service	£350–500	£30–40
Elizabeth II 2nd type for Gallantry	£600–800	£40–50
Elizabeth II 2nd type for Meritorious Service	£300–450	£30–40

63. QUEEN'S / KING'S GALLANTRY MEDAL

Instituted: 20 June 1974.
Ribbon: Blue with a central pearl-grey stripe bisected by a narrow rose-pink stripe.
Metal: Silver.
Size: 36mm.
Description: (Obverse) the Queen's effigy; (reverse) St. Edward's crown above THE QUEEN'S GALLANTRY MEDAL flanked by laurel sprigs.
Comments: *Awarded for exemplary acts of bravery. Although intended primarily for civilians, it is also awarded to members of the armed forces for actions which would not be deemed suitable for a military decoration. With the introduction of the QGM the gallantry awards in the Order of the British Empire came to an end. To date, almost 1,100 QGMs have been awarded, including 18 bars. A bar is added for a second award. A post-1990 SAS QGM and bar group sold at a recent auction for £26,000.*

Second award bar.

VALUE:		Miniature
Service award	From £5000	£15–20
Civilian award	From £3500	

64. ALLIED SUBJECTS' MEDAL

Instituted: November 1920.
Ribbon: Bright red with a light blue centre, flanked by narrow stripes of yellow, black and white (thus incorporating the Belgian and French national colours).
Metal: Silver or bronze.
Size: 36mm.
Description: (Obverse) the effigy of King George V; (reverse) designed by C. L. J. Doman, the female allegory of Humanity offering a cup to a British soldier resting on the ground, with ruined buildings in the background.
Comment: *Shortly after the cessation of the First World War it was proposed that services rendered to the Allied cause, specifically by those who had helped British prisoners of war to escape, should be rewarded by a medal. The decision to go ahead was delayed on account of disagreement between the War Office and the Foreign Office, but eventually the first awards were announced in November 1920, with supplementary lists in 1921 and 1922. Medals were issued unnamed and almost half of the total issue, namely 56 silver and 247 bronze medals, were issued to women.*

VALUE:		Miniature
Silver (134)	£1000–1250	£40–50
Bronze (574)	£500–600	£45–55

NB These prices are for unattributable awards.

65. KING'S MEDAL FOR COURAGE IN THE CAUSE OF FREEDOM

Instituted: 23 August 1945
Ribbon: White with two narrow dark blue stripes in the centre and broad red stripes at the edges.
Metal: Silver.
Size: 36mm.
Description: (Obverse) the crowned profile of King George VI; (reverse) inscribed, within a chain link, THE KING'S MEDAL FOR COURAGE IN THE CAUSE OF FREEDOM.
Comments: *Introduced to acknowledge acts of courage by foreign civilians or members of the armed services "in the furtherance of the British Commonwealth in the Allied cause" during the Second World War. Like its First World War counterpart, it was intended mainly to reward those who had assisted British escapees in enemy-occupied territories. About 3200 medals were issued, commencing in 1947.*

VALUE: £600–700 (unattributable)   *Miniature* £30–40

66. KING'S MEDAL FOR SERVICE IN THE CAUSE OF FREEDOM

Instituted: 23 August 1945.
Ribbon: White with a central red stripe flanked by dark blue stripes.
Metal: Silver.
Size: 36mm.
Description: (Obverse) effigy of King George VI; (reverse) a medieval warrior in armour carrying a broken lance, receiving nourishment from a female.
Comments: *Introduced at the same time as the foregoing, it was intended for foreign civilians who had helped the Allied cause in other less dangerous ways, such as fund-raising and organising ambulance services. 2490 medals were issued.*

VALUE: £250–300 (unattributable)   *Miniature* £15–20

67. SEA GALLANTRY MEDAL

Instituted: 1855, under the Merchant Shipping Acts of 1854 and 1894.
Ribbon: Bright red with narrow white stripes towards the edges.
Metal: Silver or bronze.
Size: 58mm or 33mm.
Description: (Obverse) Profile of the reigning monarch; (reverse) a family on a storm-tossed shore reviving a drowning sailor. Both obverse and reverse were sculpted by Bernard Wyon.
Comments: *Exceptionally, this group of medals was authorised not by Royal Warrant but by Parliamentary legislation, under the terms of the Merchant Shipping Acts of 1854 and 1894. The 1854 Act made provision for monetary rewards for life saving at sea, but in 1855 this was transmuted into medals, in gold, silver or bronze, in two categories, for gallantry (where the rescuer placed his own life at risk) and for humanity (where the risks were minimal). The gold medal, if ever awarded, must have been of the greatest rarity. These medals, issued by the Board of Trade, were 58mm in diameter and not intended for wearing. The only difference between the medals lay in the wording of the inscription round the circumference of the obverse. In 1903 Edward VII ordered that the medal be reduced to 1.27 inches (33mm) in diameter and fitted with a suspension bar and ribbon for wearing. Both large and small medals were always issued with a minimum of the recipient's name and date of rescue round the rim. The last medal was awarded in 1989 and it appears to have fallen into disuse although the award has not been cancelled. Only one second award clasp has ever been issued—that to Ch.Off. James Whiteley in 1921.*

VALUE:

	Silver	Bronze	Miniature
Victoria Gallantry	£1000–1500	£550–750	£100–150
Victoria Humanity (to 1893)	£1000–1250	£500–650	
Edward VII Gallantry (large)	£1750–2000	£1500–1650	
Edward VII Gallantry (small)	£850–1000	£550–650	£100–150
Edward VII (2nd small type)	£750–950	£450–550	
George V	£500–650	£350–450	£50–75
George VI 1st type	£1200–1500	—	
George VI 2nd type	—	—	
Elizabeth II	—	—	

68. SEA GALLANTRY MEDAL (FOREIGN SERVICES)

Instituted: 1841.

Ribbon: Plain crimson till 1922; thereafter the same ribbon as the SGM above.

Metal: Gold, silver or bronze.

Size: 36mm or 33mm.

Description: The large medal had Victoria's effigy (young head) on the obverse, but there were five reverse types showing a crowned wreath with PRESENTED BY (or FROM) THE BRITISH GOVERNMENT inside the wreath. Outside the wreath were the following variants:

1. Individually struck inscriptions (1841-49 but sometimes later).
2. FOR SAVING THE LIFE OF A BRITISH SUBJECT (1849-54)
3. FOR ASSISTING A BRITISH VESSEL IN DISTRESS (1849-54)
4. FOR SAVING THE LIVES OF BRITISH SUBJECTS (1850-54)

There are also unissued specimens or patterns with a Latin inscription within the wreath VICTORIA REGINA CUDI JUSSIT MDCCCXLI.

The small medal, intended for wear, has five obverse types combined with four reverse types: as 2 above (1854-1906), as 3 above (1854-1918), as 4 above (1854-1926), or FOR GALLANTRY AND HUMANITY (1858 to the present day).

Comments: *Although intended to reward foreigners who rendered assistance to British subjects in distress some early awards were actually made for rescues on dry land. Originally a special reverse was struck for each incident, but this was found to be unnecessarily expensive, so a standard reverse was devised in 1849. Medals before 1854 had a diameter of 45mm and were not fitted with suspension. After 1854 the diameter was reduced to 33mm and scrolled suspension bars were fitted. Of the large medals about 100 gold, 120 silver and 14 bronze were issued, while some 10 gold and 24 bronze specimens have been recorded. The small bronze medal is actually the rarest of all, only six medals being issued.*

Type 4 rev.

Original ribbon

Post-1922 ribbon

VALUE:	Gold	Silver	Bronze
Victoria large	—	£650–750	£450–550
Victoria small	£2000–2500	£350–450	—
Edward VII	£2000–2750	£450–550	—
George V	£1750–2000	£350–450	—
George VI	—	—	—
Elizabeth II	—	—	—
Miniature			£175–225

69. BRITISH NORTH BORNEO COMPANY'S BRAVERY CROSS

Instituted: 1890.

Ribbon: Gold (later yellow) watered silk 34mm.

Metal: Silver or bronze.

Size: 36mm.

Description: The cross pattée has a central medallion bearing a lion passant with the Company motto PERGO ET PERAGO (I carry on and accomplish) within a garter. The arms of the cross are inscribed BRITISH NORTH BORNEO with FOR BRAVERY in the lower limb. Three crosses have been recorded with the lower inscription for bravery omitted.

Comments: *Manufactured by Joseph Moore of Birmingham. The silver version bears the Birmingham hallmark for 1890. The reverse of the bronze medal is smooth. The cross was awarded for bravery in some 17 actions between 1883 and 1915, to the Company's Armed Constabulary. Several of these actions involved fewer than 40 combatants, but at the other extreme 144 men took*

69. BRITISH NORTH BORNEO COMPANY'S BRAVERY CROSS *continued*

part in the major battle at Tambunan in 1900. Only five silver and four bronze crosses are known to have been awarded. Jemadar Natha Singh was the only officer to win both bronze (1892) and silver (1897). Examples with the word STERLING on the reverse are modern copies.

VALUE:

Silver	£1000–1500	*Not known in miniature.*
Bronze	£500–750 (but much more in either case if attributable)	
Specimens/Copies	£100–150	

70. KING'S MEDAL FOR NATIVE CHIEFS

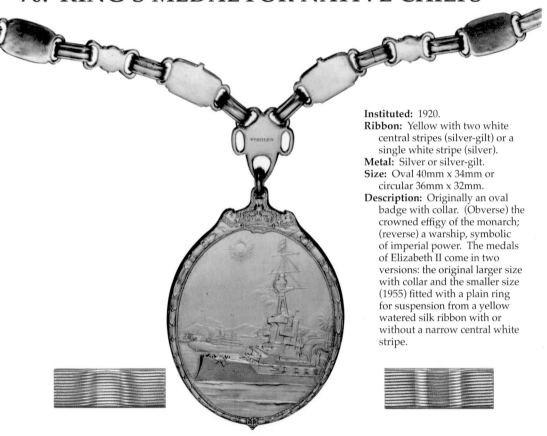

Instituted: 1920.
Ribbon: Yellow with two white central stripes (silver-gilt) or a single white stripe (silver).
Metal: Silver or silver-gilt.
Size: Oval 40mm x 34mm or circular 36mm x 32mm.
Description: Originally an oval badge with collar. (Obverse) the crowned effigy of the monarch; (reverse) a warship, symbolic of imperial power. The medals of Elizabeth II come in two versions: the original larger size with collar and the smaller size (1955) fitted with a plain ring for suspension from a yellow watered silk ribbon with or without a narrow central white stripe.

Comments: *Various large silver medals were struck for award to native chiefs in various parts of the world, from the eighteenth century onwards, and of these the awards to American Indian chiefs are probably the best known. In 1920, however, a standard King's Medal for Chiefs was instituted. It was awarded exceptionally in silver-gilt (first class), and usually in silver (second class). The oval medal was worn round the neck from a silver collar. The more modern issues, however, are smaller and intended for wear with a ribbon from the breast. The medal is normally returned on the death of the recipient.*

VALUE:

	Silver-gilt	Silver
George V		
First (couped) type	£1200–1500	£800–1000
Second (larger bust) type	£1000–1200	£750–850
George VI	£1000–1200	£650–750
Elizabeth II		
First type	£1000–1200	£650–750
Second (small) type	£400–500	£350–450

MENTIONS
and Commendations

A description of the various emblems denoting Mentions in Despatches and King's (or later Queen's) Commendations was published as a Supplement to the London Gazette, July 27, 1951. A special emblem to signify a Mention in Despatches was first instituted during World War I and continued to be awarded for active service in that conflict up to August 10, 1920. It was worn on the ribbon of the Victory Medal (no. 170) or the British War Medal if no Victory Medal is awarded and consisted of a bronze spray of oak leaves.

For Mentions in Despatches after August 10, 1920, or a King's Commendation for Brave Conduct or Valuable Service in the Air, a bronze emblem consisting of a single oak leaf was worn on the appropriate medal ribbon, either a General Service Medal or the War Medal, 1939–45. King's or Queen's Commendations for Brave Conduct or Valuable Service in the Air, in cases where no campaign or war medal was awarded, were worn on the breast in the position where an appropriate medal ribbon would have been worn, generally on the uniform tunic after any medal ribbons.

King's or Queen's Commendations in respect of bravery, granted to civilians for acts during or since the Second World War, are denoted by a silver emblem in the form of a spray of laurel leaves (this was originally a plastic oval badge). The emblem was worn on the ribbon of the Defence Medal (no. 185) for bravery in situations earning the medal. Where no medal was awarded, it was sewn directly on to the coat. For civilians the King's or Queen's Commendation for Valuable Service in the Air, during the Second World War and subsequently, consisted of an oval silver badge, worn on the coat below any medals or medal ribbons, or in civil airline uniform, on the panel of the left breast pocket.

Since 2003 all MiD and Commendation emblems may be worn on UK, UN, NATO or EC/EU medal ribbons.

Mention in Despatches emblem 1914–20

King's Commendation for Brave Conduct plastic badge for civilians (1942–45).

King's Commendation for Valuable Service in the Air silver badge for civilians (1942–93).

Mention in Despatches emblem 1920–94

The emblems for Mentions and Commendations were revised in 1994, as shown in the table below.

FOR GALLANTRY			FOR VALUABLE SERVICE
IN ACTION WITH THE ENEMY (ALL ENVIRONMENTS)	NOT IN ACTION WITH THE ENEMY or OUT OF THEATRE (EXCEPT FLYING)	NOT IN ACTION WITH THE ENEMY or OUT OF THEATRE (FLYING)	IN-THEATRE BUT NOT IN ACTION WITH THE ENEMY
MENTION IN DESPATCHES	QUEEN'S / KING'S COMMENDATION FOR BRAVERY	QUEEN'S / KING'S COMMENDATION FOR BRAVERY IN THE AIR	QUEEN'S / KING'S COMMENDATION FOR VALUABLE SERVICE
A single oak leaf in SILVER	A spray of laurel leaves in SILVER	A new emblem in SILVER	A spray of oak leaves in SILVER

CAMPAIGN
Medals

The evolution of medals struck to commemorate, and later to reward participants in, a battle or campaign was a very gradual process. The forerunner of the modern campaign medal was the Armada Medal, cast in gold or silver, which appears to have been awarded to naval officers and distinguished persons after the abortive Spanish invasion of 1588. The obverse bears a flattering portrait of Queen Elizabeth (thought to have been designed by Nicholas Hilliard, the celebrated miniaturist) with a Latin inscription signifying "enclosing the most precious treasure in the world" (i.e. the Queen herself). On the reverse, the safety of the kingdom is represented by a bay tree growing on a little island, immune from the flashes of lightning which seem to strike it. This medal, and a similar type depicting the Ark floating calmly on a stormy sea, bore loops at the top so that a chain or cord could be passed through it for suspension from the neck of the recipient.

The Civil War produced a number of gallantry medals, mentioned in the previous section; but in 1650 Parliament authorised a medal which was struck in silver, bronze or lead to celebrate Cromwell's miraculous victory over the Scots at Dunbar. This was the first medal granted to all the participants on the Parliamentary side, and not restricted to high-ranking officers, or given for individual acts of heroism.

The Dunbar Medal thus established several useful precedents, which were eventually to form the criteria of the campaign medal as we know it today. After this promising start, however, the pattern of medals and their issue were much more restrictive. Naval medals were struck in gold for award to admirals and captains during the First Dutch War (1650–53), while the battle of Culloden (1746) was marked by a medal portraying the "Butcher" Duke of Cumberland, and granted to officers who took part in the defeat of the Jacobites.

In the second half of the eighteenth century there were a number of medals, but these were of a private or semi-official nature. The Honourable East India Company took the lead in awarding medals to its troops. These medals were often struck in two sizes and in gold as well as silver, for award to different ranks. The siege of Gibraltar (1779–83) was marked by an issue of medals to the defenders, but this was made on the initiative (and at the expense) of the garrison commanders, Generals Eliott and Picton, themselves.

During the French Revolutionary and Napoleonic Wars several medals were produced by private individuals for issue to combatants. Alexander Davison and Matthew Boulton were responsible for the medals granted to the officers and men who fought the battles of the Nile (1798) and Trafalgar (1805). Davison also produced a Trafalgar medal in pewter surrounded by a copper rim; it is recorded that the seamen who received it were so disgusted at the base metal that they threw it into the sea! At the same time, however, Government recognition was given to senior officers who had distinguished themselves in certain battles and engagements and a number of gold

medals were awarded. The events thus marked included the capture of Ceylon (1795–96) and the battles of Maida, Bagur and Palamos.

Towards the end of the Napoleonic Wars an Army Gold Medal was instituted in two sizes—large (generals) and small (field officers). Clasps for second and third battles and campaigns were added to the medal, but when an officer became eligible for a third clasp the medal was exchanged for a Gold Cross with the names of the four battles engraved on its arms. Clasps for subsequent campaigns were then added to the cross (the Duke of Wellington receiving the Gold Cross with nine clasps). A total of 163 crosses, 85 large and 599 small medals was awarded, so that, apart from their intrinsic value, these decorations command very high prices when they appear in the saleroom.

The first medal awarded to all ranks of the Army was the Waterloo Medal, issued in 1816 shortly after the battle which brought the Napoleonic Wars to an end. No action was taken to grant medals for the other campaigns in the Napoleonic Wars until 1847 when Military and Naval General Service Medals were awarded retrospectively to veterans who were then still alive. As applications were made, in some cases, in respect of campaigns more than fifty years earlier, it is hardly surprising that the number of medals awarded was comparatively small, while the number of clasps awarded for certain engagements was quite minute. The Military General Service Medal was restricted to land campaigns during the Peninsular War (1808–13), the American War (1812–14) and isolated actions in the West Indies, Egypt and Java, whereas the Naval GSM covered a far longer period, ranging from the capture of the French frigate La Cleopatra by HMS Nymphe in June 1793, to the naval blockade of the Syrian coast in 1840, during the British operations against Mehemet Ali. Thus Naval Medals with the clasp for Syria are relatively plentiful (7057 awarded) while in several cases clasps were awarded to one man alone, and in seven cases there were no claimants for clasps at all. It is worth bearing in mind that applications for the medals and clasps resulted mainly from the publicity given by printed advertisements and notices posted up all over the country. With the poor general standard of literacy prevalent at the time, many people who were entitled to the medals would have been quite unaware of their existence.

The Naming of Medals

The Military and Naval GSMs, with their multitudinous combinations of clasps, have long been popular with collectors, but the other campaign medals of the past century and a half have a strong following as well. With the exception of the stars and medals awarded during World War II, all British campaign medals have usually borne the name of the recipient and usually his (or her) number, rank and regiment, unit or ship as well. This brings a personal element into the study of medals which is lacking in most other branches of numismatics. The name on a medal is very important for two reasons. It is a means of testing the genuineness, not only of the medal itself, but its clasp combination, and secondly it enables the collector to link the medal not only with the man who earned it, but with his unit or formation, and thus plays a vital part in the development of naval or military history, if only a small part in most cases.

Much of the potential value of a medal depends on the man who won it, or the unit to which he belonged. To form a coherent collection as opposed to a random accumulation of medals, the collector would be well advised to specialise in some aspect of the subject, restricting his interests perhaps to one medal (the Naval GSM) or a single group (British campaigns in India), or to medals awarded to the men of a particular regiment. The information given on the rim or back of a medal is therefore important in helping to identify it and assign it to its correct place. Even this has to be qualified to some extent. Some regiments are more popular than others with collectors and much depends on the part, active or passive, played by a unit in a particular battle or campaign for which the medal was awarded. Then again, the combination of event with the corps or regiment of the recipient must also be considered.

At one extreme we find the Royal Regiment of Artillery living up to its motto Ubique (everywhere) by being represented in virtually every land action (and not a few naval actions, as witness the Atlantic Star worn by former Maritime Gunners), so that a comprehensive collection of medals awarded to the RA would be a formidable feat.

At the other extreme one finds odd detachments, sometimes consisting of one or two men only, seconded from a regiment for service with another unit. The Indian IGS medal with clasp Hazara 1891, was also issued to five men of the 1st Dragoon Guards, these men were part of the "Government Telegraph Department", Punjab Division, whose names appear on Roll WO100/75 page 269, together with other soldiers serving as Signallers from other regiments. Whereas a specimen of the IGS medal with this clasp is not hard to find named to a soldier in one of the Bengal units, it constitutes a major rarity when awarded to one of the "odd men" and its value is correspondingly high.

As the personal details given on a medal regarding the recipient are so important, it is necessary for the collector to verify two facts—that the person whose name is on the medal was actually present at the action for which either the medal or its clasps were awarded, and

secondly, that the naming of the clasp and the attachment of the clasps is correct and not tampered with in any way. As regards the first, the National Archives at Kew, London, is a goldmine of information for all naval and military campaigns. Apart from despatches, reports and muster rolls covering the actions, there are the medal rolls compiled from the applications for medals and clasps. Transcriptions of the medal rolls are held by regimental museums and also by such bodies as the Military Historical Association and the Orders and Medals Research Society and, of course, many of these can be found on-line. Details of these and other clubs and societies devoted to medal collecting can be found in the later chapters.

The presence of a name on the roll does not mean that a medal or clasp was inevitably awarded; conversely authenticated medals are known to exist named to persons not listed on the medal roll. There are often divergences between the muster and medal rolls. Moreover, discrepancies in the spelling of recipients' names are not uncommon and clasps are sometimes found listed for regiments which were not even in existence when the battle was fought! This is explained, however, by the fact that a man may have been serving with one unit which took part in the campaign and subsequently transferred to another regiment. When claiming his medal he probably gave his present unit, rather than the one in which he was serving at the time of the action.

Unfortunately cases of medals having been tampered with are by no means rare, so it is necessary to be able to recognise evidence of fakery. A common device of the faker is to alter the name and personal details of the recipient and to substitute another name in order to enhance the medal's value. This is done simply by filing the inscription off the rim and adding a new one. In order to check for such alterations a similar medal of proven genuineness should be compared with a pair of fine callipers. Take the measurements at several points round the rim so that any unevenness should soon be apparent.

We cannot stress too much the importance of being closely familiar with the various styles of naming medals. Over the past 150 years an incredible variety of lettering—roman, italic, script, sans-serif, seriffed in all shapes and sizes—has been used at one time or another. In some cases the inscription was applied by impressing in raised relief; in others the inscription was punched in or engraved by hand. If a medal is normally impressed and you come across an engraved example you should immediately be on your guard. This is not an infallible test, however, as medals have been known with more than one style of naming, particularly if duplicates were issued at a much later date to replace medals lost or destroyed.

A rather more subtle approach was adopted by some fakers in respect of the Naval GSM. The three commonest clasps—Algiers (1362), Navarino (1137) and Syria (7057)—were awarded to many recipients possessing common names such as Jones or Smith which can be matched with recipients of some very rare clasps. In the case of the Naval GSM the ship on which the recipient served is not given, thus aiding the fraudulent substitution of clasps. It is necessary, therefore, to check the condition of clasps, even if the naming appears to be correct. Points to watch for are file or solder marks on the rivets which secure the clasps to each other and to the suspender of the medal. This test is not infallible as clasps do occasionally work loose if subject to constant wear (particularly if the recipient was a cavalryman, for obvious reasons). But clasps whose rivets appear to have been hammered should automatically be suspect, until a check of the medal rolls pass them as authentic. Examples of the earlier medals, particularly those awarded to officers may be found with unorthodox coupling. Major L. L. Gordon in his definitive British Battles and Medals, mentions a Naval GSM awarded to one of his ancestors with clasps for Guadaloupe and Anse la Barque in a large rectangular style which must have been unofficial. The medal is quite authentic, so it must be presumed that officers were allowed a certain degree of latitude in the manner in which they altered their medals.

Medals with clasps awarded for participation in subsequent engagements are invariably worth much more than the basic medal. In general, the greater number of clasps, the more valuable the medal, although, conversely, there are a few instances in which single-clasp medals are scarcer than twin-clasp medals. There is no short answer to this and individual rare clasps can enhance the value of an otherwise common medal out of all proportion. Thus the Naval GSM with clasp for Syria currently rates about £1000, but one of the two medals known to have been issued with the Acheron clasp of 1805 would easily rate 12 times as much. Again, relative value can only be determined by reference to all the circumstances of the award.

The person to whom a medal was issued has considerable bearing on its value. If the recipient belonged to a regiment which played a spectacular part in a battle, this generally rates a premium. The rank of the recipient also has some bearing; in general the higher the rank, the more valuable the medal. Medals to commissioned officers rate more than those awarded to NCOs and other ranks, and the medals of British servicemen rate more as a rule than those awarded to native troops. Medals granted to women usually command a relatively good premium. Another grim aspect is that medals issued to personnel who were wounded or killed in the campaign also rate more highly than those issued to servicemen who came through unscathed.

With the collector of British campaign medals the person to whom the medal was awarded tends to become almost as important as the medal itself. It is often not sufficient to collect the medal and leave it at that. The collector feels that he must investigate it and delve into the archives to find out all that he can about the recipient. Nowadays there is a plethora of information available on-line and the National Archives and regimental museums have already been mentioned, but do not overlook the usefulness of such reference tools as the monumental Mormon International Genealogical Index (now on microfiche and available in good public libraries and county record offices). All of these should help you to flesh out the bare bones of the details given in the muster and medal rolls.

Medal Groups

Apart from the combination of clasps on a medal and the significance of the recipient, there is a third factor to be considered in assessing the value of medals, namely the relationship of one medal to another in a group awarded to one person. Just as the number of clasps on a medal is not in itself a significant factor, so also the number of medals in a group is not necessarily important per se. Groups of five or more medals, whose recipient can be identified, are by no means uncommon. For example, a fairly common five medal group would consist of 1914–15 Medal, War Medal and Victory Medal (for World War I) and the Defence Medal and War Medal (for World War II). Thousands of men served throughout the first war survived to do duty, in a less active role, during a part at least of the second, long enough to qualify for the latter pair of medals.

It should be noted that none of the medals awarded for service in World War II was named to the recipient, so that groups comprising such medals alone cannot be readily identified and are thus lacking in the interest possessed by those containing named medals. Six-medal groups for service in World War II are not uncommon, particularly the combination of 1939–45 Star, Africa Star, Italy Star, France and Germany Star, Defence Medal and War Medal awarded to Army personnel who served from any time up to late 1942 and took part in the campaigns of North Africa and Europe.

Conversely it would be possible for troops to have served over a longer period and seen more action and only been awarded the 1939–45 Star, Burma Star (with Pacific clasp) and the War Medal. Naval groups consisting of the 1939–45 Star, Atlantic Star (with clasp for France and Germany), Italy Star and War Medal are less common and therefore more desirable (with, of course, the rider that it must be possible to identify the recipient), while the most desirable of all is the three-medal group of 1939–45 Star (with Battle of Britain clasp), Air Crew Europe Star (with clasp for France and Germany) and the War Medal. Such a group, together with a Distinguished Flying Cross awarded to one of The Few, is a highly coveted set indeed, providing, as always, that one can prove its authenticity. In any event, the addition of a named medal to a World War II group (e.g. a long service award, a gallantry medal, or some other category of medal named to the recipient), together with supporting collateral material (citations, log-books, pay-books, service records, newspaper cuttings, etc), should help to establish the provenance of the group.

71. LOUISBURG MEDAL

Date: 1758.

Campaign: Canada (Seven Years War).

Branch of Service: British Army and Navy.

Ribbon: 32mm half yellow, half blue, although not originally intended for wear and therefore not fitted with suspension or ribbon.

Metals: Gold, silver or bronze.

Size: 42mm.

Description: (Obverse) the globe surrounded by allegorical figures of victory and flanked by servicemen; (reverse) burning ships in the harbour.

Comments: *More in the nature of a decoration, this medal was only given to certain recipients for acts of bravery or distinguished service in the capture in July 1758 of Louisburg in Canada during the Seven Years War. James Wolfe and Jeffrey Amherst commanded the land forces and Edward Boscawen the fleet.*

VALUE:

Gold	Rare
Silver	£4500–5500
Bronze	£1750–2500

72. CARIB WAR MEDAL

Date: 1773.

Campaign: Carib rebellion, St Vincent.

Branch of Service: Local militia or volunteers.

Ribbon: None.

Metal: Silver.

Size: 52mm.

Description: (Obverse) bust of George III in armour; (reverse) Britannia offering an olive branch to a defeated Carib, the date MDCCLXXIII in the exergue.

Comments: *The Legislative Assembly of St Vincent in the West Indies instituted this award to members of the militia and volunteers who served in the campaign of 1773 which put down a native rebellion that had been fomented by the French.*

VALUE:

Silver	£2500–3500

73. DECCAN MEDAL

Date: 1784.

Campaign: Western India and Gujerat 1778-84.

Branch of Service: HEIC forces.

Ribbon: Yellow cord.

Metals: Gold or silver.

Size: 40.5mm or 32mm.

Description: (Obverse) a rather languid Britannia with a trophy of arms, thrusting a laurel wreath towards a distant fort. (Reverse) an inscription in Farsi signifying "As coins are current in the world, so shall be the bravery and exploits of these heroes by whom the name of the victorious English nation was carried from Bengal to the Deccan. Presented in AH 1199 [1784] by the East India Company's Calcutta Government".

Comments: *The first medals struck by order of the Honourable East India Company were conferred on Indian troops for service in western India and Gujerat under the command of Warren Hastings. They were struck at Calcutta in two sizes; both gold and silver exist in the larger size but only silver medals in the smaller diameter.*

VALUE:

40.5mm gold	£5000–6500
40.5mm silver	£1800–2000
32mm silver	£1200–1400

74. DEFENCE OF GIBRALTAR

Eliott's medal   Picton's medal

Date: 1783.

Campaign: Siege of Gibraltar 1779–83.

Branch of Service: British and Hanoverian forces.

Ribbon: None.

Metal: Silver.

Size: 49mm (Eliott) and 59mm (Picton) .

Description: Eliott's medal was confined to the Hanoverian troops, hence the reverse inscribed BRUDERSCHAFT (German for "brotherhood") above a wreath containing the names of the three Hanoverian commanders and General Eliott. The obverse, by Lewis Pingo, shows a view of the Rock and the naval attack of 13 September 1782 which was the climax of the siege. Picton's medal, awarded to the British forces, has a larger than usual diameter, with a map of the Rock on the obverse and a 22-line text—the most verbose British medal—above a recumbent lion clutching a shield bearing the castle and key emblem of Gibraltar on the reverse.

Comments: *Several medals of a private nature were struck to commemorate the defence of Gibraltar during the Franco-Spanish siege of 1779–83, but those most commonly encountered are these silver medals which were provided by George Augustus Eliott and Sir Thomas Picton, the military commanders.*

VALUE:

Eliott medal	£850–1250
Picton medal	£1000–1500

75. MYSORE MEDAL

Date: 1792.
Campaign: Mysore 1790-92.
Branch of Service: HEIC forces.
Ribbon: Yellow cord.
Metal: Gold or silver.
Size: 43mm or 38mm.
Description: (Obverse) a sepoy of the HEIC Army holding British
and Company flags over a trophy of arms with the fortress of
Seringapatam in the background; (reverse) a bilingual inscription (in
English and Farsi). The medal has a ring for suspension round the
neck by a cord.
Comments: *Indian officers and men who served under Marquis Cornwallis
and Generals Abercromby and Meadows received this medal for service
in the campaign which brought about the downfall of Tippoo Sultan of
Mysore.*

VALUE:

43mm gold (subadars)	£15,000–25,000
43mm silver (jemadars)	£2500–2800
38mm silver (other ranks)	£1500–1800

76. ST VINCENTS BLACK CORPS MEDAL

Date: 1795.
Campaign: Carib rebellion 1795.
Branch of Service: Local militia volunteers.
Ribbon: None.
Metal: Bronze.
Size: 48.5mm.
Description: (Obverse) the winged figure of Victory brandishing a
sword over a fallen foe who has abandoned his musket; (reverse)
native holding musket and bayonet, BOLD LOYAL OBEDIENT
around and H.G.FEC. in exergue.
Comments: *Awarded to the officers and NCOs of the Corps of Natives raised
by Major Seton from among the island's slaves for service against the
rebellious Caribs and French forces.*

VALUE:

Bronze	£1000–1250

77. CAPTURE OF CEYLON MEDAL

Date: 1796.
Campaign: Ceylon 1795.
Branch of Service: HEIC forces.
Ribbon: Yellow cord.
Metal: Gold or silver.
Size: 50mm.
Description: The plain design has an English inscription on the
obverse, and the Farsi equivalent on the reverse.
Comments: *Awarded for service in the capture of Ceylon (Sri Lanka) from
the Dutch during the French Revolutionary Wars. It is generally believed
that the gold medals were awarded to Captains Barton and Clarke while the
silver medals went to the native gunners of the Bengal Artillery.*

VALUE:

Gold (2)	—	
Silver (121)	£2500–3500 (original striking)	£800–1000 (later striking)

78. DAVISON'S NILE MEDAL

Date: 1798.
Campaign: Battle of the Nile 1798.
Branch of Service: Royal Navy.
Ribbon: None, but unofficially 32mm, deep navy blue.
Metal: Gold, silver, gilt-bronze and bronze.
Size: 47mm.
Description: (Obverse) Peace caressing a shield decorated with the portrait of Horatio Nelson; (reverse) the British fleet at Aboukir Bay. The edge bears the lettering "A TRIBUTE OF REGARD FROM ALEX^r DAVISON, ESQ^r ST JAMES'S SQUARE=".
Comments: *Nelson's victory at the mouth of the Nile on 1 August 1798 was celebrated in a novel manner by his prize agent, Alexander Davison, whose name and London address appear in the edge inscription of the medal designed by Kuchler. Originally issued without a suspender, many recipients added a ring to enable the medal to be worn. Admiral Nelson's medal was stolen in 1900 and is believed to have been melted down. Prices quoted below are for unnamed specimens, contemporary engraved medals are usually worth about twice as much.*

VALUE:	
Gold (Nelson and his captains)	£12,000–15,000
Silver (junior officers)	£1500–2000
Gilt-bronze (petty officers)	£550–750
Bronze (ratings)	£300–450

79. SERINGAPATAM MEDAL

Date: 1808.
Campaign: Seringapatam, India, 1799.
Branch of Service: HEIC forces.
Ribbon: 38mm gold.
Metal: Gold, silver-gilt, silver, bronze and pewter.
Size: 48mm or 45mm.
Description: (Obverse) the British lion defeating Tiger of Mysore (Tippoo Sultan) with the date of the capture of the fortress IV MAY MDCCXCIX (1799) in the exergue; (reverse) the assault on Seringapatam.
Comments: *The British and native troops who took part in the renewed campaign against Tippoo Sultan were awarded this medal in 1808 in various metals without suspension (a number of different types of suspenders and rings were subsequently fitted by individual recipients). The medal was designed by Kuchler and struck in England (48mm) and Calcutta, the latter version being slightly smaller (45mm). There are several different strikings of these medals.*

VALUE:

British Mint	
Gold 48mm (30)	£8000–10,000
Silver-gilt 48mm (185)	£1500–1750
Silver 48mm (850)	£1000–1500
Bronze 48mm (5000)	£450–550
Pewter 48mm (45,000)	£350–450
Calcutta Mint	
Gold 45mm (83)	£5000–6500
Silver 45mm (2786)	£1000–1500
Miniature	Silver £230–290

80. EARL ST. VINCENT'S MEDAL

Date: 1800.   **Campaign:** Mediterranean.
Branch of Service: Royal Navy.
Ribbon: None.
Metal: Gold or silver.   **Size:** 48mm
Description: (Obverse) left-facing bust of the Earl in Admiral's uniform; (reverse) a sailor and marine.
Comments: *A private medal presented by Earl St Vincent, when he struck his flag and came ashore in 1800, to the petty officers and men of his flagship* Ville de Paris *as a token of appreciation to his old shipmates. Contemporary engraved and named pieces with researched provenance are worth at least twice as much as unnamed specimens.*

VALUE:
Gold	£6000–7500
Silver	£850–1000

81. EGYPT MEDAL 1801

Date: 1801.
Campaign: Egypt 1801.
Branch of Service: HEIC forces.
Ribbon: Yellow cord.
Metal: Gold or silver.
Size: 48mm.
Description: (Obverse) a sepoy holding a Union Jack, with an encampment in the background. A four-line Farsi text occupies the exergue; (reverse) a warship and the Pyramids.
Comments: *Issued by the Honourable East India Company to British and Indian troops in the Company's service who took part in the conquest of Egypt under Generals Baird and Abercromby.*

VALUE:
Gold (16)	—	
Silver (2200)	£1800–2000 (original striking)	£400–500 (later striking)

82. SULTAN'S MEDAL FOR EGYPT

Date: 1801.
Campaign: Egypt 1801.
Branch of Service: British forces.
Ribbon: The gold medals were originally suspended by gold hook and chain as shown. The silver medals were hung from a sand-coloured ribbon.
Metals: Gold or silver.
Size: Various (see below).
Description: The very thin discs have an elaborate arabesque border enclosing the *toughra* or sign manual of the Sultan.
Comments: *This medal was conferred by Sultan Selim III of Turkey on the British officers and NCOs who took part in the campaign against the French. It was produced in five gold versions for award to different ranks of commissioned officers, as well as one in silver for award to sergeants and corporals.*

VALUE:

Gold 54mm studded with jewels	—
Gold 54mm plain (less than 100 issued)	£8500–10,000
Gold 48mm	£5500–6500
Gold 43mm	£4500–5500
Gold 36mm	£4000–5000
Silver 36mm	£2500–3500

Miniature

Gold	£175–230
Silver	£125–175

83. HIGHLAND SOCIETY'S MEDAL FOR EGYPT 1801

Date: 1801.
Campaign: Egypt 1801.
Branch of Service: British forces.
Ribbon: None.
Metals: Gold, silver and bronze.
Size: 49mm.
Description: The medal was designed by Pidgeon. (Obverse) the right-facing bust of General Sir Ralph Abercromby, with a Latin inscription alluding to his death in Egypt; (reverse) a Highlander in combat with the Gaelic inscription NA FIR A CHOISIN BUAIDH SAN EPHAIT(These are the heroes who achieved victory in Egypt) and the date 21 MAR 1801. On the edge is the inscription "On choumun Chaeleach D'on Fhreiceadan Dubh Na XLII RT" (From the London Highland Society to the Black Watch or 42nd Regt.).
Comments: *The Highland and Agricultural Society (now Royal) was founded in 1784 to promote the development of agriculture in Scotland generally and the Highlands in particular. General Abercromby (born at Tullibody, 1734) commanded the British expedition to Egypt, and the landing at Aboukir Bay on 2 March 1801 in the face of strenuous French opposition, is justly regarded as one of the most brilliant and daring exploits of all time. The French made a surprise attack on the British camp on the night of 21 March and Abercromby was struck by a ricochet; he died aboard the flagship seven days later. Medals in gold were presented to the Prince Regent and Abercromby's sons, but silver and bronze medals were later struck and awarded to senior officers of the expedition as well as soldiers who had distinguished themselves in the campaign.*

VALUE:

Gold	—
Silver	£650–850
Bronze	£250–300

84. BOULTON'S TRAFALGAR MEDAL

Date: 1805.
Campaign: Battle of Trafalgar 1805.
Branch of Service: Royal Navy.
Ribbon: None, but unofficially 32mm navy blue (originally issued without suspension).
Metals: Gold, silver, white metal, gilt-bronze or bronze.
Size: 48mm.
Description: (Obverse) bust of Nelson; (reverse) a battle scene.
Comments: *Matthew Boulton of the Soho Mint, Birmingham, originally struck about 15,000 examples of this medal in white metal on his own initiative for presentation to the survivors of the battle of Trafalgar, but bronze and gilt-bronze specimens also exist. It was subsequently restruck on at least two occasions, the first and second strikings have the inscription impressed in large capitals around the rim TO THE HEROES OF TRAFALGAR FROM M:BOULTON, the later having the inscription omitted. As the original dies were used for each striking, they had to be polished before reuse, so the fine detail on Nelson's uniform and in the battle scene is less pronounced in the second and subsequent strikings. Examples of the original striking can sometimes be found engraved in various styles, but great care should be taken over checking the authenticity of such pieces. All gold specimens are restrikes. Silver medals were later ordered from Boulton's successors by officers who wished to have a medal to form a group with the 1848 NGS.*

VALUE:

Gold (c. 1905)	£4500–5500	Gilt-bronze	£750–850
Silver (1820–50)	£1750–2500	Bronze	£250–500
White metal	£450–600		

NB These prices are based on medals issued from the original striking and are dependent on attribution and generally in EF to Mint condition.

85. DAVISON'S TRAFALGAR MEDAL

Date: 1805.
Campaign: Battle of Trafalgar 1805.
Branch of Service: Royal Navy.
Ribbon: None, but unofficially 32mm navy blue.
Metal: Pewter with a copper rim.
Size: 52mm.
Description: (Obverse) bust of Nelson; (reverse) a man-of-war surrounded by an appropriate biblical quotation from Exodus "The Lord is a Man of War" and below: "Victory off Trafalgar over the combined Fleets of France and Spain Oct.21.1805".
Comments: *Alexander Davison, Nelson's prize agent, had this medal struck for award to the ratings of HMS Victory who took part in the battle.*

VALUE: £1750–2000

86. CAPTURE OF RODRIGUEZ, ISLE OF BOURBON AND ISLE OF FRANCE

Date: 1810.
Campaign: Indian Ocean 1809-10.
Branch of Service: HEIC forces.
Ribbon: Yellow cord.
Metal: Gold or silver.
Size: 49mm.
Description: (Obverse) a sepoy in front of a cannon with the Union Jack; (reverse) a wreath with inscriptions in English and Farsi.
Comments: *The East India Company awarded this medal to native troops of the Bengal and Bombay Armies for the capture of three French islands in the Indian Ocean (the latter two being better known today as Mauritius and Reunion) between July 1809 and December 1810.*

VALUE:	Original striking	Later striking
Gold (50)	£8500–10,000	—
Silver (2200)	£2000–2500	£550–650

87. BAGUR AND PALAMOS MEDAL

Date: 1811.
Campaign: Peninsular War 1810.
Branch of Service: Royal Navy.
Ribbon: Red with yellow edges (illustration at right has faded ribbon).
Metal: Gold or silver.   **Size:** 45mm.
Description: (Obverse) the conjoined crowned shields of Britain and Spain in a wreath with ALIANZA ETERNA (eternal alliance) round the foot; (reverse) inscription in Spanish GRATITUDE OF SPAIN TO THE BRAVE BRITISH AT BAGUR 10 SEPT. 1810, PALAMOS 14 SEPT. 1810.
Comments: *Awarded by the Captain General of Catalonia to General Sir Charles Doyle and the Royal Marines and a limited number of officers and seamen from the British frigate* Cambrian, *for two actions on the coast of Catalonia in September 1810. Only awarded to those who actually went ashore: General Doyle, the Royal Marines, Captain Francis Fane and three of his officers received the medal for their participation in the attack on Bagur, while Lieutenant Benjamin Baynton and the launch crew received the medal for their participation at Palamós. Awarded in gold to officers and silver to other ranks.*

VALUE: **Gold (8)**   £8500–10,000   **Silver (72+)**   £2750–3500

88. JAVA MEDAL

Date: 1811.
Campaign: Java 1811.
Branch of Service: HEIC forces.
Ribbon: Yellow cord.
Metals: Gold or silver.
Size: 49mm.
Description: (Obverse) the assault on Fort Cornelis; (reverse) inscriptions in English and Farsi.
Comments: *Awarded by the HEIC for the seizure of Java from the Dutch. The 750 British officers and men who took part in the operation were not only awarded this medal but were eligible for the Military GSM with Java clasp, issued 38 years later. Senior officers of the Company were given the gold medal, while junior officers, NCOs and sepoys received the silver version.*

VALUE:	Original striking	Later striking
Gold (133)	£8500–10,000	£3500–4000
Silver (6519)	£1600–1800	£500–600

89. NEPAL MEDAL

Date: 1816.
Campaign: Nepal 1814-16.
Branch of Service: HEIC native troops.
Ribbon: Yellow cord.
Metal: Silver.
Size: 51mm.
Description: (Obverse) a fortified mountain-top with a cannon in the foreground; (reverse) Farsi inscription.
Comments: *This medal marked the campaign to pacify Nepal led by Generals Marley, Ochterlony and Gillespie (the last named being killed in action). At the conclusion of the war Ochterlony began recruiting Gurkha mercenaries, a policy which has continued in the British Army to this day. The clasp "Nepaul" was granted with the Army of India Medal to British forces in 1851.*

VALUE: Original striking £2000–2750
                Later striking £450–500 (as illustrated)

90. CEYLON MEDAL

Date: 1818.
Campaign: Ceylon (Sri Lanka) 1818.
Branch of Service: British and HEIC forces.
Ribbon: 38mm deep navy blue.
Metal: Gold or silver.
Size: 35mm.
Description: The very plain design has "Ceylon 1818" within a wreath (obverse) and REWARD OF MERIT at top and bottom of the reverse, the personal details being engraved in the centre.
Comments: *Awarded by the Ceylon government for gallant conduct during the Kandian rebellion. Only selected officers and men of the 19th, 73rd and 83rd Foot, the 1st and 2nd Ceylon Regiments and 7th, 15th and 18th Madras Native Infantry received this medal.*

VALUE:

Gold (2)	—
Silver (45)	£2000–3000

91. BURMA MEDAL

Date: 1826.
Campaign: Burma 1824-26.
Branch of Service: HEIC native forces.
Ribbon: 38mm crimson edged with navy blue.
Metals: Gold or silver.
Size: 39mm.
Description: (Obverse) the Burmese elephant kneeling in submission before the British lion; (reverse) the epic assault on Rangoon by the Irrawaddy Flotilla.
Comments: *Granted to native officers and men who participated in the campaign for the subjugation of Burma. This was the first of the HEIC campaign medals in what was to become a standard 1.5 inch (38mm) diameter. The medal was fitted with a large steel ring for suspension and issued unnamed. British troops in this campaign were belatedly (1851) given the clasp "Ava" to the Army of India Medal.*

VALUE:

		Miniature
Gold (750)	£4500–5500	—
Silver-gilt	£1500–2000	—
Silver (24,000)	£850–1250	£300–350

92. COORG MEDAL

Date: 1837.
Campaign: Coorg rebellion 1837.
Branch of Service: HEIC loyal Coorg forces.
Ribbon: Yellow cord.
Metals: Gold, silver or bronze.
Size: 50mm.
Description: (Obverse) a Coorg holding a musket, with kukri upraised; (reverse) weapons in a wreath with the inscription FOR DISTINGUISHED CONDUCT AND LOYALTY TO THE BRITISH GOVERNMENT COORG APRIL 1837, the equivalent in Canarese appearing on the obverse.
Comments: *Native troops who remained loyal during the Canara rebellion of April-May 1837 were awarded this medal by the HEIC the following August. Bronze specimens were also struck but not officially issued and may have been restrikes or later copies. Bronzed and silvered electrotype copies are also known.*

VALUE:	Original striking	Later striking
Gold (44)	**£7500–8500**	—
Silver (300)	**£2000–2500**	**£500–600**
Bronze	**£300–400**	—

93. NAVAL GOLD MEDAL

Date: 1795.
Campaign: Naval actions 1795-1815.
Branch of Service: Royal Navy.
Ribbon: 44mm white with broad dark blue edges.
Metal: Gold.
Size: 51mm and 38mm.
Description: The medals were glazed on both sides and individually engraved on the reverse with the name of the recipient and details of the engagement in a wreath of laurel and oak leaves. (Obverse) the winged figure of Victory bestowing a laurel wreath on the head of Britannia standing in the prow of a galley with a Union Jack shield behind her, her right foot on a helmet, her left hand holding a spear.
Comments: *Instituted in 1795, a year after Lord Howe's naval victory on "the glorious First of June", this medal was awarded continually till 1815 when the Order of the Bath was expanded into three classes. Large medals were awarded to admirals and small medals went to captains. As medals were awarded for separate actions it was possible for officers to wear more than one; Lord Nelson himself had three. Two miniatures are recorded and would probably fetch at least £1000 if they came on to the market.*

VALUE:	
Large medal (22)	**From £85,000**
Small medal (117)	**From £60,000**
Miniature	**£350–450**

94. NAVAL GENERAL SERVICE MEDAL

Date: 1847.

Campaign: Naval battles and boat actions 1793-1840.

Branch of Service: Royal Navy.

Ribbon: 32mm white with dark blue edges.

Metal: Silver.

Size: 36mm.

Description: (Obverse) the Young Head profile of Queen Victoria by William Wyon; (reverse) Britannia with her trident seated on a sea horse.

Clasps: No fewer than 230 different clasps for major battles, minor engagements, cutting-out operations and boat service were authorised. These either have the name or date of the action, the name of a ship capturing or defeating an enemy vessel, or the words BOAT SERVICE followed by a date. No fewer than 20,933 medals were awarded but most of them had a single clasp. Multi-clasp medals are worth very considerably more. The greatest number of clasps to a single medal was seven (three awards made); four medals had six clasps and 26 medals had five clasps. For reasons of space only those clasps which are met with fairly often in the salerooms are listed below. At the other end of the scale it should be noted that only one recipient claimed the clasps for *Hussar* (17 May 1795), *Dido* (24 June 1795), *Spider* (25 August 1795), *Espoir* (7 August 1798), *Viper* (26 December 1799), *Loire* (5 February 1800), *Louisa* (28 October 1807), *Carrier* (4 November 1807), *Superieure* (10 February 1809), *Growler* (22 May 1812) and the boat actions of 15 March 1793, 4 November 1803, 4 November 1810 and 3-6 September 1814. In several cases no claimants came forward at all. The numbers of clasps awarded are not an accurate guide to value, as some actions are rated more highly than others, and clasps associated with actions in the War of 1812 have a very strong following in the USA as well as Britain. Clasps for famous battles, such as Trafalgar, likewise command a high premium out of all proportion to the number of clasps awarded. A medal to HMS *Victory* would be worth in excess of £15,000.

Comments: *Instituted in 1847 and issued to **surviving** claimants in 1848, this medal was originally intended to cover naval engagements of the French Revolutionary and Napoleonic Wars (1793-1815) but was almost immediately extended to cover all naval actions of a more recent date, down to the expedition to Syria in 1840. It was fitted with a straight suspender.*

VALUE (for the most commonly encountered clasps):

v.	1 June 1794 (583)	£3500–4500	cxxviii.	Guadaloupe (484)	£1500–2000
ix.	14 March 1795 (114)	£3500–4500	cxli.	Lissa (124)	£3000–3500
xv.	23 June 1795 (200)	£3500–4500	cxlvi.	Java (695)	£2000–2500
xxxi.	St Vincent (364)	£3500–4500	clxi.	Shannon wh Chesapeake (42)	£6500–7500
xxxiv.	Camperdown (336)	£4000–5000	clxiii.	St Sebastian (288)	£4000–5000
xxxvi.	Mars 21 April 1798 (26)	£6500–8500	clxv.	Gluckstadt 5 Jany 1814 (45)	£5000–6500
xxxviii.	Lion 15 July 1798 (23)	£6500–8500	clxxvi.	Gaieta 24 July 1815 (89)	£5000–6000
xxxix.	Nile (351)	£3500–4000	clxxvii.	Algiers (1,362)	£1500–2500
xli.	12 Octr 1798 (79)	£4000–5000	clxxviii.	Navarino (1,137)	£1500–2500
xlv.	Acre 30 May 1799 (50)	£4500–5500	clxxix.	Syria (7,057)	£1000–1500
lxii.	Egypt (618)	£2000–2500			
lxiii.	Copenhagen (545)	£4500–6000	**Boat Service**		
lxv.	Gut of Gibraltar (144)	£4000–5000	cxcii.	16 July 1806 (52)	£3500–4500
lxxv.	Trafalgar (1,710)	£8000–8500	ccvi.	1 Novr 1809 (110)	£3000–4000
lxxvi.	4 Novr 1805 (297)	£3000–4000	ccx.	28 June 1810 (27)	£4500–5500
lxxvii.	St Domingo (406)	£3500–4500	ccxxiii.	29 Sepr 1812 (25)	£4500–5500
lxxix.	London 13 March 1806 (27)	£5000–6000	ccxxvii.	Ap and May 1813 (51)	£4500–5500
lxxxv.	Curacao 1 Jany 1807 (67)	£4000–5000	ccxxviii.	2 May 1813 (48)	£4500–5500
xcvii.	Stately 22 March 1808 (31)	£5000–6500	ccxxix.	April 1814 (24)	£5500–6500
cxiii.	Martinique (506)	£2000–2500	ccxxx.	24 May 1814 (14)	£6000–7000
cxvii.	Basque Roads (551)	£3000–3500	ccxxxiii.	14 Decr 1814 (205)	£2500–3000

Miniature **Without clasp** £125–175, for each clasp add £75+ depending on the action.

Below are listed all of the clasps authorised for wear on the Naval General Service Medal. As they were not issued until some years after the events, in some cases very few were ever claimed and in some instances there were no claimants at all. The numbers issued are indicated in brackets.

i.	Nymphe 18 June 1793 (4)	lxiv.	Speedy 6 May 1801 (7)
ii.	Crescent 20 Octr 1793 (12)	lxv.	Gut of Gibraltar 12 July 1801 (144)
iii.	Zebra 17 March1794 (2)	lxvi.	Sylph 28 Septr 1801 (2)
iv.	Carysfort 29 May 1794 (0)	lxvii.	Pasley 28 Octr 1801 (4)
v.	1 June 1794 (583)	lxviii.	Scorpion 31 March 1804 (4)
vi.	Romney 17 June 1794 (2)	lxix.	Beaver 31 March 1804 (0)
vii.	Blanche 4 Jany 1795 (5)	lxx.	Centurion 18 Septr 1804 (12)
viii.	Lively 13 March 1795 (6)	lxxi.	Arrow 3 Feby 1805 (8)
ix.	14 March 1795 (114)	lxxii.	Acheron 3 Feby 1805 (2)
x.	Astraea 10 April 1795 (2)	lxxiii.	San Fiorenzo 14 Feby 1805 (13)
xi.	Thetis 17 May 1795 (2)	lxxiv.	Phoenix 10 Aug 1805 (29)
xii.	Hussar 17 May 1795 (1)	lxxv.	Trafalgar (1,710)
xiii.	Mosquito 9 June 1795 (0)	lxxvi.	4 Novr 1805 (297)
xiv.	17 June 1795 (42)	lxxvii.	St. Domingo (406)
xv.	23 June 1795 (200)	lxxviii.	Amazon 13 March 1806 (30)
xvi.	Dido 24 June 1795 (1)	lxxix.	London 13 March 1806 (27)
xvii.	Lowestoffe 24 June 1795 (6)	lxxx.	Pique 26 March 1806 (8)
xviii.	Spider 25 August 1795 (1)	lxxxi.	Sirius 17 April 1806 (20)
xix.	Port Spergui (4)	lxxxii.	Blanche 19 July 1806 (22)
xx.	Indefatigable 20 April 1796 (8)	lxxxiii.	Arethusa 23 Aug 1806 (17)
xxi.	Unicorn 8 June 1796 (4)	lxxxiv.	Anson 23 Aug 1806 (11)
xxii.	Santa Margarita 8 June 1796 (3)	lxxxv.	Curacoa 1 Jany 1807 (67)
xxiii.	Southampton 9 June 1796 (8)	lxxxvi.	Pickle 3 Jany 1807 (2)
xxiv.	Dryad 13 June 1796 (6)	lxxxvii.	Hydra 6 Aug 1807 (12)
xxv.	Terpsichore 13 Oct 1796 (3)	lxxxviii.	Comus 15 Aug 1807 (9)
xxvi.	Lapwing 3 Decr 1796 (2)	lxxxix.	Louisa 28 Octr 1807 (1)
xxvii.	Minerve 19 Decr 1796 (4)	xc.	Carrier 4 Novr 1807 (1)
xxviii.	Blanche 19 Decr 1796 (4)	xci.	Ann 24 Novr 1807 (0)
xxix.	Indefatigable 13 Jany 1797 (8)	xcii.	Sappho 2 March 1808 (4)
xxx.	Amazon 13 Jany 1797 (6)	xciii.	San Fiorenzo 8 March 1808 (17)
xxxi.	St Vincent (364)	xciv.	Emerald 13 March 1808 (10)
xxxii.	San Fiorenzo 8 March 1797 (8)	xcv.	Childers 14 March 1808 (4)
xxxiii.	Nymphe 8 March 1797 (5)	xcvi.	Nassau 22 March 1808 (31)
xxxiv.	Camperdown (336)	xcvii.	Stately 22 March 1808 (31)
xxxv.	Phoebe 21 Decr 1797 (5)	xcviii.	Off Rota 4 April 1808 (19)
xxxvi.	Mars 21 April 1798 (26)	xcix.	Grasshopper 24 April 1808 (7)
xxxvii.	Isle St. Marcou (3)	c.	Rapid 24 April 1808 (1)
xxxviii.	Lion 15 July 1798 (23)	ci.	Redwing 7 May 1808 (7)
xxxix.	Nile (351)	cii.	Virginie 19 May 1808 (21)
xl.	Espoir 7 Aug 1798 (1)	ciii.	Redwing 31 May 1808 (7)
xli.	12 Octr 1798 (79)	civ.	Seahorse wh Badere Zaffer (32)
xlii.	Fisgard 20 Octr 1798 (9)	cv.	Comet 11 Aug 1808 (4)
xliii.	Sybille 28 Feby 1799 (12)	cvi.	Centaur 26 Aug 1808 (42)
xliv.	Telegraph 18 March 1799 (0)	cvii.	Implacable 26 Aug 1808 (44)
xlv.	Acre 30 May 1799 (50)	cviii.	Cruizer 1 Novr 1808 (4)
xlvi.	Schiermonnikoog 12 Aug 1799 (9)	cix.	Amethyst wh Thetis (31)
xlvii.	Arrow 13 Sept 1799 (2)	cx.	Off the Pearl Rock 13 Decr 1808 (16)
xlviii.	Wolverine 13 Sept 1799 (0)	cxi.	Onyx 1 Jany 1809 (5)
xlix.	Surprise wh Hermione (7)	cxii.	Confiance 14 Jany 1809 (8)
l.	Speedy 6 Novr 1799 (3)	cxiii.	Martinique (506)
li.	Courier 22 Novr 1799 (3)	cxiv.	Horatio 10 Feby 1809 (13)
lii.	Viper 26 Decr 1799 (2)	cxv.	Supérieure 10 Feby 1809 (1)
liv.	Harpy 5 Feby 1800 (4)	cxvi.	Amethyst 5 April 1809 (27)
lv.	Fairy 5 Feby 1800 (4)	cxvii.	Basque Roads 1809 (551)
lvi.	Peterel 21 March 1800 (2)	cxviii.	Recruit 17 June 1809 (7)
lvii.	Penelope 30 March 1800 (11)	cxix.	Pompee 17 June 1809 (47)
lviii.	Vinciego 30 March 1800 (2)	cxx.	Castor 17 June 1809 (13)
lix.	Capture of the Désirée (24)	cxxi.	Cyane 25 and 27 June 1809 (5)
lx.	Seine 20 August 1800 (7)	cxxii.	L'Espoir 25 and 27 June 1809 (5)
lxi.	Phoebe 19 Feby 1801 (6)	cxxiii.	Bonne Citoyenne wh Furieuse (12)
lxii.	Egypt (618)	cxxiv.	Diana 11 Septr 1809 (8)
lxiii.	Copenhagen 1801 (545)	cxxv.	Anse la Barque 18 Decr 1809 (51)

cxxvi.	Cherokee 10 Jany 1810 (4)		cliii.	Griffon 27 March 1812 (3)
cxxvii.	Scorpion 12 Jany 1810 (8)		cliv.	Northumberland 22 May 1812 (63)
cxxviii.	Guadaloupe (484)		clv.	Growler 22 May 1812 (1)
cxxix.	Thistle 10 Feby 1810 (0)		clvi.	Malaga 29 May 1812 (18) (the date should
cxxx.	Surly 24 April 1810 (1)			have been 29 April 1812)
cxxxi.	Firm 24 April 1810 (1)		clvii.	Off Mardoe 6 July 1812 (47)
cxxxii.	Sylvia 26 April 1810 (1)		clviii.	Sealark 21 July 1812 (4)
cxxxiii.	Spartan 3 May 1810 (30)		clix.	Royalist 29 Decr 1812 (4)
cxxxiv.	Royalist May and June 1810 (3)		clx.	Weasel 22 April 1813 (8)
cxxxv.	Amanthea 25 July 1810 (23)		clxi.	Shannon wh Chesapeake (42)
cxxxvi.	Banda Neira (68)		clxii.	Pelican 14 Aug 1813 (4)
cxxxvii.	Staunch 18 Septr 1810 (2)		clxiii.	St. Sebastian (288)
cxxxviii.	Otter 18 Septr 1810 (8)		clxiv.	Thunder 9 Octr 1813 (9)
cxxxix.	Boadicea 18 Septr 1810 (15)		clxv.	Gluckstadt 5 Jany 1814 (45)
cxl.	Briseis 14 Octr 1810 (2)		clxvi.	Venerable 16 Jany 1814 (42)
cxli.	Lissa (124)		clxix.	Cyane 16 Jany 1814 (7)
cxlii.	Anholt 27 March 1811 (40)		clxx.	Eurotas 25 Feby 1814 (32)
cxliii.	Arrow 6 April 1811 (0)		clxxi.	Hebrus wh L'Etoile (40)
cxliv.	Off Tamatave 20 May 1811 (87)		clxxii.	Phoebe 28 March 1814 (36)
cxlv.	Hawke 18 Aug 1811 (6)		clxxiii.	Cherub 28 March 1814 (7)
cxlvi.	Java (695)		clxxiv.	The Potomac 17 Aug 1814 (108)
cxlvii.	Skylark 11 Novr 1811 (4)		clxxv.	Endymion wh President (58)
cxlviii.	Locust 11 Novr 1811 (2)		clxxvi.	Gaieta 24 July 1815 (89)
cxlix.	Pelagosa 29 Novr 1811 (74)		clxxvii.	Algiers (1,362)
cl.	Victorious wh Rivoli (67)		clxxviii.	Navarino (1,137)
cli.	Weasel 22 Feby 1812 (6)		clxxix.	Syria (7,057)
clii.	Rosario 27 March 1812 (7)			

BOAT SERVICE

These clasps have the words BOAT SERVICE separating the month and the years of the dates. They were only awarded for actions which culminated in an officer or the senior member present being promoted.

clxxx.	15 March 1793 (1)		ccvii.	13 Decr 1809 (9)
clxxxi.	17 March 1794 (29)		ccviii.	13 Feby 1810 (20)
clxxxii.	29 May 1797 (3)		ccix.	1 May 1810 (15)
clxxxiii.	9 June 1799 (4)		ccx.	28 June 1810 (27)
clxxxiv.	20 Decr 1799 (3)		ccxi.	27 Sept 1810 (36)
clxxxv.	29 July 1800 (4)		ccxii.	4 Novr 1810 (1)
clxxxvi.	29 Aug 1800 (25)		ccxiii.	23 Novr 1810 (42)
clxxxvii.	27 Octr 1800 (5)		ccxiv.	24 Decr 1810 (6)
clxxxvii.	21 July 1801 (7)		ccxv.	4 May 1811 (10)
clxxxviii.	27 June 1803 (5)		ccxvi.	30 July 1811 (4)
clxxxix.	4 Novr 1803 (2)		ccxvii.	2 Aug 1811 (9)
cxc.	4 Feby 1804 (11)		ccxviii.	20 Sept 1811 (6)
cxci.	4 June 1805 (10)		ccxix.	4 Decr 1811 (19)
cxcii.	16 July 1806 (52)		ccxx.	4 April 1812 (4)
cxciii.	2 Jan 1807 (3)		ccxxi.	1st Sept 1812 (21)
cxciv.	21 Jan 1807 (8)		ccxxii.	17 Sept 1812 (11) (Bars are known dated
cxcv.	19 April 1807 (0)			17 Decr 1812 in error)
cxcvi.	13 Feby 1808 (2)		ccxxiii.	29 Sept 1812 (25)
cxcvii.	10 July 1808 (8)		ccxxiv.	6 Jany 1813 (25)
cxcviii.	11 Aug 1808 (17)		ccxxv.	21 March 1813 (3)
cxcix.	28 Novr 1808 (2)		ccxxvi.	29 April 1813 (2)
cc.	7 July 1809 (35)		ccxxvii.	Ap and May 1813 (51)
cci.	14 July 1809 (7)		ccxxviii.	2 May 1813 (48)
ccii.	25 July 1809 (36)		ccxxix.	8 April 1814 (24)
cciii.	27 July 1809 (10)		ccxxx.	24 May 1814 (14)
cciv.	29 July 1809 (11)		ccxxxi.	Aug and Septr 1814 (1)
ccv.	28 Aug 1809 (15)		ccxxxii.	3 and 6 Septr 1814 (1)
ccvi.	1 Novr 1809 (100)		ccxxxiii.	14 Decr 1814 (205)

95. ARMY GOLD CROSS

Date: 1813.
Campaigns: Napoleonic and Peninsular War.
Branch of Service: British Army.
Ribbon: 38mm crimson edged with dark blue.
Metal: Gold. **Size:** 38mm.
Description: A cross pattée with a laurel border having a rose at the centre on each of the four flat ends. At the centre of the cross appears a British lion statant. The scrolled top of the cross is fitted with an elaborate ring decorated with laurel leaves looped through a plain swivel ring fitted to the suspender. The arms of the cross on both obverse and reverse bear the names of four battles in relief.
Clasps: Large borders of laurel leaves enclosing the name of a battle in raised relief within an elliptical frame, awarded for fifth and subsequent battles.
Comments: *Arguably the most prestigious award in the campaign series, the Army Gold Cross was approved by the Prince Regent in 1813. It was granted to generals and officers of field rank for service in four or more battles of the Peninsular War. Four crosses were also awarded for Maida, seven Martinique and three Guadeloupe. A total of 164 crosses and 244 clasps were awarded. Three crosses had six clasps, two had seven, while the Duke of Wellington himself had the unique cross with nine clasps, representing participation in thirteen battles.*

VALUE:

Gold cross without clasp (61)	From £25,000
Miniature	£520–635

The Duke of Wellington.

96. MAIDA GOLD MEDAL

Date: 1806.
Campaign: Battle of Maida 1806.
Branch of Service: British Army.
Ribbon: 38mm crimson edged with navy blue.
Metal: Gold.
Size: 39mm.
Description: (Obverse) laureated profile of George III; (reverse) winged figure of Victory hovering with a laurel wreath over the head of Britannia, shield upraised, in the act of throwing a spear. The name and date of the battle appears on Britannia's left, with the *trinacria* or three-legged emblem on the right.
Clasps: None.
Comments: *This small gold medal was authorised in 1806 and awarded to the thirteen senior officers involved in the battle of Maida in Calabria when a small British force under General Sir John Stuart defeated a much larger French army with heavy loss. A small unknown number of gold and silver specimens are known to exist.*

VALUE: From £45,000

97. ARMY GOLD MEDAL

Date: 1810.
Campaigns: Peninsular War 1806-14 and War of 1812.
Branch of Service: British Army.
Ribbon: 38mm crimson edged with navy blue.
Metal: Gold.
Size: 54mm and 33mm.
Description: (Obverse) Britannia seated on a globe, holding a laurel wreath over the British lion and holding a palm branch in her left hand while resting on a shield embellished with the Union Jack. The name of the first action is generally engraved on the reverse.
Clasps: For second and third actions.
Comments: *The Maida medal (no. 96) established a precedent for the series of medals instituted in 1810. The name of the battle was inscribed on the reverse, usually engraved, though that for Barossa was die-struck. These medals were struck in two sizes, the larger being conferred on generals and the smaller on officers of field rank. Second or third battles were denoted by a clasp appropriately inscribed, while those who qualified for a fourth award exchanged their medal and bars for a gold cross. The award of these gold medals and crosses ceased in 1814 when the Companion of the Bath was instituted.*

VALUE*:
Large medal	From £30,000
Small medal	From £18,500

*Medals to British officers in the Portuguese Service generally sell for 20% less. Only one miniature is known to exist.

98. MILITARY GENERAL SERVICE MEDAL

Date: 1847.

Campaigns: French Revolutionary and Napoleonic Wars 1793-1814.

Branch of Service: British Army.

Ribbon: 31mm crimson edged with dark blue.

Metal: Silver.

Size: 36mm.

Description: (Obverse) the Wyon profile of Queen Victoria; (reverse) a standing figure of the Queen bestowing victor's laurels on a kneeling Duke of Wellington. The simple inscription TO THE BRITISH ARMY appears round the circumference, while the dates 1793-1814 are placed in the exergue. Despite this, the earliest action for which a clasp was issued took place in 1801 (Abercromby's Egyptian campaign).

Clasps: Only 29 battle or campaign clasps were issued but multiple awards are much more common than in the naval medal, the maximum being fifteen. While it is generally true to say that multi-clasp medals are worth more than single-clasp medals, there are many in the latter category (noted below) which command higher prices. The figures quoted below are based on the commonest regiments. Clasps awarded to specialists and small detached forces rate more highly than medals to the principal regiment in a battle or campaign. In particular, it should be noted that one naval officer, Lieut. Carroll, received the Military GSM and clasp for Maida, while a few other officers of the Royal Navy and Royal Marines received the medal with the clasps for Guadaloupe, Martinique or Java, and these, naturally, are now very much sought after. Paradoxically, the clasps for Sahagun and Benevente alone are very much scarcer than the clasp inscribed Sahagun and Benevente, awarded to surviving veterans who had participated in both battles. The clasps are listed below in chronological order. Medals to officers rate a premium.

Comments: *Like the Naval GSM, this medal was not sanctioned till 1847 and awarded the following year. Unlike the Naval medal, however, the Military GSM was confined to land actions up to the defeat of Napoleon in 1814 and the conclusion of the war with the United States. The regiment is now having a bearing on price, with medals to the 52nd, 88th or 95th Foot worth a good premium.*

VALUE:

i.	Egypt	£1250–1500	xxi.	Chateauguay	£6000–7000
ii.	Maida	£1550–2000	xxii.	Chrystler's Farm	£7000–8000
iii.	Roleia	£1150–1350	xxiii.	Vittoria	£1000–1250
iv.	Vimiera	£1000–1250	xxiv.	Pyrenees	£1000–1250
v.	Sahagun	£2000–2500	xxv.	St Sebastian	£1100–1300
vi.	Benevente	£4500–6000	xxvi.	Nivelle	£1000–1250
vii.	Sahagun and Benevente	£2000–2500	xxvii.	Nive	£950–1100
viii.	Corunna	£1000–1250	xxviii.	Orthes	£950–1100
ix.	Martinique	£1500–1750	xxix.	Toulouse	£950–1100
x.	Talavera	£1100–1300	2 clasps		from £1250
xi.	Guadaloupe	£1000–1250	3 clasps		from £1500
xii.	Busaco	£1000–1250	4 clasps		from £1750
xiii.	Barrosa	£1000–1250	5 clasps		from £2000
xiv.	Fuentes D'Onor	£1000–1250	6 clasps		from £2250
xv.	Albuhera	£1250–1500	7 clasps		from £2500
xvi.	Java	£1000–1250	8 clasps		from £3000
xvii.	Ciudad Rodrigo	£1000–1250	9 clasps		from £3500
xviii.	Badajoz	£1300–1550	10 clasps		from £4000
xix.	Salamanca	£1000–1250	11 clasps		from £4500
xx.	Fort Detroit	£7000–8000	12 or more clasps		from £7500

Miniature without clasp £125–175, for each clasp add £75+ depending on the action.

99. WATERLOO MEDAL

Date: 1815.

Campaign: Waterloo 1815.

Branch of Service: British Army.

Ribbon: 38mm, crimson edged in dark blue.

Metal: Silver.

Size: 37mm.

Description: (Obverse) the profile of the Prince Regent; (reverse) the seated figure of Victory above a tablet simply inscribed WATERLOO with the date of the battle in the exergue.

Comments: *This was the first medal awarded and officially named to all ranks who took part in a particular campaign. It was also issued, however, to those who had taken part in one or more of the other battles of the campaign, at Ligny and Quatre Bras two days earlier. The ribbon was intended to be worn with an iron clip and split suspension ring but many recipients subsequently replaced these with a more practical silver mount which would not rust and spoil the uniform. Some 39,000 medals were issued. The value of a Waterloo medal depends to a large extent on the regiment of the recipient. Medals awarded to those formations which saw the heaviest action and bore the brunt of the losses are in the greatest demand, whereas medals named to soldiers in General Colville's reserve division which did not take part in the fighting, are the least highly rated.*

VALUE:

Heavy Cavalry	£3750–4750
Scots Greys	£8500–10,000
Light Cavalry	£2750–3750
Royal Artillery	£2500–3000
Royal Horse Artillery	£2500–3000
Foot Guards	£2250–2850
1st, 27th, 28th, 30th, 42nd, 44th, 52nd, 73rd, 79th, 92nd, 95th Foot	£4000–5000
Other Foot regiments	£2250–2750
Colville's division (35th, 54th, 59th, 91st Foot)	£1750–2250
King's German Legion	£1500–1850

Miniature
Original	£60–250

100. BRUNSWICK MEDAL FOR WATERLOO

Date: 1817.

Campaign: Battle of Waterloo 1815.

Branch of Service: Brunswick troops.

Ribbon: 38mm wide, yellow with light blue stripes towards the edges.

Metal: Bronze.

Size: 35mm.

Description: (Obverse) Duke Friedrich Wilhelm of Brunswick who was killed in the battle; (reverse) a wreath of laurel and oak leaves enclosing the German text "Braunschweig Seinen Kriegern" (Brunswick to its warriors) and the names of Quatre Bras and Waterloo.

Comments: *The Prince Regent authorised this medal for issue to the contingent from the Duchy of Brunswick who served at Quatre Bras or Waterloo. The next of kin of those killed in action at either battle where awarded the medal disc only with no ring, clip, suspension or ribbon. It is thought that approximately 700 medals are still extant.*

VALUE: £600–800
Casualty £2000–2500

Miniature —

101. HANOVERIAN MEDAL FOR WATERLOO

Date: 1818.
Campaign: Battle of Waterloo 1815.
Branch of Service: Hanoverian troops.
Ribbon: Maroon edged with light blue.
Metal: Silver.
Size: 35mm.
Description: (Obverse) the Prince Regent, his name and title being rendered in German. (Reverse) a trophy of arms below the legend HANNOVERISCHER TAPFERKEIT (Hanoverian bravery), with the name and date of the battle wreathed in the centre.
Comments: *The Prince Regent authorised this medal on behalf of his father George III in his capacity as Elector of Hanover and this was conferred on survivors of the battle. Suspension was by iron clip and ring similar to the British Waterloo Medal.*

VALUE:	£700–800
Miniature	£125–175

102. NASSAU MEDAL FOR WATERLOO

Date: 1815.
Campaign: Battle of Waterloo 1815.
Branch of Service: Nassau forces.
Ribbon: Dark blue edged in yellow.
Metal: Silver.
Size: 28mm.
Description: (Obverse) Duke Friedrich of Nassau; (reverse) the winged figure of Victory crowning a soldier with laurels, the date of the action being in the exergue.
Comments: *Friedrich Duke of Nassau distributed this medal on 23 December 1815 to all of his own troops who had been present at the battle.*

VALUE:	£450–550

103. SAXE-GOTHA-ALTENBURG MEDAL

Date: 1816.
Campaign: Germany and Waterloo 1814-15.
Branch of Service: Saxe-Gotha-Altenburg Foreign Legion.
Ribbon: Green with black edges and gold stripes.
Metal: Gilt bronze or bronze.
Size: 42mm.
Description: (Obverse) a crown with the legend IM KAMPFE FUER DAS RECHT (in the struggle for the right); (reverse) an ornate rose motif with the name of the duchy and the dates of the campaign in roman numerals.
Comments: *Gilded medals were issued to officers, NCOs received bronze medals with gilt raised points and other ranks a bronze version.*

VALUE:	
Gilt-bronze	£1000–1250
Bronze	£650–750

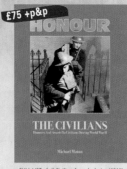
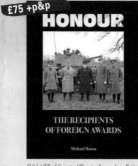
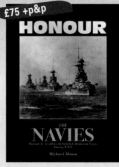
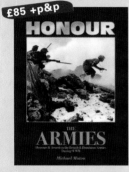

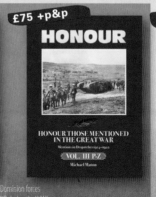

104. ARMY OF INDIA MEDAL

Date: 1851.
Campaigns: India 1803–26.
Branch of Service: British and HEIC troops.
Ribbon: 32mm pale blue.
Metal: Silver.
Size: 35mm.
Description: (Obverse) the Wyon profile of Queen Victoria; (reverse) the seated figure of Victory beside a palm tree, with a wreath in one hand and a laurel crown in the other. The medal is fitted with an ornamental scroll suspender.
Clasps: The medal was not awarded without a campaign clasp and, unusually, in multi-clasp medals, the last clasp awarded was mounted closest to the medal itself, so that the battle roll has to be read downwards. There were two dies of the reverse, leading to the long- or short-hyphen varieties, both of comparable value. In all, some 4500 medals were awarded, but there is a very wide divergence between the commonest and rarest bars. Multi-clasp medals are rare, and medals awarded to Europeans are much scarcer than those to Indian troops.
Comments: *The last of the medals authorised in connection with the Napoleonic Wars, it was instituted and paid for by the Honourable East India Company in March 1851 for award to surviving veterans of the battles and campaigns in India and Burma between 1803 and 1826. Despite the dates 1799–1826 in the exergue, the medal was in fact awarded for service in one or other of four wars: the Second Mahratta War (1803–4), the Nepal War (1814–16), the Pindaree or Third Mahratta War (1817–18) and the Burmese War (1824–26), together with the siege of Bhurtpoor (1825–26). The medal is scarce, and examples with the clasps for the Second Mahratta War are much sought after, partly because few veterans were still alive 48 years after the event to claim their medals, and partly because of the war's association with Arthur Wellesley, the Duke of Wellington, who died in the very year in which the medal was awarded. Medals to the Royal Navy with the Ava clasp are very rare.*

Rev. die a, short hyphen

Rev. die b, long hyphen

VALUE:
Prices for medals bearing the following clasps are for European recipients. Medals to Indians are generally less expensive.

i.	Allighur (66)		£3000–3500
ii.	Battle of Delhi (40)		£3500–4500
iii.	Assye (87)		£3000–3500
iv.	Asseerghur (48)		£3500–4500
v.	Laswarree (100)		£3000–3500
vi.	Argaum (126)		£2500–3000
vii.	Gawilghur (110)		£3000–3500
viii.	Defence of Delhi (5)		—
ix.	Battle of Deig (47)		£3500–4500
x.	Capture of Deig (103)		£3000–3500
xi.	Nepaul (505)		£1500–1800
xii.	Kirkee (5)		—
xiii.	Poona (75)		£3000–3500
xiv.	Kirkee and Poona (88)		£3000–3500
xv.	Seetabuldee (2)		—
xvi.	Nagpore (155)		£2500–3000
xvii.	Seetabuldee and Nagpore (21)		£6000–8000
xviii.	Maheidpoor (75)		£3000–3500
xix.	Corygaum (4)		£6000–10,000
xx.	Ava (2325)		£1000–1200 (Army)
xxi.	Bhurtpoor (1059)		£1200–1500
2 clasps (300)			from £3500
3 clasps (150)			from £7500
4 clasps (23)			from £10,000
5 or more clasps (10 x 5, 2 x 6, 1 x 7)			—
Glazed gilt specimen			£850–1000

Miniature*
One clasp Ava	£275–300
Further clasps	£125–175 each

*Note there are many silver reproductions and clasps on the market, value £10–20.

105. GHUZNEE MEDAL

Date: 1839.
Campaign: Ghuznee 1839.
Branch of Service: British and HEIC forces.
Ribbon: 35mm half crimson, half dark green (originally green and yellow)
Metal: Silver.
Size: 37mm.
Description: (Obverse) the impressive gateway of the fortress of Ghuznee; (reverse) a mural crown enclosed in a laurel wreath with the date of capture.
Comments: *This was the second medal awarded for a particular campaign (after Waterloo) and was granted to both British and Indian troops who took part in the assault on Ghuznee in July 1839 which brought the first Afghan War to a close, overthrew the pro-Russian Dost Mohamed and restored Shah Soojah who instituted the Order of the Dooranie Empire (awarded to British generals and field officers) in appreciation. The Ghuznee medal was issued unnamed by the Honourable East India Company, but many recipients subsequently had their names impressed or engraved in various styles. No clasps were issued officially, but unauthorised clasps are occasionally encountered.*

VALUE:

British recipient	£850–1000
Indian recipient	£750–850
Unnamed as issued	£500–600
Miniature	£175–330

Original type ribbon.

Taking the Ghuznee fortress.

105A. BRITISH LEGION MEDAL

Date: 1836.

Campaign: First Carlist War.

Branch of Service: British Auxiliary Legion, plus a battalion of Royal Artillery seconded to the forces loyal to Queen Isabella.

Ribbon: Broad blue with narrow yellow stripes towards the edges.

Metal: Silver or white metal.

Size: 36mm.

Description: (Obverse) A cross pattee with the word TUJO in a laurel wreath at the centre; (reverse) ESPANA / AGRADECIDA (Grateful Spain) with a British lion enclosed by the cordon of the Golden Fleece. The medal is fitted with a ring for suspension from a double-looped bar and has a brooch fitment at the top of the ribbon. The medal was struck in Birmingham.

Comments: *The British Auxiliary Legion, commanded by General Sir George De Lacey Evans (1787–1870), volunteered for service in Spain in support of Isabella II who, at the age of three (1833) succeeded her father as monarch. Her uncle, Don Carlos, opposed this and triggered off a war which lasted till 1840 and was largely fought in the northern provinces. The inscription on the obverse alludes to the battle at Laguna del Tujo near Castilla la Mancha.*

VALUE:		
Silver		£400–450
(one Continental size miniature example with engraved details to reverse is known)		
White metal		£150–200

106. ST. JEAN D'ACRE MEDAL

Date: 1840.

Campaign: Syria 1840.

Branch of Service: Royal Navy, Royal Marines and British Army.

Ribbon: Red with white edges.

Metal: Gold (22gms), silver or copper (bronzed).

Size: 30mm.

Description: (Obverse) a fortress flying the Ottoman flag, with six five-pointed stars round the top. A commemorative inscription and date in Arabic appear at the foot; (reverse) the Toughra of the Sultan in a laurel wreath.

Comments: *Awarded by the Sultan of Turkey to British, Austrian and Turkish forces under Sir Charles Napier, taking part in the liberation of this important city on the Syrian coast after eight years of Egyptian occupation. The medal has a plain ring suspension. The clasp "Syria" to the Naval GSM was awarded in 1848 in respect of this operation, and this medal generally accompanies the St Jean d'Acre medal.*

VALUE:		*Miniature*
Gold (captains and field officers)	£4500–5000	—
Silver (junior officers)	£400–450	£200–250
Copper (petty officers, NCOs and other ranks)	£200–250	—

107. CANDAHAR, GHUZNEE, CABUL MEDAL

Date: 1842.
Campaign: Afghanistan 1841–42.
Branch of Service: British and HEIC troops.
Ribbon: 40mm watered silk of pink, white, yellow, white and blue representing an eastern sky at sunrise.
Metal: Silver.
Size: 36mm.
Description: Although the medals have a uniform obverse, a profile of the Queen captioned VICTORIA VINDEX, reverses are inscribed with the names of individual battles, or combinations thereof, within wreaths surmounted by a crown.
Comments: *The Honourable East India Company instituted this series of medals in 1842 for award to both HEIC and British troops who took part in the First Afghan War. The issue of this medal to units of the British Army, to Europeans serving in the Company's forces, and to Indian troops is further complicated by the fact that unnamed medals are generally common. In addition, the medal for Cabul is known in two versions, with the inscription CABUL or CABVL, the latter being a major rarity as only fifteen were issued. Only 160 medals with Candahar reverse were issued to Europeans. Beware of modern copies of the Candahar and Cabul medals.*

VALUE:	Imperial Regiments	Indian Units	Unnamed
i. Candahar	£850–1000	£500–650	£400–550
ii. Cabul	£650–850	£450–650	£400–550
iii. Cabvl (15)	—	—	—
iv. Ghuznee/Cabul	£850–1000	£500–650	£400–550
v. Candahar/Ghuznee/ Cabul	£1200–1500	£500–650	£400–550
Miniature	from £265 (depending on reverse)		

108. JELLALABAD MEDALS

Type 1

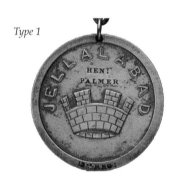

Date: 1842.
Campaign: Afghanistan 1841-42.
Branch of Service: British and HEIC forces.
Ribbon: 44mm watered silk red, white, yellow, white and blue representing an eastern sky at sunrise.
Metal: Silver.
Size: 39mm and 35mm.
Description: There are two different types of this medal, awarded by the HEIC to surviving defenders of the fortress of Jellalabad between 12 November 1841 and 7 April 1842. The first, struck in Calcutta, has a mural crown and JELLALABAD on the obverse, with the date of the relief of the garrison on the reverse; the second type shows the Wyon profile of Victoria (obverse) and the winged Victory with mountain scenery in the background and JELLALABAD VII APRIL round the top and the year in roman numerals in the exergue (reverse).
Comments: *The first type, struck in Calcutta, was considered to be unsuitable and holders were invited to exchange their medals for the second, more attractive, issue which was produced in London, although very few recipients took up the offer. The latter type was also awarded to the next of kin of soldiers killed in action.*

VALUE:	Imperial Regiments	Indian Units	Unnamed	*Miniature*
i. First type (Crown)	£850–1000	£750–850	£600-800	£350–400
ii. Second type (Victory)	£1200–1500	—	£900–1000	£250–350

109. MEDAL FOR THE DEFENCE OF KELAT-I-GHILZIE

Date: 1842.
Campaign: Afghanistan 1842.
Branch of Service: European and native troops, HEIC.
Ribbon: 40mm watered silk red, white, yellow, white and blue representing an eastern sky at sunrise.
Metal: Silver.
Size: 36mm.
Description: (Obverse) a shield bearing the name of the fort, surmounted by a mural crown and encircled by laurels; (reverse) a trophy of arms above a tablet inscribed INVICTA (unbeaten) and the date in roman numerals.
Comments: *Awarded to those who took part in the defence of the fort at Kelat-i-Ghilzie in May 1842, it is the rarest medal of the First Afghan War. No British imperial regiments took part, but 55 Europeans in the Company's service received the medal. It was also awarded to 877 native troops (including a contingent supplied by Shah Soojah) but few of their medals appear to have survived.*

VALUE:

European recipients	£5500–6500
Indian recipients	£3500–4500
Unnamed	£1800–2000
Miniature	£500–600

110. CHINA WAR MEDAL

Issued reverse

Date: 1842.
Campaign: China 1841-42.
Branch of Service: British and HEIC forces.
Ribbon: 39mm crimson with deep yellow edges the heraldic colours of Britain and China respectively.
Metal: Silver.
Size: 35mm.
Description: The medal has the usual Wyon obverse, but the reverse was to have shown a British lion with its forepaws on a dragon. This was deemed to be offensive to the Chinese and was replaced by an oval shield bearing the royal arms and a palm tree flanked by a capstan, anchor and naval cannon representing the Royal Navy (left) and a field gun, drum and regimental flag representing the Army (right), with the Latin motto ARMIS EXPOSCERE PACEM (to pray for peace by force of arms) round the top and CHINA 1842 in the exergue.
Comments: *Originally intended for issue to all ranks of the Honourable East India Company, it was subsequently awarded by the British government in 1843 to all who had taken part in the campaign in China popularly known as the First Opium War which ended with the seizure of Nanking.*

VALUE:

Royal Navy	£850–1250
Indian and Bengal marine units	£650–750
British imperial regiments	£750–850
Indian Army	£600–700
Specimens of the original reverse	£800–1000
Miniature	£200–275

111. SCINDE MEDAL

Date: 1843.
Campaign: Scinde 1843.
Branch of Service: HEIC forces and 22nd Foot.
Ribbon: 44mm watered silk red, white, yellow, white and blue representing an eastern sky at sunrise.
Metal: Silver.
Size: 36mm.
Description: The usual Wyon profile obverse was married to three different reverse types showing a crowned laurel wreath inscribed with the name of one or two campaigns and the date.
Comments: *Authorised in September 1843, this silver medal marked Sir Charles Napier's conquest of Scinde. The two major battles in the campaign, at Meeanee and Hyderabad, accomplished the complete rout of the forces of the Amirs of Scinde. The medals were originally issued with steel suspenders but the commanding officer of the 22nd Foot had the medals awarded to his men fitted with silver suspenders, at his own expense. Medals to the Indus Flotilla are particularly sought after by collectors.*

VALUE:

	22nd Foot	Indian units	HEIC ships
i. Meeanee	£1200–1500	£650–750	£1750–2500 (38)
ii. Hyderabad	£1100–1500	£650–750	£1750–2500 (52)
iii. Meeanee/Hyderabad	£1200–1500	£650–750	—
Miniature	£175–275		

112. GWALIOR STAR

Date: 1843.
Campaign: Gwalior 1843.
Branch of Service: British and HEIC forces.
Ribbon: 44mm watered silk red, white, yellow, white and blue representing an eastern sky at sunrise.
Metals: Bronze, with a silver centre.
Size: Max. width 45mm; max. height 52mm.
Description: Six-pointed bronze star with a silver centre star. The silver stars in the centre bear the name of one or other of the battles and the date 29 December 1843 on which both battles were fought. The plain reverse bears the name and regiment of the recipient.
Comments: *Bronze from guns captured at the battles of Maharajpoor and Punniar during the Gwalior campaign was used in the manufacture of these stars, thus anticipating the production of the Victoria Cross in the same manner. They were presented by the Indian government to all ranks who took part in these actions. When first issued, these stars were fitted with hooks to be worn like a breast decoration, but later ornate bar or ring suspensions were fitted to individual fancy and worn with the standard Indian ribbon of the period.*

VALUE:

	British units	Indian units	Miniature
i. Maharajpoor	£750–850	£800–1000	£250–350
ii. Punniar	£750–850	£800–1000	£350–450

113. SUTLEJ MEDAL

Date: 1846.
Campaign: Sutlej 1845-46.
Branch of Service: British and HEIC forces.
Ribbon: Dark blue with crimson edges.
Metal: Silver.
Size: 36mm.
Description: (Obverse) Wyon profile of Queen Victoria; (reverse) standing figure of Victory holding aloft a laurel crown, with a pile of captured weapons at her feet. The legend ARMY OF THE SUTLEJ appears round the top. The medal was fitted with an ornamental scroll suspender.
Clasps: Mounted above the suspender with roses between: Ferozeshuhur, Aliwal or Sobraon.
Comments: *The practice of issuing medals inscribed with different battles now gave way to the style of medals with specific battle or campaign clasps which set the precedent for the Naval and Military GSMs and later awards. As a compromise, however, the exergue of the reverse bears the name and date of the action for which the medal was first granted, and thus several different types are known.*

VALUE:	British regiments	Europeans in HEIC units	Indian units
i. Moodkee	£400–475	£300–500	£325–375
Moodkee 1 clasp	£500–575	£400–550	£375–425
Moodkee 2 clasps	£700–825	£600–750	£475–575
Moodkee 3 clasps	£1500–1800	£950–1150	£750–950
ii. Ferozeshuhur	£400–475	£300–400	£325–375
Ferozeshuhur 1 clasp	£500–575	£400–500	£375–425
Ferozeshuhur 2 clasps	£700–825	£600–750	£475–575
iii. Aliwal	£350–425	£300–400	£325–375
Aliwal 1 clasp	£500–575	£400–550	£375–475
iv. Sobraon	£400–525	£350–450	£375–475
Glazed gilt specimen	£500–750		
Miniature	£125–175, for each clasp add £50		

114. PUNJAB MEDAL

Date: 1849.
Campaign: Punjab 1848-49.
Branch of Service: British and HEIC forces.
Ribbon: Dark blue with yellow stripes towards the edges.
Metal: Silver.
Size: 36mm.
Description: (Obverse) Wyon profile of Queen Victoria; (reverse) Sir Walter Gilbert receiving the Sikh surrender. TO THE ARMY OF THE PUNJAB appears round the top and the year in roman numerals in the exergue. The medal has a scroll suspender.
Clasps: Mooltan, Chilianwala, Goojerat. Unusually the clasps read downwards from top to bottom
Comments: *This medal was granted to troops taking part in the campaigns which ended in the annexation of the Punjab. Unlike the Sutlej medal, however, this silver medal had a standard design. Large numbers of this medal were awarded to native troops, however many were melted down and therefore surprisingly few remain on the market in comparison with medals to European recipients.*

VALUE:	British units	Europeans in HEIC units	Indian units
No clasp	£400–450	£400–450	£350–375
i. Mooltan	£450–550	£400–450	£375–400
ii. Chilianwala	£450–550	£400–450	£375–400
iii. Goojerat	£450–550	£400–450	£375–400
iv. Mooltan/Goojerat	£650–750	£650–700	£475–550
v. Chilianwala/Goojerat	£650–750	£650–700	£475–550
24th Foot casualty at Chilianwala	£1200–1650	—	—
Glazed gilt specimen	£350–500		
Miniature	£90–125, for each clasp add £25		

115. SOUTH AFRICA MEDAL

Date: 1854.

Campaigns: Southern Africa 1834–53.

Branch of Service: Royal Navy and Army.

Ribbon: Gold with broad and narrow deep blue stripes towards each end.

Metal: Silver.   **Size:** 36mm.

Description: (Obverse) Wyon profile of Queen Victoria; (reverse) an African lion crouching in submission beside a protea shrub, the date 1853 being in the exergue.

Clasps: None.

Comments: *Authorised in November 1854, this medal was awarded in respect of three campaigns in southern Africa: 1834–35, 1846–47 and 1850–53, but as the medal was issued with a standard reverse and no campaign clasps it is impossible to tell when and where the recipient served without reference to the medal rolls. The majority of recipients were British troops but several hundred sailors of the Royal Navy also received the medal and a much smaller number of local forces. Medals to proven recipients who took part in well-known sieges or battles such as the siege of Port Natal (1842), Fort Cox (1850) or the battles of Zwartkopje (1845) or Boomplaats (1848) for example, are worth a considerable premium. Also of particular interest are medals awarded to men who survived the sinking of the troopship Birkenhead on its way to the Eastern Cape from Simons Town and medals awarded to those in clashes with Boer forces.*

VALUE:

British Army	£550–650
Royal Navy	£700–800
HMS *Birkenhead*	From £2000
Local forces (levies, burghers and colonial units)	From £550
Miniature	£90–125

116. SIR HARRY SMITH'S MEDAL FOR GALLANTRY

Date: 1851.

Campaign: Eighth Kaffir War 1850-51.

Branch of Service: Army and Colonial Forces.

Ribbon: Dark blue with crimson edges.

Metal: Silver.

Size: 34mm.

Description: (Obverse) British lion passant gardant with a laurel wreath over its head; date 1851 in the exergue. (Reverse) PRESENTED BY round top and FOR GALLANTRY IN THE FIELD round the foot. HIS EXCELLENCY SIR H. G. SMITH and the name of the recipient appear across the centre.

Comments: *Sir Harry Smith (1787–1860) served with distinction in the Kaffir War of 1834–35, gained his KCB in the Gwalior campaign and a baronetcy for his decisive victory at Aliwal in the Sikh War. In 1847 he returned to South Africa as governor of Cape Colony. Although short of troops he conducted the eighth Kaffir War (1850–53) with great resourcefulness but was recalled to England in 1852 before the Xhosas had been subdued. Harrismith in the Orange Free State was named in his honour, while Ladysmith in Natal was named after his beautiful and spirited Spanish wife Juanita, the forces' sweetheart of her day. Sir Harry had this medal struck at his own expense and, according to unconfirmed accounts, awarded to troopers of the Cape Mounted Rifles who took part in the epic ride through the enemy lines from Fort Cox to Kingwilliamstown in 1851. Only 31 medals were presented, of which 22 are believed to be still extant.*

VALUE:

Unnamed	£3000–4000
Named and appearing on 1853 medal roll or muster rolls	£7500–10,000

One contemporary miniature example is known

117. INDIA GENERAL SERVICE MEDAL

Date: 1854.
Campaigns: Indian 1854-95.
Branch of Service: British and Indian forces.
Ribbon: Three crimson and two dark blue stripes of equal width.
Metal: Silver or bronze.
Size: 36mm.
Description: (Obverse) Wyon profile of Queen Victoria; (reverse) Victory crowning a semi-nude seated warrior.
Clasps: 24 (see below).
Comments: *This medal was the first of four general service medals issued to cover minor campaigns in India. It was instituted in 1854 and continued for forty-one years, retaining the original Wyon profile of Queen Victoria throughout the entire period. Although the medal itself is quite common, some of its clasps are very rare, notably* Kachin Hills 1892–93 *awarded to the Yorkshire Regiment and* Chin Hills 1892–93 *awarded to the Norfolk Regiment. The maximum number of clasps to one medal recorded is seven. At first the medal was awarded in silver to all ranks regardless of race or branch of the services, but from 1885 onwards it was issued in bronze to native support personnel such as bearers, sweepers and drivers.*

VALUE:		RN/RM	British Army	Indian Army	Bronze
i.	Pegu	£350–450	£300–350	£225–300*	—
ii.	Persia	—	£650–850	£350–400	—
iii.	Northwest Frontier	—	£300–360	£225–275	—
iv.	Umbeyla	—	£325–375	£225–275	—
v.	Bhootan	—	£360–385	£225–275	—
vi.	Looshai	—	—	£400–550	—
vii.	Perak	£350–450	£360–385	£250–275	—
viii.	Jowaki 1877–8	—	£300–350	£200–250	—
ix.	Naga 1879–80	—	—	£375–450	—
x.	Burma 1885–7	£350–450	£185–250	£150–175	£150–185
xi.	Sikkim 1888	—	£380–440	£175–200	£200–250
xii.	Hazara 1888	—	£235–260	£175–200	£160–200
xiii.	Burma 1887–89	—	£200–230	£165–185	£160–200
xiv.	Burma 1887–9	—	£225–275	—	—
xv.	Chin Lushai 1889–90	—	£300–350	£200–250	£220–275
xvi.	Lushai 1889–92	—	£600–650	£225–275	£425–500
xvii.	Samana 1891	—	£300–350	£185–200	£175–200
xviii.	Hazara 1891	—	£250–300	£185–200	£175–200
xix.	NE Frontier 1891	—	£385–425	£175–200	£175–200
xx.	Hunza 1891	—	—	£500–550	£850–1000
xxi.	Burma 1889–92	—	£200–250	£175–200	£150–185
xxii.	Chin Hills 1892–93	—	£1100–1300	£385–475	£875–1000
xxiii.	Kachin Hills 1892–93	—	£850–1000	£400–500	£875–1000
xxiv.	Waziristan 1894–95	—	£275–300	£175–200	£175–200

Miniature £25–35, for each clasp add £15–20 (Hunza, Chin Hills and Kachin Hills clasps are rare)

* *In addition a number of Indian ships were present—medals to Indian naval or marine recipients are rare.*

118. BALTIC MEDAL

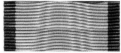

Date: 1856.
Campaign: Baltic Sea 1854–55.
Branch of Service: Royal Navy, Royal Marines and Royal Sappers and Miners.
Ribbon: Yellow with light blue edges.
Metal: Silver.
Size: 36mm.
Description: (Obverse) Wyon profile of Queen Victoria; (reverse) Britannia seated on a plinth decorated by a cannon, with a coastal scene in the background and BALTIC round the top.
Comments: *Authorised in 1856, this medal was granted to officers and men of the Royal Navy and Royal Marines for operations against Russia in the Baltic at the same time as the war in the Crimea. It was also awarded to about 100 members of the Royal Sappers and Miners engaged in the demolition of Russian fortifications of Bomarsund and Sveaborg. Medals were generally issued unnamed but often privately named afterwards, the exception being medals to the Sappers and Miners which were officially impressed.*

VALUE:

Unnamed	£200–250
Privately named	£200–250
Officially impressed to Sappers and Miners	£1000–1500
Miniature	£75–100

119. CRIMEA MEDAL

Date: 1854.
Campaign: Crimea 1854–56.
Branch of Service: Royal Navy and Marines, British Army.
Ribbon: Pale blue with yellow edges.
Metal: Silver.
Size: 36mm.
Description: (Obverse) Wyon profile of Queen Victoria; (reverse) a Roman soldier, armed with circular shield and short sword, being crowned by a flying Victory.
Clasps: Unusually ornate, being shaped like oak leaves with acorn finials: Alma, Balaklava, Inkerman, Sebastopol, Azoff, but the maximum found on any medal is four. Recipients of the Balaklava clasp were invariably entitled to other clasps. Unofficial clasps for Traktir, Mamelon Vert, Malakoff, Mer d'Azoff and Kinburn are sometimes found on medals awarded to French troops.
Comments: *Medals may be found unnamed, unofficially or regimentally named, or officially impressed. Medals awarded to participants in the most famous actions of the war—the Thin Red Line (93rd Foot) and the Charge of the Light and Heavy Brigades—rate a very high premium. The prices quoted are for medals named to the Army. Clasps awarded to the Royal Navy and Royal Marines (Azoff, Balaklava, Inkerman, Sebastopol) rate a good premium, especially those named to personnel on board HM Ships* London, Niger, Rodney *and* Wasp.* No fewer than 19 VCs were awarded for gallantry at Inkerman alone, the largest number for a single action.*

VALUE :	Unnamed	Engraved	Regimentally impressed	Officially impressed Army
No clasp	£150–200	£175–200	£175–200	£200–250
i. Alma	£150–200	£200–250	£200–250	£250–350
ii. Balaklava	£200–250	£200–250	£200–250	£350–400
93rd Foot*	—	£500–575	£800–1000	£1000–1500
Heavy Brigade*	—	£850–1500	£1000–1750	£1500–2000
Light Brigade (Charger)*	—	£2500–3500	£4500–5500	£10,000–15,000
iii. Inkerman	£175–200	£200–250	£200–250	£225–275
iv. Sebastopol	£175–200	£200–250	£200–250	£275–350
v. Azoff	£300–375	£350–400	—	£525–650
2 clasps	£250–300	£300–350	£300–375	£450–600
3 clasps	£325–400	£400–450	£400–475	£750–1000
4 clasps	£400–500	£500–750	£565–700	£1500–2000
Miniature	£25–35, for each clasp add £15			

*It is always difficult to price scarce or rare medals such as those marked * as we have seen many engraved or Depot-style impressing that were probably named in the past 30 to 40 years. Also an engraved Crimea, together with a Mutiny and/or LS&GC would be worth considerably more than the prices indicated. Buyer beware!

120. TURKISH CRIMEA MEDAL

Date: 1855.
Campaign: Crimea 1855-56.
Branch of Service: British, French and Sardinian forces.
Ribbon: Crimson with green edges (originally 18mm wide).
Metal: Silver.
Size: 36mm.
Description: (Obverse) a cannon, weapons and the four Allied flags
   with the name and date in the exergue; (reverse) the Toughra and
   Arabic date according to the Moslem calendar.
Clasps: None.
Comments: *Instituted by the Sultan of Turkey, this silver medal was
   conferred on troops of the three Allies who fought in the Crimea. The
   obverse types differed in the arrangement of the flags, corrsponding with
   the inscription in English, French or Italian in the exergue. Although
   the medals were intended to be issued to British, French and Sardinian
   troops respectively, they were issued haphazardly due to most of the British
   version being lost at sea. They were unnamed, but many were privately
   engraved or impressed later. There are a number of dangerous copies
   known to be circulating.*

VALUE:		*Miniature*
i. CRIMEA (British Issue)	£150–175	£45–50
ii. LA CRIMEE (French Issue)	£220–250	Not seen
iii. LA CRIMEA (Sardinia Issue)	£125–150	£35–45

120A. TURKISH MEDAL FOR GLORY

Date: 1853.
Campaign: Crimea.
Branch of Service: British forces.
Ribbon: Crimson with green edges.
Metal: Gold or silver.
Size: 31mm.
Description: (Obverse) the Sultan's cypher in a beaded ring below a
   star and crescent with flags and wreath around; (reverse) a star with
   a smaller star in the centre, an arabic inscription below which reads
   "Medal for Glory". With ring suspension.
Clasps: None.
Comments: *Instituted by the Sultan of Turkey, it was awarded to officers and
   men of British forces who fought in the war against Russia, at Silistria and
   Giurgevo. Gold medals were awarded to high ranking officers and silver to
   others.*

VALUE:	
Gold	£1000–1500
Silver	£500–750

120B. TURKISH MEDAL FOR THE DEFENCE OF SILISTRIA

Date: 1854.
Campaign: Crimea.
Branch of Service: British and Turkish forces.
Ribbon: Crimson with green edges.
Metal: Gold or silver.
Size: 36mm.
Description: (Obverse) the Sultan's cypher within in a wreath; (reverse) a depiction of the fortress of Silistria with a flag flying from the ramparts with the river Danube in the foreground, an inscription in Turkish script below which reads "Silistria 1271 AH (1854)". With ring suspension
Clasps: None.
Comments: *Instituted by the Sultan of Turkey, it was awarded to officers and men of British forces who were present during the actual siege by 30,000 Russian troops. Only seven British officers were there at the time and qualified for the medal but the medal was issued unnamed.*

VALUE:
Gold	£1000–1500
Silver	£500–750

120C. TURKISH MEDAL FOR THE DEFENCE OF KARS

Date: 1855.
Campaign: Crimea.
Branch of Service: British and Turkish forces.
Ribbon: Crimson with green edges.
Metal: Silver.
Size: 36mm.
Description: (Obverse) the Sultan's cypher within in a wreath; (reverse) a depiction of the city of Kars with a flag flying from the citadel and the words "Kars 1272 AH (1855)" in Turkish script below. With simple ring suspension.
Clasps: None.
Comments: *Instituted by the Sultan of Turkey, it was awarded to officers and men of British forces who were present at the siege of Kars by 50,000 Russian troops. The silver medal was awarded to the British officers present including the British Commissioner, Brigadier General Sir William Fenwick Williams. Lt C. C. Teesdale was sawarded the VC for his part in the action. The medals were issued unnamed.*

VALUE: £2000–3000

121. INDIAN MUTINY MEDAL

Date: 1858.

Campaign: Sepoy Mutiny, India 1857–58.

Branch of Service: Royal Navy, British Army and Indian forces. It was also awarded to many civilians who took part in suppressing the Mutiny.

Ribbon: White with two red stripes, representing blood and white bandages.

Metal: Silver.

Size: 36mm.

Description: (Obverse) Wyon profile of Queen Victoria; (reverse) the standing figure of Britannia bestowing victor's laurels, with the British lion alongside. INDIA appears round the top with the dates 1857–1858 in the exergue.

Clasps: Delhi, Defence of Lucknow, Relief of Lucknow, Lucknow, Central India. The maximum recorded for a single medal is four (Bengal Artillery) or three (imperial troops, 9th Lancers).

Comments: *This medal was awarded to troops who took part in operations to quell the Sepoy mutiny which had been the immediate cause of the uprising, although it also served to focus attention on the Honourable East India Company's conduct of affairs and led directly to the transfer of the administration of India to the Crown. Medals with the clasp for the defence of Lucknow awarded to the original defenders rate a considerable premium, as do medals awarded to members of the Naval Brigade which witnessed most of the fighting in the mopping-up operations. Medals to Indian recipients although scarcer on the market, generally bring a little less than their British counterparts although verified four-clasp medals to the Bengal Artillery are much sought after.*

VALUE:

	Royal Navy	British Army	Miniature
No clasp	£800–1000*	£250–350	£30-40
i. Delhi	—	£550–650	£50–60
ii. Defence of Lucknow			
original defender	—	£1750–1850	£70–95
first relief force	—	£800–1000	
iii. Relief of Lucknow	£1800–2000	£450–550	£50–60
iv. Lucknow	£1800–2000	£450–550	£60–70
v. Central India	—	£450–550	£60–70, add
2 clasps	£2000–2500	£550–750	£15 for each
3 clasps (9th Lancers)	—	£1850–2000	additional clasp
4 clasps (Bengal Arty.)	—	£3500–4500	

66 medals to HMS Shannon and 253 to HMS Pearl.

122. SECOND CHINA WAR MEDAL

Date: 1861.

Campaign: Second China War 1857-60.

Branch of Service: Royal Navy and British Army.

Ribbon: 33mm crimson with yellow edges (originally five equal stripes of green, white, red, yellow and blue, edged with red).

Metal: Silver.

Size: 36mm.

Description: As the First China War Medal (no. 110), but without the year 1842 at the foot.

Clasps: Fatshan 1857, Canton 1857, Taku Forts 1858, Taku Forts 1860, Pekin 1860.

Comments: *This medal was awarded to British sevicemen who took part, alongside the French, in the campaign against China which had been provoked by hostile acts against European nationals. The Royal Navy, under Admiral Sir Michael Seymour, destroyed a Chinese flotilla at Fatshan Creek, preparing the way for the attack on Canton whose capture brought the first phase to an end in June 1858. Reinforcements were meanwhile diverted to help put down the Indian mutiny. Fighting broke out again and this time large numbers of troops were involved in the assault on the Taku forts and the sack of Pekin (Beijing). Examples of the China medal of 1842, with or without clasps for 1857-60, have been recorded to recipients who fought in the Second China War. Medals may be found unnamed or with names officially engraved (Indian Army) or impressed (British Army, Indian Navy). Although those to the Navy were all issued unnamed, they are occasionally encountered unofficially named.*

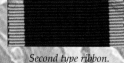

Original ribbon.

Second type ribbon.

VALUE:

	Unnamed	Army/Navy officially impressed	Miniature
No clasp	£150–180	£250–350	£45–50
i. China 1842	—	—	£130–160
ii. Fatshan 1857	£200–275	£450–500	£70–80
iii. Canton 1857	£275–300	£375–450	£70–80
iv. Taku Forts 1858	£275–300	£375–400	£70–80
v. Taku Forts 1860	£275–300	£375–400	£70–80
vi. Pekin 1860	£275–300	£375–400	£70–80
2 clasps	£350–450	£550–650	For each
3 clasps	£450–550	£650–800	clasp add
4 clasps	£600–700	—	£15
5 clasps	£650–750	—	

The storming of the Taku forts.

123. NEW ZEALAND MEDALS

Date: 1869.

Campaigns: First and Second Maori Wars 1845–47 and 1860–66.

Branch of Service: Army, Navy and local volunteers.

Ribbon: Blue with a central orange stripe.

Metal: Silver.

Size: 36mm.

Description: (Obverse) Veiled head of Queen Victoria. (Reverse) Date of service in a wreath, with NEW ZEALAND round the top and VIRTUTIS HONOR (honour of valour) round the foot. Suspender ornamented with New Zealand fern fronds.

Comments: *These medals were unusual in having the recipient's dates of service die-struck on the centre of the reverse, though medals were also issued without dates. As the medal was only awarded to surviving veterans, the numbers issued in respect of the earlier conflict are understandably small. Many of the dates are very scarce, especially those issued to naval personnel in the first war when only naval personnel received dated medals. Medals to locally-raised units are worth a considerable premium. A hitherto unknown 1845-dated medal appeared at auction in January 2010 when it sold for a hammer price of £12,800. This medal was named to Captain David Robertson, HMS Hazard.*

VALUE:		Army	RN/RM
First war			
i.	Undated	£500–600	—
ii.	1845–46 (155)	—	£1300–1600
iii.	1845–47 (36)	—	£1400–1700
iv.	1846–47 (69)	—	£1300–1600
v.	1846 (10)	—	£1500–2000
vi.	1847 (20)	£800–1000	£1500–2000
Second war			
vii.	Undated	£450–550	—
viii.	1860	£750–850	—
ix.	1860–61	£475–575	£650–750
	(to Australians)	£2000–2300	—
x.	1860–63	From £1550	—
xi.	1860–64	£450–550	—
xii.	1860–65	£450–550	—
xiii.	1860–66	£450–550	—
xiv.	1861	—	—
xv.	1861–63	—	—
xvi.	1861–64	£450–550	—
xvii.	1861–65	—	—
xviii.	1861–66	£450–550	—
xix.	1861–66		
	(Waikato Regt issues)	From £850	—
xx.	1862–66	—	—
xxi.	1863	£450–550	—
xxii.	1863–64	£450–550	£650–750
xxiii.	1863–65	£450–550	—
xxiv.	1863–66	£450–550	—
xxv.	1864	£450–550	—
xxvi.	1864–65	£450–550	—
xxvii.	1864–66	£450–550	—
xxviii.	1865	£450–550	£650–750
xxvix.	1865–66	£450–550	—
xxx.	1866	£450–550	—

Miniature		
Undated		£100–125
Dated		£85–£95

124. ABYSSINIAN WAR MEDAL

Date: 1869.
Campaign: Abyssinia (Ethiopia) 1867–68.
Branch of Service: Royal Navy, British and Indian Armies.
Ribbon: Red with broad white edges.
Metal: Silver.
Size: 33mm diameter.
Description: (Obverse) the veiled portrait of Victoria framed by a zigzag pattern with floral ornament alternating with the letters of the name ABYSSINIA. The recipient's name and unit were embossed in the centre of the reverse except most to Indian troops which were impressed. Suspension is by a ring via a large crown standing proud from the top of the medal.
Clasps: None.
Comments: *The imprisonment of British subjects by King Theodore of Abyssinia precipitated a punitive expedition under General Sir Robert Napier involving ships of the Royal Navy, a naval brigade and troops of the British and Indian armies. Because casualties were unusually light (only two killed and 27 wounded), medals from this campaign are not so highly rated as those from other nineteenth century wars.*

VALUE:
British troops	£375–475
Royal Navy	£375–475
RN Rocket Brigade	£575–650
Indian troops	£300–400
Miniature	£125–175

125. CANADA GENERAL SERVICE MEDAL

Date: 1899.
Campaign: Canada 1866–70.
Branch of Service: Royal Navy, British Army and Canadian units.
Ribbon: Three equal stripes of orange-red, white and orange-red.
Metal: Silver.
Size: 36mm.
Description: (Obverse) crowned and veiled Old Head bust of Queen Victoria by Sir Thomas Brock (reflecting the very late issue of the medal). (Reverse) Canadian flag surrounded by maple leaves.
Clasps: Fenian Raid 1866, Fenian Raid 1870, Red River 1870.
Comments: *This medal was not authorised until January 1899, thirty years after the event, and was issued by the Canadian Government to British and Canadian local forces who took part in operations to put down the Fenian raids of 1866 and 1870 and the Red River rebellion of the latter year. Of the 16,100 medals awarded, 15,000 went to local forces. Naval medals command a premium.*

VALUE:
	Canadian forces	British Army	Royal Navy	*Miniature*
i. Fenian Raid 1866	£350–400	£475–600	£650–750	£65–70
ii. Fenian Raid 1870	£350–400	£475–600	—	£70–75
iii. Red River 1870	£3500–4000	£4000–4500	—	£90–115
2 clasps*	£750–850	£950–1000	—	£85–110
3 clasps	Rare	—	—	—

*Two 2-clasp medals were awarded to men of the 1st Bn 60th Foot (KRRC) and ten to the 4th Bn.

126. ASHANTEE MEDAL

Date: 1874.
Campaign: Gold Coast 1873–74.
Branch of Service: Royal Navy, Army and native troops.
Ribbon: Yellow with black stripes at the sides and two narrow black stripes towards the centre.
Metal: Silver. **Size:** 36mm.
Description: The obverse and reverse are similar to the East and West Africa Medal of 1887–1900, differing solely in thickness and the method of naming. The veiled profile of Victoria graces the obverse while the reverse, designed by Sir Edwin Poynter, shows a skirmish in the jungle between British soldiers and Ashantee warriors.
Clasps: Coomassie.
Comments: *All ranks who took part in operations against King Kalkali of Ashantee, Gold Coast, were awarded this medal, approved in June 1874. The campaign was fought in difficult and hostile terrain, requiring the building of a road through dense rain forest, the construction of many staging posts, camps, bridges and a telegraph. The movement of troops and supplies was met with skirmishes and ferocious battles developed as the column approached Kumasi in the final four weeks and resulted in the award of four VCs. There was also a very high incidence of sickness and disease among the troops, notably the naval contingent. Unusually the medals are named in engraved capitals filled in with black.*

VALUE	Royal Navy	Army	Natives	Miniature
No clasp	£350–400	£350–400	£250–300	£50–55
i. Coomassie	£450–550	£450–550	£300–350	£70–75

127. SOUTH AFRICA MEDAL

Date: 1879.
Campaign: South Africa 1877–79.
Branch of Service: Royal Navy, Army and colonial units.
Ribbon: Gold with broad and narrow deep blue stripes towards each end.
Metal: Silver.
Size: 36mm.
Description: The same design as no. 115, except that the date 1853 in the exergue is replaced by a Zulu shield and four crossed assegais.
Clasps: 1877, 1877–8, 1877–9, 1877–8–9, 1878, 1878–9, 1879.
Comments: *The campaign began in 1877 with an attack on the Fingoes by the Galeka and Gaika tribes and culminated in the showdown between the Zulus and the British when Lord Chelmsford's column was annihilated at Isandhlwana. When the 3,000 Zulus advanced on Rorke's Drift, however, they were checked with heavy losses by a tiny garrison of 139 men. During the defence no fewer than eleven VCs were won—a very large number for a single action. The campaign concluded with the defeat of Cetshwayo's warriors at Ulundi. A number of recipients of the medal stayed on in the country and took part in the first Anglo-Boer War of 1880–81. Medals confirmed to these men, particularly those who took part in the sieges of Wakkerstroom, Rustenburg, Standerton, Marabastadt or Lydenburg or well-known battles such as Swartkoppies, are worth a considerable premium.*

VALUE:	RN	Army	Colonial	Miniature
No clasp	£550–650	£650–750	£550–650	£35–40
i. 1877	—	Unique	£3500–4500	£110–160
ii. 1877–8	£950–1250	£850–1000	£850–950	£70–80
iii. 1877–9	—	Unique	£4500–6000	—
iv. 1877–8–9	£850–1000	£1000–1200	£850–1000	£70–80
v. 1878	—	£850–1200	£850–1000	£70–80
vi. 1878–9	—	£850–1200	£850–1000	£70–80
vii. 1879	£850–1000	£850–1500	£850–1000	£75–85

Isandhlwana casualty	From £10,000
Isandhlwana escapee	From £10,000
Rorke's Drift participant	From £35,000

128. AFGHANISTAN MEDAL

Date: 1881.
Campaign: Afghanistan 1878–80.
Branch of Service: British and Indian Armies.
Ribbon: Dark green, the sacred colour of the prophet with broad crimson edges, the heraldic colour of Britain.
Metal: Silver.
Size: 36mm.
Description: (Obverse) veiled profile of Queen Victoria. (Reverse) a column on the march, with an elephant carrying cannon. The dates 1878–79–80 appear in the exergue.
Clasps: Ali Musjid, Peiwar Kotal, Charasia, Kabul, Ahmed Kel, Kandahar. Maximum number of clasps per medal is four.
Comments: *This medal was awarded to all who took part in the campaigns against Afghanistan known as the Second Afghan War. In 1877 the Amir refused to accept a British resident and the following year raised an army which began harrassing the Indian frontier. A treaty with Russia, however, granting it protective rights in Afghanistan, precipitated an armed response from Britain. In 1880 General Roberts led a column from Kabul to Kandahar to relieve General Burrows and the resulting battle led to the defeat of the Afghans and the conclusion of the war. Medals awarded to the 66th Foot (Berkshire Regiment) and E Battery of B Brigade, Royal Artillery rate a high premium as these units sustained the heaviest casualties at the battle of Maiwand in July 1880.*

VALUE:	British units	Indian units	Miniature
No clasp silver	£275–350	£175–250	£25–35
i. Ali Musjid	£375–450	£250–300	£35–45
ii. Peiwar Kotal	£375–450	£250–300	£35–45
iii. Charasia	£375–450	£250–300	£35–45
iv. Kabul	£375–450	£250–300	£30–35
v. Ahmed Khel	£375–450	£250–300	£35–45
vi. Kandahar	£375–450	£250–300	£30–35
2 clasps	£550–650	£350–400	£60–70
3 clasps	£650–850	£400–550	£80–90
4 clasps	£800–1500	£500–850	£95–100
Maiwand casualties:			
66th Foot	£3250–3750	—	
E Bty, B Bde RHA	£2750–3500	—	

Richard Caton Woodville's famous depiction of Saving the Guns at Maiwand.

129. KABUL TO KANDAHAR STAR

Date: 1881.
Campaign: Afghanistan 1878–80.
Branch of Service: British and Indian Armies.
Ribbon: 40mm watered silk of pink, white, yellow, white and blue representing an eastern sky at sunrise.
Metal: Bronze from captured guns.
Size: Height 60mm, width 45mm.
Description: (Obverse) a rayed five-pointed star surmounted by a crown with a ring for suspension. The centre is inscribed KABUL TO KANDAHAR with 1880 at the foot and the VRI monogram of the Queen Empress in the centre. Stars were either issued unnamed, or had the recipient's name impressed (to British) or engraved (to Indian) troops on the reverse.
Clasps: None.
Comments: *This star, struck by Jenkins of Birmingham, was awarded to those who took part in the epic 300-mile march from the Afghan capital to Kandahar, led by General Roberts to relieve the beleaguered forces of General Burrows.*

VALUE:

Unnamed	£200–250
Impressed (British troops)	£400–450
Engraved (Indian troops)	£250–300

Miniature	Early pierced crown £75–85
	Later solid crown £50–65

130. CAPE OF GOOD HOPE GENERAL SERVICE MEDAL

Date: 1900.
Campaign: Uprisings in Transkei, Basutoland and Bechuanaland 1880-97.
Branch of Service: Local forces and volunteers.
Ribbon: Dark blue with a central yellow stripe.
Metal: Silver.
Size: 36mm.
Description: (Obverse) Jubilee bust of Queen Victoria by Sir Joseph Boehm; (reverse) arms of Cape Colony.
Clasps: Transkei, Basutoland, Bechuanaland.
Comments: *Instituted by the Cape government, this medal acknowledged service in putting down the Transkei (September 1880–May 1881), Basutoland (September 1880–April 1881) and Bechuanaland (December 1896–July 1897) rebellions in those areas. The medal was awarded, with one or more campaign clasps, to local forces and volunteer regiments. Recent research has shown that the medal could not be awarded without a clasp. The previously held notion that ten medals were awarded without clasps, was brought about by an error in transcribing the medal rolls.*

VALUE:

			Miniature
i.	Transkei (562)	£375–450	£50–60
ii.	Basutoland (1589)	£250–350	£50–60
iii.	Bechuanaland (2483)	£225–300	£50–60
	2 clasps (585)	£350–475	£65–80
	3 clasps (23)	£3000–4000	—

131. EGYPT MEDAL 1882–89

Dated rev.

Undated rev.

Date: 1882.

Campaign: Egypt 1882–89.

Branch of Service: Royal Navy and Army.

Ribbon: Three blue and two white stripes, (the Blue and White Niles).

Metal: Silver.

Size: 36mm.

Description: (Obverse) the veiled profile of Queen Victoria; (reverse) the Sphinx.

Clasps: 14, listed below. Maximum number for one medal is 7, but only one such award was made. Common two-clasp combinations are denoted below by /.

Comments: *British involvement in Egypt deepened after the opening of the Suez Canal in 1869, many British officers being seconded to the Khedive's Army. When the Army mutinied in 1882 and triggered off a general anti-European uprising, an Anglo-French expedition was mounted. Subsequently the French withdrew before a landing was effected. Trouble erupted in the Sudan (under Anglo-Egyptian administration) in 1884 where General Gordon was besieged at Khartoum. Further campaigns aimed at the overthrow of the Mahdi and the reconquest of the Sudan. These prolonged operations created immense logistical problems. Nile transportation in particular was a matter resolved only when Canadian voyageurs were recruited to handle the river-boats. In addition, a contingent of troops from New South Wales "answered the Empire's call" and medals awarded to them for the Suakin campaign of 1885 are much sought after. Except where noted, the prices quoted below are for medals awarded to British Army personnel. Medals awarded to Indian or Egyptian troops are generally worth about 25 per cent less than comparable awards to British Army units.*

VALUE:

			Miniature
i.	No clasp (dated)	£125–200	£30–35
ii.	No clasp (undated)	£125–200	£30–35
iii.	Alexandria 11th July	£275–350	£45–50
iv.	Tel-el-Kebir	£250–300	£45–50
v.	El-Teb	£325–375	£45–50
vi.	Tamaai	£325–375	£45–50
vii.	El-Teb–Tamaai	£300–350	£45–50
viii.	Suakin 1884	£250–300	£45–50
ix.	The Nile 1884–85	£250–300	£45–50
x.	The Nile 1884–85/Abu Klea	£900–1200	£45–50
xi.	The Nile 1884–85/Kirbekan	£350–400	£45–50
xii.	Suakin 1885	£250–300	£45–50
xiii.	Suakin 1885/Tofrek	£350–400	£45–50
xiv.	Gemaizah 1888	£300–350	£45–55
xv.	Toski 1889	£450–650	£55–65
xvi.	Gemaizah 1888/Toski 1889		
	Egyptian troops	£260–300	
	20th Hussars	£350–450	
2 clasps		£275–350	Add £15
3 clasps		£375–475	for each
4 clasps		£475–600	clasp
5 clasps		£1250–2000	—
Canadian boatmen		£2500–3000	
NSW units (Suakin 1885)		£2600–2900	

132. KHEDIVE'S STAR

Date: 1882.
Campaign: Egypt 1882–91.
Branch of Service: Royal Navy and Army.
Ribbon: 37mm deep blue.
Metal: Bronze.
Size: Height 60mm; width 45mm.
Description: A five-pointed star with a circular centre showing the Sphinx and Pyramids surrounded by a band inscribed EGYPT followed by a year round the top, with "Khedive of Egypt" and the year in the Moslem calendar in Arabic at the foot. (Reverse) the Khedive's monogram surmounted by a crown. The star is suspended by a ring from an ornamental clasp in the centre of which is a star and crescent.
Clasps: Tokar.
Comments: *This star, struck by Jenkins of Birmingham, was conferred by Khedive Tewfik of Egypt on those who qualified for the Egypt medal and it was invariably worn alongside, to the detriment of the silver medal which suffered abrasion from the points of the star. There was also an undated version found with or without a campaign clasp for Tokar, awarded in 1891. These stars were issued unnamed.*

VALUE:			Miniature
i.	1882	£80–100	£15–20
ii.	1884	£80–100	£14–18
iii.	1884-86	£80–100	£20–25
iv.	Undated	£80–100	£20–25
v.	Undated with Tokar bar	£250–300	£75–120

133. GENERAL GORDON'S STAR FOR THE SIEGE OF KHARTOUM

Date: 1884.
Campaign: Mahdist uprising, Sudan 1884.
Branch of Service: British and Sudanese forces.
Ribbon: Deep blue or red.
Metal: Silver or pewter.
Size: Height 80mm; maximum width 54mm.
Description: Star with three concentric circles and seven groups of rays on which are superimposed seven crescents and stars. Suspension by a ring from a Crescent and Star ornament.
Clasps: None.
Comments: *To boost the morale of the defenders Charles Gordon, commanding the garrison at Khartoum, had this star cast locally in a sand mould, using his own breast star of the Order of Mejidieh as the model. Exceptionally, recipients had to purchase their medals, the proceeds going to a fund to feed the poor.*

VALUE:

Silver gilt	£1500–2000
Silver	£1000–1200
Pewter	£1000–1200

134. NORTH WEST CANADA MEDAL

Date: 1885.
Campaign: Riel's rebellion 1885.
Branch of Service: Mainly local forces.
Ribbon: Blue-grey with red stripes towards the edges.
Metal: Silver.
Size: 36mm.
Description: (Obverse) bust of Queen Victoria; (reverse) the inscription NORTH WEST CANADA 1885 within a frame of maple leaves.
Clasps: Saskatchewan,
Comments: *Paradoxically, while the medal for the Fenian Raids of 1866–70 was not sanctioned till 1899, this medal for service in the North West was authorised immediately after the conclusion of operations against the Metis led by Louis Riel. It was issued unnamed, with or without the clasp for Saskatchewan where the bulk of the action took place. Of particular interest are medals to officers and men aboard the steamship* Northcote *involved in a boat action; exceptionally, their medals were impressed. Other medals may be encountered with unofficial naming. The medal was awarded to sixteen British staff officers but the majority of medals (5600 in all) went to local forces.*

VALUE:			Miniature
i.	No clasp named	£900–1200	—
ii.	No clasp unnamed	£500–600	£65–75
iii.	Saskatchewan	£2000–2500	£80–100
Northcote recipient		£3500–4000	

135. ROYAL NIGER COMPANY'S MEDAL

Date: 1899.
Campaign: Nigeria 1886–97.
Branch of Service: Officers and men of the Company's forces.
Ribbon: Three equal stripes of yellow, black and white.
Metal: Silver or bronze.
Size: 39.5mm.
Description: (Obverse) the Boehm bust of Queen Victoria; (reverse) the Company's arms in a laurel wreath.
Clasps: Nigeria 1886-97 (silver), Nigeria (bronze).
Comments: *This medal was issued in silver to Europeans and bronze to natives for service in the vast territories administered by the Royal Niger chartered company. Silver medals were impressed in capitals, but those in bronze were more usually stamped with the recipient's service (constabulary) number. Specimens of both versions were later struck from the original dies but these lack name or number.*

VALUE:

		Miniature
Silver named (85)	£3000–4000	no clasp £175–220
Silver specimen	£80–100	—
Bronze oficially numbered (250)	£650–850	Nigeria clasp £210–260
Bronze specimen	£60–80	—

136. IMPERIAL BRITISH EAST AFRICA COMPANY'S MEDAL

Date: 1890.
Campaign: East Africa (Kenya and Uganda) 1888–95.
Branch of Service: Company forces.
Ribbon: Plain dark blue.
Metal: Silver.
Size: 40mm.
Description: (Obverse) the Company badge, a crowned and radiant sun, with a Suaheli inscription in Arabic round the foot signifying "the reward of bravery"; (reverse) plain except for a wreath. Suspension is by a plain ring or an ornamental scroll.
Comments: *The rarest of the medals awarded by the chartered companies, this medal was originally intended solely as a gallantry award; but after the BEA Company was wound up in 1895 further issues were authorised by the Foreign Office for service in Witu (1890) and the Ugandan civil war (1890-91). Fewer than thirty medals are known.*

VALUE: £4000–5000   *Miniature* £330–460

137. EAST AND WEST AFRICA MEDAL

Date: 1892.
Campaigns: East and West Africa 1887–1900.
Branch of Service: Royal Navy, Army and native forces.
Ribbon: As 126.
Metal: Silver or bronze.
Size: 36mm.
Description: As the Ashantee Medal (no. 126), distinguished only by its clasps.
Clasps: 22 (see below). A 22nd operation (Mwele, 1895–96) was denoted by engraving on the rim of the medal.
Comments: *This medal was awarded for general service in a number of small campaigns and punitive expeditions. Though usually awarded in silver, it was sometimes struck in bronze for issue to native servants, bearers and drivers. British regiments as such were not involved in any of the actions, but individual officers and NCOs were seconded as staff officers and instructors and their medals bear the names of their regiments. Units of the Royal Navy were also involved in many of the coastal or river actions. Especially sought after are naval medals with the bar for Lake Nyassa 1893 in which the ships* Pioneer *and* Adventure *were hauled in sections overland through 200 miles of jungle.*

VALUE:		Royal Navy	Europeans	Natives	Miniature
i.	1887–8	£850–1250	£425–625	£400–450	£45–50
ii.	Witu 1890	£200–250	£200–250	£150–180	£50–55
iii.	1891–2	£225–275	£200–250	£150–180	£50–55
iv.	1892	£1250–1500	£200–250	£150–180	£50–55
v.	Witu August 1893	£225–250	—	£150–180	£65–75
vi.	Liwondi 1893	£2500–3500	—	—	—
vii.	Juba River 1893	£3000–4000	—	—	—
viii.	Lake Nyassa 1893	£3000–4000	—	—	—
ix.	1893–94	£750–900	£200–250	£150–180	£55–65
x.	Gambia 1894	£325–375	—	£150–180	£55–65
xi.	Benin River 1894	£350–400	£200–250	£150–180	£45–55
xii.	Brass River 1895	£325–375	—	—	£50–55
xiii.	M'wele 1895–6	£400–450	£300–350	£200–250	£110
	(Bronze)			£800–1000	
xiv.	1896–98	—	£375–475	£220–300	£35–50
xv.	Niger 1897	—	£375–425	£220–300	£50–60
xvi.	Benin 1897	£300–350	£200–250	£220–300	£40–50
xvii.	Dawkita 1897	—	—	—	£110
xviii.	1897–98	—	£325–425	£220–250	£50–55
xix.	1898	£725–950	£325–425	£220–250	£50–55
xx.	Sierra Leone 1898–9	£225–275	£325–425	£220–250	£50–55
xxi.	1899	£925–1250	£325–375	£500–700	£50–55
xxii.	1900	—	£325–375	£220–250	£50–55
	2 clasps	£475–525	£325–375	£250–300	
	3 clasps	£575–675	—	£350–400	—
	4 clasps	—	—	£450–500	—

138. BRITISH SOUTH AFRICA COMPANY'S MEDAL

1st type rev.

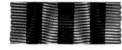

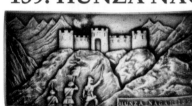

Mashonaland (2nd) rev.

Date: 1896.
Campaign: South Africa 1890-97.
Branch of Service: British Army and colonial units.
Ribbon: Seven equal stripes, four yellow and three dark blue.
Metal: Silver.
Size: 36mm.
Description: (Obverse) the Old Head bust of Queen Victoria; (reverse) a charging lion impaled by a spear, with a mimosa bush in the background and a litter of assegais and a shield on the ground.
Clasps: Mashonaland 1890, Matabeleland 1893, Rhodesia 1896, Mashonaland 1897.
Comments: *Originally instituted in 1896 for award to troops taking part in the suppression of the Matabele rebellion of 1893, it was later extended to cover operations in Rhodesia (1896) and Mashonaland (1897). The medal, as originally issued, had the inscription MATABELELAND 1893 at the top of the reverse. The medal was re-issued with RHODESIA 1896 or MASHONALAND 1897 inscribed on the reverse, but holders of medals for their first campaign only added clasps for subsequent campaigns. Rather belatedly, it was decided in 1927 to issue medals retrospectively for the Mashonaland campaign of 1890; in this instance the name and date of the campaign were not inscribed on the reverse though the details appeared on the clasp. Although 705 men were entitled, only 200 claimed the medal and clasp. An unusually ornate suspender has roses, thistles, shamrocks and leeks entwined. Only two medals are known with all four clasps, while only fifteen medals had three clasps.*

VALUE:		Miniature
a. Undated reverse with		
Mashonaland 1890 clasp	£850–1000	£55–65
i. Matabeleland 1893	Rare	—
ii. Rhodesia 1896	Rare	—
iii. Mashonaland 1897	Rare	—
b. Matabeleland 1893 rev.	£350–400	£45–50
ii.Rhodesia 1896	£500–600	£55–65
iii. Mashonaland 1897	£500–600	£55–65
with 2 clasps	£850–1000	£70–80
c. Rhodesia 1896 rev.	£350–400	£55–65
iii. Mashonaland 1897	£600–700	£65–75
d. Mashonaland 1897	£350–400	£55–65
Shangani Patrol confirmed member £1800–2200		

139. HUNZA NAGAR BADGE

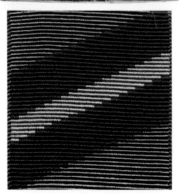

Date: 1891.
Campaign: Hunza and Nagar 1891.
Branch of Service: Jammu and Kashmir forces.
Ribbon: Large (46mm x 32mm) with a broad red diagonal band and white centre stripe and green upper left and lower right corners.
Metal: Bronze.
Size: 55mm x 27mm.
Description: A uniface rectangular plaque featuring three soldiers advancing on the crenellated hill fort of Nilt, with mountains in the background. The inscription HUNZA NAGAR 1891 appears lower right. It was intended to be worn as a brooch at the neck but subsequently many were fitted with a suspender for wear with a red and green ribbon. The reverse is impressed "Woodstock St."
Clasps: None.
Comments: *Gurney of London manufactured this badge which was awarded by the Maharajah of Jammu and Kashmir to his own troops who served in the operation against the border states of Hunza and Nagar and qualified for the Indian general service medal with clasp for Hunza 1891. The punitive expedition was led by Colonel A. Durand in response to the defiant attitude of the Hunza and Nagar chiefs towards the British agency at Gilgit.*
VALUE: £500–650

140. CENTRAL AFRICA MEDAL

Date: 1895.
Campaigns: Central Africa 1891–98.
Branch of Service: Mainly local forces.
Ribbon: Three equal stripes of black, white and terracotta representing the Africans, Europeans and Indians.
Metal: Silver or bronze.
Size: 36mm.
Description: Obverse and reverse as the East and West Africa (Ashantee) medal, distinguished only by its ribbon.
Clasps: Originally issued without a clasp but one for Central Africa 1894–98 was subsequently authorised.
Comment: *Though generally issued in silver, a bronze version was awarded to native servants. The first issue of this medal had a simple ring suspension and no clasp. For the second issue a clasp, Central Africa 1894–98 was authorised and the medal was issued with a straight bar suspender, which is very rare.*

VALUE:		Miniature
Without clasp (ring suspension)		£75–100
To natives	£800–1200	
To Europeans	£2000–3000	
With clasp (ring suspension)		£85–120
To natives	£1500–2000	
To Europeans	£2500–3500	
With clasp (bar suspension)	£1200–1500	£85–120
To Navy native	£2500–3000	
Bronze, unnamed	**From £500**	—

141. HONG KONG PLAGUE MEDAL

Date: 1894.
Campaign: Hong Kong, May-September 1894.
Branch of Service: Royal Navy, Royal Engineers, KSLI and local personnel.
Ribbon: Red with yellow edges and two narrow yellow stripes in the centre.
Metal: Silver.
Size: 36mm.
Description: (Obverse) a Chinese patient lying on a trestle table being supported by a man warding off the winged figure of Death while a woman tends the sick man. The year 1894 appears on a scroll in the exergue, while the name of the colony in Chinese pictograms is inscribed on the left of the field. (Reverse) inscribed PRESENTED BY THE HONG KONG COMMUNITY round the circumference, and FOR SERVICES RENDERED DURING THE PLAGUE OF 1894 in seven lines across the centre. It was fitted with a plain ring for suspension.
Clasps: None.
Comments: *The colonial authorities in Hong Kong awarded this medal to nurses, civil servants, police, British Army and Royal Navy personnel who rendered assistance when the crown colony was stricken by a severe epidemic of bubonic plague in May 1894. Despite stringent measures, over 2500 people died in the ensuing three months. About 400 medals were issued in silver and awarded to 300 men of the King's Shropshire Light Infantry, 50 petty officers and ratings of the Royal Navy and NCOs and other ranks of the Royal Engineers, as well as about the same number of police and junior officials, while 45 were struck in gold for award to officers, nursing sisters and senior officials. However, the medal was not authorised for wear on uniform by British troops.*

VALUE:

		Miniature
Gold (45)	£6500–10,000	£225–310
Silver (400)	£1600–1800	£175–250

142. INDIA MEDAL

Date: 1896.

Campaign: India 1895–1902.

Branch of Service: British and Indian forces.

Ribbon: Crimson with two dark green stripes—the heraldic colour of Britain and the sacred colour of the prophet.

Metal: Silver or bronze.

Size: 36mm.

Description: Issued with two different obverses, portraying Queen Victoria (1895–1901) and King Edward VII in field marshal's uniform (1901–02). (Reverse) British and Indian soldiers supporting a standard. The Edward VII reverse is undated.

Clasps: Seven, mainly for actions on the North West Frontier (see below).

Comments: *This medal replaced the India GSM which had been awarded for various minor campaigns over a period of four decades from 1854. Combatant troops were given the medal in silver but native bearers and servants received a bronze version. Although the clasp Waziristan 1901–2 is rare to British recipients it was awarded to a number of regiments.*

VALUE:

		British regiments	Indian Army	Bronze	Miniature
i.	Defence of Chitral 1895	£3500–4500	£2400–3000	£3500–4500	£90–110
ii.	Relief of Chitral 1895	£200–225	£175–200	£135–185	£30–35
iii.	Punjab Frontier 1897–98	£200–225	£175–200	£125–160	£25–30
iv.	Malakand 1897*	£500–700	£200–275	£160–225	£55–65
v.	Samana 1897*	£200–225	£185–225	£125–160	£40–45
vi.	Tirah 1897–98*	£200–250	£185–225	£125–160	£50–55
vii.	Waziristan 1901–2	£350–450	£185–225	£125–160	£60–70
3 clasps		£275–350	£275–350	£185–260	£55–65
4 clasps		—	£325–375	—	£65–85

These clasps are always paired with clasp iii.

143. JUMMOO AND KASHMIR MEDAL

Date: 1895.

Campaign: Defence of Chitral 1895.

Branch of Service: Native levies.

Ribbon: White with red stripes at the edges and a central green stripe.

Metal: Bronze, silver.

Size: 35mm high; 38mm wide.

Description: This medal, by Gurney of London, has a unique kidney shape showing the arms of Jummoo (Jammu) and Kashmir on the obverse. (Reverse) a view of Chitral fort with troops in the foreground.

Clasps: Chitral 1895.

Comments: *Awarded by the Maharajah of Jummoo (Jammu) and Kashmir to the Indian troops who participated in the defence of Chitral (a dependency of Kashmir) during the siege of 4 March to 20 April by Chitralis and Afghans led by Umra Khan and Sher Afzul. It always comes with the clasp. with the name of the maker (GURNEY LONDON) on the back. The medal in bronze was presumably awarded to other ranks and those in silver to officers.*

VALUE:	Silver	Bronze
Named	—	£500–700
Unnamed	1200–1600	£400–600

144. ASHANTI STAR

Date: 1896.
Campaign: Gold Coast 1896.
Branch of Service: British forces.
Ribbon: Yellow with two black stripes.
Metal: Bronze.
Size: 44mm.
Description: A saltire cross with a four-pointed star in the angles, surmounted by a circular belt inscribed ASHANTI 1896 around a British crown. The plain reverse is simply inscribed FROM THE QUEEN.
Clasps: None.
Comments: *Issued unnamed, but the colonel of the West Yorkshire Regiment had the medals of the second battalion engraved at his own expense. Some 2000 stars were awarded to officers and men serving in the expedition led by Major-General F.C. Scott against the tyrannical King Prempeh. It is believed that the star was designed by Princess Henry of Battenberg whose husband died of fever during the campaign.*

VALUE:

Unnamed	£200–250
Named to West Yorkshire Regiment	£650–750
In attributable group	£850–1000
Miniature	£50–60

145. QUEEN'S SUDAN MEDAL

Date: 1899.
Campaign: Reconquest of the Sudan 1896–97.
Branch of Service: Royal Navy, Army and local forces.
Ribbon: Half-yellow and half-black representing the desert and the Sudanese nation, divided by a thin crimson stripe representing the British forces.
Metal: Silver or bronze.
Size: 36mm.
Description: (Obverse) the bust of Queen Victoria similar to the Jubilee bust but with sceptre; (Reverse) a seated figure of Victory holding palms and laurels with flags in the background, the word SUDAN appearing on a tablet at her feet.
Clasps: None.
Comments: *Unusually, no clasps were granted for individual actions which included the celebrated battle of Omdurman in which young Winston Churchill charged with the cavalry. Medals named to the 21st Lancers are especially desirable on that account.*

VALUE:

Bronze	
unnamed	£250–300
named	£300–350
Silver	
unnamed	£225–275
named to British Regt	£375–450
Indian Regt	£325–375
21st Lancers	£2500–3500
Confirmed charger*	£3500–4000
RN/RM (46)	£3000–3500
War correspondent	£1500–2000

* Dependent on which Company the recipient served in.

Miniature	£40–50

146. KHEDIVE'S SUDAN MEDAL 1896–1908

(reverse)

Date: 1897.
Campaign: Sudan 1896-1908.
Branch of Service: Royal Navy and British and Egyptian Armies.
Ribbon: 38mm yellow with a broad central deep blue stripe, symbolising the desert and the River Nile.
Metal: Silver or bronze.
Size: 39mm.
Description: (Obverse) an elaborate Arabic inscription translating as 'Abbas Hilmi the Second' and the date 1314 (AD 1897); (reverse) an oval shield surrounded by flags and a trophy of arms. Bar suspender.
Clasps: Fifteen (see below) but medals with more than the two clasps 'The Atbara' and 'Khartoum' are unusual. Inscribed in English and Arabic to British recipients.
Comments: *Instituted by the Khedive of Egypt in February 1897 and granted to those who served in the reconquest of Dongola province in the Sudan (1896-8) as well as in subsequent operations for the pacification of the southern provinces. It was awarded to officers and men of the British and Egyptian Armies and Royal Navy personnel who served on the Nile steamboats. In addition, the crews of the Royal Naval ships HMS Melita (139) and HMS Scout (149) were awarded silver medals with no clasps for Dongola 1896 (but were not awarded the Queen's Sudan Medal 1896–98). Medals to Royal Naval personnel with clasps are rare and command a high premium: Hafir (16), The Atbara (6), Sudan 1897 (12), Khartoum (33), Gedaref (9), Gedid (5) and Sudan 1899 (6).*

VALUE:

No clasp silver		ix. Sudan 1899	£160–185
Unnamed	£130–150	x. Bahr-el-Ghazal 1900–2	£195–235
named to British regt	£200–250	xi. Jerok	£160–185
named to Indian regt	£160–185	xii. Nyam-Nyam	£185–210
named to Royal Navy	£375–475	xiii. Talodi	£185–210
No clasp bronze	£160–185	xiv. Katfia	£185–210
i. Firket	£160–185	xv. Nyima	£185–210
ii. Hafir	£160–185	2 clasps	£200–250
iii. Abu Hamed	£160–185	3 clasps	£250–275
iv. Sudan 1897	£160–185	4 clasps	£275–350
v. The Atbara	£155–175	5 clasps	£375–450
vi. Khartoum	£250–275	6 clasps	£400–500
vii. Gedaref	£160–185	7 clasps	£500–550
viii. Gedid	£160–185	8 clasps	£525–600

Miniature

No clasp silver	£40–55
With any single clasp	£55–85
Add £15 for each additional clasp	

A young, fresh-faced Winston Churchill aged 24 poses in his brand new 4th Hussars dress uniform. He was to be involved in action in the Sudan and his detailed accounts of his experiences there provide an important eye-witness view of this turbulent time in the history of the British Empire.

147. EAST AND CENTRAL AFRICA MEDAL

Date: 1899.
Campaigns: East and Central Africa 1897–99.
Branch of Service: British, Indian and local forces.
Ribbon: Half yellow, half red.
Metal: Silver or bronze.
Size: 36mm.
Description: (Obverse) the bust of Queen Victoria similar to the Jubilee bust but with sceptre; (reverse) a standing figure of Britannia with the British lion alongside.
Clasps: Four (see below).
Comments: *Instituted for service in operations in Uganda and the southern Sudan, it was awarded in silver to combatants and in bronze to camp followers. Most of the medals were awarded to troops of the Uganda Rifles and various Indian regiments. The few British officers and NCOs were troop commanders and instructors seconded from their regiments and their medals are worth very much more than the prices quoted, which are for native awards.*

VALUE:

	Europeans	Natives	Miniature
No clasp			
silver	—	£260–285	£50–60
bronze	—	£335–435	—
i. Lubwa's (with clasp Uganda 1897–98)	—	£750–900	£80–90
ii. Uganda 1897–98	£800–1000	£450–550	£70–80
iii. 1898 (silver)	—	£450–550	£70–80
iv. 1898 (bronze)	—	£550–650	—
v. Uganda 1899	—	£450–550	£70–80

147A. UGANDA STAR

Instituted: 1897–98.
Campaign: Mutiny of Sudanese troops in Uganda.
Branch of Service: African civilians and soldiers.
Ribbon: None.
Metal: Silver.
Description: An eight-pointed uniface star surmounted by a crown, with the dates 1897 and 1898 on a circular rim enclosing the Old Head or Veiled Bust of Queen Victoria. Brooch-mounted. Manufactured by Carrington of London and issued in a blue plush-lined case.
Comments: *This award, approved by the Foreign Office and sanctioned by Queen Victoria, acknowledged the loyalty of African tribal leaders but, in a few cases, was also awarded to Sudanese troops (one, in fact, a Tunisian) who fought gallantly in quelling the serious mutiny of Sudanese troops of the Uganda Rifles. It was for this action that British, Indian and Local forces were awarded the East and Central Africa Medal with the bar for Lubwa's (see above). Only 39 stars were awarded.*

VALUE: From £2500

148. BRITISH NORTH BORNEO COMPANY'S MEDAL 1888–1916

Instituted: 1897.

Campaign: North Borneo (now Sabah, Malaysia), 1897-1916.

Ribbon: Initially gold (later yellow) watered silk 32mm, replaced in 1917 by a 32mm ribbon with maroon edges, two yellow stripes and a dark blue central stripe. The central stripe was originally 6mm wide but modern ribbons have a 10mm stripe.

Metal: Silver or bronze.

Size: 38mm, with a thickness of 5mm.

Description: (Obverse) the shield of the Company, supported by a warrior on either side. The Company motto at the foot is PERGO ET PERAGO (I carry on and accomplish); (reverse) the British lion facing left, standing in front of a bush adorned with the Company flag, with a small wreath in the exergue.

Clasps: Punitive Expedition (1897), Punitive Expeditions (1898-1915), Rundum (1915). The Punitive Expeditions clasp was awarded to those who took part in two or more actions, but it also replaced the earlier single Expedition clasp in due course.

Comments: *These medals were awarded for service in the 15 minor expeditions between 1883 and 1915, excluding the major action at Tambunan. The manufacturers, Spink, supplied 12 silver medals in 1898–9 for award to officers (only three being named). In 1906 a further 74 silver medals were issued, to be exchanged for the bronze medals initially awarded to other ranks. A further 11 silver medals were supplied later on, all unnamed. A total of 75 bronze medals were supplied, 25 of them stamped with a name and sometimes rank and number as well, and issued, both stamped and engraved, to other ranks.*

First type ribbon.

Second type ribbon.

VALUE:

	Type	Officially named	Unnamed original	Stamped "Specimen"	Miniature
i. Punitive Expedition	Silver	£1500–2000	£350–500	£60–80	£180–200
	Bronze	£1500–2000	£350–500	£60–80	
ii. Punitive Expeditions	Silver	£1500–2000	£350–500	£60–80	£180–200
	Bronze	£1500–2000	£350–500	£60–80	
iii. Rundum	Silver	£1500–2000	£350–500	£60–80	£180–200

148A. BRITISH NORTH BORNEO COMPANY'S MEDAL 1899–1900

Instituted: 1900.
Campaign: The final expedition in the Tambunan Valley against Mat Salleh.
Ribbon: 32mm yellow with a 10mm green stripe down the centre.
Metal: Silver or bronze.
Size: 38mm. Officially named medals are 5mm thick.
Description: (Obverse) the shield of the British North Borneo Company with BRITISH NORTH BORNEO round the top and the date 1900 below; (reverse) a wreath enclosing a device of one clothed and one naked arm supporting the Company's flag. The motto PERGO ET PERAGO is inscribed outside the wreath. The inscription SPINK & SON, LONDON appears in very tiny lettering at the foot.
Clasps: Tambunan.
Comments: *Instituted for award to those officers and men who took part in the expedition of January-February 1900 against Mat Salleh who had roused the Tegas against the Tiawan Dusuns in the Tambunan Valley. Salleh was killed on February 1, 1900 when Company forces stormed his stronghold and his followers were dispersed or killed. Eight silver medals were originally awarded to officers, but in 1906 some 106 were issued to be exchanged for the bronze medals initially issued to other ranks. A further 22 silver medals were later supplied, unnamed. A total of 125 bronze medals were supplied, 118 of them stamped with a name and sometimes also a rank and number, and issued, both stamped and engraved, to other ranks. Only 36 are recorded as replaced by silver medals, but it is known that some of these bronze medals were not returned to the authorities.*

VALUE:

Type	Officially Named	Unnamed original	Spink copy	Stamped "Specimen"
Silver	£1800–2000	£300–500	£50–60	£60–80
Bronze	£1000–1500	£300–500	£50–60	£60–80

Miniature	£175–200

149. SULTAN OF ZANZIBAR'S MEDAL

Date: 1896.
Campaign: East Africa 1896.
Branch of Service: Sultan's forces.
Ribbon: Plain bright scarlet.
Metal: Silver.
Size: 36mm.
Description: (Obverse) a facing bust of Sultan Hamid bin Thwain surrounded by a Suaheli inscription in Arabic; (reverse) same inscription set in four lines.
Clasps: Pumwani, Jongeni, Takaungu, Mwele (inscribed only in Arabic).
Comments: *Awarded to the Zanzibari contingent who served under Lieut. Lloyd-Matthews RN in East Africa alongside British and Imperial forces.*

VALUE: £400–500   *Miniature* £580–680

150. QUEEN'S SOUTH AFRICA MEDAL

Date: 1899.

Campaign: Anglo-Boer War 1899-1902.

Branch of Service: British and Imperial forces.

Ribbon: Red with two narrow blue stripes and a broad central orange stripe.

Metal: Silver or bronze.

Size: 36mm.

Description: (Obverse) the Jubilee bust of Queen Victoria; (reverse) Britannia holding the flag and a laurel crown towards a large group of soldiers, with warships offshore. The words SOUTH AFRICA are inscribed round the top.

Clasps: 26 authorised but the maximum recorded for a single medal is nine to the Army and eight to the Navy.

Comments: *Because of the large number of British and imperial forces which took part and the numerous campaign and battle clasps awarded, this is one of the most popular and closely studied of all medals, offering immense scope to the collector. A total of 250,000 medals were awarded. Numerous specialist units were involved for the first time, as well as locally raised units and contingents from India, Canada, Australia and New Zealand. Of particular interest are the medals awarded to war correspondents and nurses which set precedents for later wars. Although nurses received the medal they were not issued with clasps to which they were entitled. A small number of bronze medals without a clasp were issued to bearers and servants in Indian units. The original issue of the QSA depicts Britannia's outstretched hand pointing towards the R of AFRICA and bears the dates 1899–1900 on the reverse field. Less than 70 of these were issued to Lord Strathcona's Horse who had returned to Canada before the war ended, but as the war dragged on the date was removed before any other medals were issued, although some medals can be found with a "ghost" of this date still to be seen. On the third type reverse there is again no date but Britannia's hand points towards the F. The prices for clasps given overleaf are for clasps issued in combination with others. Some clasps are much scarcer when issued singly than combined with other clasps and conversely some clasps are not recorded on their own. Verified ten-clasp medals to South African units are known. It is important to note that the following list is very basic and represents the value of straightforward medals and clasps. Confusion can sometimes occur as single clasps and combinations of two or three clasps can command higher premiums than medals with a greater number of clasps. It is beyond the remit of this book to give the value of every possible combination of clasps. A very rough guide would be to take the most valuable clasp as a starting point and add 25% of this value for each Battle clasp and 10% for each State clasp, however, this is by no means infallible. An example would be to take a three-clasp medal which has Elandslaagte (£350–400), Belfast (£80–100) and Relief of Kimberley (£200–275) which as a simple 3-clasp medal would be valued at £100–165 — however, on the rough guide system it would be valued at c. £650. Certain clasp combinations will always command a higher premium, for example Relief of Ladysmith/ Relief of Mafeking, Defence of Ladysmith/Relief of Mafeking, Elandslaagte/Defence of Ladysmith, Defence of Kimberley/Paardeberg, etc. Clasps for Natal and Cape Colony cannot appear on the same medal.*

1st type rev.

2nd type rev.
(occasionally ghost
dates can be seen)

3rd type rev.

150. QUEEN'S SOUTH AFRICA MEDAL *continued*

VALUE:	RN	British Army	SA/Indian	Aus/NZ	Canadian
No clasp bronze	—	—	£150–250	—	—
No clasp silver	£150–160	£75–85	£85–150	£150–200	£125–175
i. Cape Colony	£180–200	£75–85	£80–100	£150–200	£125–175
ii. Rhodesia	£1000–1250	£400–450	£300–350	£375–450	£350–400
iii. Relief of Mafeking	—	—	£400–450	£425–550	£400–450
iv. Defence of Kimberley	—	£350–450	£250–300	—	—
v. Talana	—	£350–400	£250–350	—	—
vi. Elandslaagte	—	£350–450	£300–350	—	—
vii. Defence of Ladysmith	£750–850	£375–500	£200–250	—	—
viii. Belmont	£300–350	£125–150	—	£250–300	—
ix. Modder River	£300–350	£125–150	—	£250–300	—
x. Tugela Heights	£300–350	£100–125	—	—	—
xi. Natal	£300–350	£100–160	£120–150	—	£220–250
xii. Relief of Kimberley	£750–950	£200–275	£85–100	£150–185	—
xiii. Paardeberg	£250–300	£100–125	£85–100	£125–175	£175–200
xiv. Orange Free State	£180–225	£85–125	£75–100	£125–175	£175–200
xv. Relief of Ladysmith	£450–500	£125–150	£80–100	—	—
xvi. Driefontein	£240–260	£85–125	—	£125–175	£225–275
xvii. Wepener	—	£800–1000	£400–450	—	—
xviii. Defence of Mafeking	—	—	£1500–2250	—	—
xix. Transvaal	£450–600	£85–100	£75–100	£120–155	£225–275
xx. Johannesburg	£250–300	£85–100	£85–100	£125–175	£125–175
xxi. Laing's Nek	£500–650	£85–100	—	—	—
xxii. Diamond Hill	£250–300	£85–100	£85–100	£125–175	£200–225
xxiii. Wittebergen	£1000–1200	£85–100	£85–100	£125–175	—
xxiv. Belfast	£250–300	£85–100	£85–100	£125–175	£125–175
xxv. South Africa 1901	£125–150	£75–90	£75–85	£85–125	£100–150
xxvi. South Africa 1902	£750–850	£75–90	£65–75	£85–125	£100–150
2 clasps (*see Comment above*)	£200–250	£150–200	£100–150	£175–200	£175–200
3 clasps „	£250–280	£100–175	£125–175	£185–225	£185–225
4 clasps	£300–350	£150–275	£130–185	£225–275	£225–275
5 clasps*	£380–450	£150–200	£130–185	£275–300	£225–275
6 clasps*	£550–650	£165–250	£225–275	£325–375	£325–375
7 clasps*	£800–900	£475–550	£450–500	£850–1000	—
To Royal Marines	£1600–1800				
8 clasps*	£1800–2000	£850–1000	£2000–3000	—	—
9 clasps	—	—	£3500–4000	—	—
Relief dates on reverse (Lord Strathcona's Horse)	—	—	—	—	£4000–5000
Nurses	—	£500–650	—	—	—
War Correspondents	—	£1500–1750	—	—	—

* excluding date clasps

Miniature
From £20 with no clasp to £50 with 6 fixed clasps—"slip-on" style clasps approx. 20% less.
With dated reverse £125–175

151. QUEEN'S MEDITERRANEAN MEDAL

Date: 1899.
Campaign: Mediterranean garrisons 1899-1902.
Branch of Service: British militia forces.
Ribbon: Red with two narrow dark blue stripes and a central broad orange stripe (as for Queen's South Africa Medal).
Metal: Silver.
Size: 36mm.
Description: Similar to the Queen's South Africa Medal but inscribed MEDITERRANEAN at the top of the reverse.
Clasps: None.
Comments: *Awarded to officers and men of the militia battalions which were sent to Malta and Gibraltar to take over garrison duty from the regular forces who were drafted to the Cape.*

VALUE:

Silver (5,000)	£350–400	*Miniature* £75–85

152. KING'S SOUTH AFRICA MEDAL

Date: 1902.
Campaign: South Africa 1901–02.
Branch of Service: British and imperial forces.
Ribbon: Three equal stripes of green, white and orange.
Metal: Silver.
Size: 36mm.
Description: (Obverse) bust of King Edward VII in field marshal's uniform; (reverse) as for Queen's medal.
Clasps: Two: South Africa 1901, South Africa 1902.
Comments: *This medal was never issued without the Queen's medal and was awarded to all personnel engaged in operations in South Africa in 1901–02 when fighting was actually confined to numerous skirmishes with isolated guerrilla bands. Very few medals were awarded to RN personnel as the naval brigades had been disbanded in 1901. Apart from about 600 nurses and a few odd men who received the medal without a clasp, this medal was awarded with two clasps—most men were entitled to both clasps, single clasp medals being very rare. Only 137 were awarded to New Zealand troops.*

VALUE:

No clasp (Conductors and associated ranks in the ASC (106) and nurses (587))	£300–400
Two clasps:	
i. South Africa 1901	
ii. South Africa 1902	
RN (33)	£1500–1800
Army	£95–125
Canada (160)	£175–200
Australia (*not issued on its own, in a pair with any QSA to an Australian*)	£2500–2600
New Zealand	£300–350
South African units	£85–125
St John Ambulance Brigade (12)	£300–350
Single clasp 1902 (ii) (502 to Imperial troops, none known for Colonial troops)	From £200
Miniature	
No clasp	£15–20
2 clasps	£20–25

152A. ST ANDREW'S AMBULANCE ASSOCIATION MEDAL FOR SOUTH AFRICA

Date: 1902.

Campaign: South Africa 1899–1902.

Branch of Service: St Andrew's Ambulance Association.

Ribbon: Plain white silk.

Metal: Silver.

Size: 31x20mm.

Description: An oval medal: (obverse) the Geneva cross surmounted on a rayed star in red enamel with SOUTH AFRICA above and 1900 below surrounded by the inscription SCOTTISH NATIONAL RED CROSS HOSPITAL; (reverse) the arms of the Association: St Andrew in front of the cross, with ST ANDREW'S AMBULANCE ASSOCIATION around.

Clasps: None.

Comments: *This small medal was awarded in 3 classes, Bronze, Silver and Gold. The Gold medal was given to senior staff of the 160-strong Scottish Hospital, including Sir George Cayley (late IMS) who commanded; the Silver to Officers, Nurses, and Civil Surgeons and the Bronze to the OR's who served. The Bronze variety has been seen named in small impressed capitals on the rim at 6 o'clock. All Varieties of the medal are rare.*

VALUE: Rare   *Miniature* —

153. ST JOHN AMBULANCE BRIGADE MEDAL FOR SOUTH AFRICA

Date: 1902.

Campaign: South Africa 1899–1902.

Branch of Service: St John Ambulance Brigade.

Ribbon: Black with narrow white edges.

Metal: Bronze.

Size: 37mm.

Description: (Obverse) King Edward VII; (reverse) the arms of the Order and SOUTH AFRICA and the dates 1899 and 1902 with the legend in Latin around.

Clasps: None.

Comments: *Issued by the Order of St John of Jerusalem to the members of its ambulance brigade who served during the Boer War or who played an active part in the organisation, mobilisation and supply roles. Medals were engraved on the edge with the recipient's name and unit. It is most often associated with the two South Africa medals, but 14 members who went on from South Africa to serve during the Boxer Rebellion were also awarded the China Medal.*

VALUE: Bronze (1,871) £300–350   *Miniature* £175–200 *(in silver slightly less)*

153A. NATIONAL FIRE BRIGADE'S UNION MEDAL FOR SOUTH AFRICA

Date: 1902.

Campaign: South Africa 1899–1902.

Branch of Service: National Fire Brigade's Union.

Ribbon: Red with narrow orange edges and two orange stripes near the centre.

Metal: Silver.

Size: 36mm.

Description: (Obverse) King Edward VII; (reverse) A bust of a helmeted fireman with a Geneva cross in the sky above. Around the circumference a spray of laurel leaves between the dates 1899 and 1902 and SOUTH AFRICA at top.

Comments: *Awarded to a small detachment of volunteers of the National Fire Brigades Union (Ambulance Department) who served in South Africa as stretcher bearers and ambulance personnel. Each volunteer also received the St John Ambulance Medal for South Africa and the Queen's South Africa Medal with the clasp Cape Colony. Only 42 were awarded.*

VALUE: £1200–1500   *Miniature* (silver) £220–350

154. KIMBERLEY STAR

Date: 1900.
Campaign: Defence of Kimberley 1899–1902.
Branch of Service: British and local forces.
Ribbon: Half yellow, half black, separated by narrow stripes of red, white and blue.
Metal: Silver.
Size: Height 43mm; max. width 41mm.
Description: A six-pointed star with ball finials and a circular centre inscribed KIMBERLEY 1899–1900 with the civic arms in the middle. (Reverse) plain, apart from the inscription MAYOR'S SIEGE MEDAL 1900. Suspended by a plain ring from a scrolled bar.
Clasps: None
Comments: *The Mayor and council of Kimberley awarded this and the following medal to the defenders of the mining town against the Boer forces. Two medals were struck in gold but about 5000 were produced in silver. Those with the "a" Birmingham hallmark for 1900 rate a premium over stars with later date letters.*

VALUE:

Hallmark "a"	£450–550	*Miniature*	£145–175
Later date letters	£350–450		

155. KIMBERLEY MEDAL

Date: 1900.
Campaign: Defence of Kimberley 1899–1900.
Branch of Service: Local forces.
Ribbon: As above.
Metal: Silver
Size: 38mm.
Description: (Obverse) the figure of Victory above the Kimberley Town Hall, with the dates 1899–1900 in the exergue. (Reverse) two shields inscribed INVESTED 15 OCT. 1899 and RELIEVED 15 FEB. 1900. The imperial crown appears above and the royal cypher underneath, with the legend TO THE GALLANT DEFENDERS OF KIMBERLEY round the circumference.
Comments: *Although awarded for the same purpose as MYB154, this silver medal is a much scarcer award.*

VALUE: £1800–2000

156. YORKSHIRE IMPERIAL YEOMANRY MEDAL

Date: 1900.
Campaign: South Africa 1900–02.
Branch of Service: Yorkshire Imperial Yeomanry.
Ribbon: Dark blue with a central yellow stripe.
Metal: Silver.
Size: 38mm.
Description: Three versions were produced. The first two had the numeral 3 below the Prince of Wales's feathers and may be found with the dates 1900–1901 or 1901–1902, while the third type has the figures 66, denoting the two battalions involved. The uniform reverse has the white rose of Yorkshire surmounted by an imperial crown and enclosed in a laurel wreath with the legend A TRIBUTE FROM YORKSHIRE.
Comments: *Many medals were produced locally and awarded to officers and men of county regiments. The medals struck by Spink and Son for the Yorkshire Imperial Yeomanry, however, are generally more highly regarded as they were much more extensively issued, and therefore more commonly met with.*

VALUE:

		Miniature
3rd Battalion 1900–1901	£300–350	£130–150
3rd Battalion 1901–1902	£300–350	£110–130
66th Company 1900–1901	£300–350	Not seen

157. MEDAL FOR THE DEFENCE OF OOKIEP

Date: 1902.
Campaign: Defence of Ookiep 1902.
Branch of Service: British and colonial forces.
Ribbon: Dark brown with a central green stripe.
Metal: Silver or bronze.
Size: 36mm.
Description: (Obverse) a miner and copper-waggon, with the Company name and date of foundation (1888) round the circumference; (reverse) a thirteen-line text. Fitted with a scroll suspender.
Clasps: None.
Comments: *Commonly known as the Cape Copper Co. Medal, this medal was awarded by the Cape Copper Company to those who defended the mining town of Ookiep in Namaqualand when it was besieged from 4 April to 4 May 1902 by a Boer commando led by Jan Christian Smuts, later Field Marshal, Prime Minister of South Africa and a member of the Imperial War Cabinet. The defence was conducted by Lt-Col W. A. D. Shelton, DSO, and Maj J. L. Dean of the Namaqualand Town Guard, the Company's manager. The garrison consisted of 206 European miners, 660 Cape Coloureds, 44 men of the 5th Warwickshire militia and twelve men of the Cape Garrison Artillery.*

VALUE:

Silver (officers)	£6000–8000
Bronze (other ranks)	£1200–1500

158. CHINA WAR MEDAL 1900

Date: 1901.
Campaign: Boxer Rebellion 1900.
Branch of Service: British and imperial forces.
Ribbon: Crimson with yellow edges.
Metal: Silver or bronze.
Size: 36mm.
Description: (Obverse) bust of Queen Victoria; (reverse) trophy of arms, similar to the 1857-60 China Medal but inscribed CHINA 1900 at the foot.
Clasps: Taku Forts, Defence of Legations, Relief of Pekin.
Comments: *Instituted for service during the Boxer Rebellion and the subsequent punitive expeditions, this medal was similar to that of 1857-60 with the date in the exergue altered to 1900. There are three types of naming: in small, impressed capitals for European troops, in large impressed capitals for naval recipients, and in engraved cursive script for Indian forces. The medal was issued in silver to combatants and in bronze to native bearers, drivers and servants. The international community was besieged by the Boxers, members of a secret society, aided and abetted by the Dowager Empress. The relieving force, consisting of contingents from Britain, France, Italy, Russia, Germany and Japan, was under the command of the German field marshal, Count von Waldersee. The British Legation Guard, comprising 80 Royal Marines and a number of "odd men", won the clasp for Defence of Legations, the most desirable of the campaign bars in this conflict.*

VALUE:	Royal Navy	Army	Indian units	*Miniature*
Silver no clasp	£200–250	£250–300	£185–250	£25–30
Australian naval forces	£1500–2000 (approx. 550 issued)			
HMS *Protector*	£4000–4500			
Bronze no clasp	—	—	£185–250	—
i. Taku Forts	£800–1000	—	—	£35–45
ii. Defence of Legations	£9000–12,000	—	—	£55–65
iii. Relief of Pekin:				
Silver	£450–500	£700–750	£285–350	£30–35
Bronze	—	—	£300–350	—
2 clasps	£800–1000	—	—	£45–55
No-clasp medal to a nurse	£1500–2000			
To a war correspondent (9)	£1500–2000			
ditto Relief of Pekin (1)	—			

159. TRANSPORT MEDAL

Date: 1903.
Campaigns: Boer War 1899-1902 and Boxer Rebellion 1900.
Branch of Service: Mercantile Marine.
Ribbon: Red with two blue stripes.
Metal: Silver.
Size: 36mm.
Description: (Obverse) bust of King Edward VII in the uniform of an Admiral of the Fleet; (reverse) HMST *Ophir* below a map of the world with a Latin inscription at the foot OB PATRIAM MILITIBUS PER MARE TRANSVECTIS ADJUTAM (For carrying troops across the sea).
Clasps: S. Africa 1899-1902, China 1900.
Comments: *The last of the medals associated with the major conflicts at the turn of the century, it was instituted for award to the officers of the merchant vessels used to carry troops and supplies to the wars in South Africa and China. The medal was discontinued as from August 4, 1914.*

VALUE:

		Miniature
i. South Africa 1899–1902 (1219)	£900–1100	£80–110
ii. China 1900 (322)	£1200–1500	£80–110
Both clasps (178)	£1500–1700	£110–160

160. ASHANTI MEDAL

Date: 1901.
Campaign: Gold Coast 1900.
Branch of Service: British and local forces.
Ribbon: Black with two broad green stripes.
Metal: Silver or bronze.
Size: 36mm.
Description: (Obverse) bust of King Edward VII in field marshal's uniform. (Reverse) a lion on the edge of an escarpment looking towards the sunrise, with a native shield and spears in the foreground. The name ASHANTI appeared on a scroll at the foot.
Clasps: Kumassi.
Comments: *A high-handed action by the colonial governor provoked a native uprising and the siege of the garrison at Kumassi. The medal was awarded to the defenders as well as personnel of the two relieving columns. Very few Europeans were involved as most were in South Africa fighting the Boers. The medal was awarded in silver to combatants and bronze to native transport personnel and servants.*

VALUE:

	Silver	Bronze	Miniature
No clasp	£350–400	£400–500	£45–65
i. Kumassi	£650–750	Rare	£65–80

161. AFRICA GENERAL SERVICE MEDAL

Date: 1902.
Campaigns: Minor campaigns in Africa 1902 to 1956.
Branch of Service: British and colonial forces.
Ribbon: Yellow with black edges and two thin central green stripes.
Metal: Silver or bronze.
Size: 36mm.
Description: (Obverse) effigies of Edward VII, George V and Elizabeth II; (reverse) similar to that of the East and Central Africa medal of 1897–99, with AFRICA in the exergue.
Clasps: 34 awarded in the reign of Edward VII, ten George V and only one Elizabeth II (see below).

continued overleaf

161. AFRICA GENERAL SERVICE MEDAL *continued*

Comments: *This medal replaced the East and West Africa Medal 1887–1900, to which 21 clasps had already been issued. In turn, it remained in use for 54 years, the longest-running British service medal. Medals to combatants were in silver, but a few bronze medals were issued during the 1903–04 operations in Northern Nigeria and the Somaliland campaigns of 1902 and 1908 to transport personnel and these are now much sought after, as are any medals with the effigy of George V on the obverse. With the exception of the 1902–04 Somali campaign and the campaign against the Mau Mau of Kenya (1952–56) European troops were not involved in any numbers, such personnel consisting mostly of detached officers and specialists.*

VALUE:		RN units	British regiments	African/Indian
i.	N. Nigeria	—	—	£200–225
ii.	N. Nigeria 1902	—	—	£180–200
iii.	N. Nigeria 1903	—	—	£170–190
iv.	N. Nigeria 1903–04	—	—	£240–280
v.	N. Nigeria 1903–04 (bronze)	—	—	£230–250
vi.	N. Nigeria 1904	—	—	£225–250
vii.	N. Nigeria 1906	—	—	£200–225
viii.	S. Nigeria	—	—	£280–320
ix.	S. Nigeria 1902	—	—	£240–280
x.	S. Nigeria 1902–03	—	—	£240–280
xi.	S. Nigeria 1903	—	—	£220–260
xii.	S. Nigeria 1903–04	—	—	£280–320
xiii.	S. Nigeria 1904	—	—	£210–230
xiv.	S. Nigeria 1904–05	—	—	£280–320
xv.	S. Nigeria 1905	—	—	£400–500
xvi.	S. Nigeria 1905–06	—	—	£240–280
xvii.	Nigeria 1918	—	—	£180–200
xviii.	East Africa 1902	—	—	£380–420
xix.	East Africa 1904	—	—	£300–350
xx.	East Africa 1905	—	—	£240–280
xxi.	East Africa 1906	—	—	£280–320
xxii.	East Africa 1913	—	—	£280–320
xxiii.	East Africa 1913–14	—	—	£220–240
xxiv.	East Africa 1914	—	—	£280–320
xxv.	East Africa 1915	—	—	£250–270
xxvi.	East Africa 1918	—	—	£220–250
xxvii.	West Africa 1906	—	—	£250–300
xxviii.	West Africa 1908	—	—	£250–300
xxix.	West Africa 1909–10	—	—	£320–370
xxx.	Somaliland 1901	—	—	£320–370
xxxi.	Somaliland 1901 (bronze)	—	—	£300–350
xxxii.	Somaliland 1902–04	£175–225	£220–280	£160–190
xxxiii.	Somaliland 1902–04 (bronze)	—	—	£350–450
xxxiv.	Somaliland 1908–10	£175–225	—	£150–175
xxxv.	Somaliland 1908–10 (bronze)	—	—	£250–300
xxxvi.	Somaliland 1920	£450–550	—	£170–200
	as above but RAF (225 awarded)	—	£700–900	—
xxxvii.	Jidballi (with Somaliland 1902–04)	—	£350–450	£210–270
xxxviii.	Uganda 1900	—	—	£250–300
xxxix.	B.C.A. 1899–1900	—	—	£250–300
xl.	Jubaland	£300–350	—	£210–250
xli.	Jubaland (bronze)	—	—	£550–650
xlii.	Jubaland 1917–18	—	—	£230–250
xliii.	Jubaland 1917–18 (bronze)	—	—	£250–300
xliv.	Gambia	£600–800	—	£300–350
xlv.	Aro 1901–1902	£800–900	—	£250–300
xlvi.	Lango 1901	—	—	£350–400
xlvii.	Kissi 1905	—	—	£400–450
xlviii.	Nandi 1905–06	—	—	£200–250
xlix.	Shimber Berris 1914–15	—	—	£300–350
l.	Nyasaland 1915	—	—	£250–300
li.	Kenya	£350–500	£150–175	£75–125
lii.	Kenya (to RAF)	—	£200–250	—
	2 clasps	£250–300	£350–400	£175–300
	3 clasps	—	—	£250–450
	4 clasps	—	—	£350–500
	5 clasps	—	—	£450–650
	6 clasps	—	—	£850–1200
	Medal to war correspondent	£1200–1500		

Miniature
Range from £35 to £90 depending upon clasp. "Slip-on" clasps are approx. 20% cheaper. Add £15 for each additional clasp.

162. TIBET MEDAL

Date: 1905.
Campaign: Tibet 1903–04.
Branch of Service: British and Indian regiments.
Ribbon: Green with two white stripes and a broad maroon central stripe.
Metal: Silver or bronze.
Size: 36mm.
Description: (Obverse) bust of King Edward VII; (reverse) the fortified hill city of Lhasa with TIBET 1903–04 at the foot.
Clasps: Gyantse.
Comments: *The trade mission led by Colonel Sir Francis Younghusband to Tibet was held up by hostile forces, against whom a punitive expedition was mounted in 1903. This medal was awarded mainly to Indian troops who took part in the expedition, camp followers being awarded the medal in bronze. A clasp was awarded to those who took part in the operations near Gyantse between 3 May and 6 July 1904.*

VALUE:

	British	Indian	Bronze	Miniature
Without clasp	£500–700	£350–400	£125–150	£45–55
i. Gyantse	£1200–1500	£550–650	£350–450	£65–75

163. NATAL REBELLION MEDAL

Date: 1907.
Campaign: Natal 1906.
Branch of Service: Local forces.
Ribbon: Crimson with black edges.
Metal: Silver.
Size: 36mm.
Description: (Obverse) right-facing profile of King Edward VII. (Reverse) an erect female figure representing Natal with the sword of justice in her right hand and a palm branch in the left. She treads on a heap of Zulu weapons and is supported by Britannia who holds the orb of empire in her hand. In the background, the sun emerges from behind storm clouds.
Clasp: 1906.
Comments: *The Natal government instituted this medal for services in the operations following the Zulu rebellion. Local volunteer units bore the brunt of the action and it is interesting to note that one of the recipients was Sergeant-Major M. K. Gandhi who later led India to independence. Medals to officers are engraved in running cursive script.*

VALUE:

		Miniature
No clasp (2000)	£175–200	£45–55
i. 1906 (8000)	£225–275	£55–70
Natal Naval Corps		
without clasp (67)	£175–250	
clasp 1906 (136)	£275–300	

163A. MESSINA EARTHQUAKE COMMEMORATIVE MEDAL

Date: 1908.
Campaign: Messina earthquake relief.
Branch of Service: Royal Navy.
Ribbon: Green with white edges and central white stripe.
Metal: Silver.
Size: 31.5mm.
Description: (Obverse) left-facing profile of King Victor Emanuel III; (reverse) A wreath of oak leaves within which are the words MEDAGLIA COMMEMORATIVA / TERREMOTO CALABRO SICULO 28 DICEMBRE 1908.
Comments: *The King of Italy rewarded Royal Naval and other personnel who went to the aid of victims of the tragic earthquake that hit Messina in December 1908 with this silver medal. Officers and men serving on certain ships were eligible for the award as well as members of the Mercantile Marine and others who were engaged in relief operations. The Admiralty's published list of RN ships is as follows: HMS Duncan, HMS Euralyus, HMS Exmouth, HMS Lancaster, HMS Minerva and HMS Sutlej. However 52 medals were also awarded to personnel from HMS Boxer, which was omitted from the original list and a further 35 medals were awarded to the officers and men of HMS Philomel who had actually "been engaged in work which was directly attributable to the rescue operations". The medal was issued unnamed. In addition to the commemorative medal a special Messina Earthquake Merit Medal was awarded in two sizes (40mm and 30mm) bronze, silver and gold to organisations, vessels and various key individuals who played a part in the rescue operations and examples are known in miniature, in silver.*

VALUE:

		Miniature
Unattributed single medal	£120–150	£65–85
Royal Navy (c. 3500)	£200–300	
Royal Marines (481)	£250–400	
Mercantile Marine (c. 400)	£300–400	
Other	£200–300	
Merit medal	Rare	£125–£155

The aftermath of the devastating earthquake at Messina.

164. INDIA GENERAL SERVICE MEDAL

Date: 1909.
Campaigns: India 1908 to 1935.
Branch of Service: British and Indian forces.
Ribbon: Green with a broad blue central stripe.
Metal: Silver.
Size: 36mm.
Description: Three obverse types were used: Edward VII (1908–10), George V Kaisar-i-Hind (1910–30) and George V Indiae Imp (1930–35). (Reverse) the fortress at Jamrud in the Khyber Pass, with the name INDIA in a wreath at the foot.
Clasps: Twelve, plus two in bronze (see below).
Comments: *This medal was awarded for a number of minor campaigns and operations in India before and after the First World War. The medals were struck at the Royal Mint in London and by the Indian government in Calcutta, the only difference being in the claw suspenders, the former being ornate and the latter plain. Medals with the clasps* North West Frontier 1908 *and* Abor 1911–12 *were also issued in bronze to native bearers.*

VALUE:

		British Army	RAF	Indian regiments	Miniature
i.	North West Frontier 1908	£150–200	—	£80–100	£25–30
	bronze clasp	—	—	£200–220	
ii.	Abor 1911–12	—	—	£250–300	£30–35
	bronze clasp	—	£275–350	—	
iii.	Afghanistan NWF 1919	£85–100	£150–180	£50–75	£20–25
iv.	Waziristan 1919–21	£125–150	£180–200	£50–75	£20–25
iva*	Mahsud 1919–20	£125–150	£550–650 (175)	£75–100	£20–25
v.	Malabar 1921–22	£175–200	—	£125–175	£35–40
vi.	Waziristan 1921–24	£85–100	£150–180	£50–75	£20–25
vii.	Waziristan 1925 (254)	—	£1400–1600	—	£25–30
viii.	NW Frontier 1930–31	£85–100	£150–180	£50–75	£20–25
ix.	Burma 1930–32	£125–150	£1000–1500	£75–100	£20–25
x.	Mohmand 1933	£200–250	£500–600	£45–65	£20–25
xi.	NW Frontier 1935	£85–100	£150–200	£45–65	£25–30

*Usually found in combination with Waziristan 1919-21, but 10 medals were awarded either with this clasp alone or with the Afghanistan NWF clasp.

Royal Mint striking.

Calcutta striking.

165. KHEDIVE'S SUDAN MEDAL 1910

Date: 1911.
Campaign: Sudan 1910 to 1922
Branch of Service: British and Egyptian forces.
Ribbon: Black with thin red and green stripes on either side.
Metal: Silver or bronze.
Size: 36mm.
Description: (Obverse) an Arabic inscription signifying the name of Khedive Abbas Hilmi and the date 1328 in the Moslem calendar (1910 AD) (type I). He was deposed in December 1914 when Egypt was declared a British protectorate, and succeeded by his nephew who was proclaimed Sultan. Sultan Hussein Kamil changed the Arabic inscription and date to AH 1335 (1916–17) on later issues of the medal (type II) . (Reverse) a lion poised on a plinth with the sunrise in the background.
Clasps: 16, inscribed in English and Arabic.
Comments: *Introduced in June 1911 as a replacement for the previous Khedive's Sudan medal of 1896–1908, it was awarded for minor operations in the southern Sudan between 1910 and 1922. The silver medal was issued with clasps to combatants, and without a clasp to non-combatants, while the bronze version was granted to camp followers. The medal is usually found unnamed although a few British recipients' medals are found named in small impressed capitals or Arabic script. The prices below are for unnamed examples.*

VALUE:
Silver without clasp type I	£350–400	
Silver without clasp type II	£300–350	
Bronze without clasp type I	£400–450	
Bronze without clasp type II	£300–350	
i.	Atwot	£450–500
ii.	S. Kordofan 1910	£450–500
iii.	Sudan 1912	£450–500
iv.	Zeraf 1913-14	£450–500
v.	Mandal	£450–500
vi.	Miri	£450–500
vii.	Mongalla 1915-16	£450–500
viii.	Darfur 1916	£450–500
ix.	Fasher	£450–500
x.	Lau Nuer	£450–500
xi.	Nyima 1917-18	£450–500
xii.	Atwot 1918	£450–500
xiii.	Garjak Nuer	£450–500
xiv.	Aliab Dinka	£450–500
xv.	Nyala	£450–500
xvi.	Darfur 1921	£550–600
	2 clasps	£600–700
Miniature		
	Silver type I	£40–60
	Silver type II	£40–60
	With any single clasp	£60–95

For each additional clasp add £15–30 (slip-on clasps approx. 20% less)

165A. BRITISH RED CROSS SOCIETY MEDAL FOR THE BALKAN WARS 1912–13

Date: 1913.
Campaign: Balkan Wars 1912–13.
Branch of Service: British Red Cross Society.
Ribbon: White with a central red stripe.
Metal: Silver gilt.
Size: 30mm.
Description: (Obverse) an enamelled design of a red cross on a white shield with the legend THE BRITISH RED CROSS SOCIETY around; (Reverse) blank for naming and hallmark. Ribbon suspended from a top white enamel brooch with indented ends and BALKAN WAR 1912–13, 1912 or 1913. The medal has a swivel scroll bar suspender
Clasps: White enamelled Bulgaria, Greece, Montenegro, Servia, Turkey.
Comments: *This medal, manufactured by J. R. Gaunt of Birmingham, was given to all members of the Society who rendered first aid service to the belligerents also to others who gave help to those units. A total of 198 medals were awarded to members of the Society and a further 72 to others for services rendered. An additional 14 medals were awarded to Turkish nationals but these carried the Red Crescent emblem in place of the Red Cross. A complete roll of all recipients is held by the BRCS.*

VALUE: £250–300

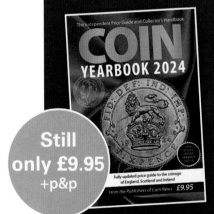

FIRST WORLD WAR MEDALS

The increased popularity in family history research, accompanied by the vast digitisation of records and the on-line resources such as *Ancestry, Find My Past* etc., has gone a long way to encouraging more and more people to find out about their ancestors' military service and as World War I was the first war that touched every family there is plenty of interest in this conflict out there. This interest is inevitably reflected in the prices of World War I medals that have held firm particularly among popular units and whilst the prices we have quoted are broadly similar to previous editions of the *Yearbook*, there are instances of World War I medals being offered for far more than listed here—whether they actually make that amount is a matter of conjecture. Certain medals will command a premium, of course, as with any medals a connection to the more famous actions, in this case particularly the Somme, Gallipoli, the Retreat from Mons, and the battles of Loos and Jutland will increase the price of the group (the prices paid for First Day of the Somme casualties continue to be strong) and gallantry and complete "sets" to casualties all continue to sell exceptionally well. It should also be noted that medals to Imperial forces, particularly Australian, Canadian and New Zealanders are also very popular. As always in the MEDAL YEARBOOK the prices listed in this section are intended as a guide for a non-casualty private in a line regiment. The medals to an officer killed on the First Day of the Somme for example will, of course, be worth more.

166. 1914 STAR

Date: 1917.
Campaign: France and Belgium 1914.
Branch of Service: British forces.
Ribbon: Watered silk red, white and blue.
Metal: Bronze.
Size: Height 50mm; max. width 45mm.
Description: A crowned four-pointed star with crossed swords and a wreath of oak leaves, having the royal cypher at the foot and a central scroll inscribed AUG NOV 1914. Uniface, the naming being inscribed incuse on the plain reverse.
Clasps: 5th Aug.–22nd Nov. 1914. The clasp was sewn on to the ribbon of the medal, the first of this type. A silver rosette is worn on the ribbon strip if the bar was awarded.
Comments: *Awarded to all those who had served in France and Belgium between 5 August and 22 November 1914. In 1919 King George V authorised a clasp bearing these dates for those who had actually been under fire during that period. The majority of the 400,000 recipients of the star were officers and men of the prewar British Army, the "Old Contemptibles" who landed in France soon after the outbreak of the First World War and who took part in the retreat from Mons, hence the popular nickname of Mons Star by which this medal is often known. Approximately 1000 were awarded to members of the Royal Flying Corps of which about 300 received the bar, hence they command a premium. A significant number of Indian Army troops were engaged on the Western Front in 1914 and earned the 1914 Star.*

VALUE:		Miniature
1914 Star	From £75	£5–10
To RN	£225–350	
RM	£125–200	
RND	£175–300	
1914 Star/BWM/Victory trio		
Corps	From £85	
British Regiments	From £125	
Canadian Regiments	From £850	
Australian Regiments	From £1500	
1914 trio with plaque (no. 172)		
Corps	From £200	
Regiments	From £275	
RFC	From £1500	
i. 5th Aug.–22nd Nov. 1914 ("Mons") clasp	From £125	£5–7
Clasp alone	£50–60	

The single 1914 Star named to Private J. Parr of the 4th Battalion Duke of Cambridge's Own (Middlesex Regiment) accepted as being the first fatal casualty of the war, was sold at auction by DNW in August 2021 for £24,000.

167. 1914–15 STAR

Date: 1918.
Campaign: First World War 1914–15.
Branch of Service: British and imperial forces.
Ribbon: Watered silk red, white and blue (as above).
Metal: Bronze.
Size: Height 50mm; max. width 45mm.
Description: As above, but AUG and NOV omitted and scroll across the centre inscribed 1914–15.
Clasps: None.
Comments: *Awarded to those who saw service in any theatre of war between 5 August 1914 and 31 December 1915, other than those who had already qualified for the 1914 Star. No fewer than 2,350,000 were awarded, making it the commonest British campaign medal up to that time.*

VALUE:

1914–15 Star	From £25	*Miniature*	£5–8
1914–15 Star/BWM/Victory trio			
Corps	From £50		
RN	From £60		
Regiments	From £65		
1914–15 trio with plaque (no. 172)			
Corps	From £150		
RN	From £200		
Regiments	From £200		

168. BRITISH WAR MEDAL 1914–20

Date: 1919.
Campaign: First World War, 1914–20.
Branch of Service: British and imperial forces.
Ribbon: Orange watered centre with stripes of white and black at each side and borders of royal blue.
Metal: Silver or bronze.
Size: 36mm.
Description: (Obverse) the uncrowned left-facing profile of King George V by Sir Bertram Mackennal. (Reverse) St George on horseback trampling underfoot the eagle shield of the Central Powers and a skull and cross-bones, the emblems of death. Above, the sun has risen in victory. The figure is mounted on horseback to symbolise man's mind controlling a force of greater strength than his own, and thus alludes to the scientific and mechanical appliances which helped to win the war.
Clasps: None.
Comments: *This medal was instituted to record the successful conclusion of the First World War, but it was later extended to cover the period 1919–20 and service in mine-clearing at sea as well as participation in operations in North and South Russia, the eastern Baltic, Siberia, the Black Sea and Caspian. Some 6,500,000 medals were awarded in silver, but about 110,000 in bronze were issued mainly to Chinese, Indian and Maltese personnel in labour battalions. It was originally intended to award campaign clasps, but 79 were recommended by the Army and 68 by the Navy, so the scheme was abandoned as impractical. The naval clasps were actually authorised (7 July 1920) and miniatures are known with them, though the actual clasps were never issued.*

VALUE:		*Miniature*
Silver (6,500,000)	From £15*	£5–10
Bronze (110,000)	£135–155	£15–20
BWM/Victory pair		
Corps	From £25	
Regiments/RN	From £35	
Pair with plaque (no. 172)		
Corps	From £140	
Regiment/RN	From £200	

* Current prices are dictated by world silver markets. The BWM being 1oz of silver, as the price of silver fluctuates so will the minimum price of the BWM.

169. MERCANTILE MARINE WAR MEDAL

Date: 1919.
Campaign: First World War 1914–18.
Branch of Service: Mercantile Marine.
Ribbon: Green and red with a central white stripe, symbolising port and starboard and masthead steaming lights.
Metal: Bronze.
Size: 36mm.
Description: (Obverse) Mackennal profile of King George V; (reverse) a steamship ploughing through an angry sea, with a sinking submarine and a sailing vessel in the background, the whole enclosed in a laurel wreath.
Clasps: None.
Comments: *Awarded by the Board of Trade to members of the Merchant Navy who had undertaken one or more voyages through a war or danger zone.*

VALUE:

Bronze (133,000)	£35–65
To woman	£250–350
With BWM	From £85
With WWI pair	From £125
With 1914–15 trio	From £175
With 1914 trio	From £250
To Australians	Add 50 per cent
To South Africans	Add 75 per cent
With plaque (no. 172)	Add £100+
Miniature	£25–40

170. VICTORY MEDAL

Date: 1919.
Campaign: First World War 1914–19.
Branch of Service: British and imperial forces.
Ribbon: 38mm double rainbow (indigo at edges and red in centre).
Metal: Yellow bronze.
Size: 36mm.
Description: (Obverse) the standing figure of Victory holding a palm branch in her right hand and stretching out her left hand. (Reverse) a laurel wreath containing a four-line inscription THE GREAT WAR FOR CIVILISATION 1914–1919.
Clasps: None.
Comments: *Issued to all who had already got the 1914 or 1914–15 Stars and most of those who had the British War Medal, some six million are believed to have been produced. It is often known as the Allied War Medal because the same basic design and double rainbow ribbon were adopted by thirteen other Allied nations (though the USA alone issued it with campaign clasps). The Union of South Africa produced a version with a reverse text in English and Dutch (not Afrikaans as is often stated).*

VALUE:

British pattern	£10–25
South African pattern	£25–35
Dark "Chocolate" colour issue	£20–25
Miniature	
Normal	£5–6
"CIVILIZATION" variety	£25–30
South African pattern	£75–85

171. TERRITORIAL FORCE WAR MEDAL

Date: 1919.
Campaign: First World War 1914–19.
Branch of Service: Territorial forces.
Ribbon: Watered gold silk with two dark green stripes towards the edges.
Metal: Bronze.
Size: 36mm.
Description: (Obverse) effigy of King George V; (reverse) a wreath enclosing the text FOR VOLUNTARY SERVICE OVERSEAS 1914–19.
Clasps: None.
Comments: *Awarded to all those serving with the Territorial Forces on 4 August 1914, or those who had completed four years service before this date and rejoined on or before 30 September 1914, who served overseas during the course of World War I. Those who had already qualified for the 1914 or 1914–15 Stars, however, were excluded. Around 34,000 medals were awarded, making it by far the scarcest of the First World War medals. The value of individual medals depends on the regiment or formation of the recipient. The totals awarded given below are from "The Great War Medal Collector's Companion" courtesy of Howard Williamson.*

VALUE:

Infantry/Corps (23,762)	£150–300
Artillery (6460)	£120–250
Yeomanry (3271)	£400–500
Cavalry (95)	£850–1000
RFC, RAF, RNAS (505)	£850–1000
Nurses (277)	£650–750
Miniature	£25–35

171A. BRITISH RED CROSS SOCIETY MEDAL FOR WAR SERVICE

Date: 1920.
Campaign: First World War.
Branch of Service: Members of the British Red Cross Society.
Ribbon: Plain white.
Metal: Bronze-gilt.
Size: 31mm.
Description: (Obverse) the Geneva Cross surrounded by a laurel wreath, with the legend BRITISH RED CROSS SOCIETY: FOR WAR SERVICE: 1914–1918 around; (reverse) a wreath enclosing the text INTER/ARMA/CARITAS ("Amidst the arms, charity").
Clasps: None.
Comments: *Granted to all members of the BRCS including Voluntary Aid Detachments who had performed one year or 1,000 hours voluntary service during the war and who did not receive any British War Medal for services rendered in respect of Red Cross war work. The medal was unnamed for wear only on Red Cross or similar uniform.*

VALUE: £15–25   *Miniature*   £25–35

For medals awarded by various other organisations for service during World War I see "Miscellaneous Medals" nos. 390 et seq.

172. MEMORIAL PLAQUE

Date: 1919.
Campaign: First World War.
Branch of Service: British forces.
Ribbon: None.
Metal: Bronze.
Size: 120mm.
Description: The plaque shows Britannia bestowing a laurel crown on a rectangular tablet bearing the full name of the dead in raised lettering. In front stands the British lion, with dolphins in the upper field, an oak branch lower right, and a lion cub clutching a fallen eagle in the exergue. The inscription round the circumference reads HE (or SHE) DIED FOR FREEDOM AND HONOVR. A parchment scroll was issued with each plaque giving the deceased's name and unit.
Comments: *Given, with a parchment scroll, to the next of kin of those who lost their lives on active service during the War. Originally it was thought that Naval and Army plaques differed because of the width of the "H" in "HE" however examples of narrow "H" plaques found to Army units and wide "H" plaques to the Navy indicates this to be incorrect. The most likely reason for the narrower "H" is the later decision to add an "S" to allow for female casualty plaques.*

VALUE:	"He died" (1,355,000)	From £65
	"She died" (600)	From £3000
	Parchment scroll (male)	From £35
	ditto (female)	From £1500–2500
Miniature:	Uniface/unnamed (modern manufacture)	£40–50

172A. SILVER WAR BADGE

Date: 12 September 1916.
Campaign: First World War.
Ribbon: None.
Metal: Silver.
Size: 33mm.
Description: A brooch-mounted circular badge with the crowned royal monogram in the centre and edge inscription FOR KING AND EMPIRE + SERVICES RENDERED +.
Comments: *Awarded to service personnel who sustained a wound or contracted sickness or disability in the course of the war as a result of which they were invalided out. It was worn on the lapel in civilian clothes. Each badge was numbered on the reverse. The purpose of the badge was to prevent men of military age but not in uniform from being harassed by women pursuing them with white feathers. Later in the War medical restrictions altered and some men re-enlisted and could wear the badge in uniform. Recently records for these badges have become publicly available and this research potential has inevitably had an effect on prices.*

VALUE:	From £30–40	*Miniature:*	£20–25

172B. CEYLON VOLUNTEER SERVICE MEDAL

Date: 1919.
Campaign: First World War.
Branch of Service: Ceylon volunteer forces.
Ribbon: None.
Metal: Bronze.
Size: 48mm x 44mm.
Description: An upright oval medal. (Obverse) a seated female figure bestowing a laurel crown on a kneeling soldier, with a radiant sun on the horizon; above, a six-line inscription: PRESENTED BY THE GOVERNMENT OF CEYLON TO THOSE WHO VOLUNTARILY GAVE THEIR SERVICES OVERSEAS IN THE GREAT WAR OF with the dates 1914 1919 in two lines on the right of the field; (reverse) the winged figure of Victory seated on a throne above a tablet inscribed with the name of the recipient.
Comments: *Awarded to volunteers from the Ceylon forces who served abroad during the war. Ceylon (now Sri Lanka) was the only British colony to issue such a medal for war service.*

VALUE: £125–175

173. NAVAL GENERAL SERVICE MEDAL 1909–62

Date: 1915.
Campaigns: Naval actions 1909 to 1962.
Branch of Service: Royal Navy.
Ribbon: White with broad crimson edges and two narrow crimson stripes towards the centre.
Metal: Silver.   **Size:** 36mm.
Description: (Obverse) effigy of the reigning monarch (see below). (Reverse) Britannia and two seahorses travelling through the sea.
Clasps: 17 (see below).
Comments: *Instituted for service in minor operations for which no separate medal might be issued. Five different obverses were employed: George V (1915-36), George VI Ind Imp (1936-49), George VI Fid Def (1949-52), Elizabeth II Br Omn (1952-53) and Elizabeth II Dei Gratia (1953-62). Medals issued with the first clasp include the name of the recipient's ship but this lapsed in later awards. The MALAYA clasp was issued with three types of medal: the George VI Fid Def and Elizabeth II Dei Gratia being the most common. The clasp BOMB & MINE CLEARANCE 1945–46 is very rare as it was apparently only awarded to the Royal Australian Navy. The clasp CANAL ZONE was instituted in October 2003 for service between October 1951 and October 1954.*

Bomb & Mine Clearance 1945–53 clasp

VALUE:			Miniature
			(in silver add £5)
i.	**Persian Gulf 1909-1914**		
	RN (7,127)	£185–225	
	Army (37)	£800–1000	£20-30
ii.	**Iraq 1919-20** (116)	£2000–2500	£20-30
iii.	**NW Persia 1919–20** (4)*	Rare	£35–75
iv.	**Palestine 1936–39** (13,600)	£125–155	£20-30
v.	**SE Asia 1945–46** (2,000)	£250–300	£20-30
vi.	**Minesweeping 1945–51** (4,750)	£200–250	£20-30
vii.	**Palestine 1945–48** (7,900)	£150–185	£20-30
viii.	**Malaya (George VI, Elizabeth II**		
	2nd type) (7,800)	£125–155	£20-30
	(Elizabeth II 1st type)	£145–175	£20-30
ix.	**Yangtze 1949** (1,450)	£850–1250	£20-30
	to HMS *Amethyst*	£1550–2500	
x.	**Bomb & Mine Clearance 1945–53** (145)	£1600–2000	£40–60
xi.	**Bomb & Mine Clearance 1945–46**	Very rare	£40–60
xii.	**Bomb & Mine Clearance**		
	Mediterranean (60)	£2000–2500	£40–60
xiii.	**Cyprus** (4,300)	£155–200	£12–15
xiv.	**Near East** (17,800)	£100–125	£12–15
xv.	**Arabian Peninsula** (1,200)	£225–275	£12–15
xvi.	**Brunei** (900)	£300–375	£12–15
xvii.	**Canal Zone**	£250–350	—

* The clasp NW Persia 1920 was withdrawn in favour of the clasp NW Persia 1919–20. Recipients were supposed to return their first clasp in exchange for the latter.

174. GENERAL SERVICE MEDAL 1918–62

Date: 1923.
Campaigns: Minor campaigns 1918 to 1962.
Branch of Service: Army and RAF.
Ribbon: Purple with a central green stripe.
Metal: Silver.
Size: 36mm
Description: (Obverse) six different effigies of the reigning monarch [George V coinage head (1918–30), George V crowned and robed bust (1931–36), George VI Ind Imp (1937–49), George VI Fid Def (1949–52), Elizabeth II Br Omn (1952–54) and Elizabeth II Dei Gratia (1955–62)]. (Reverse) a standing figure of Victory in a Greek helmet and carrying a trident, bestowing palms on a winged sword.
Clasps: 18 (see below).
Comments: *Awarded to military and RAF personnel for numerous campaigns and operations that fell short of full-scale war. It did not cover areas already catered for in the Africa and India general service medals. The George V crowned and robed bust was used only on the medal for Northern Kurdistan in 1931. The clasp CANAL ZONE was instituted in October 2003 for service between October 1951 and October 1954. On 29 July 2014 it was confirmed that those who served in Cyprus between 1955 and 1959 qualify for the clasp CYPRUS, also aircrew who assisted with at least one day's service in the operation between 20 June 1948 and 6 October 1948 qualify for the clasp BERLIN AIRLIFT.*

VALUE:

		British units	RAF	Indian and local units	Miniature *(in silver* add £5)
i.	S. Persia (Brit. officers)	£275–350	£3000–3500	£75–100	£20–30
ii.	Kurdistan	£125–150	£250–300	£75–100	£20–30
iii.	Iraq	£100–125	£200–250	£75–100	£20–30
iv.	N.W. Persia	£125–150	£300–350	£75–100	£20–30
v.	Southern Desert Iraq	—	£650–750	£1200–1500†	£20–30
vi.	Northern Kurdistan	£350–450	£2000–2500	—	£90–100
vii.	Palestine	£120–150	£150–200	£75–100	£20–30
viii.	S.E. Asia 1945–46	£120–150	£100–150	£65–75	£20–30
ix.	Bomb and Mine Clearance 1945–49	£650–750	£500–600	—	£40–60
x.	Bomb and Mine Clearance 1945–56	—	—	£500–600*	£40–60
xi.	Palestine 1945–48	£75–100	£75–100	£85–100	£20–30
xii.	Malaya (George VI)	£75–100	£75–100	£65–75	£20–30
xiii.	Malaya (Elizabeth II)	£75–100	£75–100	£65–75	£20–30
xiv.	Cyprus	£75–100	£75–100	£65–75	£12–15
xv.	Near East	£85–125	£80–120	—	£12–15
xvi.	Arabian Peninsula	£85–125	£75–100	£65–95	£12–15
xvii.	Brunei	£200–250	£200–250	£125–155	£12–15
xviii.	Canal Zone	£250–300	£250–300	—	£12–15
xvix.	Berlin Airlift	£85–100	£85–100	—	£12–15

†Indian units only *Australian units

174A. IRAQ ACTIVE SERVICE MEDAL

Date: May 1926.
Campaign: Iraq, 1924–38.
Branch of Service: Army and RAF.
Ribbon: 31mm in equal stripes of green, white and green.
Metal: Bronze.
Size: 38mm.
Description: (Obverse) a crescent forming the lower part; with an Arabic inscription above signifying "General Service" in two laurel branches. The medal is superimposed on crossed rifles, with rays in the arc between the muzzles, to which is joined a flattened loop suspender. (Reverse) The name of King Faisal I in Arabic and the date (AH) 1344 (i.e. 1926).
Clasps: Dates 1930–31, 1932, 1935 or 1936 in Arabic numerals with an Arabic inscription on the left.
Comments: *Also known as King Faisal's War Medal, it was awarded to British Army and RAF personnel stationed in Iraq or serving with the Iraq Levies. It was originally issued without a clasp, but clasps denoted subsequent actions or periods of service. By 1931, however, medals were issued with appropriate clasps from the outset.*

VALUE:

Without clasp	£85–125	*Miniature*	£50–80
With clasp	£100–150		

175. INDIA GENERAL SERVICE MEDAL 1936–39

Date: 1938.
Campaign: India 1936–39.
Branch of Service: British and Indian Armies and RAF.
Ribbon: Stone flanked by narrow red stripes, with broad green stripes at the edges.
Metal: Silver.
Size: 36mm
Description: (Obverse) crowned effigy of King George VI; (reverse) a tiger with the word INDIA across the top.
Clasps: North-West Frontier 1936–37, North-West Frontier 1937–39.
Comments: *The fourth and last of the IGS series, it was introduced when the change of effigy from George V to George VI became necessary, anticipating a similarly long life. It was not awarded after the outbreak of the Second World War, while the partition and independence of the Indian sub-continent afterwards rendered it obsolete. The medal was struck at the Royal Mint, London for award to British Army troops and RAF personnel, but the Calcutta Mint struck the medals awarded to the Indian Army.*

VALUE:

	British Army	RAF	Indian Army	*Miniature*
North West Frontier				
i. 1936-37	£100–150	£120–150	£45–50	£20–25
ii. 1937-39	£100–150	£120–150	£45–50	£20–30
2 clasps	£150–200	£180–200	£55–75	£20–35

(slip-on clasps deduct 20%)

176. BRITISH NORTH BORNEO COMPANY'S GENERAL SERVICE MEDAL 1937–1941

Instituted: 1937.

Campaign: British North Borneo (now Sabah), 1937–41.

Branch of Service: British North Borneo Company staff, Constabulary and various civilians.

Ribbon: 35mm, half dark green, half yellow. Gallantry awards were denoted by a thin red central stripe.

Metal: Silver. Copies were made in bronze.

Size: 38mm diameter, with a thickness of 3mm.

Description: (Obverse) the shield of the Company flanked by warriors as supporters. Above the shield are two arms, one clothed and the other naked, supporting the Company's flag. Below the shield is the motto PERGO ET PERAGO (I carry on and accomplish); (reverse) the seated figure of Britannia facing right, holding a trident in her left hand, with her right hand resting on a shield which bears the Union flag. NORTH BORNEO GENERAL SERVICE MEDAL is inscribed round the top and in the exergue is a branch with 11 leaves.

Clasps: None.

Comments: *Only one gallantry award was ever made, to Leong Yew Pong, aged 15, gazetted August 3, 1939. For specially valuable or long and meritorious services 44 were issued, gazetted in 1937, 1938, 1939 and 1941, with one replacement in 1947. Recipients were government officials, armed constabulary, rubber planters, the Archdeacon of North Borneo, the Chairman of the Chamber of Commerce, railway managers, businessmen and local dignitaries.*

VALUE

Medal	Type	Officially named	Unnamed original	Spink copy	Specimen
For Gallantry	Silver	Unique	Rare	£250–300	£300–350
For Service	Silver	£1500–1750	Rare	£150–200	£150–200
Miniature	£210–230				

Ribbon with red stripe denoting gallantry

176A. SUDAN DEFENCE FORCE GENERAL SERVICE MEDAL

Instituted: November 1933.

Campaign: Minor campaigns in the Sudan after 1933.

Branch of Service: Sudan Defence Force (SDF) and Police.

Ribbon: Central stripe of royal blue, edged by two yellow stripes and two black stripes at the edges.

Metal: Silver.

Size: 36mm.

Description: (Obverse) the seal of the Governor-General of the Sudan; (reverse) a stationary group of Sudanese soldiers, with "The Sudan" in Arabic below.

Clasps: None.

Comments: *The medal was awarded on the recommendation of the Kaid el'Amm (SDF Commander) to native personnel of the SDF, Police and other approved Sudanese who served in the field on such operations as might be considered by the Governor-General as being of sufficient importance to warrant the grant of the medal. It was also awarded for action against Italian forces in the southern Sudan from June 1940 to November 1941. About 9,000 were issued.*

VALUE: £175–£250

SECOND WORLD WAR STARS

Nine different campaign stars were issued for the Second World War. Apart from some Commonwealth issues notably Australia, Pakistan and South Africa, these were issued unnamed. In the cases of the Pacific Star, Burma Star and Italy Star naval personnel must have earned the 1939–45 Star before eligibility for those Stars begins. This is the same for the RAF in respect of the Air Crew Europe Star. It was decided that the maximum number of stars that could be earned by any one person was five, although this was increased to six when the Government agreed to the retrospective issue of the Arctic Star in March 2013, while those who qualified for more received a clasp to be sewn on the ribbon of the appropriate star. Only one clasp per ribbon was permitted which was the first to be earned after qualifying for that star, but this rule has been relaxed for the 1939–45 Star to allow for the new *Bomber Command* clasp. Thus the stars could bear the following clasps:

1.	1939–45 Star	Battle of Britain *and/or* Bomber Command
2.	Atlantic Star	Air Crew Europe *or* France and Germany
3.	Arctic Star	None
4.	Air Crew Europe Star	Atlantic *or* France and Germany
5.	Africa Star	North Africa 1942–43, 8th Army *or* 1st Army
6.	Pacific Star	Burma
7.	Burma Star	Pacific
8.	Italy Star	None
9.	France and Germany Star	Atlantic

Most of the ribbons are believed to have been designed by King George VI personally and have symbolic significance in each case. When ribbons alone are worn, the clasp is usually denoted by a silver rosette. However, the Battle of Britain clasp is represented by a gilt rosette and the 8th Army and 1st Army clasps by small silver numerals. As the clasps were sewn on to the ribbon and the stars issued unnamed, it is difficult to put valuations on examples with campaign clasps, however, the prices quoted are for medals with the *original* clasps. When purchasing expensive groups it is advisable that the medals be supported by documentary provenance or form part of a group in which at least one of the medals is named to the recipient.

Many of the medals and stars of the Second World War are still being officially produced, therefore there are a number of different die varieties available. There are also a number of dangerous copies in existence so care should be taken when purchasing expensive items. In the past few years a number of lapel badges or emblems have also been produced for award to veterans—see MYB nos. 242C et seq.

177. 1939–45 STAR

Date: 1945.
Campaign: Second World War 1939–45.
Branch of Service: British and Commonwealth forces.
Ribbon: Equal stripes of dark blue, red and light blue symbolising the Royal and Merchant Navies, Army and RAF respectively. The 1939–43 ribbon was authorised in November 1943 and worn by those awarded this proposed Star which became the 1939–45 Star when finally issued.
Metal: Bronze.
Size: Height 44mm; max. width 38mm.
Description: The six-pointed star has a circular centre with the GRI/VI monogram, surmounted by a crown and inscribed THE 1939-1945 STAR round the foot.
Clasps: Battle of Britain, Bomber Command, sewn directly on to the ribbon.
Comments: *The first in a series of nine bronze stars issued for service in the Second World War, it was awarded to personnel who had completed six months' service in specified operational commands overseas, between 3 September 1939 and 2 September 1945, though in certain cases the minimum period was shortened. Any service curtailed by death, injury or capture overseas also qualified, as did the award of a decoration or a mention in despatches. Clasps were awarded to RAF aircrew who took part in the Battle of Britain and, as a result of constant lobbying, in 2013 a clasp was also granted to aircrew members of Bomber Command. The clasps are denoted by a gilt rosette when the ribbon is worn alone. Surprisingly RAF ground crews who kept the Battle of Britain fighters in the air did not qualify for the 1939–45 Star, although those who assisted with the evacuation of troops from the beaches of Dunkirk did qualify.*

VALUE:		*Miniature*
1939–45 Star	£12–15	£5–7
Battle of Britain clasp	£2000–3000	£8–10
Bomber Command clasp	£40–60	£6–8

178. ATLANTIC STAR

Campaign: Atlantic 1939-45.
Branch of Service: Mainly Royal and Commonwealth Navies.
Ribbon: Watered silk blue, white and green representing the ocean.
Metal: Bronze.
Size: Height 44mm; max. width 38mm.
Description: As above, but inscribed THE ATLANTIC STAR.
Clasps: Air Crew Europe, France and Germany.
Comments: *This star was awarded in the Royal Navy for six months' service afloat between 3 September 1939 and 8 May 1945 in the Atlantic or home waters, and to personnel employed in the convoys to North Russia and the South Atlantic. Personnel must have already qualified for the 1939–45 Star with the qualifying period for this not counting towards the Atlantic Star. Merchant Navy personnel also qualified, as did RAF and Army (maritime gunners and air crews—the latter only requiring 2 months service) who served afloat. In the last six months of operational service up to 8 May 1945, the Atlantic Star was awarded but not the 1939–45 Star. Entitlement to the France and Germany or Air Crew Europe stars was denoted by clasps to that effect, if the Atlantic Star was previously awarded. Only one clasp could be worn. Only two awards were made to WRNS: to an officer and a rating.*

VALUE:		Miniature
Atlantic Star	£30–35	£5–7
Air Crew Europe clasp	Add £80-100	£8–10
France and Germany clasp	Add £25–30	£8–10

178A. ARCTIC STAR

Campaign: Arctic convoys 1939–45.
Branch of Service: British and Commonwealth forces.
Ribbon: A central white stripe with fine black edging bordered either side by equal stripes of pale blue, dark blue and red.
Metal: Bronze.
Size: Height 44mm; max. width 38mm.
Description: As above, but inscribed THE ARCTIC STAR.
Clasps: None.
Comments: *As the direct result of constant lobbying by veterans and associated organisations over the years, the Government finally agreed to issue the Arctic Star retrospectively from March 2013. Large numbers of surviving veterans or their next of kin have successfully applied for the medal. The Star is intended primarily to commemorate those who assisted or saw service on the ships of the convoys that sailed to North Russia in support of the Russian allies. Any member of the Royal Navy or Merchant Navy, as well as members of the Army and the RAF and certain civilian units are eligible if they served on or over the Arctic Circle for any length of time.*

VALUE:		Miniature
Arctic Star	£400–500	£8–10

179. AIR CREW EUROPE STAR

Campaign: Air operations over Europe 1939-44.
Branch of Service: RAF and Commonwealth aircrew.
Ribbon: Pale blue (the sky) with black edges (night flying) and a narrow yellow stripe on either side (enemy searchlights).
Metal: Bronze.
Size: Height 44mm; max. width 38mm.
Description: As above, but inscribed THE AIR CREW EUROPE STAR.
Clasps: Atlantic or France and Germany.
Comments: *Awarded for operational flying from UK bases over Europe, for a period of two months between 3 September 1939 and 4 June 1944. Entitlement to either the Atlantic Star or France and Germany Star was denoted by the appropriate bar. This star is by far the most coveted of all the Second World War stars. Officially named stars to South Africans are the rarest of all the Second World War medals.*

VALUE:		Miniature
Air Crew Europe Star	£350–400	£5–10
Atlantic clasp	Add £90	£12–15
France and Germany clasp	Add £25–30	£12–15

180. AFRICA STAR

Campaign: Africa 1940-43.
Branch of Service: British and Commonwealth forces.
Ribbon: Pale buff symbolising the sand of the desert, with a broad red central stripe, a dark blue stripe on the left and a light blue stripe on the right symbolising the three services.
Metal: Bronze.
Size: Height 44mm; max. width 38mm.
Description: As above, but inscribed THE AFRICA STAR.
Clasps: North Africa 1942-43, 8th Army, 1st Army.
Comments: *Awarded for entry into an operational area in North Africa between 10 June 1940 (the date of Italy's declaration of war) and 12 May 1943 (the end of operations in North Africa), but service in Abyssinia (Ethiopia), Somaliland, Eritrea and Malta also qualified for the award. A silver numeral 1 or 8 worn on the ribbon denoted service with the First or Eighth Army between 23 October 1942 and 23 May 1943. A clasp inscribed North Africa 1942-43 was awarded to personnel of the Royal Navy Inshore Squadrons and Merchant Navy vessels which worked inshore between these dates. RAF personnel also qualified for this clasp, denoted by a silver rosette on the ribbon alone.*

VALUE:		Miniature
Africa Star	£20–25	£3–5
8th Army clasp	Add £20	£8–10
1st Army clasp	Add £20	£8–10
North Africa 1942–43 clasp	Add £20	£10–12

181. PACIFIC STAR

Campaign: Pacific area 1941-45.
Branch of Service: British and Commonwealth forces.
Ribbon: Dark green (the jungle) with a central yellow stripe (the beaches), narrow stripes of dark and light blue (Royal Navy and RAF) and wider stripes of red (Army) at the edges.
Metal: Bronze.
Size: Height 44mm; max. width 38mm.
Description: As above, but inscribed THE PACIFIC STAR.
Clasps: Burma.
Comments: *Awarded for operational service in the Pacific theatre of war from 8 December 1941 to 15 August 1945. Service with the Royal and Merchant navies in the Pacific Ocean, Indian Ocean and South China Sea and land service in these areas also qualified. Personnel qualifying for both Pacific and Burma Stars got the first star and a clasp in respect of the second.*

VALUE:		Miniature
Pacific Star	£35–40	£3–5
Burma clasp	Add £40	£6–8

182. BURMA STAR

Campaign: Burma 1941-45.
Branch of Service: British and Commonwealth forces.
Ribbon: Three equal bands of dark blue (British forces), red (Commonwealth forces) and dark blue. The dark blue bands each have at their centres a stripe of bright orange (the sun).
Metal: Bronze.
Size: Height 44mm; max. width 38mm.
Description: As above, but inscribed THE BURMA STAR.
Clasps: Pacific.
Comments: *Qualifying service in the Burma campaign counted from 11 December 1941 and included service in Bengal or Assam from 1 May 1942 to 31 December 1943, and from 1 January 1944 onwards in these parts of Bengal or Assam east of the Brahmaputra. Naval service in the eastern Bay of Bengal, off the coasts of Sumatra, Sunda and Malacca also counted.*

VALUE:		Miniature
Burma Star	£25–30	£3–5
Pacific Clasp	Add £40	£6–8

183. ITALY STAR

Campaign: Italy 1943-45.
Branch of Service: British and Commonwealth forces.
Ribbon: Five equal stripes of red, white, green, white and red (the Italian national colours).
Metal: Bronze.
Size: Height 44mm; max. width 38mm.
Description: As above, but inscribed THE ITALY STAR.
Clasps: None.
Comments: *Awarded for operational service on land in Italy, Sicily, Greece, Yugoslavia, the Aegean area and Dodecanese islands, Corsica, Sardinia and Elba at any time between 11 June 1943 and 8 May 1945.*

VALUE:		*Miniature*
Italy Star	£20–25	£3–5

184. FRANCE AND GERMANY STAR

Date: 1945.
Campaign: France and Germany 1944-45.
Branch of Service: British and Commonwealth forces.
Ribbon: Five equal stripes of blue, white, red, white and blue (the national colours of the United Kingdom, France and the Netherlands).
Metal: Bronze.
Size: Height 44mm; max. width 38mm.
Description: As above, but inscribed THE FRANCE AND GERMANY STAR.
Clasps: Atlantic.
Comments: *Awarded for operational service in France, Belgium, the Netherlands or Germany from 6 June 1944 to 8 May 1945. Service in the North Sea, English Channel and Bay of Biscay in connection with the campaign in northern Europe also qualified. Prior eligibility for the Atlantic or Air Crew Europe Stars entitled personnel only to a bar for France and Germany. Conversely a first award of the France and Germany Star could earn an Atlantic bar.*

VALUE:		*Miniature*
France and Germany Star	£20–25	£3–5
Atlantic clasp	Add £90	£6–8

185. DEFENCE MEDAL

Date: 1945.
Campaign: Second World War 1939-45.
Branch of Service: British and Commonwealth forces.
Ribbon: Two broad stripes of green (this green and pleasant land) superimposed by narrow stripes of black (the black-out), with a wide stripe of orange (fire-bombing) in the centre.
Metal: Cupro-nickel or silver.
Size: 36mm.
Description: (Obverse) the uncrowned effigy of King George VI; (reverse) two lions flanking an oak sapling crowned with the dates at the sides and wavy lines representing the sea below. The words THE DEFENCE MEDAL appear in the exergue.
Clasps: None, but the King's Commendation for Brave Conduct emblem is worn on the ribbon.
Comments: *Awarded to service personnel for three years' service at home, one year's service in a non-operational area (e.g. India) or six months' service overseas in territories subjected to air attack or otherwise closely threatened. Personnel of Anti-Aircraft Command, RAF ground crews, Dominion forces stationed in the UK, the Home Guard, Civil Defence, National Fire Service and many other civilian units* qualified for the medal. The medal was generally issued unnamed in cupro-nickel, but the Canadian version was struck in silver.*

VALUE:		*Miniature*
Cupro-nickel (32g)	£15–20	£8–10
Silver (Canadian) (36g)	£25–30	£12–15

*The definitive list of eligible recipients was published by the Ministry of Defence in 1992—Form DM1/DM2 and Annexe. This lists 50 different organisations and 90 sub-divisions of eligible personnel.

186. WAR MEDAL 1939–45

Date: 1945.
Campaign: Second World War 1939-45.
Branch of Service: British and Commonwealth forces.
Ribbon: Narrow red stripe in the centre, with a narrow white stripe on either side, broad red stripes at either edge and two intervening stripes of blue.
Metal: Cupro-nickel or silver.
Size: 36mm.
Description: (Obverse) effigy of King George VI; (reverse) a triumphant lion trampling on a dragon symbolising the Axis powers.
Clasps: None.
Comments: *All fulltime personnel of the armed forces wherever they were serving, so long as they had served for at least 28 days between 3 September 1939 and 2 September 1945 were eligible for this medal. It was granted in addition to the campaign stars and the Defence Medal. A few categories of civilians, such as war correspondents and ferry pilots who had flown in operational theatres, also qualified. No clasps were issued with this medal but a bronze oak leaf denoted a mention in despatches. The medal was struck in cupro-nickel and issued unnamed, but those issued to Australian and South African personnel were officially named with SA prefixes (see MYB189). The Canadian version of the medal was struck in silver.*

VALUE:

		Miniature
Cupro-nickel (32g)	£10–15	£8–10
Officially named	£20–25	
Silver (Canadian) (36g)	£25–35	£12–15

186A. KING'S BADGE

Date: 1941.
Campaign: Second World War.
Ribbon: None.
Metal: Silver.
Size: 26mm.
Description: A circular buttonhole badge with the crowned monogram GRI in script capitals in the centre, inscribed FOR LOYAL SERVICE.
Comments: *Awarded to personnel who had been invalided out of the services and were in receipt of a war disablement pension. The badges are not numbered or named. For further information see MEDAL NEWS, September 2008.*

VALUE: £15–20   *Miniature* £15–20

187. INDIA SERVICE MEDAL

Date: 1945.
Campaign: India 1939-45.
Branch of Service: Indian forces.
Ribbon: Dark blue with two wide and one central thin pale blue stripes. The colours of the Order of the Indian Empire and the Order of the Star of India
Metal: Cupro-nickel.
Size: 36mm.
Description: (Obverse) the effigy of the King Emperor; (reverse) a map of the Indian sub-continent with INDIA at the top and 1939–45 at foot.
Clasps: None.
Comments: *Awarded to officers, men and women of the Indian forces for three years' non-operational service in India. In effect, it took the place of the Defence Medal in respect of Indian forces.*

VALUE: £15–20   *Miniature* £10–12

188. CANADIAN VOLUNTEER SERVICE MEDAL

Date: 22 October 1943.
Campaign: Second World War 1939-45.
Branch of Service: Canadian forces.
Ribbon: Narrow stripes of green and red flanking a broad central stripe of dark blue.
Metal: Silver.
Size: 36mm.
Description: (Obverse) seven men and women in the uniforms of the various services, marching in step; (reverse) the Canadian national arms.
Clasps: Maple leaf clasp to denote overseas service. A clasp inscribed DIEPPE and surmounted by the Combined Operations emblem, was instituted on 28 April 1994 for award to all servicemen who took part in the Dieppe raid of 19 August 1942. A clasp inscribed Hong Kong, with the letters HK entwined within a circle, was instituted on 28 April 1994 for award to those involved in the Battle of Hong Kong, 8–25 December 1941. A clasp showing an ascending heavy bomber was instituted on 11 April 2013 to be awarded to members of an air crew and non-flying personnel for operational service with a Bomber Command squadron engaged in or supported bombing operations over Continental Europe from September 3, 1939 to May 8, 1945.
Comments: *Awarded for eighteen months' voluntary service in the Canadian forces from 3 September 1939 to 1 March 1947. The seven marching personnel are based on real people taken from National Defence photographs, representing the land, sea and air forces plus a nurse. The individuals are: first row: centre, 3780 Leading Seaman P. G. Colbeck, RCN; left, C52819 Pte D. E. Dolan, 1 Can. Para Bn; right, R95505 F/Sgt K. M. Morgan, RCAF. Second row: centre, W4901 Wren P. Mathie, WRCNS; left, 12885 L/Cpl J. M. Dann, CWAC; right, W315563 LAW O. M. Salmon, RCAF; back row: Lt N/S E. M. Lowe, RCAMC. 650,000 have been awarded including 525,500 with the overseas clasp.*

VALUE:		*Miniature*
Silver medal	£30–35	£8–10
i. Maple Leaf clasp	£30–35	£12–15
ii. Dieppe clasp	£35–45	£15–18
iii. Hong Kong clasp	£35–45	

188A. CANADIAN MEMORIAL CROSS

Instituted: 1 December 1919.
Branch of Service: Relatives of deceased Canadian forces.
Ribbon: Violet 11mm with ring suspension only.
Metal: Dull silver.
Size: 32mm.
Description: A Greek cross with the royal cypher at the centre, superimposed on another with arms slightly flared at the ends. Maple leaves adorn three of the arms while the top arm has a crown surmounted by a suspension ring. (Reverse) The service number, rank, initials and name of the person being commemorated are engraved. There is also a sterling mark on the lower arm. Four versions of the cross exist: the original, with GRI cypher (1914–19), with GVIR cypher and ring suspension (1940–45), GVIR cypher with suspension bar (1945–52) and an EIIR version for Korea and later conflicts.
Comments: *Issued to wives and mothers of servicemen who had died during World War I. A second version was introduced in August 1940 for award to widows and mothers of World War II servicemen, but this was extended to include those of merchant seamen and civilian firefighters. Newfoundland service personnel became eligible after April 1, 1949. The current version was introduced in 1950 for the Korean War and peacekeeping operations. All service-related deaths since 7 October 2001 are eligible and up to three Crosses are now granted to persons previously designated by the deceased.*

VALUE:	Named	Unnamed
GVR, ring suspension (58,500)	From £120	£55–65
GVIR, ring suspension } (32,500)	From £120	£55–65
GVIR, bar suspension	From £120	£55–65
EIIR, bar suspension (1,000)	From £150	£65–75

Miniature £70–90

189. AFRICA SERVICE MEDAL

Date: 1943.
Campaign: Second World War 1939-45.
Branch of Service: South African forces.
Ribbon: A central orange stripe, with green and gold stripes on either side.
Metal: Silver.
Size: 36mm.
Description: (Obverse) a map of the African Continent, inscribed AFRICA SERVICE MEDAL on the left and AFRIKADIENS-MEDALJE on the right; (reverse) a leaping Springbok.
Clasps: None, but a Protea emblem is worn on the ribbon by recipients of the King's Commendation.
Comments: *Awarded to Union service personnel who served at home and abroad during the War for at least thirty days. Medals were fully named and gave the service serial number of the recipient, prefixed by various letters, for example N (Native Military Corps), C (Cape Corps), M (Indian and Malay Corps), etc., no prefix indicated a white volunteer.*

VALUE:
Silver medal (190,000)   £25–45   *Miniature* £10–12

Protea emblem.

190. AUSTRALIA SERVICE MEDAL 1939–45

Date: 1949.
Campaign: Second World War 1939-45.
Branch of Service: Australian forces.
Ribbon: Dark blue representing the Royal Australian Navy, Khaki representing the Army, light blue representing the R.A.A.F and red representing the Mercantile Marine.
Metal: Cupro-nickel.
Size: 36mm.
Description: (Obverse) the effigy of King George VI; (reverse) the Arms of the Commonwealth of Australia surrounded by the inscription "THE AUSTRALIA SERVICE MEDAL 1939–45".
Clasps: None.
Comments: *Awarded to all Australian personnel who had seen at least 18 months' full time or three years part-time service. The medals were named to the recipients. In the case of Army personnel, their service numbers were prefixed by the initial of their state or territory of enlistment: D (Northern Territory), N (New South Wales), NG (New Guinea), P (Papua), Q (Queensland), S (South Australia), T (Tasmania), V (Victoria) and W (Western Australia). X prefix is for Volunteer Overseas Services, that is service with the 2nd AIF (Second Australian Imperial Force). In 1996 time served for eligibility was reduced to 30 days full-time, 90 days part-time.*

VALUE:
    Cupro-nickel medal (600,000)   £55–65   *Miniature* £12–15

191. NEW ZEALAND WAR SERVICE MEDAL

Date: 1946.
Campaign: Second World War 1939-45.
Branch of Service: New Zealand forces.
Ribbon: Black with white edges.
Metal: Cupro-nickel.
Size: 36mm.
Description: (Obverse) effigy of King George VI; (reverse) the text FOR SERVICE TO NEW ZEALAND 1939-45 with a fern leaf below. Suspension was by a pair of fern leaves attached to a straight bar.
Clasps: None.
Comments: *Issued unnamed, to all members of the New Zealand forces who completed one month full-time or six months part-time service between September 1939 and September 1945, provided the applicant carried out the prescribed training or duties. This included Home Guard service and Naval Auxiliary Patrol service.*

VALUE:
    Cupro-nickel medal (240,000)   £30–35   *Miniature* £12–15

191A. NZ MEMORIAL CROSS

Instituted: 1960.
Campaign: Second World War, 1939–45.
Branch of Service: Relatives of deceased New Zealand forces personnel.
Ribbon: 12mm royal purple
Metal: Dull Silver.   **Size:** 32 mm.
Description: A cross surmounted by a crown, with fern leaves on each arm, in the centre, within a wreath, the Royal Cypher; (reverse) details of the person in respect of whose death the cross is granted.
Comments: *First announced in the New Zealand Gazette dated at Wellington, September 12, 1947 and approved by the King but not instituted until August 16, 1960. Originally granted to the next-of-kin of persons who had lost their lives on active service with the New Zealand forces during the Second World War, or who had subsequently died of wounds or illness contracted during that conflict. Provision was made for the grant of crosses to the parent(s) as well as the wife or eldest surviving daughter or son. It was subsequently awarded in respect of postwar campaigns: Korea (47), Malaya, South Vietnam (37), and East Timor (3).*

VALUE: Officially named   Unnamed
               From £100   £75–85

192. SOUTH AFRICAN MEDAL FOR WAR SERVICES

Date: 1946.
Campaign: Second World War 1939–46.
Branch of Service: South African forces.
Ribbon: Three equal stripes of red, white and blue, the South African national colours.
Metal: Silver.
Size: 36mm.
Description: (Obverse) South African arms; (reverse) a wreath of protea flowers enclosing the dates 1939 and 1945. Inscribed in English and Afrikaans: SOUTH AFRICA FOR WAR SERVICES on the left and SUID AFRIKA VIR OORLOGDIENSTE on the right.
Clasps: None.
Comments: *Men and women who served for at least two years in any official voluntary organisation in South Africa or overseas qualified for this medal so long as the service was both voluntary and unpaid. Those who already had the Africa Service Medal were ineligible, but exceptions exist. The medals are unnamed but were issued with a named certificate.*

VALUE: Silver (17,500) £40–50   *Miniature* £15–18

192A. SOUTH AFRICAN MEMORIAL PLAQUE

Date: 1946.
Campaign: Second World War 1939–46.
Branch of Service: South African forces.
Metal: Bronze.
Size: Wood backing 135x106.4mm.
Description: The South African arms in a wreath superimposed on a Maltese cross with torches in the angles. Below is a separate panel containing the details of the deceased. Mounted on a wooden panel.
Comments: *The plaque was given to the next of kin to personnel who lost their lives whilst on active service. The name and the cause of death are inscribed thereon. A numbered brooch of a similar design was also issued. Plaques to personnel killed in famous actions or in well-known theatres of war are worth a considerable premium, as are those named to SAAF aircrew, SANF personnel or plaques named to women. Plaques bearing the Star of David signifying that the person was of the Jewish faith are extremely rare.*

VALUE: **Plaque from £50, brooch from £25**

193. SOUTHERN RHODESIA SERVICE MEDAL

Date: 1946.
Campaign: Second World War 1939-45.
Branch of Service: Southern Rhodesian forces.
Ribbon: Dark green with black and red stripes at each edge.
Metal: Cupro-nickel.
Size: 36mm.
Description: (Obverse) King George VI; (reverse) the Southern Rhodesian national arms. FOR SERVICE IN SOUTHERN RHODESIA round the top and the dates 1939-1945 at the foot.
Clasps: None.
Comments: *This very scarce medal was awarded only to those who served in Southern Rhodesia during the period of the War but who were ineligible for one of the campaign stars or war medals. 5,000 medals were struck but only 3,908 were awarded.*

VALUE:
Cupro-nickel (3908) £300–350   *Miniature* £25–30

194. NEWFOUNDLAND VOLUNTEER WAR SERVICE MEDAL

Date: 1981.
Campaign: Second World War 1939-45.
Branch of Service: Newfoundland forces.
Ribbon: Deep claret with edges of red, white and blue.
Metal: Bronze.
Size: 37mm
Description: (Obverse) the royal cypher of George VI surmounted by a crown topped by a caribou, the Newfoundland national emblem; (reverse) Britannia on a scallop shell background guarded by two lions.
Comments: *While the Second World War was being fought, Newfoundland was still a separate British colony which did not enter the Canadian Confederation till 1949. Consequently Newfoundland servicemen did not qualify for the Canadian Volunteer Service medal, and this deficiency was not remedied until July 1981 when the Newfoundland provincial government instituted this medal. Those who had served with the Canadian forces, on the other hand, and already held the Canadian medal, were not eligible for this award. The medal could be claimed by next-of-kin of those who died in or since the war.*

VALUE: Bronze (7500)   £450–550   *Miniature*   £65–75

194A. THE ELIZABETH CROSS

Instituted: 2009.
Campaign: Post World War II.
Branch of Service: Relatives of deceased UK forces personnel.
Ribbon: None.
Metal: Oxidised silver.
Size: 31 mm.
Description: A Greek cross superimposed on another cross, with a crowned Royal cypher at its centre, within a wreath. The arms of the outer cross bear the national emblems of the British Isles: the Rose (England), Thistle (Scotland), Shamrock (Ireland) and the Daffodil (Wales).
Comments: *The Cross was first announced in July 2009 and complements the existing Canadian Memorial Cross (MYB 188A) and the New Zealand Memorial Cross (MYB 191A). Only one Cross will be available to the next of kin of any service personnel who died whilst on operational duty or as a consequence of an act of terrorism. Awards of the Cross have been back-dated to 1 January 1948 to cover deaths that occurred after World War II or as a result of service in Palestine since 27 September 1945. It is accompanied by a memorial scroll, except in the case of Korean War casualties, as a scroll has already been issued for that conflict—in this instance the Cross alone will be issued. Crosses are named to the individual commemorated.*

VALUE: From £400

195. KOREA MEDAL

Date: July 1951.
Campaign: Korean War 1950-53.
Branch of Service: British and Commonwealth forces.
Ribbon: Yellow, with two blue stripes .
Metal: Cupro-nickel or silver.
Size: 36mm.
Description: (Obverse) Right-facing bust of Queen Elizabeth II by Mary Gillick; there are two obverse types, with or without BRITT: OMN; (reverse) Hercules wrestling with the Hydra, KOREA in the exergue.
Clasps: None.
Comments: *Awarded to all British and Commonwealth forces who took part in the Korean War between July 1950 and July 27, 1953. British and New Zealand medals were issued in cupro-nickel impressed in small capitals, medals to Australian forces were impressed in large capitals and the Canadian version was struck in silver and has CANADA below the Queen's bust. Particularly prized are medals issued to the "Glorious Gloucesters" who played a gallant part in the battle of the Imjin River.*

VALUE:		*Miniature*
British		
Regiments	£160–180	£12–15
Corps	£120–150	
RN	£100–150	
RAF	£600–850	
To Gloucester Regiment	£550–750	
Australian or New Zealand naming	£250–300	
Canadian, silver (over 20,000)	£100–150	£15–20

196. SOUTH AFRICAN MEDAL FOR KOREA

Date: 1953.
Campaign: Korea 1950-53.
Branch of Service: South African forces.
Ribbon: Sky blue central stripe flanked by dark blue stripes and edges of orange.
Metal: Silver.
Size: 38mm.
Description: (Obverse) maps of South Africa and Korea with an arrow linking them and the words VRYWILLIGERS and VOLUNTEERS in the field. (Reverse) the then South African arms surmounted by the crowned EIIR.
Clasps: None.
Comments: *Awarded to the 800 personnel in the contingent sent to Korea by the Union of South Africa. Suspension is by a ring and claw.*

VALUE:			
Silver (800)	£450–550	*Miniature*	£40–50
Pilot's issue	£1500–2000		

197. UNITED NATIONS KOREA MEDAL

Date: December 1950.
Campaign: Korea 1950-53.
Branch of Service: All UN forces.
Ribbon: Seventeen narrow stripes alternating pale blue and white.
Metal: Bronze.
Size: 35mm.
Description: (Obverse) the wreathed globe emblem of the UN;
(reverse) inscribed FOR SERVICE IN DEFENCE OF THE
PRINCIPLES OF THE CHARTER OF THE UNITED NATIONS.
Clasps: Korea.
Comments: *National variants were produced, but the British type was
granted to all personnel of the British and Commonwealth forces who
had served at least one full day in Korea or in support units in Japan.
Moreover, as those who served in Korea after the armistice in July 1953
were also entitled to the UN medal it is sometimes found in groups without
the corresponding British medal. The award was extended to cover the
period up to July 27, 1954, the first anniversary of the Panmunjom Truce.
Issues to Australian, South African and Canadian personnel were named
on the rim.*

VALUE: £20–25   *Miniature* £10–15

198. GENERAL SERVICE MEDAL 1962–2007

Date: 1964.
Campaign: Campaigns and operations since 1962.
Branch of Service: British forces.
Ribbon: Deep purple edged with green.
Metal: Silver.
Size: 36mm.
Description: (Obverse) a crowned bust of Queen Elizabeth II; (reverse)
an oak wreath enclosing a crown and the words FOR CAMPAIGN
SERVICE. It has a beaded and curved suspension above which are
mounted campaign clasps.
Clasps: 14. The maximum number of clasps awarded appears to be six.
Comments: *This medal, also commonly known as the Campaign Service
Medal 1962, was instituted for award to personnel of all services, and thus
did away with the need for separate Army and Navy general service medals.
Awards range from a mere 70 for South Vietnam to over 130,000 for service
in Northern Ireland. The eligibility for the Northern Ireland clasp ceased at
midnight on 31 July 2007—the eligibility period having been from 14 August
1969, almost 38 years, the longest period for any individual clasp. In July 2014
it was confirmed that those who served between 21 December 1963 and 26
March 1964 qualify for the clasp CYPRUS 1963–64.*

VALUE:			*Miniature*
			for silver add £5
i.	Borneo	£85–100	£12–15
ii.	Radfan	£90–120	£12–15
iii.	South Arabia	£75–100	£12–15
iv.	Malay Peninsula	£75–100	£12–15
v.	South Vietnam	Rare	£15–20
vi.	Northern Ireland	£75–100	£12–15
vii.	Dhofar	£220–250	£12–15
viii.	Lebanon	£2000–2500	£12–15
ix.	Mine Clearance, Gulf of Suez (250)	£1800–2000	£12–15
x.	Gulf	£250–300	£12–15
xi.	Kuwait	£400–450	£12–15
xii.	N. Iraq & S. Turkey	£375–475	£12–15
xiii.	Air Operations Iraq	£350–450	£15–20
	2 clasps	£100–125	£15–20
	3 clasps	£150–200	£25–30
	4 clasps	£250–300	£30–35
xiv.	Cyprus 1963–64	£75–95	£15–25

198A. OPERATIONAL SERVICE MEDAL 2000

Date: 1999.
Campaign: Operations after May 5, 2000.
Branch of Service: All branches of the armed forces.
Ribbon: Broad central red stripe, flanked by royal blue and light blue with green edge stripes (Sierra Leone), buff edge stripes (Afghanistan) or ochre edge stripes (Congo). The colours represent the three services.
Metal: Silver.
Size: 36mm.
Description: (Obverse) crowned profile of Queen Elizabeth; (reverse) an eight-pointed star with different crowns impaled on each alternate point, the centre having the Union flag in a circle surrounded by the inscription FOR OPERATIONAL SERVICE. The medal has a scrolled suspender with ornamental finials.
Clasp: Afghanistan (three distinctly different officially issued types), Operation Pitting, D.R.O.C. (Congo), Iraq & Syria, silver rosette.
Comments: *Intended for minor campaigns for which a separate medal is not awarded. It replaces the General Service Medal 1962–2007, except for Northern Ireland and Air Operations Iraq. It has so far been awarded for operations in Afghanistan (from 11 September 2001 to the conclusion of Operation Pitting), Sierra Leone (5 May 2000–31 July 2002), the Democratic Republic of the Congo (14 June–10 September 2003) and Iraq and Syria. The award of a clasp is denoted by the a silver rosette on the ribbon when only the ribbon is worn—for Afghanistan two rosettes can be worn if the two clasps (Afghanistan and Operation Pitting) are awarded. For operations Maidenly and Barras (Sierra Leone) a "South Atlantic" type rosette is worn with the medal, and a smaller version on the ribbon alone. The D.R.O.C. clasp is especially sought after.*

Sierra Leone

Congo

Afghanistan   *Iraq & Syria*

VALUE:

Cavalry	£400–600
Line regiment	£250–350
Corps	£200–300
Royal Marines	£300–500
Royal Navy	£300–500
RAF	£300–500
RFA	£300–500
Miniature	**£12–15** (silver add £5)

198B. ACCUMULATED CAMPAIGN SERVICE MEDAL

Instituted: January 1994.
Branch of Service: All branches of the armed services.
Ribbon: Purple with green edges and a central gold stripe.
Metal: Silver.
Size: 36mm.
Description: (Obverse) crowned effigy of Queen Elizabeth; (reverse) the inscription FOR ACCUMULATED CAMPAIGN SERVICE set within a four-part ribbon surrounded by a branch of oak leaves with laurel and olive leaves woven through the motto ribbon.
Comments: *The ACSM was awarded for aggregated service since August 14, 1969 in those theatres of operations where the General Service Medal (GSM) 1962 with clasp was awarded. The GSM (MYB198) has subsequently been replaced by the Operational Service Medal. The following medals count towards the award: Iraq Medal, GSM 1962–2007 with the clasps for Northern Ireland, Dhofar, Lebanon, Mine Clearance–Gulf of Suez, Gulf, Kuwait, Northern Iraq and Southern Turkey, Air Operations Iraq; the Operational Service Medal awarded since 2000 for Sierra Leone, Afghanistan and the Democratic Republic of Congo. Further periods of 36 months accumulated campaign service are denoted by a clasp, indicated as a silver rosette when the ribbon alone is worn. A gilt rosette is worn on the ribbon alone to denote the award of four silver clasps. A further gilt rosette was awarded for a further three silver clasps and a third gilt rosette for another two silver clasps. Service on UN, NATO EC or EU missions is not allowed to count towards the qualifying service. This was the first British medal put out to competitive tendering, a contract won by the Royal Mint. As such, the medal is not only silver but hallmarked (believed to be the first medal, although hallmarking is a feature of certain decorations and orders). In July 2011 the medal was superseded by the Accumulated Campaign Service Medal 2011 (MYB 198C).*

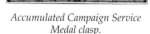

Accumulated Campaign Service Medal clasp.

VALUE: £300–350   *Miniature*   £10–12

198C. ACCUMULATED CAMPAIGN SERVICE MEDAL 2011

Instituted: July 2011.
Branch of Service: All branches of the armed services.
Ribbon: Purple with green edges and two central gold stripes.
Metal: Silver.
Size: 36mm.
Description: (Obverse) crowned effigy of Queen Elizabeth; (reverse) the inscription FOR ACCUMULATED CAMPAIGN SERVICE set within a four-part ribbon surrounded by a branch of oak leaves with laurel and olive leaves woven through the motto ribbon.
Comments: *On July 1, 2011 the Accumulated Campaign Service Medal (no. 198B) was superseded by the Accumulated Campaign Service Medal 2011, with the qualifying time to be reduced from 36 months (1,080 days) to 24 months (720 days). Although the medal design remains identical to the previous issue it will not be hallmarked on the rim and the ribbon carries two gold stripes. The range of qualifying service has also been amended to reflect the current operational conditions and the need for medallic recognition. The new medal will mean that holders of an existing operational service medal (whether military, MOD civilian or Contractors on Deployed Operations) or other specifically designated multi-national campaign medal, who are or were serving on or after January 1, 2008 (whether currently serving or retired), are eligible for the ACSM 11 provided they have completed more than 24 months (720 days) campaign service. Bars are to be awarded for each additional period of 720 days approved operational service.*

The following campaign service counts towards the ACSM 11 and holders of the following medals, if they have completed enough service, may be eligible for the new medal: General Service Medal: Northern Ireland August 14, 1969–July 31, 2007; Dhofar October 1, 1969–September 30, 1976; Lebanon February 7, 1983–March 9, 1984; Mine Clearance Gulf of Suez August 15, 1984–October 15, 1984; Gulf November 17, 1986–February 28, 1989; Kuwait March 8, 1991–September 30, 1991; N Iraq & S Turkey April, 6, 1991–July 17, 1991; Air Operations Iraq (South) July 16, 1991–March 18, 2003, and Iraq (North) July 16, 1991–April 30, 2003. Operational Service Medal: Sierra Leone May 5, 2000–July 31, 2002; Afghanistan September 11, 2001 to a date to be decided; Democratic Republic of Congo June 14, 2003– September 10, 2003. The Iraq Medal January 20, 2003–May 22, 2011. And any Multinational campaign medals approved since April 1, 2000. Certain service does not count towards the ACSM 11, this includes any service prior to August 14, 1969, service in Kuwait during Op TELIC after August 10, 2003; service in the Balkans; service in the British Embassy in Iraq; service on Op BANDOG with the exception of Afghanistan; service in the First Gulf War and service in the Falklands Conflict.

VALUE:	£300–350	*Miniature*	£10–15

198D. GENERAL SERVICE MEDAL 2008

Date: 2016.
Campaign: Campaigns and Operations since 2008.
Branch of Service: British forces.
Ribbon: 32mm, green with two 5mm purple stripes 5mm from the edges.
Metal: Silver .
Size: 36mm.
Clasps: Southern Asia, Arabian Peninsula, Northern Africa, Western Africa, Eastern Africa, Gulf of Aden.
Description: (Obverse) Effigy of the reigning monarch; with the legend REGINA FID DEF ELIZABETH II DEI GRATIA around; (reverse) A standing figure of Britannia holding a shield and trident, in front of a lion with the words FOR CAMPAIGN SERVICE below, the whole surrounded by a wreath of oak.
Comments: *Instituted for minor campaigns since 2008. The first awards were made by the Secretary of State for Defence, Michael Fallon, in June 2016. The clasps are named for geographic locations as opposed to specific Operations with Southern Asia, Arabian Peninsula each covering two Operations to date.. East Africa covers Operations in Somalia. The Western Africa clasp covers service there in the period 13 January 2013–22 May 2013 with the Northern Africa clasp covering service in that region from 1 November 2012 onwards. The British sailors of HMS Daring who braved the threat of missile attack in the Middle East were the first to receive the Gulf of Aden clasp in August 2018.*

VALUE:	—	*Miniature*	£12–15

199. UNITED NATIONS EMERGENCY FORCE MEDAL

Date: 1957.
Campaign: Israel and Egypt 1956–67.
Branch of Service: All UN forces.
Ribbon: Sand-coloured with a central light blue stripe and narrow dark blue and green stripes towards each edge.
Metal: Bronze.
Size: 35mm.
Description: (Obverse) the UN wreathed globe emblem with UNEF at the top; (reverse) inscribed IN THE SERVICE OF PEACE. Ring suspension.
Clasps: None.
Comments: *Awarded to all personnel who served with the UN peace-keeping forces on the border between Israel and Egypt following the Sinai Campaign of 1956. These medals were awarded to troops from Brazil, Canada, Colombia, Denmark, Finland, Indonesia, Norway, Sweden and Yugoslavia.*

VALUE:

Bronze original issue	£35–45	*Miniature*	£10–15

200. VIETNAM MEDAL

Date: July 1968.
Campaign: Vietnam 1964-73.
Branch of Service: Australian and New Zealand forces.
Ribbon: A broad central stripe of bright yellow surmounted by three thin red stripes (the Vietnamese national colours) and bordered by broader red stripes, with dark and light blue stripes at the edges, representing the three services.
Metal: Silver.
Size: 36mm.
Description: (Obverse) the crowned bust of Queen Elizabeth II; (reverse) a nude male figure pushing apart two spheres representing different ideologies.
Clasps: None.
Comments: *Awarded to personnel who served in Vietnam a minimum of one day on land or 28 days at sea after 28 May 1964. The medal was impressed in large capitals (Australian) or small capitals (New Zealand).*

VALUE:

Australian recipient	£200–250
New Zealand recipient (3,312)	£250–300
Miniature	£10–12

201. SOUTH VIETNAM CAMPAIGN MEDAL

Date: May 12, 1964.
Campaign: Vietnam 1964–72.
Branch of Service: Allied forces in Vietnam.
Ribbon: White with two broad green stripes towards the centre and narrow green edges.
Metal: Bronze.
Size: Height 42mm; max. width 36mm.
Description: A six-pointed star, with gold rays in the angles. The gilt enamelled centre shows a map of Vietnam engulfed in flames; (reverse) a Vietnamese inscription in the centre.
Clasps: 1960 (bronze, cupro-nickel or silver gilt).
Comments: *Awarded by the government of South Vietnam to Australian and New Zealand forces who served at least six months in Vietnam from March 1, 1961. The original issue, of Vietnamese manufacture, was relatively crude and issued unnamed. Subsequently medals were produced in Australia and these are not only of a better quality but bear the name of the recipient. A third version, made in the USA, has the suspension ring a fixed part of the medal. The medal was always issued with a clasp.*

VALUE:
Unnamed	£15–20
Named	£25–35
Miniature	enamels £10–15, painted £5–8

202. RHODESIA MEDAL

Date: 1980.
Campaign: Rhodesia 1979–80.
Branch of Service: British and Rhodesian forces.
Ribbon: Sky blue, with a narrow stripe of red, white and dark blue in the centre.
Metal: Rhodium-plated cupro-nickel.
Size: 36mm.
Description: (Obverse) the crowned bust of Queen Elizabeth II; (reverse) a sable antelope with the name of the medal and the year of issue.
Clasps: None.
Comments: *This medal was awarded to personnel serving in Rhodesia for fourteen days between 1 December 1979 and 20 March 1980, pending the elections and the emergence of the independent republic of Zimbabwe, known as Operation Agila. Medals were issued unnamed or named in impressed capitals. It was officially named to the armed forces and RAF personnel but unnamed to participating British Police. Examples with the word COPY in raised capitals immediately below the suspension fitment are believed to have been issued as replacements for lost medals, although examples with "R" for replacement are also known to exist. There has been some discussion over whether this medal is actually a campaign medal. It seems that the Ministry of Defence includes it in its list of campaign medals whereas the Central Chancery does not include it as a campign medal but rules that it should be worn after long service awards. Further research may clarify the situation.*

VALUE:
Cupro-nickel (2500)	£450–550	*Miniature*	£15–25

203. SOUTH ATLANTIC MEDAL

Date: 1982.
Campaign: Falkland Islands and South Georgia 1982.
Branch of Service: British forces.
Ribbon: Watered silk blue, white, green, white and blue.
Metal: Cupro-nickel.
Size: 36mm.
Description: (Obverse) crowned profile of Queen Elizabeth II; (reverse) laurel wreath below the arms of the Falkland Islands with SOUTH ATLANTIC MEDAL inscribed round the top.
Clasps: None, but a rosette denoting service in the combat zone.
Comments: *Awarded to all personnel who took part in operations in the South Atlantic for the liberation of South Georgia and the Falkland Islands following the Argentinian invasion. To qualify, the recipient had to have at least one full day's service in the Falklands or South Georgia, or 30 days in the operational zone including Ascension Island. Those who qualified under the first condition were additionally awarded a large rosette for wear on the ribbon. As a result of the Sir John Holmes' Independent medal review in 2012 the 30 day qualifying period for the award of the South Atlantic Medal was extended from 12 July to 21 October 1982. Those who qualify under this condition are not entitled to wear the rosette*

VALUE:	With rosette	Without
Army (7000)	£750–850	£550–750
Scots & Welsh Guards	£1000–1500	
Parachute Regiment	£1750–2500	
Royal Navy (13,000)*	£650–750	£500–650
Royal Marines (3700)	£1200–1500	£750–1000
Royal Fleet Auxiliary (2000)	£475–550	£300–400
RAF (2000)	£550–750	£350–450
Merchant Navy and civilians (2000)	£500–700	£350–450
Gurkhas	£750–850	£500–650
Miniature	£15–20	

*Medals to the crew of HM Submarine Conqueror are worth a considerable premium.

203A. SOVIET 40th ANNIVERSARY MEDAL

40th anniversary

Date: 1985.
Campaign: Second World War.
Branch of Service: British and Canadian forces who served mainly in RN or MN ships on Arctic convoys.
Ribbon: One half red, the other orange with three black stripes, edged with pale blue. Later issues have no blue edges. Worn in the Russian style.
Metal: Bronze.
Size: 32mm.
Description: (Obverse) Group of servicemen and women in front of a five-pointed star flanked by oak leaves and the dates 1945–1985 above; (reverse) 40th anniversary of the Victory in the Great Patriotic War 1941–1945, in Russian.
Clasps: None.
Comments: *In 1994 Her Majesty the Queen approved the wearing of this medal, first awarded by the Soviet Government, to selected ex-Servicemen, mostly surviving veterans of the Arctic convoys of World War II. Similar medals have also been issued for the 50th and subsequent five year anniversaries. However, those for the 55th and subsequent anniversaries have not been authorised for wear.*

VALUE:	British striking	£15–20
	Russian striking	£10–15
	Miniature	£10–15

203AA. USHAKOV MEDAL

Date: 2013.
Campaign: Second World War.
Branch of Service: Allied forces who served on the Arctic convoys.
Ribbon: Pale blue moire edged with narrow stripes of white and dark blue. Worn in the Russian style.
Metal: Silver.
Size: 36mm.
Description: (Obverse) Central couped portrait of Marshal Ushakov with Cyrillic wording around and laurel leaves below, the circular medal surmounted on an anchor; (reverse) anchor with serial number.
Clasps: None.
Comments: *Copies of the original Soviet medal were awarded by the Russian Government, on application, to surviving veterans of the Arctic convoys of World War II. Permission to wear was granted in 2013 by HM the Queen.*

VALUE: £35–50

203B. PINGAT JASA MALAYSIA MEDAL

Instituted: 2005.
Ribbon: Central red stripe, flanked by dark blue and yellow.
Metal: Base metal (brass)-coated nickel silver.
Size: 38mm
Description: (Obverse) arms of the Republic of Malaysia with JASA MALAYSIA below; (reverse) map of Malaysia with P.J.M. below, attached to a scrolled suspension bar by two crossed fern fronds.
Comments: *Awarded by the Malaysian Government to members of the British and Commonwealth Armed Forces who were posted on strength of unit or formation and served in the prescribed operational area of Malaysia and Singapore during the "Confrontation" and "Emergency" periods in direct support of operations for: 90 days or more, in Malaysia between August 31, 1957 and December 31 1966 or Singapore between August 31, 1957 and August 9, 1965; or for 180 days for ADF outside the area but in support of operations for the first two dates. Permission to wear was officially granted in time for veterans to wear their medals at the Remembrance Day ceremonies in 2011. Several types are known, with later strikings being of poorer quality than the original and with various minor alterations to the original design.*

VALUE: £35–55   *Miniature*   £10–15

Late striking

203C. KING HUSSEIN MEDAL

Date: 1970.
Campaign: Jordan Civil War.
Branch of Service: British military medical teams.
Ribbon: Plain crimson.
Metal: Silver with red enamel emblem.
Size: 38mm.
Description: (Obverse) Emblem of the Red Cross and Red Crescent. THE HASHEMITE KINGDOM OF JORDAN and its Arabic equivalent, with the date 1970 and Arabic equivalent at the sides; (rev) seven-line inscription across the centre.
Comments: *Awarded to British and American personnel involved in relief operations codenamed Operation Shoveller during and after the Civil War of September 1970. At the end of the deployment all personnel were presented with the medal by King Hussein. Permission to wear it has never been granted.*

VALUE: £50–70

204. GULF MEDAL

Date: 1992.
Campaign: Kuwait and Saudi Arabia 1990-91.
Branch of Service: British forces.
Ribbon: Sand-coloured broad central stripe flanked by narrow stripes of dark blue, red and light blue (left) or light blue, red and dark blue (right) representing the sands of the desert and the three armed services.
Metal: Cupro-nickel.
Size: 36mm.
Description: (Obverse) crowned profile of Queen Elizabeth II; (reverse) an eagle and automatic rifle superimposed on an anchor, symbolising the three armed services. The dates of the Gulf War appear at the foot.
Clasps: 2 Aug 1990, 16 Jan to 28 Feb 1991.
Comments: *Awarded to personnel who had thirty days continuous service in the Middle East (including Cyprus) between 2 August 1990 and 7 March 1991, or seven days between 16 January 1991 and 28 February 1991, or service with the Kuwait Liaison Team on 2 August 1990, the date of the Iraqi invasion. Two clasps were sanctioned and awarded to personnel who qualified for active service with the Liaison Team or in the operations to liberate Kuwait. A rosette is worn on the ribbon alone to denote the campaign clasps. Naming is in impressed capitals. More than 45,000 medals were awarded. See also the Kuwait and Iraq-Turkey clasps awarded to the General Service Medal 1962. About 1,500 civilians, including members of British Aerospace working at Dahran, also received the medal with the clasp 16 Jan to 28 Feb 1991.*

VALUE:
No clasp	£200–250
i. 2 Aug 1990	£2000–3000
ii. 16 Jan to 28 Feb 1991	
Regiments/RN/RAF	£250–350
Corps and Artillery	£200–250
Civilians	£200–250
Miniature	£15–20

204A. BRUNEI GENERAL SERVICE MEDAL

Date: 1968.
Campaign: Service in Brunei.
Branch of Service: British personnel on loan service.
Ribbon: Blue with red edges and a central red stripe.
Metal: Silver.
Size: 40x50mm max.
Description: A radiate star with a central medallion inscribed GENERAL SERVICE MEDAL and its equivalent Pingkat Laila Tugas in Arabic script, the royal insignia of the sultanate appearing in the centre. This insignia has changed several times over the years so varieties are seen. The original versions have a white enamel cross on the star (as illustrated) but the later version has the insignia surrounded by a laurel wreath. Suspended by a plain bar.
Comments: *Awarded to British personnel who completed a minimum of 12 months service. Unrestricted permission to wear the medal has been granted to entitled members of the British forces.*

VALUE: £100–150 *Miniature* £35–40

204AA. SIERRA LEONE GENERAL SERVICE MEDAL

Date: 1965.
Campaign: Service in Sierra Leone and neighbouring countries.
Branch of Service: British forces on secondment to the Royal Sierra Leone Military Forces.
Ribbon: Broad central red stripe bordered with narrow green, white and dark blue stripes.
Metal: Bronze.
Size: 36mm.
Description: (Obverse) crowned effigy of Queen Elizabeth; (reverse) arms of Sierra Leone with inscription FOR GENERAL SERVICE / SIERRA LEONE. Fitted with a ring for suspension and a brooch bar at the top of the ribbon.
Clasps: Congo.
Comments: *Worn after medals previously earned and before the United Nations' Congo Medal and Sierra Leone Long Service and Independence medals, with restricted permission. UK personnel qualified for this medal if not eligible for any other general service medal for the same service. British personnel who served in the Congo between January 26, 1962 and February 28, 1963 qualified for the clasp.*

VALUE: £55–75 *Miniature* £15–25

204B. IRAQ MEDAL

Date: 2004.
Campaign: Operation TELIC (the Iraq War).
Branch of Service: All military and civilian personnel, including embedded media, involved in the operations for the liberation of Iraq and the overthrow of Saddam Hussein.
Ribbon: Central narrow stripes of black, white and red (symbolising the Iraq national flag) flanked by broad sand-coloured edges.
Metal: Cupro-nickel.
Size: 36mm.
Description: (Obverse) crowned effigy of Queen Elizabeth; (reverse) image of a Lamassu (ancient Assyrian statue) over the word IRAQ.
Clasps: 19 Mar to 28 Apr 2003.
Comments: *This medal was awarded to all military and civilian personnel involved in Operation TELIC in Kuwait and Iraq from January 20, 2003. Those who took part in the actual combat from March 19, 2003 were awarded the clasp, denoted by a silver rosette on the ribbon alone. The medal is awarded to those who served for 30 days continuously or an aggregate 45 days.*

VALUE:		Miniature
i. With clasp		£10–20
Corps	£300–350	
Regiments/RAF/Navy	£350–400	
Cavalry	£400–450	
ii. No clasp		£10–15
Corps	£150–175	
Regiments/RAF/Navy	£175–250	
Cavalry	£300–350	

204C. IRAQ RECONSTRUCTION SERVICE MEDAL

Instituted: January 2007.
Branch of Service: Civilians and members of the Armed Forces who have seen service in Iraq but do not qualify for the Iraq Medal.
Ribbon: Sand-coloured with a broad green central stripe and narrow blue stripes towards the edges.
Metal: Rhodium-plated cupro-nickel.
Size: 36mm.
Description: (Obverse) Rank-Broadley effigy of the Queen; (reverse) cuneiform tablet translated as 'land bringing forth life' with stylised depiction of two rivers, based on a relief carving from Mesopotamia in the British Museum.
Comments: *The qualifying period for the medal was set at 40 days continuous service since March 19, 2003, or 40 days of service on working visits within Iraq aggregated over a period of one calendar year, for a minimum of 48 hours each. The medal was decommissioned in July 2013.*

VALUE: £300—£450   *Miniature*   £15–25

204D. THE CIVILIAN SERVICE MEDAL (AFGHANISTAN)

Instituted: April 2011.
Branch of Service: Civilian.
Ribbon: As 204C but lighter blue stripes.
Metal: Rhodium-plated cupro-nickel.
Size: 36mm.
Description: (Obverse) Rank-Broadley effigy of the Queen; (reverse) a stylised depiction of the mountains of Afghanistan with the name of the country, both in English and Afghan surrounding it.
Comments: *Awarded to recognise the role of civilians and others involved in the transition of Afghanistan to democracy. The qualifying period is 30 days continuous or 45 days aggregate service provided that takes place within a single calendar year and the visits are of at least 48 hours each. Those whose service is curtailed by death or injury are also eligible. Eligible persons include any Crown Servant (including Members of Her Majesty's UK Armed Forces), under Operational Control of the Foreign and Commonwealth Office (but NOT those under the command of the UK joint task force), Police and Contractors. Locally employed civilians are not eligible. Approximately 2,800 awarded.*

VALUE: £600–800   *Miniature*   £15–25

205. SAUDI ARABIAN MEDAL FOR THE LIBERATION OF KUWAIT

Original type

Date: 1991.
Campaign: Gulf War 1991.
Branch of Service: British and Allied forces.
Ribbon: Green with edges of red, black and white (the Saudi national colours). The ribbon bar has a gold state emblem (palm tree over crossed scimitars).
Metal: White metal.
Size: approx. 45mm across
Description: The white metal medal has a star of fifteen long and fifteen short round-tipped rays, surmounted by a bronze circle bearing a crowned and enwreathed globe on which appears a map of Arabia. Above the circle is a palm tree with crossed scimitars, the state emblem of Saudi Arabia. A scroll inscribed in Arabic and English LIBERATION OF KUWAIT appears round the foot of the circle.
Clasps: None.
Comments: *Awarded by the government of Saudi Arabia to all Allied personnel who took part in the campaign for the liberation of Kuwait, although only a few of the 45,000 British servicemen were subsequently given permission by the Foreign and Commonwealth Office to wear it. The contract for production was shared between Spink and a Swiss company, but subsequently a flatter version, more practicable for wear with other medals, was manufactured in the United States.*

VALUE: Original type   £35–55   *Miniature*   £15–20
            US "flat" type   £25–35

205A. MULTINATIONAL FORCE AND OBSERVERS MEDAL

Date: March 1982.
Campaign: Sinai Peninsula.
Ribbon: 36mm orange with central white stripe flanked by 3mm dark green stripes. The civilian award ribbon is orange with two green 8mm stripes and central 8mm white stripe
Metal: Bronze.
Size: 30mm.
Description: (Obverse) a dove clutching an olive branch surrounded by the inscription MULTINATIONAL FORCE & OBSERVERS; (reverse) UNITED IN SERVICE FOR PEACE in five lines.
Comments: *Awarded to personnel of the Multinational Force and Observers (MFO) created in 1979 to monitor the peace agreement between Egypt and Israel. Eligibility for the medal was originally 90 days continuous service in the force, but this was raised to 170 days in March 1985. Subsequent awards for each completed six-month tour are indicated by a silver numeral affixed to the ribbon. It was originally awarded personally by the MFO's first commander, the Norwegian General Fredrik Bull-Hansen. The Force has 3,000 personnel drawn from the armed services of Australia, Canada, Colombia, Fiji, France, Italy, the Netherlands, New Zealand, UK, USA and Uruguay. It is now classed as a Foreign award and can only be worn if authorised, otherwise it may be accepted and retained as a keepsake*

VALUE: £25–30   *Miniature* £15–20

Civilian

206. KUWAITI LIBERATION MEDALS

4th grade

Date: 1991.
Campaign: Liberation of Kuwait 1991.
Branch of Service: Allied forces.
Ribbon: Equal stripes of green, white and red with a black quadrilateral at the upper edge, representing the Kuwait national flag.
Metal: Various.
Size: Various.
Description: The circular medals have different decorative treatments of the Kuwaiti state emblem on the obverse, enshrined in a five-petalled flower (Second Grade), a five-pointed star with radiate background (Third Grade) and a plain medallic treatment (Fourth Grade). All grades, however, have a straight bar suspender of different designs.
Clasps: None.
Comments: *This medal was issued in five grades and awarded according to the rank of the recipient. The Excellent Grade was only conferred on the most senior Allied commanders, the First Grade went to brigadiers and major-generals, the Second Grade to officers of field rank (colonels and majors), the Third Grade to junior officers (captains, lieutenants and equivalent ranks in the other services), and the Fourth Grade to all other ranks. HM Government has decreed that British personnel may accept their medals as a keepsake but permission to wear them in uniform has so far been refused. The Canadian Government has followed the same policy, but the personnel of other Allied nations are permitted to wear their medals.*

VALUE:		*Miniature*
First Grade	£100–150	£25–30
Second Grade	£40–50	£20–25
Third Grade	£20–30	£20–25
Fourth Grade	£20–30	£20–25 *(silver)*

206A. NATO SERVICE MEDALS

Instituted: December 1994.

Campaigns: Any theatre or area of operations in the service of the North Atlantic Treaty Organization.

Branch of Service: NATO military and service personnel.

Ribbon: NATO blue with narrow white stripes having central metal threads: For engagements in NATO-led Article 5 operations (gold thread): Eagle Assist (central stripe), Active Endeavour (two stripes towards the edges), Non-Article 5 (central stripe with silver thread, from January 2011 two stripes towards the edges with silver thread denote operations) with clasps.

Metal: Bronze.

Size: 36mm.

Description: (Obverse) the NATO star emblem set in a wreath of olive leaves; (reverse) the title NORTH ATLANTIC TREATY ORGANIZATION and the words IN SERVICE OF PEACE AND FREEDOM in English and French. Two versions of this medal have been recorded: (a) light bronze, broad leaves in wreath, (b) dark bronze, narrow leaves.

Clasps: Former Yugoslavia, Kosovo, Non-Article 5 (superseding the first two clasps), Balkans (replaces last), Ex Yugoslavie, Africa*, OUP Libya/Libye*, NTM-Iraq*, AMIS*, Pakistan*, ISAF*, Article 5 (Eagle Assist & Active Endeavour), Sea Guardian, Afghanistan. *Worn on the same ribbon. A multitour indicator was originally an Arabic numeral, currently it is a bronze square with the number inside.

Comments: *The NATO medal was first instituted to reward personnel who took part in the Alliance operations in the former Yugoslavia. Any person serving under NATO command or operational control is eligible for the award. UK Service personnel cannot qualify for the NATO Medal and the UNPROFOR Medal (no. 207) in respect of the same period of service. The qualifying period for the medal is to be designated by the Secretary-General, however, for the operations in the former Yugoslavia the period has been set as 30 days continuous or accumulated service within the theatre of operations inside the former Yugoslavia and the Adriatic, or 90 days within the area of operations but outside the territory of the former Yugoslavia. The medal takes precedence equal to the General Service Medal in order of date of award. Bronze Arabic numerals are worn on the ribbon to denote multiple tours. The Non-Article 5 medal (ribbon) replaces the three other NATO medals (ribbons) for services anywhere in the Balkans, commencing December 3, 2002. Article 5 of the NATO Charter states that an attack on one member state is an attack on the whole Alliance. Non-Article 5 operations are therefore those outside NATO territory. No clasp was issued for the service in Macedonia (Former Yugoslavia) due to objections from Greece which does not recognise the independent sovereignty of that country. The clasps for Kosovo and Former Yugoslavia have now been superseded by the Non Article 5 clasp. The clasp for Afghanistan bears the initials of the International Security Assistance Force. Those serving more than one tour of duty are authorised to wear a bronze Arabic numeral on their ribbon to indicate this. Eagle Assist, Active Endeavour, Afghanistan and Iraq medals are not approved or authorised for wear by UK personnel, either in full size or in miniature. If presented they may be retained as keepsake(s). NATO ISAF has now been approved for wear by Australian Forces (military and police). Service on awards for these medal(s) does not count as qualifying service towards the Accumulated Campaign Service Medal. Additionally a NATO Meritorious Service Medal has been instituted—see MYB291AA.*

Former Yugoslavia.

Kosovo.

Macedonia.

Eagle Assist.

Active Endeavour.

Non-Article 5.

Afghanistan (ISAF), Africa, Sudan (AMIS), Pakistan, Balkans, Iraq (NATO Training Mission)— denoted by clasp on ribbon.

VALUE: £25–£35   *Miniature* £10–12

206B. EUROPEAN COMMUNITY MONITORING MISSION MEDAL

Date: 1995.
Campaigns: Former Yugoslavia.
Branch of Service: EC Community Peacekeeping.
Ribbon: Navy with stripes of white and red and thin yellow.
Metal: Silver.
Size: 36mm.
Description: (Obverse) Outline map of Yugoslavia surmounted by the words EC MONITOR MISSION surrounded by a ring of stars; (reverse) a dove of peace.
Comments: *Awarded for 21 days service between July 27, 1991 and June 30, 1993, in and around the former Yugoslavia. Service for this medal does <u>not</u> count as qualifying service towards the Accumulated Campaign Service Medal.*

VALUE: £30–£35   *Miniature*   £15–20

206C. WESTERN EUROPEAN UNION MISSION SERVICE MEDAL

Date: 1997.
Campaigns: Operations in the Former Yugoslavia.
Branch of Service: Personnel serving with the Western European Union forces.
Ribbon: Bright blue with central broad bright yellow stripe.
Metal: Silver.
Size: 36mm.
Description: (Obverse) capital letters WEU arranged horizontally with U and O above and below the E to signify "Western European Union" and its French equivalent "Union de l'Europe Occidentale". Ten five-pointed stars are ranged around the lower half of the circumference; (reverse) PRO PACE UNUM ("United for peace") in three lines. A clasp signifying the area of service is worn on the ribbon.
Clasp: Ex Yugoslavie.
Comments: *This medal was instituted to award service with missions under the auspices of the Western European Union. It was awarded to personnel who had served at least 30 days in the former Yugoslavia or 90 days in the Adriatic, Hungary or Rumania. The first British recipients (March 6, 1997) were 27 police officers who had served with the WEU Police Force in Bosnia-Herzegovina. A total of 15,982 medals had been awarded by September 2000. This medal is also known as the European Union Police Mission Medal. Service for these medal(s) does <u>not</u> count as qualifying service towards the Accumulated Campaign Service Medal.*

VALUE: £50–70   *Miniature*   £10–15

206D. COMMON SECURITY AND DEFENCE POLICY SERVICE MEDAL

Reverse

Date: 2004.

Campaigns: Any military operations involving the European Union.

Branch of Service: Police.

Ribbon: Bright blue with central yellow stripe for HQ and Forces or with central white stripe for Planning and Support personnel, with an emblem denoting area of service.

Metal: Silver.

Size: 36mm.

Description: (Obverse) Twelve five-pointed stars in a circle; (reverse) PRO PACE UNUM in three lines (roughly translated as "United for peace"). The medal is fitted with a large ring for suspension. A clasp signifying the area of service is worn on the ribbon.

Clasps: Artemis, Concordia, Proxima, Althea, EUPM, EU Copps, EU NAVFOR Atalanta, EUSEC South Sudan, EUBAM Rafah, EUCAP Nestor, EUFOR RD Congo, EUFOR Tchad/RCA, EUPOL-AFG (Afghanistan), EUPOL Copps, EUSEC RD Congo, EUTM Mali, EUTM Somalia, EUMM Georgia, Kosovo (for EULEX Kosovo Mission), AMIS (AMIS EU Mission), Sophia (EUNAVFOR, the European Union Naval Force).

Comments: *This medal has been awarded to police and security personnel serving in any military operation under the auspices of the European Union. It has also been awarded to civilian police missions, as well as Canadian personnel (2005). The clasps denote service in the Democratic Republic of Congo from June to September 2003 (Artemis), with the EU Police mission in Bosnia since January 2003, for service in the former Yugoslav republic of Macedonia from March to December 2003 (Concordia) or December 2003 to December 2004 (Proxima), service in Bosnia since December 2004 (Althea) and Afghanistan since June 2007. Those serving more than one tour of duty are authorised to wear an Arabic numeral on their ribbon to indicate this. Service for these medal(s) does not count as qualifying service towards the Accumulated Campaign Service Medal. The ESDP Medal with clasp Althea has been approved for unrestricted acceptance and wearing by UK personnel—headquarters and units serving in Bosnia and Herzegovina, on this operation. The ESDP medal for planning and support for Operation Althea is not approved for acceptance or wear. Those presented may be retained as a keepsake.*

VALUE: £30–35   *Miniature*   £10–15

207. UNITED NATIONS MEDAL

Style of lettering for clasps.

For the various ribbons for the medal see ribbon charts.

Date: 1951.
Campaigns: Various supervisory or observation roles since 1948.
Branch of Service: UN forces.
Ribbons: Various (see below).
Metal: Bronze.
Size: 35mm.
Description: (Obverse) the wreathed globe emblem surmounted by the letters UN; (reverse) inscribed "IN THE SERVICE OF PEACE".
Clasps: CONGO, UNGOMAP, OSGAP, UNSMIH, MINUGUA, UNCRO, ONUMOZ, UNSCOM, UNAMIC, UNMIH, UNTMIH, UNOSGI, UNMONUA, UNOCHA, UNAMA.
Comments: *Apart from the UN Korea and UNEF medals, there have been numerous awards to personnel who served in one or other of the UN peace-keeping actions around the world since the end of the Second World War. The all-purpose medal has been awarded with various distinctive ribbons for service in many of the world's trouble spots. Two versions of the medal exist: globe flat (European) and globe raised (US version). Issues to South African Personnel are named. Eligibility is generally 90 days, but some missions were 180 days. Subsequent awards for each six month tour completed with the same mission are indicated by a silver numeral affixed to the ribbon. Those serving more than one tour of duty are authorised to wear an Arabic numeral on their ribbon to indicate this. Service for these medal(s) does not count as qualifying service towards the Accumulated Campaign Service Medal. The missions are listed below in chronological order.*

UNTSO United Nations Truce Supervision Organization (Israel, Egypt, Syria since 1948).
Blue ribbon with two narrow white stripes towards the edges.
UNOGIL United Nations Observation Group in Lebanon (1958).
Same ribbon as UNTSO.
ONUC Organisation des Nations Unies au Congo (1960–64).
Originally the same ribbon as UNTSO with clasp CONGO, but a green ribbon, with white and blue edges was substituted in 1963.
UNTEA United Nations Temporary Executive Authority (Netherlands New Guinea, 1962–63).
Blue ribbon with a white central stripe bordered dark green (left) and light green (right).
UNMOGIP United Nations Military Observer Group in India and Pakistan since 1949.
Dark green ribbon shading to light green with white and blue edges.
UNIPOM United Nations India Pakistan Observation Mission (1965–66).
Ribbon as UNMOGIP.
UNYOM United Nations Yemen Observation Mission (1963–64).
Ribbon with brown centre, yellow stripes and light blue edges.
UNFICYP United Nations Force in Cyprus (1964–).
Pale blue ribbon with central white stripe bordered in dark blue. Initially 30, then increased to 90 days.
UNEF 2 United Nations Emergency Force 2 patrolling Israeli-Egyptian cease-fire (1973– 79).
Pale blue ribbon with sand centre and two dark blue stripes.
UNDOF United Nations Disengagement Observer Force, Golan Heights (1974–).
Ribbon of burgundy, white, black and pale blue.
UNIFIL United Nations Interim Force in Lebanon (1978–).
Pale blue ribbon with green centre bordered white and red.
UNGOMAP United Nations Good Offices in Afghanistan and Pakistan.
A bronze bar inscribed UNGOMAP was issued but as the mission was made up from observers from three other missions it can only be found on these ribbons: UNTSO, UNIFIL, UNDOF.
UNIIMOG United Nations Iran-Iraq Monitoring Observation Group.
Pale blue with edges of green, white and red (left) and red, white and black (right) (1988–91).
UNAVEM United Nations Angola Verification Missions: I (1988–91), II (1991–95), III (1995–97).
Pale blue ribbon with yellow edges separated by narrow stripes of red, white and black (same for all three).
ONUCA Observadores de las Naciones Unidas en Centro América (Nicaragua and Guatemala) (1989–92).
Pale blue ribbon with dark blue edges and nine thin central green or white stripes.
UNTAG United Nations Transitional Assistance Group (Namibia, 1989–90).
Sand ribbon with pale blue edges and thin central stripes of blue, green, red, sand and deep blue.
ONUSAL Observadores de las Naciones Unidas en El Salvador (1991–95).
Pale blue ribbon with a white central stripe bordered dark blue.
UNIKOM United Nations Iraq Kuwait Observation Mission (1991–2003).
Sand ribbon with a narrow central stripe of pale blue.

MINURSO Mission des Nations Unies pour la Referendum dans le Sahara Occidental (UN Mission for the Referendum in Western Sahara) (1991–).
Ribbon has a broad sandy centre flanked by stripes of UN blue.
UNAMIC United Nations Advanced Mission in Cambodia (Oct. 1991–March 1992).
Pale blue ribbon with central white stripe bordered with dark blue, yellow and red stripes.
UNTAC United Nations Transitional Authority in Cambodia (March 1992–Sept. 1993).
Green ribbon with central white stripe edged with red, pale blue and dark blue.
UNOSOM United Nations Operations in Somalia (I: 1992–93 and II: 1993–95).
Pale yellow ribbon with central blue stripe edged with green.
UNMIH United Nations Mission in Haiti (1993–96).
Pale blue ribbon with dark blue and red central stripes edged with white.
UNPROFOR United Nations Protection Force (1992–95) operating in the former Yugoslavia, especially
Bosnia. *Blue ribbon with central red stripe edged in white and green or brown edges. See also UNCRO below.*
UNOMIL United Nations Observer Mission in Liberia (1993–97).
Pale blue ribbon flanked with white stripes with dark blue or red edges.
UNOMUR United Nations Observer Mission in Uganda/Rwanda (1993–94).
Pale blue central stripe edged by white and flanked by equal stripes of black, orange and red.
UNOMIG United Nations Observer Mission in Georgia (1993–2009). For 180 days service.
Pale blue central stripe flanked by equal stripes of white, green and dark blue.
UNAMIR United Nations Assistance Mission in Rwanda (1993–96).
Pale blue central stripe edged with white and flanked by equal stripes of black, green and red.
UNHQ General service at UN headquarters, New York.
Plain ribbon of pale blue, the UN colour.
UNPREDEP United Nations Preventative Deployment in Yugoslavia (1995–99).
Blue ribbon with central red stripe bearing four yellow lines and flanked by white edging.
UNMOP United Nations Mission of Observers in Pravlaka (1996–2002).
Dark blue ribbon with central yellow stripe edged with white, and two pale blue stripes.
UNTAES United Nations Transitional Authority in Eastern Slavonia. (1996-98)
Pale blue ribbon with yellow, red edged with white, and green stripes.
UNMOT United Nations Peacekeeping Force in Tadjikistan (1994–2000).
Blue ribbon with central green stripe flanked by white stripes.
UNMIBH United Nations Mission in Bosnia Herzegovina (1995–2002).
Blue ribbon with white central stripe, edged with one green and one red stripe.
UNMOGUA United Nations Military Observers in Guatemala (1997).
Blue ribbon with central pale blue stripe and two white stripes each with central green line.
UNSMIH United Nations Support Mission in Haiti (July 1996–97).
Same ribbon as UNMIH above, but with clasp UNSMIH.
UNCRO United Nations Confidence Restoration Operation in Croatia (1994–96).
Same ribbon as UNPROFOR above, but with clasp UNCRO.
MINUGUA Mision de las Naciones Unidas en Guatemala (1997).
Same ribbon as UNMOGUA but clasp with initials in Spanish.
ONUMOZ Operation des Nations Unies pour le referendum dans Mozambique (1992–94).
Pale blue ribbon edged with white and green stripes.
UNSSM United Nations Special Service Medal.
Awarded to personnel serving at least 90 consecutive days under UN control in operations for which no other UN award is authorised. Blue ribbon with white edges. Clasps: UNOCHA, UNSCOM, UNAMA. The medal with no clasp was awarded to Operation Cheshire aircrew who had completed 100 landings at Sarajevo or ground crew who had spent 90 days at Anacona, Split or Zagreb between July 3, 1992 and January 12, 1996.
OSGAP Office of the Secretary General for Afghanistan and Pakistan.
Silver clasp worn by Canadian personnel on the ribbons of UNTSO, UNDOF or UNIFIL.
UNOMSIL United Nations Observer Mission in Sierra Leone. (1998–99)
Awarded for 90 days service. White ribbon with blue edges and the Sierra Leone colours (light blue flanked by green stripes) in the centre. This mission was redesignated UNAMSIL on October 1, 1999.
UNPSG United Nations Police Support Group Medal.
A support group of 180 police monitors created in January 1998 initially to supervise the Croatian police in the return of displaced persons. 90 days qualifying service. White ribbon with a broad blue central stripe and narrow dark grey (left) and bright yellow (right) stripes towards the edges.
MINURCA United Nations Verification Mission in the Central African Republic (1998–2000).
Mission instituted April 15, 1998 to monitor the restoration of peace following the Bangui agreement. 90 days qualifying service. Ribbon has a broad blue central stripe flanked by yellow, green, red, white and dark blue stripes on either side.
UNSCOM United Nations Special Commission.
The UN Special Service Medal with UNSCOM clasp is awarded to personnel with a minimum of 90 days consecutive service or 180 days in all, with UNSCOM clasp, in Iraq. Ribbon is UN blue with a white stripe at each edge.
UNMIK United Nations Mission in Kosovo (1999–).
Pale blue ribbon with wide central dark blue stripe edged with white. For 180 days service.
UNAMET United Nations Mission in East Timor (1999).
Pale blue ribbon with wide central white stripe edged with yellow and claret.
UNTAET United Nations Transitional Administration in East Timor (1999–2002).
Pale blue ribbon with wide central white stripe edged with yellow and claret.

207. UNITED NATIONS MEDAL *continued*

UNMISET   United Nations Mission of Support in East Timor (2002–05).
Pale blue ribbon with wide central white stripe edged with yellow and claret.
MONUC   United Nations Mission in the Congo (1999–2010).
Pale blue ribbon with wide central dark blue stripe edged with yellow.
UNMEE   United Nations Mission in Ethiopia and Eritrea (2000–2008).
Pale blue with central band of sand bisected by narrow dark green stripe.
MIPONUH   United Nations Civil Police Mission in Haiti (1997–2000).
Central bands of dark blue and red, flanked by narrow silver stripes and broad blue bands
UNTMIH   United Nations Transitional Mission in Haiti (July–November 1997).
Same ribbon as MIPONUH but with a bar inscribed UNTMIH.
MICAH   International Civilian Support Mission in Haiti (March 2000–01).
Same ribbon as MIPONUH.
UNOSGI   The UN Office of the Secretary General in Iraq.
The UN Special Service Medal with UNOSGI clasp issued to a small police group assigned to Baghdad from February 1991 to December 1992.
UNHCR   United Nations High Commission for Refugees.
A clasp issued worldwide and still on-going.
UNAMSIL   United Nations Medal for Service in Sierra Leone (1999–2005).
Same ribbon as UNOMSIL.
UNAMA   United Nations Assistance Mission in Afghanistan (2002–).
This is a political mission. A clasp bearing UNAMA is worn on the UN Special Service Medal.
MINUCI   United Nations Mission in Cote d'Ivoire (Ivory Coast) (May 2003–April 2004).
Orange, white and green stripes with blue edges.
UNMIL   United Nations Mission in Liberia (September 2003–).
Pale blue with a broad central dark blue stripe edged in red and white.
UNOCI   United Nations Operations in Cote d'Ivoire (April 2004–).
Similar to MINUCI but central stripes very narrow and blue edges correspondingly wider.
UNOB   United Nations Operations in Burundi (June 2004–07).
Central stripes of white, red, dark green and white, flanked by broad pale blue stripes.
MINUSTAH   Mission des Nations Unies Stabilisation dans Haiti (June 2004–).
Narrow central pale blue stripe, flanked by broader equal stripes of white, dark green and dark blue.
UNMIS   United Nations Mission in Sudan (March 2005–11).
UN blue with dark blue centre divided by two narrow white stripes.
UNMIT   United Nations Integrated Mission in Timor-Leste (August 2006–12)
UN blue with red centre stripe bordered each side with narrow stripes of white, dark blue and yellow.
UNAMID   African Union/United Nations Hybrid operation in Darfur (July 2007–)
Yellow with a central stripe of half blue, half white and with dark blue narrow stripes either side <u>or</u> Blue with central white stripe bordered each side by stripes of green and yellow.
MINURCAT   United Nations Mission in the Central African Republic and Chad (September 2007–10)
UN blue with five equal narrow stripes of dark blue, white, yellow, green and red.
UNGCI   A little-known United Nations Guard Contingent Mission in Iraq (1991–2003)
UN blue with orange stripes at edges divided by black stripes.
MONUSCO   United Nations Organisational Stabilisation Mission in the Democratic Republic of the Congo (2010).
Pale blue ribbon with wide central dark blue stripe edged with yellow.
UNISFA   United Nations Mission in the Republic of Sudan (2011–).
UN blue with white, green and yellow stripes with central narrow dark blue stripe .
UNMISS   United Nations Interim Security Force for Abyei, Sudan (2011–).
UN blue with central green stripe bordered by two white stripes each edged with black.
UNSMIS   United Nations Supervision Mission in Syria (2012).
Mission abandoned. Intended ribbon UN blue with red centre stripe bordered each side by thin white stripes divided by a thin green stripe.
MINUSMA   United Nations Multidimensional Integrated Stabilisation Mission in Mali (2013).
UN blue edges with central dark blue stripe bordered by thin green, yellow and red stripes at left and single pale yellow stripe at right..
MINUSCA   United Nations Multidimensional Integrated Stabilisation Mission in the Central African Republic (2014–).
UN blue with centre narrow stripes of blue, white, red, yellow, green.
MINUJUSTH   United Nations Supervision Mission in Haiti (2017–19).
Three equal stripes of Dark blue, light blue and red divided by narrow white stripes..

VALUE:

		Miniature
Any current issue medal regardless of ribbon	£25–35	£8–10
Original striking for UNTSO	£30–45	

207A. INTERNATIONAL CONFERENCE ON THE FORMER YUGOSLAVIA MEDAL

Date: 1995.
Campaigns: Former Yugoslavia.
Branch of Service: UN Observers.
Ribbon: Central broad orange stripe, flanked by narrow blue and white stripes and broad red edges, mounted in the Danish style.
Metal: Silver.
Size: 38mm.
Description: (Obverse) the wreathed globe emblem of the United Nations surrounded by 15 five-pointed stars representing the member nations of the conference, with the inscription round the edge: INTERNATIONAL CONFERENCE ON THE FORMER YUGOSLAVIA; (reverse) the Drina River and the mountains of Serbia and Montenegro surmounted by a peace dove in flight, with the words OBSERVER MISSION round the foot.
Comments: *This medal was awarded to about 100 observers who monitored the 17 land and two rail crossings between Serbia and Montenegro and Bosnia-Herzegovina during September 1994.*

VALUE: £80–100   *Miniature*   £12–16

207B. INTERFET MEDAL—International Force East Timor

Instituted: March 7, 2000.
Ribbon: 32mm central thin red stripe, flanked by deep green, white and UN light blue.
Metal: Pewter coloured silver.
Size: 38mm.
Description: (Obverse) central raised stylised dove of peace over the island of Timor, surrounded by raised inscription INTERNATIONAL FORCE EAST TIMOR surmounted by Federation Star and plain suspension bar struck as one unit; (reverse) TOGETHER AS ONE FOR PEACE IN EAST TIMOR around outer circle, inner circle blank for naming.
Method of naming: Pantographed on reverse in capitals with regimental number, initials and surname.
Comments: *The Australian Prime Minister established a specific campaign medal for members of the Australian Defence Force in East Timor. Australia led the coalition of 17 nations and this is the first Australian medal issued to other countries. Awarded for 30 days service during the INTERFET stage of the conflict. 15,046 medals have been issued, including 8,690 to members of the ADF and 6,356 to members of other countries' military establishments.*

VALUE: To Australian personnel £500–800   *Miniature*   £12–15
                                Others   £700–1000

207C. UNITAS MEDAL

Instituted: 1994.
Ribbon: 32mm, pale blue with central green stripe of 8mm edged each side by a white stripe of 4mm.
Metal: Lacquered brass.
Size: 38mm.
Description: (Obverse) a seven pointed star with central circle enclosing the Greek letter alpha; (reverse) A small embellished coat of arms of South Africa with date 1994 below. The whole is enclosed by a circle made up of the word "Unity" in all eleven official languages of the new South Africa. Suspender is uniface and struck as one piece with the medal.
Comments: *Awarded to all those who rendered service through being members of a serving force (SA Permanent Force, Citizen Force, Commandos, members of the armed forces of the former self-governing territories, the armed wing of the ANC (the MK) and APLA) during the period of South Africa's first non-racial elections and inauguration of Mr Mandela as the first black State President in South Africa between 27 April and 10 May 1994. Those medals awarded to members of the British Military Advisory Team in South Africa at the time, for which Her Majesty Queen Elizabeth II granted permission for wear, must be considered a rarity.*

VALUE:			*Miniature*
	SA recipient	£25–35	£15–20
	BMA recipient	From £250	

A NOTE ON CAMPAIGN MEDAL CLASPS
Since Worcestershire Medal Services Ltd were awarded the MoD contract for British campaign medals, all campaign clasps have a standard background as per the *Iraq & Syria* clasp on the Operational Service Medal (MYB 198A). This will also apply to all retrospective claims where the medal is produced today; so for example, General Service Medals for Cyprus or Malaya, etc. will now have clasps with the same background as that for Operation Shader—see MEDAL NEWS, December 2019/January 2020 for further details.

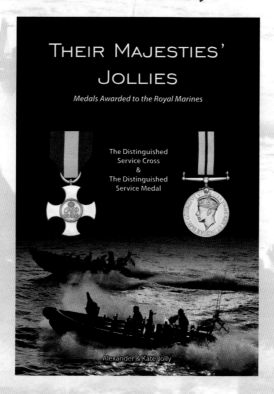

LONG
and Meritorious Service

A large, varied but until recently relatively neglected category comprises the medals awarded for long service and good conduct or meritorious service. Their common denominator is that the grant of such awards is made in respect of a minimum number of years of unblemished service—"undetected crime" is how it is often described in the armed forces. As their title implies, long service and good conduct medals combine the elements of lengthy service with no transgressions of the rules and regulations. Meritorious service, on the other hand, implies rather more. Apart from a brief period (1916–28) when awards were made for single acts of gallantry, MSMs have generally been granted to warrant officers and senior NCOs as a rather superior form of long service medal. Today long service and good conduct medals and meritorious service medals in the services can be awarded to officers as well as other ranks.

Long service and good conduct medals do not appear to excite the same interest among collectors as campaign medals. Perhaps this may be accounted for by their image of stolid devotion to duty rather than the romantic connotations of a medal with an unusual clasp awarded for service in some remote and all but forgotten outpost of the Empire. Nevertheless their importance should not be overlooked. Especially in regard to groups consisting primarily of the Second World War medals, they serve a useful purpose in establishing the provenance of the group, on account of the fact that they are invariably named to the recipient.

Service medals include not only such well known types as the Army LSGC (known affectionately as "the mark of the beast" on account of its high incidence on the chests of sergeant-majors), but also awards to the Territorial and Reserve forces, the auxiliary forces, the nursing services, and organisations such as the Royal Observer Corps and the Cadet Force, the Police, the Red Cross and St John's Ambulance Brigade. The Special Constabulary and Fire Brigades also have their own medals bestowed according to length of service and distinguished conduct. These medals may lack the glamour of naval and military awards but in recent years they have become increasingly fashionable with collectors and will certainly repay further study in their own right.

As many of these medals have been in use for eighty years or more with a standard reverse, variation usually lies in the obverse, changed for each successive sovereign. In addition, considerable variety has been imparted by the use of crowned or uncrowned profiles and busts, and changes in titles.

The following is a summary of the principal obverse types which may be encountered, referred to in the text by their type letters in brackets:

Queen Victoria (A) Young head by William Wyon
Queen Victoria (B) Veiled head by Leonard C. Wyon
Queen Victoria (C) Jubilee head by George W. de Saulles
Queen Victoria (D) Old head by Sir Thomas Brock
Edward VII (A) Bareheaded bust in Field Marshal's uniform
Edward VII (B) Bareheaded bust in Admiral's uniform
Edward VII (C) Coinage profile by George W. de Saulles
Edward VII (D) Crowned profile in Coronation robes
George V (A) Bareheaded bust in Field Marshal's uniform
George V (B) Bareheaded bust in Admiral's uniform
George V (C) Crowned bust in Coronation robes
George V (D) Crowned bust in Delhi Durbar robes
George V (E) Coinage profile by Bertram Mackennal
George VI (A) Crowned profile in Coronation robes
George VI (B) Crowned profile INDIAE: IMP 1937–48
George VI (C) Crowned profile FID: DEF 1949–52
George VI (D) Coinage profile IND: IMP 1937–48
George VI (E) Coinage profile FID: DEF 1949–52
Elizabeth II (A1) Tudor crown BR: OMN 1953–54
Elizabeth II (A) Tudor crown BR: OMN omitted 1954–80
Elizabeth II (B) Coinage bust BRITT: OMN 1953–54
Elizabeth II (C) Coinage bust BRITT OMN omitted 1954–80
Elizabeth II (D) St Edward crown 1955–
Elizabeth II (E) New bust for Diamond Jubilee Medal

PRINCIPAL OBVERSE TYPES:

Queen Victoria (A) Young Head

Queen Victoria (B) Veiled Head

Queen Victoria (C) Jubilee Head

Queen Victoria (D) Old Head

Edward VII (A) Bareheaded bust in Field Marshal's uniform

Edward VII (B) Bareheaded bust in Admiral's uniform

Edward VII (C) Coinage profile by George W. de Saulles

Edward VII (D) Crowned profile in Coronation robes

George V (A) Bareheaded bust in Field Marshal's uniform

George V (B) Bareheaded bust in Admiral's uniform

George V (C) Crowned bust in Coronation robes

George V (D) Crowned bust in Delhi Durbar robes

George V (E) Coinage profile by Bertram Mackennal

George VI (B) Crowned profile with INDIAE: IMP in legend 1937–48

George VI (C) Crowned profile with FID: DEF 1949–52

George VI (D) Coinage profile with IND: IMP 1937–48

George VI (E) Coinage profile with FID: DEF 1949–52

Elizabeth II (A1) Tudor crown with BR.OMN. (1953–54)
Elizabeth II (A) BR.OMN. omitted (as above) 1954–80

Elizabeth II (B) Coinage bust with BRITT: OMN, 1953–54

Elizabeth II (C) Coinage bust without BR: OMN.

Elizabeth II (D) St Edward crown from 1980

Elizabeth II (E) Ian Rank-Broadley coinage bust

Elizabeth II (F) Jody Clark coinage bust

Charles III (A) Crowned head (Tudor crown)

Charles III (B) Uncrowned head

Charles III (C) Crowned with Coronation robes

Charles III (D) in Admiral of the Fleet uniform

Charles III (E) in Field Marshal uniform

Charles III (F) in Air Chief Marshal uniform

208. ROYAL NAVAL MERITORIOUS SERVICE MEDAL

Instituted: 14 January 1919 until 1928 by Order in Council. Reinstituted 1977.

Branch of Service: Royal Navy.

Ribbon: Crimson with three white stripes.

Metal: Silver

Size: 36mm.

Description: (Obverse) effigy of the reigning monarch; (reverse) imperial crown surmounting a wreath containing the words FOR MERITORIOUS SERVICE. The medal was named in large seriffed capitals round the rim.

Comments: *Awarded without annuity or pension to warrant and petty officers of the Royal Navy. Originally it was awarded either for specific acts of gallantry not in the presence of the enemy or for arduous and specially meritorious service afloat or ashore in action with the enemy. Bars were granted for second awards. It was superseded in 1928 by the British Empire Medal for Gallantry or Meritorious Service, but re-instated on 1 December 1977. In this guise it has been awarded to warrant and petty officers of the Royal Navy, warrant officers and senior NCOs of the Royal Marines, and equivalent ranks in the WRNS and QARNNS, who have at least 20 years service and are already holders of the LSGC medal and three good conduct badges. The medal is not awarded automatically when these criteria are satisfied, as no more than 49 medals may be awarded annually. The revived medal is identical to the Army MSM and can only be distinguished by the naming giving rank and name of ship.*

VALUE:

		Miniature
George V (A)	—	—
George V (B) (1020)	£450–550	£25–35
Elizabeth II (B)	£350–450	£18–20

209. ROYAL MARINES MERITORIOUS SERVICE MEDAL

Original ribbon.

Instituted: 15 January 1849, by Order in Council (although medals dated 1848 are known).

Branch of Service: Royal Marines.

Ribbon: Plain dark blue, but later replaced by the RN MSM ribbon.

Metal: Silver.

Size: 36mm.

Description: (Obverse) effigy of the monarch; (reverse) a crowned laurel wreath enclosing the words FOR MERITORIOUS SERVICE.

Comments: *Annuities not exceeding £20 a year might be granted in addition to the medal for distinguished service. Sergeants with a minimum of 24 years service (the last fourteen as a sergeant), "with an irreproachable and meritorious character" were considered eligible for the award which was extended to discharged sergeants in 1872 when the service qualification was reduced to 21 years. The award of the MSM for gallantry was discontinued in 1874 when the Conspicuous Gallantry Medal was reconstituted. Only six MSMs for gallantry were ever awarded. The medal was identical with the Army MSM, distinguished solely by its ribbon and the naming to the recipient. Under the royal warrants of 1916-19 Marine NCOs became eligible for immediate awards of the MSM for arduous or specially meritorious service. The medals in this case were worn with crimson ribbons with three white stripes and had the obverse showing the King in the uniform of an Admiral or a Field Marshal, depending on whether the award was for services afloat, or with the naval brigades on the Western Front. The use of this medal ceased in 1928 following the institution of the BEM (MYB 19). Although George VI examples are known. The Royal Marines MSM was revived in 1977 solely as a long service award and is the same as the naval MSM already noted, differing only in the details of the recipient.*

VALUE:

		Miniature	
Victoria (A) dated 1848	£1200–1500		£50–65
Victoria	£750–1000		£80–90
Edward VII (C)	£600–800		£80–90
George V (A)	£600–800		£45–55
George V (B)	£400–600		£45–55
George VI (E)	£400-600		£35–40
Elizabeth II (B)	£400–600		£30–35

210. ARMY MERITORIOUS SERVICE MEDAL

Instituted: 19 December 1845.

Branch of Service: Army.

Ribbon: Plain crimson (till 1916), white edges added (1916-17), three white stripes (since August 1917).

Metal: Silver.

Size: 36mm.

Description: (Obverse) effigy of the monarch; (reverse) a crowned laurel wreath inscribed FOR MERITORIOUS SERVICE.

Comments: *A sum of £2000 a year was set aside for distribution to recipients in the form of annuities not exceeding £20, paid for life to NCOs of the rank of sergeant and above for distinguished or meritorious service. The number of medals awarded was thus limited by the amount of money available in the annuity fund, so that medals and annuities were only granted on the death of previous recipients or when the fund was increased. Until November 1902 holders were not allowed to wear the LSGC as well as the MSM, but thereafter both medals could be worn, the LSGC taking precedence. In 1979, however, the order of precedence was reversed. Until 1951 the MSM could only be awarded when an annuity became available, but since then it has been awarded without the annuity. From 1956 recipients needed at least 27 years service to become eligible, but this was reduced to 20 years in 2002. What was, in effect, a second type of MSM was introduced in October 1916 when immediate awards for exceptionally valuable and meritorious service were introduced. In January 1917 this was extended to include individual acts of gallantry not in the presence of the enemy. No annuities were paid with the immediate awards which terminated in 1928 with the institution of the Gallantry BEM. Bars for subsequent acts of gallantry or life-saving were introduced in 1916, seven being awarded up to 1928. The standard crown and wreath reverse was used but in addition to the wide range of obverse types swivelling suspension was used until 1926, and immediate and non-immediate awards may be distinguished by the presence or absence respectively of the recipient's regimental number. Recent awards of the Elizabethan second bust medals have reverted to swivelling suspension. By Royal Warrant of February 2002 the annual allocation was a maximum of 201 medals: Royal Navy (49), Royal Marines (3), Army (89) and RAF (60), but these figures are rarely, if ever, attained.*

First type ribbon.

Second type ribbon.

Third type ribbon.

VALUE:

		Miniature
Victoria (A) 1847 on edge (110)	£1000–1200	—
Victoria (A) 1848 below bust (10)	£2000–2500	—
Victoria (A) (990)	£400–450	£35–55
Edward VII (725)	£300–400	£35–45
George V (A) swivel (1050)	£175–250	£20–30
George V (A) non-swivel (400)	£175–250	£15–25
George V (A) Immediate awards 1916–28		
For Gallantry (366+1 bar)	£375–500	—
Meritorious service (25,845+6 bars)	£250–350	—
George V (E) (550)	£350–450	£20–30
George VI (B) (55)	£850–1000	£15–25
George VI (D) (1090)	£250–350	£15–25
George VI (E) (5600)	£250–350	£15–25
Elizabeth II (B) (125)	£450–650	£18–25
Elizabeth II (C) (2750+)	£350–450	£18–25

211. ROYAL AIR FORCE MERITORIOUS SERVICE MEDAL

Original ribbon.

Instituted: June 1918
Branch of Service: Royal Air Force.
Ribbon: Half crimson, half light blue, with white stripes at the centre and edges. Since 1977 the same ribbon as the Army MSM.
Metal: Silver.
Size: 36mm.
Description: (Obverse) effigy of the monarch; (reverse) a crowned laurel wreath enclosing the words FOR MERITORIOUS SERVICE. Originally medals were named in large seriffed capitals and were issued in respect of the First World War and service in Russia (1918-20), but later medals were impressed in thin block capitals. The RAF version had a swivelling suspension, unlike its military counterpart.
Comments: *Awarded for valuable services in the field, as opposed to actual flying service. This medal was replaced by the BEM in 1928, but revived in December 1977 under the same conditions as the military MSM. No more than 60 medals are awarded annually. The current issue is similar to the naval and military MSMs, differing only in the naming which includes RAF after the service number.*

VALUE:		Miniature
George V (E) (854)	£450–550	£25–35
Elizabeth II (C)	£350–450	£12–18

212. COLONIAL MERITORIOUS SERVICE MEDALS

For the various original ribbons see the ribbon charts at the end of this publication.

Instituted: 31 May 1895.
Branch of Service: Colonial forces.
Ribbon: According to issuing territory (see below).
Metal: Silver.
Size: 36mm.
Description: (Obverse) originally the trophy of arms as MYB 229 but later issues have the head of the reigning monarch; (reverse) as British type, but with the name of the dominion or colony round the top.
Comments: *Awarded for service in the British dominions, colonies and protectorates.*

Canada: Ribbon as for British Army MSM. CANADA on reverse till 1936; imperial version used from then until 1958. No medals with the Victorian obverse were awarded, but specimens exist.
Cape of Good Hope: Crimson ribbon with central orange stripe. Only one or two Edward VII medals issued.
Natal: Crimson ribbon with a central yellow stripe. Exceptionally, it was awarded to volunteers in the Natal Militia. Fifteen Edward VII medals awarded.
Commonwealth of Australia: Crimson ribbon with two dark green central stripes. Issued between 1903 and 1975.
New South Wales: Crimson ribbon with a dark blue central stripe. Issued till 1903.
Queensland: Crimson ribbon with light blue central stripe. Issued till 1903.
South Australia: Plain crimson ribbon. Issued till 1903.
Tasmania: Crimson ribbon with a pink central stripe. Issued till 1903.
New Zealand: Crimson ribbon with a light green central stripe. Issued since 1898 (see also NZ21).

VALUE	Rare	Miniature	£110–220

213. INDIAN ARMY MERITORIOUS SERVICE MEDAL 1848

Instituted: 20 May 1848, by General Order of the Indian government.
Branch of Service: Forces of the Honourable East India Company and later the Indian armed services.
Ribbon: Plain crimson.
Metal: Silver.
Size: 36mm.
Description: (Obverse) the Wyon profile of Queen Victoria; (reverse) the arms and motto of the Honourable East India Company.
Comments: *Awarded with an annuity up to £20 to European sergeants, serving or discharged, for meritorious service. It was discontinued in 1873.*

VALUE:		Miniature
Undated obverse	£650–750	£240–300
Dated obverse	Rare	—

214. INDIAN ARMY MERITORIOUS SERVICE MEDAL 1888

Original ribbon.

Instituted: 1888.
Branch of Service: Indian Army.
Ribbon: Plain crimson (till 1917); three white stripes added (1917).
Metal: Silver.
Size: 36mm.
Description: (Obverse) the sovereign's effigy; (reverse) a central wreath enclosing the word INDIA surrounded by the legend FOR MERITORIOUS SERVICE with a continuous border of lotus flowers and leaves round the circumference.
Comments: *For award to Indian warrant officers and senior NCOs (havildars, dafadars and equivalent band ranks). Eighteen years of exceptionally meritorious service was the minimum requirement, subject to the availability of funds in the annuity. At first only one medal was set aside for each regiment and thereafter awards were only made on the death, promotion or reduction of existing recipients. On promotion the medal was retained but the annuity ceased. It became obsolete in 1947.*

VALUE:		Miniature
Victoria (B)	£250–350	£100–120
Edward VII (A)	£200–250	£100–120
George V (C) Rex Et Indiae Imp	£175–250	£100–120
George V (D) Kaisar-i-Hind	£175–250	£100–120
George VI (B)	£150–200	£100–120

215. AFRICAN POLICE MEDAL FOR MERITORIOUS SERVICE

Instituted: 14 July 1915.

Branch of Service Non-European NCOs and men of the colonial police forces in East and West Africa.

Ribbon: Sand-coloured with red edges.

Metal: Silver.

Size: 36mm

Description: (Obverse) effigy of the sovereign; (reverse) a crown surmounted by a lion passant gardant within a palm wreath and having the legend FOR MERITORIOUS SERVICE IN THE POLICE and AFRICA at the foot.

Comments: *Awarded for both individual acts of gallantry and distinguished, meritorious or long service. In respect of the lastnamed, a minimum of 15 years exemplary service was required. It was superseded by the Colonial Police Medal in 1938.*

VALUE:

George V (A) IND: IMP 1915-31	£700–900
George V (A) INDIAE IMP 1931-7	£700–900
George VI (B) 1938	Rare
Miniature	£100–120

216. UNION OF SOUTH AFRICA MERITORIOUS SERVICE MEDAL

Instituted: 24 October 1914, by Government gazette.

Branch of Service: Service personnel of South Africa, Southern Rhodesia and Swaziland.

Ribbon: Crimson with blue edges and a central white, blue and white band.

Metal: Silver.

Size: 36mm.

Description: As British military MSM.

Comments: *A total of 46 awards were made for 21 years service and 300 meritorious service awards were made up to 1952 when the medal was discontinued. Of these only two were awarded to South Africans in the RNVR.*

VALUE:

George V (A)	Rare
George VI (B)	Rare

217. ROYAL HOUSEHOLD FAITHFUL SERVICE MEDALS

1st type obv.

1st type rev.

Original background ribbon.

Instituted: 1872 by Queen Victoria.
Branch of Service: Royal Household.
Ribbon: Originally Royal Stuart tartan; later, a different ribbon for each monarch: dark blue and red diagonal stripes descending from left to right (George V), the same but descending from right to left (George VI) or dark blue with three red stripes (Elizabeth II).
Metal: Silver.
Size: 27mm (Victoria); 29mm (later awards).
Description: (Obverse) the sovereign's effigy; (reverse) the personal details of the recipient engraved on it. The Victorian medal has a very elaborate suspension ornamented with the crowned royal monogram, with a laurel bar brooch fitting at the top. This medal was not originally intended to be worn with a ribbon, although it had a strip of Royal Stuart tartan behind it. The same medal, but struck in 22 carat gold, was presented to John Brown, the Queen's personal servant. The concept was revived by George V, a silver medal of more conventional appearance being struck with the text FOR LONG AND FAITHFUL SERVICE on the reverse. Thirty, forty and fifty year service bars were also awarded.
Comments: *Originally intended as a reward to servants of the Royal Household for long and faithful service of at least 25 years but during the reign of George V this was changed to 20 years cumulative service. A further 10 years merited a bar. Different ribbons are used for each monarch, corresponding to the crowned cypher joining the medal to the suspension bar on either side of which the recipient's years of service are inscribed.*

VALUE:

		Miniature
Victoria	From £500	Not seen
Edward VII	—	Not seen
George V (E)	From £400	£90–110
George VI (D)	From £400	£80–90
Elizabeth II (C)	From £450	£35–45
Charles III (B)	—	—

2nd type obv. (George V).

2nd type rev.

Charles III obverse.

GV ribbon.

GVI ribbon.

EII ribbon.

CIII Ribbon.

218. ROYAL NAVAL LONG SERVICE AND GOOD CONDUCT MEDAL

1st type obv.

1st type rev.

Instituted: 24 August 1831, by Order in Council.

Branch of Service: Royal Navy.

Ribbon: Plain dark blue (1831); dark blue with white edges (1848).

Metal: Silver.

Size: 34mm (1831); 36mm (1848).

Description: First type: (Obverse) an anchor surmounted by a crown and enclosed in an oak wreath; (reverse) the recipient's details. Plain ring for suspension.

Second type, adopted in 1848: (Obverse) the sovereign's effigy; (reverse) a three-masted man-of-war surrounded by a rope tied at the foot with a reef knot and having the legend FOR LONG SERVICE AND GOOD CONDUCT round the circumference. This medal originally had a wide suspender bar 38mm, but a narrow suspender was substituted in 1874. Normally the obverse was undated, but about 100 medals were issued in 1849-50 with the obverse of the Naval GSM, with the date 1848 below the Queen's bust. Between 1875 and 1877 a number of medals had the years of service added to the recipient's details, either engraved or impressed on the edge—these medals (about 60 known) are now sought after by collectors. Engraved naming was used from 1875 to 1877, but from then until 1901 impressed naming was adopted. Later medals used the various obverse effigies noted below.

Comments: *Originally awarded for 21 years exemplary conduct, but the period was reduced to 10 years in 1874, then later increased to 15 years. Bars for additional periods of 15 years were instituted by George V. In March 1981 commissioned officers of the naval services became eligible after 15 years service, provided at least 12 years were served in the ranks. Under changes announced in 2015 a clasp is now awarded for every 10 years served and the medal is now available to all ranks.*

2nd type rev. wide suspender

VALUE:		Miniature
Anchor type obv., 1831–47 (644)	£1200–1500	—
Victoria (A):		
1848–75, wide suspender (3572)	£650–850	—
Dated 1848 type (100)	£1500–2000	—
1875–77, narrow suspender,		
engraved naming (4400)	£175–250	£35–45
Year on edge variety (c. 40)	£450–500	—
1877–1901		
impressed naming (18,200)	£175–250	—
Year on edge variety (c. 20)	£400–500	—
Edward VII (B)	£75–100	—
George V (B) 1910–20 swivel	£75–100	£12–18
1920–30 non-swivelling bar	£65–85	£5–12
George V (E) 1931–36	£75–100	£10–15
George VI (D) 1937–48	£85–100	£10–15
George VI (E) 1949–52	£85–100	£10–15
Elizabeth II (B) 1953–54	£75–100	£10–15
Elizabeth II (C) 1954–	£75–100	£10–15

Later type ribbon.

2nd type rev. narrow suspender with non-swivelling bar.

2nd type obv. George V

219. ROYAL NAVAL RESERVE DECORATION

Instituted: 1908.
Branch of Service: Royal Naval Reserve.
Ribbon: Plain green ribbon, white edges being added from 1941 onwards.
Metal: Silver and silver-gilt.
Size: Height 54mm; max. width 33mm.
Description: A skeletal badge with the royal cypher in silver surrounded by an oval cable and reef knot in silver-gilt, surmounted by a crown and suspension ring.
Comments: *Granted for 15 years commissioned service (sub-lieutenant and above) in the Royal Naval Reserve, active service in wartime counting double. Bars are awarded for additional periods of 15 years. Recipients are entitled to the letters RD after their name. This decoration was replaced by the VRSM (No. 242A) in 2000.*

VALUE:		*Miniature*
Edward VII	£150–175	£30–35
George V	£185–200	£30–35
George VI (GRI)	£150–175	£30–35
George VI (GVIR)	£150–175	£30–35
Elizabeth II	£175–190	£15–25

2nd type ribbon.

220. ROYAL NAVAL RESERVE LONG SERVICE AND GOOD CONDUCT MEDAL

Instituted: 1908.
Branch of Service: Royal Naval Reserve.
Ribbon: Plain green, white edges and a central white stripe being added in 1941. On the amalgamation of the RNR and RNVR in 1958 the ribbon was changed to five equal stripes of blue, white, green, white and blue.
Metal: Silver.
Size: 36mm.
Description: (Obverse) effigy of the monarch; (reverse) a battleship with the motto DIUTERNE FIDELIS (faithful for ever) at the foot.
Comments: *Awarded to petty officers and ratings of the RNR for 15 years service, war service counting double, with bars for additional 15 year periods. This medal was replaced by the VRSM (No. 242A) in 2000.*

VALUE:		*Miniature*
Edward VII (B)	£55–65	£30–35
George V (B)	£50–60	£30–35
George V (E)	£35–50	£30–35
George VI (D)	£55–75	£30–35
George VI (E)	£55–75	£30–35
Elizabeth II (B)	£55–75	£10–15
Elizabeth II (C)	£55–75	£10–15

2nd type ribbon.

3rd type ribbon.

221. ROYAL NAVAL VOLUNTEER RESERVE DECORATION

Instituted: 1908.

Branch of Service: Royal Naval Volunteer Reserve.

Ribbon: 38mm originally plain dark green; dark blue with a central green stripe flanked by narrow red stripes (since 1919). Dark blue represents the sea, red represents the Royal Crimson, green represents the Old Volunteer colour

Metal: Silver and silver-gilt.

Size: Height 54mm; max. width 33mm.

Description: Similar to RNR decoration.

Comments: *Awarded to commissioned officers of the RNVR. The qualifying period was 15 years, service in the ranks counting half and war service counting double. In 1966 the decoration was replaced by the RD following the merger of the RNR and RNVR. Holders were entitled to the post-nominals letters VD, until 1947 when the letters VRD were substituted. Additional bars were awarded for each 10 years service.*

VALUE:		Miniature
Edward VII	£175–200	£30–35
George V	£150–175	£30–35
George VI GRI	£150–175	£30–35
George VI GVIR	£150–175	£30–35
Elizabeth II	£175–200	£15–25

222. ROYAL NAVAL VOLUNTEER RESERVE LONG SERVICE AND GOOD CONDUCT MEDAL

Instituted: 1908.

Branch of Service: Royal Naval Volunteer Reserve.

Ribbon: Originally plain green, but subsequently a broad central green stripe edged in red with blue stripes at the ends was adopted.

Metal: Silver.

Size: 36mm.

Description: Identical to the RNR medal, but distinguished by the ribbon and the naming which includes the letters RNVR, RCNVR (Canada), RSANVR (South Africa), etc.

Comments: *Awarded to petty officers and ratings for 12 years service with the necessary training, character assessed as "very good" throughout the period. War service counted double. The award was extended to the Colonial Navies during the Second World War.*

VALUE:		Miniature
Edward VII (B)	£350–400	£30–35
George V (B)	£50–75	£30–35
George V (E)	£50–75	£30–35
George VI (D, E)	£50–75	£30–35
Elizabeth II (B, C)	£75–100	£10–20

223. ROYAL FLEET RESERVE LONG SERVICE AND GOOD CONDUCT MEDAL

Instituted: 1919.
Branch of Service: Royal Fleet Reserve.
Ribbon: Blue bordered with thin red stripes and white edges.
Metal: Silver.
Size: 36mm.
Description: Similar to the RNR LSGC but with ring suspension instead of a bar suspender.
Comments: *Awarded for 15 years service in the Fleet Reserve. This medal was discontinued in 2000.*

VALUE:		Miniature
George V (B)	£45–55	£30–35
George V (E)	£45–55	£30–35
George VI (D)	£45–55	£30–35
George VI (E)	£45–55	£30–35
Elizabeth II (B)	£55–65	£10–20
Elizabeth II (C)	£55–65	£10–20

224. ROYAL NAVAL AUXILIARY SICK BERTH RESERVE LONG SERVICE AND GOOD CONDUCT MEDAL

Instituted: 1919.
Branch of Service: Royal Naval Auxiliary Sick Berth Reserve.
Ribbon: Plain green but later green with a white central stripe and white edges.
Metal: Silver.
Size: 36mm.
Description: Identical to the RNR equivalent, but the letters RNASBR appear after the recipient's name.
Comments: *Arguably the longest title of any British medal, it continued until the RNASBR was disbanded in 1949. The Auxiliary Sick Berth Reserve was created in 1903, members being recruited from the St John Ambulance Brigade. About 780 medals were granted prior to the Second World War and a further 715 between 1939 and 1949.*

VALUE:		Miniature
George V (B)	£100–120	£30–35
George V (E)	£100–120	£30–35
George VI (D)	£100–120	£30–35

225. ROYAL NAVAL VOLUNTEER (WIRELESS) RESERVE LONG SERVICE AND GOOD CONDUCT MEDAL

Instituted: 1939.
Branch of Service: Royal Naval Volunteer Wireless Auxiliary Reserve.
Ribbon: A broad central green stripe edged in red with blue stripes at the ends.
Metal: Silver.
Size: 36mm.
Description: Identical to the RNR equivalent, but the letters RNV(W) R after the recipient's name. The last of the service medals with a battleship reverse.
Comments: *Issued till 1957 when the RNWAR was disbanded. It was awarded for 12 years service, only about 200 having been issued.*

VALUE:		Miniature
George VI (D)	£250–350	£30–35
Elizabeth II (C)	£250–350	£30–35

226. ROYAL NAVAL AUXILIARY SERVICE MEDAL

Instituted: July 1965.
Branch of Service: Royal Naval Auxiliary Service (RNXS), formerly the Royal Naval Minewatching Service, disbanded 1994.
Ribbon: Dark blue with a narrow green central stripe and broad white stripes at the edges bisected by thin dark green stripes.
Metal: Cupro-nickel.
Size: 36mm.
Description: (Obverse) the Queen's effigy; (reverse) a fouled anchor in an oak wreath surmounted by a naval crown.
Comments: *Awarded for 12 years service. A bar was awarded for each additional 12 years service. 1,710 were awarded, 131 with one bar and 2 with two bars. Interestingly this medal was the last to be issued with a pure silk ribbon.*

VALUE: Elizabeth II (A) £180–220 *Miniature* £30–35

227. HM COASTGUARD LONG SERVICE AND GOOD CONDUCT MEDAL

First type reverse.

Second award bar.

Instituted: 1911 by the Board of Trade.
Branch of Service: Rocket Life Saving Apparatus Volunteers,
Ribbon: Originally pale blue with broad scarlet edges, in 2013 changed to scarlet with one broad central pale blue stripe and two narrow pale blue stripes.
Metal: Silver.
Size: 31mm.
Description: (Obverse) the effigy of the reigning monarch with the date below the truncation. (Reverse) exists in four types. The first refers to the Board of Trade but when that department handed over responsibility to the Ministry of Transport in 1942 the wording was amended to read ROCKET APPARATUS VOLUNTEER MEDAL round the circumference. In 1953 the inscription was changed to COAST LIFE SAVING CORPS, in 1968 to COASTGUARD AUXILIARY SERVICE and in 2012 to HM COASTGUARD.
Comments: *Awarded for 20 years' service.*

First type ribbon.

Second type ribbon.

VALUE:		*Miniature*
George V (E)	£175–200	£55–110
George VI (D/E) BoT	£175–200	£55–110
George VI (D/E) Rocket Apparatus	£175–200	£55–110
Elizabeth II (D) Coast Life Saving	£175–200	£55–110
Elizabeth II (D) Coastguard Auxiliary	£175–200	£15–25
Elizabeth II (D) HM Coastguard	£175–200	£15–25

228. HM COASTGUARD COMMENDATION

Instituted: 2000.
Branch of Service: HM Coastguard Service.
Ribbon: None.
Metal: Gilt.
Size: 35mm x 12mm.
Description: Pin badge depicting the emblem of HM Coastguard Service (left) with two-line inscription "HM Coastguard / For Meritorious Service" (right).
Comments: *Awarded to Coastguard, Auxiliary Coastguard and Coastguard rescue teams for rescuing shipwrecked mariners.*

VALUE: —

229. ARMY LONG SERVICE AND GOOD CONDUCT MEDAL

1st type obv. Trophy of Arms with badge of Hanover.

2nd type obv. with badge of Hanover omitted and swivel suspender.

GV type C obverse with fixed suspender and "Commonwealth" bar.

Pre-1917 ribbon.

Later ribbon, used from 1917.

Instituted: 1830.

Branch of Service: Army.

Ribbon: Plain crimson was used till 1917 when white stripes were added to the edges. Dominion and colonial medals formerly had crimson ribbons with a narrow central stripe in dark green (Commonwealth of Australia), dark blue (New South Wales), light blue (Queensland), pink (Tasmania), orange (Cape of Good Hope), yellow (Natal), white (Canada), light green (NZ). New Guinea had a scarlet ribbon with a light blue central stripe and South Australia had no central stripe on a plain crimson ribbon.

Metal: Silver.

Size: 36mm.

Description: Over the long period in which this medal has been in use it has undergone a number of changes. Until 1901 the obverse bore a trophy of arms with the royal arms in an oval shield in the centre while the reverse bore the inscription FOR LONG SERVICE AND GOOD CONDUCT. The first issue had the royal arms with the badge of Hanover on the obverse and small suspension ring with a plain crimson ribbon. A large ring was substituted in 1831. On the accession of Queen Victoria in 1837 the Hanoverian emblem was dropped from the arms. In 1855 a swivelling scroll suspension was substituted and in 1859 small lettering replaced the original large lettering on the reverse. From 1901, however, the effigy of the reigning sovereign was placed on the obverse although the reverse remained the same. In 1920 the swivelling scroll suspension gave way to a fixed suspender. In 1930 the title of the medal was changed to the Long Service and Good Conduct Medal (Military); at the same time the design was modified. A fixed suspension bar was added, bearing the words REGULAR ARMY or the name of a dominion (India, Canada, Australia, New Zealand or South Africa). This replaced the Permanent Forces of the Empire LSGC Medal (see below).

Comments: *Originally awarded to soldiers of exemplary conduct for 21 years service in the infantry or 24 years in the cavalry, but in 1854 the qualifying period was reduced to 18 years and in 1977 to 15 years. Under changes announced in 2015 a clasp is now awarded for every 10 years served. During World War II commissioned officers were permitted to acquire this medal so long as they had completed at least 12 of their 18 years service in the ranks. Canada discontinued the LSGC medal in 1950 when the Canadian Forces Decoration was instituted, while South Africa replaced it with the John Chard Medal later the same year. From 1930 onwards the lettering of the reverse inscription was in tall, thin letters. In 1940 bars for further periods of service were authorised. The LSGC is invariably named to the recipient. The William IV and early Victorian issues (to 1854) were impressed in the style of the Waterloo Medal and also bore the date of discharge and award. The 1855 issue was not dated, while lettering was impressed in the style of the Military General Service Medal. Later Victorian issues, however, were engraved in various styles, while medals from 1901 onwards are impressed in small capitals of various types. Medals to Europeans in the Indian Army are engraved in cursive script. Recent research by Irvin Mortensen, however, reveals that some medals after 1850 were issued unnamed, and this also accounts for various unofficial styles of naming found on later medals. In keeping with the other branches of the armed forces the medal is now available to all ranks.*

VALUE:

		Miniature
William IV small ring 1830–31	£850–1000	—
William IV large ring 1831–37	£750–950	—
Victoria without Hanoverian arms 1837–55	£250–350	—
Victoria swivelling scroll suspension 1855–74	£155–225	£35–45
Victoria small reverse lettering 1874–1901	£100–150	£30–35
Edward VII (A) 1902–10	£75–100	£30–35
George V (A) 1911–20	£65–85	£15–25
George V (A) fixed suspender 1920–30	£65–85	£15–25
George V (C) 1930–36, Regular Army bar	£65–85	£15–25
Commonwealth bar	From £75	£15–25
George VI (C) 1937–48, Regular Army bar	£55–80	£15–25
Commonwealth bar	From £75	£15–25
George VI (E) 1949–52, Regular Army bar	£65–85	£15–25
Elizabeth II 1953–54, Regular Army bar	£65–85	£15–25
Elizabeth II 1954–, Regular Army bar	£65–85	£15–25
Commonwealth bar	From £100	£15–25
To Royal Irish Regiment	£125–175	£15–25

230. ULSTER DEFENCE REGIMENT MEDAL FOR LONG SERVICE AND GOOD CONDUCT

Instituted: 1982.

Branch of Service: Ulster Defence Regiment.

Ribbon: Similar to the Military LSGC medal but with a central green stripe in addition.

Metal: Silver.

Size: 36mm.

Description: (Obverse) the imperial crowned bust of Queen Elizabeth II; (reverse) similar to the Military LSGC medal. Fitted with a fixed suspension bar inscribed UDR.

Comments: *Granted to personnel for 15 years exemplary service after 1 April 1970, with bars for additional 15-year periods. It is also awarded to officers provided that at least 12 of their 15 years service was in the ranks.*

VALUE:

Elizabeth II (B)	£300–450	*Miniature*	£12–18

231. VOLUNTEER OFFICER'S DECORATION

Instituted: 25 July 1892.

Branch of Service: Volunteer Force.

Ribbon: 38mm plain green, suspended from an oak bar brooch. Members of the Honourable Artillery Company were granted a distinctive ribbon in 1906, half scarlet, half dark blue with yellow edges—King Edward's racing colours.

Metal: Silver and silver-gilt.

Size: Height 42mm; max. width 35mm.

Description: An oval skeletal badge in silver and silver-gilt, with the royal cypher and crown in the centre, within a wreath of oak leaves. It is suspended by a plain ring with an oak leaf bar brooch fitted to the top of the ribbon. Although issued unnamed, many examples were subsequently engraved or impressed privately. Two versions of the Victorian decoration were produced, differing in the monogram— VR for United Kingdom recipients and VRI for recipients in the dominions and colonies.

Comments: *The basic qualification was 20 years commissioned service in the Volunteer Force, a precursor of the Territorial Army, non-commissioned service counting half. By Royal Warrant of 24 May 1894 the decoration was extended to comparable forces overseas, the qualifying period for service in India being reduced to 18 years. The colonial VD was superseded in 1899 by the Colonial Auxiliary Forces Officers Decoration and the Indian Volunteer Forces Officers Decoration. In the United Kingdom it was superseded by the Territorial Decoration, on the formation of the TF in 1908. A total of 4,710 decorations were awarded. Awards in Bermuda continued until 1930.*

VALUE:

		Miniature
Victoria VR	£150–175	£40–50
Victoria VRI	£300–350	£95–110
Edward VII	£150–175	£35–45
George V	£150–175	£30–40

HAC ribbon.

232. VOLUNTEER LONG SERVICE MEDAL

HAC ribbon.

Instituted: 1894.

Branch of Service: Volunteer Force.

Ribbon: 32mm plain green, but members of the Honourable Artillery Company were granted a distinctive ribbon in 1906, half scarlet, half dark blue with yellow edges—King Edward's racing colours.

Metal: Silver.

Size: 36mm.

Description: (Obverse) effigy of the reigning monarch; (reverse) a laurel wreath on which is superimposed ribbons inscribed FOR LONG SERVICE IN THE VOLUNTEER FORCE.

Comments: *This medal was awarded for 20 years service in the ranks. Officers could also receive the medal, being eligible on account of their non-commissioned service. Many officers then gained sufficient commissioned service to be awarded either the Volunteer Decoration or (from 1908) the Territorial Decoration. The medal was extended to Colonial Forces in June 1898, the titles of the monarch being appropriately expanded for this version. This medal was superseded by the Territorial Force Efficiency Medal in 1908, although it continued to be awarded until 1930 in Bermuda, India, Isle of Man (Isle of Man Vols.) and the 7th Volunteer Battalion of the King's (Liverpool) Regiment.*

VALUE:

		Miniature
Victoria Regina (C) (UK)	£75–100	
Unnamed	£45–50	£25–30
Victoria Regina et Imperatrix (C) (overseas)	£85–125	£25–30
Edwardus Rex (A)	£85–100	£18–30
Edwardus Rex et Imperator (A) (colonial)	£85–100	£18–30
Edwardus Kaisar-i-Hind (A) (India)	£100–120	£18–30
George V (A)		
India	£85–100	£18–25
Isle of Man	£250–300	£18–25
Bermuda	£150–200	£18–25

233. TERRITORIAL DECORATION

HAC ribbon.

Instituted: 29 September 1908.

Branch of Service: Territorial Force, later Territorial Army.

Ribbon: 38mm plain dark green with a central yellow stripe suspended from an oak bar brooch. Members of the Honourable Artillery Company were granted a distinctive ribbon in 1906, half scarlet, half dark blue with yellow edges—King Edward's racing colours.

Metal: Silver and silver-gilt.

Size: Height 46mm; max. width 35mm.

Description: A skeletal badge with the crowned monogram of the sovereign surrounded by an oval oak wreath, fitted with a ring for suspension.

Comments: *Awarded for 20 years commissioned service, service in the ranks counting half and war service double. It was superseded by the Efficiency Decoration in 1930. A total of 4,783 decorations were awarded.*

VALUE:

		Miniature
Edward VII (585)	£250–275	£18–25
George V (4,198)	£200–250	£18–15

234. TERRITORIAL FORCE EFFICIENCY MEDAL

Instituted: 1908.

Branch of Service: Territorial Force.

Ribbon: Originally 32mm plain dark green with a central yellow stripe but members of the Honourable Artillery Company were granted a distinctive ribbon in 1906, half scarlet, half dark blue with yellow edges—King Edward's household colours. In December 1919 the ribbon was changed to plain dark green with yellow edges.

Metal: Silver.

Size: Height 38mm; max. width 31mm.

Description: An oval medal fitted with claw and ring suspension. (Obverse) the sovereign's effigy; (reverse) inscribed with the name of the medal in four lines.

Comments: *Granted for a minimum of 12 years service in the Territorial Force. It was superseded in 1921 by the Territorial Efficiency Medal when the service was renamed. Bars were awarded for further periods of 12 years service.*

Original ribbon.

HAC ribbon.

VALUE:		Miniature
Edward VII (A) (11,800)	£150–175*	£18–25
Of these:		
With bar (537)	£200–250	
with second bars (64)	£300–350	
George V (A) (37,726)	£75–100	£18–25
George V first clasps	£130–150	

*Medals to Yeomanry regiments command a higher premium.

234A. TERRITORIAL FORCE IMPERIAL SERVICE BADGE

Instituted: 1912.

Branch of Service: Members of the Territorial Force.

Ribbon: None.

Metal: Cupro-nickel or brass.

Size: 10mm x 43mm

Description: A horizontal bar surmounted by a royal crown, the bar inscribed in raised lettering IMPERIAL SERVICE.

Comments: *Awarded to members of the Territorial Force who were prepared to serve outside the United Kingdom in defence of the Empire, mainly during the First World War.*

VALUE: £12–15

235. TERRITORIAL EFFICIENCY MEDAL

Instituted: 1921.

Branch of Service: Territorial Army.

Ribbon: 32mm plain dark green with yellow edges. Members of the HAC wear the ribbon of the Company as 234 above.

Metal: Silver.

Size: Height 38mm; max. width 31mm.

Description: As above, but with the name amended and inscribed in three lines.

Comments: *Introduced following the elevation of the Territorial Force to become the Territorial Army. It was superseded by the Efficiency Medal in 1930.*

VALUE:

George V (A)	£85–120	Miniature	£10–18

236. EFFICIENCY DECORATION

Instituted: 17 October 1930.

Branch of Service: Territorial Army (UK), the Indian Volunteer Forces and the Colonial Auxiliary Forces.

Ribbon: 38mm plain dark green with a central yellow stripe. In 1969, on the introduction of the T&AVR, the ribbon was altered to half blue, half green , with a central yellow stripe. Members of the Honourable Artillery Company wear half blue, half scarlet ribbon, with yellow edges.

Metal: Silver and silver-gilt.

Size: Height 54mm; max. width 37mm.

Description: An oval skeletal badge in silver and silver-gilt with the crowned monogram in an oak wreath, the ring for suspension being fitted to the top of the crown. It differs also from the previous decorations in having a suspender bar denoting the area of service: Territorial (UK), India, Canada, Fiji or other overseas country being inscribed as appropriate, but the previous ribbon was retained.

Comments: *Recipients in Britain were allowed to continue using the letters TD after their names, but in the Commonwealth the letters ED were used instead. The 20-year qualification was reduced to 12 years in 1949, bars for each additional 6 years being added. In 1969 the British suspender bar was changed to T & AVR, on the establishment of the Territorial and Army Volunteer Reserve. In 1982 the title of Territorial Army was resumed, so the inscription on the bar reverted to TERRITORIAL but the blue, yellow and green ribbon was retained. This decoration was superseded in the UK by the VRSM (No. 242A) in 2000. However, it is still current in some Commonwealth countries.*

Second yard bars

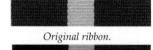

Original ribbon.

Post-1969 ribbon.

HAC ribbon.

VALUE:

	Territorial	T&AVR	Commonwealth
George V	£150–175	—	From £175
George VI (GRI)	£85–100	—	From £175
George VI (GVIR)	£85–100	—	—
Elizabeth II	£100–125	£120–150	From £175
Miniature	£20–25	£20–25	£20–25

237. EFFICIENCY MEDAL

Instituted: 17 October 1930.

Branch of Service: Territorial Army (UK), Indian Volunteer Forces and Colonial Auxiliary Forces.

Ribbon: 32mm green with yellow edges. In 1969, on the introduction of the T&AVR, the ribbon was altered to half blue, half green, with yellow edges. Members of the Honourable Artillery Company wear half blue, half scarlet ribbon, with yellow edges.

Metal: Silver.

Original ribbon.

Post-1969 ribbon.

HAC ribbon.

237. EFFICIENCY MEDAL *continued*

Aa

Ab

Size: Height 39mm; max. width 32mm.

Description: An oval silver medal. (Obverse) the monarch's effigy; (reverse) inscribed FOR EFFICIENT SERVICE. In place of the simple ring suspension, however, there was now a fixed suspender bar decorated with a pair of palm leaves surmounted by a scroll inscribed TERRITORIAL or MILITIA (for UK volunteer forces), while overseas forces had the name of the country.

Comments: *This medal consolidated the awards to other ranks throughout the volunteer forces of Britain and the Commonwealth. The basic qualification was 12 years continuous efficient service, but war service and peacetime service in West Africa counted double. Additional bars with a crown were awarded for further periods of six years continuous efficient service. The Militia bar was granted to certain categories of the Supplementary Reserve until the formation of the Army Emergency Reserve in 1951. In 1969 the bar inscribed T & AVR was introduced. The bar TERRITORIAL was resumed in 1982 but the half blue, half green ribbon with yellow edges was retained. For the distinctive medal awarded in the Union of South Africa see number 254. Instead of the second obverse of Queen Elizabeth II, Canada adopted a type showing the Queen wearing the Imperial Crown. This medal was superseded in the UK by the VRSM (No. 242A) in 2000, although it is still current in some Commonwealth countries.*

VALUE:	Territorial	Militia	T&AVR	Commonwealth
George V (C)	£75–100	£150–175**	—	From £85*
George VI (Aa)	£60–85	£85–100	—	From £85*
George VI (Ab)	£60–85	£85–100	—	From £85*
Elizabeth II (A1)	£75–100	—	—	From £150*
Elizabeth II (A)	£75–100	—	£85–120	From £150*
Miniature	from £18			£85–95

*These prices are for the commoner Commonwealth types. However, some are extremely rare as can be seen in the table below where the issue numbers are indicated in brackets (where known).
**Only RE (176), R.Signals (94) and RAMC (42).

GEORGE V (C)	GEORGE VI (Aa)	GEORGE VI (Ab)	ELIZABETH II (A1)	ELIZABETH II (A)
—	—	—	Antigua (3)	—
Australia	Australia	Australia	Australia	Australia
Barbados	Barbados	Barbados	Barbados	Barbados
Bermuda	Bermuda	Bermuda	Bermuda	Bermuda
British Guiana (15)	British Guiana	British Guiana	British Guiana	—
British Honduras (1)	British Honduras (23)	British Honduras (3)	British Honduras (13)	—
—	Burma (111)	—	—	—
Canada	Canada	Canada	Canada (Rare)	Canada (Rare)
Ceylon	Ceylon	Ceylon	Ceylon (69)	—
—	Dominica (130)	—	—	—
Falkland Islands (29)	Falkland Islands (29)	—	Falkland Islands	Falkland Islands
Fiji (29)	Fiji (35)	Fiji (9)	Fiji (7)	Fiji (33)
—	—	Gibraltar (15)	Gibraltar	Gibraltar
—	Gold Coast (275)	Gold Coast (35)	—	—
—	Grenada (1)	—	—	—
—	Guernsey (3)	Guernsey (4)	Guernsey (3)	Guernsey (35)
Hong Kong (21)	Hong Kong (50)	Hong Kong (224)	Hong Kong (145)	Hong Kong (268)
India	India	—	—	—
Jamaica	Jamaica	Jamaica	Jamaica	—
—	Jersey (40)	Jersey (7)	—	Jersey (1)

237. EFFICIENCY MEDAL continued

GEORGE V (C)	GEORGE VI (Aa)	GEORGE VI (Ab)	ELIZABETH II (A)	ELIZABETH II (B)
—	Kenya (1)	Kenya (159)	Kenya (36)	—
—	Leeward Islands (49)	Leeward Islands (14)	Leeward Islands (2)	—
—	Malaya	Malaya	Malaya (54)	—
—	Malta (320)	Malta (31)	—	Malta (36)
—	—	—	Mauritius (71)	—
—	—	—	—	Montserrat (6)
New Zealand (71)	New Zealand (34)	New Zealand	New Zealand	New Zealand
Nigeria (1)	—	Nigeria (7)	Nigeria (3)	—
—	—	—	Rhodesia/Nyasaland (7)	—
—	—	—	St Christopher Nevis (13)	—
—	St Lucia (2)	—	—	—
—	St Vincent (1)	—	—	—
S. Rhodesia (17)	S. Rhodesia (230)	S. Rhodesia (24)	S. Rhodesia (6)	—
—	Trinidad/Tobago (228)	Trinidad/Tobago (46)	Trinidad/Tobago (5)	—

238. ARMY EMERGENCY RESERVE DECORATION

Instituted: 17 November 1952.
Branch of Service Army Emergency Reserve.
Ribbon: 38mm dark blue with a central yellow stripe.
Metal: Silver and silver-gilt.
Size: Height 55mm; max. width 37mm.
Description: An oval skeletal badge, with the monarch's cypher surmounted by a crown in an oak wreath. Suspension is by a ring through the top of the crown and it is worn with a brooch bar inscribed ARMY EMERGENCY RESERVE.
Comments: *Awarded for 12 years commissioned service. Officers commissioned in the Army Supplementary Reserve or Army Emergency Reserve of Officers between 8 August 1942 and 15 May 1948 who transferred to the Regular Army Reserve of Officers after 10 years service were also eligible. War service counts double and previous service in the ranks counts half. The ERD was abolished in 1967 on the formation of the Territorial and Army Volunteer Reserve.*

VALUE:

Elizabeth II	£150–200	*Miniature*	£20–25

239. ARMY EMERGENCY RESERVE EFFICIENCY MEDAL

Instituted: 1 September 1953.
Branch of Service: Army Emergency Reserve.
Ribbon: 32mm dark blue with three central yellow stripes.
Metal: Silver.
Size: Height 39mm; max. width 31mm.
Description: This oval medal is similar to the Efficiency Medal previously noted but has a scroll bar inscribed ARMY EMERGENCY RESERVE.
Comments: *Awarded for 12 years service in the ranks or for service in the Supplementary Reserve between 1924 and 1948 prior to transferring to the Army Emergency Reserve. War service counted double. It was abolished in 1967 following the formation of the Territorial and Army Volunteer Reserve. .A very small number of awards were issued bearing the George VI effigy.*

VALUE:

Elizabeth II	£150–200	*Miniature*	£15–20

240. IMPERIAL YEOMANRY LONG SERVICE AND GOOD CONDUCT MEDAL

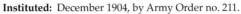

Instituted: December 1904, by Army Order no. 211.
Branch of Service: Imperial Yeomanry.
Ribbon: 32mm plain yellow.
Metal: Silver.
Size: Height 38mm; max. width 31mm.
Description: Upright oval. (Obverse) the sovereign's effigy; (reverse) inscribed IMPERIAL YEOMANRY round the top and the usual long service and good conduct inscription in four lines across the middle.
Comments: *Awarded to NCOs and troopers of the Imperial Yeomanry for 10 years exemplary service. It became obsolete in 1908 when the Territorial Force was created. Nevertheless 48 medals were awarded in 1909, one in 1910, one in 1914 and one in 1917. All medals were issued with the bust of King Edward VII on the obverse.*

VALUE:

Edward VII (A) (1674)	£450–500	*Miniature*	£60–80

241. MILITIA LONG SERVICE AND GOOD CONDUCT MEDAL

Instituted: December 1904, by Army Order no. 211.
Branch of Service: Militia.
Ribbon: 32mm plain light blue.
Metal: Silver.
Size: Height 38mm; max. width 31mm.
Description: An upright oval medal. (Obverse) the effigy of the monarch; (reverse) similar to the preceding but inscribed MILITIA at the top of the reverse.
Comments: *Qualifying service was 18 years and 15 annual camps. It was superseded by the Efficiency Medal with the Militia bar in 1930. A total of 1,587 medals were awarded between 1905 and 1930 (RGA 341, RE 15, RE Submarine Miners 8, Infantry 988, Channel Islands 89, Malta 131, Bermuda 15).*

VALUE:

		Miniature
Edward VII (A) (1446)	£450–500	£100–130
George V (C) (141)	£600–800	£100–130

242. SPECIAL RESERVE LONG SERVICE AND GOOD CONDUCT MEDAL

Instituted: June 1908, by Army Order no. 126.
Branch of Service: Special Reserve.
Ribbon: Dark blue with a central light blue stripe.
Metal: Silver.
Size: Height 38mm; max. width 31mm.
Description: As the foregoing but inscribed SPECIAL RESERVE round the top of the reverse.
Comments: *Awarded to NCOs and men of the Special Reserve who completed 15 years service and attended 15 camps. A total of 1,078 medals were awarded between 1908 and 1936 with solitary awards in 1947 and 1953. Summary of awards: RA, RFA, RGA 165, RE 9, Royal Anglesey RE 3, Royal Monmouthshire R. 5, RAMC 4, Labour Corps 4, MGC 1. North Irish Horse 16, South Irish Horse 31, King Edward's Horse 14, Infantry 823, Channel Islands 5. Of these, two awards (1 to the RGA, 1 to the South Irish Horse), were subsequently cancelled.*

VALUE:

		Miniature
Edward VII (A) (428)	£500–600	£110–135
George V (C) (650)	£500–600	£110–135

242A. VOLUNTEER RESERVES SERVICE MEDAL

Instituted: 1999.
Branch of Service: Volunteer reserves of all three armed services.
Ribbon: Dark green with three narrow central stripes of dark blue, scarlet and light blue, separated from the green by two narrow stripes of gold. Members of the Honourable Artillery Company wear half blue, half scarlet ribbon, with yellow edges.
Metal: Silver.
Size: Height 38mm; width 32mm.
Description: An oval medal. (Obverse) the sovereign's effigy; (reverse) inscribed FOR SERVICE IN THE VOLUNTEER RESERVES above a spray of oak.
Comments: *Awarded to all ranks of the volunteer reserves who complete ten years of reckonable qualifying service. Bars for additional five-year periods of reckonable qualifying service are also awarded. This medal replaces the Royal Naval Reserve Decoration, the Royal Naval Reserve Long Service and Good Conduct Medal, the Efficiency Decoration, the Efficiency Medal and the Air Efficiency Award. Since 2015 recipients are entitled to use the post-nominals VR, backdated to 1999.*

| VALUE: | £250–300 | Miniature | £10–15 |

HAC ribbon

242B. ROYAL MILITARY ASYLUM GOOD CONDUCT MEDAL

First type reverse.

Second type reverse.

Instituted: c.1850.
Branch of Service: Students in the Royal Military Asylum.
Ribbon: Plain red or crimson.
Metal: Silver or bronze.
Size: 36mm.
Description: (Obverse) the royal arms, garnished, crested and with supporters; (reverse) first type ROYAL MILITARY ASYLUM, second type: DUKE OF YORK'S ROYAL MILITARY SCHOOL round the circumference, enclosing a laurel wreath inscribed across the centre FOR GOOD CONDUCT. Fitted with a scrolled suspender and brooch. Engraved in upright capitals with the name of the recipient.
Comments: *The Royal Military Asylum was established for the education of the sons of soldiers who had been killed in action or who had died while in the service. It was renamed the "Duke of York's Royal Military School" in 1892 and subsequent medals are thus inscribed. The actual criteria for the award of the medal are not known.*

| VALUE: | "Asylum" | £125–175 |
| | "School" | £100–150 |

242C. ARMED FORCES VETERAN LAPEL BADGE

Date: May 2004.
Branch of Service: Former members of HM Armed Forces, Royal Fleet Auxiliary, Cyprus Regiment, Merchant Navy who took part in a naval action, Home Guard and Polish Forces under UK command.
Ribbon: None.
Description: Badge surmounted by a gold imperial crown with VETERAN on an enamelled scroll at the foot. The badge bears the insignia of the armed services with H.M. ARMED FORCES round the top of the circumference.
Comments: *Originally available to veterans of HM Armed Forces including the Royal Fleet Auxiliary, who served up to December 31, 1954, but later extended. It is intended for any service in the Armed Forces.*

VALUE: £10–15

242D. MERCHANT SEAFARERS VETERAN LAPEL BADGE

Instituted: 2006.
Branch of Service: Personnel of the Merchant Navy.
Ribbon: None.
Description: Similar to 242C but with the badge superimposed on the Red Ensign.
Comments: *Available to surviving veterans of the Merchant Navy who contributed to HM Armed Forces military operations in World War II. Holders of this badge are not eligible for the Armed Forces Veteran badge (242C).*

VALUE: £15–20

242E. ARCTIC EMBLEM

Instituted: 2006.
Branch of Service: Personnel of the Armed Forces and the Merchant Navy
Ribbon: None.
Description: A white five-pointed star edged in gold, with a red centre, above which is a blue arc bearing the words THE ARCTIC.
Comments: *Available to surviving veterans who served north of the Arctic Circle and west of the Urals for at least one day between 3 September 1939 and 8 May 1945. The emblem is also available to the next of kin of deceased veterans.*

VALUE: £20–25

242F. BEVIN BOYS LAPEL BADGE

Date: 2007.
Branch of Service: Former Bevin Boys.
Ribbon: None.
Description: Oval badge enamelled with the outline of a pit-head winch in white on a black background, surrounded by the words BEVIN BOYS VETERANS and with a silhouette of a miner's head with helmet.
Comments: *Available to surviving veterans of the Bevin Boys of World War II.*

VALUE: £10–15

242G. WOMEN'S LAND ARMY AND TIMBER CORPS LAPEL BADGE

Date: 2007.
Branch of Service: Former members of the Women's Land Army or Women's Timber Corps.
Ribbon: None.
Description: Enamelled replica of the original WLA badge surmounted by a crown.
Comments: *Available to surviving veterans of the Women's Land Army and Women's Timber Corps of World War II.*

VALUE: £10–15

242H. AIR TRANSPORT AUXILIARY LAPEL BADGE

Date: 2008.
Branch of Service: Former members of the Air Transport Auxiliary.
Ribbon: None.
Description: Enamelled badge depicting an eagle in flight on a turquoise background surrounded by the words AIR TRANSPORT AUXILIARY on a dark blue ribbon with laurel wreath surround.
Comments: *Available to veterans of the Air Transport Auxiliary of World War II.*

VALUE: £10–15

242 I. GC & CS LAPEL BADGE

Date: 2012.
Branch of Service: Former employees at Bletchley Park and its outstations.
Ribbon: None.
Description: Enamelled badge depicting the GCHQ emblem surrounded by a laurel wreath and the dates 1939-1945, with the legend GC&CS above, BLETCHLEY PARK AND ITS OUTSTATIONS below.
Comments: *Available to surviving personnel who worked at Bletchley Park during World War II.*

VALUE: £20–25

Statue of Women's Land Army and Timber Corps at the National Memorial Arboretum, Alrewas.

242J. MERCHANT NAVY MEDAL

Instituted: 1 June 2005.

Branch of Service: Merchant Navy.

Ribbon: Equal halves of red and green divided by a narrow white stripe. Thin gold edge stripes were added in 2011 to avoid confusion with MYB 169 and to indicate special achievement

Metal: Rhodium plated cupro-nickel.　　**Size:** 28mm.

Description: (Obverse) The bust of Admiral Nelson surrounded by the legend "THE MERCHANT NAVY MEDAL" above and "1805 - TRAFALGAR - 2005" below; (reverse) the Merchant Navy logo with the inscription "FOR MERITORIOUS SERVICE" below.

Comments: *This medal was instituted to recognise the meritorious service of British registered Merchant Seafarers. The medal was awarded annually to a maximum of 15 men or women who were judged to have made a significant contribution to merchant shipping, its operations, development, personnel, welfare or safety, or who had performed an act of bravery afloat. The names of recipients were listed in the London Gazette and the award carries the post-nominals MNM. A small silver anchor was added to the ribbon to denote an act of bravery at sea. In 2015 the medal was replaced by MYB242K.*

VALUE:　　—

242K. QUEEN'S / KING'S MERCHANT NAVY MEDAL FOR MERITORIOUS SERVICE

Instituted: 2016.

Branch of Service: Merchant Navy.

Ribbon: Equal stripes of green, red, white, red, green.

Metal: Rhodium plated cupro-nickel.

Size: 36mm.

Description: (Obverse) uncrowned bust of reigning monarch with the corresponding legend; (reverse) the Merchant Navy logo with the inscription "FOR MERITORIOUS SERVICE" below.

Comments: *Like the previous medal (MYB242J), which it replaces, this medal was instituted to recognise the meritorious service of personnel serving in the Merchant Navy or the Fishing fleets of the United Kingdom, the Isle of Man and the Channel Islands. The medal is awarded annually to a maximum of 20 men or women who are judged to have made a significant contribution to merchant shipping, its operations, development, personnel, welfare or safety and show particularly valuable devotion to duty and exemplary service so as to serve as an outstanding example to others. Recipients will typically have given 20 years of good conduct and exemplary service. The names of recipients are listed in the London Gazette and the award carries the post-nominals QMNM / KMNM.*

VALUE:　　—　　　　*Miniature*　　£12–18

243. INDIAN ARMY LONG SERVICE & GOOD CONDUCT MEDAL FOR EUROPEANS 1848

Instituted: 20 May 1848, by General Order of the Indian Government.
Branch of Service: Indian Army.
Ribbon: Plain crimson.
Metal: Silver.
Size: 36mm.
Description: (Obverse) a trophy of arms, not unlike its British counterpart, but a shield bearing the arms of the Honourable East India Company was placed in the centre. (Reverse) engraved with the recipient's name and service details. In 1859 some 100 medals were sent to India by mistake, these had the Wyon profile of Queen Victoria on the obverse and a reverse inscribed FOR LONG SERVICE AND GOOD CONDUCT within an oak wreath with a crown at the top and a fouled anchor at the foot.
Comments: *Awarded to European NCOs and other ranks of the Indian Army on discharge after 21 years meritorious service. It was discontinued in 1873 after which the standard Army LSGC medal was granted.*

HEIC arms type.

VALUE:		Miniature
HEIC arms	£500–650	£110–165
Victoria (A) (100)	£650–750	£90–110

Victoria type.

244. INDIAN ARMY LONG SERVICE & GOOD CONDUCT MEDAL (INDIAN)

Instituted: 1888.
Branch of Service: Indian Army.
Ribbon: Originally plain crimson but white edges were added in 1917.
Metal: Silver.
Size: 36mm.
Description: (Obverse) the sovereign's effigy; (reverse) the word INDIA set within a palm wreath surrounded by a border of lotus flowers and leaves. The inscription FOR LONG SERVICE AND GOOD CONDUCT appears between the wreath and the lotus flowers.
Comments: *Awarded to native Indian NCOs and other ranks for 20 years meritorious service. The medal became obsolete in 1947 when India achieved independence.*

VALUE:		Miniature
Victoria (B) Kaisar-i-Hind	£150–175	£100–110
Edward VII (A) Kaisar-i-Hind	£100–125	£100–110
George V (D) Kaisar-i-Hind	£90–100	£65–85
George V (C) Rex Et Indiae Imp	£90–100	£65–85
George VI (B)	£90–100	65–85

245. INDIAN VOLUNTEER FORCES OFFICERS' DECORATION

Instituted: May 24, 1894, by extension to the Volunteer Officer Decoration (MYB 231).

Branch of Service: Indian Volunteer Forces.

Ribbon: Plain dark green (see Comments below).

Metal: Silver and silver-gilt.

Size: Height 65mm; max. width 36mm.

Description: An oval skeletal badge with the royal cipher in the centre, surrounded by a band inscribed INDIAN VOLUNTEER FORCES and surmounted by a crown. Designed for a 32mm ribbon, the decoration is fitted with a plain straight suspender behind the crown and hung from a bar brooch with an oak leaf frieze.

Comments: *Awarded for 18 years commissioned service, with service in the ranks counting half and war service double. Replacing the VD with VRI cipher in 1903, the Indian Volunteer Decoration was modelled on the Colonial Auxiliary Forces Decoration (MYB 246) and superseded by the Efficiency Decoration (MYB 236) in 1930. A total of 1,171 decorations are known to have been awarded between 1903 and 1934. Normally issued named, with the recipient's rank, name and unit engraved on the reverse. Seven styles of engraving have been observed over the life of the award. While early and late decorations may be hallmarked, the majority are not.*

VALUE:			Miniature
Edward VII	£300–350		£55–65
George V	£300–350		£35–45

246. COLONIAL AUXILIARY FORCES OFFICERS' DECORATION

Instituted: 18 May 1899.

Branch of Service: Colonial Auxiliary Forces.

Ribbon: Plain green (see Comments below).

Metal: Silver and silver-gilt.

Size: Height 66mm; max. width 35mm.

Description: Similar to the previous decoration, with an oval band inscribed COLONIAL AUXILIARY FORCES.

Comments: *Awarded to officers of auxiliary forces everywhere except in India for 20 years commissioned service. Service in the ranks counting half and service in West Africa counting double. Although issued unnamed, it was usually impressed or engraved privately. Examples to officers in the smaller colonies command a considerable premium. It became obsolete in 1930. The suspension of the medal is by a flattened loop which is only 32mm wide although it was intended to take a 38mm ribbon—the 32mm ribbon is therefore usually worn on the medal and the 38mm on the tunic.*

VALUE:			Miniature
Victoria	£350–375		£90–100
Edward VII	£225–275		£80–90
George V	£175–250		£55–65

247. COLONIAL AUXILIARY FORCES LONG SERVICE MEDAL

Instituted: May 18, 1899.
Branch of Service: Colonial Auxiliary Forces.
Ribbon: Plain green.
Metal: Silver.
Size: 36mm.
Description: (Obverse) the effigy of the reigning monarch; (reverse) an elaborate rococo frame surmounted by a crown and enclosing the five-line text FOR LONG SERVICE IN THE COLONIAL AUXILIARY FORCES.
Comments: *Awarded for 20 years service in the ranks, West African service counting double. It was superseded in 1930 by the Efficiency Medal with the appropriate colonial or dominion bar.*

VALUE:		Miniature
Victoria (D)	£100–125	£30–40
Edward VII (A)	£80–110	£25–30
George V (A)	£80–110	£18–25

248. COLONIAL LONG SERVICE AND GOOD CONDUCT MEDALS

Instituted: May 31, 1895.
Branch of Service: Indian and other Colonial forces.
Ribbon: Crimson with a central stripe denoting the country of service (see no. 212).
Metal: Silver.
Size: 36mm.
Description: Similar to its British counterpart except that the name of the appropriate colony appeared on the reverse. The obverse of the Victorian award for the Colony of Natal depicts the Royal coat of arms.
Comments: *Awarded to warrant officers, NCOs and other ranks for meritorious service and long service and good conduct. Medals of the individual Australian colonies were superseded in 1902 by those inscribed COMMONWEALTH OF AUSTRALIA. The Colonial LSGC medal was replaced in 1909 by the Permanent Forces of the Empire Beyond the Seas LSGC award.*

VALUE:	From £750	Miniature	£85–110

249. PERMANENT FORCES OF THE EMPIRE BEYOND THE SEAS LONG SERVICE AND GOOD CONDUCT MEDAL

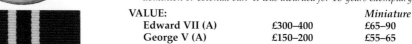

Instituted: 1909.
Branch of Service: Colonial and Dominion forces.
Ribbon: Maroon bearing a broad white central stripe with a narrow black stripe at its centre.
Metal: Silver.
Size: 36mm.
Description: (Obverse) the effigy of the reigning sovereign; (reverse) the legend PERMANENT FORCES OF THE EMPIRE BEYOND THE SEAS round the circumference, with FOR LONG SERVICE AND GOOD CONDUCT in four lines across the centre.
Comments: *This award replaced the various colonial LSGC medals, being itself superseded in 1930 by the LSGC (Military) Medal with appropriate dominion or colonial bar. It was awarded for 18 years exemplary service.*

VALUE:		Miniature
Edward VII (A)	£300–400	£65–90
George V (A)	£150–200	£55–65

250. ROYAL WEST AFRICA FRONTIER FORCE LONG SERVICE & GOOD CONDUCT MEDAL

Instituted: September 1903.
Branch of Service: Royal West Africa Frontier Force.
Ribbon: Crimson with a relatively broad green central stripe.
Metal: Silver.
Size: 36mm.
Description: (Obverse) the effigy of the reigning monarch. Two reverse types were used, the word ROYAL being added to the regimental title in June 1928.
Comments: *Awarded to native NCOs and other ranks for 18 years exemplary service.*

VALUE: £300–350   *Miniature*   £30–35

251. KING'S AFRICAN RIFLES LONG SERVICE AND GOOD CONDUCT MEDAL

Instituted: March 1907.
Branch of Service: King's African Rifles.
Ribbon: Crimson with a broad green central stripe.
Metal: Silver.
Size: 36mm.
Description: Very similar to the foregoing, apart from the regimental name round the top of the reverse.
Comments: *Awarded to native NCOs and other ranks for 18 years exemplary service.*

VALUE:		*Miniature*
Edward VII	£650–850	—
George V	£250–300	£55–65
George VI (B)	£250–300	£45–55
Elizabeth II	£500–750	£30–40

252. TRANS-JORDAN FRONTIER FORCE LONG SERVICE AND GOOD CONDUCT MEDAL

Instituted: 20 May 1938.
Branch of Service: Trans-Jordan Frontier Force.
Ribbon: Crimson with a green central stripe.
Metal: Silver.
Size: 36mm.
Description: Similar to the previous medals, with the name of the Force round the circumference.
Comments: *This rare silver medal was awarded for 16 years service in the ranks of the Trans-Jordan Frontier Force. Service in the Palestine Gendarmerie or Arab Legion counted, so long as the recipient transferred to the Frontier Force without a break in service. Only 112 medals were awarded before it was abolished in 1948.*

VALUE: £600–800

253. SOUTH AFRICA PERMANENT FORCE LONG SERVICE AND GOOD CONDUCT MEDAL

Instituted: 29 December 1939.
Branch of Service: South African forces.
Ribbon: Crimson with white stripes.
Metal: Silver.
Size: 36mm.
Description: (Obverse) Crowned effigy of King George VI; (reverse) FOR LONG SERVICE AND GOOD CONDUCT in four lines across the upper half and VIR LANGDURIGE DIENS EN GOEIE GEDRAG in four lines across the lower half. It also differs from its British counterpart in having a bilingual suspension bar.
Comments: *Awarded to NCOs and other ranks with a minimum of 18 years service.*

VALUE:		Miniature
George VI (B)	£120–140	£35–45
George VI (C)	£150–170	£35–45

254. EFFICIENCY MEDAL (SOUTH AFRICA)

Instituted: December 1939.
Branch of Service: Coast Garrison and Active Citizen Forces of South Africa.
Ribbon: 32mm plain dark green with yellow edges.
Metal: Silver.
Size: Height 38mm; max. width 30mm.
Description: An oval silver medal rather similar to the Efficiency Medal (number 237) but having a scroll bar inscribed UNION OF SOUTH AFRICA with its Afrikaans equivalent below. The reverse likewise bears a bilingual inscription.
Comments: *Awarded for 12 years non-commissioned service in the Coast Garrison and Active Citizen Forces. A bar, bearing in the centre a crown, was awarded for every six years of additional service. It was replaced in 1952 by the John Chard Medal.*

VALUE:	£65–75	Miniature	£35–45

254A. ROYAL HONG KONG REGIMENT DISBANDMENT MEDAL

Instituted: 1995.
Branch of Service: Royal Hong Kong Regiment (Volunteers).
Ribbon: Half red and half blue with a central yellow stripe.
Metal: Cupro-nickel.
Size: 38mm.
Description: (Obverse) Regimental badge with dates 1854 and 1995 either side and ROYAL HONG KONG REGIMENT THE VOLUNTEERS around. (Reverse) Coat of Arms of Hong Kong with DISBANDMENT MEDAL 3rd SEPTEMBER 1995 (date of disbandment) around.
Comment: *Available to those serving with the Regiment as the end of the Crown Colony became imminent. Recipients, however, had to purchase a full size and a miniature medal in a plush case.*

VALUE:	£75–100	Miniature	£55–65

255. CANADIAN FORCES DECORATION

Instituted: 15 December 1949.
Branch of Service: Canadian Forces.
Ribbon: 38mm orange-red divided into four equal parts by three thin white stripes.
Metal: Silver-gilt (George VI) or gilded tombac brass or bronze (Elizabeth II).
Size: Height 35mm; max. width 37mm.
Description: A decagonal (ten-sided) medal. The George VI issue has a suspension bar inscribed CANADA and the recipient's details engraved on the reverse, whereas the Elizabethan issue has no suspension bar, the recipient's details being impressed or engraved on the rim and the word "CANADA" appears at the base of the effigy. The reverse has a naval crown at the top, three maple leaves across the middle and an eagle in flight across the foot. The George VI version has the royal cypher superimposed on the maple leaves.
Comments: *Awarded to both officers and men of the Canadian regular and reserve forces for 12 years exemplary service. A bar, gold in colour, bearing the shield from the arms of Canada surmounted by the crown is awarded for each additional 10 years of qualifying service. Approximately 2,400 medals and 3,000 clasps are awarded annually.*

VALUE:		Miniature
George VI (E)	£75–100	£12–25
Elizabeth II (D)	£30–45	£12–25

256. VICTORIA VOLUNTEER LONG AND EFFICIENT SERVICE MEDAL

Instituted: 26 January 1881 but not given royal sanction until 21 April 1882.
Branch of Service: Volunteer Forces, Victoria.
Ribbon: White, with broad crimson stripes at the sides.
Metal: Silver.
Size: 39mm.
Description: (Obverse) the crowned badge of Victoria with LOCAL FORCES VICTORIA round the circumference; (reverse) inscribed FOR LONG AND EFFICIENT SERVICE. Two types of obverse exist, differing in the motto surrounding the colonial emblem. The first version has AUT PACE AUT BELLO (both in peace and war) while the second version is inscribed PRO DEO ET PATRIA (for God and country).
Comments: *Awarded to officers and men of the Volunteers in the colony of Victoria for 15 years efficient service. Awards to officers ended in 1894 with the introduction of the Volunteer Officers Decoration. This medal was replaced by the Commonwealth of Australia LSGC medal in 1902.*

1st type obv.

VALUE: £800–1200   *Miniature*   £220–330

2nd type obv.

1st and 2nd type rev.

257. NEW ZEALAND LONG AND EFFICIENT SERVICE MEDAL

Instituted: 1 January 1887.

Branch of Service: Volunteer and Permanent Militia Forces of New Zealand.

Ribbon: Originally plain crimson, but two white central stripes were added in 1917.

Metal: Silver.

Size: 36mm.

Description: (Obverse) an imperial crown on a cushion with crossed sword and sceptre and NZ below, within a wreath of oak-leaves (left) and wattle (right) and having four five-pointed stars, representing the constellation Southern Cross, spaced in the field; (reverse) inscribed FOR LONG AND EFFICIENT SERVICE. Plain ring suspension.

Comments: *Awarded for 16 years' continuous or 20 years' non-continuous service in the Volunteer and Permanent Militia Forces of New Zealand. It became obsolete in 1931 following the introduction of the LSGC (Military) medal with bar for New Zealand.*

VALUE: £100–150   *Miniature* £45–55

258. NEW ZEALAND VOLUNTEER SERVICE MEDAL

Instituted: 1902.

Branch of Service: Volunteer Forces, New Zealand.

Ribbon: Plain drab khaki.

Metal: Silver.

Size: 36mm

Description: (Obverse) a right-facing profile of King Edward VII with NEW ZEALAND VOLUNTEER round the top and 12 YEARS SERVICE MEDAL round the foot; (reverse) a kiwi surrounded by a wreath. Plain ring suspension.

Comments: *This rare silver medal (obsolete by 1912) was awarded for 12 years' service. Two reverse dies were used. In type I (1902–04) the kiwi's beak almost touches the ground, whereas in Type II (1905–12) there is a space between the tip of the beak and the ground. Only about 100 of Type I were produced, but 636 of Type II.*

VALUE: Type I   £250–350   *Miniature* £110–130
          Type II   £200–250

259. NEW ZEALAND TERRITORIAL SERVICE MEDAL

Instituted: 1912.

Branch of Service: Territorial Force, New Zealand.

Ribbon: Originally as above, but replaced in 1917 by a ribbon of dark khaki edged with crimson.

Metal: Silver.

Size: 36mm.

Description: (Obverse) left-facing bust of King George V in field marshal's uniform; (reverse) similar to the above.

Comments: *It replaced the foregoing on the formation of the Territorial Force on March 17, 1911, from which date the old Volunteer Force ceased to exist but became obsolete itself in 1931 when the Efficiency Medal with New Zealand bar was adopted.*

VALUE:
     George V   £80–100   *Miniature*   £35–55

261. ULSTER DEFENCE REGIMENT MEDAL

Instituted: 1982.
Branch of Service: Ulster Defence Regiment.
Ribbon: Dark green with a yellow central stripe edged in red.
Metal: Silver.
Size: 36mm.
Description: (Obverse) crowned head of Elizabeth II (B); (reverse) crowned harp and inscription ULSTER DEFENCE REGIMENT with a suspender of laurel leaves surmounted by a scroll bar bearing the regiment's initials.
Comments: *Awarded to part-time officers and men of the Ulster Defence Regiment with 12 years' continuous service since 1 April 1970. A bar for each additional six-year period is awarded. Officers are permitted to add the letters UD after their names. This medal is superseded by the Northern Ireland Home Service Medal (MYB 261B).*

VALUE:

Elizabeth II (B)	£350–450	*Miniature*	£20–25

261A. ULSTER DEFENCE REGIMENT MEDALLION

Instituted: 1987.
Branch of Service: Relatives of personnel of the Ulster Defence Regiment killed whilst on duty.
Ribbon: Dark green with a yellow central stripe edged in red, as MYB261.
Metal: Silver.
Size: 36mm.
Description: Uniface medal showing a crowned Irish harp flanked by sprays of shamrocks. Ring suspension. Ribbons of awards to widows and other female relatives mounted as a bow with a brooch fitment.
Comments: *Designed by Colour Sergeant Win Clark and struck by Spink & Son, it was commissioned by the Regiment for presentation to the families of UDR personnel killed during the conflict in Northern Ireland as a token of appreciation.*

VALUE: —

261B. NORTHERN IRELAND HOME SERVICE MEDAL

Instituted: 1992.
Branch of Service: Part time members of the Ulster Defence Regiment and the Royal Irish Regiment.
Ribbon: Dark green with a light blue central stripe.
Metal: Silver.
Size: 36mm.
Description: (Obverse) crowned head of Elizabeth II (B); (reverse) a scroll bearing the inscription FOR HOME SERVICE IN NORTHERN IRELAND surmounted by a crown, superimposed on a design of flax with harps below.
Comments: *Awarded to part-time officers and men of the Ulster Defence Regiment or Royal Irish Regiment with 12 years' continuous efficient service after 1 July 1980. A bar for each additional six-year period is awarded. Next of kin of eligible deceased members can apply for the medal.*

VALUE: £300–400　　　*Miniature* £15–20

262. CADET FORCES MEDAL

Instituted: February 1, 1950.

Branch of Service: Cadet Forces.

Ribbon: A broad green central band bordered by thin red stripes flanked by a dark blue stripe (left) and light blue stripe (right, with yellow edges.

Metal: Cupro-nickel.

Size: 36mm.

Description: (Obverse) the effigy of the reigning monarch; (reverse) a hand holding aloft the torch of learning with the words "THE CADET FORCES MEDAL" around. Medals are named to recipients on the rim, in impressed capitals.

Comments: *Awarded to uniformed volunteers of the Cadet Forces in recognition of long and exemplary service in the Cadet Forces. Service may reckon from September 3, 1926, with service between September 3, 1939 and September 2, 1945 counting two-fold. Until June 30, 1971, officers and non-commissioned officers only were awarded the medal, the qualification for which was 12 years' continuous service, with clasps for successive periods of 12 years' service. From July 1, 1971, cadet service over the age of 18 years of age could reckon for the medal and the qualifying period for the clasp was reduced to eight years, which need not be continuous. With effect from April 1, 1999, the qualifying period for the clasp was reduced to six years. Awards are now governed by the Royal Warrant dated November 19, 2001 which consolidates amendments to earlier Royal Warrants and extends the qualification and recognition provisions. Under JSP814 (1st edition) 2006, service for the medal did not have to be continuous; but JSP814 (final dated 31 March 2011) now states service to be continuous. Service for the clasp does not need to be continuous.*

The maximum cadet service is four years; other reckonable services includes the UK Volunteer Services, OTC, University Royal Naval Units and University Air Squadrons (maximum three years and not counted towards the Volunteer Services Medal or its predecessors), and Regular forces (maximum three years and not counted towards a long service award). When the ribbon alone is worn, the award of each clasp is denoted by a silver rose. To denote service beyond the award of three clasps, the following are to be worn: Four clasps—one gold rose, Five clasps—one gold rose and one silver rose, Six clasps—one gold rose and two silver roses, Seven clasps—two gold roses. Award of the medal and clasp is promulgated in the London Gazette. Issued to those qualifying in New Zealand under the terms of a Royal Warrant dated February 1, 1950 and the New Zealand Cadet Forces Medal Regulations dated January 13, 1954.

VALUE:		Miniature
George VI (C)	£100–125	£10–12
Elizabeth II (A1, BRITT: OMN)	£125–150	£10–12
Elizabeth II (A, DEI GRATIA)	£85–125	£10–12

263. ROYAL OBSERVER CORPS MEDAL

Long Service bar.

Instituted: 31 January 1950 but not awarded until 1953.

Branch of Service: Royal Observer Corps.

Ribbon: Pale blue with a broad central silver-grey stripe edged in dark blue.

Metal: Cupro-nickel.

Size: 36mm.

Description: (Obverse) effigy of the reigning monarch; (reverse) an artist's impression of a coast-watcher of Elizabethan times, holding a torch aloft alongside a signal fire, with other signal fires on hilltops in the background with the words "ROYAL OBSERVER CORPS MEDAL" around and the words "FOREWARNED IS FOREARMED" on a scroll below The medal hangs from a suspender of an eagle with outstretched wings. An obverse die with the effigy of George VI was engraved, but no medals were struck from it.

Comments: *Awarded to part-time officers and observers who have completed 12 years' satisfactory service and full-time members for 24 years service. A bar is awarded for each additional 12-year period. Home Office scientific officers and other non Royal Observer Corps members of the United Kingdom Warning and Monitoring Organisation were eligible for the Civil Defence Medal (no. 264) until being stood down on September 30, 1991. This entailed serving for 15 years alongside ROC members who received their own medal for 12 years' service.*

VALUE:		Miniature
Elizabeth II (B)	£300–350	—
Elizabeth II (C)	£250–300	£20–30

264. CIVIL DEFENCE LONG SERVICE MEDAL

Instituted: March 1961.
Branch of Service: Civil Defence and other auxiliary forces.
Ribbon: Blue bearing three narrow stripes of yellow, red and green.
Metal: Cupro-nickel.
Size: Height 38mm; max. width 32mm.
Description: (Obverse) the effigy of the reigning monarch; (reverse) two types. Both featured three shields flanked by sprigs of acorns and oak leaves. The upper shield in both cases is inscribed CD but the initials on the lower shields differ, according to the organisations in Britain and Northern Ireland respectively—AFS and NHSR (British) or AFRS and HSR (Northern Ireland). After 1968 a new reverse was used incorporating the words CIVIL DEFENCE and LONG SERVICE.
Comments: *Issued unnamed to those who had completed 15 years service in a wide range of Civil Defence organisations. It was extended to Civil Defence personnel in Gibraltar, Hong Kong and Malta in 1965. The medal became obsolescent in the UK after the Civil Defence Corps and Auxiliary Fire Service were disbanded in 1968, but members of the CD Corps in the Isle of Man and Channel Islands are still eligible. A bar is available for additional 15 years' service*

British reverse.

VALUE:		Miniature
British version	£35–50	£15–25
Northern Ireland version	£85–120	£110–160
Gibraltar	£100–125	
Hong Kong	£100–125	
Malta	£100–125	
Post 1968 reverse	£75–100	

Northern Ireland reverse.

Post-1968 reverse

264A. AMBULANCE SERVICE (EMERGENCY DUTIES) LONG SERVICE AND GOOD CONDUCT MEDAL

Instituted: 5 July 1996.

Branch of Service: Ambulance services in England and Wales, Scotland, Northern Ireland, the Isle of Man and the Channel Islands.

Ribbon: Green with, on either side, a white stripe on which is superimposed a narrow green stripe.

Metal: Cupro-nickel.

Size: 36mm.

Description: (Obverse) crowned effigy of the reigning monarch, ELIZABETH II DEI GRATIA REGINA F.D.; (reverse) FOR EXEMPLARY SERVICE round the top, with either the emblem of the Ambulance Services of Scotland or the remainder of the United Kingdom in the centre below. Fitted with a ring for suspension.

Comments: *Both full- and part-time members of Ambulance Services are eligible provided they are employed on emergency duties. Service prior to 1974 in ambulance services maintained by local authorities counts. For paramedics and technicians the qualifying service is 20 years. For ambulance officers and other management grades, at least seven of their 20 years' service must have been spent on emergency duties.*

VALUE:	£150–175	*Miniature*	£12–20

264B. ASSOCIATION OF CHIEF AMBULANCE OFFICERS SERVICE MEDAL

Instituted: —.

Branch of Service: Members of the Ambulance Service.

Ribbon: Dark green with twin central red stripe edged with yellow.

Metal: Bronze.

Size: 36mm.

Description: (Obverse) symbol of the Association (caduceus on a wheel) surrounded by ASSOCIATION OF CHIEF AMBULANCE OFFICERS; (reverse) FOR SERVICE surrounded by a laurel wreath.

Comments: *Issued by members of the Association to ambulance personnel who have performed exemplary service.*

VALUE:	£75–85	*Miniature*	£55–65

264C. ROYAL FLEET AUXILIARY SERVICE MEDAL

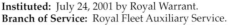

Instituted: July 24, 2001 by Royal Warrant.
Branch of Service: Royal Fleet Auxiliary Service.
Ribbon: Central band of watered royal blue flanked by narrow stripes of cypress green, yellow-gold and purple.
Metal: Cupro-nickel.
Size: 38mm.
Description: (Obverse) the crowned effigy of the Queen; (reverse) the badge of the Royal Fleet Auxiliary Service with the inscription ROYAL FLEET AUXILIARY — FOR LONG SERVICE.
Comments: *The medal is awarded to all officers, petty officers and ratings of the RFA after 20 years' service. Clasps will be granted for a further 10 years' service. The recipient's name and rank, together with date of qualification, are impressed on the rim. The first awards of this medal were made to three petty officers in 2003, a further 400 personnel being eligible.*

VALUE: £200–250   *Miniature*   £12–15

265. (WOMEN'S) ROYAL VOLUNTARY SERVICE LONG SERVICE MEDAL

Instituted: 1961.
Branch of Service: Women's Royal Voluntary Service.
Ribbon: Dark green with twin white stripes towards the end and broad red edges.
Metal: Cupro-nickel.
Size: 36mm.
Description: (Obverse) the interlocking initials WVS in an ivy wreath; (reverse) three flowers, inscribed SERVICE BEYOND SELF round the circumference.
Comments: *Issued unnamed and awarded for 15 years' service. Bars for additional 15 year periods are awarded. Although the majority of the 35,000 (approx.) medals have been awarded to women there has also been a substantial number of male recipients. Since 2013 the WRVS has simply been known as the Royal Voluntery Service. The medal design remains the same.*

VALUE: £15–20   *Miniature*   £35–45

266. VOLUNTARY MEDICAL SERVICE MEDAL

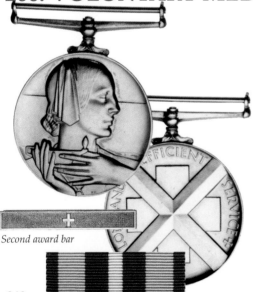

Second award bar

Instituted: 1932.
Branch of Service: British Red Cross Society and the St Andrew's Ambulance Corps (Scotland).
Ribbon: Red with yellow and white stripes.
Metal: Originally struck in silver but since the 1960s it has been produced in cupro-nickel.
Size: 36mm.
Description: (Obverse) the veiled bust of a female holding an oil lamp, symbolic of Florence Nightingale; (reverse) the crosses of Geneva and St Andrew, with the inscription FOR LONG AND EFFICIENT SERVICE.
Comments: *Awarded for 15 years' service, with a bar for each additional period of five years. The service bars are embellished with a Geneva cross or saltire (St Andrew) cross, whichever is the more appropriate.*

VALUE:		*Miniature*
Silver	£25–35	
Cupro-nickel	£15–20	£15–25

267. SERVICE MEDAL OF THE ORDER OF ST JOHN

Original type obverse.

Service Medal in Gold reverse.

Instituted: 1898.

Branch of Service: The Most Venerable Order of the Hospital of St John of Jerusalem.

Ribbon: Three black and two white stripes of equal width. The ribbon for the Service Medal in Gold has a central narrow gold stripe dividing the central black stripe.

Metal: Silver (1898-1947), silvered base metal (1947-60), silvered cupro-nickel (1960-66) and rhodium-plated cupro-nickel (since 1966). The service Medal in Gold is silver-gilt.

Size: 38mm.

Description: (Obverse) an unusual veiled bust of Queen Victoria with her name and abbreviated Latin titles round the circumference. A new obverse was adopted in 1960 with a slightly reduced effigy of Queen Victoria and less ornate lettering. (Reverse) the royal arms within a garter surrounded by four circles containing the imperial crown, the Prince of Wales's feathers and the armorial bearings of the Order and of HRH the Prince of Wales, the first Sub-Prior of the Order. Between the circles are sprigs of St John's Wort. Round the circumference is the Latin inscription MAGNUS PRIORATUS ORDINIS HOSPITALIS SANCTI JOHANNIS JERUSALEM IN ANGLIA in Old English lettering. Since 2019, in keeping with the new Service Medal in Gold, the wording is now in English reading THE MOST VENERABLE ORDER OF THE HOSPITAL OF ST JOHN OF JERUSALEM FOR SERVICE. In Canada the wording in Latin reads VENERABILISSIMI ORDNIS HOSPITALIS SANCTI JOHANNIS HIEROSOLYMITANI-PRO OFFICIO to avoid problems with the dual language in that country.

Comments: *Originally awarded for 15 years' service to the Order in the United Kingdom (12 in the Dominions and 10 in the Colonies) but the qualifying period changed to 12 years and has now been reduced to 10 years' service. The medal was designed in 1898 and first presented in 1900. A silver bar was introduced in 1911 for additional periods of five years. From then until 1924 the bar was inscribed 5 YEARS SERVICE but then a design showing a Maltese cross flanked by sprays of St John's Wort was substituted. Bars for 27 years' and each additional five years' service were subsequently instituted in silver-gilt. In 2004 a gilt laurel leaf was added to the ribbon of the Service Medal for 52 years' service in place of four gilt clasps. In 2019 a new "Gold" award was instituted—the "Service Medal in Gold"—to mark 50 years' service and, as with the silver award, clasps are added for each five years' service—these clasps are gilt. When the ribbon alone is worn a small Maltese cross is attached for each five years' service: silver for the Service Medal and gilt for the Service Medal in Gold. Suspension by a ring was changed in 1913 to a straight bar suspender. The medal is worn on the left breast.*

Although awarded for long service this medal should not be solely referred to as a long service award as it can also be awarded for conspicuous service—when so awarded it was distinguished by the addition of a silver palm leaf on the ribbon. The silver palm was discontinued in 1949, after only three years. It is believed to be the only medal still issued bearing the bust of Queen Victoria (the effigy was first sculpted by HRH Princess Louise, daughter of Queen Victoria).

Laurel leaf for 52 years' service

5-year cross

Palm leaf for conspicuous service

Voluntary Aid Detachment

Military Hospital Reserve

VAD (or MHR) now obsolete. This brooch bar can sometimes be found on the VMS Medal (MYB 266) or could be worn alone

VALUE:

		Miniature
Silver, ring suspension	£35–50	£25–30
Silver, straight bar suspension	£30–45	£15–20
Base metal, first obverse	£20–25	£10–12
Base metal, second obverse	£20–25	£10–12
Silver-gilt	—	£15–20

Ribbon bars:

5-year bar (second type)

5-year bar (silver-gilt) type

Illustrations by M. Thomas.

267A. DIPLOMATIC SERVICE MEDAL

Instituted: —
Branch of Service: Royal Diplomatic Service.
Ribbon: Garter Blue (in a bow).
Metal: Silver-gilt.
Size: 39mmx60mm.
Description: (Obverse) Royal cypher within a crowned oval frame bearing the words HER MAJESTY'S DIPLOMATIC SERVICE; (reverse) plain.
Comments: *This medal was pointed out to us by a reader with the one in his collection having apparently been awarded to an erstwhile sergeant in the Royal Tank Regiment who later went on to spend 25 years in the Diplomatic Service. Little is known about its criteria or numbers awarded. We would be pleased to learn more if any reader can help.*

VALUE: £2500–3500

268. ROYAL AIR FORCE LONG SERVICE AND GOOD CONDUCT MEDAL

Instituted: 1 July 1919.
Branch of Service: Royal Air Force.
Ribbon: Dark blue and maroon with white edges.
Metal: Silver.
Size: 36mm.
Description: (Obverse) the effigy of the reigning monarch; (reverse) the RAF eagle and crown insignia.
Comments: *Awarded to NCOs and other ranks of the RAF for 18 years' exemplary service, reduced in 1977 to 15 years. Provision for bars for further periods of service was made from 1944 onwards. A clasp is now awarded for every 10 years served and in keeping with the other armed services the medal is awarded to all ranks. Before 1945 conduct below the required standard was permitted to count if the airman had displayed higher exemplary conduct against the enemy, gallantry or some special service in times of emergency. From 1944 any prior service in the Navy and Army could be counted. Prior to this date only up to four years' service could be counted. In 1947 officers became eligible for the medal provided they had had at least 12 years' service in the ranks. Recipients' details are inscribed on the rim. Since 2016 it has been awarded to all regular members of the RAF including officers who have never served in the ranks. The later issues are of silver-plated base metal.*

VALUE:		Miniature			Miniature
George V (E)	£120–150	£25–35	Elizabeth II (B)	£60–65	£25–35
George VI (D)	£85–100	£25–35	Elizabeth II (C)	£60–65	£25–35
George VI (E)	£85–100	£25–35	RCAF recipient	£300–400	

269. ROYAL AIR FORCE LEVIES LONG SERVICE AND GOOD CONDUCT MEDAL

Instituted: 1948.

Branch of Service: RAF Levies, Iraq.

Ribbon: As the preceding.

Metal: Silver.

Size: 36mm.

Description: Similar to the previous type but was fitted with a clasp inscribed ROYAL AIR FORCE LEVIES IRAQ.

Comments: *Awarded to the locally commissioned officers and men of the RAF Levies in Iraq, for 18 years' service (the last 12 to be of an exemplary nature). The Iraq Levies were raised in 1919 and became the responsibility of the RAF in 1922, maintaining law and order by means of light aircraft and armoured cars. The force was disbanded in 1955 when the RAF withdrew from Iraq. 309 medals were issued, 115 to officers and 194 to airmen.*

VALUE:

George VI (E)	£800–1000
Elizabeth II (B)	£900–1100
Elizabeth II (C)	£900–1100

270. AIR EFFICIENCY AWARD

Instituted: September 1942

Branch of Service: AAF, RAAF and RAFVR.

Ribbon: Green with two light blue stripes towards the centre.

Metal: Silver.

Size: Height 38mm; max. width 32mm.

Description: An oval medal with a suspender in the form of an eagle with wings outspread. (Obverse) the effigy of the reigning monarch; (reverse) inscribed AIR EFFICIENCY AWARD in three lines.

Comments: *Granted for 10 years' efficient service in the Auxiliary and Volunteer Air Forces of the United Kingdom and Commonwealth. A bar was awarded for a further ten-year period. Officers are permitted to add the letters AE after their name. This award was replaced in 2000 by the VRSM (No. 242A). Of the approximately 2,500 awarded 256 were to women.*

VALUE:

George VI (D)	£145–175
George VI (E)	£175–200
Elizabeth II (C)	£150–175
Miniature (all)	£25–35
Named to officers add £40	

Second award bar

271. POLICE LONG SERVICE AND GOOD CONDUCT MEDAL

Instituted: 14 June 1951.
Branch of Service: Police Forces.
Ribbon: Dark blue with twin white stripes towards each end.
Metal: Original issue cupro-nickel, now rhodium plated
Size: 36mm.
Description: The obverse of this medal bears the effigy of the reigning monarch while the reverse has the figure of Justice with scales in her left hand and a wreath in her right surrounded by the inscription 'FOR EXEMPLARY POLICE SERVICE'. The suspender is straight and found in both swivelling and non-swivelling formats
Comments: *Originally awarded to full-time regular police officers within any UK Constabulary for 22 years' service. However, following a national campaign by Warwickshire Police Officer Kenneth Fowler, supported by Chief Officers, the Police Federations and Members of Parliament, the award point of the medal was reduced to 20 years' service on 19 January 2010, bringing it in line with the Fire, Ambulance and Prison Long Service and Good Conduct Medals which are all awarded after 20 years' service. In 1956 this medal was extended to police officers serving in Australia, Papua New Guinea and Nauru. Australia however replaced this medal in 1976 with the National Medal.*

VALUE:

		Miniature
George VI (C)	£40–50	£25–35
Elizabeth II (A)	£40–50	£10–15
Elizabeth II (D)	£40–50	£10–15

272. SPECIAL CONSTABULARY LONG SERVICE MEDAL

Special Constabulary medal.

1956 Ulster Special Constabulary medal.

Long Service bar.

Instituted: 30 August 1919.
Branch of Service: Special Constabulary.
Ribbon: A broad red stripe in the centre flanked by black and white stripes.
Metal: Bronze.
Size: 32mm.
Description: (Obverse) the effigy of the reigning monarch; (reverse) a partial laurel wreath with a six-line text inscribed FOR FAITHFUL SERVICE IN THE SPECIAL CONSTABULARY. A second reverse was introduced in 1956 for 15 years' service in the Ulster Special Constabulary, the text being modified to permit the inclusion of the word ULSTER. A third type was introduced in 1982 for 15 years' service in the RUC Reserve and is thus inscribed but, with the name change, in 2001 a fourth type inscribed Police Reserve of Northern Ireland was issued.
Comments: *Awarded to all ranks in the Special Constabulary for 9 years' unpaid service, with more than 50 duties per annum. War service with at least 50 duties counted triple. A clasp inscribed THE GREAT WAR 1914–18 was awarded to those who qualified for the medal during that conflict. Bars inscribed LONG SERVICE, with the date, are awarded for additional ten-year periods (the NI bars are not dated). To qualify during the two world wars a special constable must have served without any pay for not less than three years, and during that period have performed at least 50 duties a year, and be recommended by a chief officer of police as willing and competent to discharge the duties of special constable as required, i.e. in both world wars service counts treble.*

VALUE:

		Miniature
George V (C)	£20–25	£10–12
With Great War 1914–18 clasp	£30–35	£15–20
George V (E)	£20–25	£10–12
George VI (D)	£20–25	£10–12
George VI (E)	£55–85	£15–20
Elizabeth II (B)	£55–85	£15–20
Elizabeth II (C)	£45–55	£10–12
Northern Ireland types	£250–300	£15–20

273. ROYAL ULSTER CONSTABULARY SERVICE MEDAL

Instituted: 1982.

Branch of Service: RUC and its Reserve.

Ribbon: Green, with narrow central stripes of red, black and dark blue. Following the award of the George Cross to the RUC the ribbon of this medal was modified to reflect the award. The colour of the GC ribbon is now indicated by two vertical blue stripes at the outer edges.

Metal: Cupro-nickel.

Size: 36mm.

Description: (Obverse) the effigy of Queen Elizabeth II; (reverse) the crowned harp insignia of the RUC with the words FOR SERVICE round the foot.

Comments: *Awarded for 18 months continuous service since 1 January 1971, but the award was made immediate on the recipient also being awarded a gallantry decoration or a Queen's commendation.*

VALUE:

Elizabeth II (D)	£200–250	*Miniature*	£10–15

Original ribbon.

Post-2001 ribbon.

273A. POLICE SERVICE OF NORTHERN IRELAND (PSNI) MEDAL

Instituted: 2020

Branch of Service: Police Service of Northern Ireland

Ribbon: Light blue with central dark green stripe

Metal: Cupro Nickel

Size: 36mm

Description: (Obverse) The effigy of the reigning monarch. The QEII version used the Jody Clark coinage profile, possibly the only UK medal to do so. (Reverse) The badge of the PSNI below the motto PRO MUNERIS (For Service) and above a wreath of shamrock and laurel.

Comments: *As part of the Good Friday Agreement of 1998 the Patten review of the following year recommended that the the Royal Ulster Constabulary was disbanded and replaced with the Police Service of Northern Ireland with emphasis on recruiting from both sides of the sectarian divide. The new badge, which appears on this medal, included symbols of the crown, harp and shamrock to represent all of Northern Ireland's inhabitants and it is worth noting that the word "Royal" was dropped from the new name. The PSNI Medal is awarded to all officers of the Police Service of Northern Ireland (PSNI) who have completed five years' service since 25 February 25, 2009. This was the date that the terrorist threat level was raised from "substantial" to "severe". Those whose service has been curtailed as a result of death, disability or injury caused whilst on active duty are also eligible.*

A similar award, without suspension, the Police Service of Northern Ireland Service Medallion, was instituted at the same time for all police staff who were not serving police officers.

VALUE: *Miniature*

Medal:	—	—
Medallion:	—	

274. COLONIAL POLICE LONG SERVICE MEDAL

Instituted: 1934.
Branch of Service: Colonial police forces.
Ribbon: Green centre bordered with white and broad blue stripes towards the edges.
Metal: Silver.
Size: 36mm.
Description: (Obverse) the effigy of the reigning monarch; (reverse) a police truncheon superimposed on a laurel wreath.
Comments: *Originally awarded to junior officers who had completed 18 years' exemplary service but latterly awarded to officers of all ranks who have the required service qualification. A bar is awarded on completing 25 years' service and a second bar after 30 years. These are represented on the ribbon bar in working dress by silver rosettes. The number (where applicable), rank and name as well as (for George VI and later issues) the relevant force in which the recipient is serving at the time of the award is engraved on the rim, often locally and therefore in a variety of styles.*

VALUE:		*Miniature*
George V (C)	£100–120	£25–35
George VI (B)	£85–100	£25–35
George VI (C)	£85–100	£25–35
Elizabeth II (A)	£85–100	£20–25
Elizabeth II (B)	£85–100	£20–25

274A. OVERSEAS TERRITORIES POLICE LONG SERVICE MEDAL

Following the renaming of this and other Colonial medals in 2012 this medal is now being issued with the inscription "Overseas Territories . . ." in place of "Colonial . . .". In all other respects this medal is identical to MYB 274 above.

275. COLONIAL SPECIAL CONSTABULARY LONG SERVICE MEDAL

Instituted: 1957.
Branch of Service: Colonial Special Constabulary.
Ribbon: Two thin white stripes on a broad green centre, with broad blue edges.
Metal: Silver.
Size: 36mm.
Description: (Obverse) the effigy of the reigning monarch; (reverse) the crowned royal cypher above the words FOR FAITHFUL SERVICE in a laurel wreath.
Comments: *Awarded for nine years' unpaid or 15 years' paid service in a colonial special constabulary. A bar is awarded for further ten-year periods Since June 2012 this medal has been renamed "Overseas Service . . .".*

VALUE:

Elizabeth II (A)	£250–300	*Miniature*	£25–35

276. CEYLON POLICE LONG SERVICE AND GOOD CONDUCT MEDAL (I)

Instituted: 1925.
Branch of Service: Ceylon Police.
Ribbon: Very similar to that of the Special Constabulary Long Service Medal—a broad red stripe in the centre flanked by black and white stripes.
Metal: Silver.
Size: 36mm.
Description: (Obverse) coinage profile of King George V by Sir Bertram Mackennal; (reverse) an elephant surmounted by a crown. Ring suspension.
Comments: *Awarded for 15 years' active service. It was superseded in 1934 by the Colonial Police Long Service Medal.*

VALUE:

George V (E)	£350–400	*Miniature*	£85–95

277. CEYLON POLICE LONG SERVICE AND GOOD CONDUCT MEDAL (II)

Instituted: 1950.
Branch of Service: Ceylon Police.
Ribbon: Dark blue edged with khaki, white and pale blue.
Metal: Cupro-nickel.
Size: 36mm.
Description: (Obverse) the effigy of the reigning monarch; (reverse) similar to the foregoing, but without the crown above the elephant, to permit the longer inscription CEYLON POLICE SERVICE. Straight bar suspender.
Comments: *Awarded for 18 years exemplary service. Bars for 25 and 30 years service were also awarded. It became obsolete when Ceylon (now Sri Lanka) became a republic in 1972.*

VALUE:

		Miniature
George VI (C)	£450–500	£35–45
Elizabeth II (A)	£400–450	£35–45

278. CEYLON POLICE MEDAL FOR MERIT

Instituted: 1950.
Branch of Service: Ceylon Police.
Ribbon: Broad central khaki stripe, flanked by narrow stripes of white, light blue and dark blue.
Metal: Silver.
Size: 36mm.
Description: (Obverse) the effigy of the reigning monarch; (reverse) an Indian elephant with the legend CEYLON POLICE SERVICE at the top and FOR MERIT at the foot.
Comments: *This medal replaced, within Ceylon, the Colonial Police Medal for Meritorious Service (no. 61). It was to be awarded for "valuable service characterised by resource and devotion to duty, including prolonged service marked by exceptional ability, merit and exemplary conduct". The number awarded each year not to exceed 10. Year of issue is included in the naming, e.g. "2/69" signifying the second award of 1969.The medal became obsolete when Ceylon (now Sri Lanka) became a republic in 1972.*

VALUE		Miniature
George VI	—	—
Elizabeth II	£400–500	£35–45

278A. CEYLON POLICE MEDAL FOR GALLANTRY

Instituted: 1950.
Branch of Service: Ceylon Police.
Ribbon: As for the Medal for Merit (above) but with the addition of a very narrow red stripe superimposed on the white stripes.
Metal: Silver.
Size: 36mm.
Description: Similar to the Medal of Merit (above) but reverse inscribed FOR GALLANTRY at the foot.
Comments: *The medal became obsolete when Ceylon (now Sri Lanka) became a republic in 1972.*

VALUE:		Miniature
George VI	—	£55–65
Elizabeth II	—	£55–65

279. CYPRUS MILITARY POLICE LONG SERVICE AND GOOD CONDUCT MEDAL

Instituted: October 1929.
Branch of Service: Cyprus Military Police.
Ribbon: Yellow, dark green and yellow in equal bands.
Metal: Silver.
Size: 36mm.
Description: (Obverse) King George V; (reverse) the title of the police round the circumference and the words LONG AND GOOD SERVICE in four lines across the middle.
Comments: *Awarded to those who had three good conduct badges, plus six years exemplary service since the award of the third badge, no more than four entries in the defaulters' book and a minimum of 15 years service. Officers who had been promoted from the ranks were also eligible. No more than 7 officers and 54 other ranks were awarded this medal during its brief life before it was superseded in 1934 by the Colonial Police Long Service Medal.*

VALUE:	£800–1000

279A. ROYAL FALKLAND ISLANDS POLICE JUBILEE MEDAL

Date: 1996
Branch of Service: Royal Falkland Islands Police
Ribbon: Green with a central blue stripe edged in white.
Metal: Silver.
Size: 36mm.
Description: (Obverse) Elizabeth II (A); (reverse) arms of the colony; ROYAL FALKLAND ISLANDS POLICE round top and double dated 1846-1996 round foot. Fitted with ring suspension and a brooch clasp at the top of the ribbon.
Comments: *Awarded to all officers serving in the Royal Falkland Islands Police on 15 October 1996. Only 27 medals were awarded.*

VALUE: £1000–1500

280. HONG KONG POLICE MEDAL FOR MERIT

Instituted: May 3, 1862.
Branch of Service: Hong Kong Police.
Ribbon: Various, according to class (see below).
Metal: Gold, silver or bronze.
Size: 36mm.
Description: (Obverse) the effigy of the reigning monarch; (reverse) inscribed HONG KONG POLICE FORCE FOR MERIT within a laurel wreath and beaded circle (with various slight modifications). Examples have been recorded with the effigy of Queen Victoria as on the Abyssinian and New Zealand Medals (MY123–124), and King George V types C and E.
Comment: *Exceptionally awarded in five different classes according to the length and type of service. The 1st Class medal was struck in gold and worn with a maroon (VC) ribbon, the 2nd Class in silver with a plain yellow ribbon, the 3rd Class in bronze with a central black stripe on the yellow ribbon, the 4th Class in bronze with two central black stripes in the yellow ribbon, and the 5th Class (confined to the Police Reserve) in bronze had a green ribbon with two black central stripes. The 4th Class was engraved on the reverse above the wreath. These medals were superseded in April 1937 by the Hong Kong Police Silver Medal, only four of which were awarded before it was replaced by the Colonial Police Medal for Meritorious Service 1938.*

VALUE:	1st class	2nd class	3rd class	4th class
Victoria	Rare	£600–700	£500–550	£500–550
Edward VII	Rare	Rare	Rare	Rare
George V (B)	Rare	£500–550	£450–550	£450–500
George V (C)	Rare	£500–550	£450–550	£450–500

Miniature (all, silver or bronze)   Rare

1st Class.	*2nd Class.*	*3rd Class.*	*4th Class.*

280A. HONG KONG DISTRICT WATCH FORCE MERIT MEDAL

Instituted: 1868.
Branch of Service: District Watch Force.
Ribbon: Very dark green with a central deep red stripe.
Metal: Silver or bronze.
Size: 31mm with a prominent rim.
Description: (Obverse) four Chinese characters "Great Britain Hong Kong" above a watchman's lamp, superimposed on a cutlass and police baton, with the Chinese characters for "District Watch Force" and "Medal" at the sides; (reverse) DISTRICT WATCHMEN'S FORCE FOR MERIT within a laurel wreath.
Comment: *While the Hong Kong Police was principally a mixed force of Europeans and Indians, operated in the business and higher class residential areas, and was paid for out of the colony's revenues, the District Watch Force was a purely Chinese organisation, raised by prominent citizens of the colony to patrol and police the Chinese parts of the city. Its members had statutory powers, were uniformed and were trained and functioned in the style of the old parish constables, rather than in the gendarmerie style of the Hong Kong Police which was colonial in nature and imposed on society rather than integrated with it. The District Watch Force ceased to function at the time of the Japanese invasion in 1941 and was not revived on liberation.*

VALUE: £650–700

280B. ROYAL HONG KONG POLICE COMMEMORATIVE MEDAL

Instituted: 1996.
Branch of Service: Royal Hong Kong Police.
Ribbon: Black, magenta and old gold.
Metal: Silver.
Size: 38mm.
Description: (Obverse) the RHKP crest; (reverse) crossed tipstaves inside a laurel wreath with the dates 1844 and 1997.
Comment: *The medal, approved by Commissioner Eddie Hui Ki On, is available on purchase (originally HK$1,000, about £80) to those who served in the Hong Kong Police (1844–1969) and the Royal Hong Kong Police (1969–97). Purchasers' details are often found privately engraved in bold upright capitals in a variety of formats. The medal, worn on the left breast, has the same status as the Royal Hong Kong Regiment Disbandment Medal (254A).*

VALUE: £150–200 *Miniature* £55–80

280C. ROYAL HONG KONG AUXILIARY POLICE COMMEMORATIVE MEDAL

Instituted: 1996.
Branch of Service: Royal Hong Kong Auxiliary Police.
Ribbon: Black, magenta and old gold.
Metal: Silver.
Size: 38mm.
Description: Similar to the above, but inscribed ROYAL HONG KONG AUXILIARY POLICE FORCE.
Comment: *Similar to the above this medal is available for purchase. Some 5,000 auxiliary policemen and women are eligible for the award.*

VALUE: £150–200 *Miniature* £55-80

280D. HONG KONG MILITARY SERVICE CORPS MEDAL

Instituted: 1997.
Branch of Service: Hong Kong Military Service Corps.
Ribbon: Red, with a central yellow stripe.
Metal: Silver.
Size: 36mm.
Description: (Obverse) a Chinese dragon on a scroll bearing the initials of the Corps. HONG KONG MILITARY SERVICE CORPS inscribed round the top and 1962-1997 at the foot; (reverse) the British royal arms with inscription round the top TO COMMEMORATE DISBANDMENT and the date 31 March 1997 at the foot.
Comments: *The Military Service Corps was a unit formed in 1962 for defence of the Crown Colony and recruited locally to serve alongside and in support of the British Army. Members of the Corps were presented with this medal following its disbandment prior to the return of Hong Kong to China. A small number were also presented to previous commanding officers.*

VALUE: £100–120

281. HONG KONG ROYAL NAVAL DOCKYARD POLICE LONG SERVICE MEDAL

Instituted: 1920.
Branch of Service: Hong Kong Royal Naval Dockyard Police.
Ribbon: Yellow with two royal blue stripes towards the centre.
Metal: Gilt bronze or silver.
Size: 31mm.
Description: (Obverse) the effigy of the reigning monarch; (reverse) the title of the Police within a laurel wreath. Ring suspension (two sizes).
Comments: *Awarded for 15 years service. Although the Dockyard closed in 1961 men who transferred to other police divisions continued to be awarded the medal up to 1973. About 280 medals in all were issued.*

VALUE:		*Miniature*
George V (E)	£400–500	£110–160
George VI (C)	£400–500	£110–160
George VI (D)	£400–500	£110–160
Elizabeth II (C)	£400–500	£110–160

281A. HONG KONG DISCIPLINED SERVICES MEDAL

Instituted: 1986.
Branch of Service: Hong Kong Customs & Excise and Immigration Service.
Ribbon: Green bordered by vertical stripes of dark blue with a strip of sky blue at each edge.
Metal: Silver.
Size: 36mm.
Description: (Obverse) crowned effigy of Queen Elizabeth II (B); (reverse) armorial bearings of Hong Kong, with the inscription "For Long Service and Good Conduct".
Clasps: Awarded after 25 and 30 years, denoted by silver rosettes on riband in working dress.
Comments: *Awarded after 18 years continuous service. Engraved with name and rank on rim. Some 1,739 medals were awarded between 1987 and the return of Hong Kong to China on June 30, 1997. No other long service medal to Customs officers has been awarded in the British system.*

VALUE:	*Customs*	*Immigration*
Medal	£450–£50	£500–£550
1st clasp	£500–£550	£600–£650
2nd clasp	£600–£650	Unique

253

281B. TIENTSIN BRITISH EMERGENCY CORPS MEDAL

Instituted: —
Branch of Service: British Municipal Emergency Corps.
Ribbon: Buff with a broad central white stripe.
Metal: Silver.
Size: 36mm.
Description: (Obverse) the arms of the colony supported by a sailor and a Chinese worker surrounded by the words TIENTSIN BRITISH MUNICIPAL EMERGENCY CORPS; (reverse) a wreath surrounding a plain panel engraved FOR LONG SERVICE in three lines, with maker's name in small lettering below: STERLING / ARNOLD.
Comments: *The British Emergency Corps was presumably a paramilitary unit recruited locally. Little is known about these medals or the unit but obviously they were awarded for long service.*

VALUE: £175–225

281C. JERSEY HONORARY POLICE LONG SERVICE AND GOOD CONDUCT MEDAL

Instituted: 2014.
Branch of Service: Jersey Police.
Ribbon: Orange with narrow stripes of white, blue and yellow each side.
Metal: Silver.
Size: 36mm.
Description: (Obverse) the effigy of the reigning monarch; (reverse) an outline map of Jersey with the shield of Jersey superimposed on three ceremonial maces with HONORARY POLICE LONG SERVICE JERSEY round the circumference.
Comments: *Awarded to Honorary police officers (Centeniers, Vingteniers and Constable Officers) for 12 years service. A bar will be added for every nine years extra service.*

VALUE: £150–200   *Miniature* £12–15

282. MALTA POLICE LONG SERVICE AND GOOD CONDUCT MEDAL

Instituted: 1921.
Branch of Service: Malta Police.
Ribbon: Dark blue with a narrow central silver stripe.
Metal: Silver.
Size: 36mm.
Description: (Obverse) the effigy of King George V; (reverse) an eight-pointed Maltese cross in a laurel wreath with the title of the service and FOR LONG SERVICE AND GOOD CONDUCT round the circumference.
Comments: *Awarded to sergeants and constables with 18 years exemplary service. Officers who had had 18 years in the ranks were also eligible for the award. It was superseded by the Colonial Police Long Service Medal in 1934. No more than 112 medals were awarded, although only 99 names were published in the Police Commissioner's Annual Reports and in the Malta Gazette.*

VALUE:		*Miniature*
George V (E)	£400–500	£110–130
George V (C)	£400–500	£110–130

282A. MAURITIUS POLICE LONG SERVICE AND GOOD CONDUCT MEDAL: I

Instituted: —.

Branch of Service: Mauritius Police.

Ribbon: Three types: (a) 36mm half black, half white; (b) 33mm white with a broad royal blue central stripe; (c) blue with two narrow white stripes towards the edges.

Metal: Bronze.

Size: Oval, 40x33mm or 39x31mm.

Description: (Obverse) crown surmounting crossed tipstaves with the motto PAX NOBISCUM (Peace be with us) and the legend POLICE DE-PARTMENT round the top and MAURITIUS at the foot; (reverse) palm fronds enclosing a three-line inscription FOR GOOD CONDUCT. Fitted with a ring for suspension. Medals with 33mm ribbon fitted at top with a pin brooch by Hunt & Roskill.

Comment: *It is believed that the different ribbons indicated different periods of service, but confirmation is sought. It is presumed that this medal was superseded by no. 282B.*

VALUE:	£200–250	Miniature	£80–110

First type ribbon.

282B. MAURITIUS POLICE LONG SERVICE AND GOOD CONDUCT MEDAL: II

Instituted: —.

Branch of Service: Mauritius Police

Ribbon: Green centre flanked by white stripes and broad blue stripes towards the edges.

Metal: Silver.

Size: 36mm.

Description: (Obverse) the effigy of Queen Elizabeth II; (reverse) police truncheon on a laurel wreath.

Comments: *This medal is identical to the Colonial Police Long Service Medal (no. 274) except that the inscription substituted the name MAURITIUS for COLONIAL. It has been recorded in a medal group of 1976 and may have been introduced in or about 1968 when Mauritius attained independence.*

VALUE:	£200–250	Miniature	£18–20

283. NEW ZEALAND POLICE MEDAL

Instituted: 1886.

Branch of Service: New Zealand Police.

Ribbon: Originally plain crimson but in 1919 it was changed to a pattern very similar to that of the Permanent Forces of the Empire Beyond the Seas LSGC medal (no. 249),

Metal: Silver.

Size: 36mm.

Description: (Obverse) identical to that of the NZ Long & Efficient Service Medal (MY257); (reverse) FOR LONG SERVICE AND GOOD CONDUCT in four lines. Issued with a ring suspender until 1919 when a bar suspender was adopted. Clasps for each additional eight years service were introduced at the same time.

Comments: *Granted to sworn police staff for 14 years service. The clasp qualifying period was reduced to seven years in 1963. This medal was rendered obsolete with the introduction, in 1976, of the New Zealand Police Long Service and Good Conduct Medal (NZ26). It seems that from September 1901 this medal was also awarded to members of the NZ Prison Service and medals have WDR in front of recipient's name.*

First type obverse.

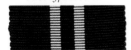

VALUE:		Miniature
Regalia obverse, bar suspension	£120–150	£25–35

Second type ribbon.

283A. SEYCHELLES POLICE LONG SERVICE AND GOOD CONDUCT MEDAL

Instituted: —.
Branch of Service: Seychelles Police.
Ribbon: Crimson.
Metal: Bronze.
Size: Oval, 40x33mm.
Description: (Obverse) crown surmounting crossed tipstaves with legend POLICE DEPARTMENT round the top and SEYCHELLES at the foot; (reverse) palm fronds enclosing a three-line inscription FOR GOOD CONDUCT. Fitted with a ring for suspension.
Comments: *This medal is similar to the Mauritius Police Medal (282A) and it is presumed that this medal also became obsolete on the introduction of the Colonial Police Long Service Medal in 1934. Details of qualifying terms of service and other regulations are sought.*

VALUE: £150–200

284. SOUTH AFRICA POLICE GOOD SERVICE MEDAL

Instituted: 1923.
Branch of Service: South Africa Police.
Ribbon: Broad black centre, flanked by white stripes and green borders.
Metal: Silver.
Size: 36mm.
Description: (Obverse) South African coat of arms; (reverse) bilingual inscriptions separated by a horizontal line. Three versions of the medal have been recorded. In the first version inscriptions were in English and Dutch, the latter reading POLITIE DIENST with VOOR TROUWE DIENST (for faithful service) on the reverse. In the second, introduced in 1932, Afrikaans replaced Dutch and read POLIESIE DIENS and VIR GETROUE DIENS respectively. In the third version, current from 1951 to 1963, the Afrikaans was modified to read POLISIEDIENS and VIR TROUE DIENS.
Comments: *Awarded to other ranks for 18 years exemplary service or for service of a gallant or particularly distinguished character. In the latter instance a bar inscribed MERIT-VERDIENSTE was awarded. The medal was replaced by the South African Medal for Faithful Service.*

VALUE:		
	1st type	£35–40
	2nd type	£30–35
	3rd type	£25–30
	Miniature	£15–20

285. SOUTH AFRICAN RAILWAYS AND HARBOUR POLICE LONG SERVICE AND GOOD CONDUCT MEDAL

Instituted: 1934.
Branch of Service: South African Railways and Harbour Police.
Ribbon: Similar to the Police Good Service Medal but with the colours reversed—a green central stripe flanked by white stripes and blue edges.
Metal: Silver.
Size: 36mm.
Description: (Obverse) the Union arms with S.A.R. & H. POLICE at the top and S.A.S.- EN HAWE POLISIE round the foot, but this was changed in 1953 to S.A.S. POLISIE at the top and S.A.R. POLICE at the foot. (Reverse) six line bilingual inscription.
Comments: *Awarded for 18 years unblemished service. Immediate awards for gallant or especially meritorious service earned a bar inscribed MERIT - VERDIENSTE (later with the words transposed). The medal was superseded in 1960 by the Railways Police Good Service Medal.*

VALUE: 1st type   £80–100   2nd type £75–100   *Miniature*   £35–45

286. FIRE BRIGADE LONG SERVICE MEDAL

Instituted: 1 June 1954.
Branch of Service: Fire Services.
Ribbon: Red with narrow yellow stripes towards the end and yellow borders.
Metal: Cupro-nickel.
Size: 36mm.
Description: (Obverse) the effigy of reigning monarch; (reverse) two firemen manning a hose. Ring suspension.
Comments: *Awarded to all ranks of local authority fire brigades, whether full- or part-time for 20 years exemplary service. Prior to the institution of this award most local authorities issued their own medals of individual design.*

VALUE:
    Elizabeth II   £45–55   *Miniature*   £12–14

286A. ASSOCIATION OF PROFESSIONAL FIRE BRIGADE OFFICERS LONG SERVICE MEDAL

Instituted: 1902.
Branch of Service: Association of Professional Fire Brigade Officers.
Ribbon: 1902–11 Orange red with narrow yellow stripe near each edge; thereafter a red central stripe flanked by narrow white stripes and broad black edges (silver medal) or grey edges (bronze medal).
Metal: Silver or bronze.
Size: 38mm.
Description: (Obverse) allegorical female figure carrying a palm frond and bestowing a laurel crown on a kneeling fireman; an early fire appliance in the background; blank exergue; (reverse) an oak wreath enclosing a four-line inscription ASSOCIATION OF PROFESSIONAL FIRE BRIGADE OFFICERS FOR LONG SERVICE. Fitted with a swivelling bar suspension.
Comments: *The medal in silver was awarded to professional fire brigade officers for a minimum of 10 years full time service and in bronze for five years, with extra clasps for further service. Engraved on the rim with the rank and name of the officer, together with the year of the award.*

VALUE: Silver £45–55   Bronze £40–50

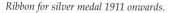

Ribbon for silver medal 1911 onwards.

286AB. NATIONAL FIRE BRIGADES UNION MEDAL

Instituted: 1895.
Branch of Service: Fire Services.
Ribbon: Mauve (originally with a narrow white central stripe for 20 years' service).
Metal: Silver or bronze.
Size: 38mm.
Description: (Obverse) similar to 286AA but with NATIONAL FIRE BRIGADES UNION round the central motif; (reverse) LONG SERVICE in minuscule lettering inside an oak wreath with space in the centre for the recipient's name. The issue number is impressed on the rim. Fitted with a suspension bar and a brooch bar denoting length of service.
Comments: *The medal in silver was awarded to fire brigade officers for a minimum of 20 years' full time service and in bronze for 10 years' service. Often engraved on the rim with the rank and name of the officer and the medal roll number. When the NFBU became the NFBA in 1918 this medal was replaced by no. 286AA.*

VALUE: Silver £50–75   Bronze £35–55

286AA. NATIONAL FIRE BRIGADES ASSOCIATION LONG SERVICE MEDAL

Instituted: 1918
Branch of Service: Fire Services.
Ribbon: Red with a central dark blue stripe flanked by very thin yellow stripes.
Metal: Silver or bronze.
Size: 38mm.
Description: (Obverse) badge of the Association: a wreathed flag within a circle surmounted by a fireman's helmet and surrounded by ladders and hoses inscribed NATIONAL FIRE BRIGADES ASSOCIATION round the central motif; (reverse) LONG SERVICE in minuscule lettering inside an oak wreath with space in the centre for the recipient's name. Fitted with a plain ring for suspension from a broad bar suspender with a clasp bearing the years of service.
Comments: *The medal in silver was awarded to fire brigade officers for a minimum of 20 years full time service and in bronze for lesser periods. Engraved on the rim with the rank and name of the officer, together with the year of the award and the roll number. The medal replaced no. 286AB.*

VALUE: Silver £45–65 Bronze £35–55

286B. BRITISH FIRE SERVICES ASSOCIATION MEDAL

Instituted: 1949.
Branch of Service: British Fire Services Association.
Ribbon: 33mm with a central silver-blue stripe flanked by black and white stripes and a broad red edge. However, the 10 year medal has a similar ribbon but with the white stripes to the edges to distinguish it from the 20 year ribbon.
Metal: Silver (20 years) or bronze (10 years).
Size: Originally 38mm, now 36mm.
Description: (Obverse) identical to the *obverse* of 286A, i.e allegorical female figure and fireman; (reverse) identical to the *obverse* of 286AA but with FOR LONG SERVICE & EFFICIENCY, round the central motif and THE BRITISH FIRE SERVICES ASSOCIATION round the circumference. The medal originally had an ornamental scrolled suspender with a bar inscribed BFSA, however it now has a simple straight suspender. The recipient's name and service number are engraved on the rim. A bar is added for each additional 5 years of service
Comments: *The British Fire Services Association was formed in 1949 by the amalgamation of the National Fire Brigades Association and the Professional Fire Brigades Association. This medal thus superseded 286A and 286AA. The silver medal of the BFSA was originally awarded for 15 years' service. Bars are awarded for holders of both medals on completion of each additional five years service. A similar medal but with a ribbon with central red stripe flanked with black and white stripes and broad silver-blue edges is awarded for Commendable Service and is not restricted to Association members.*

Original ribbon and current 20 year ribbon.

Current 10 year ribbon.

VALUE: Silver £45–65 *Miniature* £35–45
Bronze £25–35

It should be noted that a number of authorities also issued their own medals for long service and for meritorious service by members of their fire brigades. These medals are invariably well struck and are extremely collectable. However, as they are so many and so varied it is considered that these are outside of the scope of the MEDAL YEARBOOK. For a good example see the article "For Extraordinary Bravery: The London Fire Brigade Silver Medal" by Michael Pinchen in MEDAL NEWS, June/July 2015

286C. BRITISH FIRE SERVICE ASSOCIATION MERITORIOUS SERVICE MEDAL

Instituted: —
Branch of Service: British Fire Services Association.
Ribbon: Silver blue with a broad central stripe edged with thin black stripes *or* watered red with a central white stripe for gallantry.
Metal: Silver.
Size: 45mm x 36mm.
Description: A circular medallion contained within an upright oval laurel wreath suspended from an ornamental suspender with the initials B.F.S.A. on a scroll superimposed on a laurel spray. The central medallion depicts the Union Jack in a wreath with the inscription FOR MERITORIOUS SERVICE round the circumference. Reverse is plain apart from the maker's mark (foot) and the recipient's rank and name engraved on the medallion.
Comments: *Awarded for outstanding service and gallantry in fire-fighting operations. A similar medal inscribed FOR GALLANTRY is awarded for acts of outstanding gallantry.*

VALUE: Meritorious Service   £250–350
          Gallantry   —

287. COLONIAL FIRE BRIGADE LONG SERVICE MEDAL

Instituted: 1934.
Branch of Service: Colonial Fire Services.
Ribbon: Blue with twin green central stripes separated and bordered by thin white stripes.
Metal: Silver.
Size: 36mm.
Description: (Obverse) the effigy of the reigning monarch; (reverse) a fireman's helmet and axe. Ring suspension.
Comments: *Awarded to junior officers for 18 years full-time exemplary service. Bars are awarded for further periods of service. As from June 14, 2012 this medal was renamed the Overseas Territories Fire Brigade Medal.*

VALUE:		*Miniature*
George V (E)	£300–350	£35–45
George VI (D)	£300–350	£35–45
George VI (E)	£300–350	£35–45
Elizabeth II (C)	£300–350	£15–25
Elizabeth II (D)	£300–350	£15–25

288. CEYLON FIRE BRIGADE LONG SERVICE AND GOOD CONDUCT MEDAL

Instituted: 1950.
Branch of Service: Ceylon Fire Service.
Ribbon: Similar to the Police Medal (MYB277), but with a thin central white stripe through the dark blue band.
Metal: Silver.
Size: 36mm.
Description: As the Police Medal, but with a reverse inscribed CEYLON FIRE SERVICES.

VALUE:
    George VI   £300–400
    Elizabeth II   £300–400

288A. NORTHERN IRELAND PRISON SERVICE MEDAL

Instituted: 25 February 2002.

Branch of Service: Northern Ireland Prison Service.

Ribbon: Green with a broad navy blue band having at its centre a sky-blue stripe. Prison grade recipients have a ribbon with an additional thin red stripe bisecting the sky-blue stripe.

Metal: Cupro-nickel.

Size: 36mm.

Description: (Obverse) the crowned profile of the Queen with her name and titles; (reverse) a ring of flax flowers with three keys at the top, enclosing a four line inscription NORTHERN IRELAND PRISON SERVICE. The medal is fitted with a plain bar for suspension. The name of the recipient is stamped on the rim.

Comments: *The medal recognises "those who have rendered professional, committed and brave service as members of and by others in support of the Northern Ireland Prison Service". Up to July 2021 approximately 3,000 medals had been awarded which includes just 250 to civilians.*

VALUE:	Civilian issue	£200–250	*Miniature*	£20–25
	Prison service	£250–300		

288B. PRISON SERVICE MEDAL

Instituted: 17 December, 2010

Branch of Service: Operational grades in HM Prison Services of England and Wales, Northern Ireland, Jersey, Guernsey, Isle of Man and Scotland.

Ribbon: Black with twin stripes towards each end.

Metal: Cupro-nickel.

Size: 36mm.

Description: (Obverse) The effigy of the reigning monarch; (reverse) a period archway with the wording "For Exemplary Service", within the archway is the Royal cypher surmounted by a crown.

Comments: *Awarded to operational ranks of the Prison Service of the UK, after completing 20 years service on or after 29 April 2008. Naming includes rank, initials, surname and epaulette number, for uniformed ranks. Up to August 2019 almost 15,000 had been awarded.*

VALUE:	£140–160	*Miniature*	£12–15

288C. BELFAST HARBOUR POLICE MEDAL

Instituted: 1946.

Branch of Service: Belfast Harbour Police Service.

Ribbon: Deep blue with yellow edges.

Metal: Silver.

Size: 36mm.

Description: (Obverse) A mythical maritime scene—the seal of the Harbour Commissioners—with the words BELFAST HARBOUR COMMISSIONERS around; (reverse) the words WON BY across the centre above the recipient's details with BELFAST HARBOUR POLICE around the edge.

Comments: *The medal is primarily awarded for outstanding meritorious service or when awarded for gallantry a bronze anchor is worn on the ribbon. Since its inception only 16 medals have been awarded, three with the bronze anchor for gallantry, in addition four Harbour Chief Constables have received the medal for long service*

VALUE:	£300–500

289. COLONIAL PRISON SERVICE LONG SERVICE MEDAL

Instituted: October 1955.
Branch of Service: Colonial Prison Services.
Ribbon: Green with dark blue edges and a thin silver stripe in the centre.
Metal: Silver.
Size: 36mm.
Description: (Obverse) Queen Elizabeth II; (reverse) a phoenix rising from the flames and striving towards the sun.
Comments: *Awarded to ranks of Assistant Superintendent and below for 18 years exemplary service. Bars are awarded for further periods of 25 or 30 years service. As from June 14, 2012 this medal was renamed the Overseas Territories Prison Service Medal.*

VALUE:

Elizabeth II	£250–300	*Miniature*	£18–20

290. SOUTH AFRICAN PRISON SERVICE FAITHFUL SERVICE MEDAL

Instituted: September 1922.
Branch of Service: South African Prison Service.
Ribbon: Broad green centre flanked by white stripes and dark blue edges.
Metal: Silver.
Size: 36mm.
Description: (Obverse) arms of the Union of South Africa, of identical design to no. 284 except with GEVANGENIS DIENST round the top and PRISONS SERVICE round the foot. (Reverse) inscribed FOR FAITHFUL SERVICE across the upper half and in Dutch VOOR TROUWE DIENST across the lower half.
Comments: *Awarded to prison officers with 18 years exemplary service. Immediate awards for gallantry or exceptionally meritorious service received the Merit bar. In 1959 this medal was superseded by a version inscribed in Afrikaans.*

VALUE: £40–50　　　　*Miniature*　　　　£18–20

291. SOUTH AFRICA PRISONS DEPARTMENT FAITHFUL SERVICE MEDAL

Instituted: 1959.
Branch of Service: South African Prisons Department.
Ribbon: Broad dark blue centre flanked by white stripes and green edges.
Metal: Silver.
Size: 36mm.
Description: (Obverse) arms of the Union of South Africa, of identical design to no. 284 except with DEPARTEMENT VAN GEVANGENISSE round the top and PRISONS DEPARTMENT round the foot. (Reverse) VIR TROUE DIENS across the upper half and FOR FAITHFUL SERVICE across the lower half.
Comments: *The conditions of the award were similar to the previous medal, the main difference being the change of title and the substitution of Afrikaans inscriptions for Dutch. This medal was superseded by the Prisons Department Faithful Service Medal of the Republic of South Africa, instituted in 1965.*

VALUE: £35–50　　　　*Miniature*　　　　£35–45

291AA. NATO MERITORIOUS SERVICE MEDAL

Date: 1994.
Branch of Service: Personnel serving with NATO forces.
Ribbon: NATO blue with white stripes at the edges each having a vertical gold and silver thread.
Metal: Silver.
Size: 36mm.
Description: Obverse and reverse as for the other NATO medals.
Clasps: Silver bar inscribed MERITORIOUS.
Comments: *Awarded for exceptional service to NATO. It is now considered a Foreign award and can be authorised to be accepted and worn. If presented and not authorised it may be retained as a keepsake.*

VALUE: £45–55   *Miniature*   £10–15

291BB. EBOLA MEDAL FOR SERVICE IN WEST AFRICA

(now **MYB 395**—miscellaneous medals section)

291CC. THE NATIONAL CRIME AGENCY LONG SERVICE AND GOOD CONDUCT MEDAL

Instituted: March 2017
Branch of Service: Law Enforcement Agencies.
Ribbon: Central blue column with white edges and yellow stripes.
Metal: Cupronickel.
Size: 36mm
Description: The obverse shows the Ian Rank Broadley effigy of HM Queen Elizabeth II with the standard legend around the edge. The reverse has a crown above a portcullis (representing primacy and compassion) flanked by a griffin and a leopard (representing bravery, truth and valiance). The whole image is surrounded by the words "National Crime Agency" and "For Exemplary Service". Below this is an empty sphere.
Comments: *Awarded to full time members of those involved in law enforcement in the UK. Previous service in HM Revenue and Customs, the Serious Organised Crime Service and the National Crime Squad can count towards the award of this medal. The qualifying period is set at 20 aggregated years of service.*

VALUE: —   *Miniature*   £15–20

291DD. THE ROYAL NATIONAL LIFEBOAT INSTITUTION LONG SERVICE MEDAL

Instituted: 2020
Branch of Service: RNLI Volunteers.
Ribbon: Navy blue with red and yellow stripes at each edge representing the colours of a RNLI Lifeboat hull.
Metal: Cupronickel.
Size: 36mm
Description: (Obverse) the bust of William Hilary founder of the RNLI, surrounded by the name of the Institution; (reverse) a pair of arms, clasped one of which is emerging from the sea symbolising the rescue from water, be it sea, inland or flood by the RNLI operational teams. In the border is the wording WITH COURAGE NOTHING IS IMPOSSIBLE. Clasps: rectangular with a life preserver at each end and the number of years' service in raised lettering, i.e. 30 YEARS, 40 YEARS, 50 YEARS and currently to 60 YEARS.
Comments: *The medal is manufactured by Worcestershire Medal Service Ltd. and is named around the edge with the name of the recipient and year of qualification. It is available to all RNLI Volunteers for 20 years' service with clasps awarded at each additional 10-year period—see also MYB 365*

VALUE: —   *Miniature*   **£12–15**

CORONATION
Jubilee and other Royal medals

The first official royal medal was that cast by Henry Basse in 1547 for the accession of the young King Edward VI. It is known cast in gold or silver and is a curious example of bad design and poor workmanship for such an august occasion. No coronation medals were produced in honour of either Mary or Elizabeth I, but under James VI and I there was a small silver medal struck at the Royal Mint to mark the king's accession in 1603. These early medals celebrated the accession of the new sovereign, rather than the act of crowning itself.

To mark the coronation of James I, however, a small silver medalet was struck for distribution among the people who attended the ceremony, and this may be regarded as the forerunner of the modern series. This bore a Latin title signifying that James was Caesar Augustus of Britain and Heir to the Caesars. Thereafter medals in gold, silver or base metals were regularly struck in connection with the coronations of British monarchs. These were purely commemorative and not intended for wear, so they lack rings or bars for suspension.

By the early 19th century medals were being struck by many medallists for sale as souvenirs to the general public. At least fifteen different medals greeted the coronation of William IV in 1830 and more than twice that number appeared seven years later for the coronation of Queen Victoria. That paled into insignificance compared with the number produced for the coronation of Edward VII in 1902. On that occasion numerous civic authorities, organizations, industrial concerns and business firms issued medals in celebration — well over a hundred different medals and medalets were produced.

Sir George Frampton designed two silver medals, and one of these was mounted with a suspender and a blue ribbon with a thin white stripe and scarlet edges. This medal was distributed to notable personages attending the ceremony and established the precedent for subsequent coronation medals which came to be regarded as an award in recognition of services rendered in connection with the coronation, from the Earl Marshal of England to the private soldiers taking part in the ceremonial parades. In more recent times the coronation medal has even been given to people who were not present at the ceremony but who performed notable public service in the coronation year.

Other royal events have been commemorated by medals over the centuries. Royal weddings and the birth of the heir to the throne were regularly celebrated in this manner. Important anniversaries in long reigns have been the subject of numerous commemorative medals. The Golden Jubilee of George III in 1809-10, for example, resulted in over 30 different medals. Five times that number greeted the Golden Jubilee of Queen Victoria in 1887, but among them was an official medal intended for wear by those on whom it was conferred.

Even this, however, was not the first of the royal medals intended to be worn. This honour goes to a very large medal celebrating the proclamation of Victoria as Empress of India in 1877. Although fitted with a suspender bar and worn from a ribbon round the neck, it was not permitted for officers and men to wear this medal while in uniform. Later medals, however, were permitted to be worn when in uniform, but after other orders, decorations and campaign medals.

In the following listing (291A–291N) are the official Coronation Medals of James I, 1603, to Victoria, 1838. All were originally non-wearing, i.e. without suspension or ribbon, although some were later pierced or fitted with suspension for wearing. *Values of these are for silver medals only in VF (lower price) to EF condition.*

291A. JAMES I CORONATION MEDAL

Date: 1603.
Metal: Silver.
Size: 28mm.
Description: (Obverse) Bust of King James I facing right.
Legend: IAC: I: BRIT: CAE: AVG: HAE CAESArum cae
D.D. (Reverse) Lion rampant facing left. Legend: ECCE
PHA(R)OS POPVLIQ(VE) SALVS (Behold a lighthouse
and safety of the people)

VALUE: Silver   £1500–2500

291B. CHARLES I CORONATION MEDAL

Date: 1626.
Metal: Gold, silver.
Size: 28mm.
Designer: Nicholas Briot.
Description: Bust of Charles I facing right. Legend:
CAROLVS. I. DG. MAG. BRITAN. FRAN. ET. HIB. REX.
(Reverse) An arm issuing from a cloud and holding a
sword. Legend: DONEC. PAX. REDDITA. TERRIS. (As
long as Peace returns to the lands).

VALUE: Silver   £1200–1800

291C. CHARLES I CORONATION MEDAL

Date: 1633 (Scottish Coronation)
Metal: Gold, silver.
Size: 28mm.
Designer: Nicholas Briot.
Mintage: Gold (3), silver (Unknown)
Description: Bust of Charles I facing left. Legend: CAR-
OLVS DG SCOTIAE. ANGLIAE. FR. ET. HIB. REX.
(Reverse) A rose bush surmounted by a thistle. Legend:
HINC. NOSTRAE. CREVERE. ROSAE (From this our
roses abound). Exergue: CORON. 18 JVNII 1633

VALUE: Silver   £600–800

291D. CHARLES II CORONATION MEDAL

Date: 1651 (Scottish Coronation).
Metal: Gold, silver.
Size: 31mm.
Designer: Sir James Balfour.
Description: Bust of Charles II facing right. Legend:
CAROLVS.2. D.G. SCO. ANG. FRA. ET. HI. REX. FI.
DE. cor. i. ia. scon. 1651. (Reverse) Lion rampant facing
left, holding a thistle. Legend: NEMO. ME. IMPVNE.
LACESSET (No one provokes me with impunity).

VALUE: Silver   £3000–4000

291E. CHARLES II CORONATION MEDAL

Date: 1661 (English Coronation).
Metal: Gold, silver.
Size: 30mm.
Designer: Thomas Simon.
Description: Bust of Charles II facing right. Legend: CAROLVS .II.DG ANG. SCO. FR. ET. HI REX. (Reverse) Charles II, wearing royal robe, seated on throne facing left, holding sceptre. Angel hovering over him placing crown on his head. Legend: EVERSO. MISSVS. SVC-CVRRERE. SECLO. XXIII APR. 1661 (the times having been turned upside down, he has been sent to succour us)

VALUE: Silver £400–600

291F. JAMES II CORONATION MEDAL

Date: 1685.
Metal: Gold, silver, copper (?)
Size: 34mm.
Designer: John Roettier.
Mintage: Gold (200), silver (800), copper (Unknown).
Description: Bust of James II facing right, laureate. Legend: JACOBVS. II. D.G. ANG. SCO. FR. ET. HI. REX. (Reverse) Hand holding the crown above a laurel branch resting on a pillow. Legend: A. MILITARI. AD. REGIAM. (from soldiering to the palace). Exergue: INAVGVRAT. 23. AP. 1685.

VALUE: Silver £500–800

291G. WILLIAM AND MARY CORONATION MEDAL

Date: 1689.
Metal: Gold, silver, lead.
Size: 34mm.
Designer: John Roettier.
Mintage: Gold (515), silver (1,200), lead (Unknown).
Description: Conjoint busts of William and Mary facing right. Legend: GVLIELMVS. ET. MARIA. REX. ET. REGINA. (Reverse) Two-horse vehicle lower left, Jove in cloud above right. Legend: NE TOTVS ABSVMATVR. (let not the whole be consumed). Exergue: INAVGVRAT. II. AP. 1689.

VALUE: Silver £400–600

291H. ANNE CORONATION MEDAL

Date: 1702.
Metal: Gold, silver, base metal.
Size: 34mm.
Designer: John Croker.
Mintage: Gold (858), silver (1,200), base metal (Unknown).
Description: Bust of Queen Anne facing left. Legend: ANNA. D:G: MAG: BR. FR. ET. HIB: REGINA. (Reverse) Pallas Athene, left, with shield and lightning bolts, attacking recumbent monster, right. Legend: VICEM GERIT. ILLA. TONANTIS. Exergue: INAVGVRAT. XXIII. AP. MDCCII. (As, making sounds, she conducts herself).

VALUE: Silver   £300–400

291I. GEORGE I CORONATION MEDAL

Date: 1714.
Metal: Gold, silver, base metal.
Size: 34mm.
Designer: John Croker
Mintage: Gold (330), silver (1,200), base metal (Unknown).
Description: Bust of George I facing right. Legend: GEORGIVS. DG. MAG. BR. FR. ET. HIB. REX. (Reverse) Seated King, left, being crowned by Britannia standing right. Exergue: INAVGVRAT. XX. OCT. MDCCXIIII.

VALUE: Silver   £250–350

291J. GEORGE II CORONATION MEDAL

Date: 1727.
Metal: Gold, silver, base metal.
Size: 34mm.
Designer: John Croker
Mintage: Gold (238), silver (800), base metal (Unknown)
Description: Bust of George II facing left. Legend: GEORGIVS. II. D.G. MAG. BR. FR. ET. HIB. REX. (Reverse) King seated on throne, left being crowned by Britannia, standing right. Legend: VOLENTES. PER. POVLOS (through the will of the people) Exergue: CORON. XI. OCTOB. MDCCXXVII.

VALUE: Silver   £250–350

291K. GEORGE III CORONATION MEDAL

Date: 1761.
Metal: Gold, silver, bronze
Size: 34mm.
Designer: Lorenz Natter.
Mintage: Gold (858), silver (800), bronze (un-known)
Description: Bust of George III facing right. Legend: GEORGIVS. III. D.G. M. BRI. FRA. ET. HIB. REX. F.D. (Reverse) Britannia standing left, crowning King seated right. Legend: PATRIAE. OVANTI. (Crowned as the country rejoices). Exergue: CORONAT. XXII. SEPT. CI ƆI ƆCCLXI

VALUE: Silver £500–600

291L. GEORGE IV CORONATION MEDAL

Date: 1821.
Metal: Gold, silver, bronze
Size: 35mm.
Designer: Benedetto Pistrucci.
Mintage: Gold (1,060), silver (800), bronze (un-known, over 1,525)
Description: Bust of George IV, laureate, facing left. Legend: GEORGIVS IIII D.G. BRITAN-NIARUM REX F.D. (Reverse) Three standing ladies, left, facing seated King, right. Behind King stands angel holding crown above his head. Legend: PROPRIO JAM JURE ANIMO PATERNO (already by special right, inaugurat-ed in the spirit of his father). Exergue: INAU-GURATUS DIE JULII. XIX ANNO. MDCCXXI.
Comments: *A slightly smaller and thinner version of this medal was struck and pierced for suspension from a plain maroon ribbon. These medals are in-variably named to members of the Buckinghamshire Yeomanry Cavalry Hussars who took part in lining the route of the procession. This is believed to be the first coronation medal designed to be worn.*

VALUE: Silver £350–450

291M. WILLIAM IV CORONATION MEDAL

Date: 1831.
Metal: Gold, silver, bronze
Size: 34mm.
Designer: William Wyon
Mintage: Gold (1,000), silver (2,000), bronze (1,133)
Description: Head of William IV facing right. Legend: WILLIAM THE FOURTH CROWNED SEP: 8 1831 (Reverse) Head of Queen Adelaide facing right. Legend: ADELAIDE. QUEEN CONSORT. CROWNED SEP: 8 1831.

VALUE: Silver £400–500

291N. VICTORIA CORONATION MEDAL

Date: 1838.
Metal: Gold, silver, bronze.
Size: 36mm.
Designer: Benedetto Pistrucci.
Mintage: Gold (1,369), silver (2,209), bronze (1,871)
Description: Head of Queen Victoria facing left. Legend: VICTORIA D.G. BRITANNIARUM REGINA F.D. (Reverse) Three ladies symbolic of England, Scotland and Ireland, standing left, presenting crown to Queen, seated on a dais, right. A lion lies behind her chair. Legend: ERIMUS TIBI NOBILE REGNUM (We shall be a noble Kingdom to you). Exergue: INAUGURATA DIE JUNII XXVIII MDCCCXXXVIII.

VALUE: Silver £300–400

292. EMPRESS OF INDIA MEDAL

Date: 1877.
Ribbon: 42mm crimson edged in gold.
Metal: Gold or silver.
Size: 58mm.
Description: (Obverse) a left-facing bust of Queen Victoria wearing a veil and a coronet, her name and the date of her elevation being inscribed round the circumference. (Reverse) a broad zigzag border enclosing the words EMPRESS OF INDIA and its equivalent in Urdu and Hindi across the field.
Comments: *Issued to celebrate the proclamation of Victoria as Empress of India on 1 January 1877. It was awarded in gold to Indian princes and high-ranking British officials. Indian civilians and selected officers and men of the various British and Indian regiments serving in India at the time were awarded the silver medal. It was issued unnamed but many examples were subsequently engraved or impressed privately.*

VALUE:

		Miniature
Gold	£6000–10,000	£275–360
Silver	£650–850	£100–160

292A.   VISIT OF THE PRINCE OF WALES TO INDIA MEDAL 1875

(reduced)

Date: 1875–76.
Ribbon: 38mm plain white (gold), pale blue with white edges (silver).
Metal: Gold, silver or white metal with a silver crown.
Size: Oval 48mm x 77mm.
Description: (Obverse) left-facing effigy of the Prince of Wales (later King Edward VII) surrounded by a laurel wreath and surmounted by a crown fitted to a suspension ring; (reverse) Prince of Wales's emblem surrounded by the chain of the GCSI.
Comments: *A large oval medal was struck to commemorate the state visit of HRH the Prince of Wales to India. Some 48 medals were struck in gold, 165 in silver and an unknown number in white metal. The gold medals are impressed on the rim with a small numeral, and engraved with the recipient's name in block capitals. The medals were numbered and named in strict order of precedence. The silver medal has a frosted relief on a mirror table. 13 small silver badges were also presented. In addition a small silver medalet was issued to the crews of HMS* Renown *and* Terrible *and the Royal Yacht* Osborne, *with the initials A and E either side of the Prince of Wales' emblem and a reverse inscribed HRH ALBERT EDWARD PRINCE OF WALES INDIA 1875–76 (similar in style to no. 308B).*

VALUE:
Gold (48)	£7000–8000
Silver (165)	£1000–1500
White metal	£200–250
Silver badge (13)	Rare
Silver medalet	£100–150

293. JUBILEE MEDAL 1887

Date: 1887.
Ribbon: Broad central blue band with wide white stripes at the edges.
Metal: Gold, silver or bronze.
Size: 30mm.
Description: (Obverse) the bust of Queen Victoria by Sir Joseph Edgar Boehm; (reverse) an elaborate wreath in which are entwined the heraldic flowers of the United Kingdom. This encloses an eight-line inscription surmounted by a crown: IN COMMEMORATION OF THE 50th YEAR OF THE REIGN OF QUEEN VICTORIA 21 JUNE 1887. The reverse was designed by Clemens Emptmayer
Comments: *Struck to celebrate the 50th anniversary of Victoria's accession to the throne. The medal in gold was given to members of the Royal Family and their personal guests. The silver medal was given to members of the Royal Household, government ministers, senior officials, distinguished foreign visitors, naval and military officers involved in the Jubilee parade on 21 June 1887 and the captains of vessels taking part in the great Naval Review at Spithead. The bronze medal was given to selected NCOs and men who took part in the parade or the Spithead Review. All medals were issued unnamed with a ring for suspension. When the Diamond Jubilee was celebrated ten years later holders of the 1887 medal were given a clasp in the form of a cable entwined around the date 1897 and surmounted by an imperial crown. Twin loops at the ends enabled the clasp to be sewn on to the ribbon. Clasp sizes: 28mm (men), 22mm (ladies).*

VALUE:
	Without clasp	With clasp 1897	*Miniature*
Gold (133)	£1350–1500	Rare	£110–160
Silver (1,012)	£200–240	£300–350	£35–40 (add £30 for clasp)
Bronze (600)	£175–200	£300–350	£35–40 (add £30 for clasp)

294. JUBILEE (POLICE) MEDAL 1887

Date: 1887.
Ribbon: Plain dark blue.
Metal: Bronze.
Size: 36mm.
Description: (Obverse) the veiled profile of Queen Victoria; (reverse) a wreath surmounted by a crown and enclosing the inscription: JUBILEE OF HER MAJESTY QUEEN VICTORIA. The year appears at the foot and the name of the force round the top.
Comments: *Issued to all ranks of the Metropolitan and City of London Police and selected civilian staff to celebrate the Jubilee on 21 June 1887. Clasps for the 1897 Jubilee q.v. were issued to recipients of this medal still serving ten years later.*

VALUE:

	Without clasp	With 1897 clasp	Miniature
Metropolitan Police (14,000)	£45–55	£55–65	£30–35
City of London Police (900)	£75–100	£100–125	£30–35 (add £10 for clasp)

295. JUBILEE MEDAL 1897

Date: 1897.
Ribbon: Dark blue with two broad white bands and dark blue edges (as for 293).
Metal: Gold, silver or bronze.
Size: 30mm.
Description: This medal is very similar to the 1887 issue, differing solely in the date and anniversary on the reverse. Around 980 medals were awarded to army officers.

VALUE:

		Miniature
Gold (73)	£1500–1750	£150–200
Silver (3040)	£200–250	£35–45
Bronze (890)	£150–200	£25–35

296. JUBILEE MEDAL (MAYORS AND PROVOSTS) 1897

Date: 1897.
Ribbon: White with two broad dark stripes and white edges.
Metal: Gold or silver.
Size: Height 48mm; max. width 40mm.
Description: A diamond-shaped medal with ring suspension, reminiscent of the *Klippe* coinage of central Europe. Both sides had circular centres with trefoil ornaments occupying the angles. (Obverse) the Wyon profile of the young Victoria at the time of her accession; (reverse) Sir Thomas Brock's Old Head veiled bust of the Queen.
Comments: *The gold version was presented to Lord Mayors and Lord Provosts while the silver medal was granted to Mayors and Provosts. Small silver medals of more conventional circular format were produced with these motifs and sold as souvenirs of the occasion.*

VALUE:

		Miniature
Gold (14)	£1000–1500	£820–920
Silver (512)	£350–400	£210–260

297. JUBILEE (POLICE) MEDAL 1897

Date: 1897.
Ribbon: Plain dark blue.
Metal: Bronze.
Size: 36mm.
Description: Very similar to the 1887 issue with the dates suitably amended and the name of the service round the top of the reverse.
Comments: *Separate issues were made in respect of the Police Ambulance service, St John Ambulance Brigade and the Metropolitan Fire Brigade. Holders of the previous medal merely received the 1897 clasp (Metropolitan Police 8708, City of London Police 485).*

VALUE:		Miniature
Metropolitan Police (7481)	£45–55	£55–75
City of London Police (535)	£85–100	£55–75
Police Ambulance (210)	£350–450	£55–75
St John Ambulance Brigade (910)	£75–85	£55–75
Metropolitan Fire Brigade (950)	£75–85	£55–75

298. CEYLON DIAMOND JUBILEE MEDAL 1897

Date: 1897.
Ribbon: Plain red.
Metal: Gold or silver.
Size: 35mm.
Description: (Obverse) the Boehm bust of Queen Victoria with the dates 1837-1897 at the foot. (Reverse) an elephant and a stupa (dome-shaped Buddhist shrine), with two lines of concentric inscriptions: TO COMMEMORATE SIXTY YEARS OF HER MAJESTY'S REIGN and, unusually, THE RT. HON. SIR J. WEST RIDGEWAY K.C.B., K.C.M.G., GOVERNOR. A crown above the rim was fixed to a ring for suspension.
Comments: *Awarded to local dignitaries and leading officials in the Ceylon government.*

VALUE:		Miniature	
Gold	£1000–1500	£820–1020	
Silver	£200–250	£160–210	

299. HONG KONG DIAMOND JUBILEE MEDAL

Date: 1897.
Ribbon: Three equal stripes of dark blue, maroon and dark blue (also known with gold ribbon with central white stripe).
Metal Gold, silver or bronze.
Size: 36mm.
Description: (Obverse) the Boehm bust of Queen Victoria with the date 1897 at the foot; (reverse) a seascape with a British three-masted sailing ship and a Chinese junk in the background and two figures shaking hands in the foreground. The name of the colony appears at the top, while two concentric inscriptions read SIR WILLIAM ROBINSON G.C.M.G. GOVERNOR and TO COMMEMORATE SIXTY YEARS OF HER MAJESTY'S REIGN 1837-1897.
Comments: *Very little is known for certainty about this medal on account of the fact that the colonial records were destroyed during the Japanese occupation. However, it is believed that a small number of gold medals were presented to local high ranking dignitaries, silver to various civil and military personnel and bronze to others.*

VALUE:	
Gold	£2000–2500
Silver	£400–500
Bronze	£180–200

299A. LAGOS DIAMOND JUBILEE MEDAL

Date: 1897.
Ribbon: Dark blue with two broad white stripes towards the edges.
Metal Silver.
Size: 36mm.
Description: (Obverse) the veiled crowned profile of Queen Victoria (similar to the Egypt Medal 1882, No. 131) inscribed VICTORIA QUEEN AND EMPRESS with a Tudor rose at the foot; (reverse) QUEEN'S DIAMOND JUBILEE LAGOS round the circumference, with JUNE 22ND 1897 in the centre.
Comments: *Issued to civil and military personnel associated with the Diamond Jubilee celebrations in the crown colony of Lagos (1886–1906 when it was incorporated in the colony and protectorate of Southern Nigeria).*

VALUE: —

299B. INDIA DIAMOND JUBILEE MEDAL

Date: 1897.
Ribbon: White.
Metal Silver.
Size: 36mm.
Description: (Obverse) the veiled crowned profile of Queen Victoria (similar to the Egypt Medal 1882, No. 131) inscribed VICTORIA QUEEN AND EMPRESS with a Star of India at the foot; (reverse) TO COMMEMORATE THE SIXTIETH YEAR OF THE REIGN OF H.M. QUEEN VICTORIA 1897 within a laurel wreath, with royal arms above and the Star of India below.
Comments: *Issued to civil and military personnel associated with the Diamond Jubilee celebrations in India. It was also issued to Native chiefs in the colony of Natal.*

VALUE: £100–150

300. VISIT TO IRELAND MEDAL 1900

Date: 1900.
Ribbon: Plain dark blue.
Metal: Bronze.
Size: 36mm.
Description: (Obverse) a half-length version of the Boehm bust of Queen Victoria; (reverse) the female allegorical figure of Hibernia looking out over Kingstown (Dun Laoghaire) harbour in which the Royal Yacht can be seen (far left). Unusually, the medal was mounted with a suspension bar decorated with shamrocks.
Comments: *The medal designed by G. W. de Saulles commemorated Queen Victoria's visit to Ireland in 1900. It was awarded to officers of the Royal Irish Constabulary and Dublin Metropolitan Police who were involved in security and policing the various events connected with the visit. The medal was worn with the same ribbon as the Jubilee Police medals.*

VALUE:
Bronze (2285) £120–150 *Miniature* £110–130

300A. VISIT TO THE COLONIES MEDAL 1901

Date: 1901.
Ribbon: Unknown.
Metal: Gold and Silver.
Size: Oval 20 x 24mm.
Description: (Obverse) a crowned anchor with the royal garter and rose emblem inset; (reverse) inscribed T.R.H. DUKE & DUCHESS OF CORNWALL & YORK—BRITISH COLONIES 1901 H.M.S. OPHIR.
Comments: *This small medalet was issued to commemorate the visit of the Duke and Duchess of Cornwall and York to the British Colonies aboard HMS Ophir in 1901.*

VALUE:	Gold £500–600	
	Silver £150–200	Miniature £110–130

300B. TRHs THE DUKE AND DUCHESS OF YORK MEDAL 1901

Date: 1901.
Ribbon: Dark blue with a central red stripe.
Metal: Silver.
Size: 32mm.
Description: (Obverse) the left-facing conjoined busts of the Duke and Duchess surrounded by a ribboned wreath; (reverse) a crowned anchor surmounted by the garter and rose emblem T.R.H'S THE DUKE & DUCHESS OF YORK'S VISIT TO THE COLONIES 1901 surrounded by a ribboned wreath. With ring suspension
Comments: *It is believed that this attractive medal was awarded to dignitaries on the Royal Tour of 1901.*

VALUE: £125–150   *Miniature*   —

301. CORONATION MEDAL 1902

Date: 1902.
Ribbon: Dark blue with a central red stripe and white edges.
Metal: Silver or bronze.
Size: Height 42mm; max. width 30mm.
Description: (Obverse) the left-facing conjoined busts of King Edward VII and Queen Alexandra, both crowned and wearing coronation robes. (Reverse) the crowned royal cypher above the date of the actual ceremony. The medal has an elaborate raised rim decorated with a wreath culminating in a crown through which the ring for suspension was looped.
Comments: *This medal, designed by Emil Fuchs and struck by Messrs. Elkington & Co., celebrated the coronation of King Edward VII on 9 August 1902. It was presented in silver to members of the Royal Family, foreign dignitaries, high officials of the government, senior officials and service officers involved in the celebrations. Selected NCOs and other ranks of the Army and Navy taking part in the parades were awarded the medal in bronze. Both versions were issued unnamed.*

VALUE:		Miniature
Silver (3493)	£150–200	£30–35
Bronze (6054)	£100–150	£30–35

302. CORONATION MEDAL (MAYORS AND PROVOSTS) 1902

Date: 1902.
Ribbon: Dark blue with a narrow white central stripe and crimson borders.
Metal: Silver.
Size: 32mm.
Description: (Obverse) conjoined right-facing busts of the King and Queen; (reverse) the crowned cypher and date. It differed from the ordinary medal by having flat, broad borders decorated with the heraldic flowers of the United Kingdom culminating at the top in a simple suspension ring.
Comments: *The medal was designed by Emil Fuchs and struck by Messrs. Elkington & Co.*

VALUE:
Silver	£150–200	*Miniature*	£110–130

303. CORONATION (POLICE) MEDAL 1902

Date: 1902.
Ribbon: Red, with a narrow dark blue central stripe.
Metal: Silver or bronze.
Size: 36mm.
Description: (Obverse) the left-facing bust of King Edward VII; (reverse) a crown above a nosegay of heraldic flowers with the words CORONATION OF HIS MAJESTY KING EDWARD VII 1902 in the upper field. The name or initials of the service appeared round the top, LCC MFB signifying London County Council Metropolitan Fire Brigade.
Comments: *Issued to all ranks of the police and associated services to celebrate the coronation, and awarded in silver or bronze to officers and other ranks respectively. 97 bronze medals were also issued to police civilian staff. The medal was designed by G. W. de Saulles.*

VALUE:	Silver	*Miniature*	Bronze	*Miniature*
Metropolitan Police	£500–600 (51)	£25–35	£25–35 (16,709)	£25–35
City of London Police	£650–850 (5)	£25–35	£65–75 (1060)	£25–35
LCC MFB	£650–850 (12)	—	£55–65 (1000)	£55–65
St John Ambulance Brigade	—	—	£55–65 (912)	£65–75
Police Ambulance Service	Unique	—	£300–350 (204)	£95–110

304. CEYLON CORONATION MEDAL 1902

Date: 1902.
Ribbon: Plain blue.
Metal: Gold.
Size: 35mm.
Description: (Obverse) a crowned left-facing bust of King Edward VII; (reverse) the elephant and stupa motif previously used (MYB298). The concentric inscription on the reverse now tactfully omitted any reference to the governor: IN COMMEMORATION OF THE CORONATION OF H.M. KING EDWARD VII 1902. The medal was fitted with a ring for suspension.
Comments: *Like its predecessor, this rare medal was struck for presentation to local dignitaries and government officials.*

VALUE: — *Miniature* £260–310

305. HONG KONG CORONATION MEDAL 1902

Date: 1902.
Ribbon: None officially designated but it is usually seen with a red, white and blue ribbon.
Metal: Silver or bronze.
Size: 36mm.
Description: (Obverse) conjoined right-facing busts of King Edward VII and Queen Alexandra with their names round the circumference; (reverse) the maritime motif of the Diamond Jubilee medal with new inscriptions in two concentric curves: SIR HENRY A. BLAKE G.C.M.G. GOVERNOR (inner) and TO COMMEMORATE THE CORONATION OF THEIR MAJESTIES THE KING & QUEEN (outer). Usually, but not always, fitted with a suspension ring.
Comments: *Issued to all British and Indian officers and other ranks serving in the colony as well as local police. Some 6,000 medals were produced by Edmonds & Son, London, and issued in cases.*

VALUE
Silver	£150–250
Bronze	£65–85

305A. NATAL CORONATION MEDAL 1902

Date: 1902.
Ribbon: Dark blue with a central claret stripe.
Metal: Silver.
Size: 21mm, 29mm and 51mm.
Description: (Obverse) a right-facing crowned bust of King Edward VII with the inscription TO COMMEMORATE THE CORONATION OF KING EDWARD VII; (reverse) Royal coat of arms above two running wildebeests, inscribed (round top) EDWARDUS DEI GRATIA BRITANNIAR REX F:D and (round bottom) COLONY OF NATAL 26 JUNE 1902. Ring suspension.
Comments: *The small medal was distributed to schoolchildren whereas the large medal was restricted to native chiefs and is relatively scarce. It is believed that the middle-size medal was presented to local dignitaries.*

VALUE:		
	21mm	£20–30
	29mm	£85–100
	51mm	£500–600

306. DELHI DURBAR MEDAL 1903

Date: 1903.
Ribbon: Pale blue with three dark blue stripes—the colours of the Order of the Indian Empire and the Order of the Star of India..
Metal: Gold or silver.
Size: 38.5mm.
Description: (Obverse) a right-facing crowned bust of the King Emperor with DELHI DARBAR 1903 on the right side; (reverse) a three-line inscription in Farsi across the field, which translates as "By grace of the Lord of the Realm, Edward, King, Emperor of India, 1901", with an elaborate border of roses, thistles, shamrocks and Indian flowers. Ring suspension.
Comments: *Struck to celebrate the Durbar of the King Emperor at Delhi on 1 January 1903. It was awarded in gold to the rulers of the Indian princely states and in silver to lesser dignitaries, government officials, and officers and other ranks of the armed services actually involved in the celebrations.*

VALUE:			Miniature
Gold (140)	£2500–3000		—
Silver (2567)	£250–350		£35–45

307. VISIT TO SCOTLAND MEDAL 1903

Date: 1903.
Ribbon: Plain red.
Metal: Bronze.
Size: 36mm.
Description: Very similar to the Police Coronation medal but the year was changed to 1903 and the inscription SCOTTISH POLICE appeared round the top of the reverse. The medal was named to the recipient on the rim. An ornate clasp decorated with a thistle was worn above the suspension bar.
Comments: *This medal was designed by G. W. de Saulles and struck to commemorate Their Majesties' post-coronation tour of Scotland in May 1903. It was awarded to the police and troops involved in parades and escort duties, as well as the ancillary services such as the Fire Brigade and the St Andrew's Ambulance Association.*

VALUE:
    Bronze (2957)   £100–150   *Miniature*   £45–55

308. VISIT TO IRELAND MEDAL 1903

Date: 1903.
Ribbon: Pale blue.
Metal: Bronze.
Size: 36mm.
Description: (Obverse) bust of King Edward VII; (reverse) as 1900 medal with the date altered at the foot. The suspension brooch is ornamented with shamrocks.
Comments: *This medal was designed by G. W. de Saulles and struck to mark the King's visit to Ireland in July 1903. It was awarded on the same terms as the Visit to Ireland Medal 1900.*

VALUE:
    Bronze (7757)   £150–200   *Miniature*   £60–70

308A. VISIT OF THE PRINCE AND PRINCESS OF WALES TO INDIA

Instituted: 1905–06
Ribbon: Neck ribbon 55mm wide, maroon with wide blue stripes towards each edge.
Metal: Frosted silver.
Size: 51mm.
Description: (Obverse) conjoined busts of the Prince and Princess of Wales (later King George V and Queen Mary), facing right. ELKINGTON (manufacturers) inscribed minutely below busts. (Reverse) badge of the Prince of Wales surrounded by the chain of the GCSI, with legend T.R.H. THE PRINCE & PRINCESS OF WALES VISIT TO INDIA 1905-6 around with ELKINGTON LONDON in small letters below.
Comments: *Only 72 medals were struck, 70 of which were bestowed on British and Indian officials.*

VALUE: £600–800   *Miniature*   £55–65

308B. GEORGE PRINCE OF WALES MEDAL

Instituted: 1905-06.
Ribbon: 15mm, red, white and blue in equal parts.
Metal: Silver or gold.
Size: Oval 20 x 24mm.
Description: (Obverse) the Prince of Wales's plumes surrounded by the Garter and the chain and badge of the GCSI, flanked in the field by the letters G and M; (reverse) inscription T.R.H. GEORGE PRINCE OF WALES & VICTORIA MARY PRINCESS OF WALES with INDIA 1905-6 in the upper centre.
Comments: *The 26 gold medals were given by Their Royal Highnesses to their personal staff, while a total of 1,625 silver medals were presented to all hands aboard HMS* Renown *and* Terrible *and the Royal Yacht* Osborne.

VALUE:

Gold (26)	£1000–1500
Silver (1625)	£120–180

309. CORONATION MEDAL 1911

Date: 1911.
Ribbon: Dark blue with two thin red stripes in the centre.
Metal: Silver.
Size: 32mm.
Description: (Obverse) conjoined left-facing busts of King George V and Queen Mary in their coronation robes within a floral wreath; (reverse) the crowned royal cypher above the date of the coronation itself. Plain ring suspension.
Comments: *Designed by Sir Bertram McKennal, MVO, ARA, these medals were issued unnamed but may sometimes be found with unofficial engraving. Those who were also entitled to the Delhi Darbar Medal received a crowned clasp inscribed DELHI if they had previously been awarded the coronation medal. This was the first occasion that the medal might be awarded to those not actually present at the ceremony itself.*

VALUE:

		Miniature
Silver (15,901)	£80–100	£25–30
With Delhi clasp (134)	£600–800	£55–65

Delhi Durbar 1911.

309A. GUILDHALL CORONATION MEDAL 1911

Date: 1911.
Ribbon: Crimson.
Metal: Silver and enamels.
Size: 37mm.
Description: (Obverse) conjoined left-facing busts of King George V and Queen Mary with their names around, surrounded by a white enamelled ring bearing the words CORONATION RECEPTION . JUNE 1911 with laurel wreath around divided by four shields, surmounted by a crown with three semi-precious stones inset; (reverse) hallmark and pin. Suspended from an ornate clasp (with additional pin) bearing a sword and sceptre.
Comments: *The reception at the Guildhall, London, was a grand affair with members of the Royal family and a number of Heads of State in attendance. The ornate medals were presented in a plush case and were designed to be worn either as a lapel badge or as a conventional medal.*

VALUE: £250–300

310. CORONATION (POLICE) MEDAL 1911

Date: 1911.
Ribbon: Red with three narrow blue stripes.
Metal: Silver.
Size: 36mm.
Description: (Obverse) a crowned left-facing bust of King George V; (reverse) an imperial crown with an ornate surround. The inscription CORONATION 1911 appears at the foot and the name of the service at the top. Ring suspension.
Comments: *By now the number of police and ancillary services had grown considerably, as witness the various reverse types which may be encountered in this medal. The medal was designed by Sir Bertram McKennal, MVO, ARA,*

VALUE:		Miniature
Metropolitan Police (19,783)	£35–45	£20–25
City of London Police (1385)	£100–150	£25–30
County and Borough Police (2565)	£90–100	£25–30
Police Ambulance Service (130)	£650–750	£95–110
London Fire Brigade (1374)	£120–150	£95–110
Royal Irish Constabulary (585)	£175–250	£160–210
Scottish Police (1465)	£100–120	£55–65
St John Ambulance Brigade (2755)	£65–85	£65–75
St Andrew's Ambulance Corps (310)	£250–300	£110–160
Royal Parks (120)	£1000–1500	£150–170

311. VISIT TO IRELAND MEDAL 1911

Date: 1911.
Ribbon: Dark green with thin red stripes towards either end.
Metal: Silver.
Size: 36mm.
Description: Very similar to the foregoing, distinguished only by the reverse which is inscribed CORONATION 1911 round the top, with the actual date of the visit round the foot.
Comments: *This medal was designed by Sir Bertram McKennal, MVO, ARA and was granted to prominent civic dignitaries and members of the Irish police forces involved in the royal visit to Ireland which took place on 7-12 July 1911.*

VALUE:
Silver (2477)	£75–90	*Miniature*	£75–85

311A. EAST INDIAN RAILWAY COMPANY ROYAL VISIT TO INDIA MEDAL 1911

Date: 1911.
Ribbon: Dark blue with a central maroon stripe flanked by narrow gold stripes.
Metal: Gilded bronze.
Size: 32mm.
Description: (Obverse) the arms of the East Indian Railway Company surrounded by the inscription EAST INDIAN RAILWAY COMPANY with a winged wheel at the foot; (reverse) a ten-line inscription FOR SERVICES RENDERED DURING THE RAILWAY JOURNEYS OF THEIR MAJESTIES THE KING EMPEROR AND QUEEN EMPRESS IN INDIA 1911.
Comments: *Very little is known about this rare medal, but it is believed to have been awarded to members of the Honour Guard of the East Indian Railway Volunteer Rifle Corps and employees of the company present during the tour of India undertaken in 1911 by King George V and Queen Mary. It is believed that no more than 30 medals were issued.*

VALUE: £100–£120

312. DELHI DURBAR MEDAL 1911

Date: 1911.
Ribbon: Dark blue with two narrow red stripes in the middle.
Metal: Gold or silver.
Size: 38.5mm.
Description: (Obverse) the conjoined crowned busts of King George V and Queen Mary in a floral wreath; (reverse) an elaborate Farsi text which translates as "The Durbar of George V, Emperor of India, Master of the British Lands".
Comments: *This medal marked the Delhi Durbar held in the King Emperor's honour in December 1911. Most of the gold medals went to the Indian princely rulers and top government officials, 10,000 of the 30,000 silver medals were awarded to officers and other ranks of the British and Indian Armies for exemplary service, without their necessarily being present at the Durbar itself.*

VALUE:		*Miniature*
Gold (200)	£3000–4000	£320–420
Silver (30,000)	£100–130	£25–30

312AA. DELHI DURBAR MILITARY TOURNAMENT MEDAL 1911

Date: 1911.
Ribbon: None
Metal: Gold, Silver or Bronze.
Size: 44mm.
Description: (Obverse) the left-facing crowned and robed bust of King George V; (reverse) within a wreath of laurel leaves, three tablets engraved with the words DURBAR, TOURNAMENT and the event for which the medal is awarded, e.g. HOCKEY, with the legend DELHI . CORONATION . DURBAR . 1911 around
Comments: *Minted by the Calcutta Mint, and usually named on the edge with the details of the recipient. These very rare medals were awarded for specific events at the Delhi Durbar, but they are rarely seen.*

VALUE:	**Gold (6)**	£1000–1500
	Silver (15–20)	£350–400
	Bronze (40–50)	£150–200

312A. VISIT OF KING GEORGE V AND QUEEN MARY TO INDIA 1911–12

Date: 1911–12.
Ribbon: None.
Metal: Silver or gold.
Size: Oval 20 x 24mm.
Description: (Obverse): GRI entwined initials as a monogram above the word INDIA; (reverse) MRI monogram and dates 1911–12, suspended from a bar by a simple ring and scroll suspender.
Comments: *Given as a commemorative gift from the King to the crews of the "special service squadron" led by HMS* Medina *which took the King and Queen to Bombay in 1911 to proceed to Delhi for the Durbar.*

VALUE: Gold   £750–1000
                 Silver   £60–85

312AB. QUEEN ALEXANDRA'S CHILDREN'S BANQUET MEDAL 1914

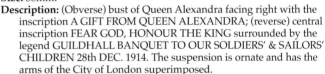

Date: 28 December 1914.
Ribbon: White, with red stripes at each edge.
Metal: Bronze.
Size: 38mm.
Description: (Obverse) bust of Queen Alexandra facing right with the inscription A GIFT FROM QUEEN ALEXANDRA; (reverse) central inscription FEAR GOD, HONOUR THE KING surrounded by the legend GUILDHALL BANQUET TO OUR SOLDIERS' & SAILORS' CHILDREN 28th DEC. 1914. The suspension is ornate and has the arms of the City of London superimposed.
Comments: *This medal, designed and manufactured by Elkington, was issued unnamed to 1,300 children and a small number of Chelsea pensioners who attended a banquet at the Guildhall on 28 December 1914. The children, between the ages of eight and thirteen, were the sons and daughters of men in the Fleet or on the Western Front. One child was chosen from each family by Sir James Gildea of the Soldiers' and Sailors' Families' Association. Relatively few medals appear to have survived.*

VALUE: £50–£70

312AC. VISIT OF THE PRINCE OF WALES TO NEW ZEALAND 1920

Date: 1920.
Ribbon: Neck ribbon 38mm maroon.
Metal: Silver, with the raised edges of the medal being milled, plain rim.
Size: 50mm.
Description: (Obverse) badge of the Prince of Wales surrounded by the chain of the GCSI; (reverse) the inscription THE VISIT OF H.R.H. THE PRINCE OF WALES TO NEW ZEALAND 1920 in seven lines, surrounded by a laurel wreath, with maker's name ELKINGTON inscribed minutely underneath the base of the wreath. Fitted with a plain suspension ring.
Comments: *This medal was awarded in connection with the visit of HRH the Prince of Wales (later King Edward VIII and Duke of Windsor) to New Zealand in the course of his tour aboard HMS* Renown *1919–20.*

VALUE: £100–150

312B. VISIT OF THE PRINCE OF WALES TO INDIA 1921–22

Date: 1921–22.
Ribbon: Neck ribbon 55mm maroon with broad blue stripes towards each edge.
Metal: Frosted silver.
Size: 50mm.
Description: (Obverse) bust of Prince of Wales facing left with inscription EDWARD PRINCE OF WALES INDIA 1921–1922; (reverse) badge of the Prince of Wales surrounded by the chain of the GCSI. Fitted with a plain suspension ring.
Comments: *Only 84 medals were awarded in connection with the visit of HRH the Prince of Wales (later King Edward VIII and Duke of Windsor) to India in the course of his world tour aboard HMS Renown.*

VALUE: £700–900   *Miniature*   £85–110

312C. WELCOME HOME MEDAL FOR THE PRINCE OF WALES

Date: 1922.
Ribbon: Green with red central stripe.
Metal: Gold, silver and bronze.
Size: Oval 43mm x 34mm.
Description: An oval medal with ornate edges. (Obverse) crowned and robed bust of the Prince of Wales with the inscription EDWARD PRINCE OF WALES KG; (reverse) The Prince of Wales's feathers with the inscription WELCOME HOME 1922. With integral ornate loop for suspension.
Comments: *Struck by F. Bowcher to mark the return of the Prince of Wales to England after his world tour.*

VALUE: Gold   £850–1000
           Silver   £120–150
           Bronze   £80–100

312D. VISIT OF THE PRINCE OF WALES TO BOMBAY MEDAL 1921

Date: 1921.
Ribbon: Watered blue with central thin white stripe.
Metal: Bronze.
Size: Oval 38mm x 30mm.
Description: An oval medal. (Obverse) bust of the Prince of Wales facing right, with the inscription EDWARD PRINCE OF WALES and surmounted by the Prince of Wales's feathers and motto ICH DIEN; (reverse) VISIT OF HIS ROYAL HIGHNESS BOMBAY NOVEMBER 1921 in six lines.
Comment: *Thought to be presented to the leading military and civil dignitaries present during the visit of the Prince of Wales. New information suggests it was also given to school children although this is unconfirmed. The number issued is not known.*

VALUE: £55–£85

312E. VISIT OF THE PRINCE OF WALES TO PATNA 1921

Date: 1921.
Ribbon: Imperial Purple.
Metal: Bronze.
Size: 40mm.
Description: (Obverse) bust of the Prince of Wales facing right with the inscription EDWARD PRINCE OF WALES, in an oval centre-piece, with an ornate floral decoration either side; (Reverse) centre blank, with the inscription VISIT OF HIS ROYAL HIGHNESS around the top half, and PATNA 22ND. DEC 1921 around the lower half of the reverse.
Comment: *Believed to have been presented to the leading military and civil dignitaries present during the visit of the Prince of Wales. The number issued is not known, but is believed to be very small.*

VALUE :   £80–£100

313. JUBILEE MEDAL 1935

Date: 1935.
Ribbon: Red with two dark blue and one white stripes at the edges.
Metal: Silver.
Size: 32mm.
Description: (Obverse) left-facing conjoined half-length busts of King George V and Queen Mary in crowns and robes of state; (reverse) a crowned GRI monogram flanked by the dates of the accession and the jubilee.
Comments: *This medal, designed by Sir William Goscombe John, RA, was issued to celebrate the Silver Jubilee of King George V and widely distributed to the great and good throughout the Empire.*

VALUE:
  Silver (85,234)   £30–45   *Miniature*   £15–20

313A. ISLE OF MAN SILVER JUBILEE MEDAL 1935

Date: 1935.
Ribbon: Three equal stripes of red, white and blue. However some medals had their ribbons substituted with black to mark the death of the King in 1936.
Metal: Nickel-plated brass or silver.
Size: 32mm.
Description: (Obverse) conjoined busts of King George V and Queen Mary in an inner circle surrounded by the legend KING GEORGE V & QUEEN MARY REIGNED 25 YEARS; (reverse) Triskelion emblem with the legend IN COMMEMORATION OF THE SILVER JUBILEE 1935. Suspended from a brooch bar of seven overlapping panels with the centre panel having the royal cypher GvR while the outer panels have two leaves in each.
Comments: *This medal was issued to celebrate the Silver Jubilee and the nickel-plated brass edition was given to all schoolchildren on the island. Just three medals are believed to have been struck in silver for presentation to civic dignitaries or officials. 8,000 medals were struck by James Fenton & Co of Birmingham.*

VALUE: Nickel-plated brass £20–30   Silver (3) £150–200

313B. GUILDHALL JUBILEE MEDAL 1935

Date: 1935.
Ribbon: None.
Metal: Enamelled silver-gilt.
Size: 38mm wide.
Description: (Obverse) Arms of the City of London within a blue enamelled garter with the date 1935 on a white panel, surmounted by the Royal cypher, crown and lion; (reverse) engraved with the date 22nd May 1935. The medal is suspended from a double scroll brooch.
Comments: *This medal was issued to selected dignitaries who attended the banquet at the Guildhall in celebration of the King's Silver Jubilee. It was made by G. Kenning & Son, London.*

VALUE: £250–300

314. CORONATION MEDAL 1937

Date: 1937.
Ribbon: Blue edged with one red and two white stripes.
Metal: Silver.
Size: 32mm.
Description: (Obverse) conjoined busts of King George VI and Queen Elizabeth in their robes of state without any inscription. The stark simplicity of this motif was matched by a reverse showing the crowned GRI over the inscription CROWNED 12 MAY 1937, with the names of the King and Queen in block capitals round the circumference.
Comments: *Issued to celebrate the coronation of King George VI on 12 May 1937.*

VALUE: Silver (90,000)   £30–50   *Miniature*   £15–20

314A. GUILDHALL CORONATION MEDAL 1937

Date: 1937.
Ribbon: None
Metal: Silver-gilt.
Size: 34mm.
Description: A rectangular medal (obverse) conjoined busts of King George VI and Queen Elizabeth in their robes of state on a shield with palm and vine sprigs below and CORONATION in a tablet. The design struck on a rectangular base with two "steps" at each side in art deco style. Reverse blank, inscribed with the name of recipient. The medal is suspended from an ornate crowned coat of arms of the City of London with GUILDHALL above
Comments: *Issued by the City of London to selected dignitaries who attended the banquet at the Guildhall to celebrate the coronation of King George VI on 12 May 1937.*

VALUE: £150–200

314B. ROYAL VISIT TO SOUTH AFRICA 1947 CHIEFS' MEDALS

Reverse i.

Reverse ii.

Date: 1947.
Ribbon: Yellow.
Metal: Silver.
Size: Oval 25mm x 32mm or 65mm x 55mm.
Description: (Obverse) conjoined busts of King George VI and Queen Elizabeth in their robes of state without any inscription. (Reverse) (i) map of South Africa surmounted by crowned GRE cypher dividing the date 1947 with KONINKLIKE BESOEK above and ROYAL VISIT below; (ii) crowned GRE with the inscription ROYAL VISIT 1947.
Comments: *Issued to celebrate the visit of King George VI to South Africa in 1947. Two distinctly different reverses have been seen but little is known about these medals which were issued in two sizes. These medals were awarded to Native Chiefs/Indabas (perhaps others also) and worn from a neck ribbon (those seen have been yellow although there are reports of others with a red ribbon). It is not known who were awarded the different sizes but it is likely that the bilingual version (Type i) was given to South African chiefs (156 comprising King Williamstown (Ciskei) 7; Umtata (Transkei) 31; Eshowe (Zululand) 40; Pietersburg (Northern Territories) 78). The unilingual version (Type ii) was probably reserved for the Protectorates and possibly Rhodesias. The number awarded is unknown.*

VALUE: Both types: Small £75–100 Large £125–175

314C. ROYAL VISIT TO SOUTH AFRICA 1947

Reverse i.

Reverse ii.

Date: 1947.
Ribbon: None
Metal: Silver gilt and silver.
Size: 38mm.
Description: (Obverse) conjoined busts of HM King George VI and HM Queen Elizabeth crowned and robed. Artists initials PM (Percy Metcalfe) on ribbon on King's left shoulder; (Reverse, two types) (i) map of South Africa surmounted by crowned GRE cypher dividing the date 1947 with KONINKLIKE BESOEK above and ROYAL VISIT below; (ii) crowned GRE with the inscription ROYAL VISIT 1947.
Comments: *Type i was issued to celebrate the visit of King George VI to South Africa in 1947. Only six medallions were struck in silver gilt (awarded to the Governor General of the Union of SA, the Prime Minister of SA and the Administrators of the four Provinces of the Union of SA). A total of 394 silver medals in red cases were awarded (Governor General's Staff, Cabinet Ministers in Attendance, Officers commanding Commands, miscellaneous persons, Inter-departmental Committee on Royal Tour, Royal Train, Pilot Train, Railway staff employed at Government Houses, Press, chauffeurs, National/Kruger Park officials, Native Indabas). The medals were distributed by the Prime Minister's Office. Type ii were issued for Northern and Southern Rhodesia as part of the African tour. The medallion, in a blue case, was given to "selected persons who have done special work in connection with the Royal Visit". They were presented to recipients on April 11, 1947, at the Provincial Commissioner's Office in Livingstone. The medallions seem to have been named in seriffed capitals.*

VALUE :

Type i (in red case)		
Silver gilt (6)	£800–1000	
Silver (394)	£200–250	
Type ii (in blue case)		
Silver gilt (8)	£800–1000	
Silver (196)	£200–250	

315. CORONATION MEDAL 1953

Date: 1953.
Ribbon: Dark red with two narrow blue stripes in the centre and narrow white edges.
Metal: Silver.
Size: 32mm.
Description: (Obverse) a right-facing bust of Queen Elizabeth II in a Tudor crown and robes of state, the field being otherwise plain. (Reverse) a similar crown over the royal monogram EIIR with the legend QUEEN ELIZABETH II CROWNED 2ND JUNE 1953 round the circumference. Ring suspension.
Comments: *This medal celebrated the coronation of Queen Elizabeth II on 2 June 1953. News that Edmund Hillary and Sherpa Tenzing had successfully attained the summit of Everest reached London on the morning of the Coronation. Subsequently the members of the Hunt Expedition were invited to Buckingham Palace on 16 July 1953 where, on Her Majesty's own initiative, they were presented with coronation medals engraved MOUNT EVEREST EXPEDITION on the rim, following the precedent of the Mwele medals of 1895–96.*

VALUE:		*Miniature*
Silver (129,000)	£50–75	£12–14
Mount Everest Expedition (37)	£850–1000	

315A. ROYAL TOUR OF THE COMMONWEALTH MEDAL 1953–54

Date: 1953
Ribbon: None
Metal: Toned bronze.
Size: 38mm.
Description: (Obverse) Right facing, bare-headed, conjoined busts of HM Queen Elizabeth and Prince Philip, with the inscription "THE ROYAL VISIT" above and "MCMLIII–IV" below; (reverse) the crowned Royal coat of arms, with the Royal cypher above and the roman numerals MCMLIII–IV at the foot.
Comments: *This circular medal, designed by Mary Gillick, was struck by the Royal Mint and issued to mark the Royal Commonwealth Tour of Queen Elizabeth and Prince Philip between November 1953 and May 1954. The medal was issued to the Royal party and to local dignitaries at numerous ports of call throughout the Commonwealth. The total number of medals issued was 1,503.*

VALUE: £75–100

In addition to the official medal illustrated above (MYB 315A), all schoolchildren in New Zealand received a medal suspended from a blue ribbon, together with a folder telling the story of the Royal Family, with pictures of the Coronation regalia, royal palaces and descriptions. For the sake of completeness this medal is included below as MYB 315AA.

Date: 1953.
Ribbon: Dark blue.
Metal: Copper-coloured alloy.
Size: 38mm.
Description: (Obverse) right-facing crowned bust of Queen Elizabeth II wearing Tudor crown; (reverse) the crowned New Zealand coat of arms surrounded by sprays of flowers and the inscription ELIZABETH II ROYAL VISIT 1953–54. The copper-coloured medal is hung by a ring from a scalloped suspender as illustrated.
Comment: *Issued to all New Zealand school-children during the Royal visit, accompanied by a folder. The medals themselves are fairly common, but those with the accompanying folder are quite rare.*

VALUE: £8–12 (with accompanying folder £20–30)

315B. ROYAL VISIT TO MALTA 1954

Date: 1954.
Ribbon: None.
Metal: Gold coloured alloy.
Size: 38mm.
Description: (Obverse) right-facing crowned bust of the Queen; (reverse) shield containing the Maltese flag with the inscription TO COMMEMORATE THE ROYAL VISIT TO MALTA G.C. 1954 round the circumference.
Comments: *Issued to all Maltese schoolchildren, teachers and municipal workers in commemoration of the Royal visit to the island.*

VALUE: £10–15

315C. ROYAL VISIT TO NIGERIA MEDAL 1956

Date: 1956.
Ribbon: None.
Metal: Toned bronze.
Size: 38mm.
Description: (Obverse) Right facing, bare-headed, conjoined busts of HM Queen Elizabeth and Prince Philip, with the inscription "THE ROYAL VISIT" above and "TO NIGERIA 1956" below; (reverse) the crowned Royal coat of arms, with the Royal cypher above and the roman numerals MCMLVI at the foot.
Comments: *This circular medal was struck by the Royal Mint and issued to mark the Royal visit of Queen Elizabeth and Prince Philip to Nigeria, between 28 January and 16 February 1956. The medal was issued to the Royal party and to local dignitaries. A total of 650 medals were issued, each contained in a red leatherette box.*

VALUE: £65–85

315D. ROYAL VISIT TO WEST AFRICA 1961

As above, but dated MCMLXI (1961) on both sides. 500 medals were struck to mark the Royal Visit to Ghana, Sierra Leone and Gambia which was originally to have taken place in 1959 but was postponed pending the birth of Prince Andrew in 1960.

VALUE: £75–100

316. JUBILEE MEDAL 1977

Date: 1977.
Ribbon: White with thin red stripes at the edges, a broad blue stripe in the centre and a thin red stripe down the middle of it.
Metal: Silver.
Size: 32mm.
Description: (Obverse) Right-facing profile of Queen Elizabeth II wearing the St Edward's crown—the first time this design was employed; (reverse) a crown and wreath enclosing the words THE 25TH YEAR OF THE REIGN OF QUEEN ELIZABETH II 6 FEBRUARY 1977. A distinctive reverse was used in Canada, showing the dates of the reign flanking the royal monogram round the foot, CANADA round the top and a large stylised maple leaf in the centre.
Comments: *The 25th anniversary of the Queen's accession was marked by the release of this unnamed medal. The total number of medals issued in the UK was relatively small at 30,000 but they were distributed to a wide range of people including members of the armed forces, crown services and a number of people engaged in important activities including industry, trade, local services, the arts, entertainment, sports, etc..*

VALUE:		*Miniature*
General issue (30,000)	£150–200	£10–12
Canadian issue (30,000)	£100–150	£10–12

318. GOLDEN JUBILEE MEDAL 2002

Date: February 2002.
Ribbon: Royal blue with thin red stripes at the edges, a broad white stripe in the centre and a thin red stripe down the middle.
Metal: Gold-plated cupro-nickel.
Size: 32mm.
Description: (Obverse) a right facing profile of Queen Elizabeth II wearing a crown; (reverse) the royal coat of arms flanked by the dates 1952 and 2002.
Comments: *Issued to celebrate the 50th anniversary of the Queen's accession. It was granted to all personnel of the armed forces who had completed five or more years service on February 6, 2002. Generals who have been Chief of the General Staff and Chief of the Defence Staff or equivalent RN and RAF ranks were awarded the medal even though retired. It was also issued to members of the police, ambulance, coastguard, fire services, RNLI and mountain rescue services, as well as members of the Royal Household including The Queen's Body Guard of the Yeomen of the Guard, who had completed five years service and holders of the VC or GC. One member on HM Customs & Excise was awarded the medal by the Ministry of Defence to mark his close co-operation in work and liaison between the two departments. Almost 400,000 medals were issued.*

VALUE: £75–100   *Miniature*   £10–12

318A. DIAMOND JUBILEE MEDAL 2012

Date: February 2012.
Ribbon: Dark red with royal blue edges and two narrow white stripes in the centre. Medals to Royal Household female recipients have a bow.
Metal: Nickel-silver.
Size: 32mm.
Description: (Obverse) right facing coinage profile of Queen Elizabeth II by Ian Rank-Broadley; (reverse) the crowned royal cypher surmounted on a faceted diamond design, with the dates 1952 – 2012 below.
Comments: *Issued to celebrate the 60th anniversary of HM the Queen's accession. Awarded to members of the armed forces (Regular and Reserve), certain emergency services and operational prison services personnel and Police Community Support Officers who have completed five years service on February 6, 2012, as well as living holders of the VC or GC and members of the Royal Household. Unusually, breaking with tradition the contract to supply the medals was awarded to Worcester Medals. An estimated 438,000 medals were issued. There are copies of this medal which at 32.4mm in diamater are slightly larger than the originals. In addition a special medal with the royal cypher reverse was struck for the Caribbean Realms.*

VALUE: £75–100   *Miniature*   £10–12

318B. DIAMOND JUBILEE MEDAL 2012— CARIBBEAN REALMS

Date: February 2012.
Ribbon: Dark red with royal blue edges, white stripe in the centre bisected by a thin black stripe.
Metal: Nickel-silver.
Size: 32mm.
Description: (Obverse) right facing coinage profile of Queen Elizabeth II by Ian Rank-Broadley with the legend DIAMOND JUBILEE H.M. QUEEN ELIZABETH II around; (reverse) the crowned royal cypher, with CARIBBEAN REALMS above and the dates 1952 – 2012 below.
Comments: *Issued by the Caribbean realms of Antigua and Barbuda (28), the Bahamas (50), Barbados (632), Grenada (5), Jamaica (3,219), Saint Kitts and Nevis (275), Saint Lucia (60), and Saint Vincent and the Grenadines (?) plus 12 to the West Indian Committee and 12 to British citizens, to celebrate the 60th anniversary of HM the Queen's accession. Similar to the British award it was awarded to members of the armed forces, certain emergency services and operational prison services personnel and Police as well as members of the public service sector for outstanding achievement.*

VALUE: £100–150   *Miniature*   £12–15

318C. PLATINUM JUBILEE MEDAL 2022

Date: February 2022.
Ribbon: Central stripe of royal blue, two broad red stripes to either side, edged with narrow silver stripes.
Metal: Nickel-silver.
Size: 32mm.
Description: (Obverse) right-facing coinage profile of Queen Elizabeth II by Ian Rank-Broadley; (reverse) the top motif from the Royal Coat of Arms showing the lion statant guardant atop a crowned Royal armorial helmet surrounded by ermine. The dates 1952–2022 appear in the field.
Comments: *Issued to celebrate the 70th Anniversary of HM the Queen's accession. Awarded to serving members of the armed forces (regular and reserve) and selected other uniformed services (including Police and Prison Service personnel) who have completed five years' service on February 6, 2022. Living holders of the VC and GC Association, and members of the Royal Household will also be eligible. It is estimated that over 400,000 will be issued.*

VALUE: —   *Miniature*   £10–12

318D. CORONATION MEDAL 2023

Date: 2023.

Ribbon: Blue with a central red stripe edged with white.

Metal: Nickel-plated nickel-silver.

Size: 32mm.

Description: (Obverse) designed by Martin Jennings (who also designed the new King's coinage profile) the obverse features the left-facing, crowned conjoined busts of King Charles III and Queen Camilla. (Reverse) Designed by Phil McDermott (who also designed the ribbon) the features the crowned cypher of His Majesty King Charles III above the date 6 MAY 2023, the whole surrounded by a laurel wreath.

Comments: *Issued to commemorate the Coronation of His Majesty King Charles III at Westminster Abbey on May 6, 2023. The first medals were not actually available until after the Coronation itself, so none were evident on the day.*

VALUE: —   *Miniature*   £10–12

For a free sample copy of COIN NEWS magazine, call 01404 46972 or visit www.tokenpublishing.com

MISCELLANEOUS
Medals

Under this heading are grouped a very disparate range of medals whose only common denominator is that they do not fit conveniently into one or other of the preceding categories. They are not without considerable interest and many of them have a very keen following and a buoyant market. They are listed and added to as we have come across them, hence they are in no particular order.

319. KING'S AND QUEEN'S MESSENGER BADGE

Date: 1722.

Ribbon: Garter blue.

Metal: Silver gilt.

Size: Earliest issues variable according to monarch and jeweller; since George V—45mm x 34mm.

Description: (Issues since George V) an upright oval fitted with a plain suspension ring and having a greyhound suspended by a ring from the foot of the rim. (Obverse) the Garter inscribed HONI SOIT QUI MAL Y PENSE enclosing the royal cypher; early issues had the Royal coat of arms; (reverse) plain, engraved with an official number of issue and, on occasion, the name of the messenger.

Comments: *Messengers can be traced back to 1199, but prior to George I badges were not issued. Few of the earlier badges can be found due to a hand in and melt down order instituted by George III in 1762. During the reign of Victoria a number of different shapes and sizes were used for the badges due to a misunderstanding whereby individual messengers obtained their insignia from different jewellers instead of the Jewel Office. Since 1870 Garrards have been responsible for the design, submission and production of Messengers' badges. From 1876 to 1951 the Foreign Office, as Controllers of the Corps of Messengers, purchased and held all badges for issue to those appointed as messengers. Since 1951 messengers, on satisfactorily completing a period of probation, are given a registered number and letter of permission to purchase their badges through the Crown Jewellers. In addition to this badge, on instruction from the Home Office during World War II, a small oval badge bearing the cypher of King George VI was issued to messengers who carried sensitive material between Government departments located in various buildings within the capital city. Garrards produced only 20 of these, thus they are extremely rare.*

VALUE:

George III	£2500–3500
George IV	£2500–3500
William IV	£2500–3500
Victoria official issue	£2500–3000
Victoria unofficial issue	£2000–3000
Edward VII	£2000–3000
George V	£1000–2000
George VI	£1000–2000
Elizabeth II	£1000–2000

King George VI Home Service Messenger Badge.

320. ARCTIC MEDAL 1857

Instituted: 30 January 1857.
Ribbon: 38mm watered white.
Metal: Silver.
Size: Height 46mm; max. width 32mm.
Description: An octagonal medal with a beaded rim, surmounted by a nine-pointed star (representing the Pole Star) through which the suspension ring is fitted. (Obverse) an unusual profile of Queen Victoria, her hair in a loose chignon secured with a ribbon. (Reverse) a three-masted sailing vessel amid icebergs with a sledge party in the foreground and the dates 1818-1855 in the exergue. The medal was issued unnamed, but is often found privately engraved.
Comments: *Awarded retrospectively to all officers and men engaged in expeditions to the polar regions from 1818 to 1855, including those involved in the on-going search for the ill-fated Franklin Expedition of 1845-8. Thus the medal was granted to civilians, scientists, personnel of the French and US Navies and employees of the Hudson's Bay Company who took part in a number of abortive search parties for Sir John Franklin and his crew. Some 1106 medals, out of 1486 in all, were awarded to officers and ratings of the Royal Navy.*

VALUE:

Unnamed	£2000–2400
Named	£3000–3500
Miniature	£1500–2000

321. ARCTIC MEDAL 1876

Instituted: 28 November 1876.
Ribbon: 32mm plain white.
Metal: Silver.
Size: 36mm
Description: A circular medal with a raised beaded rim and a straight bar suspender. (Obverse) a veiled bust of Queen Victoria wearing a small crown, dated 1876 at the foot; (reverse) a three-masted ship icebound.

Comments: *Granted to officers and men of HM ships* Alert *and* Discovery *who served in the Arctic Expedition between 17 July 1875 and 2 November 1876. The medal was later extended to include the crew on the second voyage of the private yacht* Pandora *commanded by Allen Young which cruised in Polar waters between 25 June and 19 October 1875 and from 3 June to 2 November 1876. Medals were engraved with the name, rank and ship of the recipient. Only 155 medals were awarded.*

VALUE:

Named	From £6000
Miniature	£400–600

322. POLAR MEDAL

Instituted: 1904.

Ribbon: 32mm plain white.

Metal: Silver or bronze.

Size: 33mm octagonal.

Description: (Obverse) the effigy of the reigning sovereign; (reverse) a view of the Royal Research Ship *Discovery* with a man-handling sledge party in the foreground.

Comments: *Originally issued in silver, with an appropriate clasp, to the officers and men of Captain Scott's 1902–04 Antarctic Expedition, who went out in the* Discovery *and remained throughout the stay of the ship in the Antarctic Regions, from her arrival until her departure, or to any member compulsorily invalided after 3 January 1902, or to any who joined* Discovery *during her second winter in the Antarctic. It was issued in bronze to officers and men who did not remain, for causes other than sickness, throughout the stay of the ship in Antarctic regions; and also to the officers and men of the relief ships* Morning *and* Terra Nova. *These awards continued for subsequent expeditions: the silver medal being usually awarded to officers and to men who landed or who made more than one voyage, whilst the bronze medal was awarded to those not so exposed to the dangers of the polar environment. The bronze medal ceased being awarded after those awarded for Antarctic Research Work during 1929–39. Apart from the bronze medals awarded for the British Antarctic Expedition 1902–04 and the* Aurora *Relief Expedition 1917 where the year of the expedition was on the rim of the medal, the rest all had a clasp with ANTARCTIC and the year(s) of the expedition; the exception to this being those who took part on Shackleton's expedition and who had previously been awarded the bronze medal, received a clasp to their medal. No bronze medals were awarded for the Arctic. Up to December 2005, 271 bronze awards have been made (to 259 individuals, of whom 10 received one or more additional awards); 1038 silver awards have been made (to 948 individuals, of whom 80 received one or more additional awards), 18 recipients have been awarded both the silver and bronze medals. Only six women have been awarded the medal. Names of recipients are engraved on the earlier and most recent issues, and impressed in small capitals on the earlier Elizabethan issues.*

VALUE:	Silver	Miniature	Bronze (no clasp)	Miniature (no clasp)
Edward VII	From £5000	£125–175	From £6000	£125–160
George V (B)	From £3500	£125–175	From £3000	£125–160
George V (C)	—	£125–175	From £3000	£125–160
George V (E)	From £3500	£125–175	—	£125–160
George VI	From £3000	£125–175	From £3000	£125–160
Elizabeth II	From £3000	£125–175	—	£125–160

Modern examples of miniatures £20–30

323. KING EDWARD VII MEDAL FOR SCIENCE, ART AND MUSIC

Instituted: 1904

Ribbon: 35mm scarlet with a broad central stripe of dark blue and thin white stripes towards the edges.

Metal: Silver.

Size: 32mm.

Description: The raised rim consisted of a laurel wreath and has a ring for suspension. (Obverse) the conjoined busts of King Edward VII and Queen Alexandra; (reverse) the Three Graces engaged in various cultural pursuits.

Comments: *This short-lived medal was discontinued only two years later. It was awarded in recognition of distinguished services in the arts, sciences and music. The medal was struck by Burt & Co.*

VALUE: £1250–1500

324. ORDER OF THE LEAGUE OF MERCY

Modern reverse.

Date: 1898.
Ribbon: 38mm watered white silk with a central broad stripe of black.
Metal: Originally silver, now silver-gilt.
Size: Height 51mm; max. width 39mm.
Description: Originally an enamelled red cross surmounted by the Prince of Wales's plumes enfiladed by a coronet, with a central medallion depicting the emblem of the League, a group of figures representing Charity, set within a laurel wreath. Since 1999: a silver-gilt cross with the emblem in a central medallion. Reverse: a circular plaque inscribed LEAGUE OF MERCY 1999 in four lines.
Comments: *Appointments to the Order were sanctioned and approved by the sovereign on the recommendation of the Grand President of the League of Mercy as a reward for distinguished personal service to the League in assisting the support of hospitals. Ladies and gentlemen who rendered such aid for at least five years were eligible for the award. In 1917 King George V instituted a bar to be awarded to those who gave continuing service over a period of many years after receiving the Order itself. The original Order was last awarded in 1946 and the League itself ceased to exist in 1947. However, in March 1999, 100 years after its institution, the League was re-established and today it awards silver-gilt medals for outstanding voluntary service in health and social care. Over 500 medals have been awarded since 1999.*

VALUE:
Badge of the Order	Original £70–100	Miniature	£55–65
	with bar £100–130		

325. QUEEN ALEXANDRA'S IMPERIAL MILITARY NURSING SERVICE CAPE BADGE

Date: 1902–49
Branch of Service: Queen Alexandra's Imperial Military Nursing Service.
Ribbon: Scarlet with two white outer stripes and two black inner stripes.
Metal: Silver.
Size: Oval 55mm by 36mm.
Description: A uniface oval ring surmounted by a Tudor crown fitted to a plain ring for suspension. The ring at the centre has the Cross of the Order of the Dannebrog, with an ornamental cypher of Queen Alexandra. The ring is inscribed in raised lettering QUEEN ALEXANDRA'S IMPERIAL MILITARY NURSING SERVICE.
Comments: *The cape badge was instituted in 1902 and was used until 1949 when the QAIMNS changed its name to the QARANC. It was worn on the right breast on ward dress for commissioned (qualified) nurses. It was issued through stores to each individual.*

VALUE: £80–100   *Miniature* £35–45

325A. QUEEN ALEXANDRA'S IMPERIAL MILITARY NURSING SERVICE RESERVE CAPE BADGE

Date: 1907–50

Branch of Service: Queen Alexandra's Imperial Military Nursing Service Reserve.

Ribbon: Black with two narrow outer white stripes and two inner scarlet stripes.

Metal: Silver.

Size: 38mm or 29mm.

Description: A uniface ring containing a prominent "R" surmounted by a Tudor crown fitted to a plain ring for suspension. The ring is inscribed in raised lettering QUEEN ALEXANDRA'S IMPERIAL MILITARY NURSING SERVICE RESERVE.

Comments: *The cape badge was instituted in 1907 and was used until 1950 when the QAIMNS(R) was incorporated into the QARANC. It was worn on the right breast on ward dress for commissioned (qualified) nurses. It was issued through stores to each individual.*

VALUE: *Miniature*
38mm £40–50   £35–45
29mm £30–40   £30–35

326. TERRITORIAL FORCE NURSING SERVICE CAPE BADGE

Date: 1907–21.

Branch of Service: Territorial Force Nursing Service.

Ribbon: Scarlet with a narrow central white stripe.

Metal: Silver.

Size: Oval 50mm by 34mm

Description: A uniface oval ring surmounted by a Tudor crown attached to a plain ring for suspension. The ring has at the centre two ornamental letters "A" interlocking and set at an angle. The ring is inscribed in raised lettering: TERRITORIAL FORCE NURSING SERVICE.

Comments: *The cape badge was instituted in 1907 and was used until 1921 when the TFNS was renamed the TANS. It was worn on the right breast on ward dress for commissioned (qualified) nurses. It was issued through stores to each individual.*

VALUE: £30–£40   *Miniature* £30–35

326A. QUEEN ALEXANDRA'S MILITARY FAMILIES NURSING SERVICE CAPE BADGE

Date: 1921–26.

Branch of Service: Queen Alexandra's Military Families Nursing Service.

Ribbon: Black with a wide central scarlet stripe.

Metal: Silver.

Size: Oval 44mm by 34mm

Description: A uniface oval ring containing an ornamental cypher of Queen Alexandra surmounted by a Tudor crown. Three plain rings are attached to the outer edge of the circle for suspension. The ring is inscribed in raised lettering: QUEEN ALEXANDRA'S MILITARY FAMILIES NURSING SERVICE.

Comments: *The cape badge was instituted in 1921 upon formation of the QAMFNS, and was used until 1949 when the QAMFNS was incorporated into the QARANC. It was worn on the right breast on ward dress for commissioned (qualified) nurses. It was issued through stores to each individual.*

VALUE: £80–£100   *Miniature* £25–35

326B. TERRITORIAL ARMY NURSING SERVICE CAPE BADGE

Date: 1921–50.

Branch of Service: Territorial Army Nursing Service.

Ribbon: Scarlet with a narrow central white stripe.

Metal: Silver.

Size: Oval 38mm by 28mm

Description: A uniface oval ring surmounted by a Tudor crown attached to a plain ring for suspension. The ring has at the centre two ornamental letters "A" interlocking and set at an angle. The ring is inscribed in raised lettering: TERRITORIAL ARMY NURSING SERVICE. Beneath, an ornate scroll bearing the Latin inscription: FORTITUDO MEA DEUS.

Comments: *The cape badge was instituted in 1921 upon the formation of the TANS and was used until 1950 when the TANS was incorporated into the QARANC. It was worn on the right breast on ward dress for commissioned (qualified) nurses. It was issued through stores to each individual.*

VALUE: £30–£40   *Miniature* £25–35

326C. QUEEN ALEXANDRA'S ROYAL ARMY NURSING CORPS CAPE BADGE

Date: 1949.
Branch of Service: Queen Alexandra's Royal Army Nursing Corps.
Ribbon: Scarlet with two white outer stripes and two black inner stripes.
Metal: Silver.
Size: Oval 46mm by 32mm.
Description: A uniface oval ring containing the Cross of the Order of the Dannebrog, with an ornamental cypher of Queen Alexandra, surmounted by a Tudor crown, fitted with a plain ring for suspension. The oval ring is inscribed in raised lettering QUEEN ALEXANDRA'S ROYAL ARMY NURSING COPRS.
Comments: *The cape badge was instituted in 1949 and continues to be issued today to all commissioned (qualified) nurses in the QARANC. It is worn on the right breast on ward dress for both female and, since 1992, male commissioned (qualified) nurses. It is issued through stores to each individual.*

VALUE: £80–100   *Miniature*   £35–45

327. INDIAN TITLE BADGE

Instituted: 12 December 1911.
Ribbon: Light blue edged with dark blue (1st class); red edged with dark red (2nd class); or dark blue edged with light blue (3rd class).
Metal: Silver or silver-gilt.
Size: Height 58mm; max. width 45mm.
Description: A radiate star topped by an imperial crown with a curved laurel wreath below the crown and cutting across the top of a central medallion surrounded by a collar inscribed with the appropriate title. The medallion bears the crowned profile of King George V or King George VI. From the first issue of King George V's Title Badge on June 1, 1912 until 1933, his bust faced right. As from June 1, 1933 his bust faced left for the remainder of the reign. King George VI's Title Badges had his bust facing left. (Reverse) plain, but engraved with the name of the recipient.
Comments: *Introduced by King George V on the occasion of the Delhi Durbar of 1911 and awarded in three classes to civilians and Viceroy's commissioned officers of the Indian Army for faithful service or acts of public welfare. Recipients proceeded from the lowest grade to higher grades, each accompanied by a distinctive title. Each grade was issued in Hindu and Muslim versions, differing in title: Diwan Bahadur (Muslim) or Sardar Bahadur (Hindu), Khan Bahadur (Muslim) or Rai or Rao Bahadur (Hindu) and Khan Sahib (Muslim) or Rai or Rao Sahib (Hindu), in descending order of grade. These title badges took precedence after all British and Indian orders and decorations, and before campaign medals. In miniatures (at least) the George VI versions, which all have his bust facing right, are rarer than those of King George V with left-facing bust.*

1st Class

2nd Class

3rd Class

VALUE:	Geo. V right	Geo. V left	Geo. VI
First class			
Diwan Bahadur	£150–200	£200–250	£350–400
Sardar Bahadur	£150–200	£200–250	£350–400
Second class			
Khan Bahadur	£100–175	£125–200	£300–350
Rao Bahadur	£100–175	£125–200	£300–350
Third class			
Khan Sahib	£100–175	£125–200	£300–350
Rao Sahib	£100–175	£125–200	£300–350

Miniatures
   George V   £75–85   George VI   £85–95

328. BADGES OF HONOUR (AFRICAN COUNTRIES)

Instituted: 1922.
Ribbon: Plain yellow, 38mm (neck) or 32mm (breast).
Metal: Bronze.
Size: 65mm x 48mm (neck); 45mm x 33mm (breast).
Description: Oval badges with a raised rim of laurel leaves terminating at the top in an imperial crown flanked by two lions. (Obverse) a crowned effigy of the reigning monarch; (reverse) the crowned cypher of the monarch or some emblem symbolic of the particular country with the country name in the exergue.
Comments: *The badge accompanied a certificate of honour awarded to chiefs and other persons of non-European descent who had rendered loyal and valuable service to the government of the territory. The original award was a neck badge suspended by a ribbon, but from 1954 onwards recipients were given the option of taking the award as a neck or breast badge. These awards were quite distinct from the decorations known as the Native Chiefs Medals (see number 70). They were first awarded to Ugandans but later extended to 14 other British territories in East and West Africa as well as the three High Commisson territories in Southern Africa. In particular the Badges issued for Nyasaland under Elizabeth II are rare, as Nyasaland became a Federation with Rhodesia in 1957. They are believed to have fallen into abeyance in the early 1980s.*

VALUE:

George V	£300–400
George VI	£200–275
Elizabeth II (neck)	£175–250
Elizabeth II (breast)	£175–250

329. BADGES OF HONOUR (NON-AFRICAN COUNTRIES)

Instituted: 1926.
Ribbon: 38mm watered silk mustard yellow.
Metal: Silver gilt.
Size: 41mm (George VI) or 32 mm (Elizabeth II).
Description: Circular with a raised rim of laurel leaves bearing a ring for suspension. (Obverse) crowned effigy of the reigning monarch; (reverse) the emblem of the country with the name round the foot.
Comments: *These medals accompanied certificates of honour awarded to indigenous persons who had rendered valuable service to the colony or protectorate. These awards appear to have been in abeyance since the early 1980s. Exceptionally, the New Hebrides badge was awarded to three British officers (Colonel (now General Lord) Guthrie (of Craigiebank), Lieutenant-Colonel C. H. C. Howgill, RM and HRH the Duke of Gloucester) in connection with the "Coconut War" in July 1980 instead of a campaign medal. The reverse types show the badges of 28 colonies or protectorates.*

VALUE:
George V	£1600–1800
George VI	£1800–2500
Elizabeth II	£1500–2000
Miniature	£75–100

329A. GOVERNOR GENERALS' MEDAL OF HONOUR

Instituted: 2014.

Ribbon: Yellow with three central stripes of green/light blue/green

Metal: Nickel silver: gold plated for gold award, nickel plated for silver award. Bronzed brass gilding metal (copper-zinc alloy) for bronze award.

Size: 36mm

Description: (Obverse) Crowned effigy of the reigning Monarch; (reverse) Nine stars representing the nine Caribbean Commonwealth Realms, surrounded by palm fronds with crown above. Designed by Major D Rankin-Hunt, Norfolk Herald of Arms.

Comments: *Awarded in three grades (Gold, Silver and Bronze) on the direct authority of the Governor Generals of the Caribbean realms:*

- Antigua & Barbuda
- The Bahamas
- Barbados (Prior to November 30, 2021)
- Belize
- Grenada
- Jamaica
- St Christopher and Nevis
- St Lucia
- St Vincent & The Grenadines

Used as a gift to reward islanders and others who have shown service to the country or directly in the service of the Governor General, their spouse or the Vice Regal Household.

A second award bar also exists for each grade.

VALUE: —

330. NAVAL ENGINEER'S GOOD CONDUCT MEDAL

Instituted: 1842.
Ribbon: Originally plain dark blue but later broad blue with white edges.
Metal: Silver.
Size: 35mm.
Description: (Obverse) a two-masted paddle steamer with a trident in the exergue; (reverse) a circular cable cartouche enclosing a crowned fouled anchor and the legend FOR ABILITY AND GOOD CONDUCT. Between the cable and the rim the details of the recipient were engraved round the circumference. Considering the rarity of the award, it is even more remarkable that the medals have several unique features. Shaw's medal, for example, had oak leaves in the exergue, flanking the trident, but this feature was omitted from later medals. Medals have been recorded with a straight bar suspender, a steel clip and ring suspender or fixed ring suspension with one or two intermediate rings.
Comments: *This medal was abolished five years after it was instituted, only seven medals being awarded in that period: to William Shaw (1842), William Dunkin (1842), William Johnstone (1843), John Langley (1843), J.P. Rundle (1845), George Roberts (1845) and Samuel B. Meredith (1846). Restrikes were produced in 1875 and at a later date. The original medals have a grooved rim, the 1875 restrikes a diagonal grained rim and the later restrikes a plain, flat rim.*

VALUE:
Original	Rare
1875 restrike	£125–150
Later restrike	£80–100

331. INDIAN RECRUITING BADGE (GEORGE V)

Instituted: 1917.
Ribbon: Plain dark green.
Metal: Bronze.
Size: Height 45mm; max. width 48mm.
Description: A five-pointed star with ball finials, surmounted by a wreathed gilt medallion bearing a left-facing crowned bust of King George V, inscribed FOR RECRUITING WORK DURING THE WAR.
Comments: *Awarded to Indian officers and NCOs engaged in recruitment of troops. It could only be worn in uniform when attending durbars or state functions, but at any time in plain clothes.*

VALUE: George V £100–120 *Miniature* £55–70

332. INDIAN RECRUITING BADGE (GEORGE VI)

Instituted: 1940.
Ribbon: Emerald green divided into three sections interspersed by narrow stripes of red (left) and yellow (right).
Metal: Silver and bronze.
Size: Height 42mm; max. width 39mm.
Description: A multi-rayed silver breast badge surmounted by an imperial crown with a suspension ring fitted through the top of the crown. In the centre is superimposed a bronze medallion bearing the left-facing crowned profile of King George VI, within a collar inscribed FOR RECRUITING.
Comments: *Awarded to selected civilian and military pensioners, full-time members of the Indian Recruiting Organisation, fathers and mothers having at least three children in the armed services, and wives having a husband and at least two children serving in the defence forces.*

VALUE: George VI £70–90 *Miniature* £65–80

333. NAVAL GOOD SHOOTING MEDAL

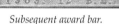

Subsequent award bar.

Instituted: August 1902.
Ribbon: Dark blue with a red central stripe edged in white.
Metal: Silver.
Size: 36mm.
Description: (Obverse) the effigy of the reigning monarch; (reverse) a nude figure of Neptune holding five thunderbolts in each hand. In the background can be seen the bows of a trireme and the heads of three horses, with a trident in the field. The Latin motto VICTORIA CURAM AMAT (Victory loves care) appears round the circumference. Fitted with a straight suspension bar. The recipient's name, number, rank, ship and calibre of gun are impressed round the rim.
Comments: *Instituted to promote excellent gunnery performances in the annual Fleet Competitions, it was first awarded in 1903 but was discontinued in 1914. Subsequent success was marked by the issue of a bar bearing the name of the ship and the date. A total of 974 medals and 62 bars were awarded. 53 men received one bar, three men got two bars and only one achieved three bars.*

VALUE:		Miniature (in silver)
Edward VII	£350–450	£65–75
George V	£350–450	£65–75
With 1 bar	£600–800	£70–80

334. ARMY BEST SHOT MEDAL

Instituted: 30 April 1869.
Ribbon: Watered crimson with black, white (or buff*) and black stripes at the edges. (*The Regulations state that the stripes should be white but recent medals have been issued with buff stripes.)
Metal: Silver.
Size: 36mm.
Description: (Obverse) the veiled diademmed profile of Queen Victoria; (reverse) Victory bestowing a laurel crown on a naked warrior armed with a quiver of arrows and a bow and holding a target, impaled with arrows, in his other hand. Fitted with a straight suspension bar.
Comments: *This medal, sometimes referred to as the Queen's Medal, was awarded annually to the champion in the Army marksmanship contests held at Bisley. It was originally struck in bronze but was upgraded to silver in 1872. The award ceased in 1882 but was revived in 1923 and thereafter known as the King's Medal. The original reverse was retained, with the appropriate effigy of the reigning sovereign on the obverse. Since 1953 it has been known as the Queen's Medal again. In the post-1923 medals a bar bears the year of the award, with additional year clasps for subsequent awards. Until 1934 a single medal was awarded each year but in 1935 two medals were granted for the champion shots of the Regular and Territorial Armies respectively. Subsequently additional medals have been sanctioned for award to the military forces of India, Canada, Australia, New Zealand, Ceylon, Rhodesia, the British South Africa Police, the Union of South Africa, Pakistan, Jamaica and Ghana.*

VALUE:		Miniature
Victoria bronze	Rare	—
Victoria silver	Rare	—
George V	£1000–1200	£40–50
George VI	£1000–1200	£40–50
Elizabeth II	£1000–1200	£25–30
Charles III	—	—

335. QUEEN'S / KING'S MEDAL FOR CHAMPION SHOTS OF THE ROYAL NAVY AND ROYAL MARINES

Instituted: 12 June 1953.
Ribbon: Dark blue with a broad red central stripe flanked by white stripes.
Metal: Silver.
Size: 36mm.
Description: (Obverse) the effigy of reigning monarch; (reverse) Neptune (as on the Naval Good Shooting Medal).
Comments: *Instituted as the naval counterpart of the Army best shot medal with a bar which bears the year of the award.*

VALUE:

Elizabeth II	£1000–1200	*Miniature*	£20–25
Charles III	—		—

336. QUEEN'S / KING'S MEDAL FOR CHAMPION SHOTS OF THE ROYAL AIR FORCE

Instituted: 12 June 1953.
Ribbon: Broad crimson centre flanked by dark blue stripes bisected by thin light blue stripes.
Metal: Silver.
Size: 36mm.
Description: (Obverse) the effigy of reigning monarch; (reverse) Hermes kneeling on a flying hawk and holding the caduceus in one hand and a javelin in the other. The medal is fitted with a straight bar suspender. A date clasp is attached to the ribbon.
Comments: *Competed for at the annual RAF Small Arms Meeting at Bisley. The medal was issued to the Champion Shot of the RNZAF under the terms of the same Royal Warrant as the RAF.*

VALUE:

Elizabeth II	£1000–1200	*Miniature*	£25–35
Charles III	—		—

337. QUEEN'S / KING'S MEDAL FOR CHAMPION SHOTS OF THE NEW ZEALAND NAVAL FORCES

Instituted: 9 July 1958.
Ribbon: Crimson centre bordered with white and broad dark blue stripes at the edges.
Metal: Silver.
Size: 36mm.
Description: (Obverse) the effigy of reigning monarch; (reverse) similar to that of the Naval Good Shooting Medal of 1903-14. Fitted with a clasp bearing the year of the award and a straight suspension bar.
Comments: *Awards were made retrospective to 1 January 1955. This medal is awarded for marksmanship in an annual contest of the New Zealand Naval Forces. Additional clasps are granted for further success. One contestant, Lt Cdr N. C. G. Peach, RNZN, has won this award ten times*

VALUE:

Elizabeth II	—	*Miniature*	£35–45
Charles III	—		—

338. UNION OF SOUTH AFRICA COMMEMORATION MEDAL

Instituted: 1910.
Ribbon: 38mm orange-yellow with a broad central dark blue stripe.
Metal: Silver.
Size: 36mm.
Description: (Obverse) the uncrowned effigy of King George V; (reverse) Mercury as God of Commerce and Prosperity, bending over an anvil, forging the links of a chain symbolic of the uniting of the four colonies (Cape Colony, Natal, Orange Free State and the Transvaal), with the date 1910 in the exergue and the legend TO COMMEMORATE THE UNION OF SOUTH AFRICA.
Comments: *This was the first medal struck in the reign of George V and resulted from the South Africa Act of 1909. This Act proclaimed the unification on 31 May 1910, of the self-governing four colonies into a legislative Union, becoming provinces of the Union of South Africa. This medal, the obverse of which was designed by Sir Bertram MacKennal, and the reverse by Mr Sydney Marsh, was struck to mark the opening of the first Parliament of the Union by HRH the Duke of Connaught. Awarded to those who took part in the inauguration of the Parliament. Additionally it was awarded to certain officers and men of HMS Balmoral Castle, a Union Castle liner specially commissioned as a man-of-war to convey HRH the Duke of Connaught as the King's representative to South Africa for the celebrations. A total of 551 medals were struck by the Royal Mint, and were issued unnamed, although privately named medals are in existence.*

VALUE:	Named	£600–800
	Unnamed	£600–800
	Miniature	£25–35

339. DEKORATIE VOOR TROUWE DIENST

The other side is similar to no. 340 illustrated opposite

Instituted: 1920.
Ribbon: A broad dark blue central stripe flanked on one side by a gold stripe with a thin red stripe superimposed towards the edge, and on the other side by a yellow stripe with a thin white stripe towards the edge. Transvaal recipients wore the ribbon with the red to the centre of the chest; Orange Free State recipients wore the ribbon with the white stripe to the centre of the chest.
Metal: Silver.
Size: 36mm.
Description: (Obverse) the arms of the Transvaal; (reverse) the arms of the Orange Free State. Fitted with a fixed suspender. Recipients wore the medal with the appropriate state arms showing.
Comments: *This medal which is correctly named the Dekoratie Voor Trouwe Dienst was awarded by the Union of South Africa to officers of the two former Boer republics for distinguished service during the Second Boer War of 1899-1902. Awards to officers and men of the former Boer Republics had to be individually claimed on prescribed forms and were named with rank, initials and surname of the individual. The late Don Forsyth published a roll listing full names and commandos/units of the recipients. This clearly identifies many recipients but cannot differentiate, for example, between any of the 10 issued ABO medals that were named "Burger P. J. Botha". However, the naming style and type of suspender can help to make positive identification possible.*

Medals issued up to October 1937 had a WWI British War Medal (MYB168) suspender and typical SA Mint WWI naming. Between October 1937 and February 1942 the WWI suspender was still used, but the naming was thinner, in a slightly smaller font as on the WWII Africa Service Medal (MYB 189). All subsequent issues have the WWII style naming as well as the "thick-necked" suspender as found on the Africa Service Medal (for details and illustrations see the article by Hent Loots in the OMRS Miscellany of Honours, No. 9, 1992). By comparing the dates on the Medal Application Forms of men with the same initials and surname a particular recipient can sometimes be pinpointed. NB Please note that these medals are often found with the suspender claw flattened to varying degrees: the SA Mint, on occasion, used rather crude methods to "fix" the pin.

VALUE:	Silver (591)	£750–900		
	Paired with matching MYB340	£1100–1500	*Miniature*	£65–75

340. ANGLO-BOERE OORLOG (WAR) MEDAL

Instituted: 1920.

Ribbon: Broad green and yellow stripes with three narrow stripes of red, white and dark blue in the centre. Transvaal recipients wore the ribbon with the green to the centre of the chest, while Orange Free State recipients wore it with the yellow towards the centre.

Metal: Silver.

Size: 36mm.

Description: Both sides inscribed ANGLO-BOERE OORLOG round the top, with the dates 1899-1902 round the foot. Medallions set in a border of a square and quatrefoil show the arms of the Orange Free State on one side and the Transvaal on the other. The medal was worn with the side showing the arms of the appropriate state uppermost. Fitted with a fixed suspender.

Comments: *Correctly named the Anglo-Boere Oorlog Medal, this was awarded by the Union government to officers and men of the former Boer republics for loyal service in the war against the British. To qualify for the medal proof had to be provided that they had fought against the British without surrendering or taking parole or the oath of allegiance prior to May 31, 1902. See note on no. 339 regarding awards to men of the former Boer Republics.*

VALUE: Silver   £240–260   *Miniature*   £65–75

Lint Voor Wonden (Wound Ribbon) Certificate value: £30; if with corresponding medal: value: £50.

341. COMMONWEALTH INDEPENDENCE MEDALS

Pakistan Independence Medal

Ceylon Police Independence Medal.

Since the partition of the Indian sub-continent in 1947 and the emergence of the Dominions of India and Pakistan, it has been customary for medals to be issued to mark the attainment of independence. As these medals are invariably awarded to British service personnel taking part in the independence ceremonies, they are appended here in chronological order of institution, the date of the actual award, where later, being given in parentheses. These medals usually have symbolic motifs with the date of independence inscribed. The distinctive ribbons are noted alongside. All are 32mm wide unless otherwise stated.

	VALUE
India 1947 (1948) Three equal stripes of orange, white and green	£20–25
Ceylon Police 1948 Three equal stripes of white, red, white with narrow black edges	£50–75
Pakistan 1947 (1950) Dark green with a central thin white stripe	£15–20
Ghana 1957 Nine alternating stripes of red, yellow and green	£60–65
Nigeria 1960 (1964) Three equal stripes of green, white and green	£25–30
Sierra Leone 1961 Three equal stripes of green, white and blue	£65–75
Jamaica 1962 Black centre flanked by yellow stripes and green edges	£60–65
Uganda 1962 (1963) Six stripes of black, yellow, red, black, yellow, red	£60–65
Kenya 1963 Yellow with two thin black stripes at the edges and a central thin green striope	£60–65

continued

341. COMMONWEALTH INDEPENDENCE MEDALS *continued*

Solomon Islands.

Sierra Leone.

Malawi.

VALUE

Malawi 1964
Three equal stripes of black, red and green — £65–75

Guyana 1966
Red centre flanked by yellow stripes and broad green
edges. The green and yellow separated (left) by a thin
black stripe and (right) by a thin pale blue stripe — £60–65

Swaziland 1968
Three equal stripes of red, yellow and blue — £60–65

Fiji 1970
Grey-blue with bars half red, half white, towards each edge — £65–75

Papua New Guinea 1975
Red bordered by thin stripes of yellow and white, with
black edges — £65–75

Transkei 1976 — £20–25

Solomon Islands 1978
Five equal stripes of blue, yellow, white, yellow and green — £65–75

Gilbert Islands (Kiribati) 1980
Half red, half black, separated by a thin white stripe, and
edged in yellow — £50–60

Ellice Islands (Tuvalu) 1980
Equal stripes of red, white and red edged yellow. the white
stripe bisected by a thin blue stripe — £30–40

Zimbabwe 1980
Silver or bronze 38mm black centre flanked by red and
yellow stripes with edges of green or blue — **Silver** £30–45
Bronze £20–25

Gambia 1981 — £35–45

Vanuatu 1980 (1981)
30mm stripes of red and green with central thinner
stripe of yellow edged by black — £20–25

St Christopher, Nevis and Anguilla 1983
Bars of green (left) and red (right) with a black central
bar having two thin white stripes, flanked by yellow
stripes — £55–75

Papua New Guinea.

Nigeria.

Zimbabwe.

*For the various ribbons see ribbon charts
on pp. 417 et seq.*

342. MALTA GEORGE CROSS 50th ANNIVERSARY COMMEMORATIVE MEDAL

Instituted: 1992.
Ribbon: Dark blue with central stripes of white and red (the Maltese national colours).
Metal: Cupro-nickel.
Size: 36mm.
Description: (Obverse) the crowned arms of the island, which include the George Cross in the upper left corner, with the date 1992 at the foot. (Reverse) a replica of the George Cross with the eight-pointed Maltese Cross at the top and the date 1942 at the foot, with a legend BHALA SHIEDA TA'EROIZMU U DEDIKAZZJONI on one side and TO BEAR WITNESS TO HEROISM AND DEVOTION on the other. Suspension is by a fixed bar decorated with laurels, attached to a ring.
Comments: *Sanctioned by the government of Malta to celebrate the fiftieth anniversary of the award of the George Cross by King George VI to the island for its heroic resistance to prolonged Axis attack during the Second World War. The medal has been awarded to surviving veterans who served in Malta in the armed forces and auxiliary services between 10 June 1940 and 8 September 1943. Permission for British citizens to wear this medal was subsequently granted by the Queen. As a number of veterans applied for the medal after the cut-off date of 15 April 1994, the Maltese Government sanctioned a second striking—these medals carry the word COPY below the right arm of the George Cross.*

VALUE:

Cupro-nickel (original striking)	£90–120	*Miniature* £20–25
Official copy	£50–60	

343. SHANGHAI VOLUNTEER CORPS MEDAL

Date: 1854.
Ribbon: Unknown—details sought.
Metal: Silver.
Size: 38mm
Description: Unknown—details sought.
Comment: *Awarded to the officers and men of the Shanghai Volunteers who took part in the battle of Soo Chow Creek (also known as the battle of Muddy Flats) which took place on April 28, 1854. Examples are of the greatest rarity and the last one to appear at auction was sold in 1991. Further details are sought.*

VALUE: —

344. SHANGHAI JUBILEE MEDAL

Instituted: 1893.
Ribbon: Watered silk half bright red, half white or red with 4mm central white stripe.
Metal: Silver or bronze.
Size: 36mm.
Description: (Obverse) triple-shield arms of the municipality surrounded by a band with thistles, shamrocks and roses round the foot and NOVEMBER 17 1843 round the top. (Reverse) a scrolled shield with the words SHANGHAI JUBILEE and NOVEMBER 17 1843 and inscribed diagonally across the centre with the recipient's name in block capitals. The shield is flanked by Chinese dragons and above is a steamship and the sun setting on the horizon. The rim is engraved "Presented by the Shanghai Municipality". Issued with a small suspension ring, but often replaced by a straight bar. This medal has also been recorded with an ornamental silver brooch bearing the dates 1843–1893.
Comments: *The British settlement in Shanghai was founded in 1843 and formed the nucleus of the International Settlement established in 1854 under the control of an autonomous Municipal Council. In effect the International Settlement functioned as an autonomous City State administered by a Municipal Committee formed from those nations comprising the Settlement. This was abolished when Shanghai was overrun by Imperial Japanese troops in 1941. Recently renewed interest from China and the Far East has vastly inflated the price of these medals at auctions. In February 2023, a silver example hammered at £6,400 at Denhams.*

VALUE:

Silver (625)	£5000–5500
Bronze (100)	£3000–4000

345. SHANGHAI FIRE BRIGADE LONG SERVICE MEDAL

Instituted: Before 1904.
Ribbon: Black with broad crimson borders.
Metal: Silver.
Size: 31mm.
Description: (Obverse) an armorial device featuring a Chinese dragon standing on a symbolic high-rise building on which is displayed a flame on a pole crossed by a hook and ladder, with MIH-HO-LOONG SHANGHAI round the top and the motto "Say the word and down comes your house" round the foot; (reverse) engraved with recipient's details. It seems strange that no Chinese characters appear on the medal. Ring and double claw suspension, with a broad silver brooch bar at the top of the ribbon.
Comment: *Awarded for a minimum of twelve years regular service with the Municipal Fire Brigade. The award was presumably in abeyance following the Japanese invasion in 1937 and the wholesale destruction of the international commercial metropolis.*

VALUE: £500–600   *Miniature* £95–110

346. SHANGHAI VOLUNTEER FIRE BRIGADE LONG SERVICE MEDAL

Instituted: 1904.
Ribbon: Red with two wide and one narrow (central) white stripes.
Metal: Gold, silver or bronze.
Size: 36mm.
Description: (Obverse) the arms and motto of the Municipality surrounded by a collar inscribed SHANGHAI VOLUNTEER FIRE BRIGADE ESTABLISHED 1866. (Reverse) originally simply engraved with name of unit, later a pair of crossed axes surmounted by a fireman's helmet under which is a horizontal tablet on which are engraved the recipient's dates of service. Round the circumference is inscribed FOR LONG SERVICE (top) and WE FIGHT THE FLAMES (foot) with quatrefoil ornaments separating the two inscriptions. Fitted with a swivelling scroll suspender.
Comments: *The medal in silver was awarded to members of the Volunteer Fire Brigade for five years service, for eight years service a clasp was added to the ribbon and for 12 years service the medal was awarded in gold. Bronze medals exist but are believed to have been specimens only.*

VALUE: £600–700   *Miniature* £95–110

347. SHANGHAI VOLUNTEER CORPS LONG SERVICE MEDAL

Instituted: 1921.
Ribbon: Equal stripes of red, white and blue, the red bisected by a thin green stripe, the white by black and the blue by yellow.
Metal: Silver.
Size: 36mm.
Description: (Obverse) an eight-pointed radiate star bearing a scroll at the top inscribed 4th APRIL 1854. The arms of the Municipality superimposed on the star and surrounded by a collar inscribed SHANGHAI VOLUNTEER CORPS. Round the foot of the medal is a band inscribed FOR LONG SERVICE. (Reverse) plain, engraved with the name of the recipient and his period of service.
Comments: *The Volunteer Corps was raised in 1853 to protect the British and other foreign settlements. The date on the scroll alludes to the Corps' first engagement, the Battle of Muddy Flat. The Corps was cosmopolitan in structure, although the British element predominated. It was disbanded in September 1942, nine months after the Japanese overran the International Settlement. Awarded for 12 years good service. The last medal was awarded in 1941.*
VALUE: £500–600   *Miniature* £95–110

348. SHANGHAI MUNICIPAL POLICE DISTINGUISHED CONDUCT MEDAL

Instituted: 1924.
Ribbon: Red with a central blue stripe (1st class); red with a blue stripe at each edge (2nd class).
Metal: Silver or bronze.
Size: 36mm.
Description: (Obverse) arms of the Municipality and the inscription SHANGHAI MUNICIPAL POLICE; (reverse) the words FOR DISTINGUISHED CONDUCT. The recipient's name and rank were engraved around the rim.
Comments: *Awarded to officers and men of the Municipal Police in two classes, distinguished solely by their ribbons and the metal used (silver or bronze). A sliding clasp was fitted to the ribbon to denote a second award; this featured the Municipal crest and was engraved on the reverse with the details of the award. It is believed that a total of 223 medals were awarded up to 1942, including 72 to foreign members of the force.*

VALUE: Silver   £950–1200   *Miniature* £95–110
         Bronze   £700–850

349. SHANGHAI MUNICIPAL POLICE LONG SERVICE MEDAL

Instituted: 1925.
Ribbon: Brown with a central yellow stripe edged in white.
Metal: Silver.
Size: 36mm.
Description: (Obverse) arms of the Municipality within a collar inscribed SHANGHAI MUNICIPAL POLICE (As MYB 348 above); (reverse) plain apart from the inscription FOR LONG SERVICE in two lines across the centre. The recipient's name and rank were engraved round the rim in upper and lower case lettering. Awards to Indians were named in cursive script with the Hindi equivalent alongside. Fitted with a swivelling scroll suspender.
Comments: *Awarded for 12 years good service in the Shanghai Municipal Police, an international force composed largely of Sikhs, Chinese and White Russians as well as British ex-soldiers and policemen. Dated clasps for further five year periods of service were awarded. The medal was abolished in 1942.*

VALUE: *Miniature*
      Without clasp   £750–1000   £50–55
      With clasp   £1500–1750   £55–65
      2 clasps   £850–1000   £65–75

350. SHANGHAI MUNICIPAL POLICE (SPECIALS) LONG SERVICE MEDAL

Instituted: 1929.
Ribbon: Dark brown with three white bars, each bisected by a thin yellow stripe.
Metal: Silver.
Size: 36mm.
Description: (Obverse) the arms of the Municipality with the motto OMNIA JUNCTA IN UNO (all joined in one) round the circumference. (Reverse) inscribed SHANGHAI MUNICIPAL POLICE (SPECIALS) FOR LONG SERVICE in six lines. A unique award to A.L. Anderson (1930) was inscribed on the reverse FOR DISTINGUISHED AND VALUABLE SERVICES.
Comments: *Awarded for 12 years active and efficient service in the Special Constabulary. Some 52 medals and 8 clasps for additional service are recorded in the* Shanghai Gazette, *but the actual number awarded was probably greater. The medal was discontinued in 1942.*

VALUE :
      Without clasp   £600–850   With clasp   £1800–2500
      Miniature   £210–260

351. SHANGHAI MUNICIPAL COUNCIL EMERGENCY MEDAL

Instituted: 1937.
Ribbon: 38mm bright red, having a broad white central stripe bordered black and yellow edges separated from the red by thin black stripes.
Metal: Bronze.
Size: 40mm.
Description: An eight-pointed star with ring suspension. (Obverse) a central medallion superimposed on the radiate star with the triple-shield arms of the Municipality surrounded by a collar inscribed SHANGHAI MUNICIPAL COUNCIL. (Reverse) a laurel wreath enclosing the words FOR SERVICES RENDERED - AUGUST 12 TO NOVEMBER 12 1937.
Comments: *Awarded to members of the Police, Volunteer Corps, Fire Brigade and civilians for services during the emergency of August-November 1937 when fighting between the Chinese and Japanese in and around Shanghai threatened to encroach on the International Settlement. Issued unnamed, but accompanied by a certificate bearing the name and unit of the recipient. Examples have been seen with the recipient's name engraved on the reverse.*

VALUE: £300–400   *Miniature* £65–85

351A. CHINESE MARITIME CUSTOMS SERVICE FINANCIAL MEDAL

Instituted:
Ribbon: Green, with yellow stripes.
Metal: Gold, silver or bronze according to class.
Size:
Description: An eight-pointed radiate star suspended by a plain ring, having an oval medallion on the obverse inscribed in Chinese and depicting a Chinese junk; (reverse) a horseshoe scroll inscribed THE CHINESE MARITIME CUSTOMS MEDAL with FINANCIAL across the foot. The recipient's name was engraved in the centre.
Comments: *The Chinese Maritime Customs Service was operated and largely staffed at the higher levels by British personnel from 1854 till 1950. Medals were awarded for five years' service or shorter service of exceptional merit and were granted in three classes, each of three grades, making nine variations in all, distinguished by the respective metals, and awarded according to the rank of the recipient.*

Obverse

VALUE: **Very Rare**   *Miniature* £100–110

351B. CHINESE MARITIME CUSTOMS SERVICE MERITORIOUS SERVICE MEDAL

Instituted:
Ribbon: Green with yellow stripes.
Metal: Gold, silver or bronze according to grade.
Size:
Description: As above, but FOR MERITORIOUS SERVICE in the tablet on the reverse.
Comments: *Awarded for 25 years continuous service, according to the rank of the recipient, but later awards in silver or gold could be made on promotion to a higher rank, or for exceptional service, notably from 1931 onwards, following the outbreak of hostilities with Japan.*

VALUE: **Very Rare**

Reverse

352. AUTOMOBILE ASSOCIATION SERVICE CROSS

Date: 1956.
Ribbon: Yellow with three narrow black stripes.
Metal: Silver.
Size: 36mm.
Description: A silver cross flory terminating in scrolls, with the AA emblem surmounted in the centre.
Comments: *Established in commemoration of the Association's Golden Jubilee, the Cross is the highest award to AA patrolmen and other uniformed members of staff for conspicuous acts of bravery involving an imminent risk of personal injury whilst on duty in uniform, or whilst engaged in an action related to duty. To date only 15 crosses have been awarded. A monetary reward accompanies the Cross.*

VALUE: £400–500

353. AUTOMOBILE ASSOCIATION SERVICE MEDAL

Date: 1956.
Ribbon: Half yellow, half black.
Metal: Silver.
Size: 36mm.
Description: A circular medal in the form of the AA badge with wings sprouting from the top and flanking a claw and ring suspension. (Obverse) AA superimposed on a wheel, with the inscription AUTOMOBILE ASSOCIATION/SERVICE MEDAL round the circumference; (reverse) details of the award.
Clasp: A silver-gilt and red enamel clasp inscribed 192064 (ie. 20 years good driving, 1964) has been reported.
Comments: *Like the Cross, the Medal of the Association was instituted in commemoration of the Association's Golden Jubilee. The medal is awarded to members of the uniformed staff for courageous or outstanding initiative and devotion to duty. To date, only 60 medals have been awarded, including four in 1997, mainly for life-saving and bravery in accidents. A monetary reward accompanies the Medal. A Service Citation is also awarded for lesser acts, a total of 63 having been bestowed so far.*

VALUE: £200–250

354. SUFFRAGETTE MEDAL

Instituted: 1909.
Campaign: Votes for women.
Ribbon: Three equal stripes of purple, silver and green.
Metal: Silver.
Size: 20mm.
Clasps: A silver dated bar, or an enamelled bar in the WSPU colours with the date on the reverse, or prison bars surmounted by a broad arrow.
Description: A small silver medal suspended by a ring from a bar with scrolled finials, engraved with the date of the award. A similarly scrolled brooch bar at the top of the ribbon is inscribed FOR VALOUR. The plain medal is engraved HUNGER STRIKE in various styles and hallmarked.
Comments: *This medal was awarded by the Women's Social and Political Union (WSPU) to those militant Suffragettes who were imprisoned for various acts of violence and who went on hunger strike while in prison. At first they were forcibly fed under the most barbaric conditions, as a result of which several died. The Government then introduced the Cat and Mouse Act, whereby hunger strikers at the point of death were released, but were then re-arrested and returned to prison when they had recovered sufficiently from their ordeal. A silver bar was awarded to those who were imprisoned and went on hunger strike whilst an enamel bar was awarded to those who were force fed in prison. The portcullis badge was given to those imprisoned in Holloway and is occasionally seen separately from the medal.*

VALUE: Boxed: From £3500
                 In personally inscribed case: From £6000

355. FLORENCE NIGHTINGALE MEDAL

Date: 1912.
Ribbon: White with narrow yellow and broad red stripes towards the edges.
Metal: Silver with enamels.
Size:
Description: An upright elliptical medal coming to a point at both ends, with a three-quarter length portrait of Florence Nightingale from the Crimean War period, inscribed MEMORIAM FLORENCE NIGHTINGALE 1820–1910 AD. The reverse bears the recipient's name.
Comments: *Instituted by the International Committee of the Red Cross for award to trained nurses, matrons, nursing organisers or voluntary aids for distinguished or exceptional service. Awards are made every other year on the anniversary of Miss Nightingale's birthday. This medal has been awarded very sparingly.*

VALUE: £500–700   *Miniature*   £410–510

356. ANZAC COMMEMORATIVE MEDAL

Date: 1967.
Ribbon: None.
Metal: Bronze.
Size: 76mm x 50mm.
Description: (Obverse) a medallion surmounted by a Royal Crown with a laurel wreath and the word ANZAC in a scroll below. In the field is the date 1915 above a picture of John Simpson and his donkey saving a wounded soldier at Gallipoli (based on a painting by 4/26A Spr Horace Moore-Jones, NZ Engineers. (Reverse) a map of Australia and New Zealand with the Southern Cross constellation. The reverse of the scroll has New Zealand fern leaves.
Comments: *This medal was instituted jointly by the governments of Australia and New Zealand and awarded to surviving veterans of the Australian and New Zealand Army Corps who served in the Gallipoli campaign, all named on the reverse. Designed by Australian artist Raymond Ewers. There is also a half-size lapel badge bearing the obverse design and numbered on the reverse.*

VALUE: Original Medal   £150–250   Lapel badge   £50–60

357. NEW ZEALAND CADET DISTRICT MEDAL

Date: 1902.
Ribbon: Plain khaki or tan with a central pink flanked by dark green stripes.
Metal: Silver.
Size: 32mm.
Description: (Obverse) profile of Edward VII or George V with inscription FOR KING AND COUNTRY: PUBLIC SCHOOL CADETS, N.Z.; (reverse) DEFENCE NOT DEFIANCE round the top, with DISTRICT PRIZE (or CHALLENGE) MEDAL AWARDED TO in three lines, leaving space for the name of the recipient to be engraved below.
Comments: *These medals were instituted following the establishment of the Public School Cadets in 1902 and were awarded in two classes in Challenge competitions or as prizes in the annual examinations.*

VALUE: District Challenge   £100–150
              District Prize   £90–100

362. CORPS OF COMMISSIONAIRES MEDAL

Date:
Ribbon: Red, white and blue.
Metal: Silver or blackened metal.
Size: 40mm.
Description: A 16-point star bearing a central medallion with the Union Jack in the centre surrounded by the Latin mottoes: VIRTUTE ET INDUSTRIA (top) and LABOR VINCIT OMNIA (foot)—"by ability and industry" and "work conquers all" respectively. Fitted with a plain ring for suspension from the ribbon which bears an elaborate brooch consisting of crossed rifle and sabre on a fouled anchor with a cannon behind, representing the armed forces from which the Corps recruits its members.
Comments: *Awarded by the Corps of Commissionaires for long and exemplary service.*

VALUE: £30–45   *Miniature*   £25–30

363. NATIONAL EMERGENCY MEDAL

Date: 1926.
Ribbon: None.
Metal: Gold or bronze.
Size: 50mm.
Description: (Obverse) Britannia seated holding a laurel branch and resting on a shield. Above the inscription across the field FOR SERVICE IN NATIONAL EMERGENCY MAY 1926 appear the national emblems of England and Scotland with the LMS emblem between; (reverse) three female figures with arms outstretched holding locomotives dividing the inscription LARGITAS MUNERIS SALUS REIPUBLICAE (the immensity of the task, the well-being of the country).
Comments: *These medals were designed by Edward Gillick and struck by the Royal Mint on behalf of the London, Midland and Scottish Railway for presentation to those volunteers who had served the company throughout the General Strike of May 1926. The medals were struck in bronze and issued in boxes unnamed to the recipients. According to Mint records, a few medals were also struck in gold, but none has so far been recorded.*

VALUE:
   Gold   —
   Bronze   £45–55

364. ROYAL WARRANT HOLDERS ASSOCIATION MEDAL

Original reverse.

1977 "Jubilee" reverse.

Instituted: 1897.

Ribbon: Dark purple with a central yellow stripe.

Metal: Silver, silver-gilt or gold.

Size: 23mm.

Description: (Obverse) crowned profile of the reigning monarch; (reverse) THE ROYAL WARRANT HOLDERS ASSOCIATION round the edge with the name of the Warrant holder engraved in the centre. The medal was surmounted by an imperial crown fitted to a ring for suspension, with a brooch bar at the top of the ribbon, for issues between those of Queen Victoria and George VI. The medal fell into abeyance in 1946 due to the scarcity of silver. In 1897 the Association issued a medal in silver to commemorate the Diamond Jubilee of Queen Victoria. In 1977, for Her Majesty Queen Elizabeth's Silver Jubilee, a new medal was struck, with the dates 1952–1977 appearing below the bust. This medal is surmounted by a Tudor crown and fitted with a ring for suspension from a bar with a brooch bar at the top of the ribbon. This issue has a special reverse bearing the Royal arms—this special reverse was used again in 2002 on the occasion of the Golden Jubilee.

Comments: *This medal was originally instituted by Queen Victoria for individuals who are granted the Royal Warrant and may be worn at formal occasions of the Association. Until 1911 medals were issued in both silver and silver-gilt to members of the Association. However, from 1911 the silver-gilt and gold medals were only awarded to Council members. Miniature medals were also authorised and are believed to have been issued but they are very rare and were discontinued in 1920. Medals were struck for the reign of Edward VIII but were never issued, however unnamed examples do exist. The 1977 Silver Jubilee medal was designed by Alex Styles of Garrard the Crown jewellers. In 2002 Her Majesty the Queen gave approval for the medal to be issued in silver-gilt or gold to mark the Golden Jubilee, but it reverted to silver in 2003. The medal may be purchased by Warrant holders only.*

VALUE:

Victoria Silver-gilt	£200–250
Jubilee	£200–250
Edward VII Silver	£100–150
Silver-gilt	£200–250
George V	£150–200
Edward VIII	£200–250
George VI	£150–200
Elizabeth II	£150–200
1977 Jubilee	£200–250
2002 Jubilee	£200–250

365. ROYAL NATIONAL LIFEBOAT INSTITUTION DECORATION

(see also 291DD and L4)

Type I.

Date: 1901, 1913.

Ribbon: Blue watered silk.

Metal: Gold or silver with enamels.

Size: 27mm (type I) or 36mm (type II).

Description: Type I: a circular uniface medal depicting a lifeboat going to the assistance of a sailing ship in distress, surrounded by a white enamelled lifebelt surmounted by a gilt crown. Type II: A wavy cross in dark blue enamel, with the initials RNLI in the angles interlaced with a rope, surmounted by a Royal Crown, fitted with a ring for suspension. First Class (gold) and Second Class (silver). Type III: an oval enamelled lapel badge depicting the Institution's emblem.

Comments: *The original decoration, suspended from a bow of blue ribbon, designed by Charles Dibdin, the RNLI Secretary, was instituted as a reward for Branch Honorary Secretaries and Lady Auxiliaries for long and devoted service. 36 awards were made initially, followed by 18 other awards in 1902–9. The medal was manufactured by Alstons & Hallam of Bishopsgate. Thereafter a new decoration in the form of a cross, awarded to men and women in two classes, gold and silver, was designed by Mr Burke of the College of Heralds and manufactured by Garrards in 1912. Objections raised by King George V led to the cross being discontinued on May 14, 1914, by which time only ten gold awards had been made and no silver awards. Today long service is rewarded with an enamelled lapel badge as illustrated below.*

VALUE:		
	Type I	—
	Type II	—
	Type III	£20–30

Type II, 2nd class in silver.

Type III lapel badge.

366. MAIDSTONE TYPHOID MEDAL

Date: 1897.
Ribbon: Purple with yellow stripes at the edges.
Metal: Silver
Size: 32mm.
Description: (Obverse) the coat of arms of the town of Maidstone with MAIDSTONE KENT on a ribbon below; (reverse) an ornate panel engraved with the recipient's name in the centre and the words WITH GRATITUDE TO . . . FOR LOVING SERVICES 1897, with an olive branch below.
Comments: *A major epidemic of Typhoid fever broke out in Maidstone, Kent during late August 1897. By 9 September 117 cases had been reported, rising to 774 by the end of the month and by 9 October the number had risen to 1,200, with 42 deaths. By the end of December when the epidemic was considered to be over a total of 132 people had died. Medals were awarded to the nursing staff who served in the town during the epidemic. Many were presented by the Mayor of Maidstone at a special ceremony held at the Museum and Technical School on Wednesday 8 December 1897.*

VALUE:	Unnamed	£150–200
	Named	£350–400

367. BOYS' LIFE BRIGADE MEDAL

Date: 1905.
Ribbon: Red.
Metal: Bronze.
Size: 34mm.
Description: (Obverse) A Geneva cross within a crowned circle and a radiate background, the circle inscribed TO SAVE LIFE; a scroll round the foot inscribed THE BOYS LIFE BRIGADE; (reverse) personal details of the recipient. Fitted with a plain suspension ring. The brooch bar is in the form of a scroll with a laurel wreath superimposed on the middle and a clasp bearing the date of the award.
Comments: *This medal was awarded for good attendance. The Boys' Life Brigade amalgamated with the Boys' Brigade in 1926 and the award of this medal was then abolished. The BLB Cross for Courage was also abolished at this time having been awarded only ten times in its history.*

VALUE: £20–30

367A. BOYS' BRIGADE SQUAD MEDAL

Date: 1896.
Ribbon: Originally dark blue, later maroon, suspended from an ornate brooch pin..
Metal: Bronze.
Size: 42mm.
Description: A multi-faceted, eight-pointed star surmounted by the Brigade badge: an anchor with the word SURE on the top cross-member of the anchor and STEADFAST on the lower limbs, the initials BB either side. When the Boys' Brigade amalgamated with the Boys' Life Brigade in 1926 the Geneva cross was added to the design.
Comments: *This medal is believed to have been awarded to the squad who achieved the highest average attendance over one year. The Boys' Brigade issued and continues to issue a large number of badges and medals, most of which are beyond the scope of this publication..*

VALUE: £25–35

368. GIRLS' LIFE BRIGADE MEDAL

Date: 1905.
Ribbon: Red.
Metal: Bronze.
Size: 34mm.
Description: Similar to MYB 367 above, but inscribed THE GIRLS' LIFE BRIGADE.
Comments: *This medal was awarded to members of the Brigade in similar circumstances to those for the Boys' Life Brigade.*

VALUE: £30–40

368A. RSPCA QUEEN VICTORIA MEDAL

Date: 1837.
Ribbon: White with two blue stripes towards each edge.
Metal: Silver.
Size: 34mm.
Description: (Obverse) a group of animals dominated by a standing horse with the legend ROYAL SOCIETY FOR THE PREVENTION OF CRUELTY OF ANIMALS FOUNDED 1824; (reverse) the throned effigy of Queen Victoria with the word PATRON below, surrounded by a floral wreath.
Comments: *This medal is awarded to people who have made a significant contribution to the Society. It was instituted in 1837 and the young Queen Victoria, an enthusiastic supporter of the Society, actually sketched a cat to be included in the reverse design. The name of the recipient is engraved in the exergue below the animals on the obverse.*

VALUE: £70–100

368B. RSPCA MERITORIOUS SERVICE TO ANIMALS MEDAL

Date: Unknown.
Ribbon: White with two blue stripes towards each edge (as 368A).
Size: 38mm.
Description: (Obverse)Two female figures one standing with an outstretched arm bearing a laurel wreath, the other kneeling by a horse with a small group of animals behind and the legend THE ROYAL SOCIETY FOR THE PREVENTION OF CRUELTY TO ANIMALS. (Reverse) A beribboned laurel wreath surmounted by the Royal arms surrounding the words PRESENTED TO (name) FOR MERITORIOUS SERVICE TO ANIMALS.
Comments: *It is uncertain where this medal sits in relation to 368A. It is possible this medal was awarded directly for animal welfare as opposed to contributing to the Society itself for which the RSPCA Queen Victoria Medal would be awarded. Any comments very welcome. See also Medals L31 and L38 in the Life Saving section.*

VALUE: £175–250

368C. RSPCA LONG SERVICE MEDAL

Date: Unknown.
Ribbon: Equal stripes of four blue, three yellow.
Metal: Bronze
Size: 36mm.
Description: (Obverse) A male figure in toga alongside a horse, cow and sheep. The rising sun in the background and the legend LONG SERVICE MEDAL.
Comments: *Little is known at this stage about the medal which was first spotted in a DNW (now Noonan's) Auction in March 2022 (picture courtesy of Noonans). Any further information on it would be gratefully received.*

VALUE: £120–150

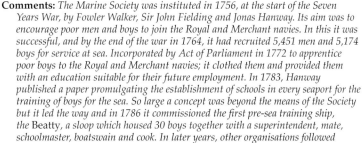

369. MARINE SOCIETY REWARD OF MERIT

Date: 1875.
Ribbon: Blue.
Metal: Silver.
Size: 47mm.
Description: (Obverse) a depiction of Britannia holding the hand of a young sailor with seascape behind , with MARINE SOCIETY INSTITUTED MDCCLVI around and INCORPORATED MDCCLXXII in exergue ; (reverse) a wreath of rose, thistle and shamrock enclosing inscription REWARD OF MERIT TO and with the name of the recipient engraved. Suspended from a thin straight bar swivel suspension.
Comments: *The Marine Society was instituted in 1756, at the start of the Seven Years War, by Fowler Walker, Sir John Fielding and Jonas Hanway. Its aim was to encourage poor men and boys to join the Royal and Merchant navies. In this it was successful, and by the end of the war in 1764, it had recruited 5,451 men and 5,174 boys for service at sea. Incorporated by Act of Parliament in 1772 to apprentice poor boys to the Royal and Merchant navies; it clothed them and provided them with an education suitable for their future employment. In 1783, Hanway published a paper promulgating the establishment of schools in every seaport for the training of boys for the sea. So large a concept was beyond the means of the Society but it led the way and in 1786 it commissioned the first pre-sea training ship, the Beatty, a sloop which housed 30 boys together with a superintendent, mate, schoolmaster, boatswain and cook. In later years, other organisations followed their example. By 1940, when the Society's training ship Warspite was broken up, the Society had trained and equipped some 36,000 boys for the Royal Navy and just under 35,000 for the Merchant Navy. Over the years, the Society was influential in the formation of several related organisations, including The Seamen's Hospital Society, Sail Training Association, Nautical Institute and Sea Cadet Corps. In 1976 the Marine Society merged with a number of other related charities: The Sailors' Home and Red Ensign Club (estab. 1830), The London School of Nautical Cookery (estab. 1893), The Incorporated Thames Nautical Training Trust (HMS Worcester) (estab. 1862), The Seafarers Education Service (estab. 1919), College at Sea (estab. 1938), The Merchant Navy Comforts Service Trust (estab. 1940) and the British Ship Adoption Society (estab. 1936). The Society continues to this day as a charity supporting maritime youth organisations.*

VALUE: £70–100

370. ROYAL BRISTOL VOLUNTEERS MEDAL

Date: 1875.
Ribbon: Plain crimson.
Metal: Silver.
Size: 37mm x 54 max.
Description: (Obverse) Arms of the city of Bristol within a garter bearing the words VIRTUTE ET INDUSTRIA surrounded by ROYAL BRISTOL VOLUNTEERS and IN DANGER READY in scroll below; (reverse) the Volunteers' edict: "IMBODIED FOR THE MAINTENANCE OF PUBLIC ORDER & PROTECTION OF THEIR FELLOW CITIZENS ON THE THREAT OF INVASION BY FRANCE MDCCXCVII. REVIVED AT THE RENEWAL OF HOSTILITIES MDCCCIII. DISBANDED WHEN THE DELIVERANCE OF EUROPE WAS ACCOMPLISHED BY THE PERSEVERENCE & MAGNANIMITY OF GREAT BRITAIN AND HER ALLIES MDCCCXIV" with scroll below bearing the words PRO PATRIA. Suspended from an integral wreath of laurel affixed to an ornamental scroll with the initials GR.
Comments: *This unusual medal was presumably given to all citizens who had volunteered for service when there was the real threat of invasion from France. The medal was worn from the neck on a crimson ribbon.*

VALUE: £150–175

371. GRANTON MEDAL FOR ZEAL

Date: 1915–19
Branch of Service: RN, RNR and RNVR.
Ribbon: Unknown.
Metal: Silver.
Size: 31mm.
Description: A thin medal (1mm) with a simple ring suspension. (Obverse) a raised laurel wreath with the words FOR ZEAL in the centre, in two lines; (reverse) plain, engraved with the recipient's details.
Comments: *Instituted personally by Commodore (later Admiral and an AM recipient) Sir James Startin, SNO of Granton Naval Base, Edinburgh, and selectively awarded to naval personnel under his command who manned the trawlers, sailing ships and coastal trading boats that were involved in extensive mine clearance and Q-ship activities ranging from the North Sea to the Bay of Biscay during the First World War. This medal was awarded to both officers and men for meritorious service in circumstances that would otherwise have gone unrecognised. Although the recipients were mainly from the RNR and RNVR, these medals were awarded at special parades by visiting dignitaries to the base, including King George V, two Prime Ministers (Asquith and Lloyd George) and the Archbishop of Canterbury. Recipients also included Admiral Lord Beatty and Admiral Lord Jellicoe and a gold medal was presented to and accepted by the King. A miniature version of the medal was also available.*

VALUE: £150–200   Miniature   £55–80

372. SECURICOR MEDAL FOR LONG SERVICE

Date: —
Ribbon: Yellow with central dark blue stripe and blue edges.
Metal: Silver.
Size: 31mm.
Description: (Obverse) the cross keys of the company's badge with the name SECURICOR above; (reverse) a laurel wreath with centrre panel engraved with the recipient's details.
Comments: *Awarded to employees of the company who exhibit a high standard of devotion to duty over a sustained period.*

VALUE: £35–40

373. SECURICOR MEDAL FOR BRAVERY

Date: —
Ribbon: Blue with central wide yellow stripe and two thin yellow stripes.
Metal: Silver.
Size: 31mm.
Description: Similar to the above .
Comments: *Awarded to employees of the company who exhibit a particularly high standard of bravery and courage when on duty.*

VALUE: £400–500

373A. SECURICOR MEDAL FOR MERIT

Date: —
Ribbon: Blue with central wide yellow stripe and two thin yellow stripes.
Metal: Silver.
Size: 29mm.
Description: Similar to the above but smaller.
Comments: *Awarded for merit, to employees of the company.*

VALUE: —

374. ST. ANDREW'S ASSOCIATION MEDAL

Date: 1899
Ribbon: Dark red with three narrow yellow stripes.
Metal: Silver.
Size: 36mm.
Description: (Obverse) St Andrew standing before a diagonal cross with the words ST ANDREW'S AMBULANCE ASSOCIATION around the circumference; (reverse) a wreath of thistles surrounding the words FOR SERVICE IN THE ST ANDREW'S AMBULANCE CORPS.
Comments: *Given for long and faithful service in the Association. Originally the medal, in silver or bronze was awarded for bravery in saving life (see MYB L54) but in 1907 the medal was introduced for efficient completion of 15 years service. In 1954 the special medal illustrated left was issued in celebration of the Association's 50th anniversary and Review by HRH the Duke of Edinburgh in Glasgow, inscribed ST ANDREW'S AMBULANCE CORPS 1904–1954, with a yellow ribbon with three narrow red stripes.*

VALUE:	1907 type	£60–75
	1954 issue	£75–100

375. SALVATION ARMY SERVICE MEDAL

Date: —
Ribbon: Maroon with two narrow blue stripes and a central thin orange stripe.
Metal: Silver.
Size: Various.
Description: An ornate cross surmounted in the centre by the Army's badge in enamels and the words LONG AND FAITHFUL SERVICE on four enamel panels around.
Comments: *Originally awarded for 25 years' service. A silver star is affixed to the ribbon for each additional 10 year period of service. This attractive medal was first instituted by General William Booth and it is believed that the higher the rank, the larger the medal awarded. It was discontinued in favour of a badge after World War II (1957 in the US). There have been other medals awarded by the SA including an extremely rare "Order of the Founder".*

VALUE: From £50

376. ROYAL NORFOLK VETERANS ASSOCIATION MEDAL

Date: 1909
Ribbon: Red ribbon with central thin gold stripe, broad green stripe to the left and broad blue stripe to the right.
Metal: Bronze.
Size: 31mm.
Description: (Obverse) crowned effigy of Edward VII with a laurel branch extending from the bottom of the medal around the left side and the words EDWARD VII on the right; (reverse) the words TO COMMEMORATE THE INSPECTION OF THE ROYAL NORFOLK VETERANS ASSOCIATION BY HIS MAJESTY KING EDWARD VII 25th OCTOBER 1909 in eight lines.
Comments: *This medal was issued to commemorate the inspection of the Association by King Edward VII at Crown Point, Norwich. In 1902 the King had agreed to become Patron of the Association, granting it the Royal title. The King's continued patronage resulted in the inspection of 25 members of the Association at Sandringham in 1907. In 1909 there was a further inspection by the King which resulted in the medal being struck. It is said that the King designed the ribbon for the medal but there is no documentary proof for this. Since 1902 each successive monarch has been the Patron of the Association.*

VALUE: £40–60

377. THE SHIPPING FEDERATION MEDAL FOR MERITORIOUS SERVICE

Date: 1917
Ribbon: None
Metal: Hallmarked gold or silver
Size: 28mm.
Description: (Obverse) a standing figure of Britannia holding a trident and shield, with a submarine on one side and a merchant ship on the other; (reverse) a fouled anchor above a plaque with the words "Presented by the Shipping Federation", flanked by a fish each side. The whole is surrounded by a laurel wreath with a scroll reading "1914 For services During the War 1918" beneath.
Comments: *Awarded by the Shipping Federation for meritorious service during World War I. Each medal has the recipient's name around the rim and the date of the action for which it was awarded.*

VALUE:	Gold	£450–550
	Silver	£200–300

378. INNER TEMPLE SERVICE MEDAL 1914–18

Date: 1919.
Campaign: First World War.
Branch of Service: All members of the Inner Temple who participated in the First World War.
Ribbon: None.
Metal: Bronze.
Size: 50mm.
Description: (Obverse) A large Greek cross, with oak leaves in the four corners of the background. Inscription in eight lines: on the upper limb of the cross, in three lines, "The Inner Temple"; across the middle of the cross, in three lines, "To members of the Inn who fought for their country"; on the lower limb of the cross, in two lines, 1914, 1918"; (reverse) The flying figure of Pegasus, over clouds, facing left. Beneath his right front hoof, the dates in roman numerals, MCMXIV—MCMXVIII.
Comments: *Awarded to all members of the Inner Temple who participated in the First World War in any capacity. The name of the recipient is usually found round the edge of the medal, e.g. CAPT. H. F. HALLIFAX, GENL. LIST CAVY. ATTD. 2/8 GURKHA RIFLES AND XX DECCAN HORSE. However, unnamed medals have been seen. The medal was originally issued in a turned wooden box with the recipient's name in calligraphy written on a paper disc glued to the bottom.*

VALUE: £65–100

379. ROYAL AGRICULTURAL SOCIETY OF ENGLAND LONG SERVICE MEDAL (I)

Date: —
Ribbon: Plain royal blue.
Metal: Bronze.
Size: 38mm.
Description: (Obverse) the monarch's bust with the legend ROYAL AGRICULTURAL SOCIETY OF ENGLAND . PATRON . around (Reverse) An agricultural labourer wearing breeches and wielding a scythe with the words LONG SERVICE above.
Comments: *This medal is awarded to employees of Members of the Royal Agricultural Society of England for approved service of not less than 40 years with the same employer or on the same holding. Members can apply for no more than three such awards in any three year period—further awards must be purchased. An additional clasp can be awarded for 50 years service.*

VALUE: £100–150

379A. ROYAL AGRICULTURAL SOCIETY OF ENGLAND LONG SERVICE MEDAL (II)

Date: —
Ribbon: Plain crimson.
Metal: Bronze.
Size: 38mm.
Description: (Obverse) The cypher of the Society with the words ROYAL AGRICULTURAL SOCIETY OF ENGLAND around; (Reverse) a cluster of acorns and oak leaves, with the words FOR LONG SERVICE around.
Comments: *We believe that this medal is a later version of the above and awarded with the same criteria. The example we have seen is from the 1960s. It is possible that the change of design had something to do with the necessity to remove the monarch's head from the obverse. If any reader can tell us more please get in touch..*

VALUE: £75–100

380. CASUALTIES UNION EXEMPLARY SERVICE MEDAL

Obverse.

Date: 2012.
Ribbon: Central stripe of red (blood) flanked by broad stripes of white (training), edged with narrow stripes of blue (origin in Civil Defence), black (blackout and total war) and green (voluntary service).
Metal: Silver-coloured base metal.
Size: 36mm.
Description: (Obverse) Casualties Union Monogram; (reverse) the words FOR EXEMPLARY SERVICE within a laurel wreath with the date of the charity's formation.
Comments: *The Casualties Union was set up in 1942 in Reigate as part of the Civil Defence Training School but became a charity after the war to continue the work of making training more realistic. The medal is usually awarded for 15 years service. Clasps are awarded for 25 years and 50 years of service. When the ribbon bar alone is worn a silver rose represents the 25 year clasp and two silver roses the 50 year clasp. The award of an Exemplary service medal for less than 15 years is represented by a gilt rose on the medal bar and the medal ribbon. The recipient's name, unit and year of award are engraved on the edge.*

VALUE: —

381. CASUALTIES UNION MERITORIOUS SERVICE MEDAL

Date: 2012.
Ribbon: As above but the red and white stripes surmounted by thin stripes of gold (merit).
Metal: Gold-coloured base metal.
Size: 36mm.
Description: (Obverse) As above. Casualties Union Monogram; (reverse) the words FOR MERITORIOUS SERVICE within a laurel wreath with the date of the charity's formation.
Comments: *Awarded for meritorious service above the requirements for the Exemplary Service medal. Clasps are awarded for Life Member and For Merit. When the ribbon bar alone is worn a gilt rose represents the award of a Life Member or For Merit clasp. Two gilt roses represent the award of Life Member and For Merit clasps. No more than two gilt roses may be worn and multiple awards of the For Merit clasp are represented by a single gilt rose. The recipient's name, unit and year of award are engraved on the edge.*

Reverse.   **VALUE:**   —

382. PRIMROSE LEAGUE MEDALS

The Primrose League was an organisation set up in 1883 by admirers of the late lamented Benjamin Disraeli, to promote the idea of Conservative principles in Great Britain. It was extremely popular for many years until its demise in the 1990s. During its existence it awarded a large number of badges, medals and pseudo orders to its members, many of which are avidly collected today. Most are very attractive and well made although regretfully there are far too many to list in this Yearbook, but information is widely available. Its insignia can easily be recognised by the appearance of the League's conjoined PL logo, as can be seen at the centre of the award illustrated here.

VALUE: Various according to age and level of award.

383. BOROUGH OF HARTLEPOOL SPECIAL CONSTABLES' MEDAL FOR SERVICE

Date: 1918.
Branch of Service: Special Constabulary.
Ribbon: Dark blue.
Metal: Silver.
Size: 35mm.
Description: (Obverse) Medieval coat of arms of the city: the legend S'COMMUNITATIS: DE: HARTLEPOL around with stag in centre, with hunting dog on its back. (Reverse) the words in reducing circles: BOROUGH OF HARTLEPOOL SPECIAL CONSTABLE / BOMBARDMENT 1914, AIR RAIDS 1915-18 / ZEPPELIN DESTROYED / 1916 in centre.
Comments: *Awarded to those special constables who served during the bombardment of the town from the sea and by Zeppelin 1914–18. Approximately 120 were issued.*

Value: **£250–300**

384. ARMY TEMPERANCE ASSOCIATION AWARD OF MERIT MEDAL

Instituted: 1867.

Branch of Service: Army, members of the Army Temperance Association and Royal Army Temperance Association.

Ribbon: Maroon. Suspended from a brooch fastening with palm leaves inscribed PALMAM QUI MERUIT FERAT (Let he who has deserved it bear the palm).

Metal: Silver.

Size: 50 x 29mm.

Description: (Obverse) ATA or RATA (after 1905) monogram, in centre of a beaded oval bearing the words AWARD OF MERIT and WATCH & BE SOBER, surmounted by a five pointed star. (Reverse) officially named to recipient, with rank, unit and date in 2mm block capitals.

Comments: *The Army Temperance Association was a very active organisation dedicated to the abstinence of alcohol throughout the army and, during the Victorian era especially, it issued a large number of medals as various rewards for its members. Most of these are beyond the scope of this book but information can be found in a number of publications dedicated to the subject. However, the medal illustrated here is included as it is sometimes found among veterans' groups. The design was changed from ATA to RATA in 1905. The total number awarded was 631 (257 ATA, 374 RATA) including 4 to women. None were awarded from 1915 to 1920, and only 14 from 1921 until awards ceased in 1927. A few ATA medals have been seen inscribed as REWARD OF MERIT.*

VALUE: £65–85

Above: the medal with RATA cypher. Right: the original ATA medal.

385. CATHEDRAL CONSTABLES' ASSOCIATION MEDAL

Instituted: 2011.

Ribbon: Green and blue diagonal stripes.

Metal: Gold plated base metal.

Size: 32mm.

Description: (Obverse) the association's crest consisting of an eight pointed star bearing a window with a cross surmounted by a crown, with the words "Cathedral Constables' Association" above, all surrounded by a laurel wreath with the Royal cypher at top; (Reverse) A laurel wreath enclosing the words, "For Faithful Service", surmounted by a dove carrying a laurel sprig.

Comments: *The association's medal is issued to officers who have served their respective Cathedral faithfully for 10 years. A bar is awarded for subsequent periods of 10 years. The medal is awarded jointly by the association and an officer's Cathedral trustees.*

VALUE: —

386. BRITISH RED CROSS SOCIETY MEDALS

Instituted: 1911.
Branch of Service: British Red Cross.
Ribbon: White with thin red stripes in various configurations.
Metal: Enamelled base metal.
Size: 38mm.
Description: A red enamelled cross surmounted by a red cross on a white shield surrounded by a white circle bearing the Society's title in gold lettering.
Comments: *The British Red Cross Society has issued various "medals" known as badges over the years. That illustrated is the proficiency badge with a clasp/ suspender awarded for proficiency in first aid. Other clasps include Nursing, Hygiene & Sanitation, Cookery, Administration & Organisation, Tuberculosis Course and Infant & Child Welfare. The Society also has its own Gallantry Cross which is a simple red cross bearing the words "For Distinguished Services". See also MYB 165A, 171A, 266 and 355. More information on the numerous awards is available on the Society's website www.redcross.org.uk.*

VALUE: From £10 upwards.

387. ROYAL LIFE SAVING SOCIETY LONG SERVICE AWARD (see also L49A)

Instituted: 2002.
Ribbon: Dark blue with a narrow pale blue centre stripe suspended from a top bar enamelled with RLSS.
Metal: Enamelled base metal.
Size: 29mm.
Description: (Obverse) the emblem of the Society: crossed boathook/oar and lifebelt surmounted by the royal crown, with the words LONG SERVICE suspended below; (reverse) plain, engraved with the recipient's name and year of issue.
Comments: *Awarded by the Society for a minimum of 50 years' service.*

VALUE: £20–30

388. MEDAL FOR THE RECONSTRUCTION OF FRANCE

Instituted: 1921.
Ribbon: French Army Blue (horizon bleu) with white side stripes.
Metal: Silver.
Size: 30mm
Description: (Obverse) A shield-shaped coat of arms surmounted by a vertical sword, over an eagle with the motto "Do Right" (above) and "Fear no Man" (below). (Reverse) A left-facing wyvern with adjacent dates "1916" and "1921" and the legend "Comite Americain pour les Regions Devestees de la France".
Comments: *Issued unnamed, this silver medal was awarded to nursing and welfare staff of the "Comite Americain pour les Regions Devestees de la France" (CARD). This organisation was set up by Anne Morgan in the USA, who had previously worked in New York with the American Fund for French Wounded. She had the support of General Petain to set up an organisation to address the plight of the thousands of French families, refugees and returning forces whose homes and livelihoods had been shattered by the First World War. The headquarters of CARD was at Chateau de Blerancourt, about 75 miles north of Paris. CARD personnel operated for about two years after the Armistice. The medal was issued to all CARD members, some of whom were British, and took its design from the Blerancourt coat of arms, which showed a wyvern .*

VALUE: £100–150

389. SOLDIERS AND SAILORS FAMILIES ASSOCIATION CAPE BADGE

Instituted: 1894.
Ribbon: None.
Metal: Bronze or silver.
Size: 48 x 36mm
Description: Oval with a scroll border. The bronze medal was worn around the neck, the silver medal on the cape with suspension from a plain metal pinback bar and two rings. (Obverse) Left-facing head and shoulder effigy of Princess Alexandra. (Reverse) Inscribed "The Soldiers and Sailors Families Association MDCCCLXXXV" (1885, the date of foundation).
Comments: *The Association was founded by Colonel James Gildea in 1885 to serve Wives and families of army and navy personnel in garrison towns and seaports. Its patron was HRH Princess (later Queen) Alexandra; the nurses of the Association were known as "Alexandra Nurses". The badge in bronze was worn by nurses with up to three years service and were surrendered if the nurse left or continued to serve beyond that time, and thus are very rare. The silver version was worn by nursing staff with more than three years service and could be retained by the recipient after five years service. Male nurses of the RAMC with appropriate qualifications were entitled to wear a version of this badge, but in bronze. Due to the small number of male nurses, the badges are comparatively rare and as such attract a premium. The badge ceased to be issued upon the formation of the RAF in 1918 when the title changed to "The Soldiers, Sailors and Airmen Families Association" (SSAFA) which continues to the present day.*

VALUE:

Bronze	£250–300
Silver	£125–175

390. SCOTTISH WOMEN'S HOSPITALS MEDAL 1914

Date: 1914–19.

Ribbon: Black, green and yellow "Tartan".

Metal: Bronze.

Size: 35mm diameter, 50mm with suspender.

Description: (Obverse) A kneeling woman draws towards her a wounded man and shields him from the grim figure of death, intent on dealing a fatal blow. (Reverse) an embossed wreath around the outer edge; at the top are the letters N.U.W.S.S and at the bottom "1914". In the centre the legend SCOTTISH WOMEN'S HOSPITALS. The medal is suspended from a dark bronze suspension bar, voided, with either side a fleur de lis.

Clasps: None.

Comments: *Much has been documented about the Scottish Women's Hospitals, which were initially funded by the National Union of Women's Suffrage Societies (NUWSS) and the American Red Cross. The units served with distinction in several theatres of war including France an the Balkans. This medal was designed by Miss Hazel Armour and was intended to represent the work of the Scottish Women's Hospitals. The medal, made by John Pinches and in a purple case, was issued unnamed, but with a small card bearing the name of the recipient, which states: "Medal conferred by the Committee of the Scottish Women's Hospitals on . . . in recognition of her valuable service". Most of those who received the medal served abroad, but a few served at home in administrative and fund-raising capacities.*

VALUE:	Un-attributable	£250–300
	Attributable	£350–450

391. FIRST AID NURSING YEOMANRY MEDAL 1914–1919

Date: 1914–1919.

Ribbon: White with scarlet edges.

Metal: Bronze.

Size: 32mm.

Description: (Obverse) Head of a female Greek warrior in helmet facing right with wreath around. Top centre the date 1914; bottom centre the date 1918. (Reverse) Shield with cross moline to centre, around which the words "First Aid Nursing Yeomanry".

Clasps: None

Comments: *The First Aid Nursing Yeomanry Corps was founded in 1907 by Edward Charles Baker who recruited "respectable young women" for training in First Aid and Home Nursing, and who had to qualify in Horsemanship, Veterinary Work, Signalling and Camp Cookery. They had to provide their own uniform and first aid outfit, and pay enrolment and fees. During WWI the FANYC provided ambulance drivers and other staff, earning 95 decorations, including 11 mentions, 19 MMs and 27 Croix de Guerre. A service medal for FANYC was produced after the demobilisation of their active service units in 1920, for those who had served either abroad or at home. A bronze pinback badge was also produced for the same period (scarce). The medals were issued unnamed.*

VALUE:	Un-attributable:	£120–150
	Attributable:	£250–350

392. WOMEN'S HOSPITAL CORPS MEDAL 1914–1919

Date: 1914–1919.
Ribbon: Not known .
Metal: Bronze and enamel.
Size: 35mm diameter, 50mm high with suspender.
Description: Suspended by a ring from an oak leaf spray. (Obverse) "1914, Liberte, Egalite, Fraternite" around a central laurel wreath. (Reverse) "Women's Hospital Corps". Both sides green enamel on a white enamel background.
Clasps: None.
Comments: *The Women's Hospital Corps was formed in 1914 and 21 staff (including 2 men) proceeded to France, and subsequently qualified for the 1914 star for their work in Paris and Wimereux. The medal was awarded by former militant suffragists Louisa Garrett Anderson and Flora Murray to staff of the WHC for service in France during the early months of WWI.*

VALUE: **Extremely rare (only example known to date)**

393. MEDAL FOR SERVICE TO THE SERBIAN RED CROSS IN LONDON

Date: 1914–1919.
Ribbon: Central cream/white broad stripe, with narrower dark blue each side and red stripes to the edges.
Metal: Silver.
Size: 32mm.
Description: (Obverse) Left-facing pair of male heads in wreath with crown above, beneath the wreath the legend "Service to Serbia During War". (Reverse) Crowned double-headed Serbian eagle surmounted on a Geneva Cross with the legend around: "Serbian Red Cross Society London".
Clasps: None.
Comments: *Issued unnamed, the medal was awarded by the Council of the Serbian Red Cross Society in Great Britain in 1923 for services rendered to Serbia, and the member's name was inscribed upon the Roll of Honourable Service to Serbia. A certificate accompanied the medal. Many of those who received the medal served abroad, but most served at home in administrative and fund-raising capacities allied to the British Red Cross. It is not known how many were awarded, but the medals are very scarce, inferring only a small number were produced.*

VALUE: Unattributable: £250–300
            Attributable: £350–400

394. NATAL EXEMPTION MEDAL

Date: 1891.
Ribbon: Unknown but example seen with gold with broad and narrow blue stripes towards each edge, the same as MYB127.
Metal: Silver or bronze.
Size: 32mm.
Description: (Obverse) A patterned circle enclosing the words "EXEMPTED FROM NATIVE LAW", usually with the recipient's name engraved thereon. (Reverse) Plain.
Comments: *In 1865 a Letter of Exemption could be given to native people of important rank or lineage or in a position of authority, recommended by prominent colonists. The holder was subject to the laws of the colonists rather than native customs. After 1890 a medal, which could be purchased by recommended individuals, was struck to accompany the letter. That illustrated is also dated with the date of the recipient's original Letter of Exemption.*

VALUE: Silver £3000–4000   Bronze   —,

395. EBOLA MEDAL FOR SERVICE IN WEST AFRICA (formally 291BB)

Date: 2015.

Ribbon: Equal stripes of bright green, red, bright green, white, light blue each side of a central thin yellow stripe (the colours of the flags of the West African Nations affected).

Metal: Nickel silver.

Size: 36mm.

Description: (Obverse) The Rank-Bradley effigy of HM Queen Elizabeth II; (reverse) the eternal flame, representing the light of hope surrounded by abstract lines representing the Ebola virus. With the inscription •FOR SERVICE• WEST AFRICA EBOLA EPIDEMIC

Comments: *Awarded to an estimated 3,000 (as of July 2015) military and civilian personnel who volunteered to combat the outbreak of Ebola in Sierra Leone, Liberia, Guinea and their territorial waters. Qualification for the medal is 21 days continuous service from March 23, 2014 (the date which the World Health organisation first publicly recognised the Ebola Outbreak in West Africa) or 30 days accumulated service on working visits within the operational area provided these visits are for a minimum of 48 hours each. If qualifying service is reduced or terminated through death, serious illness, evacuation, wounding or other disability due to service in the operational area and the individual might have been expected otherwise to complete the full qualifying period then the medal will be awarded. The situation in West Africa is to be reviewed on a regular basis to determine whether the medal is still warranted.*

VALUE: —   *Miniature*   £15–20

396. NUCLEAR TEST MEDAL

Date: 2023.

Ribbon: Central white stripe, flanked by two yellow stripes, then two thinner black stripes, then equal stripes of red and blue. These represent, as follows: white and yellow for the flash of the explosion; black for the particle fallout; Red for the fireball; Blue for the sky and the Pacific Ocean where the majority of testing took place.

Metal: Nickel plated nickel-silver

Size: 36mm

Description: (Obverse) The right-facing crowned portrait of His Majesty King Charles III by Jack McDermott. (Reverse) The nuclear "atom" symbol above a laurel wreath and the words NUCLEAR TEST MEDAL.

Comments: *After a long running campaign by veterans of the nuclear tests, Prime Minister Rishi Sunak announced, in November 2022, that a medal would be awarded to UK Service and civilian personnel, and those from other nations, who served at the locations where the UK atmospheric nuclear tests were conducted, including the preparatory and clear-up phases, between 1952 and 1967 inclusive. It will also be awarded to UK personnel who served at locations where American atmospheric nuclear tests took place in 1962 under Operation DOMINIC. Qualifying service for the medal is defined as service of any length.*

VALUE: —   *Miniature*   £10–12

397. THE HUMANITARIAN SERVICE MEDAL

Date: 2023.

Ribbon: Central white stripe flanked by equal stripes of red, light blue, dark blue and purple. The colours represent: white for the civilian population; red for the first responders e.g. Red Cross, Red Crescent; pale blue of the NHS for doctors and nurses who may deploy (as in Ebola); dark blue for the blue light services (Police, Fire, Paramedics etc); purple – tri-service colour of the military as a response and protection force.

Metal: Nickel plated nickel-silver

Size: 36mm

Description: (Obverse) The right-facing crowned portrait of His Majesty King Charles III by Jack McDermott. (Reverse) A laurel wreath with an intertwined scroll bearing the words FOR HUMANITARIAN SERVICE.

Comments: *Announced in July 2023 the medal is to be awarded for serious (level 2) and catastrophic (level 3) emergencies to those in public service and members of organisations that contribute on behalf of the government, such as charities, which respond in support of human welfare during or in the aftermath of a crisis. Examples are given that include combating a life-threatening crisis or providing disaster relief or aid provision, it will be awarded for service both in the UK and internationally.*

VALUE: — Miniature £10–12

MEDAL RIBBONS

In this section we feature the majority of the ribbons for the medals included in the main sections of the book. Where the same ribbon is used for more than one medal, only one is illustrated here.
(Not all shown to scale, see reference number for actual sizes)

ORDERS OF KNIGHTHOOD MEDAL RIBBONS
(Not all shown to scale, see reference number for actual sizes)

1. The Most Noble Order of the Garter

2. The Most Ancient and Most Noble Order of the Thistle

3. The Most Illustrious Order of St Patrick

4. The Most Honourable Order of the Bath

5. The Royal Guelphic Order

6. The Most Distinguished Order of St Michael & St George

7. The Most Exalted Order of the Star of India

8. The Most Eminent Order (George V)

9. The Royal Family Order (George IV)

9. The Royal Family Order (Edward VII)

9. The Royal Family Order (George V)

9. The Royal Family Order (George VI)

9. The Royal Family Order (Elizabeth II)

11. The Imperial Order of the Crown of India

12. The Royal Victorian Order

13. The Royal Victorian Medal

13. The Royal Victorian Medal (foreign Associates)

15. Order of Merit

16. The Most Excellent Order of the British Empire (Civil 1st type)

16. The Most Excellent Order of the British Empire (Civil 2nd type)

16. The Most Excellent Order of the British Empire (Military 1st type)

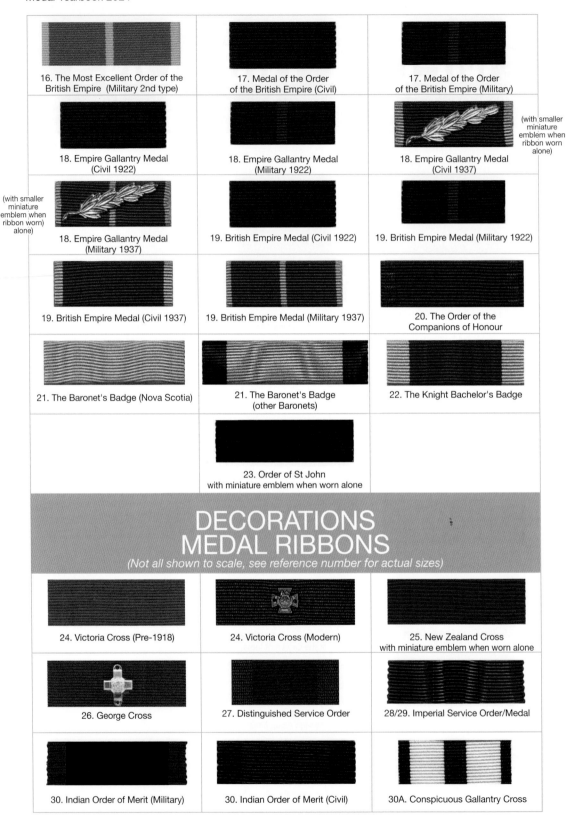

16. The Most Excellent Order of the British Empire (Military 2nd type)

17. Medal of the Order of the British Empire (Civil)

17. Medal of the Order of the British Empire (Military)

18. Empire Gallantry Medal (Civil 1922)

18. Empire Gallantry Medal (Military 1922)

18. Empire Gallantry Medal (Civil 1937)

(with smaller miniature emblem when ribbon worn alone)

18. Empire Gallantry Medal (Military 1937)

(with smaller miniature emblem when ribbon worn alone)

19. British Empire Medal (Civil 1922)

19. British Empire Medal (Military 1922)

19. British Empire Medal (Civil 1937)

19. British Empire Medal (Military 1937)

20. The Order of the Companions of Honour

21. The Baronet's Badge (Nova Scotia)

21. The Baronet's Badge (other Baronets)

22. The Knight Bachelor's Badge

23. Order of St John with miniature emblem when worn alone

DECORATIONS
MEDAL RIBBONS
(Not all shown to scale, see reference number for actual sizes)

24. Victoria Cross (Pre-1918)

24. Victoria Cross (Modern)

25. New Zealand Cross with miniature emblem when worn alone

26. George Cross

27. Distinguished Service Order

28/29. Imperial Service Order/Medal

30. Indian Order of Merit (Military)

30. Indian Order of Merit (Civil)

30A. Conspicuous Gallantry Cross

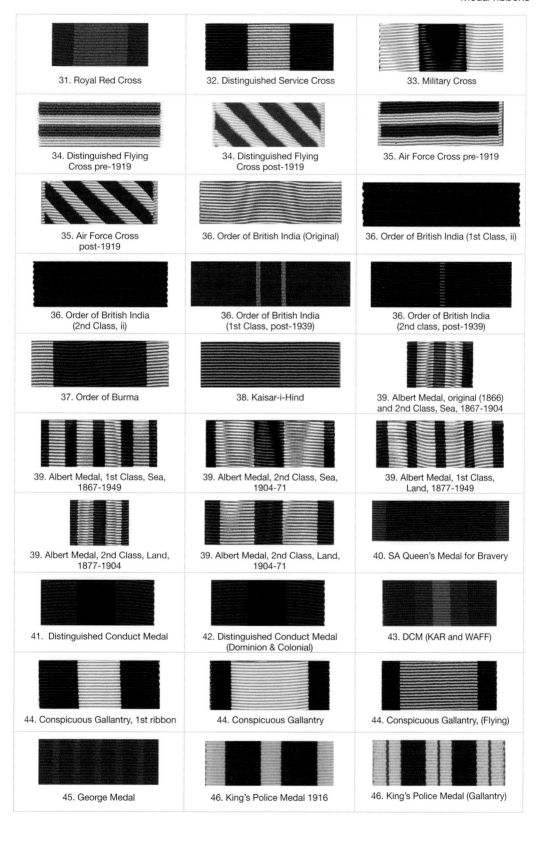

31. Royal Red Cross	32. Distinguished Service Cross	33. Military Cross
34. Distinguished Flying Cross pre-1919	34. Distinguished Flying Cross post-1919	35. Air Force Cross pre-1919
35. Air Force Cross post-1919	36. Order of British India (Original)	36. Order of British India (1st Class, ii)
36. Order of British India (2nd Class, ii)	36. Order of British India (1st Class, post-1939)	36. Order of British India (2nd class, post-1939)
37. Order of Burma	38. Kaisar-i-Hind	39. Albert Medal, original (1866) and 2nd Class, Sea, 1867-1904
39. Albert Medal, 1st Class, Sea, 1867-1949	39. Albert Medal, 2nd Class, Sea, 1904-71	39. Albert Medal, 1st Class, Land, 1877-1949
39. Albert Medal, 2nd Class, Land, 1877-1904	39. Albert Medal, 2nd Class, Land, 1904-71	40. SA Queen's Medal for Bravery
41. Distinguished Conduct Medal	42. Distinguished Conduct Medal (Dominion & Colonial)	43. DCM (KAR and WAFF)
44. Conspicuous Gallantry, 1st ribbon	44. Conspicuous Gallantry	44. Conspicuous Gallantry, (Flying)
45. George Medal	46. King's Police Medal 1916	46. King's Police Medal (Gallantry)

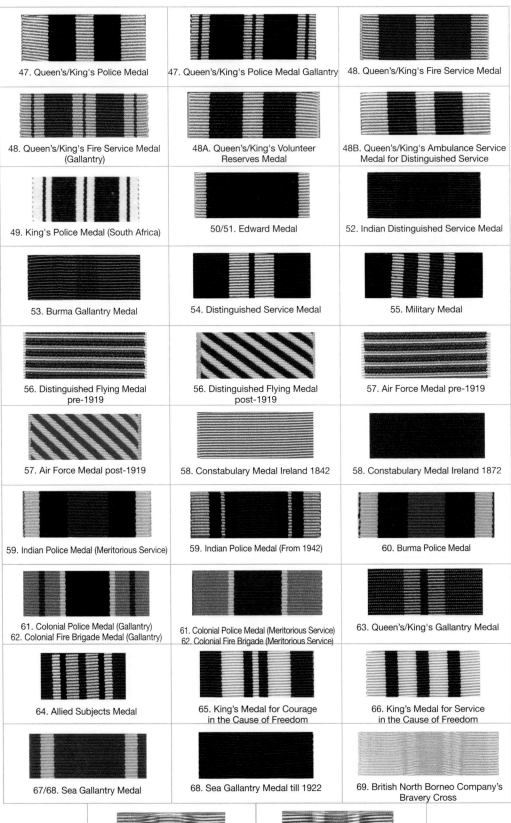

47. Queen's/King's Police Medal

47. Queen's/King's Police Medal Gallantry

48. Queen's/King's Fire Service Medal

48. Queen's/King's Fire Service Medal (Gallantry)

48A. Queen's/King's Volunteer Reserves Medal

48B. Queen's/King's Ambulance Service Medal for Distinguished Service

49. King's Police Medal (South Africa)

50/51. Edward Medal

52. Indian Distinguished Service Medal

53. Burma Gallantry Medal

54. Distinguished Service Medal

55. Military Medal

56. Distinguished Flying Medal pre-1919

56. Distinguished Flying Medal post-1919

57. Air Force Medal pre-1919

57. Air Force Medal post-1919

58. Constabulary Medal Ireland 1842

58. Constabulary Medal Ireland 1872

59. Indian Police Medal (Meritorious Service)

59. Indian Police Medal (From 1942)

60. Burma Police Medal

61. Colonial Police Medal (Gallantry)
62. Colonial Fire Brigade Medal (Gallantry)

61. Colonial Police Medal (Meritorious Service)
62. Colonial Fire Brigade (Meritorious Service)

63. Queen's/King's Gallantry Medal

64. Allied Subjects Medal

65. King's Medal for Courage in the Cause of Freedom

66. King's Medal for Service in the Cause of Freedom

67/68. Sea Gallantry Medal

68. Sea Gallantry Medal till 1922

69. British North Borneo Company's Bravery Cross

70. Native Chief's Medal (i)

70. Native Chief's Medal (ii)

CAMPAIGN MEDAL RIBBONS

(Not all shown to scale, see reference number for actual sizes)

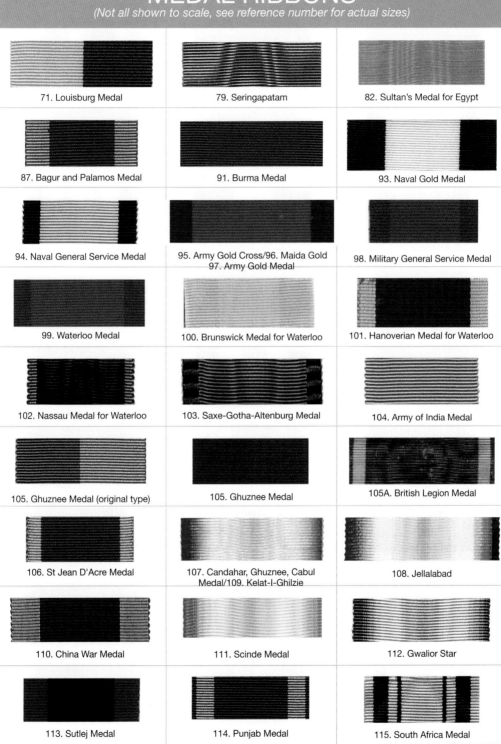

71. Louisburg Medal	79. Seringapatam	82. Sultan's Medal for Egypt
87. Bagur and Palamos Medal	91. Burma Medal	93. Naval Gold Medal
94. Naval General Service Medal	95. Army Gold Cross/96. Maida Gold 97. Army Gold Medal	98. Military General Service Medal
99. Waterloo Medal	100. Brunswick Medal for Waterloo	101. Hanoverian Medal for Waterloo
102. Nassau Medal for Waterloo	103. Saxe-Gotha-Altenburg Medal	104. Army of India Medal
105. Ghuznee Medal (original type)	105. Ghuznee Medal	105A. British Legion Medal
106. St Jean D'Acre Medal	107. Candahar, Ghuznee, Cabul Medal/109. Kelat-I-Ghilzie	108. Jellalabad
110. China War Medal	111. Scinde Medal	112. Gwalior Star
113. Sutlej Medal	114. Punjab Medal	115. South Africa Medal

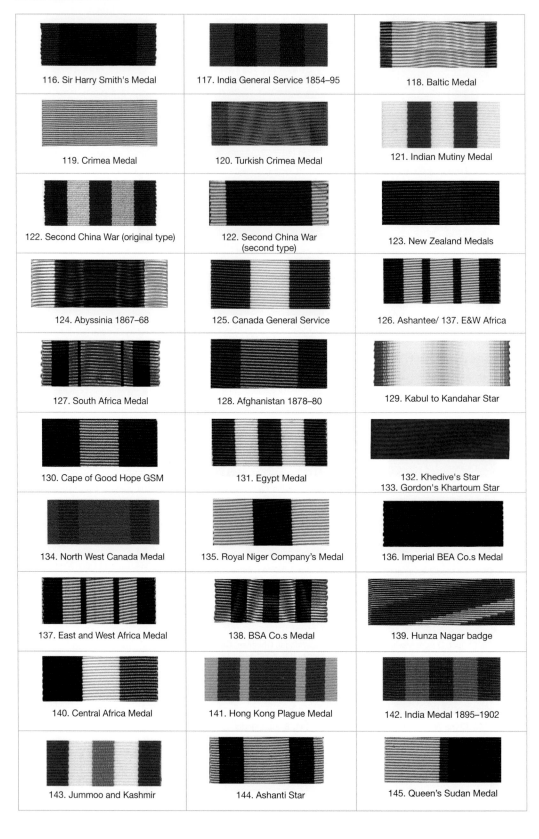

116. Sir Harry Smith's Medal

117. India General Service 1854–95

118. Baltic Medal

119. Crimea Medal

120. Turkish Crimea Medal

121. Indian Mutiny Medal

122. Second China War (original type)

122. Second China War (second type)

123. New Zealand Medals

124. Abyssinia 1867–68

125. Canada General Service

126. Ashantee/ 137. E&W Africa

127. South Africa Medal

128. Afghanistan 1878–80

129. Kabul to Kandahar Star

130. Cape of Good Hope GSM

131. Egypt Medal

132. Khedive's Star
133. Gordon's Khartoum Star

134. North West Canada Medal

135. Royal Niger Company's Medal

136. Imperial BEA Co.s Medal

137. East and West Africa Medal

138. BSA Co.s Medal

139. Hunza Nagar badge

140. Central Africa Medal

141. Hong Kong Plague Medal

142. India Medal 1895–1902

143. Jummoo and Kashmir

144. Ashanti Star

145. Queen's Sudan Medal

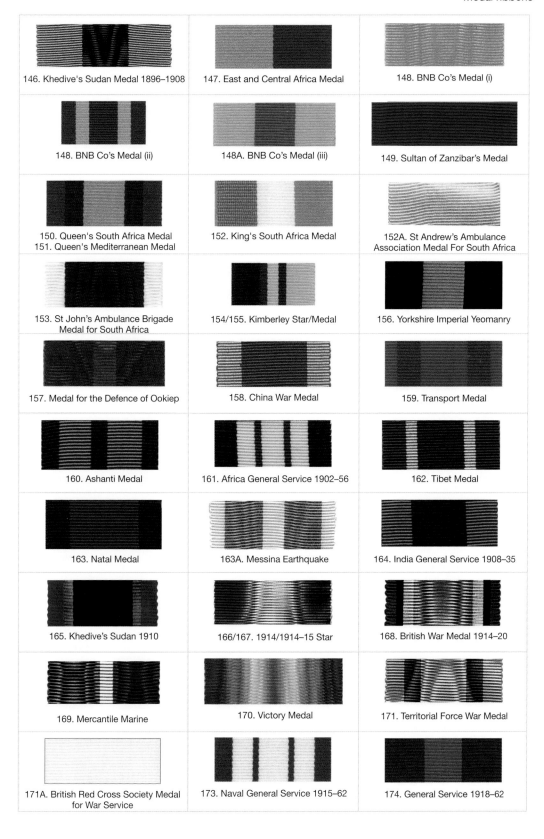

146. Khedive's Sudan Medal 1896–1908

147. East and Central Africa Medal

148. BNB Co's Medal (i)

148. BNB Co's Medal (ii)

148A. BNB Co's Medal (iii)

149. Sultan of Zanzibar's Medal

150. Queen's South Africa Medal
151. Queen's Mediterranean Medal

152. King's South Africa Medal

152A. St Andrew's Ambulance
Association Medal For South Africa

153. St John's Ambulance Brigade
Medal for South Africa

154/155. Kimberley Star/Medal

156. Yorkshire Imperial Yeomanry

157. Medal for the Defence of Ookiep

158. China War Medal

159. Transport Medal

160. Ashanti Medal

161. Africa General Service 1902–56

162. Tibet Medal

163. Natal Medal

163A. Messina Earthquake

164. India General Service 1908–35

165. Khedive's Sudan 1910

166/167. 1914/1914–15 Star

168. British War Medal 1914–20

169. Mercantile Marine

170. Victory Medal

171. Territorial Force War Medal

171A. British Red Cross Society Medal
for War Service

173. Naval General Service 1915–62

174. General Service 1918–62

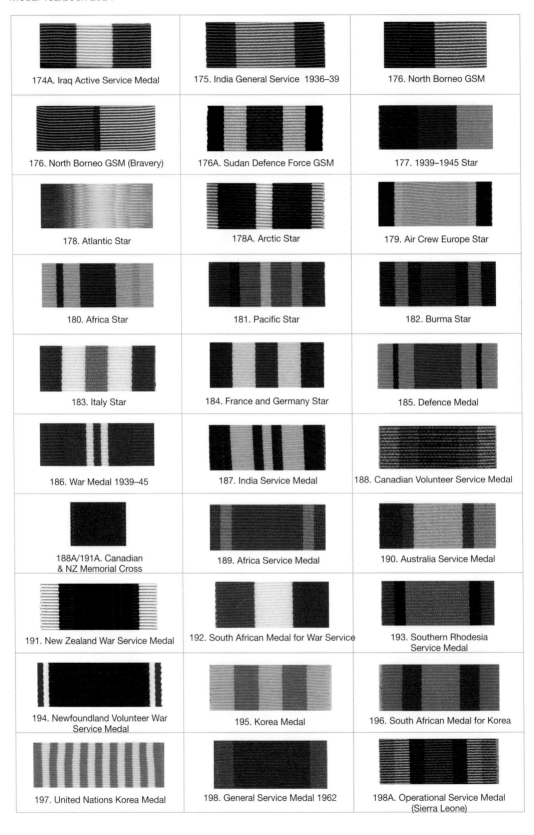

174A. Iraq Active Service Medal

175. India General Service 1936–39

176. North Borneo GSM

176. North Borneo GSM (Bravery)

176A. Sudan Defence Force GSM

177. 1939–1945 Star

178. Atlantic Star

178A. Arctic Star

179. Air Crew Europe Star

180. Africa Star

181. Pacific Star

182. Burma Star

183. Italy Star

184. France and Germany Star

185. Defence Medal

186. War Medal 1939–45

187. India Service Medal

188. Canadian Volunteer Service Medal

188A/191A. Canadian & NZ Memorial Cross

189. Africa Service Medal

190. Australia Service Medal

191. New Zealand War Service Medal

192. South African Medal for War Service

193. Southern Rhodesia Service Medal

194. Newfoundland Volunteer War Service Medal

195. Korea Medal

196. South African Medal for Korea

197. United Nations Korea Medal

198. General Service Medal 1962

198A. Operational Service Medal (Sierra Leone)

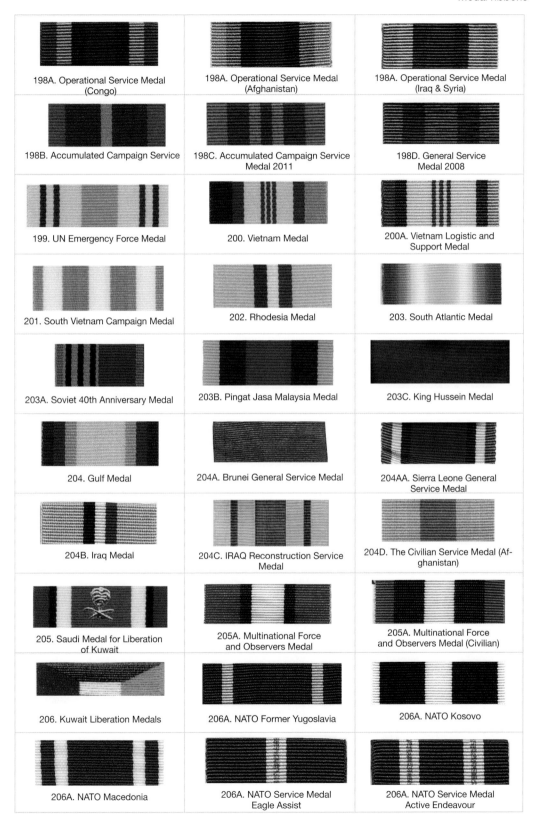

198A. Operational Service Medal (Congo)

198A. Operational Service Medal (Afghanistan)

198A. Operational Service Medal (Iraq & Syria)

198B. Accumulated Campaign Service

198C. Accumulated Campaign Service Medal 2011

198D. General Service Medal 2008

199. UN Emergency Force Medal

200. Vietnam Medal

200A. Vietnam Logistic and Support Medal

201. South Vietnam Campaign Medal

202. Rhodesia Medal

203. South Atlantic Medal

203A. Soviet 40th Anniversary Medal

203B. Pingat Jasa Malaysia Medal

203C. King Hussein Medal

204. Gulf Medal

204A. Brunei General Service Medal

204AA. Sierra Leone General Service Medal

204B. Iraq Medal

204C. IRAQ Reconstruction Service Medal

204D. The Civilian Service Medal (Afghanistan)

205. Saudi Medal for Liberation of Kuwait

205A. Multinational Force and Observers Medal

205A. Multinational Force and Observers Medal (Civilian)

206. Kuwait Liberation Medals

206A. NATO Former Yugoslavia

206A. NATO Kosovo

206A. NATO Macedonia

206A. NATO Service Medal Eagle Assist

206A. NATO Service Medal Active Endeavour

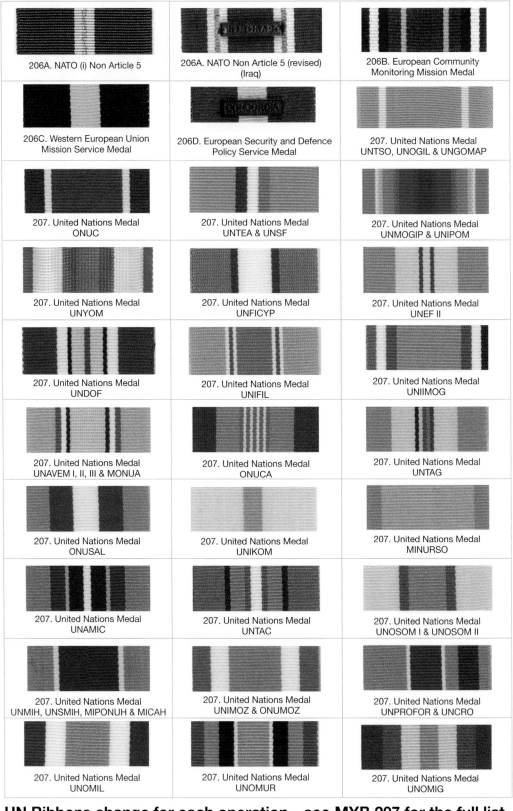

206A. NATO (i) Non Article 5	206A. NATO Non Article 5 (revised) (Iraq)	206B. European Community Monitoring Mission Medal
206C. Western European Union Mission Service Medal	206D. European Security and Defence Policy Service Medal	207. United Nations Medal UNTSO, UNOGIL & UNGOMAP
207. United Nations Medal ONUC	207. United Nations Medal UNTEA & UNSF	207. United Nations Medal UNMOGIP & UNIPOM
207. United Nations Medal UNYOM	207. United Nations Medal UNFICYP	207. United Nations Medal UNEF II
207. United Nations Medal UNDOF	207. United Nations Medal UNIFIL	207. United Nations Medal UNIIMOG
207. United Nations Medal UNAVEM I, II, III & MONUA	207. United Nations Medal ONUCA	207. United Nations Medal UNTAG
207. United Nations Medal ONUSAL	207. United Nations Medal UNIKOM	207. United Nations Medal MINURSO
207. United Nations Medal UNAMIC	207. United Nations Medal UNTAC	207. United Nations Medal UNOSOM I & UNOSOM II
207. United Nations Medal UNMIH, UNSMIH, MIPONUH & MICAH	207. United Nations Medal UNIMOZ & ONUMOZ	207. United Nations Medal UNPROFOR & UNCRO
207. United Nations Medal UNOMIL	207. United Nations Medal UNOMUR	207. United Nations Medal UNOMIG

UN Ribbons change for each operation—see MYB 207 for the full list.

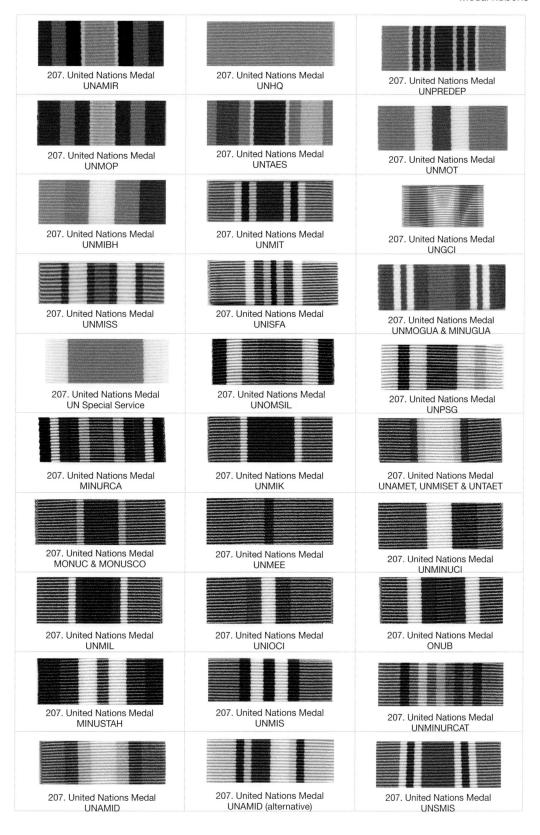

207. United Nations Medal
UNAMIR

207. United Nations Medal
UNHQ

207. United Nations Medal
UNPREDEP

207. United Nations Medal
UNMOP

207. United Nations Medal
UNTAES

207. United Nations Medal
UNMOT

207. United Nations Medal
UNMIBH

207. United Nations Medal
UNMIT

207. United Nations Medal
UNGCI

207. United Nations Medal
UNMISS

207. United Nations Medal
UNISFA

207. United Nations Medal
UNMOGUA & MINUGUA

207. United Nations Medal
UN Special Service

207. United Nations Medal
UNOMSIL

207. United Nations Medal
UNPSG

207. United Nations Medal
MINURCA

207. United Nations Medal
UNMIK

207. United Nations Medal
UNAMET, UNMISET & UNTAET

207. United Nations Medal
MONUC & MONUSCO

207. United Nations Medal
UNMEE

207. United Nations Medal
UNMINUCI

207. United Nations Medal
UNMIL

207. United Nations Medal
UNIOCI

207. United Nations Medal
ONUB

207. United Nations Medal
MINUSTAH

207. United Nations Medal
UNMIS

207. United Nations Medal
UNMINURCAT

207. United Nations Medal
UNAMID

207. United Nations Medal
UNAMID (alternative)

207. United Nations Medal
UNSMIS

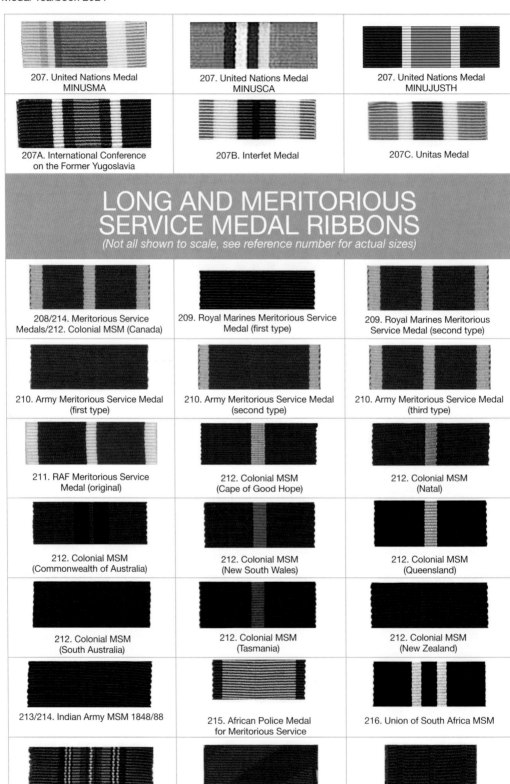

207. United Nations Medal
MINUSMA

207. United Nations Medal
MINUSCA

207. United Nations Medal
MINUJUSTH

207A. International Conference
on the Former Yugoslavia

207B. Interfet Medal

207C. Unitas Medal

LONG AND MERITORIOUS
SERVICE MEDAL RIBBONS
(Not all shown to scale, see reference number for actual sizes)

208/214. Meritorious Service
Medals/212. Colonial MSM (Canada)

209. Royal Marines Meritorious Service
Medal (first type)

209. Royal Marines Meritorious
Service Medal (second type)

210. Army Meritorious Service Medal
(first type)

210. Army Meritorious Service Medal
(second type)

210. Army Meritorious Service Medal
(third type)

211. RAF Meritorious Service
Medal (original)

212. Colonial MSM
(Cape of Good Hope)

212. Colonial MSM
(Natal)

212. Colonial MSM
(Commonwealth of Australia)

212. Colonial MSM
(New South Wales)

212. Colonial MSM
(Queensland)

212. Colonial MSM
(South Australia)

212. Colonial MSM
(Tasmania)

212. Colonial MSM
(New Zealand)

213/214. Indian Army MSM 1848/88

215. African Police Medal
for Meritorious Service

216. Union of South Africa MSM

217. Royal Household FS QV

217. Royal Household FS GVIR

217. Royal Household FS EIIR

217. Royal Household FS CIII

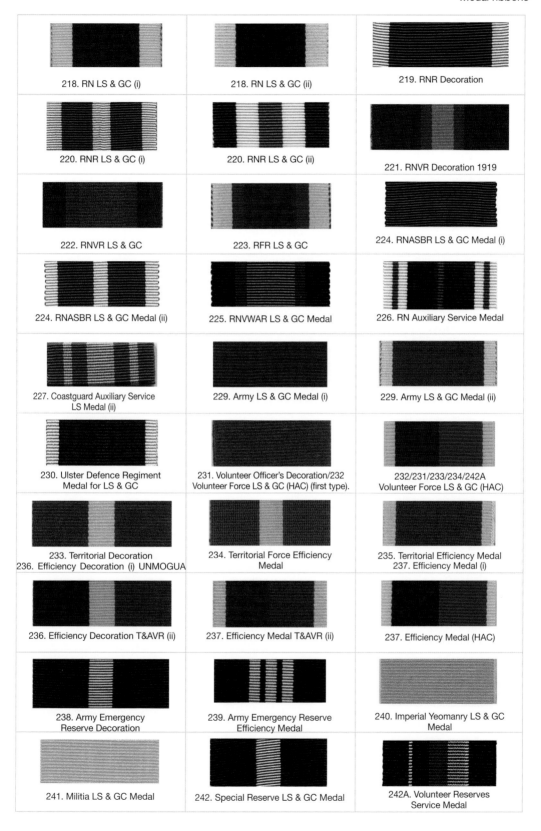

218. RN LS & GC (i)

218. RN LS & GC (ii)

219. RNR Decoration

220. RNR LS & GC (i)

220. RNR LS & GC (ii)

221. RNVR Decoration 1919

222. RNVR LS & GC

223. RFR LS & GC

224. RNASBR LS & GC Medal (i)

224. RNASBR LS & GC Medal (ii)

225. RNVWAR LS & GC Medal

226. RN Auxiliary Service Medal

227. Coastguard Auxiliary Service LS Medal (ii)

229. Army LS & GC Medal (i)

229. Army LS & GC Medal (ii)

230. Ulster Defence Regiment Medal for LS & GC

231. Volunteer Officer's Decoration/232 Volunteer Force LS & GC (HAC) (first type).

232/231/233/234/242A Volunteer Force LS & GC (HAC)

233. Territorial Decoration 236. Efficiency Decoration (i) UNMOGUA

234. Territorial Force Efficiency Medal

235. Territorial Efficiency Medal 237. Efficiency Medal (i)

236. Efficiency Decoration T&AVR (ii)

237. Efficiency Medal T&AVR (ii)

237. Efficiency Medal (HAC)

238. Army Emergency Reserve Decoration

239. Army Emergency Reserve Efficiency Medal

240. Imperial Yeomanry LS & GC Medal

241. Militia LS & GC Medal

242. Special Reserve LS & GC Medal

242A. Volunteer Reserves Service Medal

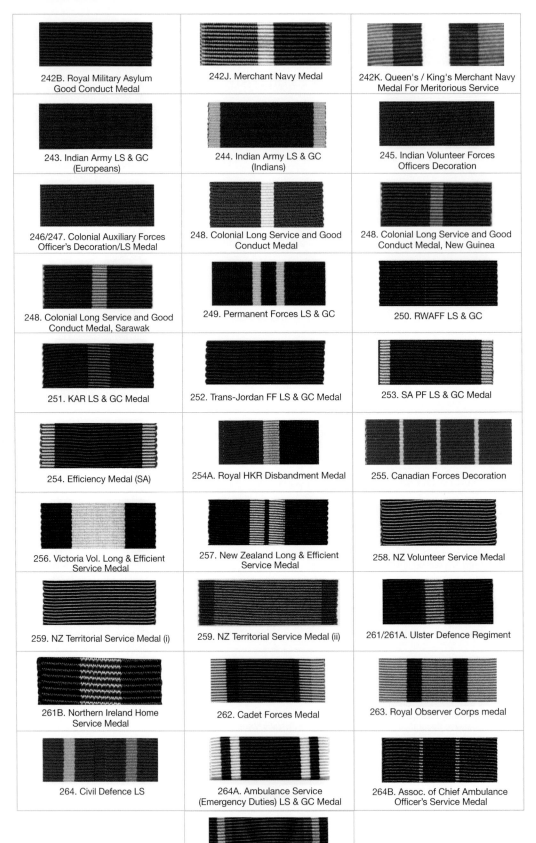

242B. Royal Military Asylum Good Conduct Medal

242J. Merchant Navy Medal

242K. Queen's / King's Merchant Navy Medal For Meritorious Service

243. Indian Army LS & GC (Europeans)

244. Indian Army LS & GC (Indians)

245. Indian Volunteer Forces Officers Decoration

246/247. Colonial Auxiliary Forces Officer's Decoration/LS Medal

248. Colonial Long Service and Good Conduct Medal

248. Colonial Long Service and Good Conduct Medal, New Guinea

248. Colonial Long Service and Good Conduct Medal, Sarawak

249. Permanent Forces LS & GC

250. RWAFF LS & GC

251. KAR LS & GC Medal

252. Trans-Jordan FF LS & GC Medal

253. SA PF LS & GC Medal

254. Efficiency Medal (SA)

254A. Royal HKR Disbandment Medal

255. Canadian Forces Decoration

256. Victoria Vol. Long & Efficient Service Medal

257. New Zealand Long & Efficient Service Medal

258. NZ Volunteer Service Medal

259. NZ Territorial Service Medal (i)

259. NZ Territorial Service Medal (ii)

261/261A. Ulster Defence Regiment

261B. Northern Ireland Home Service Medal

262. Cadet Forces Medal

263. Royal Observer Corps medal

264. Civil Defence LS

264A. Ambulance Service (Emergency Duties) LS & GC Medal

264B. Assoc. of Chief Ambulance Officer's Service Medal

264C. Royal Fleet Auxiliary Service Medal

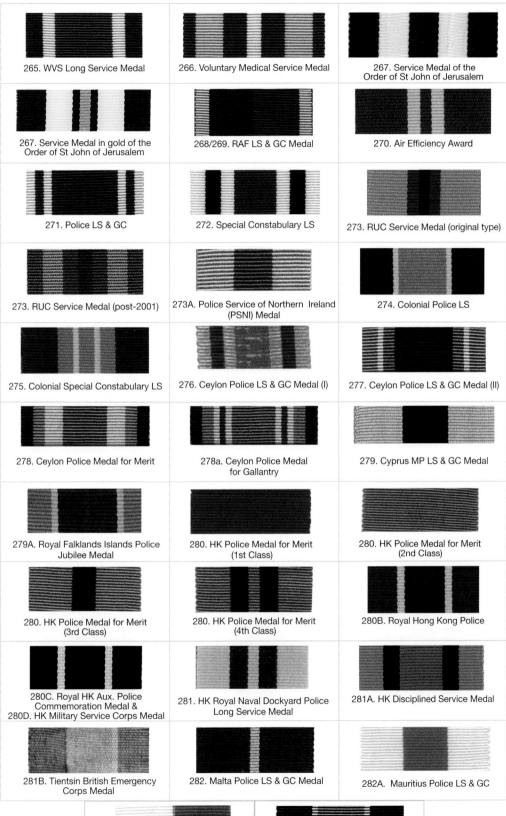

265. WVS Long Service Medal

266. Voluntary Medical Service Medal

267. Service Medal of the Order of St John of Jerusalem

267. Service Medal in gold of the Order of St John of Jerusalem

268/269. RAF LS & GC Medal

270. Air Efficiency Award

271. Police LS & GC

272. Special Constabulary LS

273. RUC Service Medal (original type)

273. RUC Service Medal (post-2001)

273A. Police Service of Northern Ireland (PSNI) Medal

274. Colonial Police LS

275. Colonial Special Constabulary LS

276. Ceylon Police LS & GC Medal (I)

277. Ceylon Police LS & GC Medal (II)

278. Ceylon Police Medal for Merit

278a. Ceylon Police Medal for Gallantry

279. Cyprus MP LS & GC Medal

279A. Royal Falklands Islands Police Jubilee Medal

280. HK Police Medal for Merit (1st Class)

280. HK Police Medal for Merit (2nd Class)

280. HK Police Medal for Merit (3rd Class)

280. HK Police Medal for Merit (4th Class)

280B. Royal Hong Kong Police

280C. Royal HK Aux. Police Commemoration Medal & 280D. HK Military Service Corps Medal

281. HK Royal Naval Dockyard Police Long Service Medal

281A. HK Disciplined Service Medal

281B. Tientsin British Emergency Corps Medal

282. Malta Police LS & GC Medal

282A. Mauritius Police LS & GC

282A. Mauritius Police LS & GC Medal (I) (first type)

282B. Mauritius Police LS & GC Medal (II)

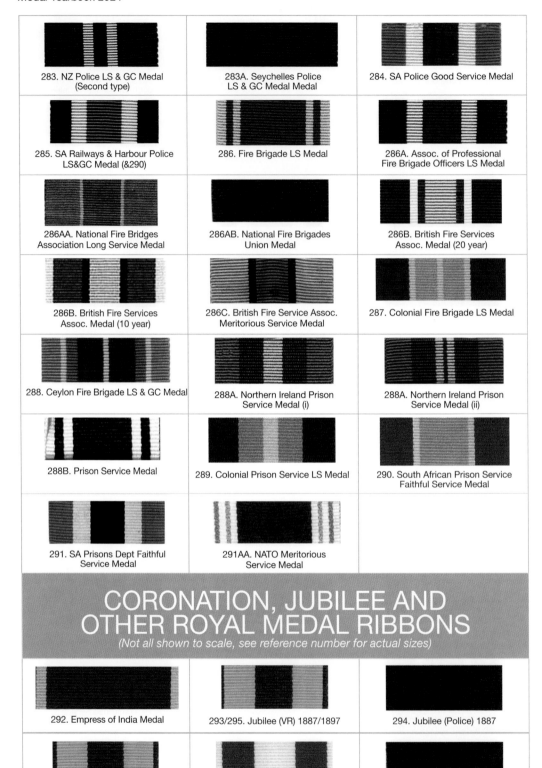

283. NZ Police LS & GC Medal (Second type)	283A. Seychelles Police LS & GC Medal Medal	284. SA Police Good Service Medal
285. SA Railways & Harbour Police LS&GC Medal (&290)	286. Fire Brigade LS Medal	286A. Assoc. of Professional Fire Brigade Officers LS Medal
286AA. National Fire Bridges Association Long Service Medal	286AB. National Fire Brigades Union Medal	286B. British Fire Services Assoc. Medal (20 year)
286B. British Fire Services Assoc. Medal (10 year)	286C. British Fire Service Assoc. Meritorious Service Medal	287. Colonial Fire Brigade LS Medal
288. Ceylon Fire Brigade LS & GC Medal	288A. Northern Ireland Prison Service Medal (i)	288A. Northern Ireland Prison Service Medal (ii)
288B. Prison Service Medal	289. Colonial Prison Service LS Medal	290. South African Prison Service Faithful Service Medal
291. SA Prisons Dept Faithful Service Medal	291AA. NATO Meritorious Service Medal	

CORONATION, JUBILEE AND OTHER ROYAL MEDAL RIBBONS
(Not all shown to scale, see reference number for actual sizes)

292. Empress of India Medal	293/295. Jubilee (VR) 1887/1897	294. Jubilee (Police) 1887
295. Jubilee Medal 1897	296. Jubilee 1897 (Mayors & Provosts)	297. Jubilee (Police) 1897

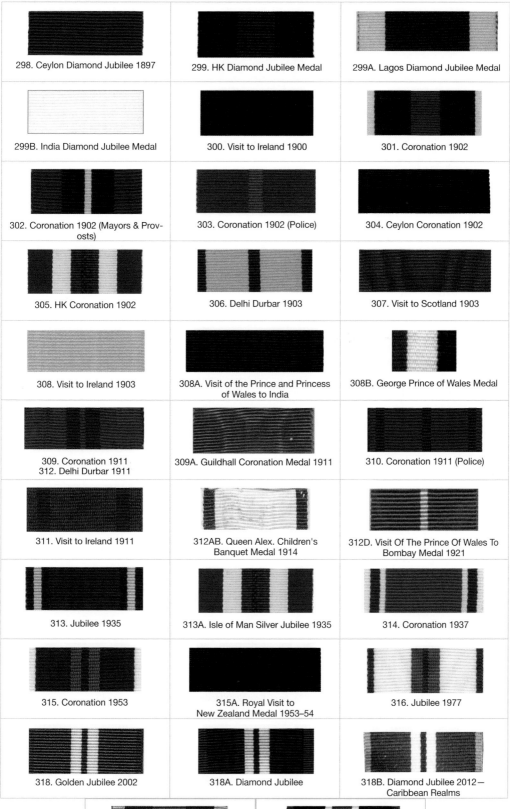

298. Ceylon Diamond Jubilee 1897

299. HK Diamond Jubilee Medal

299A. Lagos Diamond Jubilee Medal

299B. India Diamond Jubilee Medal

300. Visit to Ireland 1900

301. Coronation 1902

302. Coronation 1902 (Mayors & Provosts)

303. Coronation 1902 (Police)

304. Ceylon Coronation 1902

305. HK Coronation 1902

306. Delhi Durbar 1903

307. Visit to Scotland 1903

308. Visit to Ireland 1903

308A. Visit of the Prince and Princess of Wales to India

308B. George Prince of Wales Medal

309. Coronation 1911
312. Delhi Durbar 1911

309A. Guildhall Coronation Medal 1911

310. Coronation 1911 (Police)

311. Visit to Ireland 1911

312AB. Queen Alex. Children's Banquet Medal 1914

312D. Visit Of The Prince Of Wales To Bombay Medal 1921

313. Jubilee 1935

313A. Isle of Man Silver Jubilee 1935

314. Coronation 1937

315. Coronation 1953

315A. Royal Visit to New Zealand Medal 1953–54

316. Jubilee 1977

318. Golden Jubilee 2002

318A. Diamond Jubilee

318B. Diamond Jubilee 2012— Caribbean Realms

318C. Platinum Jubilee Service medal

318D. Coronation 2023

MISCELLANEOUS MEDAL RIBBONS
(Not all shown to scale, see reference number for actual sizes)

319. King's and Queen's Messenger Badge

320. Arctic Medal (1857)

321. Arctic Medal (1876)

322. Polar Medal

323. EVII Medal for Science, Art & Music

324. Order of the League of Mercy

325. Queen Alex. Imperial Military Nursing Service Cape Badge

325A. Queen Alex. Imperial Military Nursing Service Reserve Cape Badge

326. Territorial Force Nursing Service Cape Badge

326A. Queen Alex. Military Families Nursing Service Cape Badge

326B. Territorial Army Nursing Service Cape Badge

326C. Queen Alex. Royal Army Nursing Corps Cape Badge

327. Indian Title Badge (1st Class)

327. Indian Title Badge (2nd Class)

327. Indian Title Badge (3rd Class)

328. Badge of the Cert. of Honour

329. Badge of Honour (non-African countries)

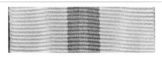

329A. The Governor Generals' Medal of Honour

330. Naval Engineers GC Medal

331. Indian Recruiting Badge (GV)

332. Indian Recruiting Badge (GVI)

333. Naval Good Shooting

334. Army Best Shot Medal

335. Queen's Medal for Champion Shot (RN/RM)

336. Queen's Medal for Champion Shot (RAF)

337. Queen's Medal for Champion Shot NZ Naval Force

338. Union of South Africa Commemoration Medal

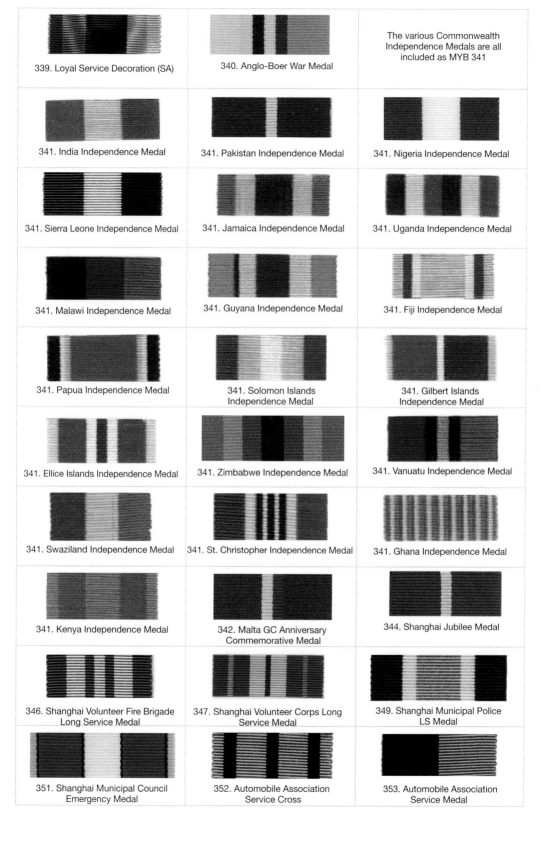

339. Loyal Service Decoration (SA)

340. Anglo-Boer War Medal

The various Commonwealth Independence Medals are all included as MYB 341

341. India Independence Medal

341. Pakistan Independence Medal

341. Nigeria Independence Medal

341. Sierra Leone Independence Medal

341. Jamaica Independence Medal

341. Uganda Independence Medal

341. Malawi Independence Medal

341. Guyana Independence Medal

341. Fiji Independence Medal

341. Papua Independence Medal

341. Solomon Islands Independence Medal

341. Gilbert Islands Independence Medal

341. Ellice Islands Independence Medal

341. Zimbabwe Independence Medal

341. Vanuatu Independence Medal

341. Swaziland Independence Medal

341. St. Christopher Independence Medal

341. Ghana Independence Medal

341. Kenya Independence Medal

342. Malta GC Anniversary Commemorative Medal

344. Shanghai Jubilee Medal

346. Shanghai Volunteer Fire Brigade Long Service Medal

347. Shanghai Volunteer Corps Long Service Medal

349. Shanghai Municipal Police LS Medal

351. Shanghai Municipal Council Emergency Medal

352. Automobile Association Service Cross

353. Automobile Association Service Medal

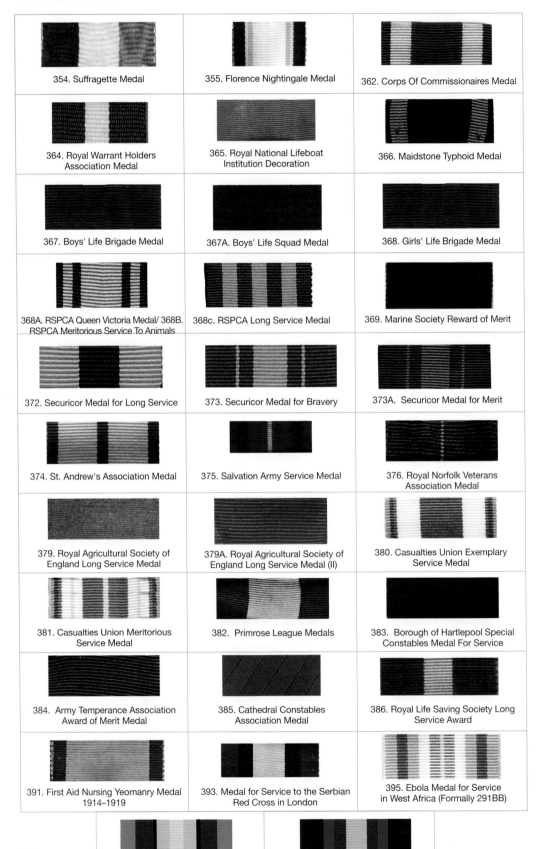

354. Suffragette Medal

355. Florence Nightingale Medal

362. Corps Of Commissionaires Medal

364. Royal Warrant Holders Association Medal

365. Royal National Lifeboat Institution Decoration

366. Maidstone Typhoid Medal

367. Boys' Life Brigade Medal

367A. Boys' Life Squad Medal

368. Girls' Life Brigade Medal

368A. RSPCA Queen Victoria Medal/ 368B. RSPCA Meritorious Service To Animals

368c. RSPCA Long Service Medal

369. Marine Society Reward of Merit

372. Securicor Medal for Long Service

373. Securicor Medal for Bravery

373A. Securicor Medal for Merit

374. St. Andrew's Association Medal

375. Salvation Army Service Medal

376. Royal Norfolk Veterans Association Medal

379. Royal Agricultural Society of England Long Service Medal

379A. Royal Agricultural Society of England Long Service Medal (II)

380. Casualties Union Exemplary Service Medal

381. Casualties Union Meritorious Service Medal

382. Primrose League Medals

383. Borough of Hartlepool Special Constables Medal For Service

384. Army Temperance Association Award of Merit Medal

385. Cathedral Constables Association Medal

386. Royal Life Saving Society Long Service Award

391. First Aid Nursing Yeomanry Medal 1914–1919

393. Medal for Service to the Serbian Red Cross in London

395. Ebola Medal for Service in West Africa (Formally 291BB)

396. Nuclear Test Medal

397. The Humanitarian Service Medal

Index Of Medals

Please note: the number indicated is the MEDAL number not the PAGE number.
356   The following medals are to be found in the deluxe version of the Medal Yearbook.

IRELAND

AUSTRALIA

AUSTRALIA *continued*

CANADA

NEW ZEALAND

SOUTH AFRICA

MEDALS
For Saving Life

Medals for Saving Life fall into two categories: those awarded by the Government (official awards) and those awarded by other organisations and individuals, of which there are a large number. The first official award by the British Government was the Sea Gallantry Medal (Foreign Services) in 1841 to be followed by the Board of Trade Medal for Saving Life from Sea, then the Albert Medal and subsequently a number of others. These will be found in the main section of this Yearbook. The current section is concerned only with non-official awards for life saving.

The Royal Humane Society (1774), National Institution for the Preservation of Life from Shipwreck (later RNLI) (1824), Society for the Protection of Life from Fire (1836) and Liverpool Shipwreck and Humane Society (1839), all of which are very active to this day, were all instituted before the first official medals. They arose due to a desire to acknowledge and reward those who put the wellbeing of others before themselves. Initially, certainly as regards the RHS, the early rewards were given for the use of life saving methods to help restore the apparently dead (drowned) but the desire to reward those who braved the dangers of drowning, fires and asphyxiation was soon implemented. The RHS supported the creation of numerous humane societies in many towns and cities of Great Britain, and this was continued overseas

In addition to the principal life saving organisations indicated above, the 19th century generated an increasing number of similar but smaller organisations whose objectives were to reward life savers. These organisations were numerous and various and the following list is indicative of those that are known to us today. As will be seen, they represent philanthropic organisations and societies, social groups, commercial companies and municipal authorities. Additionally, life saving medals were issued for specific rescues by grateful survivors or their friends and family.

These awards are of considerable human interest and together with the associated citations, diplomas, parchments and other printed material are now much more appreciated for what they represent—bravery in the face of personal danger. Each life saving award is truly a gallantry award.

A number of the life saving awards from the following list (noted with an "L" number) are described in detail in this section of the MEDAL YEARBOOK, but many of them are as yet incompletely researched. The Life Saving Awards Research Society continues its research of these awards and as the research is completed these will be included in future editions.

	Medal Yearbook no. (where applicable)		Medal Yearbook no. (where applicable)
LIFE SAVING SOCIETIES / FUNDS		Northants Humane Society	
Bath Humane Society		Plym, Tamar, Lynher & Tavy Humane Society	L4A
Bolton & District Humane Society	L33A	Port of Plymouth Humane Society	L4B
Bristol Humane Society		Royal Humane Society	49/ L1
Carnegie Hero Fund Trust	L30	Royal National Lifeboat Institution	L4
Fleetwood Humane Society		(Royal) Society for the Protection	
Glasgow Humane Society	L2	of Life from Fire	L5
Grimsby Humane Society		Royal Life Saving Society (Mountbatten Medal)	L50
Hundred of Salford Humane Society	48/L3	Sheffield Society for the Recognition of Bravery	L27
Jersey Humane Society	L10A	Shipwrecked Fishermen & Mariners Royal Benevolent	
Lancashire Humane Society		Society	L8
Liverpool Shipwreck & Humane Society	14/15/18/L7	Shropshire Society Life Saving Medal	L13
Norfolk Humane Society			

L1. ROYAL HUMANE SOCIETY MEDALS

Date: 1774

Ribbon: None or blue (1776–1867); plain navy blue (1867); thin central yellow stripe and white edges added (silver medal, 1921). Stanhope medal: plain navy blue until 1921, when changed to blue with yellow and black edges. In 2000 the ribbon was changed to grey edges instead of black. Police medal: plain navy blue with a central yellow stripe.

Metal: Gold, silver or bronze.

Size: 51mm (1774–1867); 38mm (1867–).

Description: The first Large Medal was engraved by Lewis Pingo and is described: (obverse) a cherub, nude but for a flowing cloak, blowing on a burnt-out torch explained by the Latin legend LATEAT SCINTILLVLA FORSAN (perhaps a tiny spark may be concealed). A three-line Latin text across the exergue reads SOC. LOND. IN RESVSCITAT INTERMORTVORVM INSTIT. with the date in roman numerals. (Reverse) an oak wreath containing the engraved details of the recipient and the date of the life-saving act. Round the circumference is a Latin motto HOC PRETIVM CIVE SERVATO TVLIT (He has obtained this reward for saving the life of a citizen). Around 1826, the dies were worn out and were replaced with dies of a similar design by another engraver, Benedetto Pistrucci, the main difference being a general reworking of the cherub figure on the obverse.

In 1837 a new reverse die was produced which omitted the motto HOC PRETIUM CIVE SERVATO TULIT from the circumference. This was to be awarded in the future for "unsuccessful" rescues (note—until this date no distinction had been made between "successful" and "unsuccessful" rescues). Until this time the medal had been awarded in silver (except 14 instances of an honorary gold award, three of these being the Fotheringill Gold Medal), but from now onwards bronze medals were also struck.

In 1867, the "small" version (38mm diameter) of the medal was introduced. This was a wearable version having a scroll suspender fitted with a navy blue ribbon. The reverses of the smaller medals were similar to those of the larger variety except that the area inside the wreath (previously left plain for the engraved details of the rescue) were now replaced for a successful rescue with VIT.OB.SERV.D.D. SOC.REG.HVM (The Royal Humane Society presented this gift for saving life) and for an unsuccessful rescue with VIT.PERIC.EXPOS. D.D. SOC REG.HVM (The Royal Humane Society, his life having been exposed to danger). The punctuation varies on later issues. Four types of the small version are known (Type I 1867, Type II 1867–2000, Type III 2000–2020 and Type IV 2020–)

Scrolled clasps in silver and bronze were awarded from 1869 for subsequent acts of bravery deserving of a medal; the silver and bronze clasps corresponded to the previous award (i.e. a silver medal holder would only receive a silver clasp—even if the subsequent rescue was only "bronze standard"). However, a bronze medal holder would receive a silver medal if the rescue was "silver standard". The clasp continued in use (with some variations in design) up to 1950 when the last clasp (a bronze award) was issued. Since then, only one recipient has qualified for a second medal but a second award was issued instead of a clasp. In 2020, two recipients of the Society's bronze medals qualified for second bronze awards and bronze clasps.

The Stanhope Medal in memory of Captain C. S. S. Stanhope, RN, was struck in gold and first issued in 1873. The medal was similar to the Society's silver medal but has a plaque-shaped bar fixed to the suspender embossed with the year of the award and STANHOPE MEDAL. This plaque was discontinued in 1935 or possibly earlier. The medal could be issued with either the "successful" or "unsuccessful" reverses.

Comments: *The Society was formed in 1774 for the specific purpose of diffusing knowledge about the techniques of resuscitation and saving life from drowning. Within two years of its inception, the Society's large medals were struck chiefly in silver, although 14 gold and two silver-gilt medals were also issued for extraordinary bravery or as honorary awards for non life saving activities. In addition monetary rewards and testimonials were granted to those who saved life, or attempted to save life from drowning, but later the Society's remit was broadened to include "all cases of exceptional bravery in rescuing or attempting to rescue persons from asphyxia in mines, wells, blasting furnaces or in sewers where foul air may endanger life". In 1837 a new medal specifically for unsuccessful rescues was introduced and at the same time medals were struck in bronze for both types of rescue. In December 1866 the Society was requested by the Duke of Cambridge, the Army's most senior officer that "some alteration might be made in the size of the Medal in question so as to admit of its being worn." The Society rapidly acceded to his request and by late 1867 the first "wearable" medals were being awarded. Details of the recipient and the act were engraved on the rim. Interestingly it wasn't until 1869 that the Army and Navy formally gave permission for the wearing of the Society's medals.*

Second award clasp.

The Stanhope medal (below, left) was first awarded in 1873 in memory of Captain C.S.S. Stanhope. This is the highest honour bestowed by the Society and is awarded annually for the most gallant rescue to have been rewarded by the Society. Since 1962, the Liverpool Shipwreck & Humane Society, and the Humane Societies of Australasia, Canada, New Zealand and New South Wales have also participated by submitting their most gallant rescue. Since 2014 the Foundation for Civilian Bravery, Sri Lanka, has also submitted their most gallant rescue. In January 2000, the Society introduced The Police Medal, struck in silver/gilt, to honour the police officer who has shown "courage of the highest order" during the preceding year. It is awarded to police officers who have already been awarded a Society award—usually either a Silver or a Bronze Medal.

VALUE:	Gold	Silver	Bronze
Large (Type 1, 1774–1837)	—	£500–700	—
Large successful (Type 2, 1837–67)	—	£400–600	£250–400
Large unsuccessful (Type 2, 1837–67)	—	£400–600	£250–400
Small successful (Type I)	—	£400–550	£300–400
Small successful (Type II)	—	£350–550	£180–250
Small successful (Type III)	—	£500–750	£300–500
Small successful (Type IV)	—	£500–750	£300–500
Small unsuccessful (Type II)	—	£500–750	£180–250
Small unsuccessful (Type III)	—	£500–750	£300–500
Small unsuccessful (Type VI)	—	£500–750	£300–500
Stanhope Gold Medal	£2500–4000	—	—
Police Medal (silver-gilt)	£500–750	—	—
Miniature	£400–500	£90–110	£55–85

L2. GLASGOW HUMANE SOCIETY MEDALS

Instituted: 1780.
Ribbon: None.
Metal: Gold or silver.
Size: 42mm.
Description: (Obverse) a naturalistic treatment of the elements of the Glasgow civic arms: the tree that never grew, the bird that never flew, the fish that never swam and the bell than never rang, with edge inscription GLASGOW HUMANE SOCIETY INSTITUTED 1780; (reverse) PRESENTED BY THE GLASGOW HUMANE SOCIETY TO above a horizontal tablet engraved with the name of the recipient; below: FOR INTREPIDITY OF COURAGE AND SUCCESS IN SAVING THE LIFE OF A FELLOW CITIZEN.
Comments: *Awarded mainly for saving people from drowning in the Clyde and Kelvin rivers but also for rescues in the Firth of Clyde.*

VALUE:
Gold: —   Silver: £600–850

L3. HUNDRED OF SALFORD HUMANE SOCIETY MEDALS

First type.

Second type.

Date: 1789.
Ribbon: Plain dark blue.
Metal: Gold, silver or bronze.
Size: 32mm (circular type); height 49mm, max. width 41mm (cruciform type).
Description: Circular gold, silver or bronze medals were awarded from 1874 onwards, with the recipient's name and details engraved on the reverse, and featuring a cherub kindling a spark similar to the Royal Humane Society's medal, on the obverse. Around the time of the society's centenary in 1889, however, a more elaborate type of medal was devised, with the circular medal superimposed on a cross of distinctive shape, so that the society's name could be inscribed on the arms. Recipient's details are found on the reverse.
Comments: *This society was formed in 1789 to serve the needs of the Salford and Manchester area. After a few years it was dissolved, but was revived again in 1824. These awards ceased in 1922. The Society also awarded medals for swimming proficiency in silver and in bronze—see MYBL48.*

VALUE:	Gold	Silver	Bronze	*Miniature*
Circular medal	—	£100–200	£200–250	—
Cruciform medal	£1000–1800	£185–275	—	—

L4. ROYAL NATIONAL LIFEBOAT INSTITUTION MEDALS (see also no. 365)

Date: 1824.
Ribbon: Plain blue.
Metal: Gold, silver or bronze.
Size: 36mm.
Description: The first medals bore the effigy of George IV on the obverse and it was not until 1862 that this was replaced by a garlanded profile of Victoria by Leonard C. Wyon. Medals portraying Edward VII and George V were introduced in 1903 and 1912 respectively, but when permission to portray George VI was refused in 1937 the RNLI adopted a profile of its founder, Sir William Hillary, instead. All but the Edwardian medals have a reverse showing a drowning seaman being rescued by three men in a boat with the motto LET NOT THE DEEP SWALLOW ME UP. The Edwardian medals have the seated figure of Hope adjusting the lifejacket on a lifeboatman. The earliest medals (1824) were issued without any means of suspension. Subsequent medals (1825–c. 1831) were pierced below the rim to allow a suspension ring to be fitted. Later a band of the appropriate material was added to the medal having an integral loop which allowed a larger suspension loop to be fitted. The characteristic dolphin suspension made its appearance c. 1852 and is still in use to this day. Rewards for additional rescues were initially recognised by a miniature rowing boat, gold for gold awards and silver for silver awards, suspended from short chains either being attached to the medal riband or from the medal itself. Details of the rescue were engraved on the boat. These were phased out c. 1835 for silver boats; the last gold boat was c. 1848. Additional rewards were given by issuing additional medals and this continued until c. 1852 when second, third and subsequent rewards were recognised by the award of "service clasps" fixed to the medal suspension. Details of the rescue are engraved on the reverse of the clasp.

Comments: *The RNLI was founded, as the Royal National Institution for the Preservation of Life from Shipwreck, on 4 March 1824 and began awarding medals to "persons whose humane and intrepid exertions in saving life from shipwreck on our coasts are deemed sufficiently conspicuous to merit honourable distinction". Its title changed to the Royal National Lifeboat Institution in 1854. The medals are engraved on the edge with the recipient's name and the date the recipient was voted the award.*

VALUE:	Gold (150)	Silver (1,564)	*Miniature*	Bronze (793)	*Miniature*
George IV	£2000–3500	£850–1500	—	—	—
Victoria	£2000–3500	£800–1400	£165–220	—	—
Edward VII	£2500–4000	£1300–2200	£220–280	—	—
George V	£2500–4000	£850–1200	£220–280	£450–750	£165–220
Hillary	£2500–4000	£850–1200	£220–280	£450–750	£165–220

L4A. PLYM, TAMAR, LYNHER AND TAVY HUMANE SOCIETY MEDALS

Date: 1836.
Ribbon: None.
Metal: Silver, silver-gilt and bronze.
Size: 48mm.
Description: (Obverse) a winged female figure with a star on her forehead, holding the left wrist of a man who has been raised from the water and lies against a rock. Over the man's head, she is holding an oil lamp in her right hand, with the flame flickering and uncertain. Around the upper perimeter is "LATET SCINTILLULA FORSAN". In the exergue is "MDCCCXXXI"; (reverse) an oak wreath with outside the wreath "THE PLYM TAMAR LYNHER AND TAVY HUMANE SOCIETY". Within the wreath are engraved the recipient's name and details of award. The design of the medal is attributed to Lt. Col. Charles Hamilton Smith, KH, and the medallist was Benjamin Wyon.

Comments: *The Society (initially known as the Plym and Tamar Humane Society) was based on the river systems around Plymouth. The Society owed its origin and establishment to a "medical gentleman of the town" who, during the course of his practice, observed many instances of "suspended animation" where the individuals could have been revived had the necessary apparatus and knowledge been readily available. The objective of the Society was to preserve life, to bestow rewards on all who promptly risked their own lives to rescue those of their fellow creatures; to provide assistance, as far as possible, in all cases of apparent death in the town and neighbourhood; to restore the apparently drowned and dead; and to distinguish by rewards all who may be successful in such restoration. Shortly after the Society's institution in December 1831, they began to issue medals and these were struck in silver and bronze. The medals were issued without means of suspension. There are seven known examples for the period 1832–61 which have an engraved inscription in running script detailing the recipient, place of rescue and date signed by two officials (President, Hon. Secretary or Treasurer). Additionally two examples from the 1870s are recorded, with fewer details. A small number of un-named silver and bronze examples and a presentation example to Lt.-Col. H. Smith, the designer of the medal, are known. Also at least one silver-gilt presentation example is known.*

VALUE:	Silver-gilt £400–500	Silver £450–£575	Bronze £350–£400

L4B. PORT OF PLYMOUTH SWIMMING ASSOCIATION AND HUMANE SOCIETY MEDALS

Date: 1831.
Ribbon: Blue.
Metal: Silver and bronze.
Size: 36mm (40mm widest point of star).
Description: The medals were issued in silver and bronze with further acts of gallantry by medal holders being rewarded with bars to their medals. The medal has always had the basic design of a four-armed cross surmounting a wreath, with a round centre and a crown at the top (crown varied according to the reigning monarch). The centres show the swimmer diving from the left or the right to rescue a person in the water, with different scenes in the background. In others, the centres are plain, or in the case of one known award, the initials of the rescuer.
Comments: *The society was formed in 1831 as The Plym & Tamar Humane Society but in 1862/63 it amalgamated with the Port of Plymouth Swimming Association. However, for another century the Society maintained separate sections for Swimming and the Humane Society, each with its own Chairman, Secretary and Committee. The Humane Society had responsibility for investigating any acts of bravery in rescuing persons along a section of the Plymouth, Stonehouse and Devonport coastline, with the Devonport Humane Society having responsibility for the remainder of the local coastline. As a result of these investigations the Society awarded medals, certificates, watches and other pecuniary awards in those cases felt worthy of recognition. Many of the Society's records have been lost over the years but extant medals indicate that the medals were awarded from c. 1842 to the Second World War period.*

VALUE: Silver   £350–475   Bronze   £300–350

L5. MEDALS OF THE SOCIETY FOR THE PROTECTION OF LIFE FROM FIRE

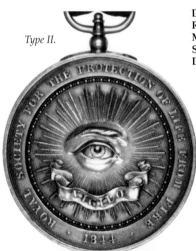

Type II.

Date: 1836.
Ribbon: Plain scarlet.
Metal: Silver or bronze.
Size: 52mm (I and II), 45mm (III), 42mm (IV &V) and 40mm (VI).
Description: The first medal (type I) had the Eye of Providence in a garter on the obverse and a reverse giving the recipient's details in an oak-leaf wreath. They were fitted with a ring suspender. The Society styled itself Royal from 1843 and a new medal (type II) was adopted the following year, with the word ROYAL added and the date at the foot of the obverse changed to 1844. In 1852 type III was introduced, with an obverse of a man carrying a woman away from a fire. This and type IV (1892) were struck in silver or bronze. As royal patronage ended with the death of Queen Victoria, a new medal (type V) was required in 1902 without the Royal title. Types IV and V show a man rescuing a woman and two children from a fire. The reverse of this medal has the words DUTY AND HONOR within a wreath, the recipient's details being placed on the rim. Type VI, awarded from 1984, has no suspension, with the recipient's details engraved on the reverse. Type VII awarded from 2013 is again suspended from a scarlet ribbon. This has a new design with the words FOR BRAVERY on the reverse.

VALUE:		Silver	Bronze
I	Eye and garter (1836)	£850–950	—
II	Eye and garter (1844)	£850–950	—
III	Man and woman (1852)	£450–600	£350–450
IV	Man, woman and children (1892)	£550–700	£400–500
V	As type IV but "Royal" removed (1902)	£300–400	£220–300
VI	As type IV but details on rev.	1 issued	£350–450
VII	FOR BRAVERY reverse	£350–500	£350–450
	Miniature **(type IV)**	£175–220	—

L6. LLOYD'S MEDALS FOR SAVING LIFE AT SEA

Date: 1836.
Ribbon: Blue, striped white, red and white in the centre.
Metal: Gold, silver or bronze.
Size: 73mm or 36mm.
Description: Both large and small medals had similar motifs. (Obverse) the rescue of Ulysses by Leucothoe; (reverse) an ornate wreath.
Comments: *The first medals, introduced in 1837, had a diameter of 73mm and were not intended for wear, but in 1896 the diameter was reduced to 36mm and a ring fitted for suspension with a ribbon.*

VALUE:

		Miniature
Small gold	Rare	
Large silver	£750–1500	—
Large bronze	£450–750	—
Small silver	£400–650	£90–110
Small bronze	£350–500	£65–90

L7. LIVERPOOL SHIPWRECK AND HUMANE SOCIETY'S MARINE MEDALS

Type I.

Date: 1839.
Ribbon: Plain dark blue.
Metal: Gold, silver or bronze.
Size: 54mm (type I), 45mm x 36mm (oval, type II) or 38mm (type III).
Description: (Obverse) a man on a spar of wreckage, taking an inert child from its drowning mother, with the stark legend LORD SAVE US, WE PERISH. This motif was retained for smaller, oval medals (type II) introduced around 1867 with the name of the Society round the edge, and a simple wreath reverse. The suspender was mounted with the Liver Bird emblem. A smaller circular version (type III) was adopted in 1874/75 and fitted with a scroll suspender. In this type the Liver Bird appeared in a wreath on the reverse. Bars engraved with the details were awarded for subsequent acts of life-saving. In addition to the general Marine medals there were distinctive awards in connection with specific marine rescues and funded separately. These had the type III obverse, but the reverse was inscribed CAMP & VILLAVERDE or BRAMLEY-MOORE. A glazed silver medal inscribed IN MEMORIAM was granted to the next of kin of those who lost their lives while attempting to save the lives of others.
Comments: *The Society was formed in 1839 to administer funds raised to help and reward those who distinguished themselves in saving life as a result of a hurricane which swept the Irish Sea in January of that year. The first medals were struck in 1844 and presented for rescues dating back to November 1839. They were large (54mm) in diameter, without suspension.*

Type II.

VALUE:

	Gold	Silver	Bronze
I. Large (54mm) 1844	—	£400–550	—
II. Oval 1867	—	£650–800	—
III. Small (38mm) 1874/5	£1500–2200	£250–400	£150–200
Camp & Villaverde	—	£500–650	£450–550
Bramley-Moore	Rare	£500–650	£450–550
In Memoriam	—	£800–1200	—
Miniature (type II)	£165–250	£110–165	£110–130
(type III)	£165–250	£110–165	£110–130

L8. SHIPWRECKED FISHERMEN AND MARINERS ROYAL BENEVOLENT SOCIETY MEDALS

Date: 1851.
Ribbon: Navy blue.
Metal: Gold or silver.
Size: 36mm.
Description: (Obverse) the Society's arms; (reverse) inscribed PRESENTED FOR HEROIC EXERTIONS IN SAVING LIFE FROM DROWNING with a quotation from Job 29: 13 at the foot. The circumference is inscribed ENGLAND EXPECTS EVERY MAN WILL DO HIS DUTY, a quotation from Lord Nelson's signal to the fleet at Trafalgar, 1805. The first medals had a straight suspender but by 1857 a double dolphin suspender had been adopted (six variations of this suspender can be identified). Details of the recipient's name and the date of the rescue are engraved on the edge. Some medals of 1860 don't have the edge engraved.
Comments: *The Society was founded in 1839 to raise funds for shipwrecked fishermen and mariners and the families of those lost at sea. The first medals were awarded in 1851 and the last award was made to Alexander Lamont in 1965.*

VALUE	Gold	Silver
Straight suspender	**£2500–3000**	**£400–550**
Dolphin suspender	**£2500–3000**	**£350–500**
Miniature	**£350–475**	**£165–230**

L9. TAYLEUR FUND MEDALS

Date: 1861.
Ribbon: Dark blue edged with white stripes.
Metal: Gold or silver.
Size: 45mm.
Description: (Obverse) a sinking ship with the legend TAYLEUR FUND FOR THE SUCCOUR OF SHIPWRECKED STRANGERS; (reverse) details of the award engraved.
Comments: *In January 1854 the emigrant ship* Tayleur *foundered on Lamtray Island, Dublin, Ireland. A fund was started for the relief of the survivors and the surplus used to issue silver life-saving medals. The first awards were made in 1861. Medals are known to have been awarded for 11 separate rescues, the last in 1858. In December 1913 the residue of the Tayleur Fund was transferred to the RNLI and the issue of medals terminated.*

VALUE:

Gold (3)	**Rare**
Silver (48)	**£750–1100**

L10. HARTLEY COLLIERY MEDALS

Date: 1862.
Ribbon: None.
Metal: Gold or silver.
Size: 53mm.
Description: (Obverse) an angel with mine rescuers and disaster victims. Details of the award were engraved on the reverse.
Comments: *Some 204 miners perished in the disaster which overtook the Hartley Colliery, Northumberland on 10 January 1862. This medal was awarded to those involved in the rescue operations.*

VALUE:

Gold (1)	—
Silver (37)	**£850–1200**

L10A. JERSEY HUMANE SOCIETY MEDALS

Date: 1865.
Ribbon: Silver medal—purple 32mm wide;
Bronze medal—royal blue 32mm wide.
Metal: Gold, silver or bronze.
Size: 38mm.
Description: The medal has a plain swivel type suspension, curved, 40mm wide. (Obverse) the escutcheon of Jersey—(Three lions passant guardant heraldic "leopards"), around "HUMANE SOCIETY OF JERSEY" embossed in large capital letters: Below a naked mariner astride a ship's spar in heavy seas waving for assistance. (Reverse) a wreath around "PRESENTED TO (NAME) FOR COURAGE AND HUMANITY" embossed in capital letters.
Comments: *The first society meeting to award medals took place in June 1865 when one gold (Philip Ahier Jnr.), and two silver medals (Alex. J. Bellis and Howard Morris) were awarded. Since then, the Society has remained active with only a break during the German Occupation 1940–45, when the Military Authorities ordered the Society to cease its function and hand over all documents and medals to the Germans. These were, however, hidden by the then Secretary until the Liberation.*

VALUE:
Gold (2)	—
Silver (approx. 55)	£800–1000
Bronze (approx. 110)	£500–700

L11. MERCANTILE MARINE SERVICE ASSOCIATION MEDALS

Date: 1872.
Ribbon: Blue.
Metal: Gold (2) and silver (74).
Size: 38mm.
Description: (Obverse) a border with the legend "MERCANTILE MARINE SERVICE ASSOCIATION". In the centre are two seated figures of Neptune and Britannia. Neptune has a shield decorated with an anchor; Britannia a shield decorated with a sailing ship. Between the two figures are Cornucopias, Mercury's staff and a Liver bird. Beneath the two figures are the words "INCORPORATED BY SPECIAL ACT OF PARLIAMENT", and the maker's name Elkington & Co. Liverpool. The reverse bears a wreath containing the engraved details of the incident and the recipient's name.
Comments: *The medal was instituted by the MMSA in 1875 but the first awards were made retrospectively for rescues in 1872. The award was generally given to the Master and senior officers of ships engaged in life saving actions, but towards the end of its issuance some of the recipients were not officers. The medal was also awarded (in gold and in silver) to the students on the school ship* Conway *(Boy's training ship on the River Mersey) who had demonstrated "the greatest proficiency in all branches of training and education". The reverse of the medal was engraved with full details of the award. The last known award was made in 1906.*

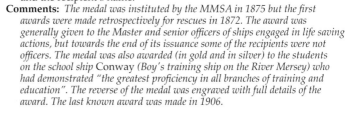

VALUE:
Gold	—
Silver	£350–500

L11A. THE LEANDER MEDAL

London version.

Date: The Serpentine Swimming Club of London—1863 and The Birmingham Leander Swimming Club—1877.

Ribbon: No standard ribbon exists but the colours of the London Club are red and white and some combination of these colours is most common.

Metal: Silver, rarely gold.

Size: Approx 45mm.

Description: Circular, either with a ring or straight suspensory bar. (Obverse) a depiction of Leander swimming across the Hellespont (which we now know as the Dardanelles) towards the temple of Sestos where his lover, Hero, awaits. In the exergue are the words LEANDER MEDAL and sometimes, in the upper sky PERGE ITA UT FIT (continue on your present course). (Reverse) a wreath and space for engraving details. A slight difference can be seen in the illustrated London medal (upper) and the Birmingham medal (lower).

Comments: *The Leander medal was awarded many times for swimming, but only very rarely for saving life—the engraving on the reverse gives the clue.*

VALUE: (for life saving)

Gold	—
Silver	£250–375

Birmingham version.

L11B. WRECK OF THE *CHUSAN*

Date: 1874.

Ribbon: No ribbon but an elaborate suspension consisting of a fouled lifebelt surmounted by an anchor.

Metal: Silver.

Size: 50mm.

Description: (Obverse) within a rope and beaded circle, an engraved depiction of a vessel (the *Chusan*) in the Ardrossan harbour, a rough sea, mountains in the background, a jetty in the lower left foreground; (reverse)within the same type of border as the obverse, the engraved words: "Subscribers Medal—PRESENTED TO (NAME) FOR HEROIC EFFORTS IN SAVING LIFE AT THE WRECK OF THE CHUSAN IN ARDROSSAN HARBOUR—21ST OCT. 1874".

Comments: *This private life saving medal provided by the residents of Ardrossan, Scotland, was awarded to four seamen for life saving rescues from the paddle steamer* Chusan *wrecked in Ardrossan Harbour on October 21, 1874.*

VALUE: £900–1100

L12. LIFE SAVING MEDALS OF THE ORDER OF ST JOHN

First type reverse.

Original ribbon.

Third type ribbon.

Date: 1870.

Ribbon: Black, embroidered with the eight-point cross in white (1870), black watered silk (1888), white inner and red outer stripes added, separated by a black line (1950) which was subsequently removed in 1954.

Metal: Gold, silver or bronze.

Size: 36mm.

Description: The first medals (1870) had a plain eight-pointed cross of the Order on the obverse with the legend AWARDED BY THE ORDER OF ST. JOHN OF JERUSALEM IN ENGLAND; (reverse) a sprig of St John's wort bound by two ribbons, the upper bearing JERUSALEM ACRE and the lower bearing CYPRUS RHODES MALTA, within a circular border the words FOR SERVICE IN THE CAUSE OF HUMANITY. A second type of medal was adopted in 1888 and showed two tiny lions and two tiny unicorns in the interstices of the cross, with the legend FOR SERVICE IN THE CAUSE OF HUMANITY; the reverse shows sprigs of St John's wort bound with a ribbon bearing JERUSALEM ENGLAND, within a circular border AWARDED BY THE GRAND PRIORY OF THE ORDER OF THE HOSPITAL OF ST. JOHN OF JERUSALEM. A third type was adopted in 1980 in the same style as the 1888 type but with the reverse wording changed to read AWARDED BY THE MOST VENERABLE ORDER OF THE HOSPITAL OF ST. JOHN OF JERUSALEM. The current 4th type, introduced in about 2011, has the reverse wording: "AWARDED BY THE GRAND PRIORY OF THE HOSPITAL OF ST JOHN OF JERUSALEM". Bars to the medal were authorised to recognise further acts of gallantry from 1963.

Comments: *The medal was sanctioned in 1870 and awarded for gallantry in saving life, these medals were originally granted in bronze or silver, but gold medals were also struck from 1907. Of the first type only 34 silver and 18 bronze were awarded. The bar to the medal has only been awarded twice, once in gold and once in silver.*

VALUE:

	Gold	Silver	Bronze
1st type 1874	—	£900–1500	£850–950
2nd type 1888	£1600–2200	£700–1200	£400–1000
3rd type 1980	—	£800–1000	£500–750
4th type 2011–todate	—	£750–900	£500–700

L12A. MAHARAJAH OF BURDWAN'S MEDAL FOR GALLANT CONDUCT— BURNING OF HMS *GOLIATH* 1875

Date: 1875

Ribbon: Blue.

Metal: Silver. Bronze specimens are known

Size: 36mm.

Description: The medal has a fixed ring suspender. (Obverse) Bust of Queen Victoria wearing a coronet and veil draped behind, she wears the Order of the Star of India. Below "J. S. & A. B. Wyon". Around "VICTORIA REGINA". (Reverse) Surrounding: "THE GIFT OF THE MAHARAJAH OF BURDWAN"; within "PRESENTED BY THE LORD MAYOR OF LONDON FOR GALLANT CONDUCT AT THE BURNING OF H.M.S. GOLIATH 22nd DECr 1875",

Comment: *HMS Goliath was a training ship lent by the Royal Navy to Forest Gate School Board in 1870. Moored off Grays, Essex, it held some 450 orphan boys, mostly from the East End of London and was used for training in Naval Service. On December 22, 1875 a fire accidentally broke out in the lamp-room and the ship was completely destroyed. One officer and 19 boys are believed to have died in the disaster. Such was the conduct of the boys that the Maharajah of Burdwan wrote to The Times expressing his desire to award a medal, through the Lord Mayor of London, to those boys who had particularly distinguished themselves. The medals were presented at the Mansion House in a private ceremony by the Lord Mayor.*

VALUE: £650–885

L13. SHROPSHIRE SOCIETY IN LONDON LIFE SAVING MEDAL

Date: —
Ribbon: 30mm with two equal stripes of blue and yellow.
Metal: Silver.
Size: 51mm.
Description: (Obverse) a left-facing profile of Captain Matthew Webb whose name appears round the top, with the inscription •BORN IN SHROPSHIRE 1848•SWAM THE CHANNEL 1875• around; (reverse) two draped females holding wreath above panel with a swimmer in waves below, with legend •PRESENTED FOR BRAVERY BY THE SHROPSHIRE SOCIETY IN LONDON. Panel inscribed with recipient's details. Fitted with a plain ring for suspension and a brooch bar at the top of the ribbon.
Comment: *Struck by John Pinches and presented by the Shropshire Society in London (instituted in 1916) for outstanding acts of bravery in Shropshire. It is not known how many were awarded.*

VALUE: £400–650

L14. LIVERPOOL SHIPWRECK AND HUMANE SOCIETY'S FIRE MEDALS

Date: 1883.
Ribbon: Plain scarlet.
Metal: Gold, silver or bronze.
Size: 38mm.
Description: (Obverse) a fireman descending the stairs of a burning house carrying three children to their kneeling mother, her arms outstretched to receive them, with FOR BRAVERY IN SAVING LIFE in the exergue; (reverse) the wreathed Liver Bird previously noted for the third type of Marine medal (L7 type III). The medal is fitted with a scroll suspender. Clasps engraved with the details are awarded for subsquent acts.
Comments: *The first recipient was William Oversby in November 1883, for rescuing a child from a burning house. The first woman recipient was Miss Julia Keogh (12 February 1895) who saved two children in a house fire.*

VALUE:

	Gold (2)	Silver	Bronze
	Rare	£350–500	£250–350
Miniature	£280–350	£220–320	£165–220

L15. LIVERPOOL SHIPWRECK AND HUMANE SOCIETY'S SWIMMING MEDALS

Date: 1885.
Ribbon: Five equal stripes, three blue and two white.
Metal: Silver or bronze.
Size: Height 44mm; max. width 30mm.
Description: This extremely ornate medal has a twin dolphin suspender and a free form. (Obverse) a wreath surmounted by crossed oars and a trident, with a lifebelt at the centre enclosing the Liver Bird emblem on a shield; (reverse) plain, engraved with the recipient's name and details.
Comments: *Not granted for life-saving as such, but for proficiency in swimming and life-saving techniques.*

VALUE:

Silver	£100–185	Bronze	£75–100

L15A. ALLY SLOPER'S MEDAL

Date: 1884.
Ribbon: Equal stripes of red, white and blue.
Metal: Silver.
Size: 36mm.
Description: (Obverse) Ally Sloper parodying Britannia with an umbrella converted into a trident and a barrel with the words "FOR VALOUR" in place of Britannia's shield. (Reverse) A wreath around the circumference with at the base Ally Sloper's initials intertwined. The centre is plain in which details of the recipient and details of the act which led to the award are engraved. Various suspender types to the medal are known, being either a ring and claw or a bar and claw suspender, with the bar being plain or ornate.
Comments: *"Ally Sloper's Half Holiday" was a comic satirical magazine published from 1884 to 1916 and was revived in three separate periods thereafter. The medal was awarded for bravery. It was awarded to the famous (i.e. the explorer H. M. Stanley and Piper Findlater, VC) and to the more humble (David Buchanan, a journeyman painter, William J. Osborn, a coastguard and John Jones, a miner). Full details of the awards can be found in copies of the magazine which are available at the British Library.*

VALUE: £600–1000

L16. ANSWERS MEDAL FOR HEROISM

Date: 1892.
Ribbon: Equal stripes of blue, white, blue, white and blue.
Metal: Silver.
Size: 38mm.
Description: (Obverse) a wreath enclosing a lion crouching on a plinth with the words FOR BRAVERY, a sunburst in the background; (reverse) HONORIS CAUSA within a wreath surrounded by the legend PRESENTED BY THE PROPRIETORS OF ANSWERS. Fitted with a scroll suspender.
Comments: *This medal is typical of the many awards made by newspapers and magazines in the late 19th century. The medals were accompanied by a first class diploma. Second class diplomas were projected but never issued. It was also intended to issue a gold medal but no trace of such award has been found.*

VALUE: £400–700

L17. LLOYD'S MEDALS FOR MERITORIOUS SERVICE

Date: 1893.

Ribbon: Red with blue stripes towards the edges (1893); blue with broad white stripes towards the edges (since 1900).

Metal: Silver or bronze.

Size: 36mm x 38mm (star), 39mm x 29mm (oval), 36mm (circular).

Description: The original medal was a nine-pointed rayed star in bronze with the arms of Lloyd's on the obverse, suspended by a ring from a red ribbon with blue stripes towards the edge. A silver oval medal was introduced in 1900 with Lloyd's arms on the obverse and details of the recipient engraved on the reverse. This medal was fitted with a twin dolphin suspender and a blue ribbon with broad white stripes towards the edge. A third type, introduced in 1913, was a circular medal, struck in silver and bronze (from 1917), with Lloyd's shield on the obverse. The fourth type, still current, was introduced in 1936 and has the full arms, with crest, motto and supporters, on the obverse. The ribbon is suspended by a ring. Type I was issued un-named; type 2–4 were issued named.

Comments: *These medals have been awarded to officers and men for extraordinary services in the preservation of vessels and cargoes from peril.*

2nd type.

4th type.

VALUE:

	Silver	Bronze
1st type: Star 1893	—	£150–200
2nd type: Oval 1900	£500–600	—
3rd type: Circular 1913	£400–500	£300–350
4th type: Circular 1936	£350–500	£250–350
Miniature **(oval)**	£275–350	—
(circular)	£220–275	—

L18. LIVERPOOL SHIPWRECK AND HUMANE SOCIETY'S GENERAL MEDALS

Date: 1894.

Ribbon: Five equal stripes, three red and two white.

Metal: Gold, silver or bronze.

Size: 38mm.

Description: (Obverse) a cross pattée with a wreathed crown at the centre and the legend FOR BRAVERY IN SAVING LIFE with the date 1894 at the foot; (reverse) the wreathed Liver Bird of the Marine medal, type III. Fitted with a scrolled or an ornate bar suspender. Bars for subsequent awards are granted.

Comments: *The first award was made on 9 June 1894 to Constables Twizell and Dean who were both injured whilst stopping runaway horses.*

VALUE:

	Gold	Silver	Bronze
General medal	1 issued	£300–450	£250–350
Miniature	£330–400	£165–250	£110–165

L19. TODAY GALLANTRY FUND MEDALS

Date: 1894
Ribbon: Red with a central white stripe.
Metal: Silver and bronze.
Size: 38mm.
Description: (Obverse) standing figure of Britannia, lion and shield within a wreath; (reverse) the heraldic emblems of the United Kingdom with the legend ABSIT TIMOR (let fear depart) and AWARDED BY THE GALLANTRY FUND. The name of the recipient and date of the award are engraved within a wreath. The medal is fitted with a silver ornamental suspension bar for both the bronze and silver medals.
Comments: *This medal was awarded by the magazine "To-Day", published between 1893 and 1903. Its first editor was the novelist Jerome K. Jerome who enthusiastically promoted the idea of the Gallantry Fund, but when he gave up the editorship in 1897 the Fund soon fell into disuse. About 30 medals were issued.*

VALUE:
Silver	£200–300
Bronze	£200–350

L20. IMPERIAL MERCHANT SERVICE GUILD MEDALS

Date: c. 1895.
Ribbon: Blue
Metal: Silver with a silver-gilt rope and enamelled flag on a gold centre.
Size: 40mm and 63mm.
Description: A cross pattée in the centre of which, within a rope ring, is the Guild flag with the initials M.S.G. superimposed. (Reverse) plain but for the details of the recipient engraved with the formula "Presented by the Merchant Service Guild to . . . for heroism at sea (date)". The cross is suspended by a ring and hook, from a rod with a ball and point at each end. There is a brooch of similar design.
Comments: *Only three examples of this medal are known. The medal to C. Wood Robinson is 63mm and those to John H. Collin and W. Nutman are 40mm. No definite dates of issue for this award have been determined, but the rescues for which the known recipients got these awards were in 1895 and 1896.*

VALUE: All known examples are in large medal groups. No value for a single medal.

L21. PLUCK MEDAL FOR HEROISM

Date: 1895
Ribbon: Blue
Metal: Silver (Bronze specimens are known)
Size: 32mm
Description: (Obverse) sprig of laurel and palm on left and right, with a cross pattée in the centre inscribed FOR HEROISM; (reverse) a sprig of laurel on the left of a scroll engraved with the recipient's name alongside the words PRESENTED BY PLUCK.
Comments: *"Pluck" was an adventure magazine for boys published from 1895 to 1916. Medals were issued from the inception of the periodical. In issue 8 it was announced that the award was to be known as the Answers— Pluck Award and until issue 24 the medal was similar to that given by Answers. From number 25 onwards the distinctive Pluck award was used. The last medals appear to have been issued in 1897.*

VALUE: £350–550

L22. TYNEMOUTH MEDALS

Date: 1895.
Ribbon: Dark blue, or burgundy
Metal: Gold or silver.
Size: Silver 51mm (gold smaller).
Description: Silver: (obverse) a scene viewed from the north of King Edward's Bay at Tynemouth, with Pen Bal Crag surmounted by a lighthouse. In the left foreground is a ship, sinking by the stern and a lifeboat putting off into stormy seas to the rescue. Around the top is the inscription PALAM QUI MERUIT and around the bottom TYNEMOUTH MEDAL; (reverse) recipient's engraved name surrounded by a laurel wreath. The medal is suspended by a scroll suspender with an ornate bar. **Gold:**. The obverse is similar to the silver medal but has no motto and there are numerous changes to the scene. The reverse carries the motto on a large lifebuoy within which are the details of the recipient.
Comments: *The Tynemouth Medal Trust was formed in response to a request from Mr E. B. Convers, a New York lawyer, who had witnessed a rescue in the Tynemouth area. He was so impressed that he had a medal designed and produced and sent 100 silver medals to the Trustees to be awarded for acts of heroism to Tynesiders worldwide, or for acts of heroism in the Tyne and the surrounding area. A variant to the silver medal exists in which the reverse of the medal is not inverted in relation to the suspender—this is known as the Tynemouth Extension Medal. The original medal has the reverse inverted.*

VALUE:		
	Gold	£1500–2000
	Silver (approx. 100)	£400–600

L23. *DRUMMOND CASTLE* MEDAL

Date: 1896.
Ribbon: Plain crimson.
Metal: Silver.
Size: 38mm.
Description: (Obverse) the veiled profile of Queen Victoria; (reverse) a wreath enclosing the name of the ship and the date of its sinking with the legend FROM QUEEN VICTORIA A TOKEN OF GRATITUDE. Fitted with a scrolled suspender.
Comments: *Presented on behalf of Queen Victoria by officials from the British Embassy in Paris to inhabitants of Brest, Ushant and Molene for their generosity and humanity in rescuing and succouring the survivors of the SS* Drummond Castle *which struck a reef off Ushant on 16 June 1896. Of the 143 passengers and 104 crew, all but three perished. 282 medals were struck and 271 of these were awarded to those who helped save the living and assisted in the recovery and burial of the victims.*

VALUE: £350–500

L24. NEWFOUNDLAND SILVER STAR FOR BRAVERY

Date: 1897.
Ribbon: Two equal stripes of dark blue and crimson.
Metal: Silver.
Size: 36mm max.
Description: A six-pointed radiate star with ball ornaments in the interstices, surmounted by a circular medallion showing a ship in distress and having the inscription FOR BRAVERY AT SEA in a collar. Fitted with a plain ring for suspension.
Comment: *Originally instigated by the Governor of Newfoundland, Sir Terence O'Brien, in 1893, as a bravery award. A total of 27 were made. In 1897 three were awarded to those who assisted in putting out a fire on the SS* Aurora *which, loaded with dynamite, was docked in St John's Harbour, Newfoundland. These three were altered to have the name of SS* Aurora *added to the legend.*

VALUE: £850–1300

L25. QUIVER MEDALS

Date: c.1897.
Ribbon: Dark blue for water rescues, red for land, both with a broad diagonal white stripe from lower left to upper right.
Metal: Gold, Silver and Bronze.
Size: 38mm.
Description: A thick medal weighing two ounces. (Obverse) a naked figure holding a rescued child, with the winged skeletal figure of Death hovering over a stormy sea in the background; (reverse) a laureated tablet bearing the name of the recipient and the date of the act. The circumference is inscribed round the top: FOR HEROIC CONDUCT IN THE SAVING OF LIFE and THE QUIVER MEDAL round the foot. The very elaborate suspension ring is in the form of a laurel wreath and is fitted to the suspender bar by means of a scroll inscribed THE QUIVER MEDAL. Brooch mounting at top of ribbon.
Comments: *The popular Victorian magazine "Quiver" took a keen interest in rewarding heroic deeds and encouraged its readers to submit details of such bravery "to include rescues by land and water, and in any part of the world". "Quiver" also took a particular interest in promoting safety at sea and organised a Lifeboat Fund which provided not only a number of lifeboats named "Quiver" but also this gallantry award. At least 58 silver and bronze medals were awarded of which four were presented to the survivors of the Margate surf boat disaster on December 2, 1897. A specially struck gold medal (of a different design) was awarded by "Quiver" to Captain Inch of "Volturno" fame.*

VALUE:		
	Gold (1)	RARE
	Silver (29)	£450–600
	Bronze (30)	£350–450

If you know of a British Life Saving medal that is not included in the MEDAL YEARBOOK we would be delighted to hear from you.

Or if you can supply us with a photograph of any of the medals not illustrated in this publication we would be pleased to include it next year.

If you can help, please contact the Editorial Team, telephone 01404 46972 or at the address on page 1. Thank you!

L25A. WHITWICK COLLIERY DISASTER MEDAL

Date: 1898.
Ribbon: No ribbon—medal suspended by a pin through top loop.
Metal: Bronze 26mm x 26mm
Description: A bronze cross pattée bearing a chased likeness of the Whitwick pit with Whitwick Colliery Disaster 1898 on the four arms of the cross. The reverse is plain with the inscription PRESENTED TO [space for recipient's name] FOR BRAVERY APRIL 22 1898. The recipient's first name and surname are engraved in capitals.
Comments: Instituted following the underground fire at the Whitwick pit on 19/20 April 1898, to reward the 119 men who entered the mine in dangerous conditions to initially rescue the survivors but latterly to recover the dead. Of the 42 miners in the mine only seven survived.

VALUE: £100–150

L26. HUMANE SOCIETY OF NEW ZEALAND MEDALS

Date: 1898.
Ribbon: Scarlet edged with broad beige stripes on which was embroidered gold fern leaves (1898–1914) or 32mm plain royal blue (from, 1915).
Metal: Gold, silver and bronze versions.
Size: 38mm.
Description: Originally an eight-pointed cross with ball points, with a circular medallion at the centre showing two figures surrounded by an inscription ROYAL HUMANE SOCIETY at the top and NEW ZEALAND round the foot, the cross mounted on an oak wreath surmounted by a Royal Crown fitted with a plain ring for suspension. The reverse was engraved with the recipient's name, date and details of the award. The second type consists of a circular medal with (obverse) an allegorical life-saving scene, name of the Society round the top and FOR LIFE SAVING in two lines in the field; (reverse) a laurel wreath with the recipient's name and details engraved in the centre. Early versions of this medal had a scrolled swivel suspension bar but later versions had a plain suspension bar. The top of the ribbon is fitted with a plain brooch.
Comments: *Presented by the Governor General as Patron of the Royal Humane Society of New Zealand. Only one or two awards are made each year. The medal is worn on the right breast. Until 1913 the Society also awarded a special gold medal, known as the Stead Medal, for acts of outstanding bravery. It was similar to the gold medal but had a suspension bar inscribed STEAD MEDAL. It was revived in 1963 for award to unsuccessful nominees for the Stanhope Gold Medal.*

Second type.

VALUE:	Gold	Silver	Bronze
Type I	£2500–3850 (6)	£1250–1800 (73)	£650–£800 (89)
Type II	£2000–2750 (10)	£650–800 (82)	£450 –550 (449)
Stead Medal	—		

L26A. PORT SUNLIGHT ORDER OF CONSPICUOUS MERIT

Date: 1901.

Ribbon: None.

Metal: Gold (15 carat).

Size: 45mm high x 42mm wide.

Description: The medals were only issued in 15 carat gold (Birmingham hallmarks). The medal is in the form of a cross pattée with a ring suspender (to allow attachment of a chain or similar for suspension). The obverse has a central legend "PORT SUNLIGHT ORDER OF CONSPICUOUS MERIT". The reverse is plain upon which the details of the recipient, the act of bravery and the date and time of the incident are engraved. The hallmark is also impressed on the reverse.

Comments: *In 1887, William Hesketh Lever (later Lord Leverhulme) began looking for a new site on which he could expand his soap-making business, at that time based in Warrington. He purchased 56 acres of unused marshy land at the site which became Port Sunlight (after his best-selling brand of soap), which was relatively flat, allowed space for expansion, and had a prime location between the River Mersey and a railway line. The garden village was founded to house his factory workers. Lever personally helped to plan the village, and employed nearly 30 different architects. He introduced schemes for welfare, education and the entertainment of his workers, and encouraged recreation and organisations which promoted art, literature, science or music. His stated aims were "to socialise and Christianise business relations and he also decided to instigate a form of recognition for the various acts of bravery that they had shown in rescuing those in distress. To this end he founded the Port Sunlight Order of Conspicuous Merit. The first medals were presented at a meeting held in the Hume Hall, Port Sunlight on 26 August 1901, where five awards were made for acts of bravery during that year. The final award was made in 1923—a total of only 19 awards having been made.*

VALUE: £400–600

L27. THE SHEFFIELD SOCIETY FOR THE RECOGNITION OF BRAVERY MEDAL

Date: c. 1903.

Ribbon: Blue.

Metal: Gold, silver and bronze.

Size: 38 mm.

Description: (Obverse) a laurel branch and an oak leaf branch, tied to form a wreath, surmounted by a crown with inside the wreath an array of arrows above three sheaves of corn; (reverse) a laurel wreath upon which is a shield on which are inscribed details of the recipient and the act of bravery, with SHEFFIELD SOCIETY FOR RECOGNISING BRAVERY around.

Comments: *The Society owes its inception to Colonel Sir John E. Bingham, Bt. The rewards were intended to be given to any person residing in the city of Sheffield or within a radius of six miles from the Sheffield Parish Church, including the borough of Rotherham, for a conspicuous act of bravery, but not for rescues or attempted rescues from drowning and rescue or attempted rescues from asphyxia in mines, wells, sewers, and the like, or for any act of bravery that received an award from the Royal Humane Society.*

VALUE:		
	Gold (1)	Rare
	Silver	£400–550
	Bronze	£300–400

L28. BOYS' BRIGADE CROSS FOR HEROISM

Date: September 1902.
Ribbon: Originally royal blue with two equal white stripes, but changed to plain royal blue in 1941.
Metal: Bronze.
Description: A cross pattée formed of four V-shaped finials linked to a circular disc inscribed the BOYS' BRIGADE CROSS FOR HEROISM and enclosing the emblem of the Boys' Brigade. The cross has a suspension ring and a plain brooch bar at the top of ribbon. There are two types, with or without a Geneva cross behind the anchor in the emblem (added in 1926 when the Boys' Life Brigade amalgamated with the Boys' Brigade).
Comments: *First awards were made in 1904, the cross was awarded only 194 times up to the end of 1985, including five posthumous awards. Simon Herriott, aged 8, became the youngest holder in 1980.*

VALUE:	First type (without central cross)	£750–1200
	Second type (with central cross)	£600–800

L29. GOLDEN PENNY MEDAL

Date: 1901
Ribbon: None
Metal: Bronze
Size: 36mm
Description: (Obverse) Britannia as found on pre-decimal British currency, with the legend THE GOLDEN PENNY but without a date in the exergue; (reverse) THE GOLDEN PENNY above AWARDED TO . . . FOR BRAVERY, with the recipient's name engraved or impressed .
Comments: *The medal appears to have been issued at irregular intervals between November 1901 and June 1904. It is estimated that approximately 33 medals were issued during this period. A variant of this medal is known where the reverse legend "THE GOLDEN PENNY" is replaced by "HOUR GLASS". An example of this medal is known in its John Pinches case of issue. This corresponds with the fact that the "Golden Penny" magazine changed its name to "Hour Glass" for a short period in 1904 then reverted back to "Golden Penny".*

VALUE: £500–800

L30. CARNEGIE HERO FUND MEDAL

Date: 1908.
Ribbon: None.
Metal: Bronze.
Size: 90mm.
Description: UK version: (Obverse) an angel and a nude male figure surrounded by an inscription "HE SERVES GOD BEST WHO MOST NOBLY SERVES HUMANITY"; (reverse) two wreaths surrounding a central tablet inscribed "FOR HEROIC ENDEAVOUR TO SAVE HUMAN LIFE..." surrounding a further inscription "PRESENTED BY THE TRUSTEES OF THE CARNEGIE HERO FUND". Details of the recipient are engraved on the rim.
Comments: *The Carnegie Hero Fund Trust was established by Andrew Carnegie, first in the USA and Canada in 1904 and in Scotland in 1908 followed by eight other countries. The first UK medallion was awarded posthumously on 26 November 1909 to Thomas Wright for a life saving act on 23 September 1908. To date fewer than 200 medallions have been awarded in the UK. The design above is that of the UK medal but there are other designs for each of the 11 countries who administer the funds.*

VALUE:

UK		
Bronze	£1000–1500	

USA & Canada		
Gold	£6000–10,000	
Silver	£1000–2000	
Bronze	£750–1000	

Details of recipients are embossed here.

Design of the US & Canadian version

L30A. HAMSTEAD COLLIERY MEDAL 1908

Date: 1908.

Ribbon: Pale blue (30mm).)

Metal: Gold (24) and Silver (16).

Size: 38mm.

Description: A circular medal suspended from an ornamental bar joined to the medal by a ring. The ribbon has a top suspender bar with a pin back of the same ornamental design as the lower bar. (Obverse) within a wreath a heroic figure effecting the rescue of a miner, rubble and mining implements are in the background. To the sides a wreath partially surrounding. (Reverse) on a surrounding band the words: HAMSTEAD COLLIERY DISASTER . MARCH 1908., whilst within the band are the words: PRESENTED TO (name engraved) FOR CONSPICUOUS BRAVERY IN ATTEMPTING TO RESCUE THE ENTOMBED MINERS.

Comments: *The Hamstead Colliery, near Birmingham, suffered a disastrous fire on 4 March 1908, whereby 24 miners were entombed. Rescue attempts by the Hamstead men were augmented by the efforts of the Tankersley (Barnsley) and Altofts (Normanton) mine rescue brigades. One of them, a Yorkshireman named John Welsby, lost his life in the subsequent rescue attempts, and in spite of their valorous efforts all 24 trapped miners died. The Committee charged with the administration of the Hamstead Colliery Disaster Relief Fund decided that 25 gold medals would be awarded to the Hamstead miners who attempted to reach their trapped colleagues before the arrival of the Yorkshire rescue parties. Silver medals plus £10 would be presented to each of the local miners who assisted in the later exploration work. The Government Inspectors and higher mining officials who directed underground operations at great personal risk would each receive gold medals. In addition to the above, five Edward Medals (Mines) in silver and two in bronze were also awarded. John Welsby's widow received £262 from a special fund and his Edward Medal (posthumous award).*

VALUE: Gold   £2000–3500   Silver   £1500–1800

L30B. BOLTON & DISTRICT HUMANE SOCIETY MEDAL

Date: 1895.

Ribbon: Plain dark blue.

Metal: Silver and bronze.

Size: 51.3mm (general medal) or 35mm (Hulton Colliery medal).

Description: The Society's general medal is described thus: (Obverse) a vertical figure of flying angel holding a wreath in her left hand, with "VIRTUTE ET PATIENTIA" around the border. There is a small flower at the six o'clock position, beneath which is the maker's name "JENKINS . BIRMM". (Reverse) around the border is "BOLTON AND DISTRICT HUMANE SOCIETY". The centre is blank for the recipient's name and the date of the act. In 1911 the Society additionally issued the Hulton Colliery variety medal, which is a smaller medal in bronze, with the same obverse and reverse design, albeit with the legend "HULTON COLLIERY DISASTER DECEMBER 21ST 1910" in the reverse centre. The latter variety medal was issued unnamed. The suspender consists of ornamental laurel leaves, very similar to that on the Crimea Medal.

Comments: *Established in Bolton in 1895, the Society issued its own silver and bronze medals and testimonials for acts of lifesaving in Bolton and neighbouring areas. Between 1895 and 1911 the Society awarded approximately 19 silver and 48 bronze medals. The Hulton Colliery variety of the Society's medal was created following the explosion of 21 December 1910 at Hulton Colliery (Pretoria Pit), which killed at least 344 miners. Large numbers of their colleagues were involved in rescue efforts and the grim and dangerous work of recovering the bodies. Rescuers efforts were recognized by awards of the Edward Medal (Mines) 2nd class, the Order of St John Life Saving Medal, Royal Humane Society medals, the Lancashire and Cheshire Coal Owners Rescue Station Medal with "Hulton 1911" clasp, and the Bolton Society's own special medal, the latter going to approximately 165 recipients.*

VALUE: General medal in silver: £500–800
General medal in bronze: £300–600
Hulton Colliery variety medal in bronze: £300–450

L31. RSPCA LIFE-SAVING MEDALS

Date: 1909.
Ribbon: Blue with three white stripes in the centre, the central stripe being narrower than the others (silver); blue with a central white stripe flanked by narrow red and white stripes (bronze).
Metal: Silver or bronze.
Size: 36mm.
Description: (Obverse) originally (Type I) the Royal coat of arms with "For Animal Life Saving" below and the name of the Association around the edge; (reverse) a seated female figure surrounded by a cow, sheep, cat, dog, goat and horse; later issues (Type II) portray the seated female figure surrounded by a cow, sheep, cat, dog, goat and horse, with R.S.P.C.A. below; (reverse) plain, with an inscription. The recipient's name usually appears on the rim. Both medals have a brooch bar inscribed FOR HUMANITY or FOR GALLANTRY
Comments: *Instituted in 1909 by the Royal Society for the Prevention of Cruelty to Animals, this medal is awarded in silver or bronze for acts of gallantry in saving the lives of animals, the early bronze awards are gilt. See also 368A, 368B and L38.*

VALUE:	Type I	Type II
Silver	£350–450	£300–450
Bronze	£250–350	£200–300

L31A. NATIONAL CANINE DEFENCE LEAGUE MEDAL

Date: c. 1891.
Ribbon: Red.
Metal: Silver or bronze.
Size: 30mm.
Description: (Obverse) Victory standing with sword in hand over vanquished dragon, her right hand resting on a dog; NATIONAL CANINE DEFENCE LEAGUE inscribed round the top; (reverse) spray of oak leaves with a placard engraved with the name of the recipient and date of the award. Fitted with a plain ring for suspension
Comments: *Awarded for acts of bravery or exceptional humanity in the rescue of dogs from dangerous situations. Medals in bronze were intended for award to dogs for brave acts.*

VALUE:		
	Silver (early issue)	£800–1200
	Silver (late issue)	£300–375
	Bronze	£250–350

L31B. THE PEOPLE'S DISPENSARY FOR SICK ANIMALS CROSS

Date: 1917
Ribbon: Broad red band with a narrow blue central stripe and broad white edges.
Metal: Silver.
Size: 32mm.
Description: A plain cross pattée with the initials PDSA on the arms. At the centre is a medallion bearing the figure of St Giles. The reverse is plain except for the name of the recipient and date of the award.
Comments: *Awarded to people who have performed acts of bravery involving animals. The PDSA also award medals to animals, the Dickin Medal (no. 358) being the most important.*

VALUE: £250–400

L31C. OUR DUMB FRIENDS LEAGUE MEDAL

Date: 1897
Ribbon: Plain red.
Metal: Silver.
Size: Heart-shaped, 45mm x 50mm.
Description: (Obverse) Figures of a horse, dog, cat and donkey within a heart-shaped ribbon inscribed OUR DUMB FRIENDS LEAGUE A SOCIETY FOR THE ENCOURAGEMENT OF KINDNESS TO ANIMALS; (reverse) engraved with the name of the recipient and date of the award.
Comments: *Awarded for acts of bravery involving the rescue of animals. Founded as "Our Dumb Friends League" the charity's fund raising body was called the Blue Cross Fund. This was particularly active in WWI and eventually the ODL was renamed the Blue Cross. Medals are known to have been awarded between 1910 and 1946, although further research may expand this date range. Certificates were also awarded for lesser acts of bravery.*

VALUE:
Silver	£400–550
Bronze	£350–400

L32. SCOUT ASSOCIATION GALLANTRY MEDALS

Date: 1909.
Ribbon: Red (bronze), blue (silver) or half red, half blue (gilt).
Metal: Bronze, silver and gilt.
Size: 33mm.
Description: The medal is in the form of a cross pattée with the fleur-de-lys emblem at the centre. *Type 1* 1909–19 (obverse) FOR SAVING LIFE and the motto BE PREPARED; (reverse) (i) indent of Scout emblem and motto with ridge underneath; (ii) plain. *Type 2* 1920–66 (obverse) FOR GALLANTRY with motto BE PREPARED, (reverse) plain with maker's name "Collins, London". *Type 3* 1966–date (obverse) FOR GALLANTRY with the new Scout emblem with inverted "V", no emblem; (reverse) plain. The Type 1 medal is suspended from a ring suspender and Types 2 and 3 have a fixed bar suspender.
Comments: *The Scout movement began informally in 1907 and the Boy Scouts Association was founded a year later. The Scout Association's highest award is the Cornwell Scout badge, named after "Boy" Cornwell of Jutland fame. However, gallantry awards were instituted in 1908 and 1909. The bronze cross is the highest award of the Association for gallantry, granted for special heroism or action in the face of extraordinary risk. The silver cross is awarded for gallantry in circumstances of considerable risk. The gilt cross is awarded for gallantry in circumstances of moderate risk. In Canada, the order is reversed, with gilt (with red ribbon) being the highest and bronze (with red/blue ribbon) being the lowest. A clasp may be awarded to the holder of any gallantry award for further acts of gallantry in circumstances of similar risk. Collective awards may also be made to Troops, Groups or other Units within the Scout Movement and in 1943 the Boy Scouts of Malta & Gozo received the unique distinction of being awarded the Bronze Cross.*

Bronze award ribbon.

Silver award ribbon.

Gilt award ribbon.

VALUE: (British)
Bronze (148)	£1000–1500
Silver (1343)	£650–1000
Gilt	£450–650

L32A. CORNWELL SCOUT BADGE

Date: 1916.
Ribbon: None.
Metal: Bronze.
Size: 30 x 25mm.
Description: The fleur de lys of the Scout Association surrounded by a large stylised capital C, suspended by a brooch pin with attached safety chain.
Comments*: This award was named after John Travers Cornwell who won a posthumous Victoria Cross at the Battle of Jutland. At the age of 16 Jack Cornwell was one of the youngest winners of the VC and had been a Scout before entering the Navy. It was originally awarded "in respect of pre-eminently high character and devotion to duty, together with great courage and endurance" but is now reserved exclusively to members of a training section of the Scout Association under 25 years of age (until 2002, under 20 years of age) who have an outstanding record of service and efficiency. It is very rarely awarded, the last occasion being in 1998. To date a total of 634 badges have been awarded.*

VALUE: £350–535

L33. C.Q.D. MEDALS

Date: 1909.
Ribbon: Plain dark blue or crimson (*).
Metal: Silver-gilt, silver, bronze.
Size: 45mm.
Description: (Obverse) the SS *Republic* with the initials C.Q.D. at the top; (reverse) the words FOR GALLANTRY across the middle, with a very verbose inscription round the circumference and continued in eight lines across the field. Ring suspension. Issued unnamed, but examples are known with the recipient's name and ship privately engraved.
Comments: *This medal takes its curious name from the CQD signal (All Stations Distress) sent out by the stricken White Star steamship* Republic *after it collided with the Italian steamer* Florida *on January 21, 1909. The liner* Baltic *responded to the call. The* Republic *was the more severely damaged vessel, but all of her passengers and crew were transferred, first to the* Florida *and then to the* Baltic, *before she sank. The saloon passengers of the* Baltic *and* Republic *subscribed to a fund to provide medals to the crews of all three ships in saving more than 1700 lives. Silver-gilt examples without suspender were presented to senior officers of the three ships involved and to Jack Binns, the Marconi operator aboard the* Republic *who sent out the CQD radio signal. Silver medals with ring suspenders were presented to the officers and crews. Binns became a hero when the survivors reached New York and was given a welcome parade. This was the first time that radio was used to effect a rescue at sea and indirectly sealed the fate of the* Titanic *three years later, as the White Star Line wrongly assumed that any larger liner would take several hours to sink and radio would obtain help quickly within well-used shipping lanes and lifeboats would only be required to effect the transfer of passengers and crew. As a result the number of lifeboats on the* Titanic *was severely reduced. Coincidentally, Jack Binns was offered the post of wireless officer on board the new* Titanic *but declined. It is believed that bronze examples exist but the Editor would be pleased to learn of any definite sightings of these.*
   * Originally it was believed this medal was awarded with a dark blue ribbon. However, many examples have appeared on the market with a plain crimson ribbon. The Times *of February 8, 1909 carried a report that described the medal as being "fitted with a ring for suspension, from a crimson ribbon 1½" wide."*

VALUE:
   Silver-gilt   £1000–1500
   Silver   £400–600

L34. *CARPATHIA* AND *TITANIC* MEDALS

Date: 1912.
Ribbon: Maroon.
Metal: Gold, silver or bronze.
Size: Height 40mm; max. width 35mm.
Description: The ornately shaped medal, in the best Art Nouveau style, has the suspension ring threaded through the head of Neptune whose long beard flows into two dolphins terminating in a fouled anchor and ship's spars. (Obverse) the *Carpathia* steaming between icebergs; (reverse) a twelve-line inscription, with the name of the recipient and the name of the manufacturer at the foot. The ribbon hangs from a straight bar suspender.
Comments: *This medal recalls one of the greatest tragedies at sea, when the White Star liner* Titanic *struck an iceberg on her maiden voyage and sank with the loss of 1,490 lives. The 711 survivors were picked up by the* Carpathia *whose officers and men were subsequently awarded this medal in gold, silver or bronze according to the rank of the recipient.*

VALUE:		
Gold (14)		£35,000–45,000
Silver (110)		£12,000–15,000
Bronze (180)		£3500–5500

L35. LLOYD'S MEDALS FOR SERVICES TO LLOYD'S

Date: November 1913.
Ribbon: Blue with broad white stripes towards the edge.
Metal: Gold or silver.
Size: 36mm.
Description: (Obverse) Neptune in a chariot drawn by four horses; (reverse) an oak-leaf wreath enclosing a scroll inscribed FOR SERVICES TO LLOYD'S. Fitted with ring suspension.
Comments: *Instituted by Lloyd's Committee, this medal was intended to reward services of a general nature.*

VALUE:		*Miniature*
Gold (14)	£2000–5000	—
Silver (10)	£1000–1250	£200–250

L35A. *ERINPURA* AND *TOPAZE* MEDAL

Date: June 1919.
Ribbon: None.
Metal: Silver or bronze.
Size: 32mm.
Description: (Obverse) simple inscription . 526 . MEN, WOMEN AND CHILDREN . TAKEN OFF . S.S. BRINPURA . AGROUND ON . MUSHEGERA REEF BY H.M.S.TOPAZE . 15.6.19; (reverse) an oak-leaf wreath with A MEMENTO PRESENTED BY THE PASSENGERS within.
Comments: *In a severe dust storm on 15 June 1919 the SS* Erinpura *went aground at full speed on the Mushegera Reef in the Red Sea. HMS* Topaze, *a Gem Class scout cruiser, came to her aid and took off the passengers and most of the crew, leaving a few men on board to maintain the engines. Attempts to refloat her were unsuccessful as the bow section was stuck fast and eventually had to be cut away and completely replaced. The medals were struck on behalf of the grateful passengers and presented to the officers and crew of HMS* Topaze. *The medals are known in bronze although there are unconfirmed reports of examples in silver—perhaps presented to the officers (?). The obverse is incorrectly inscribed* BRINPURA *as the ship has been confirmed as the* Erinpura, *built for the British India Steam Navigation Co. Ltd in 1910 and sunk by German bombers en route to Malta in World War II.*

VALUE:		Bronze £100–165		Silver —

L36. ORDER OF INDUSTRIAL HEROISM

Date: 1923.
Ribbon: Bright watered red.
Metal: Bronze.
Size: 28mm.
Description: (Obverse) a modern interpretation of St Christopher carrying Christ (by Eric Gill); (reverse) inscription ORDER OF INDUSTRIAL HEROISM around the perimeter and in the upper half AWARDED BY THE DAILY HERALD above the recipient's name and date of award.
Comments: *Created by the "Daily Herald" and first issued in 1923. It was given as a reward to the "workers" who demonstrated bravery in the workplace and was initially only to be awarded to members of a Trade Union. However, there are numerous examples of the awards being given to non Union members and the definition of "workplace" was wide. The award was intimately associated with the "Daily Herald" throughout the lifetime of the newspaper and when it ceased publication in 1963 the award was discontinued. The medal was always awarded with a certificate and a monetary award. 440 were awarded.*

VALUE: £800–1200

L36AA. COUNTY BOROUGH OF
SOUTHEND ON SEA PIER DEPARTMENT
LIFE SAVING AWARD

Date: 1926.
Ribbon: Dark blue with two silver stripes on each side and a central gold stripe.
Metal: Silver.
Size: 37.5mm.
Description: Type 1: A circular medal with a ring soldered to the edge through which a second ring is fitted for the ribbon. The ribbon is suspended from an ornate gold brooch bar. Type 2: The ring suspender is replaced with a fixed bar suspender and the ornate gold brooch bar is no longer present. (Obverse) Type 1: "COUNTY BOROUGH OF SOUTHEND ON SEA PIER DEPARTMENT" around the circumference in an ornate garter, within which is the Borough coat of arms. Type 2: Similar to type 1 but "COUNTY BOROUGH OF SOUTHEND ON SEA PIER AND FORESHORE DEPARTMENT" around the circumference, but with no ornate garter which has been removed. (Reverse) Types 1 and 2: "AWARDED FOR SAVING LIFE" around the circumference, with a plain central area with "TO" and space for the recipient's name and date of the rescue to be added. A hallmark is located above "TO".
Comments: *During 1926, the Pier Department recognising the numerous acts of life saving that had occurred at the pier over the preceding years, decided that a special medal should be struck, to be called the "PIER LIFE SAVING MEDAL". This was later modified (sometime before 1939) as described above.*

VALUE: Type 1   £400–500   Type 2   £400–500

L36A. COLONEL WOODCOCK'S SWIMMING PRIZES TRUST MEDAL

Date: Approx. 1925.
Ribbon: Seen as dark blue—25mm.
Metal: Silver.
Size: 28mm.
Description: Circular with a ring suspension. (Obverse) a swimmer in the centre with the words COLONEL WOODCOCK'S SWIMMING MEDAL around; (reverse) a wreath, open at the top, with space for engraving details in the centre.
Comments: *The Bristol City and County Council, on the recommendation of the Baths and Education Committees, award twelve medals each year—eight for swimming and four for life saving. About 1950 the medals were discontinued and lapel badges instituted instead.*

VALUE: (for life saving)   £150–250

L37. CORPORATION OF GLASGOW BRAVERY MEDALS

Type I obverse.

Date: 1924
Ribbon: Green with red edges.
Metal: Gold, silver or bronze.
Size: 38mm (type I), 33mm (type II), 30mm (type III).
Description: Type I: (obverse) Fame blowing a trumpet and holding a laurel wreath in front of a circular scrolled cartouche inscribed FOR BRAVERY; (reverse) plain, engraved with the name and details of the recipient. Type II: (obverse) wreath enclosing the words FOR BRAVERY; (reverse) Arms of the Corporation of Glasgow and details of the recipient. Type III: (obverse) Arms of the Corporation of Glasgow with FOR BRAVERY above and two sprigs of laurel below; (reverse) plain for details of the recipient. Fitted with a ring suspension and an ornate thistle brooch inscribed GALLANTRY in a scroll.
Comments: *Following the reorganisation of local government in Scotland in 1975, the award ceased and was replaced by the Strathclyde Regional Council Medal for Bravery.*

VALUE:	Type I	Type II	Type III
Gold	—	—	£350–500
Silver	£280–380	£100–200	—

L37A. IMPERIAL CHEMICAL INDUSTRIES BRAVERY AWARD

Date: 1930.
Ribbon: Dark blue suspended from a brooch bar bearing the word "Fortis".
Metal: Gold (9ct) (pre-war), later bronze.
Size: 38mm x 26mm
Description: (Obverse) "Awarded for Bravery" with a lion rampant bearing the letters "I.C.I."; (reverse) inscription in raised letters (name, location and date of incident).
Comments: *A meeting of the ICI Central Council in 1929 proposed an award to be given for outstanding acts of bravery by ICI workers whilst at work. Originally awarded in 9ct gold but after World War II issued in bronze. The first award was made to Harry Smithies in 1929 and the last to James Nicol in 1975. 36 medals were awarded. ICI were taken over in 2008.*

VALUE:		
	Gold	£1000–1750
	Bronze	£800–1000

L38. RSPCA MARGARET WHEATLEY CROSS

Date: 1936.
Ribbon: 32mm blue with a white stripe towards each edge.
Metal: Bronze.
Size: 33mm square.
Description: Cross pattée with a central circular cross with rounded ends superimposed. R.S.P.C.A. across the top arm of the outer cross and INSTD. 1936 across the lower arm. THE MARGARET WHEATLEY CROSS inscribed in four lines across the centre. (Reverse) central circle inscribed FOR BRAVING DEATH ON BEHALF OF ANIMALS, above and below a raised horizontal panel engraved with the details of the award. Fixed ring for suspension.
Comments: *The RSPCA's highest award, it was named in memory of 16 year-old Margaret Wheatley who was killed by a train at Grange-over-Sands on June 4, 1936 while saving her dog that had got trapped on the railway line. She was posthumously awarded the RSPCA's Silver Medal and was also the first recipient of the cross named in her honour. To date, a total of 70 crosses have been awarded, at least 32 of them posthumously.*

VALUE: Rare

L38A. DUNDEE CORPORATION MEDAL FOR GALLANTRY

Date: 1937.
Ribbon: Blue with silver top bar bearing the word GALLANTRY.
Metal: Silver.
Size: 38mm.
Description: A circular medal with plain ring suspension bearing (obverse) the coat of arms of the City and Corporation of Dundee. (Reverse) a thistle flower and leaves with the words AWARDED TO . . . FOR BRAVERY above.
Comments: *Awarded for acts of gallantry within the city of Dundee irrespective of whether or not the person was a citizen of Dundee. Manufactured and supplied by the local firm of Laurence W. Strachan. Only 41 medals were awarded between its institution in 1937 and 29 September 1951.*

VALUE: £550–650

L39. LLOYD'S MEDAL FOR BRAVERY AT SEA

Date: 1940.
Ribbon: White with broad blue stripes at the sides.
Metal: Silver.
Size: 36mm.
Description: (Obverse) a seated nude male figure holding a laurel wreath, extending his hand towards a ship on the horizon; (reverse) a trident surmounted by a scroll inscribed BRAVERY, enclosed in a wreath of oak leaves. It has a ring suspender.
Comments: *Instituted by Lloyd's Committee, it was awarded to officers and men of the Merchant Navy and fishing fleets for exceptional bravery at sea in time of war. A total of 523 medals was awarded up to December 1947 when it was discontinued.*

VALUE:
Silver £800–1200 *Miniature* £200–250

L40. LONDON, MIDLAND AND SCOTTISH RAILWAY MEDAL

Date: 1940.
Ribbon: Dark blue.
Metal: Silver.
Size: 38mm.
Description: (Obverse) Three different steam locomotive chimneys with a radiant sun in the right background with the inscription LONDON, MIDLAND AND SCOTTISH RAILWAY round the circumference; (reverse) a locomotive driving wheel on which is superimposed at the left a sprig of laurel, with the inscription FOR COURAGE or FOR MERIT round the top of the circumference. The date 1940 appears in the exergue. Fitted with a plain ring for suspension.
Comments: *Instituted by the Chairman of the LMS Company for acts of gallantry or meritorious service, hence the two different reverse types. The Chairman, Lord Stamp, was killed in an air raid in 1941 and it is believed that many of the records relating to this medal perished with him. Although the exact number of awards is not known, it is believed that about 20 awards were made.*

VALUE: £1800–2500

L41. SOUTHERN RAILWAY MERITORIOUS SERVICE MEDAL

Date: 1940.
Ribbon: Green with railway track and sleepers in gold.
Metal: Silver gilt.
Size: 32mm.
Description: (Obverse) a cross formy with SR in a circle at the centre, superimposed on a laurel wreath surrounded by a locomotive driving wheel; (reverse) FOR MERIT in seriffed capitals over a space for the recipient's name and SOUTHERN RAILWAY across the foot. The ornamental suspension bar is in the form of a vehicle spring. This medal was designed by Kruger Gray and struck at the Royal Mint.
Comments: *Instituted by the Directors of the Company for award to those employees considered to have performed outstanding deeds in the performance of their duties. 18 medals were awarded at a ceremony on August 16, 1940, and a further six medals were subsequently awarded.*

VALUE: Rare

L42. THE DALE AWARD

Instituted: November 1940.
Ribbon: White with broad blue and narrow black stripes towards the edges.
Metal: Silver.
Size: 33mm.
Description: (Obverse) a central medallion enamelled in white bearing the spires of Coventry Cathedral, surrounded by an inscription: THE DALE AWARD / COVENTRY.NOV.14.1940; (reverse) a laurel wreath enclosing a ten-line inscription across the middle: AWARDED BY THE COVENTRY HOSPITAL FUND FOR DEVOTION TO HOSPITAL & AMBULANCE DUTY DURING THE COVENTRY AIR RAID NOVEMBER 14th 1940. The medal bears the Birmingham assay marks and maker's mark of Thomas Fattorini. The medal was not named.
Comments: *This medal was awarded by the Coventry and Warwickshire Hospital Saturday Fund to ambulance drivers and others for devotion to duty during the air raid of 14 November 1940. It is believed that 32 awards were made. A fascinating recollection by a recipient can be found on the website www. coventrymemories.co.uk.*

VALUE: £450–575

L43. LONDON PASSENGER TRANSPORT BOARD MEDAL FOR BRAVERY

Instituted: 1940.

Ribbon: Red with green central stripe and four narrow white stripes on either side.

Metal: Cupro-nickel.

Size: 38mm.

Description: (Obverse) a naked man kneeling and turning a large wheel; (reverse) the words LONDON TRANSPORT above a sprig of laurel, with a space for the recipient's name and a three-line inscription across the foot: FOR BRAVERY AND DEVOTION TO DUTY. Plain suspension bar and an ornamental brooch fitment at the top of the ribbon.

Comments: *This medal was instituted by Lord Ashfield, Chairman of the LPTB, to reward "special deeds of bravery" undertaken by LPTB staff during the Blitz. Only nine medals were awarded (all presented on February 21, 1941) before the medal was discontinued, after some government pressure, to encourage nominations for the official civilian bravery awards of the George Cross and George Medal. A few unnamed specimens are known, possibly reaching the market from the stock of John Pinches when they ceased business.*

VALUE:
Named (9)	£2500–3000
Unnamed	£250–350

L44. LONDON AND NORTH EASTERN RAILWAY GALLANTRY MEDAL

Date: 1941.

Ribbon: Dark blue with a central white stripe flanked by narrow white stripes.

Metal: Silver with a matt finish.

Size: 38mm.

Description: (Obverse) a shield containing the arms of the company, superimposed on a laurel wreath surrounded by the inscription LONDON AND NORTH EASTERN RAILWAY on a raised band; (reverse) a scroll for the recipient's name superimposed on a laurel wreath with the rising sun in the background. The raised band is inscribed FOR COURAGE AND RESOURCE. Fitted with a plain suspension bar and an ornamental brooch bar at the top of the ribbon.

Comments: *Awarded "for outstanding acts of gallantry and resource which are not connected with enemy action, but which are of such a standard as would warrant recommendations for Government recognition had the acts been connected with enemy action". As some of the medals were awarded for actions resulting from enemy air raids the phrase "not connected with enemy action" was very liberally interpreted. A total of 22 medals were awarded, the last in 1947.*

VALUE: £1800–2800

The hugely emotive PDSA Dickin Medal for Gallantry (MYB L44A), together with the RSPCA Red Collar for Valour awarded to War Dog Rob, for his gallantry and outstanding service during World War II, during which he undertook 20 parachute descents, was sold for a world record price of £140,000 (hammer) at Noonans in October 2022. Accompanied by an archive of photographs and other related items, it had been estimated at £20,000–30,000. The entire proceeds were donated to the Taylor McNally Foundation, a childrens' educational charity in Northern Ireland.

L44A. DICKIN MEDAL

Date: 1943.
Ribbon: Three equal bands of green, dark brown and pale blue.
Metal: Bronze.
Size: 36mm.
Description: (Obverse) a laurel wreath enclosing the inscription "For Gallantry" in raised cursive script over the motto WE ALSO SERVE in block capitals; the initials PDSA in a tablet at the top of the wreath; (reverse) the date, name of recipient and details of the award. Fitted with a plain ring for suspension.
Comments: *Awarded by the People's Dispensary for Sick Animals to recognise acts of bravery by birds and animals in wartime, and consequently popularly known as the Animals' VC. Originally, Maria Dickin, founder of the PDSA, also instituted a lesser award for acts of bravery by animals, known as the PDSA Silver Medal. The Dickin Medal has been awarded 75 times since 1943 plus two Honorary Dickin Medals. The recipients comprise 39 dogs, 32 pigeons, four horses and one cat (Simon). The most recent award was to Belgian Malinois "Bass" for his life-saving devotion to duty as a Multi-Purpose Canine in the US Marine Special Operation Command. He received the award in recognition of his devotion to service while deployed in Afghanistan in May 2019, where his actions saved many lives.*

VALUE:　　From £20,000 (see previous page)

L44B. PDSA GOLD MEDAL

Date: 2002.
Ribbon: Dark blue.
Metal: Gold.
Size: 36mm.
Description: (Obverse) a laurel wreath enclosing the inscription "Gold Medal" in raised cursive script below the initials "pdsa"; (reverse) the date, name of recipient and details of the award. Fitted with a plain ring for suspension.
Comments: *The PDSA Gold Medal is the non-military counterpart to the PDSA Dickin Medal and is known as the animals' "George Cross". Instituted in 2002, it rewards civilian acts of animal bravery and exceptional devotion to duty. The PDSA Gold Medal has been awarded 30 times. The most recent recipient is "Magawa", an African giant pouched rat, who was awarded the honour on September 25, 2020 for his work in Cambodia where he detected 39 landmines and 28 unexploded ordnance and other munitions. He is the first rat to receive the award.*

VALUE:　　—

L45. BINNEY MEMORIAL MEDAL

Date: 1947.
Ribbon: None.
Metal: Bronze.
Size: 48mm.
Description: (Obverse) a bust of Captain R.D. Binney, CBE, RN; (reverse) inscription FOR COURAGE IN SUPPORT OF LAW AND ORDER and AWARDED TO above the recipient's name on a raised tablet.
Comments: *Instituted in memory of Captain Ralph Douglas Binney who was killed on 8 December 1944 in the City of London while attempting to apprehend two armed robbers single-handedly. It is awarded annually to the British citizen who displays the greatest courage in support of law and order within the areas under the jurisdiction of the Metropolitan Police and the City of London Police. The medal is not intended for wear. See MEDAL NEWS, August 1998 for a detailed article on the medal by Victor Knight.*

VALUE:　£750–1000

L46. SEA CADET GALLANTRY CROSS

Date:

Ribbon: Red with a central white stripe and blue stripes towards the edges.

Metal: Silver.

Size: 36mm.

Description: (Obverse) a fouled anchor within a wreath superimposed on a cross pattée inscribed FOR GALLANTRY with initials N and L on the left and right arms of the cross to signify the Navy League; (reverse) blank.

Comments: *Awarded by the Sea Cadet Association, originally the Navy League, for gallantry in saving or attempting to save life under circumstances of exceptional danger and personal risk to the saver. It has been very rarely awarded.*

VALUE: £600–1000

L47. SEA CADET GALLANTRY MEDAL

Date:

Ribbon: Red with a central white stripe and blue stripes towards the edges.

Metal: Bronze.

Size: 36mm.

Description: A circular medal with a plain ring suspension. (Obverse) an image of the cross as above but without the initials on the arms; (reverse) blank.

Comments: *Awarded for gallantry in saving or attempting to save life under circumstances of considerable danger and personal risk to the saver. Both the cross and the medal are manufactured by Spink & Son. Gallantry certificates and commendations are also awarded for life saving in lesser circumstances.*

VALUE: £400–600

L47A. GALLANTRY MEDALLISTS' LEAGUE GOLD MEDAL FOR COURAGE

Date: 2006

Ribbon: Red with a dark blue stripe towards the right and light blue towards the left, representing the colours of the Gallantry Medallists League.

Metal: 9ct white gold and gilded.

Size: 36mm.

Description: The medal is made in two pieces. (Obverse) a six-pointed star with a central disc hand painted in enamels surrounded by a red enamel ring bearing the words "FOR COURAGE". The central disc depicts a hand at the top pulling up another hand, symbolising rescue, the upper hand has wings symbolising the innocence of youth. These wings are carried over into the design of the suspension. (Reverse) inscribed with the name of the medal, the recipient and details of the act for which the award is made.

Comments: *The medal is to be presented each year to the most deserving recipient of the* Woman's Own *"Children of Courage" award—a ceremony which was instituted in 1973 to honour ten of the UK's most deserving children who have acted heroically over the previous year. The heroism can take many forms from courage in the face of disability or steadfast devotion to bravery in saving life. The first award was made in December 2006 to nine-year-old Lewis Woodruffe who calmly led his young brothers and sisters to safety during a disastrous fire at the family home.*

VALUE: —

L48. HUNDRED OF SALFORD HUMANE SOCIETY SWIMMING PROFICIENCY MEDALS

Date: 1889.

Ribbon: Special Proficiency Medal and Proficiency Medal issued without a ribbon, although often seen with a blue ribbon.

Metal: Both silver.

Size: Special Proficiency Medal—irregular shape with small ring suspender. Proficiency Medal—circular 26mm with a small ring suspender.

Description: Special Proficiency Medal: (obverse) an ornamental pattern of three shields, bearing the arms of Salford backed by crossed tridents. An intertwined blue enamel band around the medal carries the legend HUMANE SOCIETY FOR THE HUNDRED OF SALFORD; (reverse) plain. Proficiency Medal: (obverse) a single shield carrying the arms of Salford surrounded by a blue enamel band that carries the words HUMANE SOCIETY FOR THE HUNDRED OF SALFORD, the whole is encircled by a wreath and is surmounted by a crown; (reverse) plain.

Comments: *Following the discontinuing of awards for life saving in 1921, the Society began to run competitions for children with the object of encouraging swimming proficiency with a view to life saving. Two medals were awarded, the Special Proficiency Medal and the Proficiency Medal. Each year there are a number of winners of the Proficiency Medal and the best boy and girl are selected to receive the Special Proficiency Medal.*

VALUE:

Special Proficiency Medal	£75–125
Proficiency Medal	£50–90

L49. ROYAL HUMANE SOCIETY SWIMMING PROFICIENCY MEDAL

Date: 1882.

Ribbon: None.

Metal: Silver.

Size: 51mm.

Description: (Obverse) a life saving scene, circumscribed by the motto NARE EST ALIENAM NOSSE SALUTEM in sans serif capitals and by a heavily beaded border. The exergue is blank to allow the engraved details of the school and the date of award to be entered; (reverse) "Awarded FOR PROFICIENCY IN SWIMMING EXERCISE with reference to saving life from DROWNING". Above this "ROYAL HUMANE SOCIETY", and below "INST: 1774" and again circumscribed by heavy beading.

Comments: *In February 1882, the RHS received a letter from Dr Dukes, the physician at Rugby School, relating to the establishment of a prize "for swimming and for a knowledge of the treatment of the apparently drowned". The Society saw merit in this and by the end of the year the medal was awarded to seven winners of competitions held at seven public schools. The competition grew in popularity and for many years 20 to 30 medals per year were awarded. However, with increasing competition from the Royal Life Saving Society the RHS award declined in popularity and the last awards were made in 1948. The medal was awarded only in silver, although a bronze specimen is known.*

VALUE: £40–100

L49A. ROYAL LIFE SAVING SOCIETY PROFICIENCY MEDALS (see also no. 387)

Diploma with Honours.

First type Award of Merit.

Date: Bronze Medallion—1892.
　　　Award of Merit (silver)—1908.
　　　Diploma (gold)—1896.
Ribbon: 33mm—light blue with centre white stripe and two intermediate dark blue stripes.
Metal: Bronze; Silver; Gold.
Size: Differing designs: 25–32mm.
Description: First type (1891–1904) (obverse) a water rescue with THE LIFE SAVING SOCIETY ESTABLISHED 1891 around; (reverse) the name of the recipient in the centre with QUEMCUNQUE MISERUM VIDERIS HOMINEM SCIAS (WHOMSOEVER YOU SEE IN DISTRESS, RECOGNIZE IN HIM A FELLOW MAN), the motto of the Society, around. Second type (1905–37) (obverse) the name of the Society with added ROYAL. Third type (1938–54) (obverse) the name of the Society within a circle with a boathook and an oar crossed and tied with a bow. Fourth type (1955–80) same as third type but reduced in size from 32mm to 25mm. Fifth type (1981 to date) reinstated to 32mm size. (Reverse) plain, engraved with the name of the recipient. The Award of Merit comes in three types: type I silver, depicting a rescue, type II the same but with a wreath around and type III the Lifebelt and crossed boathook/oar design—since 1952 this has been awarded in gilt metal with blue and white enamelled centre. The Diploma medal is a gold coloured medal bearing a blue enamelled shield.
Comments: *The awards of this society are very complex, for example silver awards of merit fall into at least five classes, which are outside the scope of this Yearbook. These medals were awarded for various stages of proficiency in swimming and lifesaving. In 1945 a further exam medal, the Bronze Cross in two sizes to go between the Bronze Medallion and Award of Merit, was established. From 1955 to about 1990 the medals were reduced to 25mm diameter.*

VALUE:

Bronze Medal	£5–15
Bronze Cross	£10–20
Award of Merit	£20–35
Diploma	£80–100

Second type Bronze Medallion.

Second type Award of Merit.

Bronze Cross.

L50. THE ROYAL LIFE SAVING SOCIETY MOUNTBATTEN MEDAL

Date: 1951.
Ribbon: None.
Metal: Silver.
Size: 51mm.
Description: A circular medal without suspender. The medal is cased. The obverse has the family crest of the Mountbatten family and on the reverse is "The Mountbatten Medal of the Royal Life Saving Society for the award holder who makes the best rescue of the year—Presented by the President RLSS The Earl Mountbatten of Burma". The name of the recipient and the year of the award is engraved on the lower rim of the medal.
Comments: *Earl Mountbatten instituted the medal in 1951 and it was to be awarded annually for a rescue adjudged by RLSS Commonwealth Council to be the bravest performed in that year by an award holder of the RLSS who, in the opinion of the Commonwealth president, makes the best rescue of the year. Originally, the conditions of the award required that the potential recipient should, "not have been otherwise signally honoured". This effectively disqualified many worthy recipients for consideration of the award, so, in 1965 this condition was removed. Since its inception the medal has generally been awarded annually, but occasionally no award was made, as the rescues in those years were adjudged not to have met the high standard necessary to qualify for the medal. Exceptionally, in 1955, 2004 and 2006 there were two recipients. To date 36 awards have been made.*

Value: £500–800

L51. TYNE & WEAR FIRE AND CIVIL DEFENCE AUTHORITY MEDAL FOR BRAVERY

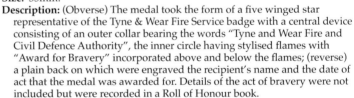

Date: 1986
Ribbon: Three blue and two white stripes.
Metal: Base metal with colouring according to class.
Size: 35mm.
Description: (Obverse) The medal took the form of a five winged star representative of the Tyne & Wear Fire Service badge with a central device consisting of an outer collar bearing the words "Tyne and Wear Fire and Civil Defence Authority", the inner circle having stylised flames with "Award for Bravery" incorporated above and below the flames; (reverse) a plain back on which were engraved the recipient's name and the date of act that the medal was awarded for. Details of the act of bravery were not included but were recorded in a Roll of Honour book.
Comments: *The medal was awarded in three classes: Gold, Silver and Bronze to recognise acts of bravery by members of the public in emergency situations in Tyne & Wear. It was also awarded to members of the Fire Service for acts of bravery outside their normal firefighting duties. In 1992 the award was replaced by a scroll.*

VALUE:

Gold (21)	£200–275
Silver (45)	£100–175
Bronze (84)	£75–125

Because of the nature of Lifesaving medals and the fact they were often issued by private organisations, more are coming to light all the time. This being the case trying to put them all in chronological order within this book is a difficult task and thus it has been decided that when new information comes to light from now on, the medals will be listed and numbered sequentially rather than chronologically. Thus it is important to check the list at the beginning of this section to ascertain the relevant MYB number.

L52. MORAY FLOODS MEDAL

Date: 1829
Ribbon: None
Metal: Silver
Size: 41mm
Description: (Obverse) A wreath enclosing a view of the bridge over the River Spey at Fochabers, partially destroyed by the flooded river. (reverse) A wreath enclosing raised lettering, PRESENTED BY THE CENTRAL COMMITTEE FOR THE FLOOD FUND TO . . . (space for impressed details of recipients name and location). AS AN HONORARY REWARD FOR HIS COURAGE AND HUMANITY SHEWN AT THE GREAT FLOOD AUGUST 4th 1829.
Comments: *After the severe storm on the night of August 3/4, 1829 and the ensuing floods in the region of Morayshire, Scotland, a flood fund committee was formed and it was agreed that a silver medal be awarded to those fellows who were engaged in that perilous work of mercy. The amount of rain that fell that night was estimated to be around one sixth of a normal year's downfall. In some places the height of the water reached forty feet above the normal. Many bridges were broken and washed away, whole fields of crops and soil disappeared, acres of trees were uprooted and many houses were washed away leaving whole families marooned on higher ground or on the roofs of houses. The majority of medals were to those men that took to their cobles and other small boats and rowing out to perform their acts of heroism. Loss of human life was minimal but cattle and animals were not so lucky. To date there is no known medal roll of the recipients but it is thought that around 50 medals were awarded.*

VALUE: £600–850

L53. CASTLEFORD EXPLOSION DEVOTION TO DUTY MEDAL

Date: 1930
Ribbon: Black with two orange stripes.
Metal: Bronze.
Size: 36mm.
Description: (Obverse) A fireman in a burning building with smoke, flames and falling beams, wielding an axe and wearing typical early uniform and helmet.
Comments: *The medal was awarded to firefighters who fought a fire at the acid mixing plant of Hickson and Partners in Castleford on July 4, 1930. 13 workers at the factory were killed in the explosion and around 50 others received injuries. Houses in the locality had to be evacuated and many windows were blown in and roofs damaged by the initial blast. Steps were taken to prevent toxic material escaping and in addition to the local fire brigade others from the surrounding area were called upon to assist. .*

VALUE: £800–1000

L54. ST ANDREWS AMBULANCE ASSOCIATION LIFE SAVING MEDAL

Date: 1904

Ribbon: Alternate stripes of equal width of yellow, white, red, white and yellow.

Metal: Silver and bronze.

Size: 36mm.

Description: (Obverse) the figure of St Andrew standing in front of a cross saltire, encircled by the legend "ST ANDREW'S AMBULANCE ASSOCIATION" around the circumference.(Reverse) within a wreath of oak leaves the inscription, "AWARDED FOR SAVING LIFE ON LAND" and below the manufacturer's mark and hallmarks. Around the outside of the wreath is "INCORPORATED BY ROYAL CHARTER 1899". The name of recipient and date of rescue is engraved on the rim of the medal

Comments: *Awarded for saving life. The St Andrew's Ambulance Association was Incorporated in 1899 and its Royal Charter of 1899 stated that one of the objects and purposes of the Association to be the award of medals, badges or certificates of honour for special services in the cause of humanity, especially for saving life on land at imminent personal risk. This medal should not be confused with a separate medal (MYB 374) which was instituted to reward long service. In addition to silver and bronze medals, Certificates of Honour and of Merit were also awarded for life saving actions. To date 13 silver medals, 15 bronze medals, 41 Certificates of Honour and 42 Certificates of Merit have been awarded (these numbers are currently being researched). The first silver and bronze medals were awarded in 1904 and the last known awards were 1934 (silver) and 1937 (bronze).*

VALUE:

	Silver	Rare
	Bronze	Rare

A firefighter in the aftermath of the destruction after the blaze at the acid-mixing plant of Hickson & Partners in Castleford 1930 (courtesy Castleford Museum).

FOREIGN MEDALS
Found in British Groups

In this section we have included a selection of the most common "foreign" medals found in British Groups, i.e. those medals issued by a foreign authority to British or Commonwealth personnel which they in turn have sought permission to wear alongside those medals awarded by their own government. Quite often these medals, when found, were awarded for gallantry where the recipient was directly involved in action with allies from the country who conferred the medal, either fighting alongside them or in an act of heroism involving one of their countrymen.

As always it must be stressed that the prices given here are for single examples as found in dealers' lists and websites, when found in an attributable group their value dramatically increases.

Apart from medals given by "foreign" governments in wartime, various awards are also given by overseas authorities for attendance on particular occasions or for valuable service rendered, these are far too diverse and numerous to include in this publication, although many do receive restricted permission to wear. A good example is the medal illustrated left, awarded by the Sultan of Johore in 1955 on the occasion of his Diamond Jubilee: this medal is typical of the type of medal awarded to British citizens by overseas authorities and given restricted permission to wear by Her late Majesty Queen Elizabeth II. In this instance permission was granted to wear: *a.* In the presence of the Sultan; *b.* In the presence of any member of the Ruling House; *c.* On all official occasions whilst in Johore.

This and other medals awarded by "foreign" governments are detailed in the book *Honour the Recipients of Foreign Awards* which lists every gazetted British and Dominion recipient of such an honour from 1914 until 1968. This is another title in the "Honour" series by Michael Maton published in 2013 by Token Publishing Ltd.

It must be stressed that included in this section of the Yearbook are only the most common medals found in British and Commonwealth groups and the list is by no means exhaustive. It has always been common practice amongst high ranking officers of all countries to, in effect, "swap" orders and decorations with allies, some of which would never be received by the ordinary fighting soldier, sailor or airman. Because of the rarity of these awards within British groups it has been decided to exclude them at this stage, although we are grateful for all examples of "one-offs" that have been sent in. Should any reader have their own examples of such awards please let us know, with an illustration if possible. It is our intention to look in depth at the matter of Foreign awards and medals that are found alongside their British counterparts and to this end we intend to include a new section within the pages of MEDAL NEWS magazine in order to highlight some of the medals not hitherto included here. We will then, hopefully, use this new information to expand this section in the future. However, it must be remembered that there have been literally thousands of awards given to British personnel over the years and it would be impossible to include them all.

BELGIUM

As with most orders, these are awarded in various classes. In this section we have concentrated on those most commonly encountered.

Order of Leopold II, Officer's breast badge.

Order of the Crown, Commander's badge.

ORDER OF LEOPOLD II
Commander's neck badge	£200–350
Knight's badge	£65–85
Officer's badge	£55–75
Miniature	£30–40

ORDER OF THE CROWN
Commander's badge	£250–350
Officer's badge	£45–65
Knight's badge	£35–50
Miniature	£30–40

CROIX DE GUERRE
WWI	£35–50
WWII	£40–55
Miniature	£14–17

DECORATION MILITAIRE
	£40–55
Miniature	£12–16

FRANCE

LEGION d'HONNEUR 1870–1951
Commander's neck badge	£350–450
Officer's badge	£150–175
Knight's badge	£75–100
Miniature	£30–45

LEGION d'HONNEUR 1951 to date
As awarded to British veterans	£100–150

MÉDAILLE MILITAIRE 1870 £35–45

Miniature £30–40

CROIX DE GUERRE
1914–15 reverse	£35–50
1914–16 reverse	£35–50
1914–17 reverse	£35–50
1914–18 reverse	£25–45
WWII	£45–55
for each star or palm add £5	
Miniature	£14–18

MEDAILLE d'HONNEUR DES AFFAIRE ETRANGERE

	Military with swords	Civil
First class "en vermeil"	£250–300	£150–200
2nd class "en argent"	£100–150	£50–75
3rd class "en bronze"	£50–75	£30–45
Miniature	£20–25	£15–20

GREECE

ORDER OF THE REDEEMER
   Commander's badge   £400–650
   Knight's badge   £250–350
   Officer's badge   £150–200

   Miniature   £50–60

GREEK WAR CROSS   £50–100

   Miniature   £15-20

ITALY

AL VALORE (unnamed)
   Bronze   £30–45
   Silver   £45–55
   Silver-gilt   £55–65

   Miniature   *bronze*   £20–25
                   silver   £30–35
                   gilt   £30–35

ORDER OF THE CROWN
   Commander's badge   £150–250
   Officer's badge   £75–100
   Knight's badge   £55–75

   Miniature   £45–65

Restrikes are also known. They can be distinguished from the originals by the omission of the initials FG at the bottom on the obverse.

ITALY *continued*

WAR MERIT CROSS   £20–30

Miniature   £15–20

In addition to the above medals, the Messina Earthquake Medal, awarded by the King of Italy in 1908 to British personnel who went to the aid of victims of the tragic earthquake at Messina, can be found under Medal No. 163A

IRAQ

IRAQ FLOOD MEDAL 1954.
Widely distributed amongst the Iraqis but rare to British units with only 66 being awarded.

Value :   Rare

JAPAN

ORDER OF THE RISING SUN	
3rd Class	£550–650
4th Class	£400–500
5th Class	£250–300
6th Class	£200–250
7th Class	£55–75
8th Class	£35–55
Miniature	£40-60

ORDER OF THE SACRED TREASURE	
3rd Class	£475–600
4th Class	£250–350
5th Class	£150–250
6th Class	£100–175
7th Class	£40–50
8th Class	£35–45
Miniature	£45-65

LUXEMBOURG

**CROIX DE GUERRE
WWII** £65–85

Miniature £20–25

NORWAY

**KING HAAKON VII
FREEDOM CROSS** £175–250

Miniature £20–25

**KING HAAKON VII
FREEDOM MEDAL** £120–180

Miniature £20–25

OMAN

SULTAN'S COMMENDATION MEDAL £35–45
Miniature £20–25

GENERAL SERVICE MEDAL £20–35
Miniature £20–25

AS SUMMOOD MEDAL £30–45
Miniature £20–25

OMAN PEACE MEDAL £20–35
Miniature £20–25

These and other Omani medals were awarded to British personnel seconded to the Sultanate following periods of unrest in that country. For more information on them and on the role of British Forces see *Awards of the Sultanate of Oman* by Lt-Col Ashley Tinson.

POLAND

CROSS OF VALOUR
WWII	£65–85
Miniature	£15–20

ORDER OF POLONIA RESTITUTA
WWI	From £100
WWII	£75–100
Miniature	£15–20

ROMANIA

ORDER OF THE STAR OF ROMANIA WITH SWORDS (1864–1931) £75–150

Miniature	£40–55

ORDER OF THE CROWN (1881–1932) £75–150

Miniature	£30–40

RUSSIA

ORDER OF ST STANISLAUS
Gold	From £5000+
Silver-gilt	£1500–2000

Miniature   £170–290

ORDER OF ST ANNE

Gold	From £6000+
Miniature	£170–290

CROSS OF ST GEORGE
3rd Class	£350–525
4th Class	£250–400

Miniature   £85–110

MEDAL OF ST GEORGE
3rd Class	£150–265
4th Class	£100–210

Miniature   £35–55

MEDAL FOR ZEAL
Silver	£225–325

Miniature   £35–55

See also MYB 203A and 203AA.

SOVIET UNION

The Soviet Union awarded some 160 orders and medals to British Servicemen either during or immediately after World War II. The most numerous of these being the Order of the Patriotic War (1st and 2nd class), the Medal for Valour, the Medal for Meritorious Service in Battle and the Order of the Red Star. However, the numbers of these awarded to British personnel were still less than 30 in each case and as such documented examples come on the market very rarely making it extremely difficult to give accurate valuations. For more information see MEDAL NEWS June/July 2001.

SERBIA

ORDER OF KARAGEORGE (1904–15)
   4th Class   £450–575

   Miniature   £60–75

ORDER OF THE WHITE EAGLE (1882–1915)
   Knight's badge   £350–475

   Miniature   £90–110

TURKEY

ORDER OF THE OSMANIEH
   1st Class   £550–675
   2nd Class   £450–550
   3rd Class   £250–350
   4th Class   £95–150
   5th Class   £65–85

ORDER OF THE MEDJIDIEH
   Commander's badge   £550–750
   Knight's badge   £250–300

   Miniature   £45–65

   Miniature   £35–60

UNITED STATES

DISTINGUISHED SERVICE CROSS   from £75
(Army)

US NAVY CROSS   from £75

US AIR FORCE CROSS   from £75

DISTINGUISHED SERVICE MEDAL   from £75
(Army)

Miniatures of US medals are available, prices range from £5–10 for "plain" examples to £10–20 for more sophisticated "fancy" pieces.

UNITED STATES *continued*

US DISTINGUISHED SERVICE MEDAL   £25–35
(Navy-Marine Corps)

US DISTINGUISHED FLYING CROSS   £25–35

Legionnaire

LEGION OF MERIT
Commander	£150–250
Officer	£120–175
Legionnaire	£75–100

US SILVER STAR   £35–50

US BRONZE STAR   £25–35

US AIR MEDAL   £25–35

MEDALS
Of the Irish Republic (Eire)

Since 1921 Ireland has been divided into two distinct countries: the Irish Free State in the south and Ulster in the north, both as separate countries within the British Empire. However, in 1949 the Irish Free State proclaimed itself a republic and became known as Eire. Since that time it has issued its own medals and honours, including a number of retrospective awards for the troubled times prior to independence and for the period before it became a republic. Irish men and women served with the British armed forces at home and overseas and many Irish regiments famously took part in many of the fiercest actions of World War I. Medals and awards for these actions will be found in the main section of this book. During World War II the Irish Defence Forces remained neutral although the Dublin Government assisted the British war effort in many ways. Today Irish troops regularly serve with the United Nations and have been in action on a number of occasions. Interestingly in the 1950s the Irish Government decided to standardise the Irish language and introduced An Caighdean Ofigiuil, which was a change in the Irish alphabet. The earlier Irish medals carry inscriptions in the old Irish alphabet but to simplify matters we have given the modern Irish equivalent in these listings where possible.

E1. 1916 MEDAL

Instituted: January 1941.
Ribbon: Two equal stripes of green (left) and orange, suspended from an ornate clasp of Celtic design.
Metal: Bronze.
Size: 38mm, max.
Description: (Obverse) based on the cap badge of the Irish Republican Army, viz. an eight-pointed star with "flames" between the points, surmounted by a double circle on which is a depiction of "Cuchulainn", the memorial erected at the General Post Office, Dublin, to commemorate the 1916 uprising; (reverse) central medallion inscribed SEACTMAIN NA CASGA (Easter Week) curved above 1916. With plain ring suspension.
Comments: *The medal, which takes precedence over all other Irish medals, was instituted by the Irish Republican Government to commemorate the Easter Uprising in Dublin, April 1916. Recipients, who were mostly members of the Dublin Brigade of the Irish Republican Army, also received a pension in respect of this medal. Of the 2,000 medals originally struck some 1,906 were issued. Of these 266 were named and presented to the next of kin of those who had died before the date of issue, including the 88 who were killed in the rebellion and 16 executed afterwards; the remainder were issued unnamed. Another 450 medals were struck and issued later.*

VALUE:		
	Original named 1916 casualty (88)	From £65,000
	1941 issue named medal	From £15,000
	Post 1941 named late issue medal	From £6500
	Unnamed	£2500–3750
	Miniature	£500–1,000
	Contemporary miniature	£185–275

E2. MILITARY MEDAL FOR GALLANTRY

Instituted: 4 December 1944.

Ribbon: Dark green with a central stripe of crimson (1st Class), dark green with crimson edges (2nd Class), dark green with crimson edges and central crimson stripe (3rd Class).

Metal: Silver (1st Class), light bronze (2nd Class), dark bronze (3rd Class).

Size: 36mm.

Description: (Obverse) a Celtic cross with a longer lower limb, surrounded by a laurel wreath with the words DE BARR CALMACTA (For Gallantry) in the centre; (reverse) inscribed AN BONN MILEATA CALMACTA (The Military Gallantry Medal) above a scroll bearing the recipient's name.

Comments: *The medal is intended to be awarded in three different classes to members of the Defence Forces who have performed actions of outstanding gallantry in the course of their military duty whilst not on war service. Only seven medals have so far been awarded in 2nd or 3rd Class. The 1st Class has never been awarded, making this probably one of the rarest gallantry awards.*

1st class.   *2nd class.*     *3rd class.*

VALUE: —

E3. DISTINGUISHED SERVICE MEDAL

Instituted: February 1964.

Ribbon: Dark green with 6mm black centre stripe (1st Class), 5mm black edges (2nd Class) or 3mm black edges and black centre stripe (3rd Class), suspended from a clasp with a stylised Celtic design.

Metal: Silver (1st Class) or bronze (2nd and 3rd Class).

Size: 36mm.

Description: (Obverse) a figure of Cuchulainn driving a two-horse chariot; (reverse) legend AN BONN SEIRBISE DEARSCNA (The Distinguished Service Medal) around. With simple ring suspension.

Comments: *Awarded in three classes for acts of bravery or special devotion to duty which do not merit the award of the Military Medal for Gallantry (MYBE2).*

VALUE:	
1st class	—
2nd class	£575–850
3rd class	£475–675

E4. CIVIL MEDAL FOR BRAVERY

Instituted: —.

Ribbon: Crimson with two narrow white stripes 3mm apart at centre (gold), dark green with two narrow white stripes 3mm apart at centre (silver) or dark blue with two narrow white stripes 3mm apart at centre (bronze).

Metal: gold (1st Class), silver (2nd Class) and bronze (3rd Class).

Size: 36mm.

Description: (Obverse) a winged figure brandishing a flaming sword standing over another winged figure representing death and the inscription MIR GAILE GNIOM TARRTALA (The Council for Deeds of Bravery) below; (reverse) the words ARNA BRONNAD AG COMAIRLE NA MIR GAILE AR (Awarded by the Council for Deeds of Bravery to) in the top half with the recipient's name engraved to the right of an olive branch below.

Comments: *Awarded by the Department of Justice. The gold and silver medals are awarded for an individual act of bravery in saving life; the bronze is awarded to civilians for brave deeds which do not merit the other awards.*

VALUE:	1st class	2nd class	3rd class
	—	£1200–1800	£575–950

E5. GENERAL SERVICE MEDAL 1917–21

Instituted: January 1941.

Ribbon: Two equal stripes of black (left) and orange, suspended from an ornate clasp of Celtic design.

Metal: Bronze.

Size: 38mm.

Clasp: COMRAC (this word has two meanings, combat or action).

Description: (Obverse) a standing figure of a soldier holding a rifle surrounded by the crests of the four provinces of Ireland and bisecting the word "EIRE", at the foot COGAD NA SAOIRSE (War of Independence); (reverse) plain except for a laurel wreath around.

Comments: *Awarded to those who took part in the struggle for independence between the Easter Uprising of 1916 to ratification of the treaty which ensured independence from Britain and the establishment of the Irish Free State in 1921. The COMRAC clasp was awarded to those who took an active part in the military operations. When this clasp is worn the simple ring suspender is exchanged for one of an ornate triangular design. Approximately 15,000 medals were issued with a clasp, and 40,000 without, of these 1,080 Comrac medals and 1,360 no clasp medals were issued named.*

VALUE:	Unnamed	Named	*Miniature*
With clasp	£600–800	From £1500	£65–90
Without clasp	£385–550	£395–650	£42–65

E6. THE EMERGENCY SERVICE MEDAL 1939–46

Instituted: 6 October 1944.

Ribbon: Orange-red with two white 4.5mm stripes 1.5mm apart at centre or with one central 10mm stripe, suspended from a bar bearing the words SEIRBHIS NAISIUNTA (National Service).

Metal: Bronze.

Size: 38mm.

Clasp: Laurel spray between the dates 1939 and 1946 for each two years extra service.

Description: (Obverse) a female figure of Ireland holding a sword, with Irish wolf hound on a leash at her side and the legend RE NA PRAINNE (Emergency Period) above and around; (reverse) a branch of laurel and the dates 1939 and 1946, with the recipient's unit above.

Comments: *The medal was instituted to reward Defence Service personnel who served between September 3, 1939 and March 31, 1946. A total of 11 different units were recorded and medals are inscribed on the reverse with the unit in which each recipient served. The most popular unit for collectors is the 26th Battalion which was comprised of veterans from the 1916 Uprising. The qualifying period was one year's service with the Defence Forces, the Chaplaincy Service, the Army Nursing Service or the Local Defence Forces (the ribbons for which have two stripes) or two years with the Air Raid Precautions Service, the Irish Red Cross Society or the Local Security Force (the ribbons for which have one stripe). A clasp was awarded for each extra two years service, with a maximum of two being available.*

VALUE:	
Army, Air Corps, Navy (Na Forsai Cosanta)	£85–120
Naval Reserve (An Sluag Muiri)	£300–385
26th Battalion IRA (An 26u Cathlan)	£350–485
Chaplaincy Service (An Seirbhis Seiplineachta)	£850–1400
Local Defence Force (An Forsa Cosanta Aitiuil)	£75–135
Volunteer Reserve (Forsa na n-Oclac, 2u Line)	£100–175
Army Nursing Service (Seirbis Altranais an Airm)	£600–1000
Volunteer Aid (Red Cross) (Ranna Cabair Deontaca Cumann Croise Deirge na h-Eireann)	£110–185
First Aid (Red Cross) (Ranna Cead-Cabair Cumann Croise Deirge na h-Eireann)	£130–180
Air Raid Precautions (Na Seirbisi Reamcuraim In Agaidh Aer-Ruatar)	£85–165
Local Security Force (Na Caomnoiri Aitiula)	£50–95
Miniature	£35–55

E7. MERCHANT SERVICE MEDAL 1939–46

Instituted: 6 October 1944.

Ribbon: Blue with central white stripe, suspended from a clasp bearing the words SEIRBHIS NAISIUNTA (National Service).

Metal: Bronze.

Size: 38mm.

Clasp: Laurel spray between the dates 1939 and 1946 for each two years extra service.

Description: (Obverse) as MYB E6 above,—a female figure holding a sword, with Irish wolf hound at her side and RE NA PRAINNE (Emergency Period) above; (reverse) a steamship sailing left and a sailing ship in the background with the words AN TSEIRBHIS MUIR-TRACTALA (The Merchant Marine Service) above and the dates 1939–1946 over a laurel branch below.

Comments: *Awarded for six months' continuous service on Irish registered merchant ships between September 1939 and March 1946. A total of just over 500 of these medals were issued, including 127 with single extra service bars, 37 with two bars and a further 57 with three bars.*

VALUE:

Without bar	£900–1200
One bar	£1200–1500
Two bars	£1400–1850
Three bars	£1600–2000

E8. PERMANENT DEFENCE FORCES SERVICE MEDAL

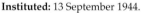

Instituted: 13 September 1944.

Ribbon: There are two types of ribbon for this medal: plain blue for NCOs and other ranks but with a central gold stripe when a bar is awarded; officers, members of the Chaplaincy Service and the Army Nursing Service also have the ribbon with gold stripe. Both types are suspended from a bar bearing the word SEIRBIS.

Metal: Bronze.

Size: 38mm.

Clasps: Bronze bar with a cross and laurel design for extra service.

Description: (Obverse) Eire, represented as a female figure, placing a wreath on a kneeling soldier and AN BONN SEIRBISE (For good service) to left; (reverse) the words THE SERVICE MEDAL (in English) around with the recipient's details inscribed in the centre.

Comments: *Awarded to members of the Chaplaincy Service and the Army Nursing Service and to officers of the Permanent Defence Forces for a minimum of 15 years satisfactory and continuous service with a bar awarded for additional 5 years service. Officers can only qualify for one bar. The qualifying period for NCOs and other ranks is 10 years with a bar awarded for further 6 years service. Second award bars bear the inscription "21".*

VALUE:

Without bar	£120–175
With bar	£160–230

E9. PERMANENT DEFENCE FORCES SERVICE FOR GOOD CONDUCT

This medal, instituted in 1987 is exactly the same as E8 but inscribed **AN BONN BEA IOMPAIR (For good conduct)** and is suspended from a ribbon of diagonal green and orange stripes.

E10. ST JOHN AMBULANCE BRIGADE OF IRELAND SERVICE MEDAL

Instituted: September 1945.

Ribbon: Watered white with a single black centre stripe with two thinner black stripes each side and green edges.

Metal: Silver or silver-gilt.

Size: 38mm.

Description: (Obverse) the Maltese Cross emblem of the Brigade with sprigs of shamrock in the angles, surrounded by the legend THE ST JOHN AMBULANCE BRIGADE OF IRELAND; (reverse) the words FOR SERVICE inside a wreath of St John's wort leaves and flowers.

Comments: *Awarded in silver to members of the Brigade in Ireland for 15 years service and in silver-gilt for 50 years service.*

VALUE:	Silver	£45–75
	Silver-gilt	£125–165

E11. THE UNITED NATIONS PEACEKEEPERS MEDAL

Instituted: 3 October 1989

Ribbon: 32mm wide with central vertical stripe of United Nations blue, 3mm wide, flanked by orange vertical stripes, 4.5mm wide, flanked by white vertical stripes, 5mm wide, with vertical green stripe, 5mm wide each side.

Metal: Nickel-plated brass (silver appearance).

Size: 35mm.

Description: (Obverse) female figure of Eireann standing on a shoreline releasing a dove of peace into the sky with an olive branch in its beak and three wild geese flying into the distance; (reverse) NÁ NÁISIUN AONTAITE DON TSÍOCÁIN—FOR PEACE UNITED NATIONS.

Comments: *The official name of this medal is An Bonn Chosantoiri Síochána na Naisiun Aontaithe (The United Nations Peacekeeper's Medal). Any member of the Irish Defence Forces who is entitled to a United Nations Service medal, is entitled to this medal. Only one United Nations Peacekeeper's Medal is awarded irrespective of how many peacekeeping tours the recipient has taken part in and there are no bars or other indicators to show how many tours the recipient has been on.*

VALUE: £125–220

E12. 1916-1966 "SURVIVORS" MEDAL

Instituted: 1966.

Ribbon: Green with 5mm orange edges and a white 1mm central stripe.

Metal: Hallmarked silver (gilded).

Size: 38mm max.

Description: The same type of ring suspender as the 1916 medal, MYB E1 (qv), with a similar wearing brooch, which has the maker's name stamped on the reverse. (Obverse) as 1916 medal; (reverse) plain circular back with 1916/Ca'isc/1966 (1916 Easter 1966) in three lines.

Comments: *Issued to the recipients of the 1916 medal who were still alive in 1966 on the 50th Anniversary of the Easter Rising. 964 medals were issued. None of these medals were officially named.*

VALUE: £3000–5000

E13. 1921-71 "SURVIVORS" MEDAL

Instituted: 1971.
Ribbon: Orange with green edges and a black central stripe.
Metal: Gilt bronze.
Size: Significantly smaller than the 1917–21 medal.
Description: A circular medal with the same type of ring suspender as the 1917–21 medal (MYB E5) and with a similar wearing brooch. (Obverse) same as 1917–21 medal; (reverse) as the 1917-21 medal except with "1921–71" in the area where the blank space is on the 1917-21 medal.
Comments: *Issued to the recipients of the 1917–21 medal who were still alive in 1971 on the 50th Anniversary of the Truce. There is no difference between the medals issued to combatants and non-combatants. None of these medals were officially named.*

VALUE: £400–565

E14. RESERVE DEFENCE FORCES LONG SERVICE MEDAL

Instituted:
Ribbon: Blue ribbon with yellow edges (7 years), and blue ribbon with yellow edges and a central yellow stripe (12 and 21 years).
Metal: A golden coloured medal.
Size: 38mm.
Description: Circular medal with suspender similar to the Irish UN Service Medal. (Obverse) a Celtic warrior with shield and spear surrounded by the words Cus Na Saoirse/Faire Biodgac; (reverse) plain circle with around the edges An Bonn Seirbise/F.C.A. 7 S.M.
Comments: *Awarded to members of An Forsa Cosanta Aitiuil (Local Defence Force) and An Slua Muiri (Naval Reserve) after 7 years service. A bar is awarded after 12 years service and a further bar is awarded after 21 years service. This medal is no longer issued as it is to be replaced by a new medal to reflect the fact that following the reorganisation of the reserve forces the FCA has been replaced by the RDF and the Slua Muiri by the NSR. The reverse of the new medal will read An Bonn Seirbhise - na hOglaig Cultaca (The Service Medal Reserve Forces).*

VALUE:	7 years	12 years	21 years
	£100–175	£135–200	£200–295

MEDALS OF AN GARDA SÍOCHÁNA

E15. SCOTT MEDAL FOR VALOR

Instituted: 1923.

Ribbon: 34mm wide. Three equal stripes of green, white and orange.

Metal: Gold (first class), Silver (second class) and Bronze (third class).

Size: 44mm.

Description: The medal is in the form of a Celtic cross. (Obverse) the entwined GS of the Garda crest in the centre with "Walter Scott Medal" on the top arm of the cross and "For Valor" on the bottom arm; the left arm carries the shield and eagle crest of the United States and the right arm the harp and sunburst of Ireland; (reverse) New York City coat of arms surrounded by the coats of arms of each of the four Irish provinces (Leinster, Munster, Connacht, Ulster), one in each of the arms of the cross with the words "Garda Síochána na h-Éireann". The medals are suspended from a pin brooch, on which is engraved the name of the recipient.

Comments: *In 1923, the then Commissioner of the Garda Síochána, General Eoin O'Duffy met Colonel Walter Scott, an Honorary Commissioner of the New York City Police and a well known philanthropist. Colonel Scott expressed the wish to assist in some way with what was, at the time, the world's youngest Police Force, namely the Garda Síochána. He presented to An Garda Síochána a $1,000 gold bond, the interest from which would pay, in perpetuity, for a gold medal. The one condition attached to the award of the Scott Medal was: "No action, however heroic, will merit the award of the Scott medal unless it takes the shape of an act of personal bravery, performed intelligently in the execution of duty at imminent risk to the life of the doer, and armed with full previous knowledge of the risk involved". In 1925, Colonel Scott presented a further $500 bond to provide silver and bronze medals to members who, during the year performed similar acts in the execution of duty but with less risk to their lives and who are next in order of merit. A Scott medal ceremony is held annually when recipients are formally presented with their medals by the Minister for Justice, Equality and Law Reform. The ceremony usually takes place at the Garda College.*

VALUE: **From £3000**

E16. GARDA SÍOCHÁNA LONG SERVICE MEDAL

Instituted: 1972.

Ribbon: Green ribbon with two white central stripes.

Metal: Silver coloured.

Size: 34mm.

Description: (Obverse) The scales of justice surrounded by the words "Garda Síochána" which are at the centre of a star with 22 points (one for each year of service); (reverse) the words "Seirbhís Fhada" (Long Service) with a Celtic design.

Comments: *Awarded to members of An Garda Síochána after 22 years service. Issued unnamed.*

VALUE: **£125–185**

E17. GARDA SÍOCHÁNA GOLDEN JUBILEE MEDAL

Instituted: 1972.
Ribbon: Three equal stripes of yellow, blue, yellow.
Metal: Gold coloured.
Size: 34mm.
Description: (Obverse) The entwined GS of the Garda Síochána crest surrounded by a pentagon with 10 stars; (reverse) a pillar of justice with a scroll going through and around it with the words "Jubaile Orga 1922-1972" (Golden Jubilee 1922-1972).
Comments: *Struck to commemorate the 50th Anniversary of the founding of the force in 1972. The medal was given to anyone serving in the police that year (approx 9,000) and was issued unnamed.*

VALUE: £80–100

E18. GARDA SÍOCHÁNA MILLENNIUM MEDAL

Instituted: 2000.
Ribbon: Pale blue with a broad central yellow stripe edged with white stripes with red edges.
Metal: Gold coloured.
Size: 34mm.
Description: (obverse) Scales suspended from the Garda crest with MM in the left pan and a dove in the right with the inscription "Garda Siochana" and the date "2000" below.
Comments: *Issued unnamed to all serving officers in commemoration of the Millennium.*

VALUE: £85–110

E19. GARDA UNITED NATIONS SERVICE MEDAL

Instituted:
Ribbon: Dark blue central stripe with equal white stripes each side and narrow light blue edges.
Metal: A gold coloured medal
Size: 34mm.
Description: (Obverse) The entwined GS of the Garda Síochána crest in a circle below a dove of peace with an olive branch in its beak and the words "Seirbhis Thar Lear" (Overseas Service); (reverse) plain back with the words "Garda Siochana – don tSiochain – Na Naisiuin Aontaithe" (Garda Siochana – for Peace – United Nations).
Comments: *The medal was given to a very few members of the force who served with the United Nations overseas. Issued unnamed*

VALUE: £265–375

E20. CIVIL DEFENCE LONG SERVICE MEDAL

Instituted: 1961.

Ribbon: Pale blue with a single red stripe in the centre for ten years service or two red stripes for twenty years service.

Metal: Gold coloured.

Size: 36mm.

Description: (Obverse) The Celtic Cross with the words "Seirbhis Fada—Long Service" inscribed between the arms of the cross. The centre of the Cross has the International CD badge of a blue triangle on an orange background inset in coloured enamel; (reverse) is concave and blank for recipient's details.

Comments: *The medal is issued by the Minister of Defence and was first awarded in 1997. Suspension is from a straight bar.*

VALUE: £110–180

E21. CIVIL DEFENCE MILLENNIUM MEDAL

Instituted: 2000

Ribbon: Orange with two pale blue stripes separated by a central green stripe with clasp "1950–2000".

Metal: Gold coloured

Size: 36mm

Description: (Obverse) An Irish harp in the centre surrounded by the words "Cosaint Sibhalta—Civil Defence"; (reverse) blank space for recipient's details surrounded by a rope pattern around the edge.

Comments: *The medal was issued by the Civil Defence Officers Association initially in the year 2000 to mark the 50th anniversary of the Civil Defence. Suspension is from a straight bar.*

VALUE: £95–125

E22. THE BATTLE OF JADOTVILLE MEDAL

Instituted: 2017
Ribbon: Central Irish tricolour edged in UN blue.
Metal: Alloy
Size: 34mm.
Description: (Obverse) image of a standing Celtic warrior carrying sword and shield to one side and the shoulder badge worn by all Irish UN soldiers in the Congo to left, with the words "COSAINT CHALMA" ("valiant defence") and "MISNEACH" ("courage") around. Issued with the clasp "Jadotville".
Comments: *Issued to the 156–158 Irish UN peacekeepers of "A" Company, 35th Irish Infantry Battalion for their heroic defence in the Congo against nearly 4,000 armed Katangese gendarmeries and mercenaries between 13 and 17 September 1961. The action became known as the "Siege of Jadotville".*

VALUE: —

"This medal recognises the leadership, courage, bravery and professional performance of 'A' Company 35 Infantry Battalion and its attachments who, under challenging circumstances at Jadotville, while besieged by overwhelming numbers of Katanganese Gendarmerie and cut-off from support and reinforcements, did valiantly defend their position from 13 Sept 1961 to 17 Sept 1961."

The Siege of Jadotville occurred during Ireland's peacekeeping mission in the Congo in 1961. At the UN post at Jadotville, "A" Company of the 35th Infantry Battalion took responsibility on 3 September. On 9 September 9 they were surrounded by a large force of Katangese gendarmerie and early on the morning of 13 September, they came under attack. They endured almost continuous attacks from ground and air until 17 September. Despite their courageous resistance "A" Company was taken into captivity on 17 September, where they remained until finally released on 25 October 1961. The UN operation in the Congo was the first peacekeeping mission in which significant numbers of Irish soldiers took part. A total of 6,000 Irish troops served in the Congo from 1960 until 1964.

UNOFFICIAL
Medals

Interest has been steadily growing in recent years in unofficial medals, a subject on the fringes of medal collecting. The term is deliberately vague and encompasses a very wide range of medals, medalets and medallions of a commercial, private or local nature. Such a generic term would, for example, include regimental medals awarded for marksmanship or good conduct, often associated with official medal groups of the 19th century. This is a very esoteric group, often consisting of medals which were specially engraved for the occasion and therefore exceedingly difficult to quantify.

On the other hand, many of the earlier medals, now highly regarded as forerunners of the general campaign series, were unofficial in origin, and relied upon the enterprise of public-spirited individuals and prize agents such as Alexander Davison (MYB78 and 85) or Matthew Boulton (MYB84), generals such as Elliot (MYB 74), Earl St Vincent (MYB80) or Gordon of Khartoum (MYB 133) or even private bodies such as the Highland Society (MYB83).

Then there is the large and fascinating group of civic or institutional medals which were presented to volunteers returning from the Boer War of 1899–1902. M. G. Hibbard, in his splendid monograph Boer War Tribute Medals (1982), recorded no fewer than 78 such medals, 40 from towns and cities in England, 25 from other parts of the United Kingdom and 13 from Commonwealth countries. Some of these were fitted with ribbons and were obviously intended for wear alongside the official medals of the war; others were 'danglers' intended to be fitted to watch-chains; and others still were not fitted with any form of suspension and were thus in the nature of commemorative medals intended purely as a memento of volunteer service.

So far as can be ascertained, such tribute medals were not produced in previous conflicts, which were predominantly fought by regular troops; and such was the scale of the involvement of volunteers and later conscripts in the First World War that the cost of providing civic medals of this nature would have been prohibitive. Instead, returning soldiers had to be content with some form of paper testimonial, at best. A notable exception was the gold medal presented by the Lord Mayor of London to the members of the anti-aircraft gun crews which shot down the first Zeppelin (listed below).

Apart from that, the Boer War group therefore constitutes a unique, but clearly defined group. They are, however, generally outside the scope of this YEARBOOK, although it should be noted that several medals in this category have long been accepted in the regular canon: the Kimberley Star (MYB154), the Kimberley Medals (MYB155), the Yorkshire Imperial Yeomanry Medal (MYB156) and the Medal for the Defence of Ookiep (MYB157). The reason for their acceptance is quite arbitrary, and just why the Yorkshire Imperial Yeomanry medal should be so highly regarded while others are not seems to rest on the fact that this medal is more commonly met with than the others—which is hardly a valid criterion.

For the sake of completing the record we have endeavoured to introduce a number of unofficial medals, particularly as groups including certain of these medals are coming onto the market and inevitably some purchasers are curious to know their origins.

In addition there are a number of other unofficial medals available to veterans such as the "Battle for Britain" medal with its various clasps but it is not the intention to make this a definitive guide, so we have decided to limit this section to those medals that were initially commissioned or supported by the relevant veterans associations and mainly produced in recent years in order to fill the gap left in the official series*.

Credit for reviving such medals must go to the Mayor of Dunkirk on whose initiative the medal awarded to survivors of the 1940 evacuation was instituted in 1965. Subsequently distribution of this medal was taken over by the Dunkirk Veterans' Association, applications being strictly limited to those who could prove that they had taken part in that historic event. This practice continued with the commissioning of the Bomber Command Medal by their Association (following a design competition in MEDAL NEWS) in response to the long-standing grievance of veterans of the Second World War who felt that their contribution to the ultimate victory had been deliberately ignored for political reasons. The success of this medal encouraged the production of similar awards for other categories of servicemen, or for campaigns which many felt should have had a distinctive campaign medal. However, it must be stressed that most of these modern medals are available for purchase only by bona-fide veterans or their proven next of kin with sales also benefitting related charities. The wearing of these medals has always been a contentious issue, with many veterans choosing to wear them below but never alongside their official decorations.

*As many of the modern medals are still being struck, it has been decided not to give valuations for these.

Do you know about the Commemorative Medals available?

Pictured from left to right:
Allied Special Forces
Arabian Service
Arctic Campaign
Battle for Malta 60th Anniversary
Bomber Command WWII
British Forces Campaign
British Nuclear Weapons Tests
Cadet Forces
Cold War
Hong Kong Service
Hors de Combat
International Submarine Service
King's Coronation Medal
Malta G.C. 50th Anniversary
Merchant Naval Service
National Service
Normandy Campaign
Allied Ex.-Prisoners of War
Queen Elizabeth II
65th Anniversary Coronation
Queen's Diamond Jubilee
Queen's Sapphire Jubilee
Queen's Platinum Jubilee
RAF Apprentices 1920-1993
Regimental & Service
Restoration of Peace 1945
Royal Naval Patrol Service
Suez (Canal Zone)
Territorial Army Centennial
Uniform Service
Veteran's Star
Victory & Peace 75
Vietnam Veterans

Plus Medal Replacements

AWARD is proud to have produced and issued thirty three commemorative medals, most at the request of, or in conjunction with a veteran group or charity.

Each full size medal is produced and struck in the United Kingdom to the exacting standards for which AWARD has become internationally renowned and is fitted with a uniquely woven ribbon, complete with a concealed individual suspender bar ready to wear. Cost approximately £59.50.

AWARD provide a comprehensive and professional replacement, cleaning and mounting service. For details of available commemorative and replacement full-size and miniature medals and related items contact:

AWARD, PO Box 300, Shrewsbury SY5 6WP Telephone: 01952 510053
Fax: 01952 510765 E-mail: info@awardmedals.com or visit

www.awardmedals.com

AWARD
PROUD TO SERVE

Proud supporter of Veteran Groups & Charities since 1986

U1. CHERRY MEDAL

Date: 1904.
Campaign: China, 1900–4
Branch of Service: Royal Navy.
Ribbon: Cherry red.
Metal: Silver.
Size: 38mm.
Description: (Obverse) a bare cherry tree with five naval officers in the foreground and a large number of other officers, all in frock coats, moving up in single file, with a scroll across the foot inscribed in Latin SUB HOC CERESO MANEMUS (under this cherry tree we remain); (reverse) a fouled anchor flanked by the Golden Fleece and a Chinese Dragon with the legend ARGONAUT CHINA 1900–1904 round the circumference. The medal is fitted with a plain suspension ring.
Comments: *The name of the medal and the colour of ribbon allude to Captain George Henry Cherry RN, commander of HMS* Argonaut *which served on the China Station in 1900-4. The five officers on one side of the tree represent the only ones remaining of the original number when the ship was paid off: Lieutenant Arthur Vernon Ross, Captain T. H. Hawkins RM, Chief Engineer A. W. Turner, Senior Engineer T. W. Cleave and Chaplain T. A. Dexter. The other line represents those officers who left the ship during the commission. The obverse motto contains a spelling error: CERESO instead of CERASO. This medal started off as a joke. Captain Cherry was a terrible martinet and his disgruntled officers felt that they deserved a medal for having to put up with him. It was designed by Miss Ross, sister of the senior watchkeeper, and struck by Gamage's of London. Only 100 medals were struck. Originally it was intended to be given only to the five officers who had stuck it out to the bitter end, but others complained and thus were awarded the medal with a bar indicating each year of service. Many years later, Admiral Cherry was offered one of the medals and graciously received it.*

VALUE: £250–350

U1A. EMIN RELIEF EXPEDITION STAR

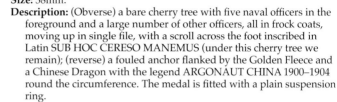

Date: 1889.
Campaign: Sudan.
Ribbon:
Metal: Sterling silver.
Size: 50mm.
Description: A five-pointed star with a plain reverse and a central medallion bearing the monogram of the Royal Geographical Society, surrounded by an incuse inscription EMIN RELIEF EXPEDITION / 1887-9.
Comments: *This medal was awarded mainly to the Zanzibaris forming the bulk of the expedition organised in 1889 to discover the whereabouts of Emin Pasha, Governor of Equatoria, who had retreated south with Egyptian troops, officials and their families in the aftermath of the Mahdist revolt and the fall of Khartoum. The expedition, led by H. M. Stanley, located Emin and his followers in April 1888. Emin, in fact, refused to be relieved and the expedition not only failed in its primary objective but was a disaster, most Europeans and many Zanzibaris perishing before they returned empty-handed. The Royal Geographical Society commissioned the medals from Carrington. Some 200 were produced and of these 178 were issued to surviving members of the expedition. Of these, only nine were named to the recipients.*

VALUE: £450–550

423

U2. SECOND CRUISER SQUADRON MEDAL

Date: 1908.
Campaign: Goodwill tour of South America and South Africa.
Branch of Service: Royal Navy.
Ribbon: Pale blue.
Metal: Bronze.
Size: 36mm.
Description: (Obverse) a right-facing lady in Edwardian dress waving to distant ships, with the words SOUTH AFRICA and SOUTH AMERICA round the edge on either side of the suspender; (reverse) a seven-line inscription: 2ND CRUISER SQUADRON—GOOD HOPE, DEVONSHIRE, ANTRIM, CARNARVON—1908. The words CLOSER UNION appear at the sides.
Clasps: 14—Buenos Aires, Monte Video, Rio de Janerio, St Helena, Capetown, Simonstown, Port Elizabeth, East London, Ladysmith, Bloemfontein, Johannesburg, Pretoria, Pietermaritzburg, Durban.
Comments: *Privately issued and named to members of the goodwill cruise. It is uncertain how many medals were issued but they can be encountered with various combinations of clasps or none at all. It appears that there were two distinct strikings, the named examples being on a slightly thicker flan. The thinner, unnamed versions are believed to have been restrikes for specimen purposes. It is not known who funded or manufactured these medals.*

VALUE: £150–350 dependent on number of clasps

U2A. NATIONAL SERVICE LEAGUE MEDAL

Date: 1912.
Ribbon: White with a narrow central red stripe and narrow blue edges.
Metal: Bronze, silver or gold.
Size: 32mm (bronze) or 26mm (others).
Description: (Obverse) Standing figure of Britannia, helmeted and cloaked, her hands resting on the pommel of an unsheathed broadsword, with the inscription FOR KING AND COUNTRY round the upper part of the circumference. Fitted with a plain ring for suspension, with a brooch bar at the top of the ribbon inscribed NATIONAL SERVICE LEAGUE; (reverse) THE PATH OF DUTY IS THE PATH OF SAFETY and wreath.
Comments: *The National Service League was founded by Field Marshal Lord Roberts in the aftermath of the Boer war. The aim of the League was to warn Britain of the German menace and encourage young men to become proficient marksmen. Its wider aims were "to secure the legislative adoption of universal naval and military training for national defence". Ironically, Lord Roberts was proved right all too soon, and the League was dissolved in 1921.*

VALUE: Gold £450–600   Silver £250–350   Bronze £50–75

U2B. EMDEN MEDAL

Date: 1915.
Campaign: First World War.
Branch of Service: Royal Australian Navy.
Ribbon:
Metal: Silver.
Size: 60mm x 36mm.
Description: Mexican silver dollar surmounted by a crown and two concentric scrolls at the top inscribed NOV. 9. 1914 and HMAS SYDNEY / SMS EMDEN.
Comments: *Shortly after the outbreak of the War the Australian cruiser* Sydney *located the German light cruiser* Emden *in the Cocos Islands. After a brief engagement the* Emden *was boarded and captured. A quantity of Mexican silver dollars were found on board and these were subsequently mounted by the firm of W. Kerr of Sydney and presented to the crew of the* Sydney *as a memento of the action.*

VALUE: £1000–1500

U3. LORD MAYOR OF LONDON'S MEDAL FOR THE DESTRUCTION OF ZEPPELIN L15

Date: 1916.
Campaign: First World War.
Branch of Service: Royal Artillery.
Ribbon:
Metal: 9 carat gold.
Size: 29mm.
Description: (Obverse) the arms of Sir Charles Wakefield within a double ring inscribed PRESENTED BY THE LORD MAYOR round the top and COLONEL SIR CHARLES WAKEFIELD round the foot; (reverse) An anti-aircraft gun and two scrolls inscribed WELL HIT and MARCH 31st and number L15. It is engraved near the top with the rank and name of the recipient. It was issued unmounted but various ornamental suspensions loops were later fitted privately.
Comments: *The Lord Mayor of London offered a reward of £500 to the first gun crew to shoot down a Zeppelin. On 3 April 1916 Capt. J. Harris submitted a claim on behalf of the Purfleet gun crew that they were responsible for the bringing down of the airship L15, but it later transpired that gun crews from Abbey Wood, Dartford, Erith, North Woolwich, Plumstead and the Royal Arsenal, among others, were also involved. It was decided to use the prize money in procuring these medals, a total of 353 being awarded.*

VALUE: £1000–1500

U3A. HMAS *SYDNEY* MEDAL

Date: 1941.
Campaign: World War II.
Branch of Service: Royal Australian Navy.
Ribbon: none.
Metal: Oxidised silver.
Size: 57mm.
Description: (Obverse) HMAS *Sydney* in action; (reverse) 13-line inscription surmounted by a crowned anchor and flanked by laurel leaves at top and bottom.
Comments: *This medal, struck by Amor of Sydney, was presented by the citizens of Sydney to the officers and crew of HMAS* Sydney *which resulted in the sinking of the Italian cruiser* Bartolomeo Colleoni *on July 19, 1940. Some 640 medals were issued but most of them were lost when the* Sydney *sank in 1941.*

VALUE: £450–500

U4. DUNKIRK MEDAL

Date: 1960.
Campaign: Dunkirk evacuation, 1940
Branch of Service: All British and Allied forces.
Ribbon: Chrome yellow with one thin and one wide red stripe each side with two very thin black lines bisecting both sides.
Metal: Bronze.
Size: 36mm wide.
Description: (Obverse) a shield bearing the arms of Dunkirk (a lion passant above a heraldic dolphin) mounted on an anchor; (reverse) a circle bearing a burning lamp with DUNKERQUE 1940 beneath, surrounded by a laurel wreath and surmounted by crossed swords; the whole mounted on and surrounded by a laurel wreath.
Comments: *This medal was first made available to veterans of the Dunkirk evacuation and later administered by the now disbanded Dunkirk Veterans Association. It was created by the French National Association of Veterans of the Fortified Sector of Flanders and of Dunkirk and awarded in recognition of the sacrifice of 30,000 combatants between 29 May and 3 June 1940.*

VALUE: £60–70 *Miniature* £15–20

U5. BOMBER COMMAND MEDAL

Date: 1985.
Campaign: Second World War.
Branch of Service: RAF Bomber Command.
Ribbon: Midnight blue with a central flame stripe and blue-grey edges.
Metal: Cupro-nickel.
Size: 36mm.
Description: (Obverse) A Tudor crown surmounting a laurel wreath containing the letters RAF, flanked by smaller wreaths containing the brevet letters of the aircrew signifying courage, team spirit and leadership; (reverse) a Lancaster bomber flanked by the dates 1939 and 1945 with inscription A TRIBUTE TO THE AIRCREW OF BOMBER COMMAND round the circumference.
Comments: *Produced at the behest of Air Vice Marshal Donald Bennett following a design competition in MEDAL NEWS. The competition was the brainchild of author Alan Cooper campaigning on behalf of Bomber Command veterans. The first medal was struck by Lady Harris (widow of the wartime commander of Bomber Command). Now available from Award Productions Ltd.*

U5A. ARMY CADET FORCE ANNIVERSARY MEDAL

Instituted: 1985.
Branch of Service: Army Cadet Force.
Ribbon: Red and blue separated by a thin yellow stripe.
Metal: Enamelled white metal.
Size: 55 x 85mm.
Description: (Obverse) the insignia of the ACF superimposed by figures of an officer and cadet shaking hands, the dates 1860 and 1985 flanking the motto at the foot. Fitted with a ring above the crown for suspension. (Reverse) plain, apart from the manufacturer's mark of Reu & Company of Heubach, Wurttemberg, Germany. A brooch bar in the form of a scroll 20mm deep is fitted to the top of the ribbon and bears a three-line inscription: ARMY CADET FORCE 125H ANNIVERSARY ONE DAY MARCH 26TH OCTOBER 1985.
Comments: *The medal was awarded to all members of the ACF who took part in the one-day march to celebrate the 125th anniversary of the Force.*

U6. NORMANDY CAMPAIGN MEDAL

Date: 1987.
Campaign: Service in the Normandy campaign between June 6 and August 20, 1944.
Branch of Service: All British and Allied forces.
Ribbon: Dark red with deep navy blue stripes towards the edges and light blue edges, symbolising the three services.
Metal: Cupro-nickel.
Size: 36mm.
Description: (Obverse) insignia of the combined services surrounded by 13 stars (representing the USA) and the inscription BLESSENT MON COEUR D'UNE LANGUEUR MONOTONE ("wounds my heart with monotonous languor"), a quotation from Verlaine broadcast by the BBC at 21.15 on June 5, 1944 to signal the start of the D-Day operations. (Reverse) a tank landing craft with its ramp on the beaches of France symbolised by fleurs-de lys; NORMANDY CAMPAIGN round the top and the date of the campaign inscribed on the ramp. The medal is fitted with a plain suspension bar while the ribbon bears a clasp inscribed NORMANDY between oak leaves.
Comments: *Commissioned by the Normandy Veterans Association, now defunct, whose Welfare and Benevolent Fund has been taken over by The Spirit of Normandy Trust which benefits from the proceeds of sales.*

U7. ARCTIC CAMPAIGN MEDAL

Date: 1991.
Campaign: Second World War.
Branch of Service: Personnel of the Russian convoys.
Ribbon: 32mm watered weave in equal stripes of blue and white representing ice and sea.
Metal: Cupro-nickel.
Size: 36mm.
Description: (Obverse) a liberty ship framed in the cross-hair of a U-boat periscope, with the inscription FOR SERVICE IN THE ARCTIC ZONE 1939-45 round the top; (reverse) four figures representing merchant seamen, Royal Naval, Army and RAF personnel, with the inscription THE ARCTIC CAMPAIGN round the top.
Comments: *This award was proposed by the Russian Convoy Club in conjunction with the North Russian Club.*

U8. MERCHANT NAVAL SERVICE MEDAL

Date: 1998.
Campaign: —
Branch of Service: Merchant Navy and DEMS Gunners.
Ribbon: Dark blue with a central narrow white stripe flanked by broader green and red stripes, representing the navigation lights of an approaching ship.
Metal: Cupro-nickel.
Size: 36mm.
Description: (Obverse) a stockless anchor encompassed by its heavy cable, surmounted by the initials MN; (reverse) a capstan surmounted by a naval crown and flanked by grotesque sea monsters, the whole encircled by a rope tied at the foot in a reef knot. The outer circumference is inscribed FOR MERCHANT NAVAL SERVICE. The medal is fitted to a plain suspension bar by an ornamental scroll.
Comments: *Veterans were eligible for this medal in respect of at least two years' service in the Merchant Navy. The award was inspired by the fact that although service in the mercantile marine was recognised after World War I and during World War II, it was ignored after World War II.*

U9. ALLIED EX-PRISONERS OF WAR MEDAL

Date: 1991.
Campaign: All wars of the 20th century.
Branch of Service: Prisoners of war.
Ribbon: Green with red edges. The centre has a broad black stripe edged in white, having a white strand of barbed wire running down the middle.
Metal: Cupro-nickel.
Size: 36mm.
Description: (Obverse) a young bird trapped by barbed wire, against a globe of the world, with the inscription INTERNATIONAL PRISONERS OF WAR; (reverse) a twisted barb of wire whose four strands divide the inscription INTREPID AGAINST ALL ADVERSITY. Fitted with a plain suspension bar.
Comments: *This award proposed by the National Ex Prisoners of War Association is applicable to any former PoWs whose countries were allies of Britain at the time of their capture irrespective of whether the United Kingdom was itself involved in the conflict.*

U10. RESTORATION OF PEACE MEDAL

Date: 1995.
Campaign: Second World War.
Branch of Service: Armed forces and civilians involved in the war effort.
Ribbon: Rich claret with a central broad gold stripe.
Metal: High-security HS1 gold-coloured alloy.
Size: 36mm.
Description: (Obverse) the letter V enclosing the date 1945, superimposed on a globe with the inscription A TIME FOR PEACE round the circumference; (reverse) a simple wreath enclosing the inscription FOR ALL WHO STRIVED FOR PEACE. The plain suspension bar is fitted to the medal by a peace dove on both sides.
Comments: *Produced at the behest of the British Red Cross Society to mark the 50th anniversary of the cessation of hostilities in the Second World War.*

U11. SUEZ CANAL ZONE MEDAL

Date: 1995.
Campaign: Suez Canal Zone, 1945-57.
Branch of Service: British and French forces.
Ribbon: Sand-coloured edged with narrow stripes of red, white and blue. A broad central crimson stripe has a light blue stripe down the middle.
Metal: High-security HS1 gold-coloured alloy.
Size: 36mm.
Description: (Obverse) the Sphinx and Pyramid flanked by the dates 1951-54 and 1956-57, representing the two most recent periods of conflict; (reverse) stylised papyrus grass with the words TO MARK SERVICE IN THE CANAL ZONE at left. Fitted with an ornamental suspension bar in the form of Pharaonic wings.
Comments: *The Ex-Services Mental Welfare Society (Combat Stress) was the beneficiary of this project.*

U12. NATIONAL SERVICE MEDAL

Date: 1991.

Campaign: Period of conscription, 1939-60.

Branch of Service: National Service, both military and civilian.

Ribbon: Dark blue with a narrow central gold stripe and narrow white and red stripes at the edges representing the involvement of the Royal British Legion.

Metal: Cupro-nickel.

Size: 36mm.

Description: (Obverse) the seated figure of Britannia supported by a lion, with the inscription NATIONAL SERVICE 1939-1960; (reverse) a wreath enclosing the inscription FOR CROWN AND COUNTRY. Fitted with scrolled suspension.

Comments: *Between January 1939 when the National Service Act was passed, and December 1960 when it was repealed, some 5,300,000 young people were conscripted into the armed services. The medal was proposed by the Royal British Legion and over 140,000 have been issued to date.*

U13. JORDAN SERVICE MEDAL

Instituted: April 1997.

Branch of Service: British ex-service personnel who served in the Hashemite Kingdom of Jordan between 1948 and 1957 and again during the 1958 emergency, i.e. the 16th Independent Parachute Brigade and attached units.

Ribbon: Golden sand, edged on both sides with four thin stripes of the Jordanian national colours (black, white, green and red).

Metal: Gilt brass.

Size: 36mm.

Description: (Obverse) Effigy of King Hussein; (reverse) inscription in raised lettering: FOR SERVICE IN THE HASHEMITE KINGDOM OF JORDAN, with or without the date 1958 below.

Comments: *This medal was produced on the initiative of G. E. Harris of Haverfordwest with the approval of the late King Hussein. Sales of the medal benefit the SSAFA Forces Help charity. It was manufactured by the Bigbury Mint, Ermington, Devon. To date nearly 2,000 veterans have applied for the medal (either version), including two of the four female nurses who served in Jordan.*

U14. HONG KONG SERVICE MEDAL

Instituted: 1999.

Branch of Service: All former civil and military personnel who served for a minimum of six months in the Crown Colony of Hong Kong, or their next of kin.

Ribbon: Pale blue with a central yellow stripe.

Metal: Gilt metal.

Size: 36mm.

Description: (Obverse) Bird of Paradise surounded by the words HONG KONG SERVICE MEDAL 1841–1997; (reverse) HONG KONG in Cantonese characters surrounded by a circular wreath. The medal is suspended from a unique suspender depicting two mythical Chinese dragons.

Comments: *SSAFA, the Armed Forces charity was the beneficiary of this project.*

U15. BRITISH FORCES GERMANY MEDAL

Instituted: 1999.
Branch of Service: All British service personnel in Germany, 1945–89.
Ribbon: 32mm NATO blue with central narrow stripes of black, red and gold (the German national colours).
Metal: Rhodium-plated cupro-nickel.
Size: 36mm.
Description: (Obverse) Standing figures of a soldier and airman holding the Union Jack, BRITISH FORCES GERMANY round the top with ARMY 1945–1989 RAF round the foot; (reverse) a laurel wreath incorporating the recipient's name, rank and service number over the years of service. Plain suspension bar.
Comments: *All men and women who served with the British Forces in Germany from the end of World War II until 1989 are eligible for this medal designed by Martin Duchemin.*

U16. ROYAL NAVAL PATROL SERVICE MEDAL

Instituted: 1989.
Branch of Service: Royal Naval Patrol Service of World War II.
Ribbon: Watered dark and light green with a central orange stripe edged with black.
Metal: Cupro-nickel.
Size: 36mm.
Description: (Obverse) The badge of the RNPS with a shark swimming around it.
Comments: *Commissioned by the Royal Naval Patrol Service Association to commemorate service. Available only to veterans or their next of kin.*

U17. HORS DE COMBAT MEDAL

Instituted: 2001.
Branch of Service: All uniformed British service personnel.
Ribbon: Rich red bordered by narrow bands of blue with wider outer edges of white. A poppy is attached to the ribbon if the medal is issued to next of kin to those killed in action.
Metal: Cupro-nickel.
Size: 36mm.
Description: (Obverse) A gladiator kneeling before a female figure with the legend IN THE LINE OF DUTY; (reverse) a stylised rendering of the surgeon's knot with the same legend.
Comments: *For all those who sustained wounds or injury in the line of duty. Also available to next of kin.*

U18. INTERNATIONAL SUBMARINE SERVICE MEDAL

Instituted: 2002.
Branch of Service: Submariners of all nations.
Ribbon: Navy blue with a thin red stripe flanked by thin black and white stripes.
Metal: Cupro-nickel
Size: 36mm.
Description: (Obverse) a modern submarine viewed from the bow, with inscription INTERNATIONAL SUBMARINE SERVICE; (reverse) a depth gauge with the inscription BY SKILL AND STEALTH WE COME UNSEEN.
Comments: *Commissioned by London Submariners and the International Submarine Association in recognition of the men who have served, and continue to serve, beneath the world's oceans.*

U19. QUEEN'S GOLDEN JUBILEE COMMEMORATIVE MEDAL

Instituted: 2002.
Branch of Service: All service personnel, past or present, including police, coastguard, ambulance and other services.
Ribbon: Broad gold bands at the edges, with thin white, purple and white stripes in the centre.
Metal: Gilt brass.
Size: 36mm.
Description: (Obverse) left-facing robed bust of the Queen inscribed QUEEN ELIZABETH II GOLDEN JUBILEE 2002; (reverse) royal arms.
Comments: *This attractive medal was produced for the benefit of the SSAFA (Soldiers, Sailors and Air Forces Association) on the initiative of G. E. Harris who also instigated the Jordan Service Medal (no. U13) and is manufactured by the Bigbury Mint. It provides a need for those who were not entitled to the official medal.*

U20. NORTH AFRICA SERVICE MEDAL

Instituted: 1999.
Branch of Service: Veterans of the North African campaigns of World War II.
Ribbon: Yellow and sky-blue stripes at the edges, with navy blue, red and air force blue in the centre representing the armed services.
Metal: Bronze.
Size: 36mm.
Description: (Obverse) a camel standing beside a desert rat, with the inscription FOR SERVICE IN NORTH AFRICA, M.E.L.F.; (reverse) ornamental edge with centre blank for engraving with the name of the recipient.
Comments: *Designed and manufactured by the Bigbury Mint on the initiative of Ron Skeates of Aveton Gifford.*

U21. CAMERONIANS (SCOTTISH RIFLES) MEDAL

Instituted: 1999.
Branch of Service: Those who served in the regiment either as regulars or on National Service, including wives.
Ribbon: Three stripes of blue, black and dark green taken from the regimental tartan.
Metal: Silver-plated brass.
Size: 36mm.
Description: (Obverse) regimental badge of the Cameronians; (reverse) FOR SERVICE IN THE CAMERONIANS SCOTTISH RIFLES.
Comments: *The regiment was named in memory of the Covenanting leader Richard Cameron and was raised at Douglas, Lanarkshire in 1689. It later merged with the 90th (Perthshire) Regiment, at which point it adopted the Government tartan. However, in 1891 they were authorised to use the Douglas tartan.*

U22. BRITISH NUCLEAR WEAPONS TEST MEDAL

Instituted: October 3, 2004.
Branch of Service: Australian and British personnel involved in the testing of nuclear weapons in Australia from 1952 onwards.
Ribbon: White with a narrow central black stripe flanked by two shades of red.
Metal: Cupro-nickel.
Size: 36mm.
Description: (Obverse) depicts the nuclear symbol surrounded by the words "British Nuclear Weapons Test in Australia & Pacific". Fitted with a straight bar for suspension.
Comments: *The medal was produced by Award Productions in conjunction with the Australian and British Nuclear Tests Veterans' Associations.*

U23. ARABIAN SERVICE MEDAL

Instituted: 2005.
Branch of Service: Civil and Military personnel who served in Aden and other parts of Arabia.
Ribbon: Three equal stripes of blue, yellow and green.
Metal: Cupro-nickel.
Size: 36mm.
Description: Crossed daggers within a Saracenic arch border inscribed ARABIAN SERVICE / 1839-1967. A crescent and star attaches the medal to the bar suspension.
Comments: *Instituted by the Aden Veterans Association it commemorates British involvement in South Arabia from 1839 till the withdrawal of British forces in 1967.*

U24. BATTLE FOR MALTA MEDAL

Instituted: September 2005.
Branch of Service: Veterans who served in Malta or supplied the island between 1940 and 1943.
Ribbon: Two equal stripes of white and red.
Metal: Cupro-nickel.
Size: 36mm.
Description: The George Cross with inscription REUNION & 60TH COMMEMORATION OF VICTORY IN MALTA IN WORLD WAR II.
Comments: *Commissioned by the Battle of Malta International Veterans Committee.*

U25. VIETNAM VETERANS MEDAL

Instituted: 2005.
Branch of Service: Commonwealth forces who served in Vietnam between 1960 and 1972.
Ribbon: Broad central yellow stripe with three thin red stripes superimposed, and green and dark blue stripes at the edges.
Metal: Gold-coloured alloy.
Size: 36mm.
Description: Dragon and soldier in combat gear, with VIETNAM VETERANS MEDAL round the circumference.
Comments: *Produced by Award Productions for the Vietnam Veterans of Australia.*

U26. ACTIVE SERVICE MEDAL

Instituted: 2003.
Branch of Service: British and Commonwealth Forces.
Ribbon: Central white stripe, with red edges surrounded by yellow.
Metal: Gold plated bronze.
Size: 36mm.
Description: (Obverse) A serviceman draws his sword ready for action. Alongside him is the dove of peace. A number of clasps are available for this medal, stating where the recipient has seen his/her active service.
Comments: *This medal is produced for the benefit of SSAFA Forces Help on the initiative of G. E. Harris. It is manufactured by Bigbury Mint Ltd.*

U27. GENERAL SERVICE CROSS

Instituted: 1992.
Branch of Service: British and Commonwealth Forces who have served. in peacetime or during hostilities.
Ribbon: Equal bands of blue, white and red.
Metal: Hallmarked silver.
Size: 36mm.
Description: A Winged Lion carrying a trident is surrounded by the words "For General Service".
Comments: *The War Widows have benefited from the sale of this medal. The medal is manufactured by Bigbury Mint Ltd.*

U28. RAF BOY ENTRANTS COMMEMORATIVE MEDAL

Instituted: 2004.
Branch of Service: Royal Air Force.
Ribbon: Maroon.
Metal: Hallmarked sterling silver.
Size: 36mm.
Description: (Obverse) badge of the Royal Air Force Boy Entrants Association with 1994 10TH ANNIVERSARY RAFBEA 2004 round the circumference; (reverse) a four-bladed propeller with 1934-2004 70th ANNIVERSARY OF FOUNDATION OF BOY ENTRANT SCHEME round the circumference.
Comments: *Medal struck on behalf of the Boy Entrants Association by the Pobjoy Mint.*

U29. BORDER SERVICE MEDAL

Instituted: August 2006.
Branch of Service: British and Commonwealth forces on frontier duty throughout the world (Germany, Hong Kong, Cyprus, Northern Ireland, Malaysia, Borneo, Gibraltar, Belize, etc).
Ribbon: Green with a central red band.
Metal: Antique bronze.
Size: 36mm.
Description: (Obverse) a watch tower with a fortified border in the background; (reverse) the recipient's number, rank and name and place of service. .
Comments: *Produced by Martin Duchemin on behalf of Royal British Legion Industries.*

U30. OPERATION VIBRATTO COMMEMORATIVE MEDAL

Instituted: June 21, 1981.
Branch of Service: Military personnel of Allied Forces Southern Europe who came to the aid of victims of the earthquake of November 23, 1980 in Campania and Baslilicata, Italy.
Ribbon: A narrow blue central stripe, flanked by white stripes, with red, yellow and red, stripes on either side.
Metal: Bronze.
Size: 36mm.
Description: (Obverse) a female, fireman and soldier with arms raised in a supportive gesture towards the earthquake region; (reverse) equestrian statue and public building in Naples with the word BENEMERONZA (Merit) above and COMMISSARIATO STRAORDINARIO DELLA CAMPANIA E DELLA BASILICATA (Office of the Special Commissioner of Campania and Basilicata) round the circumference.
Comments: *About 100 medals were awarded to members of the Tri-Service British contingent based at Naples. Although accepted by the Ministry of Defence it may not be worn on the uniform of serving personnel.*

U31. BLACK WATCH MEDAL

Instituted: 2006.
Branch of Service: Service in the Black Watch (Royal Highland Regiment).
Ribbon: Dark blue, red and green.
Metal: Cupro-nickel.
Size: 37mm.
Description: (Obverse) the regimental badge with inscription THE BLACK WATCH / ROYAL HIGHLAND REGIMENT round the circumference; (reverse) FOR SERVICE TO THE BLACK WATCH x ROYAL HIGHLAND REGIMENT, 1739-2006. The ribbon is fitted with a brooch bar and suspended by a ring attached to the medal.
Comments: *The medal was struck by the Bigbury Mint.*

U32. ROYAL HIGHLAND FUSILIERS MEDAL

Instituted: 2009.
Branch of Service: Service in the Royal Highland Fusiliers.
Ribbon: Dark green and blue bisected by a thin yellow line.
Metal: "Golden" alloy.
Size: 36mm.
Description: (Obverse) the Royal Highland Fusiliers badge with the date 1959; (reverse) the new regimental badge of the Royal Regiment of Scotland with inscription ROYAL HIGHLAND FUSILIERS 50th ANNIVERSARY 1959–2009 round the circumference. The ribbon is fitted with a brooch bar.
Comments: *The medal was produced by ScotMint of Ayr to celebrate the 50th anniversary of the formation of the Royal Highland Fusiliers (after the amalgamation of the Highland Light Infantry and the Royal Scots Fusiliers).*

U33. LOWER SAXONY FIREFIGHTING MEDAL 1975

Instituted: 2009.
Branch of Service: Royal Engineers.
Ribbon: Red with a white stripe at centre.
Metal: Bronze coloured base metal.
Size: 30mm.
Description: (Obverse) a depiction of flames roaring through a forest; (reverse) the words WALDBRAND KATASTROPHE IN NIEDERSACHSEN AUGUST 1975. With ring suspension.
Comments: *This medal was officially presented by the Lower Saxony Land Ministry to members of the team of Royal Engineers who, with their Centurion tanks and bulldozers, helped dig fire breaks to stop a forest fire from spreading on Luneburg Heath in August 1975.*

U34. ROYAL GREEN JACKETS COMMEMORATIVE MEDAL

Date: 2007.
Branch of Service: Royal Green Jackets.
Ribbon: Green with one red and one black stripe.
Metal: Silver.
Size: 36mm.
Description: (Obverse) Insignia of the Royal Green Jackets; (reverse) RGJ emblem with inscription and date of "coming out of the line" when the new regiment The Rifles were formed.
Comments: *Struck by the Bigbury Mint as an initiative with the RGJRA and available to all past members of the RGJ, RGJ-TA. Eligibility extends to members of the past regiments which made up the RGJ (43 & 52 The Ox & Bucks LI, KRRC and RB).*

U35. RHODESIAN INDEPENDENCE COMMEMORATIVE MEDAL

Date: 2009.
Branch of Service: Available to all those who lived in Rhodesia during its independence from November 11, 1965 until December 11, 1979.
Ribbon: Dark green with a central, wide white stripe.
Metal: Silver.
Size: 36mm.
Description: Roaring lion's head with inscription over.
Comments: *This unofficial medal was commissioned on behalf of the joint committee of the Rhodesian Army, Rhodesian Air Force and British South Africa Police Associations.*

U36. AFPS MEDAL

Date: 2009.
Branch of Service: Members of Parliament.
Ribbon: One stripe of crimson and one of green separated by a thinner yellow stripe, representing the House of Commons, the House of Lords and the Monarch.
Metal: Silver.
Size: 36mm.
Description: The Combined Services emblem surmounted by the Parliamentary portcullis badge.
Comments: *This unofficial medal was instituted by the Armed Forces Parliamentary Scheme to reward MPs who have carried out at least four annual 22-day commitments with the armed forces over a period of ten or more years.*

U37. CADET FORCES COMMEMORATIVE MEDAL

Date: 2010.
Branch of Service: Available to all those who served in the Cadet Forces, their next of kin or direct descendants.
Ribbon: Outer stripes of red, dark blue and light blue representing the Army, Air Force and Navy bounded by equal bands of yellow with a central green stripe.
Metal: Silver.
Size: 36mm.
Description: (Obverse) A fouled anchor, the L98-A1 Cadet GP Rifle and propellor with year dates; (reverse) mottoes of the various Cadet Forces.
Comments: *Produced by Award Productions Ltd to mark the 150th anniversary since the first Cadet Corps formed at Rossall School in 1860 as an army contingent to help the country's defence numbers following heavy losses in the Crimean War.*

U38. COLD WAR COMMEMORATIVE MEDAL

Date: 2010.
Branch of Service: For those who served in the Armed Forces of any country opposing the totalitarian regimes of the Communist Pact between 1945 and 1991 (next of kin or direct descendants also eligible).
Ribbon: Red, white and blue strip on the left representing the Allies and the bright red of the Soviet flag on the right.
Metal: Silver.
Size: 36mm.
Description: (Obverse) Rolled up flags of the three main players in the Cold War—the Soviet Union contained by the UK and US and dates 1945–91; (reverse) The Russian Bear on a wall clutching a missile with the Lion of the UK and the Eagle of the US repelling.
Comments: *Produced by Award Productions Ltd to pay tribute to those who served during this tense period of history.*

U39. BEVIN BOYS MEDAL

Date: 2009.
Branch of Service: The Bevin Boys Medal was commissioned by the Bevin Boys Association and as such is their official medal.
Ribbon: Black edged on both sides by a pale blue and green stripe.
Metal: Silver.
Size: 36mm.
Description: Colliery gantry with inscription over.
Comments: *The Bevin Boys medal is available to ballotees, optants, volunteers or next of kin called up between 1942 and 1948. There is no minimum length of service to be eligible for this medal but details of the training colliery and name of colliery worked, if known has to be provided. Struck by Bigbury Mint, a donation is made to the Bevin Boys Association from the sale of each medal.*

U40. THE TERRITORIAL ARMY CENTENNIAL MEDAL

Date: April 2008

Campaign: Available to all those who served or are currently serving in the TA or TAVR, their next of kin or direct descendants

Branch of Service: Territorial Army.

Ribbon: Diagonal green and yellow stripes representing the TA and the blue stripe the period 1967-1979 when the TAVR (Territorial Army and Volunteer Reserve) units were formed.

Metal: Gilt nickel.

Size: 36mm.

Description: An antique bronzed oval medal: (obverse) the monogram TA with the year dates 1908 and 2008 in an oak wreath; (reverse) the Army crossed swords symbol with the inscription TERRITORIAL ARMY CENTENNIAL MEDAL.

Comments: *Struck in association with The Resolution Project.*

U41. THE COMMEMORATIVE SERVICE MEDAL

Date: September 2008

Campaign: Available to all those who served or are currently serving in any of the 19 Regiments and Services detailed below, their next of kin or direct descendants.

Branch of Service: Royal Navy, Army, Royal Air Force, Royal Marines, Royal Artillery, Royal Army Service Corps, Royal Engineers, REME, Royal Signals, Army Catering Corps, Light Infantry, Parachute Regiment, Royal Army Medical Corps, Royal Army Ordnance Corps, Royal Army Pay Corps, Royal Corps of Transport, Royal Military Police, Royal Tank Regiment and RAF Regiment.

Ribbon: Red for Army and Regiments, Navy Blue for Royal Navy, Green for Royal Marines and Air Force Blue for the RAF and RAF Regiment.

Metal: Silver-plated nickel.

Size: 36mm.

Description: (Obverse) Each medal bears the appropriate Regimental or Service emblem in the nickel silver plated centre framed by a 24 ct gold plated border; (gold plated reverse) a laurel wreath encasing the words FOR CROWN AND COUNTRY.

Comments: *Produced by Award Productions Ltd to pay tribute to and display affinity to Regiment or Service.*

Bevin Boys working with an older, experienced miner at Ollerton Colliery, Nottinghamshire, February 1945 (image Wikipedia public domain).

U42. THE CADET FORCES FIRST AID MEDAL

Date: 2010.

Branch of Service: Cadet Forces.

Ribbon: Three stripes of dark blue (RN), red (Army) and light blue (ATC). The central red stripe edged with thin yellow stripes.

Metal: Nickel silver or gilt.

Size: 32mm.

Description: (Obverse) a Maltese cross surrounded by a laurel wreath and an outer legend; (reverse) blank but named to the qualifying participant.

Comments: *The gilt medal was awarded to winning teams in the ACF, ATC, CCF and SCC Cadet 150 2010 national first aid competitions. Nickel silver medals were awarded to qualifying participants in Cadet 150 Festival of First Aid 2010, or trained or supported teams for Cadet 150 Festival of First Aid 2010. Cadet 150 Festival of First Aid signifies any of the events held over the period October 16–17, 2010 including the national first aid competitions of each of the ACF, ATC, CCF and SCC, the Inter Services and St John Ambulance Young Grand Prior events. Nickel silver medals without Cadet 150 reverse engraving may also be issued for qualifying events in 2011 or later years. The medal is unofficial and may not be worn in uniform.*

U43. ALLIED SPECIAL FORCES MEDAL

Date: 2011.

Branch of Service: Available to any member of an elite or special force of Britain or ally of Britain, their next of kin or direct descendants.

Ribbon: The green, sky blue and sea blue stripes represent involvement.

Metal: Silver.

Size: 36mm.

Description: (Obverse) A dagger and wings surmount a globe of the world. The words ALLIED SPECIAL FORCES surround the globe; (reverse) a globe with lightning bolts and mottoes of the various branches of service.

Comments: *Produced by Award productions Ltd to pay tribute to all of the Special and Elite forces of the United Kingdom and those of their allies around the world.*

U44. COMMEMORATIVE QUEEN'S DIAMOND JUBILEE MEDAL

Date: 2012.

Branch of Service: Available to all those who have served Queen Elizabeth II from 6 February 1952 including current serving members of the Armed Forces, Emergency Services, Prison Service, Police Community Support Officers, holders of the Victoria Cross and George Cross and members of the Royal Household. Next of kin and direct descendants may also apply.

Ribbon: Rich purple broad stripes, central white "diamond" white, bordered with red, white and blue narrow stripes.

Metal: Silver.

Size: 36mm.

Description: (Obverse) Multi layered textured diamond, central crown and traditional surround; (reverse) English Rose, Scottish Thistle, Irish Shamrock and Welsh Leek framed with a traditional laurel.

Comments: *Produced by Award Productions Limited to commemorate the 60th anniversary of the reign of Queen Elizabeth II.*

U45. BRITISH FORCES CAMPAIGN SERVICE MEDAL

Date: 2013.
Branch of Service: British Forces.
Ribbon: Central red stripe flanked by narrow white and wide blue stripes.
Metal: Silver.
Size: 36mm.
Description: (Obverse) a compass-like design representing the global dominance of the British Forces, surmounted by a crown representing the monarch's place as the head of the armed forces and framed with BRITISH FORCES FOR CROWN & COUNTRY around. (Reverse) laurel wreath surrounding the crowned words FOR BRITISH FORCES CAMPAIGN SERVICE.
Comments: *Produced by Award Productions Ltd to pay tribute to and to recognise the contributions of British Forces involved in campaigns and operations otherwise unrecognised. Qualifying criteria for this medal is one or more days service or posting in one or more of the qualifying regions or operations in FALKLANDS, NORTHERN IRELAND, GERMANY, GIBRALTAR, SINGAPORE; service alongside NATO forces or as part of a NATO-led initiative, protection of a BORDER and/or COASTAL PATROL. A total of 17 clasps are available.*

U46. HOME SERVICES MEDAL

Date: 2013.
Branch of Service: Civil.
Ribbon: Black with a central yellow stripe.
Metal: Silver coloured
Size: 36mm.
Description: (Obverse) The points of the compass surmounted by clasped hands with HOME SERVICES MEDAL around; (reverse) Laurel wreath enclosing a crown and the words FOR SERVICES TO HUMANITY.
Comments: *This medal, marketed by Medals of Distinction, is intended as a reward for any civilian who served in Northern Ireland during the "Toubles". A donation to the charities SANDS and Pilgrim Bandits is made for each purchase.*

U47. ARMED FORCES VETERAN MEDAL

Date: 2013.
Branch of Service: British Armed Forces.
Ribbon: Green with three equal stripes of dark blue, red and light blue. stripe.
Metal: Silver coloured.
Size: 36mm.
Description: (Obverse) A globe surrounded by emblems of the armed forces with ARMED FORCES VETERAN around; (reverse) Laurel wreath enclosing the words FOR SERVICES RENDERED.
Comments: *This medal, marketed by Medals of Distinction, is intended as a reward for any person who served in the British armed forces in any capacity. A number of different clasps are available to denote the area of involvement. A donation to the charities SANDS and Pilgrim Bandits is made for each purchase.*

U48. THE VETERANS STAR

Date: 2014.

Branch of Service: British and Commonwealth Forces.

Ribbon: Army red, Navy blue and Air Force blue framed between red, white and blue stripes representing Great Britain and The Commonwealth.

Metal: Silver.

Size: 36mm.

Description: The obverse of the medal comprises the flag of Great Britain surrounded by the words "For Crown and Country". The distinctive star formation has been inspired by the First and Second World War Stars. Unlike other UK medals it has a highly polished nickel-plated finish. The reverse of the star has a sandblasted finish.

Comments: *Produced by Award Productions Ltd, the Veterans Star is available to veterans who served in any of our Great British and Commonwealth Forces for a minimum period of two years. Next of kin or direct descendants may also apply.*

U49. THE UNIFORM SERVICE MEDAL

Date: 2016.

Branch of Service: All uniformed services.

Ribbon: Pale blue with a central darker blue stripe..

Metal: Silver.

Size: 33mm octagonal.

Description: The obverse of the medal is inspired by the shape of the Union flag represented by members of the uniformed services coming together to the same centre point, united in their services. The reverse of the medal has a satin finish suitable for naming with the service details of the recipient. Fitted with a suspension bar featuring a crown.

Comments: *Produced by Award Productions Ltd, the Uniform Service medal is available to those who have served or are currently serving for a minimum period of two years in any of the uniformed services: Armed Forces, Border Control, Coast Guard, Fire and Rescue, Nursing, Police, Ambulance and Prison services, etc. Next of kin and direct descendants may also apply.*

U50. COMMEMORATIVE QUEEN'S SAPPHIRE JUBILEE MEDAL

Date: 2017.

Branch of Service: Available to all those who have served Queen Elizabeth II from 6 February 1952 including current serving members of the Armed Forces, Emergency Services, Prison Service, Police Community Support Officers, holders of the Victoria Cross and George Cross and members of the Royal Household. Next of kin and direct descendants may also apply.

Ribbon: A central stripe in sapphire blue with light blue and silver white stripes highlighting the reflective facets of the gem and medal.

Medal: Silver.

Size: 36mm.

Description: (Obverse) A multi-faceted design to reflect the sapphire cut gemstone with an English rose, Scottish thistle, Irish clover and Welsh leek, representing the plants of the United Kingdom; (reverse) a regal crown sits at the top of the medal with wording ELIZABETH II SAPPHIRE JUBILEE and 1952-65-2017, encircling the bottom.

Comments: *Produced by Award Productions Ltd to commemorate the 65th anniversary of the reign of Queen Elizabeth II.*

U51. COMMEMORATIVE QUEEN ELIZABETH II 65th ANNIVERSARY CORONATION MEDAL

Date: 2018.

Branch of Service: Available to all those who have served Queen Elizabeth II from June 1953 including current serving members of the Armed Forces, Emergency Services, Prison Service, Police Community Support Officers, holders of the Victoria Cross and George Cross and members of the Royal Household. Next of kin and direct descendants may also apply.

Ribbon: Regal purple with gold stripe at each edge.

Metal: Silver.

Size: 36mm.

Description: (Obverse) HM the Queen invested with regalia and sat upon the Coronation Chair with legend ANNIVERSARY OF THE CORONATION OF HER MAJESTY ELIZABETH II 1953–2018; (reverse) four quarters of the medals peeled away to reveal a crown at its heart. Surrounding the design is the wording SIXTY FIFTH ANNIVERSARY OF THE 1953 CORONATION.

Comments: *Produced by Award Productions Ltd. SSAFA, the Armed Forces charity is the beneficiary of this medal.*

U52. HEREFORDSHIRE REGIMENT "SUVLA 100" MEDAL

Date: 2015.

Branch of Service: Members of the Regiment, their families and descendants.

Ribbon: Black, green and red, the Regimental colours.

Metal: Silver plated base metal.

Size: 36mm.

Clasps: A silver rosette is added to the ribbon for family and descendants whose members served during the Great War 1914–18.

Description: (Obverse) Regimental cap badge of the Herefordshire Regiment with the legend "8 August 1915 - Suvla Bay - 8 August 2015; Gallipoli 1915". (Reverse) the words "The Divisional Commander speaks with appreciation of the 1/1st Herefordshire Regiment which attacked with impetuosity and courage on the extreme right of the Line."

Comments: *Commissioned by the Herefordshire Light Infantry Museum to commemorate the 100th Anniversary of the 1/1st Herefordshire Regiment landing at Suvla Bay, Gallipoli on 8th August 1915. The reverse quotation was made in despatches by General Sir Ian Standish Monteith Hamilton, GCB, GCMG, DSO, TD, Commander in Chief Mediterranean Expeditionary Force during the Gallipoli Campaign. The medal is produced by Worcester Medal Services Ltd in a limited batch of 250, each being individually numbered on the rim and a roll kept by the Museum. The medal is currently available with the Museum benefitting from the sale of this medal.*

U53. OPERATION CROWN MEDAL

Date: 2018.

Branch of Service: A commemorative medal commissioned by the Operation Crown Association to pay tribute to former UK service personnel who served in North East Thailand between 1963 and 1968 under Operation Crown.

Ribbon: Comprises colours of the flag of Thailand.

Metal: Silver plated nickel

Size: 36mm.

Description: (Obverse) The Thai Great Crown of Victory encompassed by the word OPERATION CROWN and THAILAND and the years 1963–1968; (reverse) features the words "UK Armed Forces deployed in support of SEATO and SLAT 1963–1968" surrounded by a laurel leaf wreath symbolising victory and honour.

Comments: *Produced by Award Productions Ltd.*

U54. THE WORLD WAR II 75th ANNIVERSARY VICTORY & PEACE MEDAL

Date: 2020.

Branch of Service: Armed forces and civilians involved in the war efforts and their next of kin.

Ribbon: Outer bands of red and blue represent the services, Merchant Navy and the involvement of SSAFA, two diamond white bands reflect the 75th anniversary of victory and peace. The theme of the Restoration of Peace Medal (U10) is continued with the two centre bands of rich claret separated by a band of gold.

Metal: Silver plated nickel

Size: 36mm.

Description: (Obverse) The dove of peace rising in flight from the "V" for victory carrying in its beak a palm branch, the symbol of victory and peace surrounded by the wording 75TH ANNIVERSARY OF THE DECLARATION OF PEACE; (reverse) features the iconic design of the Restoration of Peace Medal issued to mark the 50th anniversary.

Comments: *Produced by Award Productions Ltd. SSAFA, the Armed Forces charity, is the beneficiary of this medal.*

443

U55. ROYAL AIR FORCE APPRENTICES 1920–1993 MEDAL

Date: 2021.

Branch of Service: All those who successfully completed the RAF Apprentice training course under the RAF Apprentice Training Scheme, preparatory to commencing adult service in the Royal Air Force. Next of kin and direct descendants may also apply.

Ribbon: An amalgam of hatband colours generally worn by RAF Apprentices during their period of training at a RAF Apprentice Training School.

Description: (Obverse) Each medal bears a 28mm minted, nickel silver plated RAF badge set in the centre, framed by a 24ct gold plated border. (Reverse) the gold-plated reverse features the Royal Air Force Apprentice Wheel surrounded by the words ROYAL AIR FORCE APPRENTICES and the years 1920–1993 when the RAF Apprentice Training Schemes was in force.

Metal: Gold and silver-plated nickel.

Size: 36mm.

Comments: *Commissioned by the RAF Administrative Apprentices' Association and produced by Award Productions Ltd.*

U56. COMMEMORATIVE QUEEN'S PLATINUM JUBILEE MEDAL

Date: 2022.

Branch of Service: Available to all those who have served Queen Elizabeth II from February 6, 1952, including current members of the Armed Forces, Emergency Services, Prison Service, Police Community Support Officers, holders of the Victoria Cross and George Cross, and members of the Royal Household. Next of kin and direct descendants may also apply.

Ribbon: Red, white and blue central stripes reflecting the Country's flag between royal blue and platinum stripes representing the Platinum Jubilee.

Description: (Obverse) Leaves and acorn of an oak tree behind a regal crown symbolising strength,. wisdom and endurance. (Reverse) A royal crown sits at the top of the medal with the wording ELIZABETH II PLATINUM JUBILEE and 1952-70-2022, encircling the bottom.

Metal: Silver plated nickel.

Size: 36mm.

Comments: *Produced by Award Productions Ltd to commemorate the 70th anniversary of the reign of Queen Elizabeth II. SSAFA, the Armed Forces charity is the beneficiary of this medal.*

U57. COMMEMORATIVE KING'S CORONATION MEDAL

Date: 2023

Branch of Service: Available to all those who served the crown to commemorate the King's Coronation and all those who are currently serving members of the Armed Forces, Emergency Services personnel (paid, retained or volunteers), Prison Service, Police Community Support Officers, holders of the Victoria Cross and George Cross and members of the Royal Household. Next of kin and direct descendants may also apply.

Ribbon: Two broad rich purple stripes representing royalty edged by two patriotic red stripes representing power, leadership and courage, and a centre green stripe reflecting the King's interest in the environment, sustainability and peace.

Description: (Obverse) The symbols of the Monarchy—the crown, the Orb and the Sceptre surrounded by the wording THE CORONATION OF HIS MAJESTY CHARLES III and the date 6th May 2023. (Reverse) A stylish designed Charles III cypher surrounded by the wording PROTECTOR OF ALL FAITHS to reflect the King's desire to protect the free practise of all faiths and the date of the Coronation.

Metal: Silver-plated nickel.

Size: 36mm.

Comments: *Produced by Award Productions Ltd in support of SSAFA, the Armed Forces charity, to commemorate the Coronation of King Charles III.*

AWARDS

of the British Commonwealth

In recent years many countries of the British Commonwealth have created their own individual systems of Honours and Awards. However, some British awards are still recognised within these systems. The medals and awards of these countries instituted prior to their own systems being introduced, are included in the main section of this book. In the following sections of the YEARBOOK we include the latest honours and awards of AUSTRALIA, CANADA, NEW ZEALAND and SOUTH AFRICA, together with their current Orders of Precedence encompassing their own and former British honours and awards.

"The Australian and New Zealand troops have indeed proved themselves worthy sons of the Empire."

GEORGE R.I.

AUSTRALIAN
Medals

Since 1975 Australia has instituted a number of Australian awards. Medals and decorations pertaining to Australia, instituted prior to 1975 will be found in chronological sequence within the main text of this book. The Australian system was inaugurated on February 14, 1975 the first steps to establishing its own honours and awards. In 1991 a range of awards to recognise gallantry and distinguished service was introduced to the Australian system to replace Imperial awards. The only award retained from the former Imperial system is the Victoria Cross, which was renamed Victoria Cross for Australia.

There are several key differences between the Australian awards and those of the Imperial system:

Awards are applied to all the Services, and the level of the award is not restricted by rank but is determined by the quality of the action or service.

The establishment of unit awards for gallantry and meritorious service, which were not previously available under the Imperial system.

The establishment of campaign medals that differentiate warlike and non-warlike service.

The establishment of retrospective campaign medals that differentiate warlike and non-warlike service, and in some cases for service that has been previously recognised by Imperial campaign medals.

These differences have made collecting Australian medals difficult to appreciate. However, with careful study, it can be an equally rewarding collecting subject. Further information on Australian gallantry and distinguished service awards can be found in Australians Awarded by Clive Johnson (2008) (2nd Edition published in 2014) and The National Honours & Awards of Australia by Michael Maton (1995). There is also a website for Australian Honours and Medals, maintained by the Honours, Symbols and Legal Policy Branch in Canberra, ACT: www.pmc.gov.au/government/its-honour. The site is constantly being updated and, apart from listing the Australian honours and awards, has a search facility to enable researchers to trace medal details of Australians back to 1901, the year of Federation. It is also possible to search for awards by localities, defined by postcodes. This is an essential tool for military historians, medal collectors and family historians.

THE ORDER OF PRECEDENCE IN AUSTRALIA (including British awards)

Victoria Cross (VC)
George Cross (GC)
Cross of Valour (CV)
Knight/Lady of the Garter
Knight/Lady of the Thistle
Knight/Dame Grand Cross of the Order of the Bath
Order of Merit
Knight/Dame of the Order of Australia (AK/AD)
Knight/Dame Grand Cross of the Order of St Michael
and St George
Knight/Dame Grand Cross of the Royal Victorian
Order
Knight/Dame Grand Cross of the Order of the British
Empire
Companion of the Order of Australia   (AC)
Companion of Honour
Knight/Dame Commander of the Order of the Bath
Knight/Dame Commander of the Order of St
Michael and St George
Knight/Dame Commander of the Royal Victorian
Order
Knight/Dame Commander of the Order of the
British Empire
Knight Bachelor
Officer of the Order of Australia (AO)
Companion of the Order of the Bath
Companion of the Order of St Michael and St
George
Commander of the Royal Victorian Order
Commander of the Order of the British Empire
Star of Gallantry (SG)
Star of Courage (SC)
Companion of the Distinguished Service Order
Distinguished Service Cross (DSC)
Member of the Order of Australia (AM)
Lieutenant of the Royal Victorian Order
Officer of the Order of the British Empire
Companion of the Imperial Service Order
Member of the Royal Victorian Order
Member of the Order of the British Empire
Conspicuous Service Cross (CSC)
Nursing Service Cross (NSC)
Royal Red Cross (1st Class)
Distinguished Service Cross
Military Cross
Distinguished Flying Cross
Air Force Cross
Royal Red Cross (2nd Class)
Medal for Gallantry (MG)
Bravery Medal (BM)
Distinguished Service Medal (DSM)
Public Service Medal (PSM)
Australian Police Medal (APM)
Australian Fire Service Medal (AFSM)
Ambulance Service Medal (ASM)
Emergency Services Medal (ESM)
Australian Corrections Medal (ACM)
Australian Intelligence Medal (AIM)
Medal of the Order of Australia (OAM)

Order of St John
Distinguished Conduct Medal
Conspicuous Gallantry Medal
Conspicuous Gallantry Medal (Flying)
George Medal
Conspicuous Service Medal (CSM)
Australian Antarctic Medal (AAM)
Queen's Police Medal for Gallantry
Queen's Fire Service Medal for Gallantry
Distinguished Service Medal
Military Medal
Distinguished Flying Medal
Air Force Medal
Sea Gallantry Medal
Queen's Gallantry Medal
Royal Victorian Medal
British Empire Medal
Queen's Police Medal for Distinguished Service
Queen's Fire Service Medal for Distinguished
Service
Commendation for Gallantry
Commendation for Brave Conduct
Queen's Commendation for Brave Conduct
Commendation for Distinguished Service
War Medals
Campaign Medals
Active Service Medals
Service Medals
Police Overseas Service Medal
Humanitarian Overseas Service Medal
National Emergency Medal
Civilian Service Medal 1939-1945
National Police Service Medal
Polar Medal
Imperial Service Medal
Coronation, Jubilee, Remembrance and
Commemorative Medals (in order of date receipt)
80th Anniversary Armistice Remembrance Medal
Australian Sports Medal
Centenary Medal
Defence Force Service Medal
Reserve Force Decoration (RFD)
Reserve Force Medal
Defence Long Service Medal
National Medal
Australian Defence Medal
Australian Cadet Forces Service Medal
Champion Shots Medal
Long Service Medals (Imperial)
Anniversary of National Service 1951-1972 Medal
Independence and Anniversary Medals (in order of
date of receipt)
Foreign Awards (in order of date of authorisation of
their acceptance and wearing).

A1. VICTORIA CROSS FOR AUSTRALIA

Instituted: 15 January 1991.
Ribbon: Crimson 38mm wide.
Metal: Bronze.
Size: 35mm at each axis.
Description: As per MYB 24 (UK VC)
Method of naming: The reverse of the suspension bar is engraved with the name, rank and ship, regiment or squadron of the recipient. The circular panel is engraved with date/s of the act for which the decoration was awarded.
Comments: *The Australian VC was established as part of the Australian System of Honours and awards on January 15, 1991. The Victoria Cross for Australia is identical to the original British VC. Recipients are entitled to the post nominal letters VC. Five have been awarded to date: the first to Trooper Mark Donaldson of the Australian SASR on 16 January 2009 for gallantry in Afghanistan in 2008; the second, awarded on 24 January 2011 to Corporal Benjamin Roberts-Smith, MG, of the Australian SASR for conspicuous gallantry in Afghanistan in 2010; the third, awarded to Corporal Daniel Keighran of Six Battalion, the Royal Australian Regiment for conspicuous gallantry in Afghanistan in 2010 and the fourth, awarded posthumously to Corporal Cameron Stewart Baird, MG, of the 2nd Commando Regiment who was killed during engagement with insurgents in southern Afghanistan in 2013. On August 12, 2020, Her Majesty the Queen approved a retrospective award to Ordinary Seaman Edward Sheean for his actions aboard HMAS* Armidale *in the Timor Sea on December 1, 1942. Sheean's VC was officially Gazetted on December 1, 2020.*

VALUE: —

A2. CROSS OF VALOUR

Instituted: 14 February 1975.
Ribbon: Magenta 38mm wide with a blood-red central band of 16mm.
Metal: 22 carat gold.
Size: 42mm.
Description: A straight-armed Greek cross with diminishing rays between the arms; surmounted by St Edward's crown and an integral suspension bar inscribed FOR VALOUR. The Cross is surmounted by the shield and crest from the Arms of the Commonwealth of Australia.
Method of naming: Recipient's full name pantographed in capital letters on the reverse of the bar. Topped by the Federation Star.
Comments: *Intended to replace the British civilian award of the George Cross. Five have been awarded to date: D. J. Tree (saved a child from electrocution); V. A. Boscoe (apprehension of armed robbers); A. Sparkes (rescuing a child from a flooded drain); R. T. Joyes and T. Britten (Bali Bombing). Recipients are entitled to the post nominal letters CV.*

VALUE: From £25,000 (Obviously value is dependent on the reason for the award and would attain upward of £30,000, especially in a group with other medals).

A3. ORDER OF AUSTRALIA

Instituted: 14 February 1975.
Ribbon: Royal blue bearing scattered gold mimosa blossoms of various sizes (General Division); similar, but with gold edges (Military Division)

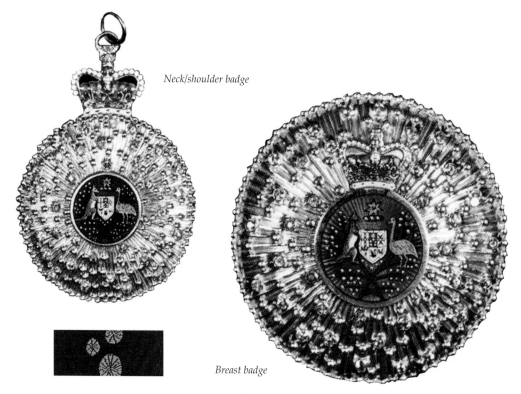

Neck/shoulder badge

Breast badge

KNIGHTS AND DAMES OF THE ORDER

Instituted: 24 May 1976.
Ribbon: Royal blue bearing scattered gold mimosa blossoms of various sizes (General Division); similar, but with gold edges (Military Division).
Metal: 18 carat gold.
Size: Neck badge: 60mm disk; Breast badge: 80mm disk; miniature badge 20mm disk; lapel badge 10mm diameter; ribbon bar 38mm.
Description: The insignia consists of a neck badge and breast badge.
Neck badge: Jewelled and having at its centre the arms of Australia enamelled in full colour on a blue background decorated with two branches of mimosa. The whole is surmounted by the St Edward Crown in full colour with a suspension ring at the top.
  In the case of a Dame there was the option of a neck badge or a shoulder badge, the latter being identical in every respect save the mounting. The neck badge is worn with a 16mm ribbon, while the shoulder badge of the Dame is worn with a 28mm ribbon.
Breast badge: The emblem of the Order is jewelled, and has the arms of Australia at the centre, surmounted by the St Edward Crown. The breast badge is worn on the left side of a coat or outer garment.
Miniature badge: worn with 16mm ribbon.
Lapel badge: for ordinary civilian wear.
Ladies' badge: mounted on a brooch bar.
Method of naming: Pantographed in the centre of the reverse of the medal.
Comments: *Knights and Dames are entitled to the prefix "Sir" or "Dame" and the use the post nominal letters AK or AD respectively. Between May 24, 1976, when the grade of Knights and Dames was introduced, and March 3, 1986, when these grades were abolished, a total of 12 Knights (including the Prince of Wales) and two Dames were created, excluding the Queen (Sovereign of the Order). On March 19, 2014, the grade of Knights and Dames was reinstated. A further three Knights (including His Royal Highness The Prince Philip, Duke of Edinburgh) and two Dames were created before the provision to appoint Knights and Dames was again removed on October 29, 2015.*

VALUE: From £12,000

Companion's badge.

COMPANION OF THE ORDER

Instituted: 14 February 1975.

Ribbon: Royal blue bearing scattered gold mimosa blossoms of various sizes (General Division); similar, but with gold edges (Military Division).

Metal: 18ct gold.

Size: 60mm diameter.

Description: The insignia consists of a gold neck badge or shoulder badge, similar to the Knight's badge but having at its centre a circlet of blue enamel edged in gold containing two sprigs of mimosa and inscribed AUSTRALIA at the foot. Miniature, lapel and brooch badges with jewelled centres identical to those of the Knights and Dames are also worn.

Neck badge: Worn with 16mm neck ribbon.

Shoulder badge: Worn with 38mm shoulder bow.

Method of naming: Pantographed in the centre of the reverse of the medal.

Comments: *Companions have the post nominal letters AC after their name. Awarded to civil and military for eminent achievement and merit of the highest degree in service to Australia or to humanity at large. Medals awarded through third party recommendation, which involves in depth information, references and research. Awards published in Australian Honours List on Australia Day, 26 January, and the Queen's Birthday. 594 (566 Civil and 28 Military) have been awarded to date.*

VALUE:	Civil	£2500–3500
	Military	**£3000–5000**
	Miniature	£120–140

OFFICER OF THE ORDER

Instituted: 14 February 1975.

Ribbon: Royal blue bearing scattered gold mimosa blossoms of various sizes (General Division); similar, but with gold edges (Military Division).

Metal: Gold plated silver.

Size: 55mm diameter.

Description: The insignia of the badge is similar to that of the Companion. The miniature, lapel badge and brooch badges have a blue enamel centre.

Method of naming: Pantographed in the centre of the reverse of the medal.

Comments: *Officers have the postnominal letters AO after their name. Awarded to civil and military for distinguished service at a high degree to Australia or to humanity. Medals awarded through third party recommendation, which involves in depth information, references and research. Awards published in Australian Honours List on Australia Day, January 26 and the Queen's Birthday. 3,359 (3,063 Civil and 296 Military) have been awarded to date. This award can also be awarded as "honorary" to non-Australians. Medals conferred are termed "Honorary AO".*

VALUE:	Civil	£1450–1600
	Military	**£1850–2500**
	Miniature	£110

Officer's badge.

MEMBER OF THE ORDER

The insignia is a badge consisting of the emblem of the Order, 45mm in diameter in silver-gilt but without the enamelled centre, although the miniature, lapel badge and brooch badges have a blue enamel centre. Members have the postnominal letters AM.

For further details of Members badge see no. A7.

This award, along with all other Australian awards can now be awarded as "honorary" to non-Australians. Medals conferred are termed "Honorary AC, Honorary AO", etc.

For the Medal of the Order of Australia see no. A18.

A4. STAR OF GALLANTRY

Instituted: 15 January 1991.

Ribbon: 32mm deep orange with chevrons of light orange, points upwards.

Metal: Silver gilt.

Size: 37mm.

Description: A seven pointed Federation Star surmounted by St Edward's Crown affixed to a suspension bar inscribed FOR GALLANTRY with (obverse) a smaller Federation Star 22mm across, surrounded by stylized flames representing action under fire; (reverse) central horizontal panel on a stepped background.

Method of naming: Full name pantographed on the reverse.

Comments: *Second and subsequent awards are denoted by a silver-gilt 34mm bar with the Federation Star at the centre. Recipients are entitled to the post nominal letters SG. The Star of Gallantry is awarded for acts of great heroism or conspicuous gallantry in action in circumstances of great peril. An amendment was made to include actions in operations in circumstances similar to armed combat or actual operations. The Star of Gallantry has been awarded eight times to date: Sergeant A from 4RAR (Commando) (2006); Lt Col Harry Smith (2008)(retrospective for his leadership and gallantry during the Battle of Long Tan in the Vietnam War in August 1966); Private S from 2nd Commando (2010) and Sergeant P for actions in Afghanistan (2011). On 13 June 2011, two special forces soldiers, identified only as Sergeant D and Private S, were awarded the Star of Gallantry in the 2011 Queen's Birthday Honours for "conspicuous gallantry in circumstances of great peril" while serving with the Special Operations Task Group. On 9 June 2014, a soldier identified as Private B was awarded the Star of Gallantry for service on operations in Afghanistan. The most recent award was announced on 17 July 2017 to the late Captain Raymond Allsopp, for conspicuous gallantry in action in Borneo on 1 July 1945, during World War II.*

VALUE: £25,000–30,000

A5. STAR OF COURAGE

Instituted: 14 February 1975.

Ribbon: Blood red 32mm with a magenta central band 16mm wide.

Metal: Sterling silver.

Size: 50mm.

Description: A seven-pointed, ribbed star surmounted by the shield and crest from the Arms of the Commonwealth of Australia and surmounted by a St Edward Crown affixed to a suspension bar inscribed FOR COURAGE.

Method of naming: Full name pantographed on reverse of bar.

Comments: *Subsequent awards are denoted by a silver bar bearing a replica of the star. Recipients are entitled to the post nominal letters SC. Awarded for acts of conspicuous courage in circumstances of great peril. Primarily a civilian award, but can be awarded to military personnel. The award can be made posthumously. 182 have been awarded to date.*

VALUE: **£2500–3500 (civil)**
           £9000–12,000 (military)

Miniature £55–85

A6. DISTINGUISHED SERVICE CROSS

Instituted: 15 January 1991.
Ribbon: Ochre-red flanked by silver-blue bands.
Metal: Nickel-silver.
Size: 41mm.
Description: (Obverse) a modified Maltese cross with a seven-pointed Federation Star at the centre and flames in the interstices. It is surmounted with a St Edward Crown affixed to a plain suspension bar. (Reverse) plain but for the horizontal panel giving details of the award.
Method of naming: Pantographed service number, initials and surname of recipient.
Clasps: Subsequent awards are denoted by nickel-silver bars with a replica of the Federation Star at the centre.
Comments: *Recipients are entitled to the post nominal letters DSC. 115 have been awarded to date, including eight first bars indicating a second award, and one second bar indicating a third award. This includes two retrospective award for an action in the Vietnam War.*

VALUE: £4500–6750

A7. MEMBER OF THE ORDER OF AUSTRALIA

Member's badge.

Instituted: 14 February 1975.
Ribbon: Royal blue bearing scattered gold mimosa blossoms of various sizes (General Division); similar, but with gold edges (Military Division).
Metal: Gold plated silver.
Size: 45mm diameter.
Description: The insignia is a badge consisting of the emblem of the Order, 45mm in diameter in silver-gilt but without the enamelled centre, although the miniature, lapel badge and brooch badges have a blue enamel centre. The badge is worn as a medal or as a shoulder badge by ladies in civilian dress.
Method of naming: Pantographed in the centre of the reverse of the medal.

Comments: *Members have the post nominal letters AM. Awarded to civil and military for service in a particular locality or field of activity to a particular group. Medals awarded through third party recommendation, which involves in depth information, references and research. Awards published in Australian Honours List on Australia Day, January 26 and the Queen's Birthday. 12,205 (10,896 Civil and 1,309 Military) have been awarded to date. This award can also be awarded as "honorary" to non-Australians. Medals conferred are termed "Honorary AM".*

VALUE:

Civil	**£450-650**
Military	**£800-1000**
Honorary	**£400–500**

Miniature £60–90

A8. CONSPICUOUS SERVICE CROSS

Instituted: 18 October 1989.
Ribbon: 32mm wide, with alternate diagonal stripes of bush green and sandy gold 6mm wide.
Metal: Nickel-silver.
Size: 38mm.
Description: A modified Maltese Cross with fluted rays between the arms. (Obverse) the constellation of the Southern Cross within laurel leaves, surmounted with a St Edward's Crown affixed to a plain suspension bar. (Reverse) a horizontal panel for details of the award.
Method of naming: Pantographed service number, initials and surname of recipient on reverse.
Clasps: Subsequent awards are denoted by nickel-silver bars with a replica of the cross flanked by laurel leaves at the centre.
Comments: *Recipients are entitled to the post nominal letters CSC. Awarded for outstanding devotion or outstanding achievement in the application of exceptional skills, by members of the Australian Defence Force. Can be awarded posthumously. 1,319 have been awarded to date, including 26 first bars indicating a second award.*

VALUE: £2500–3000   *Miniature*   £60–75

A9. NURSING SERVICE CROSS

Instituted: 18 October 1989.
Ribbon: 32mm red flanked by broad white stripes with yellow edges.
Metal: Silver, with enamel.
Size: 43mm.
Description: A stepped cross with straight arms, with a red enamelled plain cross at the centre and surmounted with the St Edward Crown affixed to a plain suspension bar. (Reverse) a horizontal panel superimposed on a pattern of fluted rays.
Method of naming: Pantographed service number, initials and surname of recipient.
Comments: *For members of the Nursing Service of the Army, RAN and RAAF. Recipients are entitled to the post nominal letters NSC. Awarded for outstanding devotion and competency in the performance of nursing duties in support of the armed forces. Presented by the Governor-General on recommendation from the Minister of Defence. Can be awarded posthumously. 29 have been awarded to date, including 1 second award bar. Nominations for the NSC have been discontinued until further notice. Nominations for other operational or non-operational awards, as appropriate, are being made instead.*

VALUE: £4200–6500   *Miniature*   £45–65

A10. MEDAL FOR GALLANTRY

Instituted: 15 January 1991.
Ribbon: 32mm light orange with chevrons of deep orange, points upwards.
Metal: Gold plated silver.
Size: 38mm.
Description: (Obverse) Federation Star surrounded by flames and surmounted by a St Edward Crown affixed to a suspension bar inscribed FOR GALLANTRY; (reverse) horizontal panel on a background of fluted rays.
Method of naming: Pantographed service number, initials and surname of recipient.
Comments: *Recipients are entitled to post nominal letters MG. Awarded to all ranks of the armed services for acts of gallantry in action in hazardous circumstances. Can be awarded posthumously. 76 have been awarded to date. This includes 28 awarded in recognition of service in the Vietnam War, arising from a review of the Vietnam End of War List conducted in 1998 and 1999, and later independent recognition review processes ; and one retrospective award each for World War I and World War II actions.*

VALUE: £9000–13,000   *Miniature* £60–75
    SAS/Special Forces from £14,000   End of Vietnam list: £4500–7500

A11. BRAVERY MEDAL

Instituted: 14 February 1975.
Ribbon: 32mm with 15 alternating stripes of blood-red and magenta.
Metal: Bronze.
Size: 38mm.
Description: (Obverse) the shield and crest from the Arms of the Commonwealth of Australia on a circular zigzag border; (reverse) zigzag pattern.
Method of naming:
Comments: *Recipients are entitled to post nominal letters BM. Awarded to civilians and members of the armed services in non-warlike conditions for acts of bravery in hazardous circumstances. Citations are simplified for Gazette details but a full account of the incident is recorded on the certificate which accompanies the award. Types of Gazette entries include "Saved child from burning car", "Saved woman from burning home" and "Saved a swimmer caught in a rip". 1,521 have been awarded to date, including two first bars indicating a second award.*

VALUE: £2200–3500   *Miniature* £65–75

A12. DISTINGUISHED SERVICE MEDAL

Instituted: 15 January 1991.
Ribbon: 32mm silver-blue with three stripes of red ochre.
Metal: Nickel-silver.
Size: 38mm.
Description: (Obverse) Federation Star with flames in the angles; (reverse) horizontal panel on a ground of fluted rays.
Method of naming:
Comments: *Recipients are entitled to the post nominal letters DSM. Awarded to all ranks of the Australian Defence Force for distinguished leadership in action. 220 have been awarded to date, including 11 first bars indicating a second award, and one second bar indicating a third award. This includes 24 awarded in recognition of service in the Vietnam War, arising from a review of the Vietnam End of War List conducted in 1998 and 1999, and later independent recognition review processes; and one retrospectiove award each for World War I and World War II actions.*

VALUE: £3500–4500   **End of Vietnam list: £21,000+**

A13. PUBLIC SERVICE MEDAL

Instituted: 18 October 1989.

Ribbon: 32mm with 12 alternating stripes of green and gold of varying widths, the widest green on the left and widest gold on the right.

Metal: Nickel-silver.

Size: 38mm.

Description: (Obverse) an inner circle showing four planetary gears spaced equidistant from a central sun gear, surrounded by the inscription PUBLIC SERVICE. An outer circle shows 36 upright human figures representing a wide range of professions and activities. (Reverse) a wreath of mimosa surrounding the text FOR OUTSTANDING SERVICE.

Comments: *Awarded for outstanding public services at Commonwealth, State or Local Government levels. The number of medals allocated to each state and territory is limited annually to 30 (Commonwealth), 22 (New South Wales), 17 (Victoria), 11 (Queensland), 6 each (Western Australia and South Australia), 3 each (Tasmania and the Australian Capital Territory) and 2 (Northern Territory). Recipients are entitled to the postnominal letters PSM. 2,829 have been awarded to date.*

VALUE: £275–385   *Miniature*   £45–60

A14. AUSTRALIAN POLICE MEDAL

Instituted: 3 March 1986.

Ribbon: 32mm white with a central broad dark blue stripe.

Metal: Nickel-silver.

Size: 38mm.

Description: (Obverse) effigy of Queen Elizabeth within a Federation Star, with an outer pattern of fluted rays; (reverse) wreath of golden wattle enclosing the inscription AUSTRALIAN POLICE MEDAL and FOR DISTINGUISHED SERVICE on a background of flames.

Method of naming: Pantographed name and rank on edge.

Comments: *Recipients are entitled to the post nominal letters APM. Awarded for distinguished service among members of the Australian Federal Police and the forces of the states and territories. Awards are limited annually to no more than one per thousand members in each force, plus one additional medal for the whole of Australia. 2,129 have been awarded to date.*

VALUE: £900–1000   *Miniature*   £50–65

A15. AUSTRALIAN FIRE SERVICE MEDAL

Instituted: 12 April 1988.

Ribbon: 32mm central gold band bearing an irregular pattern of red flames and flanked by green stripes.

Metal: Cupro-nickel.

Size: 38mm.

Description: (Obverse) effigy of Queen Elizabeth superimposed on a Federation Star composed of flames; (reverse) inscriptions AUSTRALIA FIRE SERVICE MEDAL and FOR DISTINGUISHED SERVICE on a background of flames.

Method of naming: Pantographed on edge.

Comments: *Recipients are entitled to the post nominal letters AFSM. Awarded for distinguished service among members of the fire services on the basis of one annually for every 1000 full-time and one for every 25,000 part-time or volunteer firemen. 1,679 have been awarded to date.*

VALUE: £650–800   *Miniature*   £45–55

A16. AMBULANCE SERVICE MEDAL

Instituted: 7 July 1999.**Ribbon:** Chevrons of white, red and silver.
Metal: Silver and bronze bi-metallic.
Size: 38mm.
Description: A circular medal featuring a Maltese Cross, with the seven-pointed Federation Star at the centre, surrounded by 24 dots symbolizing 24 hour service.
Method of naming: Pantographed on edge.
Comments: *Recipients are entitled to the post nominal letters ASM. Awarded for distinguished service by members of the civilian ambulance services. 501 have been awarded to date.*

VALUE: £650–775   *Miniature £45–55*

A17. EMERGENCY SERVICES MEDAL

Instituted: 7 July 1999.
Ribbon: Orange and white chequered pattern edged in blue.
Metal: Silver and bronze, bi-metallic.
Size: 38mm.
Description: (Obverse) a triangular device containing a seven-pointed Federation Star surrounded by 24 dots representing emergency services operating around the clock.
Method of naming: Pantographed.
Comments: *Recipients are entitled to the post nominal letters ESM. Awarded for outstanding duty by members of the emergency services, including state organizations and voluntary emergency services, and to persons who render distinguished service relating to emergency management, training or education. Each Australian emergency service organization may award one ESM for every 1000 full-time members each year and in addition one for every 5000 part-time, volunteer or auxiliary members. Recommendations are made by the responsible minister in the Commonwealth and each state and territory, so defined in the medals regulation to the Governor-General for approval. 594 have been awarded to date.*

VALUE: £450–665   *Miniature £45–55*

A17A. AUSTRALIAN CORRECTIONS MEDAL

Instituted: 19 June 2017.
Ribbon: 32mm with a central band of blue flanked by white and mustard green stripes.
Metal: Nickel-silver.
Size: 38mm.
Description: (Obverse) Federation Star bearing the scales of justice surrounded by a laurel of Australian wattle, surmounted a nickel-silver suspender bar bearing the word 'CORRECTIONS'; (reverse) a laurel of Australian wattle surrounding ace to engrave the name of the recipient.
Method of naming:
Comments: *Recipients are entitled to the post nominal letters ACM. Awarded for distinguished service as a correctional serv-member. Awards are limited annually to no more than one award for each 1000, or part of 1000, full-time equivalent rrectional service members of the State or Territory. 140 have been awarded to date.*

VALUE: *Miniature*

A17B. AUSTRALIAN INTELLIGENCE MEDAL

Instituted: 24 January 2020.
Ribbon: 32mm featuring a central band of yellow 5mm in width, flanked by white graduating to midnight blue then to black.
Metal: Nickel-silver in antique finish and bronze colouring, bi-metallic.
Size: 38mm.
Description: (Obverse) a raised Federation Star, the centre of the Federation Star has a bronze-coloured raised impression of a decagon, symbolising the ten agencies of the National Intelligence Community. The Federation Star is surrounded by an indented border, representing the twenty-four hour nature of intelligence. The central emblem is encircled by a contemporary laurel of a wattle which recalls the uniquely Australian nature of the award; (reverse) a border with the raised, polished words 'Australian Intelligence Medal' surrounding a space where the recipient's name may be engraved.
Method of naming:
Comments: *Awarded for distinguished service among members of Australia's national intelligence community. The number of awards in a calendar year must not exceed one award for each 1,000, or part of 1,000, full-time equivalent members of the national intelligence community; and one additional award. Awards are made on the recommendation of the Australian Intelligence Medal Committee. Recipients are not permitted to wear the medal, or use the post nominal letters AIM, without the written permission of the Committee. 16 have been awarded to date*

VALUE: *Miniature*

A18. MEDAL OF THE ORDER OF AUSTRALIA

Instituted: 24 May 1976.
Ribbon: Royal blue bearing scattered gold mimosa blossoms of various sizes (General Division); similar, but with gold edges (Military Division).
Metal: Gold plated silver.
Size: 40mm.
Description: (Obverse) emblem of the Order of Australia surmounted by St Edward Crown affixed to a plain suspension bar.
Method of naming: Pantographed in the centre of the reverse of the medal.
Comments: *Recipients are entitled to the post nominal letters OAM. Awarded to civil and military for service worthy of particular recognition. Medals awarded through third party recommendation, which involves in depth information, references and research. Awards published in Australian Honours List on Australia Day, 26 January, and the Queen's Birthday. 28,473 (27,097 Civil and 1,376 Military) have been awarded to date. This total now includes honorary awards—see A7 for explanation.*

VALUE: Civil £300–475;   Military £650–950   *Miniature £35–45*

A19. CONSPICUOUS SERVICE MEDAL

Instituted: 18 October 1989.
Ribbon: 32mm wide with alternating 3mm diagonal stripes of bush green and sandy-gold.
Metal: Nickel-silver.
Size: 38mm
Description: (Obverse) the Southern Cross encircled by laurel leaves; (reverse) a horizontal panel on a background of fluted rays.
Method of naming:
Clasps: Subsequent awards are denoted by nickel-silver bars with a replica of the medal at the centre.
Comments: *Recipients are entitled to the post nominal letters CSM. Awarded to all ranks of the Australian Defence Force for meritorious achievement or devotion to duty in non-warlike situations. Can be awarded posthumously. 1,502 have been awarded to date, including 9 second award bars.*

VALUE: £1000–1700   *Miniature £50–65*

457

A20. AUSTRALIAN ANTARCTIC MEDAL

Instituted: 2 June 1987.

Ribbon: 32mm snow-white moiré with 3mm edges in three shades of blue merging with the white.

Metal: Nickel-silver.

Size: 38mm.

Description: An octagonal medal surmounted by an ice crystal device affixed to a plain suspension bar. (Obverse) a global map of the Southern Hemisphere showing Australia and Antarctica, and the legend FOR OUTSTANDING SERVICE IN THE ANTARCTIC; (reverse) a polar explorer outside Sir Douglas Mawson's hut, leaning into a blizzard and wielding an ice-axe.

Method of Clasp: Clasps are inscribed with the years of service.

Comments: *Originally named the Antarctic Medal, this was renamed the Australian Antarctic Medal on 18 December 1997. Awarded to persons who have given outstanding service in connection with Australian Antarctic Expeditions, with at least 12 months service in Antarctica. The Governor-General makes awards of the medal on the recommendation of the Commonwealth Minister responsible for the Antarctic Territory. 107 have been awarded to date, including one clasp indicating a second award. Holders of this award are entitled to the post nominal AAM.*

VALUE: From £2500+   *Miniature £50–60*

A21. COMMENDATION FOR GALLANTRY

Instituted: 15 January 1991.

Ribbon: Plain orange 32mm wide and 90mm long.

Metal: Silver-gilt.

Size: 22mm.

Description: The insignia consists of a row of flames tapering towards the ends, with a seven-pointed Federation Star superimposed.

Method of naming: Pantographed on reverse of insignia with initials, surname and date.

Comments: *Awarded for acts of gallantry worthy of recognition considered to be of lesser magnitude than for the Victoria Cross, Star of Gallantry or Medal for Gallantry. 113 have been awarded to date. This includes 11 awarded in recognition of service in the Vietnam War, arising from a review of the Vietnam End of War conducted in 1998 and 1999, and later independent recognition review processes; and 43 claimed retrospective awards (out of 48 recommended) announced in March 2011 and August 2018 after reviews of Australian prisoners of war killed while escaping from Japanese forces during World War II. One award was made in 2011 to a member of the British SAS who served with Australian forces in Afghanistan.*

VALUE: From £3750. All must be with original citation   *Miniature £65–80*

A22. COMMENDATION FOR BRAVE CONDUCT

Instituted: 14 February 1975.
Ribbon: Blood-red 32mm wide and 90mm long.
Metal: Silver-gilt.
Size: 30mm.
Description: A sprig of mimosa, mounted diagonally near the foot of the ribbon.
Comments: *Awarded for acts of bravery worthy of recognition considered to be of lesser magnitude than for which the CV, SC, or BM would be awarded. Examples of brief citations include: "assisted in rescue of two children from burning house", "rescue during floods", "rescue of infant from crashed plane". Recipients are not entitled to post nominal letters. 2,309 have been awarded to date.*

VALUE: £600–1300
    Civil £500–600 Must be together with original citation certificate
    Mil   £900–1200 Must be together with original citation certificate

A23. COMMENDATION FOR DISTINGUISHED SERVICE

Instituted: 15 January 1991.
Ribbon: Ochre-red 32mm wide by 90mm long.
Metal: Nickel-silver.
Size: 22mm.
Description: A central Federation Star mounted on a row of flames tapering towards the end.
Comments: *Awarded for distinguished performance of duty in war-like operations. 523 have been awrded to date. This includes 36 awarded in recognition of service in the Vietnam War, arising from a review of the Vietnam End of War List conducted in 1998 and 1999 ; and one retrospective award for a World War II action. Recipients are not entitled to post nominal letters.*

VALUE: £300–500 Must be together with original citation
End of Vietnam list: £100-200 Must be together with original citation

A24. AUSTRALIAN ACTIVE SERVICE MEDAL 1945–1975

Instituted: 11 December 1997.
Ribbon: 32mm with central red stripe, flanked by narrow yellow stripes and broad stripes of pale blue, dark green and purple towards edge.
Metal: Nickel silver.
Size: 38mm.
Description: (Obverse) a seven-pointed Federation Star surrounded by the legend THE AUSTRALIAN ACTIVE SERVICE MEDAL 1945–1975; (reverse) a wreath of mimosa surrounding a plaque.
Method of naming: Pantographed in capital letters on the reverse in two lines: first line with service number, second line with initials and surname.
Clasps: Korea, Malaya, Malaysia, Thailand, Thai-Malay and Vietnam. Bars originally slide-on type but later struck as sew-on type.
Comments: *The medal is awarded to members of the Australian Defence Force who render service and who completed one day or one operational sortie within the duration of the prescribed operation. Awarded for war-like services in theatres of operation between the end of World War II and February 13, 1975. The medal is worn immediately after any World War II awards and before any other campaign medals. More than 74,000 have been issued to date.*

VALUE: £100–175   *Miniature £15–20*

A25. VIETNAM MEDAL

Instituted: 8 June 1968.

Ribbon: A broad central stripe of bright yellow surmounted by three thin red stripes and bordered by broader red stripes, with dark and light blue stripes at the edges representing the three services.

Metal: Silver.

Size: 36mm.

Description: (Obverse) the crowned bust of Queen Elizabeth II; (reverse) a naked male figure pushing apart two spheres representing different ideologies.

Method of naming: Impressed on edge with service number, initials and surname. RAAF medals can be engraved, and all issued since 1996 are pantographed.

Comments: *Awarded for 28 days in ships or craft on inland waters or off the coast of Vietnam; or for one day or more on the posted strength of a unit or formation on land; or for one operational sortie over Vietnam or Vietnam waters by aircrew posted on strength of unit; or for official visits either continuous or aggregate of 30 days between 1964 and 1972. There are some issues collectors should be aware of if collecting Vietnam medals. Some recipients have received two or more medals due to issuing errors and due to the availability of un-named specimens of this medal, examples have been seen on the market impressed with the details of prominent or desirable veterans (i.e. gallantry, KIA, SAS, etc.). Always ensure that medals come with a full complement of entitled medals, good provenance or from a reliable source.*

VALUE:

KIA, SAS or 6 RAR at Battle of Long Tan	£2500–3600
WIA	£500–950
Others	£250–400
Miniature	£20–30

A26. VIETNAM LOGISTIC AND SUPPORT MEDAL

Instituted: 24 February 1993.

Ribbon: A broad central stripe of yellow with three narrow red stripes superimposed. On the left are stripes of red and dark blue and on the right stripes of dark brown and light blue.

Metal: Nickel-silver.

Size: 36mm.

Description: (Obverse) crowned effigy of Queen Elizabeth and titles; (reverse) a naked male figure pushing apart two spheres representing different ideologies

Method of naming: Pantographed on edge in capital stylised letters.

Comments: *Awarded to personnel who served in the Vietnam War but who did not qualify for the Vietnam Medal. Recipients include QANTAS air crew who took troop flights to Saigon, civilian entertainers, war correspondents and many RAN personnel. More than 11,500 have been awarded to date. An amendment was made on January 18, 2013 to include members of the RAAF while posted or attached for service in the area of Ubon Air Base, Thailand and served there for one day's service or more during the period June 25, 1965 and ending August 31, 1968.*

VALUE: £250–435   *Miniature £15-20*

A27. AUSTRALIAN ACTIVE SERVICE MEDAL

Instituted: 13 September 1988.
Ribbon: 32mm with a central red stripe, flanked by stripes of silver-green, light-green, gold, dark green and brown.
Metal: Nickel-silver.
Size: 38mm.
Description: (Obverse) a seven-pointed Federation Star within a laurel wreath; (reverse) FOR ACTIVE SERVICE within a laurel wreath.
Method of naming: Pantographed on edge with service or PMKeys number, initials and surname.
Clasps: Balkans, Cambodia, East Timor, ICAT (International Coalition Against Terrorism), Iraq, Iraq 2003, Kuwait, Middle East, Namibia, Rwanda, Sierra Leone, Somalia, Vietnam 1975.
Comments: *Awarded for warlike service in various conflicts, denoted in each case by a campaign clasp. Since 1998 some campaigns that were determined to be non-warlike service have now been upgraded to warlike service. These include operations in Namibia, the Balkans, Cambodia, Rwanda and Sierra Leone. In 2009, the clasp 'IRAQ' was instituted to recognise Australian Defence Force members who participated in several British and United States operations enforcing Iraqi No-Fly-Zones from 1991 to 2003. In 2011, the clasp 'MIDDLE EAST' was instituted in place of the Australian Service Medal, to recognise Australian peacekeepers who served with the United Nations Truce Supervisory Organisation (UNTSO) on the Syria-Lebanon-Israel border on Operation Paladin from July 12 to August 14, 2006.*

VALUE:

Cambodia, Kuwait, Namibia, Somalia, Rwanda	£1000–1800
Iraq 2003, Iraq, ICAT	£420–650
East Timor	£300–450
Sierra Leone, Middle East	—
Vietnam 1975, Balkans	Rare

A28. INTERNATIONAL FORCE EAST TIMOR MEDAL

Instituted: 25 March 2000.
Ribbon: 32mm central thin red stripe, flanked by deep green, white and light blue.
Metal: Pewter coloured silver.
Size: 38mm.
Description: (Obverse) central raised stylised dove of peace over the island of Timor, surrounded by raised inscription INTERNATIONAL FORCE EAST TIMOR surmounted by Federation Star and plain suspension bar struck as one unit; (reverse) TOGETHER AS ONE FOR PEACE IN EAST TIMOR around outer circle, inner circle blank for naming.
Method of naming: Pantographed on reverse in capitals with service or PMKeyS number, initials and surname.
Comments: *The Prime Minister, John Howard, established a specific campaign medal for members of the Australian Defence Force in East Timor. Australia led the coalition of 17 nations and this is the first Australian medal issued to other countries. Awarded for 30 days service during the INTERFET stage of the conflict. 15,046 medals have been issued, including 8,696 to members of the ADF and 6,356 to members of foreign military establishments.*

VALUE: £600–1000   *Miniature £35–40*

A29. AFGHANISTAN MEDAL

Instituted: 30 September 2004.

Ribbon: 32mm central red line, flanked by purple, a wider khaki band, white and rimmed with light blue.

Metal: Nickel-silver plated.

Size: 37mm.

Description: (Obverse) Australian coat of arms edged by 80 pebbled circles; (reverse) is based on a portion of a snow-capped mountain range with a multi-rayed sun rising behind the mountain. The word AFGHANISTAN appears around the central device on the flan in English and in an Arabic script.

Method of naming: Pantographed around edge, with PMKeyS (identification number superseding service number in Australia), initials and surname in capital letters.

Comments: *Awarded to Australian Defence Force members who were assigned to Operation Slipper in Afghanistan, and support operations in surrounding area, from the beginning of operations on 11 October 2001 to 5 December 2002. From 6 December 2002 to 31 December 2008, and from 1 July 2014 to 31 December 2014, the Afghanistan Medal was awarded for service in Afghanistan only. From 1 January 2009 to 30 June 2014, eligibility for the medal was broadened to include service in areas outside of Afghanistan. The medal is also awarded to Australian Military Liaison Officers who served on Operations Palate and Palate II in support of the United Nations Assistance Mission in Afghanistan. Eligibility includes a specified period of 30 days service or, in the case of Air Force members, a qualifying number of sorties. For service in areas outside of Afghanistan from 1 July 2014, and for service in Afghanistan from 1 January 2015, the Afghanistan Medal has been replaced by the Australian Operational Service Medal—Greater Middle East Operation. Members awarded the Afghanistan Medal are also eligible for the clasp "ICAT" to the Australian Active Service Medal. Those who served within Afghanistan from 28 July 2006 may also be awarded the NATO Non-article 5 Medal with clasp "ISAF".*

VALUE:　　£950–1600　　　　　*Miniature £35–45*

A30. IRAQ MEDAL

Instituted: 30 September 2004.

Ribbon: 32mm with thin red central stripe, flanked by purple, with two wide bands of gold/yellow.

Metal: Nickel-silver.

Size: 38mm.

Description: (Obverse) Australian coat of arms edged by 80 pebbled circles; (reverse) a processional lion copied from a relief on the Gateway of the Temple of Ishtar in Babylon, the lion stands on a narrow plinth (for balance) and the inscription IRAQ appears below

Method of naming: Pantographed around edge, with PMKeyS (identification number superseding service number in Australia), initials and surname in capital letters.

Comments: *Awarded to Australian Defence Force personnel who have served at least 30 days in the defined area of operations. The Iraq Medal recognises service on ADF operations in and around Iraq from March 18, 2003, in Operations Falconer, Catalyst, Riverbank and Kruger.*

VALUE:　　£600–900　　　　　*Miniature £35–40*

A31. AUSTRALIAN SERVICE MEDAL 1945–75

Instituted: 22 February 1995.

Ribbon: 32mm central thin yellow stripe flanked by narrow green stripes flanked by khaki with wide navy blue stripe at left and pale blue at right.

Metal: Nickel-silver.

Size: 38mm.

Description: (Obverse) the arms of the Commonwealth of Australia surrounded by the legend THE AUSTRALIAN SERVICE MEDAL 1945 - 1975; (reverse) seven-pointed Federation Star and a plaque for recipient's details, surrounded by mimosa leaves.

Method of naming: Pantographed service number, initials and surname of recipient in capital letters.

Clasps: Berlin, FESR, Germany, Indonesia, Japan, Kashmir, Korea, Middle East, PNG, SE Asia, Special Ops, SW Pacific, Thailand, W New Guinea (multiple clasps are scarce). Originally slide on bars were issued, but proved frail and have been replaced by sew on bars.

Comments: *The medal is awarded to the members of the Australian Defence Force for 30 days service in a non-warlike theatre outside Australia between the end of WWII and February 13, 1975. The medal is worn after campaign awards and before long service and foreign awards. Can be issued as a single award, but is not issued without a clasp. 104,000 medals have been issued to date.*

VALUE:

Berlin, Germany, Indonesia, Kashmir, Middle East, WNG	£600–850
Special Ops, Thailand	£500–750
FESR, Japan, Korea, PNG, SW Pacific, SE Asia	£200–300

Miniature £35–40

A32. AUSTRALIAN SERVICE MEDAL

Instituted: 13 September 1988.

Ribbon: 32mm wide with a central brown stripe flanked by stripes of dark green, light green, gold and silver-green.

Metal: Nickel-silver.

Size: 38mm.

Description: (Obverse) a modified heraldic shield on a background of the lines of longitude, surmounted by St Edward Crown affixed to a plain suspension bar; (reverse) clusters of mimosa blossom, surrounding a Federation Star inscribed FOR SERVICE.

Method of naming: Service or PMKeyS number, initials and surname pantographed on rim. Also worthy of note, the early issues were hand engraved—primarily to RAN in crude rim to rim capitals.

Clasps: Balkans, Bougainville, Cambodia, CT/SR, East Timor, Ethiopia/Eritrea, Guatemala, Gulf, Haiti, Iran/Iraq, Iraq, Irian Jaya, Kashmir, Korea, Kuwait, Lebanon, Middle East, Mozambique, Peshawar, SE Asia, Sinai, Sierra Leone, Solomon Islands, Solomon Islands II, S. Pacific 2006, South Sudan, Special Ops, Sudan, Timor-Leste. Uganda and West Sahara.

Comments: *The medal is awarded to members of the Australian Defence Force for 30 days service with multi-national peace keeping forces within specified areas. In some instances particular clasps are awarded for lesser periods. Recipients may also be entitled to an appropriate medal issued by the United Nations or other international organisations such as the Multinational Force & Observers mission in the Sinai. The first strike of this medal produced a 7mm thick medal, crudely named. The ASM may be encountered with no service or PMKeyS number—this indicates award to a civilian.*

VALUE:

Guatemala (2), Gulf (22), Mozambique (40), Uganda (40), Irian Jaya, Ethiopia-Eritrea, West Sahara, Balkans, all considered rare clasps	£2000+
Iran-Iraq (120), Peshawar (190), Kashmir (188)	£1500+
East Timor, Timor-Leste, SE Asia, Solomon Islands and Solomon Islands II	£250–350
All others	£300–350

Miniature £35–45

For Australian Service Medal 1939–45 see Campaign Section, No. 190

A32R. AUSTRALIAN OPERATIONAL SERVICE MEDAL

Instituted: 22 May 2012.

Ribbons: Various (see Comments below) including Border Protection: equal stripes of dark blue, ochre and dark green; Greater Middle East Operation: a central black stripe, flanked by mid green and light blue stripes of equal width, edged with light sand stripes; Civilian: a central purple stripe, flanked by gold and green stripes; Special Operations: a central red stripe, flanked by back stripes of equal width; CT/SR (Counter Terrorism/Special Recovery): a central white stripe which is flanked by light blue, grey and charcoal stripes of equal width, flanked by black stripes that are three times the width of the other stripes.

Size: 38mm.

Description: (Obverse) a map of the world surrounded by attacking winds, surmounted by the Federation Star and surrounded by the words AUSTRALIAN OPERATIONAL SERVICE MEDAL, affixed to a plain suspension bar; (reverse) The words DEFENDING AUSTRALIA AND ITS NATIONAL INTERESTS, set within a ribbon surrounded by a wreath and surmounted by an hour glass.

Clasps: The Australian Operational Service Medal (Civilian) is issued with a clasp denoting the qualifying operations. Six clasps have been approved; East Timor, G.M.E. Ops (Greater Middle East Operation), ICAT (International Coalition Against Terrorism), Iraq 2003, Solomon Is II and Timor-Leste.

Method of naming: Military: PMKeyS number, initials and surname pantographed on rim. Civil: Full name pantographed on rim.

Comments: *The Australian Operational Service Medal (OSM) was established to provide recognition to Australian Defence Force personnel involved in declared operations or other service that the Chief of the Defence Force deems to be worthy of recognition and which are approved by the Governor-General. The OSM replaces the Australian Active Service Medal (MYB A27) and the Australian Service Medal (MYB A32) as the form of medallic recognition for future Australian Defence Force operations. Those operations currently recognised by the Australian Active Service Medal and the Australian Service Medal will continue to be recognised by those medals while the operations are active. For Australian Defence Force members the OSM will be awarded as a standard medal with a unique ribbon for each operation, similar to the practice in place for the United Nations Medal. Provision also exists for the award of an accumulated service device, in the form of an Arabic numeral of antique-silver finish eight millimetres high, to denote those who undertake multiple tours on a particular operation. The first service declared for the OSM comprises 11 border protection operations conducted since 1997. The OSM - Border Protection is awarded for a period of not less than an aggregate of 30 days service, or completion of 30 sorties from a unit assigned to a declared operation. In 2014, the OSM - Greater Middle East Operation was instituted to recognise Australian Defence Force members who serve for 30 days on Operations Manitou, Accordion and Okra from 1 July 2014, and on Operation Highroad in Afghanistan from 1 January 2015. An accumulated service device has been approved for the OSM - Greater Middle East Operation. The OSM – CT/SR recognises the service of Australian Defence Force personnel on counter terrorism and special recovery activities declared by the Chief of the Defence Force from November 1, 2020. The OSM (Civilian) may be awarded to Defence civilians who have been employed on Australian Defence Force operations since 2000 under the provisions of the Defence Force Discipline Act 1982. Eligible Defence civilians are issued the OSM (Civilian) with a clasp denoting the eligible operation. Further awards of the OSM (Civilian) are recognised with the issue of an additional clasp to the medal. Six clasps have been approved for the OSM (Civilian).*

Border Protection

Civilian Recognition

Greater Middle East Operation

Special Operations

Counter Terrorism / Special Recovery

VALUE: £350–525   *Miniature £30–35*

A32A. AUSTRALIAN GENERAL SERVICE MEDAL FOR KOREA

Instituted: 24 November 2009.
Ribbon: The ribbon is 32 mm wide with a central yellow stripe flanked by blue stripes and outer white stripes. The ribbon colours are representative of the colours used for the British Korea Medal and the United Nations Service Medal for Korea.
Metal: Antique coloured silver.
Size: 38mm.
Description: The suspender bar features a raised Federation Star. (Obverse) a raised map of South Korea which is superimposed over polar projection lines. The words 'AUSTRALIAN GENERAL SERVICE MEDAL KOREA' are inscribed on the inside of the medal rim with two Federation Stars included in the bottom left and right hand quadrants; (reverse) has the words 'POST ARMISTICE SERVICE 1953 – 1956' surrounded by a wreath of gum leaves and blossoms.
Method of naming: Service number, initials and surname pantographed on rim.
Comments: *The AGSM has been instituted to recognise former Defence Force personnel who completed 30 days participating in operations in South Korea, including any location 161km seaward from the coast of South Korea, during the post-armistice period from 28 July 1953 to 19 April 1956. The AGSM is worn immediately after the Australian Service Medal (ASM) 1945-1975.*

VALUE: £275–350   *Miniature* —

A33. RHODESIA MEDAL (see also no. 202)

Instituted: 1980.
Ribbon: Sky blue, with a narrow stripe of red, white and dark blue in the centre.
Metal: Rhodium-plated cupro-nickel.
Size: 36mm.
Description: (Obverse) the crowned bust of Queen Elizabeth II; (reverse) a sable antelope with the name of the medal and the year of issue.
Method of naming: unnamed (Police) or impressed capitals (RAF and armed forces); replacements show the word COPY or the letter R. Always named to Australians (impressed) as is the Zimbabwe Independence Medal.
Comments: *This medal was awarded to personnel serving in Rhodesia for 14 days between 1 December 1979 and 20 March 1980, pending the elections and the emergence of the independent Republic of Zimbabwe.Recipients also received the Zimbabwe Independence Medal. 152 medals have been awarded to Australians.*

VALUE: £2750–4000 to Australians   *Miniature* —

A34. POLICE OVERSEAS SERVICE MEDAL

Instituted: 25 April 1991.
Ribbon: 32mm with a chequerboard pattern of black and white squares.
Metal: Nickel-silver.
Size: 38mm.
Description: (Obverse) globe surmounted by a branch of wattle, the whole enclosed in a checkerboard pattern and surmounted by a St Edward's crown affixed to a plain suspension bar.
Method of naming: Pantographed in capital letters on reverse.
Clasps: Afghanistan, Bougainville, Cambodia, Cyprus, East Timor,

A34. POLICE OVERSEAS SERVICE MEDAL *continued*

Haiti, Mozambique, NPFPCP (Nauru Police Force Police Capacity Program, PNGAPP (Papua New Guinea Australia Policing Partnership), PNGECP (Papua New Guinea Enhanced Cooperation Program), RAMSI (Regional Assistance Mission to Solomon Islands), SIPDP (Solomon Islands Police Development Program, Solomon Islands, South Sudan, Sudan, Timor Leste, TLPDP (Timor Leste Police Development Program) and TPNG (Territory of Papua and New Guinea).

Comments: *Awarded to members of the Australian Federal Police and small contingents from Australian police forces serving as members of peace-keeping missions under the auspices of the United Nations in areas of conflict and unrest. Consequently recipients also receive the UN medal if their service exceeds 90 days. In 2013 two new clasps were approved. The clasp TPNG was approved for the service of Patrol Officers for the period 1 July 1949 to 30 November 1973, and the clasp Afghanistan was approved for service from 1 October 2007.*

VALUE: £400–650   *Miniature* —

A35. HUMANITARIAN OVERSEAS SERVICE MEDAL

Instituted: 16 April 1999.
Ribbon: Olive green with a central gold stripe.
Metal: Nickel-silver in matte pewter finish.
Size: 38mm.
Description: A circular medal (obverse) a stylized eucalyptus tree surrounded by a ring of gum nuts; (reverse) a ring of gum nuts.
Method of naming: Engraved in centre of reverse with recipient's name in full.
Clasps: Afghanistan, Balkans, British Columbia, British Columbia II, Cambodia, Christchurch, East Timor, Great Lakes (Africa), Haiti, Indian Ocean, Iraq, Japan, Mozambique, Nepal, Northern Iraq, Pakistan, Pakistan II, Philippines, Samoa, Somalia, South Sudan, South Vietnam (1975), Ukraine, Vanuatu and West Africa
Comments: *The medal is awarded to civilians and service personnel who have provided humanitarian service overseas and is believed to be the first medal of its kind. It is awarded to non-government employees or volunteers and may be awarded retrospectively. Following the devastating tsunami on December 26, 2004 the medal was for the first time awarded to members of the Australian Defence Force.*

VALUE: £600–750   *Miniature* —

A35A. NATIONAL EMERGENCY MEDAL

Instituted: 23 October 2011.
Ribbon: Olive green with seven central gold stripes.
Metal: Nickel-silver in matte pewter finish.
Size: 38mm.
Description: (Obverse) a stylised representation of Australia's national floral emblem, the wattle, surrounded by a ring of wattle flowers; (reverse) repeats the ring of flowering wattle and has the inscription FOR SERVICE TO OTHERS IN A NATIONAL EMERGENCY.
Clasps: BUSHFIRES 19-20, NTH QLD 2019, QLD 2010-11, TC DEBBIE 2017, VIC FIRES 09. CLASPS ARE SEW-ON TYPE.
Method of naming: Engraved in centre of reverse with recipient's name in full.
Comments: *The National Emergency Medal is awarded to members of identified organisations or individuals who render sustained service during specified dates in specified places in response to nationally-significant emergencies within Australia; or to other persons who render significant service in response to such emergencies that did not satisfy the criteria required to constitute sustained service. More than 15,000 medals have been awarded as at June 30, 2020.*

VALUE: £250–465   *Miniature* —

A36. CIVILIAN SERVICE MEDAL 1939–45

Instituted: 28 October 1994.
Ribbon: 32mm ochre-red central stripe flanked by narrow white stripes and broad stripes of opal green towards the edges.
Metal: Bronze.
Size: 38mm.
Description: (Obverse) the Southern Cross superimposed on a globe surrounded by mimosa blossoms; (reverse) horizontal panel for recipient's name, with 1939 above and 1945 below.
Method of naming: Pantographed on reverse.
Comments: *Awarded to civilians who had assisted Australia's war effort in a wide variety of organizations and who served under quasi-military conditions for at least 180 days. Can be awarded posthumously (to next-of kin). 7,083 have been awarded as at 30 June 2020.*

VALUE: £350–400   *Miniature £20–35*

A36A. NATIONAL POLICE SERVICE MEDAL

Instituted: 9 November 2010.
Ribbon: 32mm central panel of three stripes of dark blue, gold and dark blue. The central panel is flanked by white panels, each bisected by a thin red stripe.
Metal: Nickel-silver.
Size: 38mm.
Description: (Obverse) An unbroken band of Sillitoe Tartan surrounding the Federation Star with St Edward's Crown located on the suspender bar. (Reverse) Two sprays of golden wattle located immediately below a raised horizontal panel on which the recipient's details are engraved. The words 'FOR SERVICE AS AN AUSTRALIAN POLICE OFFICER' appear in capital letters around the inside of the outer rim.
Method of naming: Pantographed in centre of reverse with recipient's name in full.
Comments: *The National Police Service Medal recognises the special status that sworn police officers have because of their role protecting the community. It represents a police officer's past and future commitment to give ethical and diligent service.While a minimum of 15 years service is required to qualify for the National Police Service Medal, it does not represent a distinct period of service. A police officer must have been serving on or after 14 February 1975 in order to qualify for the National Police Service Medal. The National Police Service Medal can also be awarded to persons whose ability to complete the minimum qualifying period has been removed through death, injury or disability in the course of their police service. More than 43,000 have been awarded as at 30 June 2020.*

VALUE: £200–350   *Miniature*   —

A37. 80th ANNIVERSARY ARMISTICE REMEMBRANCE MEDAL

Instituted: 27 January 1999.
Ribbon: Red with a black central stripe and narrow black edges.
Metal: Silver.
Size: 36mm.
Description: (Obverse) a "Digger" in the uniform of World War I with the legend 80TH ANNIVERSARY ARMISTICE REMEMBRANCE MEDAL; (reverse) the words LEST WE FORGET in three lines within a wreath of ferns surmounted by a seven-pointed star. Fitted with a suspension bar with a Tudor crown on both sides.
Method of naming: Pantographed on rim.
Comments: *Awarded to all veterans of World War I who were still alive on November 11, 1998, the 80th anniversary of the Armistice. Only 71 were issued. Alec Campbell was the last surviving Gallipoli veteran for Australia and he passed away May 2002. The "Digger" on the obverse is a representation of the so-called "Bullecourt Digger", a statue that stands in a small memorial park in the French town of Bullecourt.*

VALUE: Rare

A38. AUSTRALIAN SPORTS MEDAL

Instituted: 23 December 1999.
Ribbon: Sand-coloured with four narrow dark green stripes, of varying widths, towards the right side.
Metal: Silver plated brass.
Size: 38mm.
Description: (Obverse) a stylized view of the Sydney Olympics Stadium with the Southern Cross constellation above; (reverse) the Olympic Stadium and the inscription "To commemorate Australian sporting achievement" and the date 2000. The reverse of awards made from 2021 under new regulations have the inscription "AUSTRALIAN SPORTS MEDAL".
Method of naming: Pantographed on the rim.
Comments: *This medal was initially only awarded during the year of the Sydney Olympic Games and was intended to reward Australian sporting achievement. Both current and former sports men and women have been honoured, as well as coaches, sports scientists, officials, team managers and even those who maintain playing fields and sporting facilities. More than 18,000 medals were issued. This medal was reintroduced in December 2020 to commemorate Australian sporting participation in certain multi-sport events, with eligibility backdated to the 2018 Invictus Games.*

VALUE: £100–150

A39. CENTENARY MEDAL

Instituted: 14 February 2001.
Ribbon: Deep blue with a central yellow stripe bearing three thin red stripes.
Metal: Silver.
Size: 36mm.
Description: (Obverse) a seven-pointed star with a central band inscribed CENTENARY OF FEDERATION 1901-2001.
Method of naming: Pantographed on reverse.
Comments: *The Centenary Medal was awarded to all Australian citizens who were born on or before December 31, 1901, and also acknowledges those who contributed to the success of Australia's first hundred years as a federal nation, recognising the many Australians who laid solid foundations for the nation's future. Each recipient also received a personalised warrant accompanying his or her medal. A total of 15,843 medals were issued. These included close to 1,400 medals awarded to Australian centenarians.*

VALUE: £200–350 (Centenarians)   £150–220 (Contribution to the nation)

A40. DEFENCE FORCE SERVICE MEDAL

Instituted: 20 April 1982.
Ribbon: 32mm azure blue with two gold stripes.
Metal: Cupro-nickel.
Size: 38mm.
Description: A circular chamfered medal (affectionately known as the Pizza cutter) bearing a Federation Star on which appears the Australian Defence Force emblem. The medal is surmounted by the St Edward Crown affixed to a plain suspension bar. (Reverse) inscription FOR EFFICIENT SERVICE IN THE PERMANENT FORCES.
Method of naming: Service number, initials and name engraved or pantographed on reverse. May occasionally be encountered with small ram's head engraved below naming, indicating an early issue from the Royal Australian Mint.
Clasps: Sew-on bar 4mm high decorated with sprigs of wattle, centered with EIIR cipher.
Comments: *The medal is granted for 15 years efficient remunerated service prior to 20 April 1999 and a person must have been serving on or after 14 February 1975. Clasps are awarded for each further period of 5 years efficient regular service. Reserve service and continuous full-time service in the Reserves does not qualify towards clasps for this medal. From 20 April 1999 the DFSM was replaced by the Defence Long Service Medal (DLSM).*

VALUE: £110–195 with no bar
　　add £30 for one confirmed bar, £45 (2), £85 (3), £250 (4)

A41. RESERVE FORCE DECORATION

Instituted: 20 April 1982.
Ribbon: 32mm azure blue with a broad central band of gold.
Metal: Cupro-nickel.
Size: Oval 44mm high and 36mm wide.
Description: (Obverse) the Australian Defence Force emblem on a radiating background within a wreath of wattle; (reverse) inscribed FOR EFFICIENT SERVICE IN THE RESERVE FORCES.
Clasps: Sew-on gilt bar 4mm high decorated with sprigs of wattle, centered with EIIR cipher. The bar/s awarded for further periods of five years service.
Method of naming: Service number, initials and name engraved or pantographed vertically (to fit medal design) on reverse.
Comments: *Awarded for a minimum of 15 years service as an officer in the Reserve Forces. This is the only long service medal for which recipients are entitled to post nominal letters—RFD. From 20 April 1999 the RFD was replaced by the Defence Long Service Medal. However, clasps to the RFD can still be issued in accordance with the eligibility criteria.*

VALUE:　£150–220
　　add £75 for one confirmed bar; £160 (2), £250 (3)

A42. RESERVE FORCE MEDAL

Instituted: 20 April 1982.
Ribbon: 32mm azure blue with narrow gold edges.
Metal: Cupro-nickel.
Size: Oval 44mm high and 36mm wide.
Description: (Obverse) insignia of the Australian Defence Force emblem on a rayed background; (reverse) inscription FOR EFFICIENT SERVICE IN THE RESERVE FORCES.
Method of naming: Service number, initials and name engraved or pantographed on reverse.
Clasps: Sew-on bar 4mm high decorated with sprigs of wattle, centred with EIIR cipher, awarded for further periods of five years service.
Comments: *Awarded to non-commissioned officers and other ranks of the Reserve Forces on completion of 15 years service. From 20 April 1999 the RFM was replaced by the Defence Long Service Medal. However, clasps to the RFM can still be issued in accordance with the eligibility criteria.*

VALUE: £175–250   *Miniature* —

A43. DEFENCE LONG SERVICE MEDAL

Instituted: 26 May 1998.
Ribbon: 32mm with central 10mm panel of seven narrow alternating stripes of azure blue and gold, flanked by 7mm broad azure stripes and 4mm gold edges.
Metal: Nickel-silver.
Size: 38mm.
Description: A circular medal surmounted with the St Edward Crown attached to the suspension bar. (Obverse) the Australian Defence Force emblem surrounded by two sprays of wattle leaves and blossom; (reverse) a central horizontal panel surrounded by the inscription FOR SERVICE IN THE AUSTRALIAN DEFENCE FORCE.
Method of naming: Pantographed on reverse.
Clasps: Sew-on bar 4mm high decorated with sprigs of wattle, centred with EIIR cipher, awarded for further periods of five years service.
Comments: *This medal is awarded on completion of 15 years service and supersedes the DFSM, the RFD and the RFM. This medal takes in service in both the regular and Reserve Forces, can accumulate across services and does not discriminate between rank levels.*

VALUE: £100–195   *Miniature* —
add £25 for one confirmed bar, £50 (2), £100 (3)

A44. NATIONAL MEDAL

Instituted: 14 February 1975.
Ribbon: 32mm with 15 alternating gold and blue stripes.
Metal: Bronze.
Size: 38mm.
Description: (Obverse) arms of the Commonwealth of Australia on a ground of mimosa blossom within a recessed circle. Incuse inscription round the edge THE NATIONAL MEDAL FOR SERVICE. (Reverse) plain.
Method of naming: Military (up to and including April 19, 1982) named on reverse in impressed, pantographed or engraved styles with service number, initials and surname.
Clasps: A bronze bar, 5mm high by 32mm wide, designed with 10 orbs framed in a border. The bar is awarded for additional 10 years service, and is sewn to the ribbon 10mm above the metal suspender.
Comments: *Awarded to members of the various uniformed services for long service and good conduct, being a minimum of 15 years in one service or an aggregate on 15 years in two or more services. The medal is also awarded to members of correctional services, emergency services, Royal Papua New Guinea Constabulary and Papua New Guinea service organisations (only for service before 1 December 1973), and certain approved Government organisations and approved voluntary rescue and life saving organisations.*

VALUE: £80–195 with no bars; add £25 for one bar confirmed and £100 for two.

A45. AUSTRALIAN CADET FORCES SERVICE MEDAL

Instituted: 15 December 1999.
Ribbon: 32mm stripes of blue and gold with three outer stripes navy / red / light blue.
Metal: Nickel plated bronze.
Size: 38mm.
Description: (Obverse) the emblem of the Australian Cadet Force surmounted with a St Edward's Crown; (reverse) The Federation Star overlaid by a rectangular panel for recipient details.
Method of naming: Pantographed on reverse.
Clasps: A clasp is awarded for each additional five years service.
Comments: *Awarded to officers and instructors of cadets, for efficient long service of 15 years, replacing the British Cadet Forces Medal that ceased to be issued in Australia in 1974.*

VALUE: £150–225   *Miniature* —

A46. AUSTRALIAN DEFENCE MEDAL

Instituted: 20 March 2006, revoking the original Letters Patent of 8 September 2005.
Ribbon: 32mm wide, deep red with two inner white stripes and two thin exterior stripes of black on the edge.
Metal: Nickel-silver.
Size: 38mm
Description: (Obverse) central coat of arms of Australia as Australia Service Medal 1939–45 (MYB 190), surrounded by the legend THE AUSTRALIAN DEFENCE MEDAL; (reverse) two sprigs of wattle around an imperial crown and the words FOR SERVICE. Suspended from a ring mount.
Method of naming: Pantographed on the edge with service number or PMKeyS number, initials and surname only.
Comments: *Awarded to Regular and Reserve Force members of the Australian Defence Force for four years service or completion of an initial term of enlistment, whichever is the lesser. May also be awarded to members who died in service, were medically discharged (based on individual circumstances) or who left the service due to a discriminatory Defence workplace policy. The minimum number of days service required of members of the Reserve Forces each year varies according to the member's branch of service and the era in which they served.*

VALUE: £90–135   *Miniature* —

A47. CHAMPION SHOTS MEDAL

Instituted: 13 September 1988.
Ribbon: 32mm central 8mm dark blue stripe flanked by 6mm red and 6mm light blue stripes representing the three forces.
Metal: Antiqued brass.
Size: 38mm.
Description: (Obverse) a eucalyptus wreathed vertical panel (indicating excellence) with the Southern Cross and two crossed 0.303 SMLE rifles; (reverse) plain.
Method of naming: Pantographed on the edge with service number or PMKeyS number, initials and surname only.
Clasps: show year(s) of award.
Comments: *This medal has replaced the Army Best Shot Medal (MYB334) and the Queen's Medal for Champion Shot of the Air Force (MYB336).Only three medals may be awarded annually, to the respective champions of the RAN, RAAF and Army. Notable multiple winners include Andrew Bellott and Peter Richards (four occasions each), and Brett Hartman and Andrew Munn (five occasions each). 80 awards have been made to date.*

VALUE: £1500+

A48. ANNIVERSARY OF NATIONAL SERVICE 1951–72 MEDAL

Instituted: 10 October 2001.

Ribbon: White with a central gold stripe flanked by thin royal blue stripes with bottle green, pale blue stripes and sand-coloured edges.

Metal: Bronze.

Size: 36mm.

Description: (Obverse) the emblem of the Australian Defence Force surrounded by the text ANNIVERSARY OF NATIONAL SERVICE 1951-1972; (reverse) the sun radiating towards the Southern Cross constellation with a cogwheel surround. The medal is surmounted by a St Edward Crown attached to a bar for suspension.

Method of naming: Pantographed on the edge with service number, initials and surname.

Comments: *All 325,800 National Servicemen, including the next-of-kin of the 187 who were killed on active service, are eligible for this medal. It was struck to publicly recognize all National Servicemen between 1951 and 1972 who served in the defence of Australia.*

VALUE: £150–220   *Miniature £20–35*

The Unit Citation for Gallantry, the Meritorious Unit Citation and the Group Bravery Citation (MYBA49–51) are not positioned in The Order of Wearing Australian Honours and Awards. There is a common misconception that the emblems of the awards are the actual awards. This is incorrect, the award is the signed citation certificate presented to the unit or group. The citation emblems are simply uniform dress or other clothing embellishments issued to signify that the wearer was serving with a unit or group that had been cited. For members of the uniformed services, the emblems are worn in accordance with dress rules of the particular Service concerned. Civilian personnel awarded the Group Bravery Citation should wear the insignia on the left lapel or breast. Should other honours or awards have been awarded, the Group Bravery Citation insignia should be worn centrally, approximately 10mm above. Citation valuations are based on official records accompanying a medal group.

A49. UNIT CITATION FOR GALLANTRY

Instituted: 15 January 1991.

Ribbon: Green encased in a silver-gilt rectangular frame with flame decoration. A seven-pointed Federation Star in silver-gilt is worn in the centre.

Size: 15mm by 32mm.

Comments: *This system was borrowed from the United States, many Australian formations and units receiving American unit citations during the Vietnam War. The citation is worn by all members of the unit receiving the citation for extraordinary gallantry in action, and appears on the right breast (Army and RAAF) or below the medal ribbons on the left breast (RAN). Army and RAAF members who join the unit at a later date wear the citation emblem without the Federation Star during the period of their service with the unit only. The Unit Citation for Gallantry has been awarded 6 times.*

The first Unit Citation for Gallantry was awarded to No. 1 Squadron of the SASR for gallantry in 13 major engagements in Iraq in 2003. The second to 4th Battalion, Royal Australian Regiment (now 2nd Commando) for gallantry in action in Afghanistan, from 25 August 2005 to 2 September 2006. The third Unit Citation for Gallantry was approved on 31 March 2010 to Delta Company, 6th Battalion, The Royal Australian Regiment (6RAR) for acts of extraordinary gallantry in action at the Battle of Long Tan in Vietnam on 18 August 1966. The fourth Unit Citation for Gallantry was approved on 22 March 2013 to HMAS Yarra for acts of extraordinary gallantry in action off Singapore on 5 February 1942 and in the Indian Ocean on 4 March 1942. Two further Unit Citations for Gallantry were approved in 2018, to Australian units that participated in the Battles of Fire Support Bases Coral and Balmoral, in Vietnam, from 12 May 1968 to 6 June 1968, and to the Royal Australian Navy Helicopter Flight Vietnam for service in Vietnam from October 1967 to June 1971.

VALUE: £350–685 with certificate

A50. MERITORIOUS UNIT CITATION

Instituted: 15 January 1991.
Ribbon: Gold encased in a rhodium-plated silver frame with flame decoration. A rhodium-plated silver Federation Star is mounted in the centre.
Size: 15mm by 32mm.
Comments: *Awarded to members of a unit for sustained outstanding service in warlike operations. 29 Meritorious Unit Citations have been awarded to date. Army and RAAF members who join the unit at a later date wear the citation emblem without the Federation Star during the period of their service with the unit only.*

VALUE: £275–395 with certificate

A51. GROUP BRAVERY CITATION

Instituted: 5 March 1990.
Description: Rhodium-plated rectangular insignia with bronze waratah blossom mounted in the centre.
Comments: *In addition to individual awards for bravery, a collective act of bravery by a group of persons in extraordinary circumstances may have their actions recognized by a Group Bravery Citation. 217 Group Bravery Citations (numbering more than 1,100 people) have been awarded to date.*

VALUE: £150–300 with certificate

A52. PINGAT JASA MALAYSIA

Instituted: 2005, first awards presented April 2006.
Ribbon: 35mm wide, central red stripe, flanked by dark blue and yellow.
Metal: Nickel-silver.
Size: 35mm, suspender bar 40mm.
Description: (Obverse) arms of the Republic of Malaysia with JASA MALAYSIA below; (reverse) map of Malaysia with P.J.M. below, attached to a scrolled suspension bar by two crossed fern fronds.
Method of naming: Pantographed on edge with service number, initials and surname.
Comments: *Awarded by the Government of Malaysia to members of the Australian Defence Force who were posted on the strength of a unit or formation and served in the prescribed operational area of Malaysia and Singapore in direct support of operations for 90 days or more, in Malaysia between August 31, 1957 and December 31, 1966 or Singapore between August 31, 1957 and August 9, 1965; or for 180 days outside the area but in support of operations for the first two dates. Now being issued in a case with a brass plate inserted into the lid with vote of thanks and gratitude from Malaysia. Worn in Australia as a foreign decoration. There are at least two different strikings of this medal and a number of minor differences have been noted.*

VALUE: £95–295 dependent on other service medals

State Awards

Each of the Australian States and Territories also have their own system of awards for Police, Ambulance, Fire, Prison and Emergency Services. These awards are covered fully in *Australians Awarded* published by Clive Johnson of CJ Medals in Queensland. Listed below is *a cross section* of awards to give some idea of the depth of this exciting, collectable field. Some States authorise the wearing of State Awards on the right hand side of the chest and in the reverse order, i.e. most important medal worn closest to the heart. As so few of these medals are available to the collector, it has been decided not to give valuations except where examples have been seen on the market.

Since the original introduction of this section we have been able to add many more medals but to preserve the integrity of the *Yearbook* it has been decided to maintain the original numbering for the original entries (i.e. A1 to A76) , but for the new ones we have devised a separate system listing each territory's medals with its initials as part of the prefix (i.e. A-NT, A-WA, A-T, etc., each territory numbered from 1 onwards). In this way we hope collectors will be able to catalogue their collections and add to it as more medals become listed.

A54. NEW SOUTH WALES CORRECTIVE SERVICE BRAVERY MEDAL

Instituted: 1989.
Ribbon: Dark blue with a broad crimson central stripe.
Metal: Silver-gilt.
Description: A cross pattée with radiations in the angles and surmounted by a St Edward's crown fitted to a ring for suspension. (Obverse) the arms of New South Wales within a circular band inscribed CORRECTIVE SERVICE N.S.W., with a scroll at the foot inscribed FOR BRAVERY; (reverse) plain.
Comments: *Awarded to prison officers for bravery*

VALUE: —

A55. NEW SOUTH WALES CORRECTIVE SERVICE EXEMPLARY CONDUCT CROSS

Instituted: 1989.
Ribbon: Navy blue with a broad gold central stripe.
Metal: Silver.
Description: An eight-pointed star with one point obscured by the crown, surmounted by a large St Edward's crown fitted to a suspension ring. (Obverse) the arms of New South Wales within a circular band inscribed CORRECTIVE SERVICE N.S.W., with a scroll at the foot inscribed EXEMPLARY CONDUCT; (reverse) plain.
Comments: *Awarded to prison officers for exemplary conduct.*

VALUE: —

A56. NEW SOUTH WALES CORRECTIVE SERVICE MERITORIOUS SERVICE MEDAL

Instituted: 1989.
Ribbon: Red with a broad central gold stripe.
Metal: Bronze.
Description: An elongated circle fitted with a suspension bar. (Obverse) the arms of New South Wales, with NSW CORRECTIVE SERVICE at the top and LONG SERVICE at the foot; (reverse) FOR TWENTY YEARS SERVICE in four lines within a wreath.
Clasps: A bronze clasp in the form of a five pointed star for 25 years and silver clasps for 30, 35 and 40 years service
Comments: *Awarded for 20 years service in the New South Wales prison service*

VALUE: —

A57. NEW SOUTH WALES CORRECTIVE SERVICE LONG SERVICE MEDAL

Instituted: 1989.
Ribbon: Navy blue with two silver stripes.
Metal: Bronze.
Size: 36mm.
Description: A circular medal fitted with a plain suspension bar. (Obverse) the crowned emblem of the Corrective Service with a wreath at the foot; (reverse) a laurel branch round the left side with the words FOR FIFTEEN YEARS SERVICE in four lines on the right.
Comments: *Awarded for 15 years service in the New South Wales Prison Service.*

VALUE: —

A58. COMMISSIONER'S VALOUR AWARD—NSW

Instituted: 1987.
Ribbon: Light blue with narrow white stripes towards the edges and dark blue edges.
Metal: Silver with enamelled centre.
Description: (Obverse) A cross pattée with a crowned and enamelled centerepiece bearing the insignia of the New South Wales Police Service within a wreath, inscribed NEW SOUTH WALES POLICE FOR BRAVERY.
Comments: *Awarded to police officers where an act of conspicuous merit involving exceptional bravery was in evidence. It is very sparingly awarded, only seven being awarded posthumously since it was instituted.*

VALUE: —

A59. COMMISSIONER'S COMMENDATION (COURAGE)—NSW

Instituted: 1970.
Ribbon: Light blue with a narrow central white stripe and narrow white edges.
Description: A bronze Nemesis device affixed directly to the ribbon.
Comments: *Awarded for outstanding courage in the line of duty. May be awarded posthumously. A bronze bar is awarded for additional acts. There is no restriction to the number of awards and about 90 are made annually.*

VALUE: —

A60. COMMISSIONER'S COMMENDATION(SERVICE)—NSW

Instituted: 1970.
Ribbon: Light blue with narrow white edges.
Description: A bronze Nemesis device affixed directly to the ribbon.
Comments: *Awarded to police officers for outstanding service. About ten commendations are awarded annually.*

VALUE: —

A60A. COMMISSIONER'S OLYMPIC COMMENDATION—NSW

Instituted: 2000.
Ribbon: Five equal stripes of light blue and dark blue.
Description: A bronze device of the Olympic rings affixed directly to the ribbon.
Comments: *Awarded to police officers who performed in an outstanding manner in the planning period leading up to and over the period of the Olympic games in 2000.*

VALUE: —

A60B. COMMISSIONER'S COMMUNITY SERVICE COMMENDATION—NSW

Instituted: 2002.
Ribbon: Narrow blue with narrow white edges
Description: A silver coloured Nemesis device affixed directly to the ribbon
Comments: *Awarded to sworn and unsworn salaried employees of the NSW Police Force who, as representatives of the Force raise significant funds for community causes or raise awareness of indigenous issues or volunteer in an unpaid capacity as a director in a police-related charity.*

VALUE: —

A61. COMMISSIONER'S UNIT CITATION— NSW

Instituted: 1994.

Description: A silver bar in the form of a wreath containing a light blue enamel star. For a subsequent award a star is added up to a maximum of three.

Comments: *Awarded to units, patrols, groups, squads and commands where outstanding service involving bravery or actions of obvious merit have been evident. The emblem is worn by each member of the unit, while the unit receives a framed citation for display. About five citations are awarded annually.*

VALUE: —

A61A. COMMISSIONER'S COMMUNITY SERVICE CITATION— NSW

Instituted: 1994.

Description: A silver bar in the form of a wreath containing a white insert. For a subsequent award a star is added.

Comments: *Awarded to sworn and unsworn salaried employees who, as representatives of the NSW Police Force, have demonstrated an outstanding level of service as a field officer, camp supervisor or fundraiser for a police-related charity, etc.*

VALUE: —

A61B. COMMISSIONER'S OLYMPIC CITATION— NSW

Instituted: 2000.

Description: A silver bar in the form of a wreath containing a white enamel insert with silver Olympic rings. Only one award can be conferred. .

Comments: *Awarded to officers who had significant involvement during the Olympic Games.*

VALUE: —

A61C. NEW SOUTH WALES POLICE SERVICE MEDAL

Instituted: 2002

Ribbon: Royal blue with two equal stripes of light blue.

Metal: Nickel-plated copper.

Description: (Obverse) St Edward's crown above the badge of the state of New South Wales and the Australian Wedgetail eagle carrying a scroll of Nemesis, with the words NSW POLICE MEDAL—DILIGENT AND ETHICAL SERVICE around.

Comments: *Awarded to police officers for diligent and ethical service of 10 years with the NSW Police. Clasps are awarded for each additional five years service. It can also be awarded for a member who dies in the line of duty with less than 10 years service. Pantographed on the reverse with the recipient's full name.*

VALUE: —

A62. QUEENSLAND PRISON SERVICE SUPERINTENDENT'S LONG SERVICE MEDAL

Instituted: Before 1988.
Ribbon: Dark blue with three narrow silver stripes.
Description: An eight-pointed Maltese Cross superimposed on a wreath surmounted by a St. Edward's crown attached to a ring for suspension from a rectangular bar inscribed MERITORIOUS SERVICE. The centre of the cross has the arms of Queensland.
Method of naming: The top of the ribbon has a brooch bar with the recipient's details engraved on the reverse.

VALUE: —

A63. QUEENSLAND PRISON SERVICE OFFICER'S LONG SERVICE MEDAL

Instituted: Before 1988.
Ribbon: Silver with two narrow dark blue stripes.
Description: A circular medal fitted with a loop for suspension via a ring attached to an ornamental rectangular bar. (Obverse) the crowned and wreathed insignia of the Queensland Prison Service with the inscription LONG AND MERITORIOUS SERVICE round the foot. The top of the ribbon has a brooch bar with the recipient's details engraved on the reverse.

VALUE: —

A64. QUEENSLAND POLICE SERVICE VALOUR AWARD

Instituted: 1993.
Ribbon: Maroon, light blue and dark blue in equal widths.
Metal: Silver.
Description: A Maltese Cross superimposed on a wreath, with an enamelled centerpiece featuring the St. Edward's crown within a wreath and surrounded by the inscription QUEENSLAND POLICE VALOUR AWARD.
Method of naming: Pantographed recipient details on reverse.
Clasps: In the event that an officer is awarded the Valour Award on a second occasion, the officer may be granted a silver bar.
Comments: *This award is rightfully seen as the premier award for bravery available to Queensland Police. An officer who performs an act of exceptional bravery in hazardous circumstances may be awarded the Queensland Police Service Valour Award. Including, but not restricted to "arrests of armed offenders", "hostage situation where police show sacrifice by leaving cover and drawing the offender's fire at close range","rescues in advanced fire situations", "rescues by trained personnel which required extreme sacrifice". This decoration is similar to the Queensland Police Award which was discontinued in the 1930s. May be awarded posthumously or to a person who has left the service.*

VALUE: £1200–1500

A64A. COMMISSIONER'S COMMENDATION FOR BRAVERY (QLD)

Instituted: —

Ribbon: 32mm riband alternating bands of maroon and Queensland Police Flag blue radiating inwards in decreasing widths from opposite sides with a traditional police blue coloured border.

Description: Maltese cross and crown, initially awarded with a clasp FOR BRAVERY, with subsequent awards signified by additional clasps or a rosette for the ribbon bar.

Method of naming: unnamed, but accompanied by attractive illuminated scroll.

Comments: *Awarded to an officer who performs an act of bravery in hazardous circumstances, beyond that which can be adequately recognized by a Commissioner's Certificate. Examples can include, but are not restricted to "arrests or attempted arrests of offenders in possession of firearms", "hostage situations where police intervene with considerable exposure to risk of injury", "intervention of suicidal situations", "rescues from advanced fire, floods, heavy seas, vehicles on fire, cliffs, bridges"*

VALUE: £195+ with scroll

A65. QUEENSLAND POLICE SERVICE MEDAL

Instituted: December 1998.

Ribbon: 32mm blue with broad central stripe of light blue and silver edges.

Metal: Silver.

Size: 36mm.

Description: (Obverse) the Queensland Police emblem with the inscription DILIGENT AND ETHICAL SERVICE round the circumference, surmounted by a St. Edward's crown; (reverse) QUEENSLAND POLICE SERVICE MEDAL round the circumference.

Method of naming: Name of recipient pantographed at centre of reverse.

Clasps: Awarded in five-year increments starting at 15 years service.

Comments: *Awarded to police officers after a minimum of 10 years service, but prospective candidates must demonstrate an unblemished record of diligence and ethical service. A ribbon bar with silver rosette(s) is worn on the day uniform.*

VALUE: £125–195

A65A. VICTORIA POLICE VALOUR AWARD (VA)

Instituted: December 1987.

Ribbon: Watered pale blue.

Metal: Silver and enamels.

Size: 38mm.

Description: A four armed cross with the upper arm surmounted by the Queen's crown and attached to a plain suspension bar by three small rings. (Obverse) cross enamelled in pale blue with a five pointed star on each arm surmounting a square shape made of five silver rays between each pair of arms. A central medallion with the words FOR BRAVERY in the centre and VICTORIA POLICE FORCE around the circumference completes the medal. The word "Force" was removed in 1987. (Reverse) plain

Method of naming: Full name of recipient and date of the act on reverse

Clasps: A silver bar with a central rose design is awarded for any subsequent act of courage deserving the medal.

(Old style, 1956–87)

VALUE: £1200–1500

A65B. 2010-2011 QUEENSLAND FLOOD AND CYCLONE CITATION

Instituted: 2011.

Size: 34mm.

Description: Maroon ribbon with four white vertical stripes representing the four emergency service agencies, surrounded by a bronze metallic frame. The cyclone symbols on both side of the citation represents the time-line of cyclonic events occurring between Cyclone Tasha in December 2010 and Cyclone Yasi in February 2011. The swirls on the top and bottom of the citation represents waves associated with mass flooding which occurred throughout many parts of Queensland.

Comments: *The group citation is issued to employees and volunteers of the Queensland Police Service (QPS) and the Queensland Department of Community Safety who performed duty on at least one shift at any time between 1 December 2010 and 28 February 2011. Duty performed may be in direct response to the flood and cyclone events or maintaining core business during this period. Group citations are not issued for any individual effort, but are issued to acknowledge the performance of a unit or organisation.*

Recipients of the citation receive the citation in a box set which also contains a miniature version of the citation which is worn with Mess Dress or equivalent wear at formal evening dinners or similar events. First awarded June 4, 2011.

VALUE: —

A66. A.C.T. COMMUNITY POLICING MEDAL

Instituted: 1988.

Ribbon: White with a thin central stripe and broad edges of dark blue, the central stripe flanked by two thin gold stripes.

Metal: Bronze.

Size: Upright oval 52 x 42mm.

Description: (Obverse) the arms of the Australian Capital Territory with the inscription A.C.T. COMMUNITY POLICING MEDAL round the top; (reverse) inscribed FOR DILIGENT SERVICE above a horizontal plaque, fitted with a straight suspension bar.

Method of naming: Name of recipient on reverse.

Clasps: Awarded for 20, 25 and 30 years service, but only one to be worn. A rosette showing the years served is worn on the ribbon.

Comments: *Awarded for service in the AFP ACT Community Policing, recognizing those who have dedicated 10 or more years diligent service by policing in the territory since December 6, 1988, the first day of self-government of the ACT. A ribbon bar with silver rosette(s) is worn on the day uniform.*

VALUE: £140–190

A66A. A.C.T. EMERGENCY MEDAL

Instituted: 2004.
Ribbon: 32mm, flame red with central yellow stripe bisected with a thin
blue stripe.
Metal: Bronze with antique finish.
Size: 38mm.
Description: (Obverse) a stylised flower symbolising the Canberra
Royal bluebell, surrounded by wind and flame; (reverse) inscribed
COURAGE/LEADERSHIP/TEAMWORK/PROFESSIONALISM/
INNOVATION/INTEGRITY.
Method of naming:
Clasp: 2003.
Comments: *Commissioned in March 2004 to recognise the efforts of those who*
worked tirelessly to preserve the community following the devastating bush
fires of January 2003. The medal is issued in a black case inscribed ACT
EMERGENCY MEDAL.

VALUE: £120–165

A66B. A.C.T. COMMUNITY PROTECTION MEDAL

Instituted: November 11, 2002
Ribbon: 32mm, scarlet with a central white stripe, two yellow and two blue
stripes each of 3mm.
Metal: Bronze.
Size: 36mm.
Description: (Obverse) The Coat of Arms of the Australian Capital
Territory. (Reverse) A design of eucalyptus leaves and seed pods. The
wording "For Distinguished Service" and a plinth originally for the
name of the recipient but now with the date of the award. The name
of the recipient is now engraved on the rim of the medal. A maximum
of five medals in total will be awarded by the A.C.T. Government each
year on Canberra Day (March 15).
Comments: *For sustained distinguished or outstanding service to the A.C.T.*
Community. One medal to a volunteer or employee of each of A.C.T.
Ambulance Service, A.C.T. Emergency Service or A.C.T. Emergency Services
Bureau. Also eligible are sworn or unsworn members of the Australian
Federal Police working within A.C.T. Community Policing. First presented on
Canberra Day 2003.

VALUE: —

A66C. NORTHERN TERRITORY POLICE SERVICE MEDAL

Instituted: 1998.

Ribbon: 32mm black, with a central red ochre stripe which is edged with narrow white stripes.

Metal: Bronze.

Size: 38mm.

Description: A circular medal with an edged band on the obverse circumference containing the words "NORTHERN TERRITORY POLICE SERVICE MEDAL". The central field shows the Northern Territory Police badge. (Reverse) left plain. The medal is surmounted by a round emblem showing crossed batons attached to a plain rectangular suspender.

Method of naming: Engraved to reverse.

Clasps: Bars to the medal are awarded for each consecutive 10- year period of service. The initial medal award has a plain rectangular edged bar with a central roundel depicting a stylised Sturt's Desert Rose Flower (the State floral emblem). Additional bars for 10-year increments show a small numeral (such as 10, 20, 30 etc) in the centre of the flower

Comments: *The Northern Territory Police Service Medal is recognition by the Administrator of the Northern Territory of members who have completed ten years continuous meritorious service in the Northern Territory Police Force. A bar may be awarded after each further 10-year period of service.*

10 Year Bar

30 Year Bar

VALUE: £150–225

A-NT1. NORTHERN TERRITORY POLICE VALOUR AWARD

Instituted: 1999.

Ribbon: 32mm red with three thin black stripes edged in white towards each edge.

Metal: Silver.

Size: 38mm.

Description: A circular medal with an edged band on the obverse circumference containing the words "NORTHERN TERRITORY POLICE VALOUR AWARD". The central field shows the Northern Territory Police badge. (Reverse) left plain. The medal is surmounted by a round emblem showing crossed batons attached to a plain rectangular suspender.

Method of naming: Engraved to reverse.

Clasps: Further acts of valour are recognised by the award of a rectangular bar with a raised edge containing the words "TO SERVE AND PROTECT".

Comments: *The Valour Medal is awarded by the Commissioner of Police to a member for displaying exceptional bravery in extremely perilous circumstances or who acts courageously and responsibly in the face of potential or actual danger to their life. A framed certificate is part of the award and the medal and any bar are to be worn as an unofficial honour. This award may be made posthumously and may be awarded to a member who has left the Police Force. Where an officer, who has previously been granted the Valour Award, performs an act of exceptional bravery in hazardous circumstances, that officer will be awarded a silver bar to the Valour Award.*

VALUE: —

A-NT2. NORTHERN TERRITORY POLICE COMMISSIONERS OUTSTANDING LEADERSHIP MEDAL

Instituted: 2005.

Ribbon: 32mm, white with two chequerboard bands of alternating black and white squares towards each edge, a central double line in brown and a thin white stripe at each edge.

Metal: Bronze.

Description: A circular medal with the obverse showing the raised badge of the NT Police Force in the centre, and the words "OUTSTANDING" and "LEADERSHIP" at the top and bottom circumference respectively. The medal is surmounted by a roundel containing two crossed batons, cast as part of the flat rectangular suspender. (Reverse): Left plain.

Method of naming: Engraved to the reverse.

Clasps: No clasps are awarded for this medal.

Comments: *Awarded to members of the force who demonstrate outstanding leadership and dedication to duty. The decision to award the medal rests with the Commissioner of Police.*

VALUE: —

A-NT3. NORTHERN TERRITORY TRI-SERVICE MEDAL

Lapel Badge

Instituted: 2006.

Ribbon: 32mm, white with a red central stripe flanked by narrow black stripes.

Metal: Bronze with applied toning.

Size: 38mm.

Description: The obverse of this circular medal has the words "NORTHERN TERRITORY POLICE, FIRE AND EMERGENCY SERVICES" around its circumference, while the central field has the Police badge at the top, the Emergency Services badge at the lower left and the Fire Service badge at lower right (as viewed). The medal is surmounted by a small circular connection to the plain rectangular suspender. That circular connection shows a stylised representation of the Sturt Desert Rose flower, the State's floral emblem. (Reverse) left plain.

Method of naming: Engraved to the reverse.

Clasps: Bars to the medal are awarded for each consecutive 5-year period of service. The initial medal award has a plain rectangular edged bar with a central roundel. Additional bars for 5-year increments show a small numeral (such as 15, 20, 25, 30 etc) in the centre of the roundel.

Comments: *To recognise and acknowledge unsworn personnel within the Northern Territory Police, Fire and Emergency Services who have completed ten years continuous meritorious service. A clasp may be awarded for each further five-year period of meritorious service. A similarly designed lapel button is awarded for wear out of uniform. The years of service it represents are shown in a small exergue at the bottom of the Badge.*

VALUE: —

A-NT4. NORTHERN TERRITORY FIRE & RESCUE SERVICE MEDAL

Instituted: 2006.

Ribbon: 32mm red, with a red ochre central stripe flanked with narrow white stripes, in turn flanked by 6mm black stripes.

Metal: Bronze with applied toning.

Size: 38mm.

Description: The obverse of this circular medal shows the impressed badge of the Northern Territory Fire Service. It is surmounted by crossed fire axes connected to a plain rectangular suspender. The background sections of the obverse are recessed below the badge images and have a metallic dull green overlay which accentuates the bronze colour of the images. (Reverse) left plain.

Method of naming: Engraved to the reverse.

Clasps: Bars to the medal are awarded for each consecutive 10-year period of service. The initial medal award has a plain rectangular edged bar with a central roundel. Additional bars for 10-year increments show a small numeral (such as 10, 20, 30 etc) in the centre of the roundel.

Comments: *To be eligible for the Northern Territory Fire and Rescue Service Medal and Award, a member must have completed a period of ten years continuous meritorious service as a NTFRS member. Members may be awarded a clasp for each additional 10-year period of meritorious service (i.e. 20 years, 30 years and 40 years). NTFRS auxiliaries and volunteers who are not paid employees are eligible for the Service Medal and Award after 10 years cumulative service. The Bar is mounted as follows: Full size medal—12 mm above the ribbon slot; Miniature medal—6mm above the ribbon slot.*

VALUE: —

A-NT5. BUSHFIRES NORTHERN TERRITORY VOLUNTEER LONG & MERITORIOUS SERVICE MEDAL

Instituted: 2006.

Ribbon: 32mm, white with two chequerboard bands of alternating red and white squares towards each edge, a central double line in green and a thin white stripe at each edge.

Metal: Bronze with applied toning.

Description: A circular medal with the obverse depicting a raised circle at the centre, containing the stylised image of the State flower, Sturt's Desert Rose overlaid with the rising flames logo and words "BUSHFIRES NT". A thin band with raised edges surrounds the inner circle, and contains the words "PROTECT LIFE, PROPERTY & ENVIRONMENT FROM THE THREAT OF WILDFIRE". Four small images of firefighting equipment protrude from the outer band at the 10, 2, 5 and 7o'clock positions. The medal is surmounted by a small round connector which contains the stylised image of the State flower, cast as part of the plain rectangular suspender. (Reverse): Left plain.

Method of naming: Engraved to the reverse.

Clasps: No clasps are issued for this medal.

Comments: *Awarded to active members of a Northern Territory Volunteer Bushfire Brigade (or Brigades) after 10 years' service. Active participation in the Brigade must include;*

a) operational firefighting, including fire management, hazard reduction, backburning, incident management and operational support,

b) provision of constitutional support to the Brigade(s) through ongoing participation in the committee and its formal functions,

c) general logistical support of the Brigade(s) through fundraising, provision of welfare, advocacy or promotion, on a regular basis for a minimum of 10 years.

Membership of a Brigade in and of itself is not qualification for the Medal. The volunteer must demonstrate and have verified by the Captain that they have been regular and active members of the Brigade and that their role in the Brigade has been meritorious.

The Medal shall not be awarded to a volunteer who has brought a Brigade, The Bushfires Council or Bushfires NT into disrepute.

VALUE: —

A-NT6. NORTHERN TERRITORY EMERGENCY SERVICES VOLUNTEER SERVICE MEDAL

Instituted: 2006.

Ribbon: 32mm, ochre red with 5 chequerboard bands of alternating ochre red and black squares, and a white stripe at each edge in turn bisected by a thin ochre red stripe.

Metal: Bronze with an applied aged-silver appearance.

Description: A circular medal with the obverse showing the raised badge of the NT Emergency Service in the central field, surrounded on the circumference by the words "NORTHERN TERRITORY EMERGENCY SERVICE VOLUNTEER SERVICE MEDAL". The medal is surmounted by a roundel portraying the shape of the State's floral emblem, Sturt's Desert Rose, which cast in one piece to the plain rectangular suspender. (Reverse): Left plain.

Method of naming: Engraved to the reverse.

Clasps: No clasps issued.

Comments: *To recognise NTES volunteers who have completed in excess of five years or more of meritorious service. Like most Australian States, Northern Territory fire and emergency services are largely provided by volunteers. Without these dedicated volunteers those services would not exist in small and remote communities.*

VALUE: —

A-WA1. WESTERN AUSTRALIA POLICE DIAMOND JUBILEE LONG SERVICE MEDAL

Instituted: 1897.

Ribbon: Assumed 32mm (1¼ inches) dark blue.

Metal: Gold (no hallmarks seen so possibly plated). A silver version was also issued, believed identical in form.

Size: Approximately 60mm long, 30mm wide.

Description: Oval shaped gold medal with the obverse central field bearing the left-facing veiled bust of Queen Victoria. Surmounted by the Victoria Crown which in turn connects to an ornate rectangular suspender with raised edges containing laurel leaves arranged to the left and right of a small central roundel. A plain brooch pin with an embossed line around the edge suspends the ribbon. The obverse circumference has the words "HER MAJESTY QUEEN VICTORIA'S RECORD REIGN" within a recessed band, and the inscription "1837-TO-1897" in the scrolled exergue at the bottom of the oval disc. (Reverse) The reverse is in the same style but has the name of the recipient in engraved letters inside the edge band. The central field contains the words "LONG SERVICE MEDAL" above the words "POLICE WESTERN AUSTRALIA" in the centre. The exergue has the date "JUNE 29th 1897". Method of naming: Engraved (possibly chisel or machine) letters within the reverse edge band.

Clasps: None known.

Comments: *This medal was specially struck by the firm A.W. Dobie & Company of Perth, W.A. to mark the occasion of Queen Victoria's Diamond Jubilee. It was decided that each member of the Police Force of long service and good character should receive a commemorative medal of either gold or silver, according to their rank. Sergeants and below received silver (14 issued) while gold (10 issued) was awarded to Sub-Inspectors and above, including one to a civilian, a Chief Clerk & Accountant with the Service. Of the ten gold medals issued, only two have been sighted in the market, namely that issued to Inspector E. G. Back and the one illustrated to Sub-Inspector William C. Lawrence. He became a Superintendent, second in command of the Western Australia Police Force and was born at Bunbury on June 4, 1848. In July 1871 Mr Lawrence joined the force and the records of his official career in the departmental books are without any black mark against him during the whole of his 30 years of service. Three years after he joined the force Constable Lawrence was promoted to the position of lance-corporal, a rank since abolished. In 1875 he became first-class constable, in 1879 corporal, in 1882 sergeant, in 1884 acting sub-inspector of the Perth District and detective department. In 1893 Mr Lawrence became inspector and in 1900 he reached the highest rank in the service outside the position of Commissioner—that of Superintendent. Mr Lawrence retired at the age of 64 in 1912.*

VALUE: Gold Extremely rare

Silver Rare

A-WA2. WESTERN AUSTRALIA POLICE CROSS FOR BRAVERY

Instituted: 1998.

Ribbon: 32 mm Royal blue with an 8mm gold stripe at each edge which in turn is bisected by a thin black central stripe.

Metal: Sterling silver.

Size: 38mm.

Description: Two versions of the Cross have been issued. The first comprises a plain cross with a raised panel along the horizontal arms bearing the words "FOR BRAVERY". A raised enamelled St Edward's crown is positioned at the top of the upper cross arm and a raised enamelled black swan (the State of Western Australia emblem) is at the bottom of the lower cross arm. The medal is linked by a small ring to a plain rectangular suspender with the embossed words "WESTERN AUSTRALIAN POLICE FORCE". (Reverse) Left plain. The second version is a plain cross with the arms terminating in very slight finials. The obverse edges of the cross are slightly raised and the field inside the raised edge is filled with dark blue enamel. The cross has the Western Australia Police badge at its centre, with the words "FOR" and "BRAVERY" on the horizontal arms on each side of the badge. The cross is suspended from the ribbon by a small ring connected to a rectangular suspender with rounded corners, bearing the impressed blue-enamelled words 'WESTERN AUSTRALIA -POLICE FORCE' in two lines and with a small stylised blue-enamelled laurel spray on each side of the words. (Reverse) Plain with the recipient's details shown across the horizontal arms.

Method of naming: Pantograph engraved Roman capitals showing the recipient's full name, regimental number and the date of the incident which led to the award.

Clasps: Subsequent acts of bravery are recognised by the award of a bar to the cross.Image/details required.

Comments: *Awarded to Western Australia Police Force personnel for an act of most conspicuous courage whereby the person placed themselves at peril and risk of significant personal injury or death. In 2012 a revised design was implemented. The reason for the change is given (anecdotally) as the first version, being polished Sterling silver, was prone to rapid tarnishing and damage from wear. The second version, although still Sterling silver, is protected to some extent by the enamel on the obverse.*

VALUE: Very rare

A-WA3. WESTERN AUSTRALIA POLICE STAR

WESTERN AUSTRALIA POLICE
FORCE STAR

Instituted: 2017 (second version).

Ribbon: 32mm Royal blue with a central white stripe, and a thin red stripe towards each edge.

Metal: Cupro-nickel with an "antique" finish.

Size: 38mm

Description: Two versions of this award exist. The first was a circular medal surmounted with St Edward's Crown. The obverse displays the Western Australia Coat of Arms within a five pointed star, surrounded by an edged band containing the words "WESTERN AUSTRALIA POLICE STAR". The medal is cast in one piece with the plain rectangular suspender. It was issued in about 1998 at the same time as the Victoria Police Service issued a medal for an identical purpose. Western Australia closely followed the Victorian design. The second version came about to better differentiate the WA medal from other States. It has the same ribbon and metal but is a five-pointed star with the Coat of Arms of the State in the circular central field. It is cast in one piece with the flat rectangular suspender which has the bottom edges sloping up from the star. The suspender has the impressed words "WESTERN AUSTRALIA POLICE- FORCE STAR" in two lines. (Reverse) The blank reverse is engraved at its centre with the recipient's initials, surname and police regimental number.

Method of naming: Pantograph engraved.

Clasps: *No clasps are issued for this medal. Comments: An unknown number of the first version of the medal were issued prior to implementation of the second version in 2017. The first presentation of the second version was made to Constable Ryan Marron on May 26, 2017, by the Commissioner. Constable Marron had been left severely disabled after contracting a mosquito-borne virus while stationed in the State's north-west. On the August 4,2017, 78 Police Stars were awarded to the families of deceased officers, and several serving and retired officers who had sustained a permanent injury or illness as a result of their service. The earliest officer to be recognised was Constable Patrick Hackett who was murdered in 1884. His descendants received the award.*

VALUE: Rare.

A-WA4. WESTERN AUSTRALIA POLICE COMMISSIONER'S MEDAL FOR EXCELLENCE

Instituted: 2004.

Ribbon: 32mm red with a central yellow stripe and a narrow green and yellow stripe to each side.

Metal: Copper-base metal alloy with "antiqued" finish.

Size: 38mm.

Description: A circular medal surmounted with St Edward's Crown. The obverse displays the Western Australia Police badge surrounded by an edged band containing the words "COMMISSIONER'S MEDAL FOR EXCELLENCE". The medal is cast in one piece with the plain rectangular suspender. (Reverse) The blank reverse is engraved at its centre with the recipient's initials, surname and police regimental number.

Method of naming: Pantograph engraved.

Clasps: No clasps are issued for this medal.

Comments: *The medal was established to recognise Western Australia Police members who have consistently contributed to the achievement of the goals and objectives of the Western Australia Police. Only six medals can be awarded each year. A certificate detailing the nature of the service performed to earn the medal is also issued. A lapel badge is also issued, for wear by civilian staff and sworn staff in plain clothes.*

VALUE: Rare

A-WA5. WESTERN AUSTRALIA POLICE MEDAL

Instituted: 2001.

Ribbon: 32mm blue with a central white stripe, and a thin white stripe towards each edge. The ribbon (only) is shared with the South Australia, Tasmania and Victoria Police medals issued with very similar criteria

Metal: Cupro-nickel.

Size: 38mm

Description: A circular medal surmounted with St Edward's Crown attached to a plain rectangular suspender. The medal and suspender are cast in one piece. The obverse displays the Coat of Arms of the State of Western Australia surrounded by the words "WESTERN AUSTRALIA POLICE - DILIGENT AND ETHICAL SERVICE" around the circumference. (Reverse) The blank reverse is engraved at its centre with the recipient's initials, surname and police regimental number.

Method of naming: Pantograph engraved.

Clasps: Additional bars to the medal and clasps to the ribbon bar are awarded in 5-year increments.

Comments: *The medal is issued to sworn police officers after 10 years of ethical and diligent service. Medal and ribbon bar clasps are quite varied in appearance as below:*

- *15 years—a single silver 7-pointed star*
- *20 years—two silver stars as above*
- *25 years—a gold star as above*
- *30 years—a silver wattle leaf*
- *35 years—a gold wattle leaf*
- *40 years—crossed gold wattle leaves with a roundel bearing the number 40;*
- *45 years—as above but with numeral 45*
- *A similar clasp is issued for "50 years" service and a few have been issued.*
- *A lapel badge is issued for civilian staff or plain clothes wear.*

VALUE: £170–265

Likely to be significantly higher with ascending clasps. Rarely seen in the market. Good quality reproductions/copies abound.

A-WA6. WESTERN AUSTRALIA POLICE OVERSEAS SERVICE MEDAL

Instituted: —

Ribbon: 32mm, in five bands of chequerboard pattern similar the national Police Overseas Service Medal (MYB A34) but in police blue and white rather than black and white, and with a very thin green/blue/green stripe at each edge.

Metal: Cupro-nickel with an applied aged finish.

Size: 38mm

Description: This circular medal is surmounted with the St Edward's crown attached to a rectangular plain suspender. The obverse depicts a circular globe of the earth with lines of latitude and longitude, centred on Australia. The globe is flanked by a laurel wreath with the tips of a five-pointed star showing. A scrolled panel at the top of the globe displays the words "WA POLICE" and another at the bottom of the globe shows "OVERSEAS SERVICE". (Reverse) The blank reverse is engraved at its centre with the recipient's initials, surname and police regimental number if applicable.

Method of naming: Pantograph engraved.

Clasps: Clasps are issued with this medal.

Comments: *This medal was introduced to recognise overseas service by WA Police in areas or regions not covered by the national Police Overseas Service Medal (See MYB A34). This medal is not exclusive to WA Police but can be awarded to Australian Defence Force personnel who worked alongside WA Police on these overseas operations. Recipients must have served 30 days or more in the following areas: Timor-Leste, Jordan, Papua New Guinea, Fiji, Malaysia or Maldives.*

VALUE: Rare

A-WA7. WESTERN AUSTRALIA POLICE ABORIGINAL SERVICE MEDAL

Instituted: 2018

Ribbon: 32mm black with an 11mm central red strip, which is bisected by a thin yellow stripe (displaying the political colours of the Australian Indigenous Movement).

Metal: Bronze.

Size: 38mm

Description: The obverse is a circular bronze medal surmounted with the St Edward's Crown directly attached to the suspender. The central field displays crossed feather plumes and spears overlaid with the Western Australia Police badge. An edged band around the circumference bears the words "WESTERN AUSTRALIA POLICE FORCE". The plain square suspender bears the impressed words "Aboriginal Service". Medal and suspender are cast as one piece. (Reverse) The blank reverse is engraved at its centre with the recipient's initials, surname and police regimental number if applicable.

Method of naming: Pantograph engraved.

Clasps: No clasps are issued with this medal.

Comments: *This medal is awarded to WA Police employees of proven Aboriginal descent who have served for three years or more. It recognises their role in furthering reconciliation between police and Aboriginal people after a somewhat troubled history. A small lapel badge in identical form to the medal is issued for plain clothes wear.*

VALUE: Rare

A-WA8. WESTERN AUSTRALIA POLICE CADETS MEDAL

Instituted: —
Ribbon: 32mm blue with a central red stripe and a narrow black and white stripe close to each edge.
Metal: Cupro-nickel etched finish with applied "antique" overlay.
Size: 36mm
Description: A circular medal with the obverse depicting a stylized black swan (the Western Australia State bird emblem) surrounded by an edged band bearing the words "WESTERN AUSTRALIA POLICE CADETS". The circumference of the medal comprises a wreath of laurel leaves overlaid by a five-pointed star with its tips showing. The suspender is cast as part of the medal and is plain but has the stylized embossed stars of the Southern Cross constellation at the top where it adjoins the suspender. (Reverse) The blank reverse is engraved at its centre with the recipient's initials, surname and police regimental number.
Method of naming: Pantograph engraved to the reverse.
Clasps: No clasps are issued with this medal.
Comments: *Awarded to all officers who joined the force under the Police Cadet Scheme and who served six or more months as a cadet, and on reaching the minimum entry age to the Force completed the required Police Academy training to become sworn officers and who then completed two years or more as a sworn officer.*

VALUE: Rare

A-WA9. WESTERN AUSTRALIA FIRE BRIGADES ASSOCIATION LONG SERVICE MEDALLION

Instituted: 1901
Ribbon: No ribbon issued.
Metal: —
Size: Not known.
Description: An 8-pointed silvered brass star of stylised sun rays surmounted with a brass crossed pair of fire hose nozzles and a fireman's helmet above. Inside the sun ray star is a round disc comprising a black enamelled black swan on a white ground, surrounded by a blue-enamelled band bearing the words "FIRE BRIGADES ASSOCIATION" above and "WESTERN AUSTRALIA" below. A brass wreath of laurel leaves joined at the base and open at the top surrounds the central disc. A blue enamelled exergue at the bottom of the medallion has the words "LONG SERVICE". (Reverse) Believed to be plain, with two vertical lugs fixed to accommodate a split pin.
Method of naming: Not believed named at time of issue.
Clasps: Issued in 5-year increments.
Comments: *This medal was based on the similar award available to firemen in the UK at the time of implementation. It was first awarded in 1917, for 10 years' service but a series of 5-year increment bars were created, comprising the crossed nozzles and fire helmet device from the medallion with an enamelled scroll below bearing the words "15 YEARS", "20 YEARS" etc. Only the latest bar was worn, replacing any other previously issued. Each year scroll had a different coloured enamel background. 20 years was dark blue but other colours are not known.*

VALUE: Rare.

A-WA10. WESTERN AUSTRALIA FIRE BRIGADES BOARD LONG SERVICE & GOOD CONDUCT MEDAL

Instituted: 1920.

Ribbon: 32mm maroon or deep red.

Metal: Initial issue bronze, then silver plated, then silver.

Size: (Possibly) 36 mm.

Description: A circular medal with the image of a fire engine in the central field, with the words "WEST AUSTRALIAN FIRE BRIGADES BOARD" around the circumference. A heavy scrolled and swivelling suspender is attached to the medal. The silver version suspender is less crudely cast than the bronze. (Reverse) The words "FOR LONG AND GOOD SERVICE" are in the central field in three lines, surrounded by a wreath of laurel leaves emerging from crossed fire axes and a fire helmet at the base.

Method of naming: Hand engraved on the bottom rim with the recipient's name and sometimes the date of award.

Clasps: Bars have been seen on some medals awarded in the 1940s, being a thick silvered bar bearing the words "25 YEARS" or "30 YEARS". That may indicate bars were issued at 10-year increments.

Comments: *This medal replaced the "Fire Brigades Association Long Service Medallion". It was issued after 15 years or more service. It is believed that the various medals were issued based on type of brigade membership, the silver being issued to permanent members and the bronze to volunteers (there are some claims that the reverse applied: silver to volunteers, etc.). The purpose of the (often poorly) silver-plated version is not clear.*

VALUE: Rare

A-WA11. WESTERN AUSTRALIA FIRE & EMERGENCY SERVICES OUTSTANDING ACHIEVEMENT MEDAL

Instituted: 2006.

Ribbon: 32mm with an 11mm central dark blue stripe, flanked with white stripes and an aqua blue stripe at each edge.

Metal: Nickel-base metal alloy with an applied finish. Description: A circular medal with the FESA logo at the centre of the obverse. The circumference has the words "WESTERN AUSTRALIA/OUTSTANDING" around the top circumference in two lines, and the words "ACHIEVEMENT/FIRE & EMERGENCY SERVICES" around the bottom circumference in two lines. The medal is held by a traditional style claw fitting to a plain straight suspender. (Reverse) Left plain.

Method of naming: Pantograph engraved to the reverse.

Clasps: Clasps are not thought to be issued for this medal.

Comments: *This medal has been established as the most prestigious internal FESA award. It recognises extraordinary contributions made by FESA staff and volunteers. The award is presented for outstanding achievements that would not be eligible for nomination under the Australian Honours and Awards system.*

VALUE: —

A-WA12. WESTERN AUSTRALIA EMERGENCY SERVICE DILIGENT SERVICE MEDAL

Instituted: 2005.

Ribbon: 32mm dark blue with a broad central aqua blue stripe evenly divided by two narrow dark blue stripes.

Metal: Copper-base metal alloy.

Size: 38mm

Description: A circular medal with the obverse showing a stylised black swan (the Western Australia State bird emblem) in the centre surrounded by a narrow band of chequering, with stylised flames on each side. An edged band on the circumference contains the words "EMERGENCY SERVICES WESTERN AUSTRALIA DILIGENT SERVICE'. The medal is attached to the plain straight suspender by a traditional style claw fitting. (Reverse) left plain.

Method of naming: Pantograph engraved with the recipient's initials and surname.

Clasps: Clasps are issued in 5 yearly increments.

Comments: *The WA ESDSM is awarded to Department of Fire & Emergency Services corporate staff who have achieved a minimum of 15 years diligent service. A clasp will be issued for each subsequent five years of diligent service. Service does not need to be continuous to meet this requirement. The medal can be awarded posthumously. There are no post-nominal letters for this award. Any prior service within the following former organisations will also be calculated as an eligible period of service:*

Fire and Emergency Services Authority of WA; WA Fire Brigades Board
WA Bush Fires Board
WA Fire and Rescue Service; and WA State Emergency Service
Volunteer service cannot be counted. Prior service at any other public sector agency is not considered for the ESDSM

VALUE: Rare

A-WA13. WESTERN AUSTRALIA STATE EMERGENCY SERVICE LONG SERVICE MEDAL

Instituted: —

Ribbon: 32mm yellow with a 6mm central red stripe and a 6mm black stripe on each edge.

Metal: Silver (pictured medal gives inaccurate gold appearance).

Size: 38mm.

Description: The circular silver medal obverse has the Western Australia SES symbol, the Swan with the motto "WE SERVE" in the central field. The circumference has an edged band with the words "STATE EMERGENCY SERVICE OF WESTERN AUSTRALIA" in the upper portion and the words "LONG SERVICE MEDAL" on the lower portion. (Reverse) Left plain with the recipient's name engraved on the central field. The medal has a traditional style claw fitting from a straight plain suspender.

Method of naming: Pantograph engraved.

Clasps: Clasps are awarded for this medal at each subsequent 5-year period of service.

Comments: *All active registered members of a unit, including support members are eligible for long service medallions, medals and clasps. The State Emergency Service (SES) medallion is awarded to volunteers who have completed a period of five years of diligent service. The SES long service medal is awarded for ten years of diligent service to the SES. A clasp to the medal is awarded for each subsequent five years of diligent service to the SES—up to 55 years. The length of service is calculated from the date of joining SES or registering as a volunteer. The period of service may be an aggregate amount of years, not necessarily a continuous period.*

VALUE: Rare

A-WA14. WESTERN AUSTRALIA VOLUNTEER FIRE & RESCUE SERVICE LONG SERVICE MEDAL

Instituted: —

Ribbon: 32mm red with a narrow white and blue stripe on each edge.

Metal: Gold-coloured base metal.

Size: 38mm

Description: This circular medal obverse has the badge of the WA Volunteer Fire & Rescue Service at the centre, surrounded by the words "VOLUNTEER FIRE & RESCUE SERVICE" around the circumference. It is held by a traditional-style claw fitting to a plain suspender, bearing the impressed words "FOR SERVICE". The suspender bottom bar has each side angled slightly upwards from the medal. (Reverse) Left plain.

Method of naming: Pantograph engraved.

Clasps: Clasps are awarded for each consecutive 5-year period of service. The clasp is a plain rectangular shape with a small Fireman's helmet at the centre. The first bar for 5 years' service has the helmet only, while the 10-year bar shows the black number 10 on the helmet, and so on.

Comments: *All active registered members of a brigade, including support members are eligible for long service medallions, medals and clasps. The Volunteer Fire and Rescue Services (VFRS) medallion is awarded to volunteers who have completed a period of five years of diligent service. The VFRS long service medal is awarded for ten years of diligent service to the VFRS. A clasp to the medal is awarded for each subsequent five years of diligent service to the VFRS—up to 55 years. The length of service is calculated from the date of joining VFRS or registering as a volunteer. The period of service may be an aggregate amount of years, not necessarily a continuous period.*

VALUE: —

A-WA15. WESTERN AUSTRALIA VOLUNTEER FIRE & EMERGENCY SERVICE LONG SERVICE MEDAL

Instituted: 2005.

Ribbon: 32mm navy blue with a narrow white stripe towards each edge.

Metal: Nickel- base metal alloy.

Size: 38mm

Description: This circular medal is affixed by a traditional style claw fitting to a plain suspender which bears the impressed words "FOR SERVICE". The suspender bottom bar has each side angled slightly upwards from the medal. The obverse has at the centre a raised circular disc containing the impressed symbol of the Black Swan, surrounded by a ring of cross hatching and supported at each side by a wreath-like image of rising flames. The words "VOLUNTEER FIRE & EMERGENCY SERVICE WESTERN AUSTRALIA" are shown around the circumference. (Reverse) Left plain.

Method of naming: Pantograph engraved.

Clasps: Bars/Clasps are issued with this medal, at five-year increments.

Comments: *All active registered Volunteer Fire and Emergency Services (VFES) members, including support members, are eligible for the long service medallion after completing five years of diligent service and for each subsequent five years of diligent service—up to 55 years. They become entitled to the VFES Long Service medal after 10 years' service, with a bar showing the numeral of years served awarded at each consecutive 5-year period.*

VALUE: —

A-WA16. WESTERN AUSTRALIA BUSH FIRE BRIGADES LONG SERVICE MEDAL

Instituted: 2005.
Ribbon: 32mm yellow with an 8mm green stripe at each edge which is in turn bisected by a 4mm red stripe.
Metal: Bronze.
Size: 38mm.
Description: A circular medal which has the obverse edged with a band containing a wreath of laurel leaves joined at the bottom. Inside that band is another band with the words "WESTERN AUSTRALIA" at the top and "BUSH FIRE BRIGADES" at the bottom. The central field shows the logo of the Brigades, being a tree in leaf at the left and rising flames in the right separated by a thin stripe. The medal is surmounted by the coat of arms of Western Australia, attached to a plain flat suspender. Medal and suspender are cast in one piece. The suspender bottom bar has each side angled slightly upwards from the medal. (Reverse) Left plain.
Method of naming: Pantograph engraved on the reverse.
Clasps: None known.
Comments: *All active registered members of a bush fire brigade, including support members, are eligible for the long service medal.*

VALUE: —

A-WA17. WESTERN AUSTRALIA VOLUNTEER BUSH FIRE SERVICE LONG SERVICE MEDALLION

Instituted: 2005?
Ribbon: No ribbon issued.
Metal: Silvered brass, brass and enamel.
Size: Not known.
Description: An 8-pointed silver coloured star of stylised sun rays superimposed with a round gold coloured disc containing a white enamelled ground depicting the Bush Fire Brigades logo of green leaves on the left and red flames on the right. This has the words "VOLUNTEER BUSH FIRE SERVICE" around the top of the disc and the letters "W.A." at the bottom. A blue enamelled exergue at the bottom of the medallion has the words "5 YEAR SERVICE".
Method of naming: Not believed to be named.
Clasps: None issued.
Comments: *All active registered volunteer members of a bush fire brigade, including support members, are eligible for long service medallions. The Bush Fire Service (BFS) medallions are awarded after completing five years and then ten years of diligent service.*

VALUE: —

A-WA18. WESTERN AUSTRALIA VOLUNTEER MARINE RESCUE SERVICES LONG SERVICE MEDAL

Instituted: 2005?

Ribbon: 32mm, equal stripes of green, white and red with a narrow blue stripe at each edge.

Metal: Nickel- base metal alloy.

Size: 38mm

Description: A circular medal with the obverse showing the words "VOLUNTEER MARINE RESCUE SERVICES WESTERN AUSTRALIA" around the circumference. A stylised image of waves breaking over a small boat is in the central field. The medal is attached to a plain rectangular suspender bearing the impressed words "FOR SERVICE". The medal attaches to the plain rectangular suspender by a traditional style claw fitting. The suspender bottom bar has each side angled slightly upwards from the medal, and the impressed words 'FOR SERVICE'. (Reverse) Left plain.

Method of naming: Pantograph engraved on the reverse. Clasps: Clasps are issued with this medal for increments of 10 years' service.

Comments: *All active registered marine rescue volunteers are eligible for long service awards, including rescue crews and radio operators. The Volunteer Marine Rescue Services (VMRS) medallion is awarded to volunteers who have completed a period of five and ten years of diligent service. The VMRS long service medal is awarded for 15 years of diligent service. A clasp to the medal is awarded at 15 years' service, and each subsequent ten years of diligent service— up to 55 years. The period of service counting towards the VMRS long service medal may also be with another approved volunteer emergency service. The following requirements must be met:*

- *Minimum of 15 years in total or 15 years in aggregate comprising part of that period in another approved volunteer emergency service, with no overlap in time periods. At least seven and a half years of that service shall be service in a VMRS role*
- *During the period of service active members shall have completed and maintained current applicable VMRS training standards and shall have participated in a minimum of six activities in each year; and*
- *Be physically capable of performing required duties and be rostered and available for duty for at least 50 per cent of the time required.*

VALUE: —

A-WA19. WESTERN AUSTRALIA CORRECTIONS DEPARTMENT LONG SERVICE MEDAL

Instituted: 2009.

Ribbon: 32mm green ribbon with 8 equidistant thin white stripes starting on each edge.

Metal: Zinc alloy, nickel plated with an 'antique' finish.

Size: 38mm

Description: A circular medal with the obverse having an edged band around the circumference containing the words "CORRECTIVE SERVICES WA" at the top, and "SERVICE WITH PRIDE" below. A stylised logo of a swan landing on water is in the central field. The medal is cast as one piece with its suspender. The area where the medal and suspender join shows an ornate scroll possibly depicting vines. The suspender is of plain rectangular design, with a slight downward bend at each end of the lower bar. (Reverse) Left plain.

Method of naming: Pantograph engraved on the reverse.

Clasps: No clasps are awarded for this medal.

Comments: *This medal is considered an "unofficial" award and is worn on the right uniform breast. It is awarded for 30 years of service. The maker of the medal is not known. A 51mm medallion in an identical design and metal was manufactured by Sheridan's Badges & Engraving of Perth, Western Australia for the Department and was possibly awarded to civilian or non-uniformed personnel to recognise their 30-year service.*

VALUE: —

A-SA1. SOUTH AUSTRALIA POLICE MEDAL

Instituted: —
Ribbon: 32mm blue with a white central stripe, and a thin white strip towards each edge.
Metal: Cupro-nickel rhodium plated.
Size: 38mm.
Description: The circular medal obverse has an outer edged band around the circumference containing the words "DILIGENT AND ETHICAL SERVICE". A second edged band directly inside this bears the words "SOUTH AUSTRALIA POLICE". The central field has an image of the Australian Magpie, which is the bird emblem of the State of South Australia.The medal disc is surmounted with a St Edward crown attached to a straight rectangular suspender.
Method of naming: The blank reverse is engraved at its centre with the recipient's surname and initials.
Clasps: Employees who have completed additional ten-year increments are awarded twenty, thirty, and forty-year clasps.
Comments: *The medal may be awarded to sworn and unsworn employees who have completed a period of ten years continuous, diligent and ethical service to the South Australia Police after February 14, 1975.*

VALUE: —

A-T1. TASMANIA POLICE MEDAL

Instituted: —
Ribbon: 32mm. Blue with a central white strip, and a narrow white stripe towards each edge- this ribbon (only) being identical to that of the Western Australia, South Australia and Victoria Police Medals.
Metal: Cupro-nickel Rhodium plated.
Size: 38mm.
Description: A circular medal made in identical style to those of Western Australia, South Australia and Victoria except for the obverse central field. In this medal it shows a map of Tasmania containing a heraldic lion, overlayed on to stylised ocean waves which surround the island State. The obverse is surmounted by a St Edwards crown which is attached to a plain rectangular suspender. The reverse is plain.
Method of naming: Pantograph engraved.
Clasps:
Comments:

VALUE: —

Unofficial medals

Australia, like many countries has produced a number of unofficial and semi-official medals. Although rejected by many of the ex-servicemen's institutions and RSLs, they are still a popular form of recognition, where recognition is due. Despite not having official status, these awards can still increase the desirability of a group. The Merchant Navy awards listed are an attempt to recognize the merchant seamen whose service often appears to go unrecognized, despite their involvement in both peace time and war. Although not approved within the Australian Honours System, the Merchant Navy Association is following strict protocol with regard to the issue of these medals.

A67. AUSTRALIAN MERCHANT NAVY SERVICE CROSS

Instituted: 1998.
Ribbon: Blue with narrow green, white and red central stripes and white edges.
Metal: Silver gilt.
Size: 36mm wide.
Description: A cross fourchée on which is superimposed a small circular medallion bearing the insignia of the Australian Merchant Navy, fitted with a bar suspender.
Method of naming: Usually hand engraved on reverse, or unnamed.
Clasps: A gold laurel spray is awarded for each 15 years additional service
Comments: *Created to mark United Nations Year of the Ocean, the cross is awarded for 15 years bona fide service on Articles of Agreement.*

VALUE: £85–120

A68. AUSTRALIAN MERCHANT NAVY MERITORIOUS MEDAL

Instituted: 1998
Ribbon: Watered silk, white with broad green and red edges and blue central stripe
Metal: Silver
Size: 38mm
Description: (Obverse) the crowned insignia of the Merchant Navy; (reverse) AUSTRALIAN MERCHANT NAVY MERITORIOUS MEDAL, fitted with ornamental bar suspender.
Method of naming: Hand engraved on rim or unnamed
Comments: *Awarded for exceptional contribution to the Merchant Navy over a long period of time or for an individual act of bravery by a seafarer.*

VALUE: —

A69. AUSTRALIAN MERCHANT NAVY COMMENDATION

Instituted: 1998.
Ribbon: Watered silk with a dark blue centre, white stripes and light green edges with a small laurel spray emblem attached.
Metal: Silver.
Size: 42mm.
Description: A laurel wreath joined at the top by a merchant navy crown attached to a ring for suspension.
Comments: *Awarded unnamed for an ongoing or individual contribution by a person in one of the many fields of maritime endeavour including education, research and development, maritime business, industrial relations and professional achievement. As at December 2007, only 63 had been issued—five to officers of RAN Hydrographic Service.*

VALUE: —

A70. GALLIPOLI STAR

Instituted: April 25, 1990.
Ribbon: Central broad deep blue stripe, flanked by narrow crimson stripes and broad edges of yellow and light blue respectively.
Metal: Bronze.
Size: 36mm.
Description: A small circular medal superimposed on an eight-pointed star with ring suspension. (Obverse) a Tudor crown surrounded by the inscription GALLIPOLI 1914-15.
Method of naming: Unnamed.
Comments: *This medal was originally approved by King George V but was never issued at the time. In April 1990 it was produced and presented unofficially by Mr Ross Smith, a retired army warrant officer and Canberra businessman, to the 200 surviving Gallipoli veterans to mark the 75th anniversary of the ill-fated landings on the Turkish coast. The remaining stars were sold to collectors. However, replicas of this medal have been produced and although not always marked as such, are of much lower quality than the originals, which are stamped with the letters A. J. P. in small 1mm font on the bottom arm.*

VALUE: £150–185

A71. TOBRUK T MEDAL

Ribbon: Khaki, with thin red and dark blue stripes on the left, and thin light blue and red stripes on the right.
Metal: Plated bronze.
Size: 36mm across top of T, 32mm in height.
Description: Large "T" shape, with plain suspension bar. (Obverse) laurel wreath edging and TOBRUK SIEGE 1941 in raised lettering in the centre; (reverse) plain.
Method of naming: Hand engraved usually with regimental number, initials and name on reverse—sometimes with additional information.
Comments: *Issued to Australian, British, Indian, New Zealand and Polish troops who were in action during the siege of Tobruk between April and December 1941. An unofficial award, issued by the "Rats of Tobruk" Association in 1977.*

VALUE: £100–135

A72. FRONT LINE SERVICE MEDAL

Instituted: —
Ribbon: Left half gold, right half dark green, both have a thin red stripe down the middle.
Metal: Bronze.
Size: Long rectangle 40mm by 20mm, with scroll and crossed guns to a total height of 60mm.
Description: (Obverse) A long rectangle edged with a laurel wreath and the raised words FRONT LINE SERVICE, scroll above with INFANTRY, and suspender above in the form of crossed 303 rifles; (reverse) plain.
Method of naming: Usually engraved on reverse.
Comments: *Issued by the 2/12 Battalion Association to identify those that took part in front line actions with the Infantry, thus differentiating them from other units.*

VALUE: £60–75

A73. BRITISH COMMONWEALTH OCCUPATION FORCES—BCOF

Instituted: —
Ribbon: Broad white band flanked by very narrow red bands, with narrow green on left edge and narrow blue on right edge.
Metal: Cupro-nickel.
Size: 38mm.
Description: (Obverse) central King's crown above BCOF scroll and 1946 JAPAN 1952 in raised letters around the top circumference; (reverse) sprigs of laurel, tri-services badges and the words FOR SERVICE WITH THE OCCUPATION FORCES.
Method of naming: Impressed on rim in small capitals.
Comments: *Issued by the Australian BCOF Association to any veteran who had served one day on the strength of the unit with the Commonwealth Forces. Around 8,000 have been issued.*

VALUE: £65–75   *Miniature £25*

A74. RSPCA AUSTRALIA PURPLE CROSS AWARD

Instituted: 1996.
Ribbon: 32mm purple.
Metal: Bright Nickel
Description: a circular medal featuring a resin purple cross at the centre surrounded with the inscription PURPLE CROSS AWARD; the reverse is blank.
Method of naming: Pantographed name on reverse.
Comments: *The award recognises the deeds of animals that have shown outstanding service to humans, particularly exceptional courage in risking their own safety or life to save a person from injury or death. The medal has been awarded only 8 times. 2 awards were made retrospective. The first, to "The Pikeman's Dog Wee Jack" (Eureka Stockade, 1854) and the second, to "Murphy" (on behalf of all donkeys used by John Kilpatrick Simpson at Gallipoli, 1915). The most recent award was to "Sarbi" a nine year old black Labrador. Awarded on 5 April 2011 "for her unquestioning, unwavering service to man". After being separated from her handler during the action for which Mark Donaldson was awarded his VC she was missing for 13 months wandering in Afghanistan until found by US Special Forces and returned to Australian Lines.*

VALUE: —

A75. WAR DOG OPERATIONAL MEDAL

Instituted: 2008. The Medal is backdated from 1948 (Malayan Emergency)

Ribbon: 32mm navy blue, bronze olive green and sky blue, with one blood red stripe down the centre of each colour.

Metal: Bright Nickel

Description: a square medal divided into three sections. The right section features a soldier and his dog with the words "AUSTRALIAN ACTIVE SERVICE MEDAL" underneath; the left section is for naming details; the base section displays the words "AUSTRALIAN DEFENCE FORCE TRACKERS AND WAR DOGS ASSOCIATION"; the reverse is blank.

Method of naming: Pantographed number, name and service on the obverse.

Clasps: MALAYA, MALAYSIA, BORNEO, SOUTH VIETNAM, SOMALIA, EAST TIMOR, TIMOR LESTE, THE SOLOMON ISLANDS, BOUGANVILLE, IRAQ, AFGHANISTAN. Clasps are sew-on type and multiple bars are rare. Only one dog has received three clasps.

Comments: *Although not a federally approved award the Australian Directorate of Honours and Awards of the Department of Defence has outlined that they cannot issue medals to Military Working Dogs. However, they have allowed the Australian Defence Force Trackers and War Dogs Association (ADFTWDA) to design its own medals and medal ribbons for issue to Military Working Dogs and approved them for wear by the recipient dog.*

VALUE: From £1,000

A75A. CANINE OPERATIONAL SERVICE MEDAL

Instituted: June 2017

Ribbon: 32mm purple with green, yellow and blue stripes to right.

Metal: Nickel-silver

Description: Obverse depicts Combat Assault Dog "Quake" that died in operations in Afghanistan on June 25, 2015. The reverse shows the Australian Defence Force logo.

Method of naming: Unnamed.

Clasps: EAST TIMOR, ICAT, IRAQ 03, SOLOMON IS II, TIMOR LESTE, GME OPS

Comments: *Introduced to recognise the contribution Military Working Dogs make whilst serving on operations. The Australian Defence Force is the first Defence Force to implement recognition of this nature. Awarded to Military Working Dogs that have 30 days service continuous or aggregated on a declared operation.*

VALUE: ——

A76. CANINE SERVICE MEDAL

Instituted: 2008

Ribbon: 32mm navy blue, red, and sky blue with two white stripes.

Metal: Bright Nickel

Description: a square medal divided into three sections. The right section features a soldier and his dog with the words "AUSTRALIAN SERVICE MEDAL" underneath; the left section is for naming details; the base section displays the words "AUSTRALIAN DEFENCE FORCE TRACKERS AND WAR DOGS ASSOCIATION"; the reverse is blank.

Method of naming: Pantographed number, name and service on the obverse.

Clasps: there are no clasps awarded for this medal

Comments: *Much like the War Dog Operational Medal it is not a federally approved award but is approved for issue and wear by Military Working Dogs by the ADFTWDA. The medal can also be issued to Police/Corrective Services and Customs dogs when they have served 5 years of aggregated service as a working dog on Government security details.*

VALUE: From £1,000

CANADIAN
Medals

Apart from such British campaign awards as the Louisburg Medal of 1758 (MYB71), the Canada General Service Medal (MYB125) awarded to those who helped to put down the Fenian Raids of 1866 and 1870 and the Red River rebellion of the latter year and the North West Canada Medal (MYB134), distinctive medals relating to military service in Canada date from 1902 when Canadian versions of the Meritorious Service Medal (212) and Colonial Long Service and Good Conduct Medal (MYB248) were instituted. Subsequently there were also Canadian versions of the Permanent Forces of the Empire Beyond the Seas Long Service and Good Conduct Medal (MYB249) and the military Long Service and Good Conduct Medal (MYB229). Similarly, both the Efficiency Decoration (MYB236) and the Efficiency Medal (MYB237) were issued with suspension bars denoting service in Canada. Distinctive versions of certain British medals, such as the Defence Medal (MYB185), War Medal (MYB186) and the Korea Medal (MYB195), struck in silver instead of base metal, will also be found in the appropriate sections of this volume.

Several awards which were purely Canadian in character will also be found in earlier sections of this book, as they were authorised or instituted by the imperial government. Thus the Canadian Volunteer Service Medal (MYB188), instituted to recognise volunteer service during World War II, comes under this category, as do the various types of the Canadian Memorial Cross (MYB188A) granted to the relatives of service personnel who gave their lives in both world wars and since the Korean War. Also included are awards by Newfoundland which did not enter the Confederation of Canada until 1949. For this reason Newfoundland servicemen were not eligible for the Canadian Volunteer Service Medal, and it was not until 1981 that this deficiency was remedied by the institution of a separate Newfoundland Volunteer War Service Medal (MYB194).

The move towards purely Canadian medals, however, began to develop in the inter-war period, but the earliest awards were confined to the Royal Canadian Mounted Police and include a number of medals which were authorised by the various provinces. In 1967 Canada celebrated the centenary of Confederation and the opportunity was then taken to institute the Order of Canada, with its associated Medal of Service and Medal of Courage, as well as the Centennial Medal. Five years later, Canada inaugurated a full range of honours and awards and over the intervening years this has been extended considerably.

THE ORDER OF PRECEDENCE IN CANADA

Victoria Cross (VC)
Cross of Valour (CV)
Order of Merit (OM)
Companion of the Order of Canada (CC)
Officer of the Order of Canada (OC)
Member of the Order of Canada (CM)
Commander of the Order of Military Merit (CMM)
Commander of the Order of Merit of the Police Forces (COM)
Commander of the Royal Victorian Order (CVO)
Officer of the Order of Military Merit (OMM)
Officer of the Order of Merit of the Police Forces (OOM)
Lieutenant of the Royal Victorian Order (LVO)
Member of the Order of Military Merit (MMM)
Member of the Order of Merit of the Police Forces (MOM)
Member of the Royal Victorian Order (MVO)
The Most Venerable Order of the Hospital of St John of Jerusalem (all grades)
Ordre National du Québec (GOQ, OQ, CQ) (in French only)
Saskatchewan Order of Merit (SOM)
Order of Ontario (OOnt)
Order of British Columbia (OBC)
Alberta Order of Excellence (AOE)
Order of Prince Edward Island (OPEI)
Order of Manitoba (OM)
Order of New Brunswick (ONB)
Order of Nova Scotia (ONS)
Order of Newfoundland and Labrador (ONL)
Star of Military Valour (SMV)
Star of Courage (SC)
Meritorious Service Cross (Military and Civil) (MSC)
Medal of Military Valour (MMV)
Medal of Bravery (MB)
Meritorious Service Medal (Military and Civil) (MSM)
Royal Victorian Medal (Gold, Silver & Bronze) (RVM)
Sacrifice Medal
Korea Medal
Canadian Volunteer Service Medal for Korea
Gulf and Kuwait Medal
Somalia Medal
South-West Asia Service Medal

General Campaign Star with Ribbons
General Service Medal with Ribbons
Operational Service Medal with Ribbons
Special Service Medal with Bars
Canadian Peacekeeping Service Medal
United Nations' Medals
NATO Medals
International Commission and Organisation Medals
Polar Medal
Sovereign's Medal for Volunteers
Canadian Centennial Medal, 1967
Queen Elizabeth II's Silver Jubilee Medal, 1977
125th Anniversary of the Confederation of Canada Medal, 1992
Queen Elizabeth II's Golden Jubilee Medal, 2002
Queen Elizabeth II's Diamond Jubille Medal, 2012
Royal Canadian Mounted Police Long Service Medal
Canadian Forces' Decoration (CD)
Police Exemplary Service Medal
Corrections Exemplary Service medal
Fire Services Exemplary Service Medal
Canadian Coast Guard Exemplary Service Medal
Emergency Medical Services Exemplary Service Medal
Peace Officer Exemplary Service Medal
Queen's Medal for Champion Shot
Ontario Medal for Good Citizenship (OMC)
Ontario Medal for Police Bravery
Ontario Medal for Firefighters Bravery
Saskatchewan Volunteer Medal (SVM)
Ontario Provincial Police Long Service and Good Conduct Medal
Service Medal of the Most Venerable Order of the Hospital of St John of Jerusalem
Commissionaire Long Service Medal
Newfoundland and Labrador Bravery Award
Newfoundland and Labrador Volunteer Service Medal
British Columbia Fire Services Long Service and Bravery Medal
Saskatchewan Centennial Medal
Alberta Centennial Medal
Commonwealth Orders, Decorations and Medals
Foreign Orders, Decorations and Medals

C1. VICTORIA CROSS (CANADA)

Date: 1 January 1993.
Ribbon: Crimson, with a miniature emblem when the ribbon alone is worn.
Metal: An alloy of bronze which includes metal used to make the UK VC (gunmetal from the cascabel of Chinese cannon), a bronze Confederation Metal (1867) and metal found and mined across Canada.
Size: 38mm.
Description: (Obverse) a cross pattée with raised edges having in the centre a lion standing on the royal crown partially circumscribed by a banner bearing the words PRO VALORE; (reverse) a circle containing the date of the action for which it was awarded. A straight suspender bar with a design of laurel leaves is used attached to the upper arm of the cross by a ring and "V" shaped lug.
Comments: *Available with effect from 1 January 1993 to members of the Canadian Forces or a member of an allied force serving with them for an act of supreme courage, self-sacrifice or devotion to duty in the face of an enemy. It is identical to the awards of the UK, Australia and New Zealand with the important exception of the inscription within the banner on the obverse. The two official languages of Canada (English and French) militated against the use of the English inscription FOR VALOUR as on the three other awards and the Latin translation PRO VALORE was chosen for the Canadian award. The decoration is cast by the Government of Canada in a collaboration between the Royal Canadian Mint and Natural Resources Canada. Recipients are entitled to use the post-nominals VC. None has been awarded as of 1 June, 2018.*

VALUE: —

C2. CROSS OF VALOUR

Date: 1 May 1972.
Ribbon: Light crimson—worn around the neck (men) or on a bow (women), with a miniature emblem when the ribbon alone is worn.
Metal: Gold and red enamel.
Size: 38mm.
Description: (Obverse) a cross with straight arms in red enamel edged in gold with a central medallion of a gold maple leaf on a red enamel ground encircled by a gold wreath of laurel; (reverse) the royal cypher (EIIR) surmounted by a crown on the upper arm with the words VALOUR VAILLANCE across the centre above the engraved name of the recipient and date of the incident.
Comments: *Awarded for acts of conspicuous courage in circumstances of extreme peril to Canadian citizens and foreign nationals for an act in Canada or elsewhere if the act is considered to be in the interest of Canada and merits recognition by the country. A second award is signified by a gold maple leaf worn on the larger of the two suspension rings. The first award was made on 20 May 1972. 20 have been awarded to 1 June, 2018. Recipients are entitled to use the post-nominals CV.*

VALUE: — *Miniature* £65–80

C3. ORDER OF CANADA
COMPANION (CC), OFFICER (OC), MEMBER (CM)

Date: 1 July 1967.
Ribbon: Red with a broad central stripe in white—a neck ribbon for the two higher levels (Companion and Officer) and a breast ribbon for Members. In undress uniform a small maple leaf is worn on the ribbon in red (CC) gold (OC) or silver (CM).
Metal: Silver gilt or silver with enamels.
Size: 57mm (CC), 47.5mm (OC) and 38mm (CM).
Description: (Obverse) A white enamelled stylised snowflake of six points (hexagonal in shape) edged in gold or silver with a central medallion comprising a maple leaf in red enamel (CC), gold (OC) or silver (CM) on a white enamel field all surrounded by a red enamel outer band bearing the words DESIDERANTES MELIOREM PATRIAM (they desire a better country) in gold or silver. A St Edward's crown in gold (CC and OC) or silver (CM) with red enamel is placed at the top of the central medallion on the upper point of the snowflake; (reverse) a small box in which is inscribed a serial number with the word CANADA above. The CC and OC are worn with neck ribbons, a ring suspender is used for the CM.
Comments: *Established to reward Canadian citizens who exemplify the highest qualities of citizenship which enrich the lives of their fellow citizens. Extraordinary membership includes the Governor General and their spouse and allows for the appointment of members of the Royal Family while Honorary membership is available to foreigners. There are three levels—Companion, Officer and Member—with the qualifying criteria differing for each. Appointments are made in July and December each year with a maximum of 15 (CC) Companions, 64 (OC) Officers and 136 (CM) Members appointed each year. The maximum number of living Companions at any one time will not exceed 165 although there is no limit to the number of Officers and Members. The Order initially had a single class—Companion—with the Officer and Member levels being introduced on 1 July 1972. Prior to this a Medal of Service was a part of the Order but it was discontinued in 1972 and all holders made Officers of the Order of Canada. A Medal of Courage was also attached to the Order but was never awarded and discontinued on the introduction of the Bravery Decorations (CV, SC and MB). Appointments to 1 June, 2015:*

VALUE:				
	Companion (475)	£3500–5250		
	Officer (2083)	£2500–4200		
	Member (3890)	£1000–1500	*Miniature*	£55–70

C4. ORDER OF MILITARY MERIT
COMMANDER (CMM), OFFICER (OMM), MEMBER (MMM)

Date: 1 July 1972.
Ribbon: Blue with gold edges (4.8 mm) worn around the neck (CMM) or on the breast (OMM and MMM).
Metal: Enamelled silver gilt or silver.
Size: 38mm (OMM and MMM)
Description: (Obverse) a cross pattée with the arms in blue enamel edged with gold (CMM and OMM) or silver (MMM). A central medallion has a maple leaf at the centre in red (CMM), gold (OMM) or silver (MMM) on a white background surrounded by an outer band in red enamel inscribed with the words MERIT MÉRITE CANADA in the appropriate metal and surmounted by the crown; (reverse) left plain apart from a serial number. A straight suspender bar with a laurel leaf design is used for Officers (in gold) and Members (in silver).
Comments: *Instituted to recognise conspicuous merit or exceptional service by all members of the Canadian Forces. The total of appointments (all levels) made annually cannot exceed 0.1% of the average strength of the Canadian Forces in the preceding year, which currently represents about 105 appointments or promotions a year of which 5% are CMM, 20% are OMM and 75% MMM. There is no limit to the total number at any level. Commanders are most usually of the rank of Brigadier-General/Commodore and above, Officers are Majors to Colonels and Members all those of lower rank including NCOs and junior officers. Extraordinary membership includes the Governor General and allows for the appointment of members of the Royal Family while Honorary membership is available to allied military personnel. Appointments are made in December each year. In undress uniform the level of the award is indicated by a blue cross worn on the ribbon with a maple leaf placed centrally in red, gold or silver. Prior to 1983 a maple leaf of the appropriate colour was worn alone. Appointments to 1 June, 2018:*

VALUE:				
	Commander (278)	£3500–5500		
	Officer (1295)	£1200–2000		
	Member (3286)	£750–1500	*Miniature*	£55–65

C5. ORDER OF MERIT OF THE POLICE FORCES

COMMANDER (COM), OFFICER (OOM), MEMBER (MOM)

Date: 2 October 2000.

Ribbon: Bands of blue, gold and blue, all of equal width. A neck ribbon is worn for the rank of Commander and a breast ribbon for Officers and Members.

Metal: Silver gilt or silver and enamels.

Size: 38mm (OOM and MOM).

Description: (Obverse) a cross pattée in dark blue enamel with a central medallion bearing a maple leaf and an outer band inscribed with the word MERIT (left) and MÉRITE (right) in the upper circumference and CANADA at the bottom. A St Edward's crown is on the upper arm of the cross. The maple leaf in the central medallion is red for Commanders, gold for Officers and silver for Members. The outer band is red with gold lettering for Commanders and Officers and red with silver lettering for Members. A silver suspender bar with a laurel leaf pattern and three small rings is used for the MOM, the bar is gold for the OOM.

Comments: *The Order of Merit of the Police Forces ranks immediately after the Order of Military Merit in the order of precedence. It was introduced to recognise the impact of the Police Service on society and honour those officers with careers of particular merit or who otherwise deserve formal recognition and is available in three classes— Commander (COM), Officer (OOM) and Member (MOM). In any one year there will be a maximum number of new appointees equivalent to one-tenth of one per cent of the number of police officers serving in Canada in the preceding year and is expected that they will number no more than 50. Officers from any police force in Canada are eligible although it is a living order and retired officers are not eligible, neither can it be awarded posthumously. Appointments to 1 June, 2015:*

VALUE:	Commander (22)	Rare
	Officer (156)	Rare
	Member (461)	Rare

C6. L'ORDRE NATIONAL DU QUÉBEC

GRAND OFFICIER (GOQ), OFFICIER (OQ), CHEVALIER (CQ)

Date: 20 June 1984.

Ribbon: Blue with a white central stripe, all of equal width. Worn around the neck (Grand Officier and Officier) or on the breast (Chevalier).

Metal: Gold (GOQ) or silver (OQ and CQ).

Size: 60mm (GOQ), 40mm (OQ and CQ).

Description: (Obverse) a Greek cross with very broad arms and the space between them so small that it is almost square. The upper left and lower right have an irregular highly polished area resulting in a very reflective quality with the space between the two in a matt finish giving the overall appearance of a river running between two land masses. In the bottom left corner, superimposed on the matt area is a fleur-de-lys. All the elements and ribbon colour are taken from the flag of Québec. The insignia for a Chevalier has the cross mounted on a circular silver disc with a ring suspender.

Comments: *Membership of the Order is open to any citizen of Québec without distinction to recognise outstanding work in the Province for the benefit of all. Any person can nominate any other citizen for the award. Honorary membership is available to those not resident in Québec. An award ceremony takes place once a year although special arrangements can be made if the recipient does not reside in the Province. Recipients are entitled to use the post-nominals GOQ, OQ or CQ.*

VALUE:	Grand Officier	£2500–3750
	Officier	£800–1200
	Chevalier	£600–900

C7. SASKATCHEWAN ORDER OF MERIT

Date: 5 June 1985.
Ribbon: Originally dark green with a 12mm gold central stripe. Since 2005 the colours are reversed so that the ribbon is now gold with a green central stripe.
Metal: Enamelled silver.
Size: 58mm
Description: (Obverse) a six-point star in white enamel edged in gold and with gold lines along the centre of each point. There is a central medallion in the shape of the shield from the Saskatchewan coat of arms in enamels (a lion above three sheaves of wheat) surmounted by a crown in gold. Since 2005, the shield is surrounded by the Motto of the Order "MULTIS E GENTIBUS VIRES" on a red circlet.The neck ribbon is attached to the upper point of the star by a small suspender ring.
Comments: *Awarded to recognise individual excellence and outstanding achievement to the social, cultural and economic well-being of the Province and its people. A maximum of ten appointments can be made in any one year. Any resident, past or present of Saskatchewan is eligible for membership although members of parliament, legislative assembly and judges are barred whilst in office. Recipients are entitled to use the post-nominals SOM.*

VALUE: £585–850   *Miniature*   £25–35

C8. ORDER OF ONTARIO

Date: 18 December 1986.
Ribbon: Red with a central stripe in dark green flanked by a white stripe bisected by a thin gold line.
Metal: Enamelled gold.
Size: 54mm
Description: (Obverse) a stylised version of the provincial flower (trillium) with three petals in white enamel superimposed on three dark green enamel sepals, all edged in gold. In the centre is the shield taken from the Ontario coat of arms in enamels surmounted by a crown in gold. A small ring suspender is used.
Comments: *Awarded to residents of Ontario who have shown excellence and achievement of the highest standard and whose contributions have enriched the lives of others and helped make a better society in Ontario. Recipients have the right to use the post-nominals O Ont. Elected officials at federal, provincial or municipal level are barred from membership of the Order whilst in office.*

VALUE: £585–850

C9. ORDER OF BRITISH COLUMBIA

Date: 12 April 1989.
Ribbon: Dark green with two stripes of white either side of a central dark blue stripe each bisected by a thin gold line.
Metal: Gold and enamel.
Size: 54mm
Description: (Obverse) a stylised representation of the six-petal provincial flower of British Columbia (pacific dogwood) in white and green enamels edged by gold. At the centre is the shield of the provincial coat of arms in enamels topped by a crown. A small ring suspender is used.
Comments: *Awarded in recognition of distinction and excellence in any field of endeavour for the benefit of people in British Columbia and elsewhere. Recipients are entitled to use the post-nominals OBC.*

VALUE: £585–850

C10. ALBERTA ORDER OF EXCELLENCE

Date: 16 November 1979.
Ribbon: The same design as the previous order but with the dark green replaced by dark blue.
Metal: Silver gilt and enamel.
Size: 51mm
Description: (Obverse) a cross pattée with the arms in dark blue enamel edged with gold superimposed on a circular disc visible between the arms of the cross and decorated with a design of roses and rose leaves to represent the provincial flower. A central medallion has the full achievement of arms of Alberta on a red background within an outer band of white enamel bearing the words THE ALBERTA ORDER OF EXCELLENCE in gold; (reverse) a maple leaf and sheaf of wheat.
Comments: *Awarded in October each year to Canadian citizens living in Alberta from all walks of life who have performed excellent and distinctive works at provincial, national or international level. It is the highest award that can be bestowed by the Province of Alberta. An important provision is that the work will stand the test of time. Recipients are entitled to use the post-nominals AOE.*

VALUE: £575–875   *Miniature* £50–70

C11. ORDER OF PRINCE EDWARD ISLAND MEDAL OF MERIT

Date: 29 May 1997.
Ribbon: A broad stripe of brown (left) and one of green (right) separated by a narrow white stripe and with a white line at each edge.
Metal: Enamelled gold.
Size: —
Description: (Obverse) circular with the shield from the provincial coat of arms in gold with red and white enamel on a background of gold enamel all within an outer band of blue enamel bearing the words MERIT (upper) and PRINCE EDWARD ISLAND (lower) in gold. A second version with the inscriptions in French is also available— MÉRITE (upper) and ÎLE-DU-PRINCE-EDOUARD. The ribbon, which is worn around the neck attached to the disc by two rings—one small, one large. A miniature is awarded for wear on less formal occasions— the design is the same but the ribbon is green with a central brown band, all of equal width, separated by white lines and with white edges.
Comments: *The Order is the highest that can be bestowed by the Province and given to any resident (present or former long-term) who contributes to the social, economic and cultural life of Prince Edward Island. Not more than three people can be admitted to the Order in any one year. In common with other provincial orders elected officials are not eligible whilst they remain in office. Recipients are entitled to use the post-nominals OPEI.*

VALUE: £590–750

C12. ORDER OF MANITOBA

Date: 14 July 1999.
Ribbon: White with a central stripe in red and a pale blue stripe towards each edge.
Metal: Enamelled gold.
Size: 58mm
Description: (Obverse) a stylised representation of the provincial flower (crocus) with six petals in pale blue enamel edged in gold bearing the shield from the provincial coat of arms at the centre in enamels topped by a crown in gold.
Comments: *Established to recognise current or former long-term residents of Manitoba who have demonstrated excellence and achievement in any field leading to the social, economic or cultural well-being of the Province. A maximum of eight awards can be made in any one year although the initial investiture saw 20 people honoured. Members are entitled to the use of the post-nominals OM. Certain elected officials are not eligible whilst in office.*

VALUE: £595–850

C12A. ORDER OF NEW BRUNSWICK

Instituted: December 2000
Ribbon: Red with a central blue stripe flanked by yellow stripes. Worn as a neck ribbon.
Metal: Gold and enamels.
Description: (Obverse) a stylised purple violet, the provincial floral emblem, in enamels bordered with gold. In the centre is the provincial arms surmounted by a crown, the shield depicting an ancient galley topped by a lion (an allusion to the arms of the Duchy of Brunswick, a possession of King George III in 1784 when New Brunswick was established). The ribbon is attached to the top of the crown between the two uppermost petals of the flower.
Comments: *Awarded to Canadian citizens who are present or long—term residents of New Brunswick and who have distinguished themselves in various fields. A maximum of ten awards will be made each year. Recipients are entitled to the post-nominal letters ONB.*

VALUE: £595–850

C12B. ORDER OF NOVA SCOTIA

Instituted: 2001
Ribbon: Blue with a narrow central stripe of red flanked by white, a black line and a gold line, the colours of the provincial flag. Worn as a neck ribbon.
Metal: Gold and enamels.
Description: (Obverse) in the shape of a stylised mayflower, the provincial floral emblem, in white enamel edged with gold and with green enamel between each petal. In the centre is the provincial coat of arms (a blue Saltire cross surmounted by the Scottish lion in red and gold), all surmounted by a crown on the uppermost petal to which is affixed a thin ring for suspension.
Comments: *Awarded to Canadian citizens who are present or long-term residents of Nova Scotia and who have distinguished themselves by outstanding achievement in a number of fields bringing honour and prestige to the Province. Certain public officials are not eligible while holding office. The award is available posthumously if the person is nominated within a year of death. Five appointments are made annually after the inaugural year when there were ten recipients. Recipients are entitled to the post-nominal ONS.*

VALUE: £595–800

C12C. ORDER OF NEWFOUNDLAND AND LABRADOR

Date: Instituted: 24 May 2001
Ribbon: Edged green with two stripes of white on either side of a dark blue stripe with a thin gold stripe in the center of each white stripe.
Metal: Silver gilt, Labradorite and enamel.
Size: 54mm
Description: (Obverse) a stylized version of the provincial flower (pitcher plant), the main petals are crafted with the provincial mineral, Labradorite, while the smaller petals are enamelled with similar colours. In the centre is the shield of the provincial coat of arms enamelled in colour surmounted by the Royal Crown in gold. A ring is affixed to the top petal for suspension.
Comments: *Canadian citizens who are present or former long-term residents of Newfoundland and Labrador are eligible for nomination to the Order which recognizes individuals who have demonstrated excellence and achievement in any field of endeavour benefiting in an outstanding manner Newfoundland and Labrador and its residents. The only exceptions are public officials (members of the Senate, House of Commons, House of Assembly or legislative assembly of a province, or judges), who may not be nominated while they are in office. Other Canadians and foreigners may be appointed as honorary members. A maximum of eight appointments are made annually. Members are entitled to the post-nominal letters ONL.*

VALUE: £575–825

C13. STAR OF MILITARY VALOUR

Date: 1 January 1993.
Ribbon: Crimson with a white stripe towards each edge.
Metal: Silver gilt, silver and enamel.
Size: 44mm
Description: (Obverse) a four-point star with a maple leaf between the points. A central medallion has a maple leaf placed centrally on a red background all surrounded by a circular wreath of laurel in silver; (reverse) the royal cypher (EIIR) surmounted by a crown with the inscription PRO VALORE. The rank and name of the recipient is engraved below the inscription. A suspension ring is attached to the upper point of the star.
Comments: *The second highest military valour decoration in Canada. It is awarded to any member of the Canadian Forces or allies serving with the Canadians for distinguished and valiant service in the presence of an enemy on or after January 1, 1993. Any second or subsequent award is indicated by a gold bar bearing a maple leaf in the centre. It can be awarded posthumously. Recipients are entitled to use the post-nominals SMV or ÉVM in French. 20 have been awarded to 1 June, 2018.*

VALUE: —   *Miniature* £20–35

C14. STAR OF COURAGE

Date: 1 May 1972.
Ribbon: Red with a stripe of blue towards each edge.
Metal: Silver and silver gilt.
Size: 44mm
Description: (Obverse) identical to the Star of Military Valour but in silver with a gold wreath of laurel around the central medallion bearing a gold maple leaf in its centre; (reverse) the royal cypher (EIIR) surmounted by a crown on the upper arm with the inscription COURAGE below. The name of the recipient and date of the act are engraved below.
Comments: *The second highest honour for courage awarded for acts of conspicuous courage in circumstances of great peril. It is available to Canadian citizens and foreign nationals for the performance of an act in Canada or elsewhere if the act is in the interest of Canada. The first award was made on July 20, 1972. Second or subsequent awards are indicated by a gold bar with a maple leaf at its centre. In common with several Canadian national honours the award is named in English and French and the initials of the two are not the same. The post-nominals are therefore different—SC (English) or ÉC (French "Étoile du Courage"). 447 have been awarded to 1 June 2015.*

VALUE: £2750–4200   *Miniature* £25–45

C15. MERITORIOUS SERVICE CROSS (MILITARY AND CIVIL DIVISIONS)

Date: 11 June 1984 (military) and 6 June 1991 (civil).
Ribbon: Bright blue with a white stripe (6 mm) towards each edge. The civil division is indicated by the addition of a central white stripe (1 mm).
Metal: Originally silver, then rhodium plated red brass, silver again since 2016.
Size: 38mm.
Description: (Obverse) a Greek cross with splayed ends with a wreath of laurel between the arms. A crown is attached to the upper arm of the cross to which is joined the plain straight suspender bar. A central medallion bears a maple leaf at its centre; (reverse) two concentric circles with the royal cypher (EIIR) in the centre and the words MERITORIOUS SERVICE MÉRITOIRE (separated at the bottom by a maple leaf) around the second of the two circles.
Comments: *The Cross was initially introduced for award to the military only but extended in 1991 to civilians and made retrospective to 1984. The criteria are similar for both divisions—a deed or activity performed in a highly professional manner or of a high standard bringing benefit or great honour to the Canadian Forces (military) or Canada (civil). Second or subsequent awards are indicated by a silver bar with a maple leaf in its centre. Both awards are available to Canadians and foreign nationals. The name of the recipient is engraved at the back of the suspension bar and the date on the reverse of the top arm of the cross. Recipients are entitled to use the post-nominals MSC or CSM in French. 439 MSC's have been awarded to 1 June 2018 (236 military, 203 civilian).*

VALUE: £675–1000   *Miniature*   £25–45

C16. MEDAL OF MILITARY VALOUR

Date: 1 January 1993.
Ribbon: Crimson with white stripes in the centre and at each edge.
Metal: Silver gilt.
Size: 36mm.
Description: (Obverse) circular with a maple leaf surrounded by a wreath of laurel tied at its base by a bow; (reverse) the royal cypher (EIIR) surmounted by a crown with the inscription PRO VALORE. The suspender bar is in the shape of a fleur-de-lys attached to the disc by a claw fitting. The rank and name of the recipient are engraved on the rim.
Comments: *Awarded to members of the Canadian Forces and allies serving with or in conjunction with the Canadians for an act of valour or devotion to duty in the presence of an enemy. A gold bar with a maple leaf at its centre is available for any second or subsequent award. It can be awarded posthumously. Recipients are entitled to use the post-nominals MMV or MVM in French. 89 have been awarded to 1 June 2018.*

VALUE: —   *Miniature*   £20–35

C17. MEDAL OF BRAVERY

Date: 1 May 1972.
Ribbon: Crimson with dark blue stripes in the centre and at each edge.
Metal: Silver.
Size: 36mm.
Description: (Obverse) identical to the previous award; (reverse) the royal cypher (EIIR) surmounted by a crown with the words BRAVERY (right) and BRAVOURE (left) at the circumference.
Comments: *Awarded to Canadian citizens (civilian and military) and foreign nationals as defined for previous awards for acts of bravery in hazardous circumstances. It can be awarded posthumously. The first award was made on 20 July 1972. Bars are of silver with a maple leaf placed centrally. The name of the recipient is engraved on the rim. Recipients are entitled to use the post-nominals MB. 3,129 have been awarded to 1 June 2018.*

VALUE: £675–1000   *Miniature*   £20–35

C18. MERITORIOUS SERVICE MEDAL (MILITARY AND CIVIL DIVISIONS)

Date: 6 June,1991.
Ribbon: Bright blue with two white stripes towards each edge. The civil division is indicated by the addition of a central white stripe (1mm).
Metal: Originally silver, then rhodium plated red brass, silver again since 2016.
Size: 36mm.
Description: (Obverse) a Greek cross with splayed ends with a wreath of laurel between the arms and a maple leaf in the central medallion all superimposed on a disc. A crown is attached to the upper arm of the cross to which is joined the ring suspender; (reverse) two concentric circles with the royal cypher (EIIR) in the centre and the words MERITORIOUS SERVICE MÉRITOIRE (separated at the bottom by a maple leaf) around the second of the two circles.
Comments: *The criteria are similar for both divisions—a deed or activity performed in a highly professional manner or of a high standard bringing benefit or honour to the Canadian Forces (military) or Canada (civil). Second or subsequent awards are indicated by a silver bar with a maple leaf in its centre. Both awards are available to Canadians and foreign nationals and can be awarded posthumously. The name of the recipient is engraved on the rim and the date on the top part of the reverse. 1590 MSMs have been awarded to 1 June 2018 (881 military, 709 civilian). Recipients are entitled to the use of the post-nominals MSM.*

VALUE: £350–495 | **Miniature** £20–40

C18A. SACRIFICE MEDAL

Date: 19 April 2008.
Ribbon: Two equal red stripes bisected by thin white stripes, divided by a central black stripe.
Metal: Silver.
Size: 36mm
Description: (Obverse) effigy of HM the Queen with the legend ELIZABETH II DEI GRATIA REGINA CANADA around; (reverse) a figure of "Canada" from the National Vimy Memorial and the word SACRIFICE.
Comments: *Awarded posthumously to members of the Canadian Forces who die as a result of military service after October 6, 2001. Also awarded to those who, since that date, have been wounded as a direct result of a hostile action on the condition that the wounds that were sustained required treatment by a physician and the treatment has been documented. Accidents and minor wounds are not eligible but 'friendly fire' and operational stress injuries as a direct result of hostile action are eligible under certain circumstances. Additional incidents entitle the holder to a bar. The medal is engraved with the recipient's details on the edge. 1269 medals and 21 bars have been awarded to 1 June 2018*

VALUE: £550–685 | **Miniature** £12–25

C19. CANADIAN VOLUNTEER SERVICE MEDAL FOR KOREA

Date: 12 July,1991

Ribbon: Yellow with a broad stripe in UN blue (7mm) at each edge and a central stripe of red, white and red (all 2mm).

Metal: Silver coloured copper and zinc alloy.

Size: 36mm.

Description: (Obverse) the crowned profile of Queen Elizabeth II with the word CANADA below and ELIZABETH II DEI GRATIA REGINA around the circumference; (reverse) a wreath of laurel tied at the base by a bow with a maple leaf above it. In the central field is the inscription KOREA/VOLUNTEER/1950–1954/VOLONTAIRE/COREE. A plain straight suspender was used.

Comments: *Awarded to former members of the Canadian Forces who were in the qualifying area of Korea and adjacent areas between June 27, 1950 and July 27, 1954 with four further provisos. The recipients were eligible if they were on the strength of a unit in Korea for one day, were on active service aboard a ship for at least 28 days, flew one sortie over Korea or Korean waters or had accumulated at least 28 days service in the qualifying area. The medal could be awarded posthumously and 18,611 awards were made to 1 June 2015. Issued unnamed.*

VALUE: £65–95   *Miniature*   £15–25

C20. GULF AND KUWAIT MEDAL

Date: 3 June,1991.

Ribbon: A sand coloured central stripe (8mm) flanked by stripes of dark blue (5mm), red (2mm) and light blue (5mm) to represent the three branches of the armed forces.

Metal: Silver coloured copper and zinc alloy.

Size: 36mm.

Description: (Obverse) the crowned profile of Queen Elizabeth II with the word CANADA below and ELIZABETH II DEI GRATIA REGINA around the circumference; (reverse) a wreath of laurel tied at the base by a bow with a maple leaf above it. In the central field is the inscription THE GULF/AND KUWAIT/1990–1992/LE GOLFE/ET KUWAIT in five lines. A plain straight suspender was used.

Comments: *Awarded to all members of the Canadian Forces who served in the theatre of operations between August 2, 1990 and June 27, 1991 for a minimum of 30 days cumulative service or who served during actual hostilities for at least one day between January 16 and March 30, 1991. A bar was awarded to all those who served during the hostilities for at least one day. The bar has a silver maple leaf at its centre. 4,450 medals were awarded, including 3,198 with bar to 1 June 2015. Issued unnamed*

VALUE: £95–145   *Miniature*   £15–25

C21. SOMALIA MEDAL

Date: 8 April, 1997

Ribbon: White with United Nations blue stripes (5 mm) at each edge and a central stripe of three colours (dark blue, red and light blue to represent the three armed services) flanked by stripes of a sand colour.

Metal: Gold-plated bronze.

Size: 36mm.

Description: (Obverse) three over-lapping Canadian maple leaves above two branches of laurel and with the word CANADA above; (reverse) the royal cypher (EIIR) surmounted by a crown with the words SOMALIA (left) SOMALIE (right) and the dates 1992–93 (lower) around the circumference. A ring suspender was used.

Comments: *Available to any member of the Canadian Forces or anyone attached to or working with them for a minimum of 90 days cumulative service in Somalia between November 16, 1992 and June 30, 1993. Anyone with a minimum of 60 days service who died, was evacuated or redeployed was also eligible. It was awarded posthumously. 1,425 were awarded to I June 2015, it was issued unnamed.*

VALUE: £125–175   *Miniature*   £15–25

C22. SOUTH-WEST ASIA SERVICE MEDAL

Date: 31 July, 2002
Ribbon: 32mm in width with a white stripe in the middle (12mm), on either side of which are stripes of black (4mm), red (2mm) and sand (4mm).
Metal: Originally nickel-plated red brass, since 2006 cupro-nickel.
Size: 36mm
Description: (Obverse) the Queen's effigy, wearing the King George IV State Diadem, facing right, circumscribed with the legend: ELIZABETH II • DEI GRATIA REGINA and at the base of the effigy, the word CANADA flanked by two small maple leaves; (reverse) a representation of the mythical figure of Hydra transfixed by a Canadian sword and over the design is the Latin phrase, ADVERSUS MALUM PUGNAMUS - "We are fighting evil". A claw at the top of the medal, in the form of a cluster of olive leaves representing peace is attached to a straight suspension bar.
Comments: *Awarded to Canadian Forces members deployed with, or in direct support of the operations against terrorism in South-West Asia. The medal with the AFGHANISTAN bar is awarded for 30 days cumulative service between 11 September, 2001 and 31 July, 2009 in the theatre of operations of South-West Asia while it is awarded without the bar for a minimum of 90 days cumulative service in direct support of these operations such as service with the Headquarters, Canadian Joint Task Force South-West Asia in Tampa Bay, Florida; the Stragtegic Airlift Detachment in Ramstein, Germany and other similar tasks. Rotation Bars are awarded for each period of 180 days of eligible service following eligibility for the medal with AFGHANISTAN bar (i.e. at 210 days, 390 days, etc.) The medal is issued unnamed. Over 12,736 medals and 12,409 bars have been issued to 1 June 2015.*

VALUE: £120–175   *Miniature*   £15–25

C23. GENERAL CAMPAIGN STAR

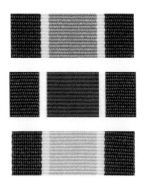

Date: 24 March 2004
*Ribbon: 32mm in width with a central stripe of 12mm specific to the theatre or task concerned (light blue for Op ALLIED FORCE, dark green for SOUTH-WEST ASIA and light grey for EXPEDITION) on either side of which are stripes of white (2mm) and dark red (8mm).
Metal: Gold-plated bronze.
Size: 44mm.
Description: A four pointed star bearing (Obverse) a wreath of maple leaves open at the top to include the Royal Crown, two crossed swords, the blades and hilts forming four additional points to the Star, an anchor and a flying eagle; (reverse) within a raised circle, the Royal Cypher ensigned by the Royal Crown, a plain space for engraving and three maple leaves on one stem. A ring is fitted to a small ball at the tip of the top point of the Star. Recipient's details are engraved on the reverse of the Star.
Comments: *Awarded to Canadian Forces members who deploy into a specific theatre of operations to take part in operations in the presence of an armed enemy. The Star is always awarded with a ribbon specific to the theatre or task being recognized, each ribbon having its own criteria. Rotation Bars are awarded for each period of 180 days of eligible service following eligibility for the Star i.e. at 210 days, 390 days, etc.*

*Ribbons: ALLIED FORCE: awarded to fighter pilots and AWACS crew members who took part in at least five missions in the theatre of operations during the air campaign in Kosovo between 24 March and 10 June, 1999. 92 issued to 1 June 2015.
SOUTH-WEST ASIA: awarded for 30 days of service in Afghanistan as part of the Canadian contribution to the International Security and Assistance Force between 24 April 2003 and 31 July 2009 and for 30 days of service in Afghanistan or the SWA naval theatre since 1 August, 2009 (naval theatre eligibility ends 14 May 2014). 32,243 issued to 1 June 2015.
EXPEDITION: awarded for 30 days in approved smaller operations conducted in the presence of an armed enemy. Service by CF members in Iraq (since 20 January 2003) and Syria (since 20 April 2015) is eligible. 155 issued to 1 June 2015.
VALUE: £185–225   *Miniature*   £15–25

C24. GENERAL SERVICE MEDAL

Date: March 24, 2004

Ribbon: 32mm in width with a dark red central stripe of 18mm on either side of which are stripes of white (2mm) and a colour specific to the threatre or task concerned (light blue for Op ALLIED FORCE, dark green for SOUTH-WEST AIA and light grey for EXPEDITION) (5mm.)

Metal: Cupro-nickel.

Size: 36mm.

Description: (Obverse) a contemporary crowned effigy of The Queen circumscribed by the inscriptions "ELIZABETH II DEI GRATIA REGINA" and "CANADA" separated by small crosses pattée; (reverse) two crossed swords, an anchor and a flying eagle surmounted by the Royal Crown and surrounded by two branches of maple leaves. The straight suspension bar is ornamented with 3 overlapping maple leaves. Recipient's details are engraved on the rim.

Comments: *Awarded to Canadian Forces members and Canadian civilians who deploy outside Canada but not necessarily into a defined theatre of operations, to provide direct support, on a full-time basis, to operations conducted in the presence of an armed enemy. The Medal is always awarded with a ribbon specific to the theatre or task being recognized, each ribbon having its own criteria. Rotation Bars are awarded for each period of 180 days of eligible service following eligibility for the Medal (i.e. at 210 days, 390 days, etc.).*

*Ribbons: ALLIED FORCE: awarded to personnel who served a least 30 days in Aviano and/or Vicenza, Italy in direct support of the air campaign in Kosovo between 24 March and 10 June, 1999. 149 issued to 1 June 2015.

SOUTH-WEST ASIA: awarded for 30 days of service in locations outside Afghanistan and the SWA naval theatre, such as at Camp Mirage, in direct support of the Canadian operations in SWA since the spring of 2003 (start dates vary depending on location). 5,774 issued to 1 June 2015.

EXPEDITION: awarded for 30 days in support of approved smaller operations conducted in the presence of an armed enemy. Support to operations in Iraq from various locations, mostly Kuwait, is eligible. Seven issued to 1 June 2015.

VALUE: £175–235   *Miniature*   £15–25

C24A. OPERATIONAL SERVICE MEDAL

Ribbon descriptions illustrated overleaf

Date: 5 July 2010

Ribbon: 32mm in width with a central stripe of 22mm specific to the theatre or task concerned (sand for SOUTH-WEST ASIA, light green for SIERRA LEONE, royal blue for HAITI, dark green for SUDAN, white for HUMANITAS and light grey for EXPEDITION) on either side of which are stripes of white (2.5mm) and red (2.5mm).

Metal: Cupro-nickel

Size: 36 mm

Description: (Obverse) a contemporary effigy of The Queen circumscribed by the inscriptions "ELIZABETH II DEI GRATIA REGINA" and "CANADA" separated by small maple leaves; (reverse) from top to bottom appear the Royal Crown on either side of which are three maple leaves conjoined on one stem, a Goode interrupted homolosine equal-area projection of the globe, and a laurel branch crossed with an oak branch. A plain straight suspender is attached by a claw fitting. Recipient's details are engraved on the rim.

Comments: *Awarded to Canadian Forces members, Canadian Police Officers, Canadian Public Servants and Government of Canada contractors, who deployed overseas to take part in, or provide direct support to, operations, or who served under dangerous circumstances, provided their service is not eligible for another medal. The Medal is always awarded with a ribbon specific to the theatre or task being recognized, each ribbon having its own criteria. Rotation Bars are awarded for each period of 180 days of eligible service following eligibility for the Medal (i.e. at 210 days, 390 days, etc.).*

1.

2.

3.   *continued overleaf*

4.

5.

6.   **515**

C24A. OPERATIONAL SERVICE MEDAL *continued*

Ribbons:

1. SOUTH-WEST ASIA: awarded for non military service in that area since 7 October 2001. 390 issued to 1 June 2015.
2. SIERRA LEONE: awarded for 30 days of service in that country since the Armistice of 31 July 2002, mainly with the British-led International Military Advisory Team (IMATT). 122 issued to 1 June 2015.
3. HAITI: awarded for 30 days of service in that country since 6 March 2004, mainly with the US-led Multinational Interim Force (6 March to 16 August 2004, as well as support from the Dominican Republic). 926 issued to 1 June 2015.
4. SUDAN: awarded for 30 days of service in that country since 15 September 2004, mainly with the African Union-Led mission in Darfur (15 September 2004 to 31 December 2007, as well as support from Ethiopia and Senegal). 125 issued to 1 June 2015.
5. HUMANITAS: replaces the HUMANITAS bar to the Special Service Medal (C25) from 1 August 2009 and is awarded for 30 days of service on approved humanitarian missions such as the earthquake relief in Haiti (12 January to 2 May 2010). 1198 issued to 1 June 2015.
6. EXPEDITION: awarded for 30 days in approved smaller operations not recognized by other medals. This currently includes service in the Middle East with the Office of the US Security Coordinator as well as naval and air antinarcotics operations in the Caribbean Sea, East Pacific and off the West coast of Africa. 4,819 issued to 1 June 2015.

VALUE: — *Miniature* **£15–25**

C25. SPECIAL SERVICE MEDAL

Date: 16 June 1984.
Ribbon: A dark green central stripe (12mm) flanked by stripes of white (5mm) and red (5mm) at the edges.
Metal: Originally rhodium-plated alloy, since 2006 cupro-nickel.
Size: 36mm.
Description: (Obverse) A wreath of laurel tied at the base by a bow with a maple leaf in the central field; (reverse) the Royal cypher (EIIR) surmounted by the Royal Crown with the words SPECIAL SERVICE SPÉCIAL around the circumference. A plain straight suspender bar is used. Issued unnamed.
Bars: PAKISTAN 1989-90: Created 6 June 1991 for 90 days of service with the Mine Awareness and Clearance Training Program in Pakistan from 15 March 1989 to 29 July 1990. 50 were awarded on 27 January 1992. Recipients can now exchange this award for the United Nations Special Service Medal.
PEACE - PAIX: Created 26 November 1992 for 180 days of service in approved peacekeeping operations since November 1947. This bar was superseded by the Canadian Peacekeeping Service Medal (C26) on 21 June 2001. 2,321 Peace Bars have been issued to 1 June 2015.
ALERT: Created 26 November 1992 for 180 days of service at Canadian Forces Station Alert since 1 September 1958. 7,902 issued to 1 June 2015.
NATO + OTAN: Created 26 November 1992 for 180 days service with NATO since 1 January 1951 or 45 days as part or in direct support of NATO operations since 19 October 2004 (some restrictions apply). 64,670 issued to 1 June 2015.
HUMANITAS: Created 9 March 1993 for 30 days of service on approved humanitarian operations between 11 June 1984 and 31 July 2009. Superseded by the HUMANITAS ribbon to the Operational Service Medal (C24A) from 1 August 2009. 1,120 issued to 1 June 2015.
JUGOSLAVIJA: Created 9 March 1993 for 90 days of service with the European Community Monitor Mission in Yugoslavia (ECMMY) from 4 September 1991. This bar was cancelled and replaced by the ECMMY Medal (206B).
RANGER: Created 1 October 1999 for 4 years service with the Canadian Rangers including completion of 3 sovereignty patrols in isolated regions of Canada since 1947. To date, more than 3,236 Ranger bars have been issued to 1 June 2015.
EXPEDITION: Created 21 May 2014 for 45 days of service overseas to participate in or provide direct support to approved operations since 1 July 2007 provided the service is not eligible for another medal. 145 issued to 1 June 2015.
Comments: *Awarded to members of the Canadian Forces for service performed under exceptional circumstances, in a clearly defined locality for a specific duration. The medal is always issued with a bar, each having its own criteria.*
VALUE: **£185–225** *Miniature* **£15–25**

C26. CANADIAN PEACEKEEPING SERVICE MEDAL

Date: 25 April 1997.
Ribbon: A light blue central stripe flanked by equal stripes of white, red and green.
Metal: Antique Silvered Copper
Size: 36mm.
Description: (Obverse) a depiction of three Canadian peacekeepers taken from the National Peacekeeping Monument in Ottawa. One figure is an unarmed UN military observer holding a pair of binoculars, another a kneeling female figure shouldering a radio and the third a guard with a rifle. The words PEACEKEEPING (upper) and SERVICE DE LA PAIX (lower) lie at the circumference; (reverse) a maple leaf with the royal cypher (EIIR) topped by a crown in the centre with a branch of laurel on either side and the word CANADA below. The plain straight suspender bar is attached by a maple leaf.
Comments: *Inspired by the award in 1988 of the Nobel Peace Prize to all UN peacekeepers. Awarded to Canadian citizens for a minimum of 30 days service on a peacekeeping or observing mission since 14 November 1947. Military personnel, police officers and civilians are eligible. Recipients are also entitled to wear any UN, NATO or other international medal issued. 75,521 have been awarded to 1 June 2015, it is issued unnamed.*

VALUE: £35–65   *Miniature*   £12–20

C26A. POLAR MEDAL

Date: 19 June 2015.
Ribbon: 32 mm, watered white.
Metal: Cupro-nickel
Size: Octagonal, 36mm across.
Description: (Obverse) a contemporary effigy of the Sovereign, circumscribed with the inscription in capital letters of the Canadian Royal Title and the word "CANADA", separated by two maple leaves. The edge of the obverse is decorated with small denticles; (Reverse) a representation of the Royal Canadian Mounted Police schooner St. Roch depicted in the Arctic near a tall iceberg and two crew members standing on the ice. A straight suspension bar is linked to a North Star at the top of the medal by two arms shaped to represent winds, water currents and the aurora borealis. Recipient's details are engraved on the rim. Additional awards are denoted by a bar bearing a single maple leaf.
Comments: *Awarded to those who have contributed to or endeavoured to promote a greater understanding of Canada's Northern communities and its people. It will also honour those individuals who have withstood the rigours of the polar climate to make significant contributions to polar exploration and knowledge, scientific research, and the securement of Canada's Northern sovereignty.*

Value: —

C26B. SOVEREIGN'S MEDAL FOR VOLUNTEERS

Date: 19 June 2015.
Ribbon: 32 mm in width with deep red edges (9.25 mm) and a centre composed of five gold stripes alternating with four blue stripes (1.5mm each).
Metal: Cupro-nickel
Size: 36mm
Description: (Obverse) a contemporary effigy of the Sovereign, circumscribed with the Canadian Royal Title and the word "CANADA", separated by two maple leaves; (Reverse) a large and a small heart interlaced, set with five maple leaves on the outer edge of the large heart which is surmounted by a coronet bearing three maple leaves. The edge is decorated with a sunburst pattern. A scroll and ball with ring suspension is used. Issued unnamed.
Comments: *Awarded to living Canadians who have made a significant, sustained and unpaid contribution to their community, in Canada or abroad. Non-Canadians are also eligible if their contribution brings benefit or honour to Canadians or to Canada.*

Value: —

C27. CANADIAN CENTENNIAL MEDAL

Date: 1 July 1967.
Ribbon: White with four red stripes (1mm) equally spaced and red stripes (5mm) at the edges.
Metal: Silver.
Size: 36mm.
Description: (Obverse) the Canadian maple leaf superimposed by the royal cypher (EIIR) surmounted by a crown and the words CONFEDERATION (left) CANADA (upper) and CONFÉDÉRATION (right) around the circumference; (reverse) the full achievement of arms of Canada above the dates 1867–1967. A plain suspender in a wide, shallow triangular shape was used.
Comments: *Awarded in celebration of the centenary of Canadian Confederation to those recommended by national and provincial governments and a variety of other bodies and associations. Approximately 29,500 medals were awarded, including 8,500 to the military.*

VALUE: £70–95   *Miniature*   £30–35

C28. QUEEN ELIZABETH II'S SILVER JUBILEE MEDAL (Canada)

Date: 6 February 1977.
Ribbon: White with thin red stripes at the edges, a broad blue stripe in the centre and a thin red stripe down the middle of it.
Metal: Silver
Size: 32mm
Description: (Obverse) Right-facing profile of Queen Elizabeth II wearing the St Edward's crown–the first time this design was employed; (reverse) a large stylised maple leaf with 'CANADA' around the top of the rim and, around the bottom of the rim, the Royal Cypher EIIR surmounted by the Crown and the dates 1952 and 1977 on each side in small lettering.
Comments: *Awarded to Canadians who have made a significant contribution to their fellow citizens, their community or to Canada on the occasion of the 25th anniversary of Her Majesty's Accession to the Throne as Queen of Canada. The recipients were selected by a number of partner organisations in every field of Canadian Life. Approximately 30,000 medals were awarded including 7,000 to the military.*

VALUE: £125–175   *Miniature*   £15–25

C29. 125th ANNIVERSARY OF THE CONFEDERATION OF CANADA MEDAL

Date: 7 May 1992.
Ribbon: White with five red stripes (1mm) equally spaced and blue stripes (4.5mm) at the edges.
Metal: Rhodium plated copper and zinc alloy.
Size: 36mm.
Description: (Obverse) the Canadian maple leaf superimposed by the royal cypher (EIIR) surmounted by a crown and the words CONFEDERATION (left) and CONFÉDÉRATION (right) and the dates 1867–1992 (lower) around the circumference; (reverse) the shield taken from the Canadian coat of arms within a belt bearing the words DESIDERANTES MELIOREM PATRIAM and surmounted by a lion. The legend A MARI USQUE AD MARE is inscribed around the lower circumference half. A plain straight suspender is used.
Comments: *Awarded to Canadian citizens who had made a significant contribution to Canada, their community or their fellow citizens in celebration of the 125th anniversary of federation. Approximately 44,000 were awarded, including 4,000 to the military.*

VALUE: £45–70   *Miniature*   £18–20

C30. QUEEN ELIZABETH II'S GOLDEN JUBILEE MEDAL (Canada)

Date: 23 February 2002.
Ribbon: 32mm in width with two outer stripes of 2mm of red, followed by 10mm stripes of royal blue, 3mm stripes of white and a central 2mm stripe of red.
Metal: Gold-plated bronze.
Size: 32mm.
Description: (Obverse) the 1990-2002 Canadian coinage effigy of HM the Queen with the legend "QUEEN OF CANADA - REINE DU CANADA"; (reverse) the Royal Crown above a stylized maple leaf bearing the Royal Cypher with 1952, 2002 and CANADA around. There is a small ring at the top of the medal, through which passes a larger ring to accommodate the ribbon which is the same as for the British Golden Jubilee Medal.
Comments: *Awarded to Canadians who have made a significant contribution to their fellow citizens, their community or to Canada on the occasion of the 50th anniversary of Her Majesty's Accession to the throne as Queen of Canada. The recipients were selected by a number of partner organisations in every field of Canadian Life. Approximately 46,000 medals were awarded including approximately 9,000 to the military. The Canadian Forces awarded its 9,000 medals proportionally through its ranks according to an automatic formula based on the component, service, rank, trade and length of service of every member of the Canadian Forces.*

VALUE: £45–75 *Miniature* £15–25

C30A. QUEEN ELIZABETH II'S DIAMOND JUBILEE MEDAL (Canada)

Date: 13 January 2012.
Ribbon: 32 mm in width with a red stripe in the centre (2 mm) on each side of which are white stripes (3 mm) followed by red stripes (10 mm) and blue edge stripes (2 mm).
Metal: Nickel-Silver
Size: 32 mm
Description: (Obverse) a contemporary crowned effigy of The Queen circumscribed by the inscriptions "ELIZABETH II DEI GRATIA REGINA" and "CANADA" separated by small maple leaves; (reverse) a diamond-cut field, on which is superimposed a lozenge inscribed with the Royal Cypher, placed on four maples leaves, incorporating the dates "1952" and "2012" at the sides, and, in base, two scrolls bearing the words "VIVAT" and "REGINA" respectively. Ring suspension.
Comments: *Awarded on the occasion of the 60th anniversary of Her Majesty's Accession to the Throne as Queen of Canada to Canadian citizens or permanent residents of Canada (alive on 6 February 2012) who have made significant contributions to Canada or to a particular province, territory, region or community within Canada, or for an outstanding achievement abroad that has brought great credit to Canada. 60,000 recipients were selected by a number of partner organizations in every field of Canadian life. 11,000 medals were allocated to the Canadian Forces, divided proportionally by command, to be awarded based on merit while respecting certain targets to ensure appropriate representation of component, ranks, gender, language, etc.*

VALUE: £95–135 *Miniature* £15-25

C31. ROYAL CANADIAN MOUNTED POLICE LONG SERVICE MEDAL

Date: 6 March 1934.

Ribbon: Dark blue with two yellow stripes towards the edges.

Metal: Silver.

Size: 36mm.

Description: (Obverse) the effigy of the reigning monarch; (reverse) the insignia of the RCMP consisting of the head of a buffalo within a buckled belt inscribed with the words MAINTIENS LE DROIT all topped by a crown. On either side of the belt are five maple leaves. The name of the Force is contained in a banner below the belt. The words FOR LONG SERVICE (above) and AND GOOD CONDUCT (below) are inscribed around the circumference. A plain straight suspender is attached by a claw fitting.

Comments: *Awarded for 20 years of service in the RCMP. Different bars exist to denote subsequent periods of service (bronze with one star for 25 years, silver with 2 stars for 30 years, gold with 3 stars for 35 years and gold and silver with 4 stars for 40 years), only the last bar awarded is worn. When Queen Elizabeth came to the throne and the medal was redesigned to display her effigy on the obverse, changes were also made to the reverse to substitute the Queen's crown for the King's that had been used from the medal's introduction. The opportunity was also taken to reduce the size of the insignia of the RCMP and move the inscription to read continuously around the circumference. In 1989 a French language version of this new design was introduced with the inscription on the reverse reading POUR ANCIENNETÉ ET BONNE CONDUITE. The recipients have the right to choose which version they would prefer. The name of the recipient is engraved on the rim. Approximately 75 Medals and close to 1,000 various bars are issued every year.*

VALUE:

George V (C)	£950–1000	
George VI (B)	£950–1000	
George VI (C)	£1000–1200	
Elizabeth II (A)	£320–575	
Elizabeth II (French)	£400–675	*Miniature* (all) £50–60

C32. CANADIAN FORCES' DECORATION

Instituted: 15 December 1949.
Branch of Service: Canadian Forces.
Ribbon: 38mm orange-red divided into four equal parts by three thin white stripes.
Metal: Silver-gilt (George VI) or gilded tombac brass or bronze(Elizabeth II).
Size: Height 35mm; max. width 37mm.
Description: A decagonal (ten-sided) medal. (Obverse) coinage bust of the reigning monarch. The George VI issue has a suspension bar inscribed CANADA and the recipient's details engraved on the reverse, whereas the Elizabethan issue has no suspension bar, the recipient's details being impressed or engraved on the rim and the word "CANADA" appears at the base of the effigy; (reverse) a naval crown at the top, three maple leaves across the middle and an eagle in flight across the foot. In the George VI version the royal cypher is superimposed on the maple leaves.
Comments: *Awarded to both officers and men of the Canadian regular and reserve forces for 12 years exemplary service. A clasp, gold in colour, bearing the shield from the arms of Canada surmounted by the crown is awarded for each additional 10 years of qualifying service. Approximately 2,400 decorations and 3,000 clasps are awarded annually.*

VALUE:		Miniature
George VI (E)	£75–125	£15–25
Elizabeth II (D)	£40–85	£20–35

C33. POLICE EXEMPLARY SERVICE MEDAL

Date: 12 August 1982.
Ribbon: Five equal stripes of dark blue (three) and yellow (two).
Metal: Rhodium plated red brass.
Size: 36mm.
Description: (Obverse) a circular medal with a maple leaf in the centre bearing a representation of the scales of justice and an outer band with the words EXEMPLARY SERVICE in the upper half and SERVICES DISTINGUÉS in the lower. It is of a skeletal design with the outer band attached to the leaves and stem of the maple leaf; (reverse) plain apart from the royal cypher (EIIR) topped by the Queen's crown in the centre of the maple leaf.
Comments: *Awarded on completion of 20 years' service to officers of any recognised Canadian police force who showed industry, efficiency and good conduct during their careers. Although members of the RCMP or Canadian Military Police are not eligible, any previous and unrecognized full-time service in either of those bodies can be counted towards the necessary number of years' service. Bars (bearing a stylised maple leaf) are available for additional periods of ten years. The medal is not a purely long service award and will be withheld if an officer with the required number of years' service does not meet the appropriate standards of behaviour necessary. It can be awarded posthumously. The name of the recipient is engraved on the rim. 44,663 have been issued to 1 June 2015.*

VALUE:	£45–65	Miniature	£15–20

C34. CORRECTIONS EXEMPLARY SERVICE MEDAL

Date: 11 June 1984.
Ribbon: Five equal stripes of green (three) and yellow (two).
Metal: Rhodium plated red brass.
Size: 36mm.
Description: (Obverse) a circular medal with a maple leaf in the centre bearing a crossed key and torch and an outer band with the words EXEMPLARY SERVICE in the upper half and SERVICES DISTINGUÉS in the lower. It is of a skeletal design with the outer band attached to the leaves and stem of the maple leaf; (reverse) plain apart from the royal cypher (EIIR) topped by the Queen's crown in the centre of the maple leaf.
Comments: *Awarded on completion of 20 years' full-time paid service to officers of the Canadian Correctional Service (federal, provincial or territorial) who showed industry, efficiency and good conduct during their careers. The service need not have been continuous. Bars (bearing a stylised maple leaf) are available for additional periods of ten years. The medal is not a purely long service award and will be withheld if an officer with the required number of years' service does not meet the appropriate standards of behaviour necessary. It can be awarded posthumously. The name of the recipient is engraved on the rim. 13,981 have been issued to 1 June 2015.*

VALUE: £45–70 *Miniature* £15–20

C35. FIRE SERVICES EXEMPLARY SERVICE MEDAL

Date: 25 August 1985.
Ribbon: Five equal stripes of red (three) and yellow (two).
Metal: Rhodium plated red brass.
Size: 36mm.
Description: (Obverse) a circular medal with a maple leaf in the centre bearing a pair of crossed axes and fire hydrant within an outer band with the words EXEMPLARY SERVICE in the upper half and SERVICES DISTINGUÉS in the lower. It is of a skeletal design with the outer band attached to the leaves and stem of the maple leaf; (reverse) plain apart from the royal cypher (EIIR) topped by the Queen's crown in the centre of the maple leaf.
Comments: *Awarded on completion of 20 years' service with a recognised Canadian fire service (including fire marshal's offices, fire commissioner's offices and the Canadian Forces Fire Service) to officers who showed industry, efficiency and good conduct during their careers. The service need not have been continuous. Bars (bearing a stylised maple leaf) are available for additional periods of ten years. The medal is not a purely long service award and will be withheld if an officer with the required number of years' service does not meet the appropriate standards of behaviour necessary. It can be awarded posthumously. The name of the recipient is engraved on the rim. 58,393 have been issued to 1 June 2015.*

VALUE: £65–85 *Miniature* £15–20

C36. CANADIAN COAST GUARD EXEMPLARY SERVICE MEDAL

Date: 14 March 1991.
Ribbon: Dark blue with a narrow white stripe in the centre and a broader yellow stripe towards each edge.
Metal: Rhodium plated red brass.
Size: 36mm.
Description: (Obverse) a solid circular medal with the crest of the Canadian Coast Guard in the centre and an outer band bearing the inscriptions EXEMPLARY SERVICE (left) and SERVICES DISTINGUÉS (right); (reverse) plain apart from the royal cypher (EIIR) topped by the Queen's crown in the centre of the maple leaf.
Comments: *Awarded on completion of 20 years' service with the Department of Transport which must include 10 years with the Canadian Coast Guard in duties with a potential risk. Officers must have shown industry, efficiency and good conduct during their careers. The service need not have been continuous. Bars (bearing a stylised maple leaf) are available for additional periods of ten years, five of which must have involved duties where there was a potential risk of danger. The medal is not a purely long service award and will be withheld if an officer with the required number of years' service does not meet the appropriate standards of behaviour necessary. It can be awarded posthumously. The name of the recipient is engraved on the rim. 456 have been issued to 1 June 2015.*

VALUE: £120–165   *Miniature*   £15–20

C37. EMERGENCY MEDICAL SERVICES EXEMPLARY SERVICE MEDAL

Date: 7 July 1994.
Ribbon: Gold with three stripes of blue all equally spaced and with a stripe of orange bisecting each of the three blue stripes.
Metal: Rhodium plated red brass.
Size: 36mm.
Description: (Obverse) a circular medal with a maple leaf in the centre bearing the star of life, staff and serpent within an outer band with the words EXEMPLARY SERVICE in the upper half and SERVICES DISTINGUÉS in the lower. It is of a skeletal design with the outer band attached to the leaves and stem of the maple leaf; (reverse) plain apart from the royal cypher (EIIR) topped by the Queen's crown in the centre of the maple leaf.
Comments: *Awarded on completion of 20 years' service in the field of pre-hospital emergency medical care. Ten of these years must have involved duties with a potential risk. Recipients must have shown industry, efficiency and good conduct during their careers. The service need not have been continuous. Bars (bearing a stylised maple leaf) are available for additional periods of ten years. The medal is not a purely long service award and will be withheld if an officer with the required number of years' service does not meet the appropriate standards of behaviour necessary. It can be awarded posthumously. The name of the recipient is engraved on the rim. 4,060 have been issued to 1 June 2015.*

VALUE: £100–165   *Miniature*   £15–20

C37A. PEACE OFFICER EXEMPLARY SERVICE MEDAL

Date: June 22, 2004
Ribbon: A central stripe of green flanked by stripes of gold, light blue and dark blue.
Metal: Rhodium plated red brass.
Size: 36mm.
Description: (Obverse) a circular medal with a maple leaf in the centre bearing a shield set on a star and an outer band with the words EXEMPLARY SERVICE in the upper half and SERVICES DISTINGUÉS in the lower. It is of a skeletal design with the outer band attached to the leaves and stem of the maple leaf; (reverse) plain apart for the royal cipher (EIIR) surmounted by the Royal Crown in the centre.
Comments: *Awarded on completion of 20 years' service as a peace officer with one or more of the following organizations: the Canada Border Service Agency; the Department of Citizenship and Immigration, Environment, Fisheries and Oceans; the Parks Canada Agency or any other organization that employs peace officers and that is deemed eligible by the Advisory Committee. Ten of these years must have involved duties with potential risk. Recipient must have shown industry, efficiency and good conduct during their careers. The service need not have been continuous. Bars (bearing a stylized maple leaf) are available for additional periods of ten years of eligible service. The medal is not a purely long service award and will be withheld if an officer with the required number of years' service does not meet the appropriate standards of behaviour necessary. It can be awarded posthumously. The name of the recipient is engraved on the rim. 4,941 have been awarded to 1 June 2015.*

VALUE: £100–165   *Miniature*   £15–18

C38. QUEEN'S / KING'S MEDAL FOR CHAMPION SHOT IN CANADA

Date: 28 August 1991.
Ribbon: Dark crimson with stripes of black, white and black (each 3mm) at the edges.
Metal: Silver.
Size: 38mm.
Description: (Obverse) the effigy of the reigning monarch with appropriate inscription around the circumference and CANADA at the bottom; (reverse) the figure of Fame on the right rising from her throne and crowning a warrior with a laurel wreath. The warrior holds a bow and quiver of arrows in his right hand and has a target with three arrows in the centre resting on his left knee. Until 2002, a plain straight suspender was used attached by a claw fitting, since then it is a straight suspender ornamented with a fleur-de-lys. The date of the award is showed on a plain silver clasp. Any subsequent award of the medal is indicated by a clasp only.
Comments: *There are two medals awarded each year, one to the regular member of the Canadian armed forces and another to the officer of the Royal Canadian Mounted Police who obtains the highest aggregate score in the two stages of the Medal Competition. The name of the recipient is engraved on the rim.*

VALUE:

Victoria bronze	—
Victoria silver	—
George V	£850–1000
George VI	£850–1000
Elizabeth II	£850–1000
Charles III	—

C39. ONTARIO MEDAL FOR GOOD CITIZENSHIP

Date: 1973.
Ribbon: White with a central stripe in gold and a broad green stripe at the edges.
Metal: Silver.
Size: 36mm.
Description: (Obverse) circular with the full achievement of arms of Ontario in the lower two-thirds and the inscription FOR GOOD CITIZENSHIP at the upper circumference; (reverse) the provincial flower—a trillium. A scrolled suspender bar is used attached to the top of the disc.
Comments: *Awarded to any citizen of Ontario to recognise good citizenship displayed by their generous, kind or self-effacing manner in improving the quality of life in the Province. It is not awarded posthumously or for acts of courage. A maximum of twelve medals are presented each year. Recipients can use post-nominals OMC.*

VALUE: £100–165

C40. ONTARIO MEDAL FOR POLICE BRAVERY

Date: 1975.
Ribbon: Royal blue with two gold stripes towards the edges.
Metal: Gold plated sterling silver with blue and white enamel.
Size: 57mm wide by 68mm high (with crown).
Description: (Obverse) a cross in blue enamel on gold with the provincial flower (white trillium) in white in a small central medallion and a maple leaf between the arms of the cross. A Queen's crown tops the upper arm; (reverse) left plain.
Comments: *Awarded to officers from any police force in the province to reward any act of superlative courage and bravery performed in the line of duty and is also intended to encourage the virtue of bravery and focus attention and support of the public behind the efforts of the police forces. The medals are presented at a special ceremony held in early November each year.*

VALUE: £140–175

C41. ONTARIO MEDAL FOR FIREFIGHTERS BRAVERY

Date: 1976.
Ribbon: Red with two gold stripes towards the edges.
Metal: Gold plated sterling silver with red and white enamel.
Size: 57mm wide by 68mm high (with crown).
Description: (Obverse) a cross in gold with a pattern on each arm in red enamel to symbolise fire and a maple leaf between the arms. The provincial flower (white trillium) in white enamel lies in a small central medallion. A Queen's crown tops the upper arm; (reverse) left plain.
Comments: *Awarded to firefighters in the Province to reward any act of superlative courage and bravery performed in the line of duty and is also intended to encourage the virtue of bravery and focus attention and support of the public behind the efforts of the firefighters. The medals are presented at a special ceremony held on 9 November each year. The medal can be awarded posthumously.*

VALUE: £125–175

C42. SASKATCHEWAN VOLUNTEER MEDAL

Date: 1995
Ribbon: Green with a gold central stripe, all of equal width.
Metal: Silver and enamel.
Size: 36mm.
Description: (Obverse) a circular silver medal with the shield from the Saskatchewan coat of arms surmounted by a crown placed in the centre. The name of the Province lies along the lower circumference and the inscription NOS IPSOS DEDIMUS (we give of ourselves) at the upper edge. The plain straight suspender bar is attached by a stylised letter "V".
Comments: *Awarded each year to a maximum of ten current or former long-term residents of Saskatchewan who have served in a voluntary capacity above and beyond the call of duty to improve daily life in the Province. Elected officials and members of the judiciary are barred from receiving the award whilst they remain in office. Recipients can use post-nominals SVM.*

VALUE: £25–45

C43. ONTARIO PROVINCIAL POLICE LONG SERVICE AND GOOD CONDUCT MEDAL

Date: 15 December 1949.
Ribbon: Crimson with two green stripes each bordered by white lines on both sides.
Metal: Silver, later in cupro-nickel
Size: 38mm.
Description: (Obverse) the Coat of Arms of the Province of Ontario with the word ONTARIO written below; (reverse) the inscription ONTARIO PROVINCIAL POLICE in three lines in the central field and FOR LONG SERVICE AND GOOD CONDUCT around the circumference and two crossed maple leaves in the exergue. An ornate, non-swivelling, suspender was attached to the top of the medal.
Comments: *Ontario is one of only two provincial police forces that remain in Canada. The medal was awarded to members of the Force who had served for not less than 20 years, the last ten of which must have been with good conduct and satisfactory service. Bars were awarded for each additional period of five years' qualifying service. For 25 and 30 years' service a plain silver bar decorated with one or two white trilliums (the provincial flower) was awarded and for 35 or 40 years qualifying service gold bars were issued also bearing one or two trillium motifs.*

VALUE: Silver   £200–325
         Cupro-nickel   £35–45

C44. COMMISSIONAIRES LONG SERVICE MEDAL

Date: August 20, 1948.
Ribbon: 32mm in width with a broad centre stripe of crimson on each side of which are stripes of white and navy blue.
Metal: Bronze, nickel-plated copper
Size: 36mm.
Description: (Obverse) within a buckled belt inscribed with the words VIRTUTE ET INDUSTRIA are superimposed on a natural maple leaf a crossed sword and anchor and a flying eagle; (reverse) the inscription THE CANADIAN CORPS OF COMMISSIONAIRES - LE CORPS CANADIEN DES COMMISSIONNARES surrounding a plain field. The medal is attached to a suspension bar bearing the inscription LABOR OMNIA VINCIT by three small rings.
Comments: *Initially awarded in bronze for 10 years but now only awarded in "silver" for 12 years of service in the Canadian Corps of Commissionaires. Bars are awarded for subsequent periods of 5 years of service, a maximum of 3 bars may be awarded to an individual.*

VALUE: £25–40

C45. SASKATCHEWAN CENTENNIAL MEDAL

Date: 2005.
Ribbon: Gold with two green stripes near the edges.
Metal: Bronzed base metal.
Size: 36mm.
Description: (Obverse) The provincial motto on a ribbon under a wreath of western red lilies, surmounted by the St. Edward's Crown, the whole circumscribed with the words "Saskatchewan 1905-2005"; (reverse) the provincial shield of arms.
Comments: *Created to commemorate the 100th anniversary of the creation of the province, the medal recognizes individuals who have made significant contributions to society and honours outstanding achievements. Approximately 4,000 medals were presented during Centennial year and up until the spring of 2006. Many recipients were members of the Canadian Forces or members of the various protective services. Persons not residing in Saskatchewan but have contributed to the province were also eligible.*

VALUE: £60–85

C46. ALBERTA CENTENNIAL MEDAL

Date: 2005
Ribbon: A central red-pink stripe flanked by stripes of white, green, gold and Royal blue.
Metal: Gold-plated bronze
Size: 36mm.
Description: (Obverse) The arms of the province surrounded by a raised circle, the whole circumscribed with the words "Alberta Centennial 1905-2005"; (reverse) the provincial shield of arms charged on a maple leaf, surrounded by a raised circle, the whole circumscribed with the words "Honouring Outstanding Albertans".
Comments: *Created to commemorate the 100th anniversary of the creation of the province, the medal recognizes Albertans whose achievements have benefited their fellow citizens, their community and their province. Approximately 8,000 medals were presented during Centennial year and up until the spring of 2006. Many recipients were members of the Canadian Forces or members of the various protective services. Eligibility was limited to Canadian citizens who reside in, or have resided in, Alberta.*

VALUE: £60–95

In addition to the medals listed in this section there are also a large number of interesting collectable medals issued by the various provinces and by numerous organisations throughout Canada. These medals are not considered official by the Government of Canada and therefore cannot be worn or mounted in conjunction with official Canadian orders, decorations and medals. Many of these are already well known whilst others are seldom seen and are very rare. Here, with the assistance of collector Jack Boddington, we include a representative selection. Others will be added in future editions. For ease of identification each has been allotted a Medal Yearbook reference number.

C57. ALBERTA MUNICIPAL ENFORCEMENT LONG SERVICE MEDAL

Date: 2005.
Ribbon: Wide central black stripe, flanked on either side by equal stripes of yellow and green with narrow white edges. The colours represent the mineral, agricultural and forestry resources of the province and the snow that caps the Rocky Mountains.
Metal: Sterling Silver.
Size: 36mm.
Description: (Obverse) the Shield of Alberta surmounted by a mural crown representing municipal authority and surrounded by 13 maple leaves representing the Canadian provinces and territories with the words MUNICIPAL ENFORCEMENT above. (Reverse) a wild rose, the provincial flower of Alberta, surmounted by a mural crown and surrounded by 13 maple leaves. The words FOR LONG SERVICE and 20 YEARS encircle the whole.
Comments: *The medal was authorised by the Province of Alberta by Ministerial Order on January 16, 2006 to recognise 20 years of service by Municipal enforcement officers. A clasp is awarded for additional five year increments. To date 24 medals have been awarded including 2 for special circumstances, 10 first clasp, and 3 second clasps have been awarded.*

Value £85–115

C58. ALBERTA EMERGENCY SERVICES MEDAL

Date: 2000

Ribbon: Blue with three central thin white pin stripes. The blue colour represents the province of Alberta and the three white stripes for good service, loyalty and good conduct, bar suspension.

Metal: Silver.

Size: 35mm.

Description: (Obverse) the Alberta shield centred around which are the words: EMERGENCY SERVICES (above) and ALBERTA (below). (Reverse) the Alberta wild rose surrounded by the words: IN THE SERVICE OF ALBERTANS

Comments: *To be eligible for the medal, the recipient must have been serving for a total of at least 12 years of service with one or more municipal emergency services or with the Alberta Emergency Management Agency or Alberta Sustainable Resource Development in the province of Alberta.*

Alberta Emergency Personnel include:

• *Members of the emergency services established by an Alberta municipality under the provisions of the Alberta Municipal Government Act (i.e. fire fighters, officers and dispatchers of full-time, part-time or volunteer Fire Services or Search and Rescue volunteers)*

• *Alberta Emergency Management Agency personnel*

• *Directors or Deputy Directors of Emergency Management appointed by municipalities under the Emergency Management Act*

• *Emergency Medical Services (EMS) Paramedicine Practitioners licensed under the Health Professions Act - Paramedic Regulation (i.e licenced Emergency Medical Responders, Emergency Medical Technicians, Emergency Medical Technologists—Paramedic)*

•*Emergency Medical Dispatchers certified through the National Academy of Emergency Medical Dispatch; or*

• *Sustainable Resource Development personnel (Fire Protection & Emergency Response).*

Value £85–115

C59. ALBERTA LAW ENFORCEMENT LONG SERVICE MEDAL

Date: 1969 (date of authorisation)

Ribbon: Royal blue with a centre green stripe with on either side, two narrow yellow stripes.

Metal: Silver.

Size: 35mm.

Description: The circular medal is suspended from a straight bar. (Obverse) the Provincial Shield of Alberta with a wheat stalk on either side and the word ALBERTA in stylised form below. (Reverse) the floral emblem of Alberta the prairie rose, with the words TWENTY FIVE YEARS above and LONG SERVICE below

Comments: *The 25 years law enforcement must have been served in Alberta. The medal was introduced by the Solicitor General of the time Roy Farran, renowned for his former SAS service and holder of the DSO, MC with two bars and Legion of Merit (USA), French Criox de Guerre and two Greek medals in addition to his British Campaign Medals. He was the author of the SAS classic "The Winged Dagger".*

Value £85–100

C60. EDMONTON POLICE SERVICE MEDAL OF VALOUR

Date: 2002 (recommendations were dated from 1961)
Ribbon: Blue with broad central white stripe, a red and gold pin line stripes in the centre
Metal: Silver.
Size: 30mm.
Description: (Obverse) round silver medal with the EPS crest centred on top of a solid "V", which symbolises Valour. The suspensory bar has "For Valour", written on it. (Reverse) a wreath surrounding a plain field with space for the engraving of the Register number, name and rank of recipient and date of occurrence.
Comments: *The Medal of Valour is the highest award that may be bestowed upon a member of the service. It is to be conferred upon members of the Edmonton Police Service for outstanding acts of personal heroism or the most conspicuous acts of courage in circumstances of extreme peril and personal hazard to life during the intelligent and appropriate execution of their duty. Nominations for the Medal of Valour would be considered for occurrences dating back to 1961: the year of amalgamation between the Edmonton Police Department and the Beverly Police Department. In the absence of specific criteria the following factors are considered in making determinations in each incident: A member found himself/herself caught in the circumstances as a result of their normal duties and engaged in a brave or heroic initiative taken on their own volition. (Incidents that do not meet these initial criteria will be considered for the officer safety award).*

Value £100–140

C61. EDMONTON POLICE SERVICE MEDAL OF HONOUR

Date: 2002.
Ribbon: Blue with central broad white stripe and three lines in red, gold and red.
Metal: Silver.
Size: 32mm.
Description: (Obverse) octagonal star shaped silver medal with the EPS Crest centred within a circle. The tip of the top point connects to the suspensory bar. The suspensory bar has "For Honour" written on it. (Reverse) a wreath surrounding a plain field with space for the engraving of the register number, name and rank of the recipient and date of occurrence.
Comments: *The criteria for this medal are as follows: "The Medal of Honour is to be conferred upon members of the Edmonton Police Service, who during the intelligent and appropriate execution of their duty, in an attempt to save or protect life suffered grievous physical injury or permanent disfigurement. The actions were performed in good faith as a peace officer, adhering to proper officer safety protocol and policy. The Medal of Honour will also be awarded posthumously, to the surviving family of Edmonton Police Service members who have lost their lives while in the lawful execution of their duties and services to the City of Edmonton".*

Value £90–120

C62. CANADIAN LIFEBOAT INSTITUTION

Date: 1981
Ribbon: Two versions—red with two blue intermediate stripes for patronage; red with two white intermediate stripes for bravery.
Metal: Gold, silver and bronze.
Size: 34mm.
Description: Circular, straight bar suspension. (Obverse) in the centre a fouled anchor surrounded by a roped border with the words CANADIAN LIFEBOAT INSTITUTION and two maple leaves. (Reverse) a cross with a crown and anchor in the centre, around a rope is the motto of the institution THE SEA SHALL NOT HAVE THEM with a maple leaf at the bottom.
Comments: *The ribbon colour identifies whether the medal is issued for patronage or for bravery in saving, or attempting to save human life, the metal distinguishing the level of service.*

	Bronze	Silver	Gold
Value for life saving	£100–135	£150–195	rare
Value for service	£60–85	£80–125	£375

C63. THE CANADIAN RED CROSS SOCIETY ORDER OF THE RED CROSS

Date: 1984.
Ribbon: Red with white stripes at outer edge.
Metal: Silver or Gold.
Size: 38mm across the arms.
Description: A cross pattée with a maple leaf in each of the four corners of the arms. Inner green enamelled wreath with a central red cross. The reverse is left plain for naming purposes (the name of the recipient and year of award are always engraved).
Comments: *The Order of the Red Cross has three grades—Companion (neck decoration in gold), Officer (breast cross in gold) and Member (breast cross in silver). The award pays tribute to volunteers and other individuals for their outstanding humanitarian service, dedication and achievements. Appointments to the Order are limited to three Companions, five Officers and twenty-five members.*

Value: —

C64. THE CANADIAN BANKS LAW ENFORCEMENT AWARD

Date: 1972.
Ribbon: Off white with wide side stripes in light purple
Metal: Gold.
Size: 35mm.
Description: Suspended from a straight bar to accommodate the ribbon. (Obverse) an antique bank vault door, the words THE CANADIAN BANKS above and LAW ENFORCEMENT AWARD below. (Reverse) within a narrow wreath the words AWARDED BY THE CANADIAN BANKERS ASSOCIATION FOR DISTINGUISHED LAW ENFORCEMENT. The medal can be worded in French if desired.
Comments: *The Canadian Banks Law Enforcement Award was established after extensive discussion between the Canadian Bankers Association and the Canadian Association of Chiefs of Police. The purpose of the award is to recognise outstanding police action in combatting crimes against banks.*

Value: £265–325

C65. THE MOOSE JAW MEDAL OF MERIT

Date: 1968.
Ribbon: Green with a wide central yellow stripe.
Metal: Gold (gilt).
Size: 34mm.
Description: A top bar in gilt carrying the words FOR MERIT. (Obverse) the civic coat-of-arms of the city of Moose Jaw, Saskatchewan surmounting the word MOOSOOCHAPISKUN which is the name of the city in the local Indian dialect, wreath of wheat stalks surround with an outer edge inscription CORPORATION OF THE CITY OF MOOSE JAW. (Reverse) plain for appropriate engraving.
Comments: *In addition to life saving, "the saving of a life where circumstances involved personal risk or heroism beyond the call of duty", the medal may also be awarded for achievements in athletics, arts and culture and civic actions.*

Value: **£80–170 depending on circumstances.**

C66. QUEEN ELIZABETH II'S PLATINUM JUBILEE MEDAL (PROVINCIAL)

Date: November 2022.
Ribbon: White with fine blue edges, bisected down the centre by two thin red parallel lines.
Metal: Nickel-silver.
Size: 32mm.
Description: (Obverse) crowned effigy of Her Majesty the Queen of Canada, facing right, circumscribed with the inscriptions "ELIZABETH II DEI GRATIA REGINA" and "CANADA", separated by small maple leaves. (Reverse) the shield of the awarding province surmounted by the Royal Cypher, on either sides of which appear the dates "1952" and "2022", the provincial flowers appear on either side of the shield and, in the base, are inscribed the words "VIVAT" and "REGINA" meaning "Long Live the Queen".
Comments: *Issued to commemorate the 70th Anniversary of the Accession of Her Majesty Queen Elizabeth II to the throne as Queen of Canada. While no national medal was created on this occasion, several Canadian provinces created their own Royal commemorative medal, uniform in design, scope and intent and aligned with previous national programmes for such anniversaries. The medals are administered by the various provinces which created them — Nova Scotia, New Brunswick, Manitoba, Prince Edward Island, Saskatchewan and Alberta.*

Value: **—.**

NEW ZEALAND
Medals

The New Zealand honours system is a uniquely New Zealand system. From 1848 to 1975, New Zealand shared in the British-based honours system. In 1975, the Queen's Service Order and accompanying Queen's Service Medal were introduced, making the system a mix of British and New Zealand honours. In 1987, the Order of New Zealand was introduced. In 1995, the system was comprehensively reviewed and a number of changes were made as a result. The most significant was the establishment of the New Zealand Order of Merit in 1996, which replaced New Zealand's use of the Order of the British Empire. In 1999 a new range of New Zealand gallantry and bravery awards were instituted, including the Victoria Cross for New Zealand.

The honours lists are approved by the King of New Zealand, as New Zealand's Head of State.

In addition, a range of campaign and long service medals have been instituted for armed forces and uniformed services. These awards are mostly administered by the respective agencies.

In 2020 the New Zealand Government made major changes to their Long Service Awards. In summary:
- All Regular Force Long Service Awards for service on or after 1 December 1977 now require 14 years for award of the Long Service Award, and 7 years for subsequent clasps.
- All attested service in any Service or arm of the NZ Armed Forces can be accumulated providing good conduct standards are maintained.
- The Long Service Award will reflect the majority of the service being recognised.
- Territorial service must be efficient but the requirement of some awards for continuous service has been removed.

Medals and decorations specific to New Zealand but made under Royal Warrants prior to 1975 are listed in the main body of this book.

In addition to those listed, a number of foreign awards have been approved for acceptance and wear by NZDF personnel and civilians. Approvals are generally made on a case-by-case basis.

Further information on New Zealand medals can found on the following websites: https://medals.nzdf.mil.nz; www.honours.govt.nz; and www.archives.govt.nz.

THE ORDER OF WEAR IN NEW ZEALAND (including British Awards)

Victoria Cross for New Zealand
New Zealand Cross
George Cross
Knight/Lady of the Order of the Garter
Knight/Lady of the Order of the Thistle
Knight or Dame Grand Cross, The Most Honourable Order of the Bath
Order of Merit
Member of the Order of New Zealand
Baronet's Badge
Knight or Dame Grand Companion of the New Zealand Order of Merit
Knight or Dame Grand Cross of the Order of St Michael and St George
Knight or Dame Grand Cross of the Royal Victorian Order
Knight or Dame Grand Cross of the Order of the British Empire
Member of the Order of Companions of Honour
Knight or Dame Companion of the New Zealand Order of Merit
Knight or Dame Commander of the Most Honourable Order of the Bath
Knight or Dame Commander of the Most Distinguished Order of St Michael and St George
Knight or Dame Commander of the Royal Victorian Order
Knight or Dame Commander of the Order of the British Empire

Knight Bachelor's badge
Companion of the New Zealand Order of Merit
Companion of the Order of the Bath
Companion of the Order of St Michael and St George
Commander of the Royal Victorian Order
Commander of the Order of the British Empire
New Zealand Gallantry Star
New Zealand Bravery Star
Companion of the Distinguished Service Order
Lieutenant of the Royal Victorian Order
Companion of the Queen's Service Order
Officer of the New Zealand Order of Merit
Officer of the Order of the British Empire
Companion of the Imperial Service Order
Member of the Royal Victorian Order
Member of the New Zealand Order of Merit
Member of the Order of the British Empire
New Zealand Gallantry Decoration
New Zealand Bravery Decoration
Royal Red Cross (First Class or Member)
Distinguished Service Cross
Military Cross
Distinguished Flying Cross
Air Force Cross
Royal Red Cross (Second Class or Associate)
Order of St John (All classes)
Distinguished Conduct Medal
Conspicuous Gallantry Medal
George Medal

Distinguished Service Medal
Military Medal
Distinguished Flying Medal
Air Force Medal
Queen's Gallantry Medal
New Zealand Gallantry Medal
New Zealand Bravery Medal
Royal Victorian Medals
Queen's Service Medal
New Zealand Antarctic Medal
New Zealand Distinguished Service Decoration
British Empire Medal
Queen's Police Medal for Distinguished Service
Queen's Fire Service Medal for Distinguished Service
War Medals in order of campaign
New Zealand Special Service Medal in order of date of award
Polar Medal in order of date of award
Coronation, Jubilee and New Zealand Commemoration Medals in date order:
  King George VI Coronation Medal 1937
  Queen Elizabeth II Coronation Medal 1953
  Queen Elizabeth II Silver Jubilee Medal 1977
  Queen Elizabeth II Golden Jubilee Medal 2002
  New Zealand 1990 Commemoration Medal
  New Zealand Suffrage Centennial Medal 1993
New Zealand Meritorious Service Medal
New Zealand Armed Forces Award
New Zealand Army Long Service and Good Conduct Medal

Royal New Zealand Navy Long Service and Good Conduct Medal
Royal New Zealand Air Force Long Service and Good Conduct Medal
New Zealand Police Long Service and Good Conduct Medal
New Zealand Fire Brigades Long Service and Good Conduct Medal
New Zealand Prison Service Medal
New Zealand Traffic Service Medal
Efficiency Decoration
Efficiency Medal
Royal New Zealand Naval Reserve Decoration
Royal New Zealand Naval Volunteer Reserve Decoration
Royal New Zealand Naval Volunteer Reserve Long Service and Good Conduct Medal
Air Efficiency Award
Queen's Medal for Champion Shots of the New Zealand Naval Forces
Queen's Medal for Champion Shots of the Military Forces
Queen's Medal for Champion Shots of the Air Forces
Cadet Forces Medal
New Zealand Defence Service Medal
Rhodesia Medal 1980
Commonwealth Independence Medals
Service Medal of the Order of St John
Other Commonwealth Members' Orders, Decorations and Medals in date of award
Approved Foreign Orders, Decorations and Medals in order of date of award

NZ1. VICTORIA CROSS FOR NEW ZEALAND

Instituted: September 20, 1999.
Ribbon: Crimson 38mm wide.
Metal: Bronze.
Size: 35mm at each axis.
Description: A cross pattée with raised edges, identical to the British and Australian Victoria Crosses (MYB24 and A1).
Comments: *Although identical to the existing VC, awards will be made under a New Zealand, as opposed to a British, Royal Warrant. Recipients are entitled to the postnominal letters VC and their name will be engraved on each award. It may be awarded posthumously. The first VC for NZ was awarded on 2 July 2007 to Corporal Apiata of the NZ SAS for gallantry in Afghanistan in 2004.*

VALUE: —

NZ2. NEW ZEALAND CROSS

Instituted: September 20, 1999.

Ribbon: Bright blue. A miniature cross is worn on the ribbon alone.

Metal: Silver with gold appliqué.

Size: Height 52mm, width 38mm.

Description: Similar to the original New Zealand Cross of 1869 (MYB25) but incorporating changes which were first proposed in 1885 and only now implemented, viz. fern fronds have replaced laurel leaves. (Reverse) inscribed FOR BRAVERY— MO TE MAIA.

Comments: *The premier civilian award for bravery, it now supersedes the George Cross so far as New Zealand citizens are concerned. Recipients are entitled to the postnominal letters NZC. To date only two crosses have been awarded, one posthumously.*

VALUE: —

NZ3. ORDER OF NEW ZEALAND

Instituted: 1987.

Ribbon: Red ochre with a narrow white stripe towards either edge. The original ribbon used on the day of investiture is 38mm wide but from that day on the medal is worn from a 15mm ribbon. The ribbon is not worn in undress uniform.

Metal: 9 carat gold.

Description: An oval medal decorated with coloured enamels bearing in the centre the heraldic shield of New Zealand within a Kowhaiwhai rafter pattern.

Comments: *Instituted as a first-level non-titular order, it is modelled on the British Order of Merit (1902) and the Order of the Companions of Honour (1917). The Order comprises the Queen as Sovereign and no more than 20 ordinary members. Additional members may be appointed in commemoration of important royal, state or national occasions. Honorary membership includes citizens of Commonwealth nations of which the Queen is not Head of State, and of foreign countries. The badge must be returned on the death of the holder. No miniature exists, but a lapel badge was instituted in 1990. Members are entitled to the post-nominal letters ONZ.*

VALUE: —

NZ4. NEW ZEALAND ORDER OF MERIT

Breast star

Instituted: May 30, 1996.
Ribbon: Plain red ochre (kokowai).
Comments: *An order of chivalry designed along British lines and intended to replace the various British orders to which New Zealanders were formerly appointed. It consists of five classes whose insignia are noted separately below. In addition, there is a collar of the order, worn only by the Sovereign of the Order and the Chancellor (the Governor-General of New Zealand). The collar is composed of links of the central badge and gold koru (in the form of the letter S) with a pendant badge featuring the New Zealand arms. Distinctive lapel badges denoting membership of the Order are worn in civilian clothes. On the abolition of Knighthoods an amending warrant dated May 18, 2000, replaced Knights and Dames with Principal and Distinguished Companions. However, in March 2009 Her Majesty approved the reinstatement of the original titles in the New Zealand honours system therefore the titles Knights and Dames are once more current.*

VALUE: —

GRAND COMPANIONS (GNZM)

Badge: A cross in white enamel set in silver-gilt with, in the centre, a medallion comprising the New Zealand arms in coloured enamel surrounded by a circle of green enamel inscribed in gold FOR MERIT / TOHU HIRANGA and surmounted by a royal crown. The badge is worn from a sash over the right shoulder and resting on the left hip.
Star: A gold breast star of eight points, each arm bearing in relief a representation of a fern frond, superimposed in the centre of which is a smaller representation of the badge of the order.
Comments: *Holders of the grades of Knight or Dame Grand Cross (GNZM) are entitled to the titles "Sir" or "Dame".*

KNIGHT AND DAME COMPANION (K/DNZM)

A badge and breast star similar to that above, except that the badge is worn from either a neck ribbon or a bow on the left shoulder. The breast star is in silver, with the badge of the order in the centre. Holders of the grades of Knight or Dame Companion are entitled to the titles "Sir" or "Dame" respectively.

Companions badge

COMPANIONS (CNZM)

A badge similar to that above (illustrated left), worn from a 38mm wide neck ribbon or a bow on the left shoulder.

OFFICERS (ONZM)

A smaller representation of the badge in silver-gilt, with the motto in green enamel. Worn from a ribbon on the left lapel or from a 38mm wide ribbon tied in a bow and worn on the left shoulder.

MEMBERS (MNZM)

Badge as for Officers but in silver.

NZ5. NEW ZEALAND GALLANTRY STAR

Instituted: September 20, 1999.
Branch of Service: New Zealand armed forces.
Ribbon: Crimson with a purple central stripe bordered by thin white stripes.
Metal: Silver and gilt.
Size: 45mm.
Description: (Obverse) faceted silver 8-pointed star of equal points surmounted by a gilt crown surrounded by a wreath of New Zealand fern. (Reverse) inscribed FOR GALLANTRY —MO TE TOANGA. With ring suspension.
Comments: *This decoration supersedes the British Distinguished Service Order, Distinguished Conduct Medal and Conspicuous Gallantry Medal. Recipients are entitled to the postnominal letters NZGS and their name will be inscribed on the reverse. The five recipients so far are Colonel N.J. Reilly for gallantry in East Timor, 1999, Cpl A. H. Moore for gallantry in Afghanistan, 2010, SSgt J. Pennell, and Cpl D.S. Askin, for gallantry in Afghanistan 2011, and Major G.M. Faraday, for gallantry in South Sudan 2014.*

VALUE: —

NZ6. QUEEN'S / KING'S SERVICE ORDER

Instituted: 1975.
Ribbon: Narrow red ochre edges with a centre of alternating diagonal steps in ochre, white and black descending from left to right. The design is based on the Maori Poutama (stepped) pattern used in Tukutuku wall panels to represent the stairway to heaven, but here denoting the steps of achievement.
Metal: Frosted sterling silver.
Description: A badge based on the stylised representation of a manuka flower, consisting of five large and five small stylised petals. Superimposed in the centre is a silver-gilt medallion bearing the crowned effigy of the monarch within a circle of red enamel originally bearing the words FOR COMMUNITY SERVICE or FOR PUBLIC SERVICES as appropriate and surmounted by St Edward's Crown. From June 2007 the two divisions of the Order have been amalgamated and the insignia now reads FOR SERVICE—MO NGA MAHI NUI. The full name of the recipient is engraved on the reverse.
Comments: *The single non-titular order was originally divided into two divisions, for Community Service and Public Services, but the divisions were abolished in 2007. Ordinary membership is limited to 30 appointments per annum. Members of the Royal Family may be appointed as Extra Companions and include so far the Duke of Edinburgh (1981), Prince Charles (1983) and the Princess Royal (1990). Recipients are entitled to the postnominal letters QSO / KSO, and appropriate lapel badges for everyday wear. A full list of the recipients of the QSO /KSO are listed on the New Zealand Honours Lists published at www.honours. govt.nz. On May 23, 2023, it was confirmed by the New Zealand Prime Minister that the Queen's Service Order would change name following the accession of King Charles III.*

VALUE: £600–895   *Miniature* £150–235

NZ7. NEW ZEALAND GALLANTRY DECORATION

Instituted: September 20, 1999.
Branch of Service: New Zealand armed forces.
Ribbon: 32mm wide. Crimson with central purple stripe and two equal white stripes.
Metal: Silver and gilt.
Size: 46mm.
Description: (Obverse) A simple faceted silver cross surmounted by the royal crown and fern frond wreath emblem; (reverse) inscribed FOR GALLANTRY —MO TE TOANGA. With ring suspension.
Comments: *This decoration supersedes the British DSC, MC, DFC, AFC, DSM, MM, DFM and AFM. Recipients are entitled to the postnominal letters NZGD. So far 12 awards have been made: two for East Timor, one each for Cambodia and Sierra Leone, and two for Afghanistan. A full list of the recipients of the NZGD is on the New Zealand Honours Lists published at www.honours. govt.nz/honours/lists/nzga.*

VALUE: —

NZ8. NEW ZEALAND BRAVERY STAR

Instituted: September 20, 1999.
Branch of Service: New Zealand police forces, fire brigades and civilians.
Ribbon: 32mm wide. Bright blue with two narrow red ochre stripes.
Metal: Silver and gilt.
Size: 46mm
Description: (Obverse) an 8-pointed faceted star with four long and four short points in the angles surmounted by a gilt royal crown and fern frond wreath emblem; (reverse) inscribed FOR BRAVERY—MO TE MAIA. With ring suspension.
Comments: *This decoration superseded the British George Medal and is the second grade award for civilian acts of bravery. Recipients are entitled to the postnominal letters NZBS. So far 21 awards (two posthumous) have been made. A full list of the recipients of the NZBS are listed on the New Zealand Honours Lists published at: www. honours.govt.nz/honours/lists/nzba.*

VALUE: —

NZ9. NEW ZEALAND BRAVERY DECORATION

Instituted: September 20, 1999.
Branch of Service: Civilians and members of the armed forces in non-combat situations.
Ribbon: 32mm wide. Bright blue with three equal stripes of red ochre.
Metal: Silver and gilt.
Size: 45mm.
Description: (Obverse) a cross pattée surmounted by a small faceted four-pointed star with the royal crown and fern frond wreath emblem; (reverse) inscribed FOR BRAVERY—MO TE MAIA. With ring suspension.
Comments: *This decoration is awarded for acts of bravery in a non-combat situation. It supersedes the British QGM, QPM, QFSM, AFC and AFM. Recipients are entitled to the postnominal letters NZBD. Recipients of the NZBD are listed on the Roll of awards published at: www.honours.govt.nz/honours/lists/nzba.*

VALUE: —

NZ10. NEW ZEALAND GALLANTRY MEDAL

Instituted: 1998.

Branch of Service: New Zealand armed forces.

Ribbon: 32mm wide. Crimson with two central purple stripes and two outer white stripes.

Metal: Bronze.

Size: 36mm.

Description: (Obverse) the Rank-Broadley effigy of Her Majesty Queen Elizabeth II with the legend ELIZABETH II QUEEN OF NEW ZEALAND; (reverse) FOR GALLANTRY / MO TE TOANGA surrounded by a fern frond wreath with the royal crown above.

Comments: *This decoration replaces the Mention in Despatches. So far 16 awards have been made: Recipients are entitled to the postnominal letters NZGM. The name of the recipient will be engraved on each award. Recipients of the NZGM are listed on the Roll of awards published at: www.honours.govt.nz/honours/lists/nzga.*

VALUE: —

NZ11. NEW ZEALAND BRAVERY MEDAL

Instituted: September 20 ,1999.

Branch of Service: Civilians or members of the New Zealand armed forces in a non-combat situation.

Ribbon: 32mm wide. Bright blue with four red ochre stripes.

Metal: Bronze.

Size: 36mm.

Description: (Obverse) the Rank-Broadley effigy of Her Majesty Queen Elizabeth II with the legend ELIZABETH II QUEEN OF NEW ZEALAND; (reverse) FOR BRAVERY / MO TE MAIA surrounded by a fern frond wreath with the royal crown above.

Comments: *This decoration replaces the Queen's Commendations for Brave Conduct and Valuable Service in the Air. Recipients are entitled to the postnominal letters NZBM. A full list of recipients of the NZBM are listed on the Roll of awards published at: www.honours. govt.nz/honours/lists/nzba.*

VALUE: —

NZ12. QUEEN'S /KING'S SERVICE MEDAL

Instituted: March 13, 1975.

Ribbon: Same as the Queen's / King's Service Order.

Metal: Silver.

Size: 36mm.

Description: (Obverse) effigy of the reigning monarch surrounded by the royal styles and titles; (reverse) New Zealand arms with THE QUEEN'S (KING'S) SERVICE MEDAL round the top with, originally, FOR COMMUNITY SERVICE or FOR PUBLIC SERVICE at the bottom, but from June 2007 the two divisions have been amalgamated and the insignia now reads FOR SERVICE— MO NGA MAHI NUI at the foot. The medal is fitted with a suspension ring.

Comments: *Awards are made for valuable voluntary service to the community or meritorious and faithful services to the Crown or similar services within the public sector. Military service is ineligible. The name of the recipient is engraved on the rim. Recipients are entitled to the postnominal letters QSM / KSM. A number of unnamed examples have surfaced following a robbery from a delivery lorry in the UK. A full list of recipients of the QSM / KSM are listed on the New Zealand Honours Lists published at www.honours.govt.nz. On May 23, 2023, it was confirmed by the New Zealand Prime Minister that the Queen's Service Medal would change name following the accession of King Charles III.*

VALUE: £350–495   *Miniature*   £70–85

NZ12A. NEW ZEALAND ANTARCTIC MEDAL

Instituted: 2006.
Ribbon: White.
Metal: Sterling silver.
Size: 36mm octagonal.
Description: (Obverse) bears the effigy of the Queen by Ian Rank-Broadley, FRBS, FSNAD, of the United Kingdom and the inscription Elizabeth II Queen of New Zealand. This effigy is also used on the New Zealand Gallantry and Bravery Awards; (reverse) shows a group of four Emperor Penguins on an Antarctic landscape with Mt Erebus in the background.
Comments: *Awarded to those New Zealanders and other persons who either individually or as members of a New Zealand programme in the Antarctic region have made an outstanding contribution to exploration, scientific research, conservation, environmental protection, or knowledge of the Antarctic region; or in support of New Zealand's objectives or operations, or both, in the Antarctic region. The Medal will not be awarded for acts of bravery, for short-term acts of extreme endurance, for long service or for service in Antarctica generally. The first three recipients were Prof. John Dudley Bradshaw, Dr. Clive Howard-Williams and Dr. Karl Erb. To date 14 awards have been made. Recipients of the NZ Antarctic Medal are listed at www.honours. govt.nz/honours/lists/nzam.*

VALUE: —

NZ12B. NEW ZEALAND DISTINGUISHED SERVICE DECORATION

Instituted: 2008.
Ribbon: Red central stripe bounded by thin yellow stripes and dark blue edges..
Metal: Sterling silver.
Size: 36mm octagonal.
Description: (Obverse) A stylised image of eight blades of a *kotiate* (lobed club) surmounted by a royal crown; (reverse) the inscription "For Distinguished Service/mo nga te mahi kahurangi" with the recipient's name engraved between.
Comments: *Awarded to members of the NZ armed forces for distinguished or meritorious service to New Zealand that consists of outstanding performance or individual efforts towards peacetime and humanitarian service. The award can be made for a single accomplishment or for cumulative efforts over a sustained period. A bar to the decoration can be awarded for further qualifying services. Foreign or Commonwealth persons can qualify for an Honorary decoration. Recipients are entitled to the post nominal letters "DSD". To date 124 awards have been made. A full list of the recipients of the New Zealand Distinguished Service Decoration are listed on the New Zealand Honours Lists published at www.honours.govt.nz/ honours/lists/dsd.*

VALUE: —

NZ12C. NEW ZEALAND DEFENCE MERITORIOUS SERVICE MEDAL

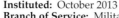

Instituted: October 2013
Branch of Service: Military and civilian employees of the New Zealand Defence Force.
Ribbon: Crimson with a narrow green central stripe flanked by narrow white stripes, with narrow gold edge stripes.
Metal: Silver.
Size: 36mm.
Description: (Obverse) the effigy of Queen Elizabeth by Ian Rank-Broadley; (reverse) a wreath of fern fronds surmounted by a Royal Crown surrounding the inscription "FOR MERITORIOUS SERVICE HE TOHU HIRANGA". A frosted finish has been applied to The Queen's effigy and all inscriptions..
Comments: *In the hierarchy of awards for distinguished and meritorious service, this medal comes after the Distinguished Service Decoration and before the Chief of Defence Force Commendation. It is awarded by the Chief of Defence Force to recognise any form of meritorious service deemed worthy of medallic recognition. Every employee of the Defence Force, including civilians, is eligible regardless of their rank, grade, Service affiliation, or length of service. The Medal can also be awarded posthumously, and with Bars for further meritorious service. The medal is always issued named.*

VALUE: — *Miniature* —

NZ12D. NEW ZEALAND POLICE MERITORIOUS SERVICE MEDAL

Instituted: October 2013
Branch of Service: Sworn and unsworn employees of the New Zealand Police Force
Ribbon: 32mm, a central stripe of dark blue and two broad stripes of crimson, separated and edged with four narrow stripes of gold.
Metal: Silver.
Size: 36mm.
Description: (Obverse) the effigy of Queen Elizabeth by Ian Rank-Broadley; (reverse) a wreath of fern fronds surmounted by a Royal Crown surrounding the inscription "FOR MERITORIOUS SERVICE HE TOHU HIRANGA". A frosted finish has been applied to The Queen's effigy Police badge and all inscriptions..

VALUE: — *Miniature* —

NZ13. NEW ZEALAND OPERATIONAL SERVICE MEDAL

Instituted: August 2002.
Branch of Service: All New Zealand personnel previously awarded an operational medal for service since September 3, 1945.
Ribbon: 32mm wide. Black with six white stripes in pairs at the edges and centre.
Metal: Silver.
Size: 36mm.
Description: (Obverse) New Zealand arms; (reverse) a kiwi on six straight lines (land) with NEW ZEALAND between two stars below and three wavy lines (sea) and the inscription FOR OPERATIONAL SERVICE below.
Comments: *Personnel who have been awarded a campaign medal for operational service for New Zealand since September 3, 1945 qualify for the award of the NZOSM, provided that the particular campaign medal has been approved for acceptance and wear by New Zealanders. The medal is worn before all post World War II campaign medals. Issued un-named until July 2009, all are now engraved on issue although medals issued before 2009 can be named on request. Over 35,000 medals have been issued to date. .*

VALUE: £75–95   *Miniature*   £35–40

NZ14A. NEW ZEALAND GENERAL SERVICE MEDAL 2002 (SOLOMON ISLANDS)

Instituted: July 2002.
Branch of Service: New Zealand civil and military personnel.
Ribbon: 32mm, dark green with a yellow central stripe flanked by narrow dark blue stripes, the national colours of the Solomon Islands.
Metal: Silver-plated base metal.
Size: 36mm.
Description: (Obverse) the effigy of Queen Elizabeth by Ian Rank-Broadley; (reverse) a wreath of New Zealand flora surmounted by a Royal Crown with the title of the medal in the middle.
Comments: *Awarded to New Zealand personnel (both military and non military) who served in the Solomon Islands and its waters between June 2000 and June 2002 and those who served with the Regional Assistance Mission in the Solomon Islands (RAMSI) since July 24, 2003 and to New Zealand Police personnel since October 6, 2002. The medal is still being issued. All medals are engraved. Over 1400 issued to date to NZDF personnel, 620 to NZ Police, and 25 to other NZ civilians on NZ Government approved deployments in support of RAMSI.*

VALUE: £325–475   *Miniature* £25–30

NZ14B. NEW ZEALAND GENERAL SERVICE MEDAL 2002 (AFGHANISTAN)

Primary operations

Instituted: July 2002.
Branch of Service: New Zealand civil and military personnel.
Ribbon: 32mm, green with a narrow central black stripe flanked by red stripes (primary operations) or with narrow blue edges (secondary operations).
Metal: Silver-plated alloy.
Size: 36mm.
Description: as NZ14A.
Comments: *Awarded to New Zealand personnel (both military and non military) who served in Afghanistan from December 2001 in one of two qualifying geographic areas. The "primary" operational area is within the borders of Afghanistan itself, while the "secondary" operational area includes areas where forces are based to support the operation. Different medal ribbons denote the primary and secondary areas. The NZGSM (Afghanistan) primary has also been awarded to over 40 New Zealand Police personnel, 25 New Zealand Red Cross aid workers, and is still being issued to New Zealand citizens deployed into Afghanistan on a range of NZ Government approved projects. When these awards were first instituted in 2002, there was a clear intention to separate the awards made to those who served within the boundaries of Afghanistan from those who served in a supporting role from outside Afghanistan. The medals are the same, but the ribbons are different colours and design. If a second tour of duty in Afghanistan was completed, they had to wear the Primary medal ribbon, regardless that in many cases the engraving on the medal reflected their first tour of duty in a Secondary location.*

In 2018 the Regulations were changed to allow personnel to wear both medals with the appropriate ribbon and it will be easily seen which tour of duty was completed first. This will also allow the engraving on both medals to be accurate for each tour of duty.

VALUE: £325–475   *Miniature* £25–30

NZ14C. NEW ZEALAND GENERAL SERVICE MEDAL 2002 (IRAQ 2003)

Instituted: 2004.
Branch of Service: New Zealand civil and military personnel.
Ribbon: 32mm, a central broad red stripe flanked by thin white stripes, then green stripes with thin black edges.
Metal: Silver-plated alloy.
Size: 36mm.
Description: As NZ14A.
Comments: *Awarded to New Zealand personnel (both military and non military) who have served in Iraq from May 27, 2003. The initial NZ Government contribution was personnel who served with the United Nations Mine Action Service's Mine Action Coordination Team based in Basrah. The qualifying period starts from May 27, 2003 for mine clearance operations, and September 17, 2003 for humanitarian and reconstruction service with the British-led Multi-National Division in (Southeast) Iraq. The medal is issued engraved. More than 215 issued to date.*

| VALUE: | £450–675 | *Miniature* | £25–30 |

NZ14D. NEW ZEALAND GENERAL SERVICE MEDAL 2002 (TIMOR-LESTE)

Instituted: 2007.
Branch of Service: New Zealand civil and military personnel.
Ribbon: 32mm, a central broad red stripe flanked by yellow, black and white stripes.
Metal: Silver-plated alloy.
Size: 36mm.
Description: As NZ14A.
Comments: *Awarded to New Zealand Defence Force, New Zealand Police and some New Zealand Government civilian personnel for service in Timor-Leste between 28 April 2006 and the cessation of awards from 31 December 2012. The medal is issued engraved. More than 1550 NZDF personnel, 185 NZ police and 20 New Zealand civilians have been issued with the medal to date.*

| VALUE: | £285–375 | *Miniature* | £25–30 |

NZ14E. NEW ZEALAND GENERAL SERVICE MEDAL 2002 (KOREA)

Instituted: September 11, 2008.
Branch of Service: New Zealand military personnel. To date this has not been awarded to any civilians.
Ribbon: 32mm, of dark blue with a red centre flanked by yellow stripes.
Metal: Silver-plated alloy.
Size: 36mm.
Description: As NZ14A.
Comments: *Awarded to NZDF personnel posted to UN Command Military Armistice Commission or the UN Honour Guard Company since 1 January 2001. Qualifying service is 30 days. Medals are issued engraved. Over 150 issued to date.*

| VALUE: | — | *Miniature* | £25–30 |

NZ14F. NEW ZEALAND GENERAL SERVICE MEDAL 2002 (COUNTER-PIRACY)

Instituted: 2009.
Branch of Service: New Zealand Defence Force.
Ribbon: 32mm width, blue with a narrow central white stripe, and edged with narrow red and wide yellow stripes.
Metal: Silver-plated base metal.
Size: 36mm.
Description: (Obverse) the effigy of Queen Elizabeth by Ian Rank-Broadley; (reverse) a wreath of New Zealand flora surmounted by a Royal Crown with the title of the medal in the middle.
Comments: *The New Zealand General Service Medal 2002 (Counter-Piracy) recognises members of the New Zealand Defence Force (NZDF) who have served for 30 days or more in counter-piracy operations in the Gulf of Aden, Western Indian Ocean, and off the eastern coasts of Somalia, Yemen and Oman, since 1 January 2009. The first large NZDF deployment was the frigate HMNZS Te Mana's November 2013 to February 2014 service as part of Combined Task Force 151 and NATO's Operation Ocean Shield. Since then Air Force, Navy and Army personnel have served on a range of maritime counter-piracy operations in this area of the world. To date 300 NZDF personnel have qualified for the award of this medal*

VALUE: £320–475   *Miniature* £20–30

NZ14G. NEW ZEALAND GENERAL SERVICE MEDAL 2002 (IRAQ 2015)

Instituted: 2015.
Branch of Service: New Zealand Defence Force.
Ribbon: 32mm width, central yellow band with red, white, green stripes either side. .
Metal: Silver-plated base metal.
Size: 36mm.
Description: (Obverse) the effigy of Queen Elizabeth by Ian Rank-Broadley; (reverse) a wreath of New Zealand flora surmounted by a Royal Crown with the title of the medal in the middle.
Comments: *This medal recognised service in building the capacity of the Iraqi Security Forces and was awarded to NZDF personnel who deployed on this training mission. Around 100 NZDF personnel and some 300 Australian Defence Force troops formed a joint training mission at Camp Taji, Iraq. In addition to the 100 personnel deployed to Camp Taji, another 40 personnel supporting operations from other locations in the Middle East, received this medal. To date over 1,300 personnel have been awarded this medal.*

VALUE: £300–465   *Miniature* £20–25

NZ14H. NEW ZEALAND GENERAL SERVICE MEDAL 2002 (GREATER MIDDLE EAST)

Instituted: 2014.
Branch of Service: New Zealand Defence Force.
Ribbon: 32mm width, central blue band with yellow, green, white stipes to either side.
Metal: Silver-plated base metal.
Size: 36mm.
Description: (Obverse) the effigy of Queen Elizabeth by Ian Rank-Broadley; (reverse) a wreath of New Zealand flora surmounted by a Royal Crown with the title of the medal in the middle.
Comments: *This medal recognised service of 30 days or more on general regional security operations in the greater Middle East from 7 December 2014. It was awarded to NZDF personnel who deploy on general regional security operations in the Middle East. It could also be awarded to those involved in supporting the training mission in Iraq from other locations in the Middle East. To date over 1,000 personnel have been awarded this medal.*

VALUE: £250–325   *Miniature* £20–25

NZ15. NEW ZEALAND SERVICE MEDAL 1946–49

Instituted: November 3, 1995.
Branch of Service: New Zealand armed forces, merchant navy and civil airline crews.
Ribbon: 32mm white with a central red stripe and black stripes at the edges.
Metal: Rhodium plated steel.
Size: 36mm.
Description: (Obverse) New Zealand arms; (reverse) FOR SERVICE TO NEW ZEALAND 1946–1949 with a fern frond below.
Comments: *Awarded to recognise New Zealand military personnel who served in the British Commonwealth Occupation Force in Japan between March 1946 and March 1949 with a minimum of 28 days service required. Sometimes referred to as the "J Force medal". Initially issued un-named, since July 2009 medals are engraved on issue. More than 5,120 issued to date.*

VALUE: £80–95   *Miniature*   £35–40

NZ16. NEW ZEALAND GENERAL SERVICE MEDAL 1992 (WARLIKE)

Instituted: May 7, 1992.
Branch of Service: New Zealand armed forces.
Ribbon: 32mm dark blue with a central black stripe flanked by red stripes.
Metal: Silver.
Size: 38mm.
Description: (Obverse) crowned effigy of Queen Elizabeth; (reverse) THE NEW ZEALAND GENERAL SERVICE MEDAL within a wreath of pohutakawa blossom, fern fronds and kowhai blossom, ensigned by a royal crown affixed to a plain suspension bar.
Clasps: Near East, Malaya 1960–64, Vietnam, Kuwait.
Comments: *Awarded to recognise service in warlike operations for which, initially, no separate New Zealand or British Commonwealth campaign medal was issued. It is worn as a campaign medal, in order of date of qualification. All medals are engraved on issue. Clasp Near East awarded for specified service between October 31, 1956 and December 22, 1956; Malaya 1960-64 between August 1, 1960 and August 16, 1964; Vietnam between December 1, 1962 and 1 May 1, 1975; and Kuwait between December 18, 1990 and March 12, 1991. The most common issue is with the clasp "Vietnam" with more than 2,650 issued to date. There are three strikings of this medal, the first (Australian) type has a weak suspension clasp, the second type made by ELM of Singapore carry the initials of the designer POS and the third type, also struck by ELM shows differences in the flowers on the reverse.*

VALUE:		*Miniature*	£25–30
Kuwait	£1200–1685		
Near East	£250–365		
Malaya 1960–64	£250–345		
Vietnam	£250–335		

NZ17. NEW ZEALAND GENERAL SERVICE MEDAL 1992 (NON-WARLIKE)

Instituted: May 7, 1992.
Branch of Service: New Zealand armed forces.
Ribbon: 32mm dark blue with a white central stripe flanked by narrow red stripes.
Metal: Bronze.
Size: 38mm.
Description: As above.
Clasps: Korea 1954-57, Korea 1958-2000, Thailand, Sinai, Indian Ocean, Peshawar, Iraq, Somalia, Mozambique, Cambodia, Rwanda, Arabian Gulf, Bougainville.
Comments: *Awarded to recognise service in non-warlike operations for which no separate New Zealand, British Commonwealth, United Nations or NATO campaign medal was issued. Thirteen clasps have been issued. The most common clasp issued is 'Sinai' with more than 1,200 issued to date. Clasp Korea 1954–57 awarded for specified service between July 27, 1954 and December 31, 1957; Korea 1958–2000 between January 1, 1958 and December 31, 2000; Thailand, May 25, 1962 and December 15, 1971; Sinai, April 25, 1982 to present; Indian Ocean, June 21, 1982 and September 20, 1983; Peshawar, April 1, 1989 and December 31, 1991; Iraq, August 1, 1991 and January 31, 2003; Somalia, December 26, 1992 and November 30, 1993; Mozambique, February 1, 1994 and June 30, 2005; Cambodia, March 1, 1994 and April 30, 2005; Rwanda, August 1, 1994 and September 17, 1994; Arabian Gulf, October 4, 1995 and December 31, 2001; Bougainville, November 19, 1997 to present. In 2002, the NZGSM 1992 was replaced by the New Zealand General Service Medal 2002. It is worn as a campaign medal, in order of date of qualification. All medals are engraved. Three clasp medals are extremely rare.*

VALUE: £325–485   *Miniature* £25–30

NZ18. EAST TIMOR MEDAL

Instituted: April 25, 2000.
Ribbon: 32mm broad green central stripe flanked by narrow red, wider black and white stripes towards the edges.
Metal: Silver-plated alloy.
Size: 36mm.
Description: (Obverse) the effigy of the Queen by Ian Rank-Broadley with ELIZABETH II QUEEN OF NEW ZEALAND round the circumference; (reverse) the head of a kiwi facing right and overshadowing a map of East Timor with the words EAST TIMOR below and a sprig of olive leaves above. Fitted with a plain suspension bar.
Clasp: A silver clasp inscribed EAST TIMOR for additional service of 365 days or more, continuous or aggregate, in the operational area.
Comments: *Awarded to recognise New Zealand personnel (both military and non military) who served in East Timor from the commencement of the New Zealand involvement in June 1999 until April 27, 2006. All medals are engraved. More than 5,000 issued to date.*

VALUE: £325–385   *Miniature* £40–45

NZ19. NEW ZEALAND SPECIAL SERVICE MEDAL (NUCLEAR TESTING)

Instituted: July 2002.
Branch of Service: New Zealand service personnel and civilians.
Ribbon: 32mm. An orange-yellow central stripe, flanked by narrow
   crimson stripes, then narrow red and white stripes and thin black
   edges.
Metal: Gold-plated.
Size: 36mm.
Description: (Obverse) the arms of New Zealand; (reverse) fern fronds and
   sprigs of pohutakawa, manuka, kowhai blossom and Mount Cook lilies.
Comments: *Awarded to recognise the service of those personnel who were part of
   an official New Zealand Government presence at an atmospheric nuclear test
   between 1956 and 1973. Initially issued unnamed, all recent medal issues are
   engraved. To date 850 have been issued.*

VALUE   £250–325   *Miniature*   £40–50

NZ19A. NEW ZEALAND SPECIAL SERVICE MEDAL (ASIAN TSUNAMI)

Instituted: December 2005.
Branch of Service: New Zealand service personnel and civilians.
Ribbon: 32mm, 11 stripes of red, white, blue, orange, green, yellow/green,
   orange, blue, white, red (colours of the six countries affected).
Metal: Gold-plated.
Size: 36mm.
Description: (Obverse) the arms of New Zealand; (reverse) fern fronds and
   sprigs of pohutakawa, manuka, kowhai blossom and Mount Cook lilies.
Comments: *Awarded to recognise New Zealanders who were involved in rescue,
   relief and rehabilitation efforts in areas devastated following the earthquake off
   the coast of Sumatra and the resulting tsunami of December 26, 2004.*
   *Qualifying service for the medal is 7 days between December 26, 2004 and
   February 28, 2005, or 14 days between December 26, 2004 and December 26,
   2005. All medals are engraved on issue. 447 issued as at June 30, 2011.*

VALUE: —   *Miniature*   £30–50

NZ19B. NEW ZEALAND SPECIAL SERVICE MEDAL (EREBUS)

Instituted: November 2006.
Branch of Service: New Zealand police.
Ribbon: 32mm, white with a central black stripe, light blue and dark blue
   stripes towards the edges.
Metal: Gold-plated.
Size: 36mm.
Description: (Obverse) the arms of New Zealand; (reverse) fern fronds and
   sprigs of pohutakawa, manuka, kowhai blossom and Mount Cook lilies.
Comments: *Awarded to recognise the service of those New Zealanders, and
   citizens of the United States of America and other countries, who were
   involved with the extremely difficult and very unpleasant, hazardous, and
   extreme circumstances associated with the body recovery, crash investigation
   and victim identification phases of Operation Overdue by the New Zealand
   Police following the crash of an Air New Zealand DC-10 aircraft on Mt.
   Erebus, Antarctica on November 28, 1979, with the loss of all 257 passengers
   and crew on board. Presentations to US citizens (mainly ex US Navy) started
   in Washington DC in June 2009 and are continuing as retired personnel are
   located. It is estimated about 70 US citizens will qualify for this award. All
   medals are engraved. To date 345 have been issued.*

VALUE: —   *Miniature*   £40–50

In 2020, the mixture of New Zealand and British awards with different eligibility criteria were all changed to New Zealand awards administered under a single set of Regulations.

All Regular Force Long Service Awards for service on or after December 1, 1977 require 14 years to qualify for the Long Service Award, and 7 years for subsequent clasps.

All attested service in any Service or arm of the NZ Armed Forces can be accumulated providing good conduct standards are maintained. The Long Service Award presented will reflect the majority of the service being recognised.

NZ20. NEW ZEALAND 1990 COMMEMORATION MEDAL

Instituted: February 9, 1990.
Ribbon: 32mm nine narrow stripes, black at the centre flanked by alternate white and red ochre.
Metal: Silver-gilt.
Size: 38mm.
Description: (Obverse) effigy of Queen Elizabeth with inscription ELIZABETH II . QUEEN OF NEW ZEALAND incuse on a raised rim; (reverse) stylised Kotuku or White Heron with inscription NEW ZEALAND 1990 COMMEMORATION.
Comments: *Awarded during the sesquicentennial year (1990) to recognise achievements of New Zealanders in community service and the public services or their contribution to the country. The medal is accompanied by a certificate. 3,632 were issued unnamed. Good quality copies exist.*

VALUE: £180–265

Miniature —

NZ21. NEW ZEALAND MERITORIOUS SERVICE MEDAL

Instituted: May 6, 1985.
Branch of Service: NCOs of the rank of sergeant or petty officer or above in the armed forces.
Ribbon: 32mm crimson with a narrow green central stripe.
Metal: Silver.
Size: 38mm.
Description: (Obverse) bare-headed effigy of Queen Elizabeth; (reverse) FOR MERITORIOUS SERVICE within a laurel wreath surmounted by a royal crown and the legend NEW ZEALAND. Reverse similar to 212.
Comments: *Awarded for a minimum of 21 years full-time service in the armed forces, although this could be reduced to 18 years in the case of those invalided out of the services on grounds of disability. The recipient must be in possession of the Long Service & Good Conduct Medal. Service before the age of 17 does not count. The medal was limited to 10 serving members of RNZN, 20 Army and 15 RNZAF per year. The medal is always issued named with number, rank, name and regiment/corps or RNZN or RNZAF. It is now discontinued in favour of MYB NZ12C.*

VALUE: From £525 *Miniature* £60–90

NZ22. NEW ZEALAND ARMED FORCES AWARD

Instituted: May 6, 1985.
Branch of Service: Officers of the armed forces.
Ribbon: 32mm dark blue, crimson and light blue with a central stripe of black.
Metal: Silver.
Size: 38mm.
Description: (Obverse) crowned effigy of Queen Elizabeth; (reverse) crossed swords, eagle and naval crown with two fronds below and inscription NEW ZEALAND ARMED FORCES AWARD.
Comments: *Awarded to Regular Force commissioned officers of the armed services for 15 years full-time service back-dated to 1977. Clasps for each additional 15 years may be awarded. Where an officer has been commissioned from the ranks at least 8 years must be commissioned service. The medal is always issued named with number, rank, name and corps/regiment, RNZN or RNZAF. For service on or after December 1, 1977 14 years are required for award of the NZ Armed Forces Award, and 7 years for subsequent clasps.*

VALUE: £325–465   *Miniature*   £25–30

NZ22A NEW ZEALAND EFFICIENCY DECORATION

Instituted: 14 August 2020
Branch of Service: Commissioned Officers of the Territorial Forces in New Zealand Army
Ribbon: 38mm plain dark green with a central yellow stripe.
Metal: Silver and silver gilt
Size: Height 54mm; maximum width 37mm.
Description: The New Zealand Efficiency Decoration consists of an oak wreath in silver tied with gold, having in the centre the Royal Cypher and Crown in gold. The height is 54mm and the maximum width is 37mm. A ring for suspension from the ribbon is fitted at the top of the Crown. A ribbon brooch bar with the words "NEW ZEALAND" is always issued with the award.
Comments: *Officers retain right to use the letters ED with this New Zealand award. For those serving on or after December 1, 1977, 12 years accumulated efficient service is required for the decoration. In addition, up to six years Regular Force service can be counted towards the required 12 years' service. For those who attest for the first time in the New Zealand Armed Forces on or after July 1, 2021, 14 years accumulated efficient service will be required for the decoration. Up to seven years Regular Force service will be able to be counted towards the required 14 years' service.*

VALUE: —

NZ22B. NEW ZEALAND EFFICIENCY MEDAL

Instituted: 14 August 2020
Branch of Service: Other ranks of the Territorial Forces in New Zealand Army
Ribbon: 32 mm green with yellow edges
Metal: Silver
Size: Height 36 mm; maximum width 32 mm
Description: An oval silver medal with Elizabeth II on obverse
Comments: *In August 2020, the decoration was renamed the New Zealand Efficiency Medal and the eligibility criteria were amended as below: For those serving on or after December 1, 1977, 12 years accumulated efficient service is now required for the medal. Up to six years Regular Force service can now be counted towards the required 12 years' service. Clasps will continue to be awarded for each six years of efficient service. For those who attest for the first time in the New Zealand Armed Forces on or after July 1, 2021, 14 years accumulated efficient service will be required for the medal. Up to seven years Regular Force service will be able to be counted towards the required 14 years' service. Clasps will be awarded for each seven years of efficient service.*

VALUE: —

NZ22C. NEW ZEALAND AIR EFFICIENCY AWARD

Instituted: 14 August 2020.
Branch of Service: Territorial Forces in the Royal New Zealand Air Force
Ribbon: Green with two light blue stripes towards the centre.
Metal: Silver
Size: Height 38 mm; maximum width 32 mm.
Description: An oval medal with a suspender in the form of an eagle with wings outspread. (Obverse) the effigy of the reigning monarch; (Reverse) inscribed AIR EFFICIENCY AWARD in three lines.
Comments: *The Air Efficiency Award was instituted in 1942. It is awarded to both officers and airmen of the Territorial Air Force and the Air Force Reserve of the Royal New Zealand Air Force.*
For those serving on or after December 1, 1977, 10 years accumulated efficient service is now required for the medal. Up to five years Regular Force service can now be counted towards the required 10 years' service. Clasps will be awarded for each ten years of efficient service.
For those who attest for the first time in the New Zealand Armed Forces on or after 1 July 2021, 14 years accumulated efficient service will be required for the medal. Up to seven years Regular Force service will be able to be counted towards the required 14 years' service. Clasps will be awarded for each seven years of efficient service.
Officers are entitled to use the post nominal letters AE after their name.

VALUE: —

NZ23. ROYAL NEW ZEALAND NAVY LONG SERVICE & GOOD CONDUCT MEDAL

Instituted: May 6, 1985.
Branch of Service: Royal New Zealand Navy.
Ribbon: 32mm dark blue edged in white.
Metal: Silver.
Size: 36mm.
Description: (Obverse) uncrowned effigy of Queen Elizabeth; (reverse) HMS *Victory* surrounded by the inscription FOR LONG SERVICE AND GOOD CONDUCT.
Comments: *For service on or after December 1, 1977 14 years are required for award of the RNZN Long Service Medal, and 7 years for subsequent clasps. Awarded to naval ratings with 15 years service. Clasps may be awarded for each additional 15 years, denoted in undress uniform by a silver rosette on the ribbon bar. Indistinguishable from the Royal Navy LS&GC Medal, apart from the recipient's details. The medal is always issued named with number, rank, name and ship.*

VALUE: £90–135   *Miniature*   £25–35

NZ24. NEW ZEALAND ARMY LONG SERVICE & GOOD CONDUCT MEDAL

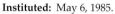

Instituted: May 6, 1985.
Branch of Service: New Zealand Army, Regular Forces.
Ribbon: 32mm crimson edged in white.
Metal: Silver.
Size: 36mm.
Description: (Obverse) crowned effigy of Queen Elizabeth; (reverse) FOR LONG SERVICE AND GOOD CONDUCT attached to an ornamental title bar bearing the words NEW ZEALAND in raised lettering.
Comments: *Similar to the British Army LS&GC Medal (229) but with a distinctive New Zealand suspension bar. For service on or after December 1, 1977 14 years are required for award of the NZ Army LS&GCM award, and 7 years for subsequent clasps. The medal is always issued named with number, rank, name and regiment/corps.*

VALUE: £95–125   *Miniature*   £25–30

NZ25. ROYAL NEW ZEALAND AIR FORCE LONG SERVICE MEDAL

Instituted: May 6, 1985.
Branch of Service: Royal New Zealand Air Force.
Ribbon: 32mm equal stripes of dark blue and crimson edged in white.
Metal: Silver.
Size: 36mm.
Description: (Obverse) uncrowned effigy of Queen Elizabeth; (reverse) an eagle with outstretched wings surmounted by a royal crown encircled by the inscription FOR LONG SERVICE AND GOOD CONDUCT.
Comments: *This medal replaces the award of the British RAF LS&GC Medal (MY 268). It is, in fact, indistinguishable from the British award except for the recipient's details engraved on the rim. For service on or after 1 December 1977 14 years are required for award of the RNZAF Long Service Medal, and 7 years for subsequent clasps.*

VALUE: £95–125   *Miniature*   £25–30

NZ26. NEW ZEALAND POLICE LONG SERVICE & GOOD CONDUCT MEDAL

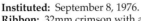

Instituted: September 8, 1976.
Ribbon: 32mm crimson with a central dark blue stripe flanked with white stripes.
Metal: Silver.
Size: 36mm.
Description: (Obverse) crowned effigy of Queen Elizabeth; (reverse) St Edward's Crown, sceptre and sword on a cushion within a wreath of oak leaves and fern fronds, surrounded by the inscription NEW ZEALAND POLICE—FOR LONG SERVICE AND GOOD CONDUCT.
Comments: *This medal replaced the New Zealand Police Medal (MYB283). It is awarded to sworn police staff on completion of 14 years service. Clasps are awarded for each additional seven years of service. All medals are issued engraved.*

VALUE: £190–285   *Miniature*   £45–50

NZ27. NEW ZEALAND FIRE BRIGADES LONG SERVICE AND GOOD CONDUCT MEDAL

Instituted: September 8, 1976.
Ribbon: 32mm vermilion with a central black stripe flanked by narrow yellow stripes.
Metal: Silver.
Size: 36mm.
Description: (Obverse) crowned effigy of Queen Elizabeth (reverse) NEW ZEALAND FIRE BRIGADES—FOR LONG SERVICE AND GOOD CONDUCT above a fern frond.
Comments: *Originally awarded for 14 years full or part time services as a fireman, but amended by Royal Warrant (October 15, 1981) to include fire brigades maintained or operated by companies as well as the forces under the control of the NZ Fire Service Commission. Clasps are awarded every additional period of seven years service. The recipient's name is engraved on the rim.*

VALUE: £175–195   *Miniature*   £45–50

NZ28. NEW ZEALAND PRISON SERVICE MEDAL

Instituted: October 15, 1981.
Ribbon: 32mm crimson with a central dark blue stripe flanked by narrow green stripes.
Metal: Silver.
Size: 36mm.
Description: (Obverse) crowned effigy of Queen Elizabeth II; (reverse) St Edward's crown and inscription NEW ZEALAND PRISON SERVICE FOR LONG SERVICE AND GOOD CONDUCT.
Comments: *Awarded for 14 years service with bars for further 7 year periods. This medal superseded the NZ Prison Service Long Service Medal originally instituted in 1901. The recipient's name is engraved on the rim.*

VALUE: £165–190   *Miniature*   £45–50

NZ29. NEW ZEALAND SUFFRAGE CENTENNIAL MEDAL 1993

Instituted: July 1, 1993.
Ribbon: 32mm purple with narrow central stripes of white, yellow and white.
Metal: Antiqued bronze.
Size: 36mm.
Description: (Obverse) crowned effigy of Queen Elizabeth; (reverse) wreath of fern and camellia enclosing the inscription 1893 THE NEW ZEALAND SUFFRAGE CENTENNIAL 1993.
Comments: *1993 was the centenary of the Electoral Act 1893 that gave women the right to vote in New Zealand. Medals awarded to 545 selected New Zealanders and persons from other countries in recognition of their contribution to the rights of women in New Zealand, or to women's issues in New Zealand, or both. A small number of men received the medal. The medals were issued unnamed with an accompanying certificate.*

VALUE: £550–765   *Miniature* £90–100

NZ30. NEW ZEALAND TRAFFIC ENFORCEMENT LONG SERVICE AND GOOD CONDUCT MEDAL

Instituted: September 28, 1970.
Ribbon: Bright blue with a narrow central white stripe flanked by black stripes.
Metal: Silver
Size: 36mm.
Description: A circular medal bearing (obverse) the coat of arms of the New Zealand Ministry of Transport; (reverse) the inscription FOR LONG SERVICE AND GOOD CONDUCT TRAFFIC ENFORCEMENT, with a suspender of stylised fern leaves.
Comments: *This award, rendered obsolete with the introduction of the New Zealand Traffic Service Medal (NZ31), was awarded to personnel of the traffic enforcement and road safety branches of the Ministry of Transport on completion of 15 years service. Clasps were awarded for each additional 10 years of service. All medals were issued engraved.*

VALUE: £220–250   *Miniature* £30–75

NZ31. NEW ZEALAND TRAFFIC SERVICE MEDAL

Instituted: December 22, 1998.
Ribbon: Bright blue with a narrow central white stripe flanked by black stripes as MYB NZ30 above.
Metal: Silver.
Size: 36mm.
Description: (Obverse) crowned effigy of Queen Elizabeth; (reverse) crowned wreath of fern fronds enclosing the word THE NEW ZEALAND TRAFFIC SERVICE MEDAL.
Comments: *Awarded to both local body and Government traffic enforcement staff who had completed 14 years service on or after January 1, 1987. Clasps were awarded for each seven years additional service. Eligibility for this medal ceased on July 1, 1992, with the merger of the Traffic Safety Service of the Ministry of Transport and the New Zealand Police.*

VALUE: £200–275   *Miniature* £40–50

NZ32. NEW ZEALAND CUSTOMS SERVICE MEDAL

Instituted: February 20, 2008.

Ribbon: Dark blue with a central stripe of bright blue bordered by yellow stripes.

Metal: Silver

Size: 36mm.

Description: (Obverse) The effigy of Queen Elizabeth by Ian Rank-Broadley and the inscription "Elizabeth II Queen of New Zealand"; (reverse) the badge of the New Zealand Customs Service. The clasp to the medal shall be of silver, oblong in shape, and bear a Royal Crown in the centre. When the ribbon is worn alone, a small silver rosette may be worn for each clasp awarded.

Comments: *Awarded to members of the New Zealand Customs Service employed on or after 1 December 2007 on completion of fourteen years service as a Customs Officer. Clasps are awarded for each additional period of seven years service. The medal is always issued engraved.*

VALUE: £160–195

NZ34. ROYAL NEW ZEALAND NAVAL RESERVE DECORATION

Instituted: May 6, 1985.

Ribbon: 38mm green edged with white.

Metal: Silver and gold.

Size: 54mm high and 33mm wide.

Description: A skeletal badge consisting of an oval loop of rope in silver surrounding the Royal Cypher in gold.

Comments: *For those serving on or after 1 December 1977, the RNZN RD is awarded for 14 years accumulated service, with clasps awarded for each 7 years accumulated service. The names of recipients are engraved on the reverse. Recipients are entitled to the postnominal letters RD. This medal replaced MYB219.*

VALUE: £175–235   *Miniature*   £30–40

NZ35. ROYAL NEW ZEALAND NAVAL VOLUNTEER RESERVE DECORATION

Instituted: May 6, 1985.

Ribbon: 38mm dark blue with a central broad green stripe flanked by narrow crimson stripes.

Metal: Silver and gold.

Size: 54mm high and 33mm wide.

Description: A skeletal badge, similar in design to the above.

Comments: *For those serving on or after 1 December 1977, the RNZN VRD is awarded for 14 years accumulated service, with clasps awarded for each 7 years accumulated service. The names of recipients are engraved on the reverse. Recipients are entitled to the postnominal letters VRD. These decorations replaced the British RD and VRD, the latter being obsolete and the organisation of the Royal New Zealand Navy being such that the British Admiralty Board regulations were no longer applicable.*

VALUE: £175–235   *Miniature*   £30–40

NZ36. ROYAL NEW ZEALAND NAVAL VOLUNTEER RESERVE LONG SERVICE AND GOOD CONDUCT MEDAL

Instituted: 1985.
Ribbon: 32mm dark blue with a central broad stripe of green between narrow crimson stripes.
Metal: Silver.
Size: 36mm.
Description: (Obverse) uncrowned effigy of Queen Elizabeth; (reverse) a battleship with the motto DIUTURNE FIDELIS (faithful of long duration).
Comments: *For those serving on or after 1 December 1977, the RNZNVR LSGCM is awarded for 14 years accumulated service, with clasps awarded for each 7 years accumulated service. This medal replaced MYB221.*

VALUE: £65–95   *Miniature* £25–35

NZ37. NEW ZEALAND DEFENCE SERVICE MEDAL

Instituted: April 2011.
Ribbon: Dark blue, red and light blue stripes. Light green stripes have been added to reflect the volunteer and territorial elements of the Services.
Metal: Antique bronze.
Size: 36mm
Description: (Obverse) The New Zealand coat of arms; (reverse) on the right one large New Zealand fern frond. On the left are the emblems of the Navy, Army and Air Force—the Naval crown, crossed swords and eagle. In the lower section the words "THE NEW ZEALAND DEFENCE SERVICE MEDAL".
Comments: *The New Zealand Defence Service Medal (NZDSM) was instituted to recognise three years attested military service since September 3, 1945. The Royal Warrant for the NZDSM allows for one or more clasps to be awarded with the medal. The number of clasps awarded to an individual will be determined by the type(s) of military service undertaken. There are four clasps which can be awarded with the NZDSM: REGULAR (illustrated), TERRITORIAL, C.M.T. and NATIONAL SERVICE. As at July 1, 2013, over 85,000 NZDSM's have been issued to serving military and ex-service personnel alike (from an estimated 160,000 possible recipients). Over 80% of awards issued are with one clasp only. Only 103 medals have been issued so far with 3 clasps.*

VALUE: £100–135   *Miniature*   £25–30

NZ38. NEW ZEALAND CHIEF OF DEFENCE FORCE COMMENDATION

Instituted: 2005.

Description: Pale blue ribbon encased in a dark blue frame, on which is superimposed the emblem of the Chief of the Defence Force, in silver, and consisting of a crown over crossed swords and fern leaves with an eagle at the centre.

Comments: *For award to members of the NZDF for performance which would be unlikely to meet the criteria for a New Zealand Honour. Commendations are available to individual military and civilian staff, and to military units. The Commendations are presented with a manuscript narrative outlining the reason for the award. Military personnel wear these commendations on their right breast in uniform. The CDF Commendation takes priority over the lower level single service Chief of Staff Commendations.*

VALUE: —

NZ39. NEW ZEALAND CHIEF OF NAVY COMMENDATION

Instituted: 2005.

Branch of Service: Navy.

Metal: Silver.

Description: A badge surmounted by a naval crown and inscribed CHIEF OF NAVY round the circumference, with twin fern fronds at the foot. The centre depicts the flag of the Chief of the Navy.

Comments: *Awarded to RNZN personnel who deliver excellent performance that is usually of benefit to the RNZN rather than NZDF as a whole.*

VALUE: —

NZ40. NEW ZEALAND CHIEF OF ARMY COMMENDATION

Instituted: 2005.

Branch of Service: Army.

Description: A crimson ribbon (similar to the Victoria Cross) but with the badge of the Army (crossed weapons—a sword and a taiaha—superimposed by a crown surmounted by a lion with NZ and NGATI TUMATAUENGA below) in gold-coloured metal.

Comments: *Awarded to NZ Army personnel who deliver excellent performance that is usually of benefit to the NZ Army rather than NZDF as a whole.*

VALUE: —

NZ41. NEW ZEALAND CHIEF OF AIR FORCE COMMENDATION

Instituted: 2005.

Branch of Service: Air Force.

Description: A blue ribbon with diagonal crimson and pale blue stripes on the left, surmounted by an eagle and two five-pointed stars.

Comments: *Awarded to RNZAF personnel who deliver excellent performance that is usually of benefit to the RNZAF rather than NZDF as a whole.*

VALUE: —

NZ41A NEW ZEALAND DEFENCE FORCE COMMENDATION

Instituted: 2017

Description: Black ribbon in which is superimposed the badge of the New Zealand Defence Force in gold and consisting of a crown over crossed swords and fern leaves with an eagle at the centre.

Comments: *The Commendation may be awarded by any Major General equivalent Awarding Authority who are not Service Chiefs in recognition of an act, conduct or service that, in their opinion is outstanding and worthy recognition, other than medallic recognition or an award of a Chief of Defence Force or Service Chief Commendation.*

VALUE: —

NZ42. NEW ZEALAND PUBLIC SERVICE MEDAL

Instituted: July 2018.

Ribbon: Red ochre with a wide central blue stripe and a narrow white stripe at both edges..

Metal: Silver.

Size: 36mm.

Description: (Obverse) effigy of Her Majesty the Queen within the Royal Styles and Titles for New Zealand; (reverse) within a circle a representation of poutama bearing the inscriptions "FOR MERITORIOUS SERVICE" and "HE TOHU HIRANGA" all within the inscriptions "TOHU RATONGA TŪMATANUI 2018/1341 O AOTEAROA" (above) and "THE NEW ZEALAND PUBLIC SERVICE MEDAL" (below), each separated by a heraldic mullet or star".

Comments: *The New Zealand Public Service Medal may be conferred for meritorious service by any employee in the New Zealand Public Service and may be conferred posthumously.*

VALUE: —

SOUTH AFRICAN
Medals

Apart from the various British campaign medals from 1834 onwards, distinctive medals relating to military service in South Africa date from 1896 when a version of the Meritorious Service Medal (MYB210) was provided with the name of the Cape of Good Hope on the reverse. This was accompanied by similar versions of the Distinguished Conduct Medal (MYB42) and the Long Service & Good Conduct Medal (MYB229). The following year similar awards were instituted for Natal.

Cape and Natal colonists received British awards from the earliest days of the British occupation, and numerous instances have been recorded of awards to South Africans of both the orders of chivalry and gallantry decorations. This situation continued after the formation of the Union of South Africa in 1910. As a rule, these were identical to the British versions in every respect but there were a few notable exceptions. The Victory Medal (MYB170) was struck with a bilingual (English and Dutch) reverse for award to South African forces. Distinctive medals for the police, railway and harbour police and prison services (MYB284–285 and 290–291) were awarded but as they were instituted by Royal Warrant they are included in the main body of this Yearbook.

Other South African awards which will be found in the main section are the King's Police Medal for gallantry or bravery (MYB49), the Africa Service Medal (MYB189), the South African Medal for War Service (MYB192) and the South African Medal for Korea (MYB196). There were also South African versions of the Efficiency Decoration (MYB236), Efficiency Medal (MYB254), the Permanent Force LS&GC (MYB253) and Air Efficiency Award (MYB270). Finally, there are three miscellaneous medals: the Union of South Africa Commemoration Medal of 1910 (MYB357), the Dekoratie Voor Trouwe Dienst of 1920 (MYB358) and the Anglo-Boere Oorlog Medal instituted at the same time (MYB359).

In 1952 the Union of South Africa instituted its own system of awards for gallantry in action, bravery in a non-combat situation and for distinguished service. Nine of these awards had a standard reverse showing the arms of the Union of South Africa surmounted by the royal cypher. In 1961, when South Africa became a republic and left the Commonwealth, the royal cypher was removed. The tenth award was the Union Medal which was completely redesigned and renamed the Permanent Force Good Service Medal (SA11 below).

For the purposes of this insertion it has been necessary to limit full coverage to military awards because of the absolute plethora of orders, decorations and medals that have made their appearance in the last 50 years while South Africa was ruled by the Nationalist Party. Not only were separate and independent award structures set up with their own orders, decorations and medals for all branches of the public service: Military, Police, Railway Police, Prisons, as well as the National Intelligence Service, but the situation was further complicated when the Nationalist Party Government in terms of its apartheid policy set up Homeland Governments that were given independence from the Republic of South Africa, each with their own set of awards for Military, Police and Prison departments—Transkei, Ciskei, KwaZulu, Bophuthatswana, Venda, Lebowa, Gazankulu and Qwa-qwa, etc. After 1994 the situation has been compounded by the issue of medals awarded retrospectively to members of the forces of freedom fighters or terrorists—MK (Mkhonto Wesizwe) and APLA (Azanian People's Liberation Army).

The awards instituted and awarded in South West Africa by the South African Government until this SA administered territory gained its independence and became Namibia in 1990 through world pressure, must not be overlooked either. The South African award system also reveals great instability through the frequent abolition of awards, their supersession and further proliferation by the introduction of new awards! Although this insertion has a primary focus on military awards, some of the awards to the South African Police, Prisons and Railway Police that may occur in medal groups with some regularity, have been included.

For information purposes a full list of orders, decorations and medals instituted since 1952 to the Police, Railway Police and Prisons, appears on the next page. The date in brackets next to each award indicates the year of gazetting of that award. The awards are listed in order of precedence for that particular compartment of the public service. These lists are preceded by a listing of South African civilian orders and decorations that are not confined to any particular public service compartment of awards.

Our grateful thanks go to Michael Kaplan of Alec Kaplan & Son CC of South Africa for updating this section.

SOUTH AFRICAN CIVILIAN AWARDS

ORDERS
Order of the Southern Cross (1986/87)—Two Classes
Order of the Star of South Africa (Non Military)
(1988)—Five Classes
Order for Meritorious Service (1986)—Two Classes
Order of Good Hope (1973/88)—Five Classes

DECORATIONS FOR BRAVERY
The Queen's Medal for Bravery (Gold and Silver) (1953)
The Woltemade Decoration for Bravery (1970/88)
Gold
The Woltemade Decoration for Bravery (1970/88) Silver
Civil Defence Medal for Bravery (1976)

MERITORIOUS SERVICE
Civil Defence Medal for Meritorious Service (1976)
State President's Sports Merit Award (1971)

SOUTH AFRICAN POLICE

ORDERS
South African Police Star for Distinguished
Leadership (1979)

DECORATIONS FOR BRAVERY
South African Police Cross for Bravery (1963)
South African Police Cross for Bravery (1989) (Gold/
Silver/ungraded)
South African Police Silver Cross for Gallantry (1985)

AWARDS FOR DISTINGUISHED, LONG AND MERITORIOUS SERVICE
South African Police Star for Distinguished Service
(1963)
South African Police Star for Distinguished Service
(1979)
South African Police Star for Outstanding Service (1979)
South African Police Star for Merit (1963)
South African Police Medal for Faithful Service (1963)
South African Police Star for Faithful Service (1979)

SERVICE
South African Police Medal for Combating Terrorism
(1974)

COMMEMORATIVE
South African Police Seventy-Fifty Anniversary
Commemorative Medal (1988)

SOUTH AFRICAN RAILWAYS POLICE

ORDERS
South African Railways Police Star for Distinguished
Leadership (1980)

DECORATIONS FOR BRAVERY
South African Railways Police Cross for Valour (1966)
South African Railways Police Cross for Valour (1980)

AWARDS FOR DISTINGUISHED, LONG AND MERITORIOUS SERVICE
South African Railways Police Star for Distinguished
Service (1980) *
Decoration for Distinguished Service in the SA
Railways Police Force (1966)
Decoration for Outstanding Service in the South
African Railways Police Force (1980)
Star for Merit in the South African Railways Police
Force (1966)
Star for Merit in the South African Railways Police
Force (1980)
South African Railways Police Star for Faithful
Service (1980)
Medal for Faithful Service in the South African
Railways Police Force (1966)
Medal for Faithful Service in the South African
Railways Police Force (1980)

SERVICE
South African Railways Police Medal for Combating
Terrorism

SOUTH AFRICAN PRISONS
(later Department of Correctional Services)

DECORATIONS FOR BRAVERY
Decoration for Valour in the South African Prisons
Service (1968)
South African Prisons Service Cross for Valour
(Diamond) (1980)
South African Prisons Service Cross for Valour (Ruby)
(1980)

AWARDS FOR DISTINGUISHED, LONG AND MERITORIOUS SERVICE
South African Prisons Service Star for Excellence
(1980)
South African Prisons Service Star for Distinction
(1980)
South African Prisons Service Star for Merit (1980)
South African Prisons Service Cross for Merit (1980)
Medal for Merit in the South African Prisons Service
(1968)
South African Prisons Service Medal for Merit
(Commissioned Officers) (1980)
South African Prisons Service Medal for Merit (Non-
Commissioned Officers) (1980)
Faithful Service Medal in the Prisons Department
(1959)
Faithful Service Medal, Prisons Department (1965)
Medal for Faithful Service in the South African
Prisons Service (1968)
South African Prisons Service Medal for Faithful
Service (1980)—Gold Medal (30 years); Silver
Medal (20 years); Bronze Medal (10 years)

* *name later changed to Star for Distinguished Devotion*

**SPECIAL NOTE ON THE PRICING OF POST-1952
SOUTH AFRICAN DECORATIONS AND MEDALS AWARDED TO MEMBERS OF
THE ARMY, NAVY AND AIR FORCE**

In 1952 the Union Defence Force made a decision to cease naming its medals. Instead each medal would be impressed with a serial number and the number, rank and name, etc. of the recipient entered against the serial number of the medal recorded down the left-hand margin of the register. The registers have since been misplaced. The register system was replaced by the computer and when a recipient received a medal, the medal number was recorded in many cases on this computerised record of service. However, these records are held by the Department of Defence and their system is not geared up to print out a full list of recipients of a particular medal with medal numbers.

    (i)   In certain cases, after the award of the medal, the recipient's number, rank, name and unit, along with the serial number of the medal awarded, was published in Part II Unit orders.

    (ii)   Since approximately 1988, the certificates of award have recorded the serial number of the medal awarded. Prior to that time, no medal serial number was printed on the certificate.

    In order to establish that the medal in the group or as a singleton was awarded to a particular recipient (i) or (ii) above, are a prerequisite = PRICE A (Medal certificate must be the original in (ii) to qualify).

    If a medal is numbered and has an un-numbered original certificate of award as supporting documentation = PRICE B.

    If a medal is numbered (or unnumbered) without any supporting documentation = PRICE C.

    It must be stressed that even if a recipient was awarded a medal, there is nothing to prove that that particular medal was actually awarded to the recipient, unless the serial number on the medal can be tied to that recipient through supporting documentation. Obviously gallantry awards must be accompanied by a copy of the citation for which the award was made.

    An A, B and C price is given for each SA Military award. For medals awarded to the Police, two prices are given: named medals and unnamed specimens, as the Police continued to name their medals (they actually impressed the day, month and year of award as well). As Prisons medals were engraved by a variety of jewellers after 1980, three prices are given for medals awarded from 1980. A: with certificate; B: named; C: unnamed. It must be stressed that all prices are given as a guide only.

SOUTH AFRICAN DEFENCE FORCE

ORDERS

SA1. STAR OF SOUTH AFRICA

Instituted: 1952.
Ribbon: 44.5mm orange with three 3mm green stripes in centre, 6mm apart.
Metal: Silver.
Description: A multi-facetted five-point star, fitted with a ring and oblong loop through which the ribbon is passed for suspension round the neck.
Comments: *Awarded for recognising exceptionally meritorious service, in time of peace or war, by officers of the SA Defence Force or of other armed forces attached to or serving with, or rendering service to the SA Defence Force. The award could recognize a particular instance or service over a period of time.*
    Further awards were denoted by a silver bar embossed in the centre with a miniature replica of the Star. None were awarded but an example of the bar is on display at the SA Museum of Military History. The reverse of the order has the embellished coat of arms of the Union of SA in relief, surmounted by the Royal cypher. After 1961 the Royal cypher was erased from existing medal stock. Those officers who were still serving in 1975 could exchange their Star of South Africa for the Order of the Star of South Africa. Post nominal title: SSA.

VALUE

	A	B	C	Miniature
With Royal cypher	£2200	£1100	£600	£110
Royal cypher erased	£1100	£500	£400	£60
Coat of arms reverse	£600	£300	£200	£50

SA2. ORDER OF THE STAR OF SOUTH AFRICA (MILITARY)

Instituted: 1975.

Ribbon: Blue, 37mm (neck ribbon), 80mm (sash), 44mm (breast ribbon) or 20mm (miniature). A narrow central white stripe denotes the second class (redesignated silver award in 1977).

Metal: Silver-gilt or silver depending on class.

Description: An eight-pointed Maltese cross with an eight-pointed star superimposed at the centre and having a circular Protea wreath behind. *First Class:* A Protea ornament at the top joins the star to a five-pointed badge in the form of a ground plan of the Castle of Good Hope, enclosing a circular device featuring the insignia of the Defence Force. This is linked by a chain to circular medallions embellished with eight-pointed stars forming the neck collar of the order. In addition to the neck badge and collar there is a gold breast star. An eight pointed multi-rayed star is surmounted by a circular protea wreath superimposed with a blue enamel Maltese Cross edged in gold, in turn surmounted by an eight pointed star with alternate long and short rays in gold. The centre of the neck badge is mounted with a diamond. The neck collar or chain was discontinued in 1978. *Second Class:* award is similar in every respect to the First Class except there is no diamond in the centre and the metal is silver and there is no neck collar.

Comments: *The Order of the Star of SA (Military) is divided into two classes:*

Class I Gold: Post nominal title: SSA. Awarded to generals and higher officers or officers of comparable rank who distinguished themselves by meritorious military service that promoted efficiency and contributed lastingly to the security of the nation.

Class II Silver: Post nominal title: SSAS. Awarded to brigadiers and higher officers or officers of comparable rank who distinguished themselves by exceptionally meritorious service of major military importance.

To all intents and purposes the award of this order was mainly confined to members of the South African Permanent Force. If an officer was promoted to Class I of the order his Class II insignia would be returnable. The 1988 amendments to the warrant eliminated the inclusion of non-South African citizens of the appropriate rank for consideration. The amendments to regulations to cover the division that was not exclusively military but could include civilians, was introduced in 1978 but space does not permit lengthy explanation of the various classes: Grand Cross, Grand Officer, Commander, Officer and Knight.

VALUE:

	A	B	C	*Miniature*
Class I Neck collar and badge and breast badge in silver-gilt	£3000	£2500	£1800	—
Class I ditto but in base metal gilt plated for presentation purposes or museums	—	—	£700	—
Class I Neck badge and breast badge.	£1200	£1000	£800	—
Class I ditto in base metal	—	—	£400	£60
Class II Neck and breast badge	£800	£600	£500	£55

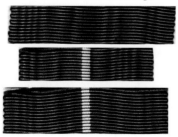

DECORATIONS FOR BRAVERY

SA3. CASTLE OF GOOD HOPE DECORATION

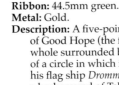

Instituted: 1952.
Ribbon: 44.5mm green.
Metal: Gold.
Description: A five-pointed star representing in outline the Castle of Good Hope (the first major fortress in South Africa) the whole surrounded by a moat. The raised centre is in the form of a circle in which is depicted the arrival of Jan Van Riebeek, in his flag ship *Drommedaris* in Table Bay on 6 April 1652 against a background of Table Mountain, surrounded by a garland of Protea (the national flower) and the inscription: CASTEEL DE GOEDE HOOF DEKORASIE round the top and CASTLE OF GOOD HOPE DECORATION round the foot. (Reverse) Serial number and Royal cypher. Recently the loop for neck wear has been replaced by a ring for breast wear.
Comments: *Awarded for a signal act of valour or most conspicuous bravery or some daring or pre-eminent act of self-sacrifice or extreme devotion to duty in the presence of an enemy. The decoration could be awarded posthumously. This is South Africa's highest gallantry award but to date it has not been awarded. As no examples of the full size decoration have been awarded, no price is given—any specimens that come on to the market should be regarded with great suspicion. A gold miniature of the decoration is worn on the ribbon on the tunic.*

VALUE:
Gold-plated base metal specimen for museums or presentation
sets of medals   £350–500

Miniature (hallmarked gold)   £350–400

SA4. LOUW WEPENER DECORATION

Instituted: 1952.
Ribbon: 35mm divided into equal stripes, six orange and five white.
Metal: Silver.
Description: Scene at the battle of Thaba Bosigo, Basutoland (now Lesotho) in 1865 in which Louw Wepener, shown in the foreground, was the hero. Inscribed LOUW WEPENER round the top and DECORATION DEKORASIE round the foot. Fitted with a scrolled suspension bar.
Comments: *It was awarded in recognition of acts of most conspicuous courage and self-sacrifice performed in the execution of or beyond the call of military duty in time of peace or war, by members of the SADF or attached troops, in saving or endeavouring to save the lives of others on land, sea or in the air or in the execution of duty for which other purely military honours are not normally granted. Post nominal title: LWD. The award was rendered obsolete by the Honoris Crux Decoration in 1975. Further awards were to have been denoted by a silver bar centred with a silver button inscribed with the initials LWD, but none were ever manufactured.*

VALUE:

	A	B	C	Miniature
Royal cypher reverse	£1700	£1300	£800	£50
Royal cypher erased	£1600	£1200	£750	£50
SA coat of arms	£1300	£750	£650	£75

SA5. VAN RIEBEECK DECORATION

Instituted: 1952.

Ribbon: 32mm sky blue.

Metal: Silver-gilt.

Description: In shape of a five-pointed star representing the outline of the Castle of Good Hope. The suspension consists of a cluster of eight protea leaves. In the centre of the obverse is the full figure of Jan Van Riebeeck (first Governor of the Cape of Good Hope) in relief against a background of three rings representing his three ships—*Drommedaris, De Rijger* and *De Goede Hoop*.

Comments: *The decoration was awarded to officers of the SA Defence Force or auxiliary services or attached troops who distinguished themselves by outstanding resourcefulness, perseverance or personal courage or by their outstanding leadership or responsibility and personal example against an enemy in the field. Post nominal title: DVR. The award was rendered obsolete by the Honoris Crux Decoration in 1975. A specimen of the bar embossed with a miniature cannon in silver gilt to denote further awards, is on display at the SA Museum of Military History.*

VALUE:

	A	B	C	Miniature
Royal cypher reverse	£1600	£1200	£600	£35
Royal cypher erased	£1600	£800	£400	£75
SA coat of arms reverse	£1600	£700	£400	£45

SA6. VAN RIEBEECK MEDAL

Instituted: 1952.

Ribbon: 32mm sky blue with 6mm white central stripe.

Metal: Silver.

Description: Very similar to the Van Riebeeck Decoration (above) but differing in the ribbon. It, too, was discontinued in August 1975.

Comments: *In all respects identical to the Van Riebeeck Decoration except the medal was awarded to Warrant Officers, NCOs and Men. The medal was rendered obsolete by the Honoris Crux Decoration in 1975. Post nominal title: VRM. Additional award bar as for the decoration, except metal is silver. Specimen on display at the SA Museum of Military History.*

VALUE:

	A	B	C	Miniature
Royal cypher reverse	£1600	£700	£400	£35
Royal cypher erased	£1600	£700	£400	£80
SA coat of arms reverse	£1600	£650	£400	£45

SA7. HONORIS CRUX

Instituted: 1952.

Ribbon: 32mm leaf-green with 3mm red outer and 2mm white inner edges.

Metal: Silver gilt and enamels.

Description: An eight-pointed Maltese Cross in silver gilt: in each angle formed by the cross is an eagle in silver gilt, facing to the right. Centre circle of the cross is enamelled in the three colours of the flag of Union of South Africa. The design was significantly influenced by the Order of the Golden Eagle that was proposed in 1894 but was rejected by the Transvaal Volksraad.

Comments: *There have been six recipients of this award. It was awarded to members of the South African Defence Force, auxiliary services, attached troops who regardless of their own safety and through personal courage and determination, perform a gallant act or deed against an enemy in the field. Subsequent deeds may entitle a recipient to a bar in silver-gilt embossed in the centre with a miniature eagle. A specimen bar is on display at the SA Museum of Military History. Post nominal title: HC.*

VALUE:

	A	B	C	Miniature
Royal cypher reverse	£1700	£750	£475	£50
Royal cypher erased	£1700	£1000	£525	£50
SA coat of arms	£1700	£900	£525	£55

SA8. LOUW WEPENER MEDAL

Instituted: 1967.

Ribbon: 35mm in width, orange divided into five broad stripes of equal width by four white stripes of 1.5mm

Metal: Bronze

Description: Identical to the Louw Wepener Decoration with the words "MEDALJE/MEDAL" substituted for"DECORATION/DEKORASIE".

Comments: *Conditions of award as for Louw Wepener Decoration for deeds of a lesser nature than those for which the Louw Wepener Decoration was awarded. The award could be made posthumously. Subsequent awards were recognized by a bar with a centred circle containing the letters LWM. Post nominal title: LWM. The medal was rendered obsolete by the Honoris Crux Decoration in 1975.*

VALUE:

A	B	C	Miniature
£1300	£850	£650	£45

SA9. HONORIS CRUX DECORATION

Instituted: 1975.

Ribbon: 32mm orange with additional white stripes according to class.

Metal: Enamelled gold or silver, according to class.

Description: An eight-pointed enamelled Maltese cross superimposed on a wreath with crossed swords in the angles, with a central roundel divided horizontally into orange, white and blue. Fitted with an ornamental suspension loop.

Comments: *This award replaced SA4, 5, 6, 7 and 8 above and was divided into four classes, distinguished by their ribbons and the embellishment of the obverse.*

Honoris Crux Diamond. *Plain orange ribbon, 32mm, with a green circular border to centre roundel mounted with eight diamonds awarded to those who distinguished themselves. Awarded for performing deeds of outstanding valour, at extreme risk to their lives*

Honoris Crux Gold. *Orange ribbon with a 1mm central white stripe. Made of silver gilt with gold border to centre roundel. Awarded for performing outstanding deeds of bravery in extreme danger.*

Honoris Crux Silver. *Orange ribbon with a 1mm white stripe 13mm from each edge. Made of silver with silver border to centre roundel. Awarded for performing exceptional deeds of bravery whilst in great danger.*

Honoris Crux. *Orange with 2mm white edges and 1mm white stripe 5mm from each edge. Made of silver. The centre roundel has a silver border but the arms of the cross are white enamel instead of green as in the other three classes. Awarded for performing deeds of bravery in dangerous circumstances.*

The post-nominal titles are: HCD, HCG, HCS and HC respectively. Further awards are denoted by a bar with miniature replica of the decoration—in gold for the first two classes and silver for the second two. Only 4 HCGs were awarded—one with a bar. In 1993 the HCD and HCG were discontinued. The crosses have a SA Mint hallmark. The first striking has voiding round the protea wreath whereas subsequent "Silver" in a narrow border strikings have no voiding at all.

VALUE:

	A	B	C	Miniature
HC (Diamond)	—	—	£1000	£150
HC (Gold)	£2600	£2200	£800	£150
HC (Silver)	£2300	£1700	£700	£150
HC	£2200	£1200	£700	£150

SA10. PRO VIRTUTE DECORATION

Instituted: 1987.

Ribbon: 32mm in width, 20mm orange central stripe edged with a narrow pale blue stripe of 6mm each.

Metal: 9ct gold.

Description: A five linked white enamelled Maltese Cross edged with gold. The centre is of dark red enamel on which is superimposed the embellished coat of arms of the Republic of South Africa. The cross is connected with the suspender by an inverted V from which extends two proteas. The reverse bears the words "PRO VIRTUTE". Awarded to officers of the SA National Defence Force who have distinguished themselves by distinguished conduct and exceptional combat leadership during military operations.

Comments: *Post Nominal Title PVD. Subsequent awards are denoted by a silver gilt bar with a miniature Protea emblem embossed in the centre of the bar.*

VALUE:

A	B	C	Miniature
£2100	£1300	£700	£100

SA11. PRO VIRTUTE MEDAL

Instituted: 1987.

Ribbon: 32mm in width, orange outer stripes of 10mm with two 4mm central light blue stripes divided by an orange 4mm central stripe.

Metal: Silver

Description: The obverse bears the outline of the cross of the Pro Virtute Decoration. The reverse bears the title PRO VIRTUTE Surmounted by the coat of arms of the Republic of South Africa and a wreath of proteas as a surround on three sides.

Comments: *Awarded to warrant officers and other ranks with a similar bar for further awards, except in silver. Conditions of award as for PVD. Post nominal title: PVM.*

VALUE:

A	B	C	Miniature
£1300	£850	£700	£100

SA12. AD ASTRA DECORATION

Instituted: 1987.

Ribbon: 30mm diagonal alternating narrow light blue and white stripes of 3mm.

Metal: Gold plated silver with hallmark.

Description: In the centre of a five-pointed star is the outline of the Castle of Good Hope in relief on which is depicted the badge of the SA Air Force in gold on a light blue background edged with white. The reverse shows the embellished coat of arms of the Republic of South Africa above the words "AD ASTRA". The star is suspended from an eagle with outstretched wings attached to a ring at the top of the star.

Comments: *This award is made to air crew members for excellent flying skill or outstanding ingenuity or skill during emergencies or unusual situations on board aircraft. Post nominal title: AAD.*

VALUE:

A	B	C	Miniature
£2100	£1300	£650	£60

SA13. THE S.A.D.F. CROSSES

Army Cross

Instituted: 1987.

Ribbons: A. Army Cross: 30mm wide. White with central 10mm guardsman red stripe; **B. Air Force Cross:** 30mm wide. White with central broad light blue stripes of 12mm divided by a narrow gold stripe of 2mm; **C. Navy Cross:** 30mm wide. White with central broad navy blue stripe of 10mm; **D. SA Medical Services Cross:** 30mm wide. White with central broad purple stripe of 10mm.

Metal: Silver

Description: A silver cross with fixed straight suspender decorated with laurel leaves. The suspender is attached to the top arm of the cross. The arms of the cross have a double border and rise to a higher point from the edge which is 2mm thick. There is a central roundel for each cross covered in shiny epoxy and bordered with three circles of laurel leaves.

A. Army Cross: orange roundel; with badge of the SA Army in gold; **B. Air Force Cross:** light blue roundel with the badge of the SA Air Force in gold; **C. Navy Cross:** navy blue roundel with the badge of the SA Navy in gold; **D. SA Medical Services Cross:** a purple roundel with the badge of the SA Medical Services in gold.

Comments: *The reverse bears the embellished coat of arms of the Republic of South Africa. A bar in silver denotes a subsequent award and bears a miniature protea. Post-nominal titles are as follows:* ***A. Army Cross:*** *CM (Crux Militere);* ***B. Air Force Cross:*** *CA (Crux Aeronautica);* ***C. Navy Cross:*** *CN (Crux Navalis);* ***D. SA Medical Services Cross:*** *CC (Crux Curationis).*

Recent events—the sinking of the Oceana *and the Mozambique floods—have seen a number of these crosses awarded, particularly to Air Force personnel. The crosses are awarded to all ranks of the SA Defence Force and auxiliary service for the SA Defence Force and other armed forces attached to or serving with or rendering service to the SA Defence Force, who have distinguished themselves by their exceptional ingenuity and skill in handling equipment, weapons, vehicles, aircraft and vessels concomitant with exemplary personal leadership, dedication and courage in peril of their lives (non-operational).*

VALUE:

A	B	C	Miniature
£2100	£1200	£500	£50

Air Force Cross

Navy Cross

SA Medical Services Cross

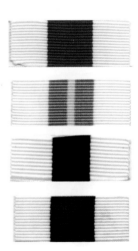

MEDALS AWARDED FOR DISTINGUISHED, LONG AND MERITORIOUS SERVICE

SA14. SOUTHERN CROSS MEDAL (1952)

Instituted: 1952.
Ribbon: 32mm dark blue with 3mm orange and white central stripes.
Metal: Hallmarked silver and enamel.
Description: A circular medal with raised 4mm rimmed border decorated with a single wreath of oak leaves with suspender also decorated with oakleaves. Within the wreath the field of dark blue enamel shows the Southern Cross constellation.
Comments: *This decoration was superseded in 1975 when it was split into two classes: the Southern Cross Decoration and the Southern Cross Medal (of different design). Recipients are entitled to the postnominal SM. The medal was awarded in times of peace or war to members of the SA Defence Force, or of an auxiliary service or other attached armed forces, irrespective of rank, who distinguished themselves by displaying outstanding devotion to duty, either in a particular instance or over a period of time.*

VALUE:

	A	B	C	Miniature
Royal cypher reverse	£1100	£700	£350	£70
Royal cypher erased	£700	£550	£400	£70
SA coat of arms	£650	£550	£300	£70

SA15. SOUTHERN CROSS DECORATION (1975)

Instituted: 1975.
Ribbon: 32mm blue with 1mm white stripes 13mm from each edge.
Metal: Silver and enamels.
Description: An eight-pointed Maltese cross superimposed on a larger, broader cross in the same form, with a beaded enamelled medallion at the centre bearing the constellation of the Southern Cross. Fitted with a protea emblem for suspension from a straight bar.
Comments: *Awarded to commissioned officers of the South African Defence Force or of related forces who contributed to the security of the nation, in recognition of outstanding service of the highest order and the utmost devotion to duty displayed in time of peace or war. In 1993 a bar (silver gilt) was authorised with a protea emblem embossed in its centre, for subsequent awards. Recipients are entitled to the post-nominal SD.*

VALUE:

A	A with bar	B	C	Miniature
£350	£370	£250	£175	£95

SA16. SOUTHERN CROSS MEDAL (1975)

Instituted: 1975.

Ribbon: (1975)—32mm in width, dark blue with 2mm white edges and 1mm white stripes 13mm from each edge. (1986)—32mm in width, divided as follows: white 4mm, dark blue 9mm, white 1mm, dark blue 4mm and then repeated in reverse.

Metal: Enamelled silver.

Description: A five-pointed radiate star with circular radiate sectors between the arms, having a beaded central medallion depicting the constellation of the Southern Cross. Fitted with a plain ring for suspension from a straight bar.

Comments: *Awarded to commissioned officers of the SA Defence Force or other armed forces attached to or serving with or rendering service to the SADF, in recognition of exceptionally meritorious service and particular devotion to duty displayed in time of peace and war. This medal replaced the Southern Cross Medal 1952 (SA14). Bar for subsequent awards as for Southern Cross Decoration (see SA15). Since 1993, recipients have been entitled to the post-nominal SM.*

VALUE:

A	A with bar	B	C	Miniature
£250	£220	£200	£160	£70

SA17. PRO MERITO MEDAL (1967)

Instituted: 1967.

Ribbon: 32mm sky blue with a dark blue centre flanked by narrow white and orange stripes.

Metal: Oxidised silver.

Description: An enamelled disa flower in relief encircled by a wreath of leafed protea flowers on the obverse. The embellished coat of arms of South Africa is on the reverse. With a foliate suspender.

Comments: *Awarded to Warrant Officers, NCOs and other ranks of the SA Defence Force and related forces for outstanding devotion to duty. 374 medals were awarded in total. Recipients are entitled to the post-nominal PMM. In 1975 this award was discontinued when it was split into two classes: The Pro Merito Decoration and The Pro Merito Medal (of different design).*

VALUE:

A	B	C	Miniature
£520	£400	£250	£65

SA18. PRO MERITO DECORATION (1975)

Instituted: 1975.

Ribbon: 32mm blue with a 4mm white central stripe.

Metal: Enamelled silver gilt.

Description: A white enamelled Maltese Cross bordered in gold with centre roundel charged with a red disa flower. The reverse has the embellished coat of arms of South Africa. At the top is a protea flower emblem for suspension from a straight bar.

Comments: *It is awarded to Warrant Officers and NCOs and other ranks of the SA Defence Force or of related forces contributing to the defence of the Republic of South Africa, who have distinguished themselves by rendering outstanding service of the highest order and displaying the utmost devotion to duty. In 1993 a silver gilt bar with protea emblem on its centre was introduced to denote a subsequent award. Recipients are entitled to the post-nominal PMD.*

VALUE:

A	B	C	Miniature
£380	£275	£200	£35

SA19. PRO MERITO MEDAL (1975)

Instituted: 1975.
Ribbon: (1975)—32mm in width, blue with 2mm white edges and 4mm white central stripe. (1986)—32mm, sky blue edged by 5mm white stripes with one 4mm white central stripe.
Metal: Oxidised silver.
Description: A five pointed radiate star with radiate sectors between the arms, having a beaded central medallion of blue enamel with a red disa flower. The reverse bears the embellished coat of arms of South Africa. In 1993, a silver bar with a protea embossed in its centre was introduced to indicate a susbequent award. In 1993 the post-nominal title of PMM was introduced. Fitted with a plain ring for suspension from a straight bar.
Comments: *This medal replaced the original Pro Merito Medal of 1976 (SA 17) when that decoration was divided into two classes. The medal was awarded for exceptionally meritorious service and particular devotion to duty in peace or war to Warrant Officers, NCOs and other ranks.*

VALUE:

	A	B	C	Miniature
	£220	£150	£120	£35

SA20. COMMANDANT GENERAL OF THE SOUTH AFRICAN DEFENCE FORCE COMMENDATION (1968)

Instituted: 1968.
Ribbon: None.
Metal: Bronze.
Description: A protea emblem sewn on to the tunic and not worn on medal ribbons.
Comments: *Awarded for mentions in despatches. It was superseded in 1974 by the Chief of the South African Defence Force Commendation Medal (SA21) for which it could be exchanged.*

VALUE:

	A	B	C	Miniature
	£75	£50	£35	£25

SA21. CHIEF OF THE SA DEFENCE FORCE COMMENDATION MEDAL (1974)

Instituted: 1974.
Ribbon: 32mm orange centre flanked by sky blue stripes and dark blue edges.
Metal: Bronze.
Description: A circular medal with concave curves between twelve points and a plain ring for suspension from a rectangular bar. In the centre, a beaded medallion of the South African Defence Force.
Comments: *Awarded to members of the SA Defence Force (an auxiliary service established to assist the SA Defence Force) who have distinguished themselves by rendering service of a high order which could not be suitably recognised in any other manner. In 1993 this medal was superseded by the Military Merit Medal.*

VALUE:

	A	B	C	Miniature
	£240	£180	£150	£25

Note: If awarded for downgraded gallantry award with citation: £200

SA22. MILITARY MERIT MEDAL

Instituted: 1993.
Ribbon: As for chief of SA Defence Force Commendation Medal (SA21).
Metal: Bronze plated brass.
Description: As for Chief of SA Defence Force Commendation Medal (SA21) but with fixed suspender.
Comments: *The medal replaced SA21 but with greatly enhanced status. The medal is now awarded to members of the SA Defence Force who have rendered outstanding service of vital importance/permanent significance of the highest order. Because of the anomaly of the previous title of the medal—only the State President and not the Chief of Defence Force could institute the medals, those who had been awarded the Chief of the SA Defence Force Commendation Medal were empowered to change the name of their medal to the new title and like the recipients of the new awards, could enjoy the post-nominal MMM. In 1993 a bar to denote a subsequent award was introduced. The bronze bar carries a centrally placed embossed protea emblem.*

VALUE:

A	A with bar	B	C	Miniature
£215	£275	£150	£95	£20

SA23. DANIE THERON MEDAL

Instituted: 1970
Ribbon: 32mm green with three narrow yellow stripes.
Metal: Silver.
Description: An eagle hovering over mountain peaks, with three stars on either side and DANIE THERON round the top and MEDALJE MEDAL at the foot. Scrolling spurs secure the medal to the plain suspension bar.
Comments: *This medal was named after the most famous Boer scout of the Anglo-Boer War 1899–1902. From 1970 to 1975, this medal was awarded to officers who were members of the commandos of the SA Defence Force, had completed not less than 10 years service in the SA Defence Force and had not yet received any other awards in recognition of outstanding devotion to duty or exceptionally diligent and outstanding service. In 1975, on the abolition of the Jack Hindon Medal, the Danie Theron Medal now covered the provisions of the Jack Hindon Medal. Recipients of the award are entitled to use the post-nominal DTM.*

VALUE:

A	B	C	Miniature
£285	£230	£195	£35

SA24. JACK HINDON MEDAL

Instituted: 1970
Ribbon: 32mm yellow with a narrow central green stripe and broad
green stripes at the edges.
Metal: Bronze.
Description: An upright oval medal showing the sun rising over a
mountain peak. In the foreground Jack Hindon and two companions
unfurling the Vierkleur (Boer flag) during the battle of Spion Kop
on January 24, 1900. Inscription JACK HINDON round the top, with
MEDALJE MEDAL at the foot. Fitted with scrolled spurs to a plain
suspension bar.
Comments: *This medal was named in honour of Captain Oliver John Hindon
who fought for the South African Republic (Transvaal) against the British
in the Boer war. (He was born in Stirling, Scotland on 20 April 1874 and
he deserted from the British Army while serving in Natal in 1888, after
severe treatment at the hands of an NCO of his unit. During the early part
of the Anglo-Boer war, Hindon, now a citizen of the Transvaal Republic,
was a member of Danie Theron's scout corps and was appointed to head a
special corps whose function was to disrupt British lines of communication
through the derailment of British trains and the cutting of telegraph lines.
So successful was he that he became one of the Boer heroes of the war.)The
conditions of this award are as the Danie Theron Medal (SA23) but the Jack
Hindon medal was awarded to Warrant Officers, NCOs and other ranks.
The medal was superseded by the Danie Theron Medal in 1975. Recipients
are entitled to the post-nominal JHM.*

VALUE:

A	B	C	Miniature
£285	£200	£140	£25

SA25. COMMANDANT GENERAL'S MEDAL

Instituted: 1956.
Ribbon: 32mm in with, orange with 6.4mm sky blue edges and 6.4mm
dark blue central stripe.
Metal: Oxidised silver.
Description: A laurel wreath enclosing a five-sided polygon divided
into sectors. In the centre is a circle enclosing crossed rifles above a
circular target and bushveld scenery. In the exergue is the inscription
KOMMANDANT GENERAALS MEDALJE COMMANDANT
GENERALS MEDAL. The top of the polygon has a fluted bar
connecting it to the suspension bar decorated with laurel sprays.
Comments: *This medal was awarded for outstanding marksmanship.
Subsequent awards of the medal are denoted by bars with a centrally placed
silver button inscribed with the year of award. This medal was superseded
in 1975 by the SADF Champion Shot Medal (SA26).*

VALUE:

A	B	C	Miniature
£195	£150	£80	£30

SA26. SADF CHAMPION SHOT MEDAL

Instituted: 1975.
Ribbon: As SA25.
Metal: Oxidised silver.
Description: Identical to SA25 except for the inscription in the exergue which now reads SAW
KAMPIOENSKUTMEDALJE / SADF CHAMPION SHOT MEDAL.
Comments: *Awarded annually to the champion shot. Subsequent awards of the medal are denoted by bars with centrally
placed silver button inscribed with the year of award. The award replaced the Commandant General's Medal (SA25).*

VALUE:

A	B	C	Miniature
£190	£150	£80	£30

SA27. CADET CORPS CHAMPION SHOT MEDAL

Instituted: 1987.
Ribbon: 32mm orange ribbon each side edged with a 6mm green stripe.
Metal: Silver.
Description: Obverse: A prancing springbok facing to the left enclosed on three sides by a wreath of laurels. Reverse: In semicircular format—top: GROOTKAMPIONSKUT, bottom: GRAND CHAMPION SHOT and centrally placed in two lines: KADETKORPS and CADET CORPS.
Comments: *The imaginative concept was that winners' achievements would not be lost on leaving school but they could mount this medal along with their SA Defence Force awards in after years. In 1994 the School Cadet Corps were abolished by the President of South Africa, so the award became obsolete. By that date, 16 awards had been made and these were backdated to 1978.*

VALUE:

A	B	C	Miniature
£130	£110	£95	£35

SA28. UNION MEDAL

Instituted: 1952.
Branch of service: Union of South Africa Permanent Defence Force.
Ribbon: 32mm equal stripes of orange, white and navy blue repeated three times to make a total of 9 stripes.
Metal: Silver.
Description: A scalloped medal with an ornamental suspender of wattle leaves and mimosa flowers. Obverse: Coat of arms of South Africa and the inscription UNION MEDAL—UNIE MEDALJE. Reverse: the Royal Cypher EIIR with crown.
Comments: *This medal was awarded to members of the Union Defence Force Permanent Force, irrespective of rank, for a minimum of 18 years service of an impeccable character. It was superseded in 1961 by the Permanent Force Good Service Medal. This medal replaced no. 253 except its award was extended to include commissioned officers as well. Approximately 1,400 medals were awarded. Those completing an extra 12 years service were eligible for a silver bar with centrally embossed coat of arms of South Africa. When the ribbon alone was worn the bar to the awards was represented by a miniature silver coat of arms.*

VALUE:	A	B	C	Miniature
	£120	£85	£75	£25
with bar	£135			

Bar for 12 years   *Ribbon emblem*

SA29. PERMANENT FORCE GOOD SERVICE MEDAL

Instituted: 1961.
Ribbon: As for Union Medal (SA28)
Metal: Silver.
Description: A scalloped medal. Obverse as for SA28 except "UNION MEDAL—UNIE MEDALJE" has been removed. Reverse: carries details over seven lines: VIR LANGDURIGE DIENS EN GOEIE GEDRAG / FOR LONG SERVICE AND GOOD CONDUCT.
Comments: *Awarded for a minimum of 18 years service. A silver bar in the form of the republican arms was added to the ribbon for further periods of 12 years service (as for SA28). About 2,700 of these medals were awarded.*

VALUE:	A	B	C	Miniature
	£50	£40	£30	£20
With bar	£60			

SA30. SOUTH AFRICAN DEFENCE FORCE GOOD SERVICE MEDAL

1st striking

Instituted: 1975.

Ribbon: 32mm green with different stripes according to the class and branch of service. In 1986 the nine ribbons were reduced to three: gold medal—green with two 7mm yellow stripes 6mm from each edge; silver medal—green edged with 7mm white stripes with a central 6mm white stripe; bronze medal—green edged with two 10mm bronze brown stripes.

Metal: Silver gilt/gilt coated brass for 30 years; silver/silver coated brass for 20 years; bronze/bronze coated brass/bronze sprayed on brass for 10 years. Some of the first issue were struck in 9ct gold.

Description: A scalloped medal bearing (obverse): the coat of arms of the Republic. (Reverse) the inscription VIR TROUE DIENS/FOR GOOD SERVICE. Ornamental suspender of wattle leaves and mimosa flowers.

Comments: *This medal superseded the Permanent Force Good Service Medal of 1961 (see SA29) and was divided into three classes, each having distinctive ribbons as follows:*

Gold Medal:
Permanent Force. Three narrow white stripes towards each edge
Citizen Force. Three narrow blue stripes towards each edge
Commandos. Three narrow orange stripes towards each edge

Silver Medal:
Permanent Force. Two narrow white stripes towards each edge
Citizen Force. Two narrow blue stripes towards each edge
Commandos. Two narrow orange stripes towards each edge

Bronze Medal:
Permanent Force. One narrow white stripe 2mm from edge
Citizen Force. One narrow blue stripe 2mm from edge
Commandos. One narrow orange stripe 2mm from edge.

Members of the Citizen Force or Commandos had the option of choosing this series instead of the John Chard series for Citizen Force or the De Wet series for the Commandos. A silver gilt bar identical to the bar mentioned in SA28 and SA29 was awarded for 40 years service and this was sewn on to the ribbon of the 30 year medal. The reverse of the medal bears the title: VIR TROUWE DIENS/ FOR GOOD SERVICE in relief. In the first two strikings of this medal the suspender was decorated with wattle leaves and mimosa flowers on the obverse while the reverse of the suspension was plain.

There are three strikings to each medal:
1st striking: SA Mint marks.
2nd striking: No Mint marks, no rim to the reverse while the bronze medal is brass coated with bronze and the gauge of the medals is almost 50 per cent thinner.
3rd striking: No Mint marks, reverse rim restored and medal of proper thickness with double faced suspension bar. Brass coated in gold, silver and bronze sprayed-on paint.

VALUE:

	A	B	C	Miniature
First striking:				
SA Mint Mark Gold (9ct)	£750	£600	£400	£105
Gilt:	£60	£45	£40	£20
Silver:	£40	£35	£30	£20
Bronze:	£35	£30	£25	£10
Second striking:				
Gilt:	£50	£40	£35	£20
Silver:	£40	£35	£30	£12
Bronze:	£35	£30	£25	£10
Third striking:				
Gilt:	£45	£35	£30	£20
Silver:	£40	£35	£30	£15
Bronze:	£35	£30	£25	£10

SA31. SOUTH AFRICAN DEFENCE FORCE MEDAL FOR 40 YEARS DISTINGUISHED CONDUCT AND LOYAL SERVICE

Instituted: 1986.

Ribbon: 32mm green with central portion 1mm white, 3mm black, 3mm white, 3mm orange and 1mm white. In 1994 the ribbon was changed however, reducing the central portion to 10mm, 5x2mm stripes of blue, yellow, black, white and red.

Metal: 9 carat gold.

Description: Obverse: The embellished coat of arms of South Africa. Reverse: The Roman numerals XL within a circular laurel wreath open at the top and the medal suspended from a double faced scrolled suspender.

Comments: *This medal is awarded to all members of the South African Permanent Force, Citizen Force or Commandos for 40 years of meritorious and irreproachable service.*

VALUE:

A	B	C	Miniature
£575	£475	£350	£45

SA32. JOHN CHARD DECORATION

Instituted: 1952.

Ribbon: 32mm dark red with 3mm dark blue (outer) and 2mm white (inner) edges.

Metal: Silver/chromed brass.

Description: An upright oval medal fitted with a ring for suspension. The centre shows a view of Rorke's Drift in 1879. At the top is the inscription JOHN CHARD and at the foot DECORATION: DEKORASIE. See descriptions below for details of the various reverses.

Comments: *This decoration was named in memory of Lieutenant John Chard, VC, who commanded the garrison at the defence of Rorke's Drift during the Zulu War, 1879. The medal ribbon is worn with a silver button embossed with the initials JCD. The measurement from the top to bottom of the upright oval was designed to exactly match the proportions of the Efficiency Decoration (No. 236). A silver bar with crown (as for the Efficiency Medal) was awarded to denote an extra 10 years, i.e. 30 years service up until 1961. In 1962 a bar of silver with centred circle enclosing the initials JCD was awarded for 30 years service. Silver emblems indicate the branch of service: a fouled anchor on the ribbon for the navy, crossed swords for the army and an eagle with outstretched wings for the air force. Holders are entitled to the post-nominals JCD.*

VALUE:

Type	Description	A	B	C	Miniature
I	*Royal cypher EIIR above SA coat of arms*	£250	£125	£100	£35
II	*Royal cypher erased*	£100	£80	£60	£25
III	*Large coat of arms of SA —voided acorn*	£65	£60	£40	£15
IV	*Unvoided acorn suspender and no rim on reverse, with coat of arms*	£60	£50	£40	£10
V	*As for IV but metal chromed brass, with coat of arms*	£45	£40	£30	—
VI	*Reverse rim, voided acorn of poor detail and medal stamped silver, with coat of arms*	£60	£50	£45	£10

SA33. JOHN CHARD MEDAL

Instituted: 1952.
Ribbon: As for John Chard decoration (SA32).
Metal: Bronze; bronze coated brass; brass sprayed with bronze paint.
Description: Identical to SA32 but with inscription MEDALJE: MEDAL round the foot.
Comments: *This medal replaced the Efficiency Medal and Air Efficiency Award. Silver emblems indicate the branch of service as in SA32.*

VALUE:

Type	Description	A	B	C	Miniature
I	Royal cypher EIIR on SA coat of arms	£185	£65	£45	£25
II	Royal cypher erased	£80	£50	£40	£12
III	Large coat of arms, solid bronze medal	£50	£28	£25	£5
IV	Unvoided acorn and no rim on reverse, bronze coated brass, with coat of arms	£50	£25	£20	£5
V	Poor detailed voided acorn, brass sprayed with bronze paint, with coat of arms	£35	£25	£20	£5

SA34. DE WET DECORATION

Instituted: 1965.
Ribbon: 32mm orange with a broad central blue stripe and 3mm green edges separated from the orange by narrow white stripes.
Metal: Silver.
Description: Two sprays of protea blossom enclose a vignette of General Christiaan De Wet, leader of Boer Forces in 1901–02, on horseback with the inscription DEKORASIE—DE WET—DECORATION round the top of the field, enclosed in a wreath of protea blossom. Foliate spurs link the top of the rim to a plain suspension bar.
Comments: *Awarded to all ranks of Commandos for 20 years service. An additional 10 years service is denoted by a silver bar with centrally placed circle with embossed initials DWD. Holders are entitled to the post nominals DWD.*

VALUE:

A	B	C	Miniature
£440	£370	£95	£20

SA35. DE WET MEDAL

Instituted: 1987.
Ribbon: 32mm central panel (made up of 7mm stripes of navy blue, yellow and navy blue), flanked by 3mm green and 2mm white stripes on either side.
Metal: Brass with lacquered bronze paint.
Description: As for De Wet Decoration (SA34) except inscribed MEDALJE—DE WET—MEDAL on the obverse. Suspender of similar design but double width and uniface.
Comments: *Awarded for 10 years service in the Commandos.*

VALUE:

A	B	C	Miniature
£85	£60	£40	£10

SA36. CADET CORPS MEDAL

Instituted: 1966.
Ribbon: 32mm orange with 5mm blue edges separated from the orange by 1.5mm white stripes.
Metal: Oxidised silver.
Description: A prancing springbok enclosed in a laurel wreath with the inscription CADET CORPS MEDAL and KADETKORPS MEDALJE at the sides.
Comments: *Awarded for 20 years service as an officer in the Cadet Corps. Those who had completed 30 years service were eligible for a silver bar with a prancing springbok embossed in the centre of the bar. It was abolished in August 1976 when the Cadet Corps ceased to exist as a separate force, being absorbed into the Commandos or Citizen Force.*

VALUE:

A	B	C	Miniature
£110	£70	£60	£25

SERVICE MEDALS

SA37. PRO PATRIA MEDAL

Instituted: 1974.
Ribbon: 32mm orange with a broad band of dark blue divided by a thin central orange stripe, with narrow white stripes towards the edges.
Metal: Brass with gilt finish.
Clasp: Cunene clasp awarded for operations into Angola in 1976, sewn on to the ribbon of the Pro Patria Medal.
Description: An eight sided medal with rectangular motifs in each sector with a central dark blue medallion depicting a stylised aloe plant in gold. It has a plain ring attached to a straight suspension bar with a protean emblem flanked by laurel sprays—type I and II have a link suspender whereas type III has a fixed suspender.
Comments: *Awarded for service in the defence of the Republic of South Africa or for suppression or prevention of terrorism with specified conditions of award. There are a number of variations in manufacture for type III.*

VALUE:

Type	Description	A	B	C	Miniature
I	Link suspender. SA Mint striking—serial numbers 1.25mm high	£525	£325	£210	
II	Link suspender	£75	£55	£40	£10
III	Fixed suspender	£55	£45	£35	£10
	With Cunene clasp	£85	£55	£45	£15

(This value should be added to types I, II and III if there is a Cunene clasp)

SA38. SOUTHERN AFRICA MEDAL

Instituted: 1989.

Ribbon: 32mm, central black stripe of 12mm centred with 2mm white stripe, flanked on either side with a 5mm red and 5mm yellow stripe.

Metal: Nickel silver.

Description: An eight sided medal with suspender ornamented with protea flower on each scrolled arm. Obverse: A leopard on the prowl beneath an acacia tree to indicate the strike power of the South African Defence Force. Reverse: A laurel wreath open at its uppermost point to embrace a small embellished coat of arms of South Africa, below are the words SUIDER-AFRICA/SOUTHERN AFRICA.

Comments: *The medal was awarded for participation in specified cross-border activites in defence of the Republic of South Africa. The award was to have originally been called the "Trans Jati Medal", the "Jati" being the cut line. The medals were to have been made from the metal of a captured Russian T34 tank but the metal was found to be unsuited for the purpose. Instead a small amount of melted metal from the tank was mixed with nickel silver. There were two strikings of the medal—the first with a uniface suspender struck as an integral part of the medal, the second with a double faced suspender attached to the medal.*

VALUE:	A	B	C	Miniature
Type I uniface suspender	£75	£55	£45	£15
Type II double faced	£160	£100	£65	—

SA39. GENERAL SERVICE MEDAL

Instituted: 1989.

Ribbon: 32mm, 6mm navy blue stripe, 2mm white stripe, 7mm orange stripe, 2mm navy blue stripe, then the first three stripes repeated in reverse.

Metal: Nickel silver.

Description: Obverse: A laurel wreath open at its uppermost point and enclosing the badge of the South African Defence Force which combines the swords, wings and anchor of the Army, Air Force and Navy, on an outline of the Castle of Good Hope. Reverse: The embellished coat of arms of South Africa with GENERAL SERVICE/ALGEMENE DIENS to the right and left of the coat of arms. Suspenders/strikings as for SA38.

Comments: *Originally the medal was awarded for service within the borders of South Africa from August, 19 1983, i.e. all members of the SADF. It was later extended to members of the SANDF who were involved in specific operations. These operations, which had to have a specific name, included service in Lesotho 1998–99 for which a silver bar "Maluti", sewn to the medal ribbon, was issued. Other operations included township duty as well as service in the Democratic Republic of the Congo, Burundi, Algiers, Mozambique, Zimbabwe and the Comorres.*

VALUE:	A	B	C	Miniature
Type I uniface suspender	£15	£10	£8	£12
Type II double faced	£120	£85	£55	—

With Maluti bar: £50–70 with certification; £40 without certification. Documentary proof of service in the areas mentioned above would enhance the value of the medal. It is regrettable that no other bars were issued for the operational service mentioned.

SA39A. SOUTH AFRICA SERVICE MEDAL

Instituted: —
Ribbon: 32mm, central 8mm red stripe with 1mm white stripe either side, flanked by 10mm yellow and 5mm blue stripes both sides.
Metal: Nickel silver.
Description: A circular medal with straight suspender. Obverse: an outline map of South Africa with shield and crossed spears above. Reverse: coat of arms of South Africa.
Comments: *Awarded to former MK/APLA members who served in a military capacity within the borders of the Republic of South Africa. Medals are numbered on the reverse below the coat of arms.*

VALUE: £35–50

SA39B. OPERATIONAL MEDAL FOR SOUTHERN AFRICA

Instituted: —
Ribbon: 32mm, central 8mm black stripe with 1mm white stripe either side, flanked by 10mm green and 5mm red stripes both sides.
Metal: Nickel silver.
Description: A circular medal with straight suspender. Obverse: A skeletal tree within a six-sided chain. Reverse: coat of arms of South Africa.
Comments: *Awarded to former MK/APLA members who rendered services in a military operational capacity beyond the borders of the Republic of South Africa for at least 60 days. Medals are numbered on the reverse below the coat of arms.*

VALUE: £35–50

COMMEMORATIVE

SA40. UNITAS MEDAL

Instituted: 1994.
Ribbon: 32mm, pale blue with central green stripe of 8mm edged each side by a white stripe of 4mm.
Metal: Lacquered brass.
Description: Obverse: A seven pointed star with central circle enclosing the Greek letter Alpha. Reverse: A small embellished coat of arms of South Africa with date 1994 below. The whole is enclosed by a circle made up of the word "Unity" in all eleven official languages of the new South Africa. Suspender is uniface and struck as one piece with the medal.
Comments: *Awarded to all those who rendered service through being members of a serving force (Permanent Force, Citizen Force, Commandos, members of the armed forces of the former self-governing territories, the armed wing of the ANC (the MK) and APLA) during the period of South Africa's first non-racial elections and inauguration of Mr Mandela as the first black State President in South Africa between 27 April and 10 May 1994. Those medals awarded to members of the British Military Advisory Team in South Africa at the time, for which Her Majesty Queen Elizabeth II granted permission for wear must be considered a rarity.*

VALUE:	A	B	C	Miniature
	£40	£30	£20	£12

MISCELLANEOUS

SA41. MENTION IN DESPATCHES

Instituted: 1967.
Metal: Gilt or bronze.
Description: A miniature replica of the embellished coat of arms of South Africa.
Comments: *Worn either on the ribbon of the Pro Patria Medal or General Service Medal. Prior to the institution of these medals, a bronze version was worn on uniform fabric of the tunic and not affixed to a medal.*

VALUE: A with Citation	A	B	C	Miniature
£40 to £50	£35	£25	£15	£10

SOUTH AFRICAN NATIONAL DEFENCE FORCE INTERIM AWARDS: 1996 TO 2003

In 1994 South Africa entered a new era when the ANC came into power after the Nationalist Government ceased to hold the reins of government. The armed forces underwent a period of transformation where former so called terrorists who had formed part of the armed wing of the African National Congress (MK, Mkhonto Wesizwe), and the Azanian People's Party (APLA, Azanian People's Liberation Army) had to be integrated into the armed forces of South Africa. In keeping with this, the South African Defence Force now became the South African National Defence Force.

Former MK and APLA members entered the SANDF with ribbonless chests. To remedy the situation 18 new medals were instituted for award to members of MK and APLA in 1996—two years after these forces had been disbanded. The awards recognised deeds of bravery or service before 27 April 1994. This decision had a South African precedent as in 1913 members of the armed forces of the old Boer republics of the Orange Free State and Transvaal had been absorbed into the newly formed Union Defence Force. Because of the outbreak of the First World War in 1914, an initiative to recognise the service and meritorious service of former members of the Boer Forces was postponed until 1920. That year the Dekoratie Voor Troue Dienst (see MYB 339) and the Anglo-Boere Oorlog Medalje (MYB 340) were instituted.

The new awards for former MK and APLA members consisted of three bravery awards in three classes for MK with a corresponding allocation for APLA. Similarly three merit and three long service awards were allocated to MK and APLA. A list of the 18 new awards (illustrated opposite) with post nominal titles is as follows:

•	Bravery. MK 1. Star for Bravery in Gold (SBG) 2. Star for Bravery in Silver (SBS) 3. Conspicuous Leadership Star (CLS) £35	•	Bravery. APLA 10. Gilt Star for Bravery (GSB) 11. Bravery Star in Silver (BSS) 12. Star for Conspicuous Leadership (SCL) £35
•	Excellent Service, MK 4. Gold Decoration for Merit in Gold (DMG) 5. Merit Medal in Silver (MMS) 6. Merit Medal in Bronze (MMB) £15	•	Excellent Service, APLA 13. Gold Decoration for Merit (GDM) 14. Silver Medal for Merit (SMM) 15. Bronze Medal for Merit (BMM) £15
•	Long Service, MK 7. Service Medal in Gold (SMG) (30 yrs) 8. Service Medal in Silver (SMS) (20 yrs) 9. Service Medal in Bronze (SMB) (10 yrs) £15	•	Long Service, APLA 16. Gold Service Medal (GSM) (30 yrs) 17. Silver Service Medal (SSM) (20 yrs 18. Bronze Service Medal (BSM) (10 yrs) £15

COMMENTS
1. Orange and red were used as the basic ribbon colour for the bravery awards; blue for merit and green for long service.
2. The design of the medals and structure of the award system was modelled on that of the SADF instituted in 1975 (see MYB SA9 for bravery; MYB SA15, 16, 22 for merit and MYB SA30 for long service.)
3. The bravery awards design was a new departure: the MK awards being a five pointed star and the APLA awards a ten pointed star. The centre of the bravery awards has a roundel with the South African Lion.
4. The official coat of arms of the Republic of South African was placed on the reverse of all the new awards.
5. The obverse of the merit and long service awards carry the symbols of MK (African shield with wheel of industry plus vertical spear and angled AK47 assault rifle) and APLA (African shield with crossed spear and AK47 assault rifle).
6. The metal used for the bravery awards and "gold" merit and "gold" long service awards is silver, plated in gold. "Enamel" work is in fact not enamel but epoxy covered paint. The obverse of all the medals was struck with a very shallow die so that the design is virtually flat, on a level with the surface of the medal. The medal series gives the over-all impression of hasty preparation which was exactly what had occurred.
7. The medals were issued with a serial number and certificate (see introduction to SA Decorations and Medals regarding the pricing of medals).
8. These interim awards have aroused very little interest. The prices given are based on actual instances of sales. In a few years after more have been offered for sale, the prices of interim awards may have to be revised.

SOUTH AFRICAN NATIONAL DEFENCE FORCE NEW AWARDS 2003

The new honours and awards system was instituted on April 27, 2003. All recommendations after that date are to be for the new honours. The new decorations and medals will be issued to all ranks of the SANDF, to any auxiliaries of the SANDF and in certain circumstances to foreign military personnel.

1. Three decorations for bravery are as follows with post nominal titles: Golden Leopard (NG); Silver Leopard (NS); Bronze Leopard (NB). Bars are awarded for subsequent awards of the same decoration.

2. Three decorations for leadership, meritorious conduct or devotion to duty are awarded. Golden Protea (PG); Silver Protea (PS); Bronze Protea (PB) As is the case with the bravery awards, further awards of the same decoration are indicated by bars.

3. A single bronze long service medal replaces the previous awards for 10, 20 and 30 years service, in bronze, silver and gold. The Medal for Loyal Service will be awarded for ten years service, characterised by good conduct. For each additional period of ten years qualifying service, to a maximum of 40 years, extra bars will be awarded to represent each ten year period. For Reserve Force members, a monogram of the letters RD will be attached to the ribbon. These letters stand for "Reserve Distinction" to accord special recognition to part time members of the Reserves.

4. A campaign medal, the General Service Medal, will reward recipients for periods of operational service, minor campaigns and other operations

NOTE: As so few of these medals have been seen on the market, it has been decided not to include them until more details are available.

POLICE AWARDS

All the awards listed have the words "SOUTH AFRICAN POLICE in their titles. Those listed here are the medals most commonly encountered by collectors. The information is taken from *Gallantry Awards of the South African Police 1913–1994* by Terence King assisted by Audrey Portman, by courtesy of Rhino Research. The book contains in-depth details of the gallantry medals listed.

SA42. STAR FOR OUTSTANDING SERVICE

Instituted: 1979
Ribbon: 36mm green divided by two stripes of yellow, blue and white.
Metal: Gilded silver
Description: A star composed of the cross of St Cuthbert, each limb notched of four and in each angle, an engrailed ray. (Obverse): in the centre, a white roundel bearing an aloe with three racemes. (Reverse): the unembellished coat of arms of the Republic of South Africa within the legend *STELLA OFFICII ENGREGII* SA POLICE. A bar denoting subsequent awards depicts an aloe with three racemes. A miniature replica of this clasp is attached to the ribbon when the ribbon alone is worn by a recipient who has been awarded a bar. All decorations and bars were issued named to the recipient and stamped with the serial number, rank and name.
Comments: *Awarded to a member of the South African Police or reserve police who: (a) in the execution of his duties in protecting or saving, or endeavouring to protect or save, life or property, has displayed particular gallantry, exceptional ingenuity, skill or perseverance; (b) in the execution of his duties has rendered outstanding services to members of a dynasty or to Heads of State or of Governments; (c) has distinguished himself through outstanding resourcefulness, leadership, and sense of responsibility or by setting a personal example in any branch of the Force. In addition, it could be awarded to any other persons who distinguished themselves through outstanding services rendered to the South African Police. This decoration was also awarded to*

recognize *acts of gallantry as well as acts of outstanding service. In 1989 all references to gallantry were removed where they occurred in the original warrant, and the award was to officers of the general staff. This was in consequence of the institution of the 1989 version of the South African Police Cross for Bravery. Recipients of this decoration are entitled to use the post nominal letters SOE (STELLA OFFICII EGREGII). Please note: Medals were stamped up to 1979. Thereafter they were machine engraved. The stamps caused a lot of damage*

VALUE: Named £195–230 Unnamed £100–125 Awards for gallantry From £1600 *Miniature* £45

SA43. STAR FOR MERIT

Instituted: 1963.
Ribbon: 32mm, orange with white central stripe edged with blue.
Metal: Silver.
Description: (Obverse): two forearms with hands overlaying the letter V resting on the letter M and holding aloft a flame. (Reverse): the badge of the South African Police, with the words VERDIENSTE above and MERIT below. A silver bar with an embossed letter V resting on an M was authorised to denote a subsequent award or completion of 30 years service. When the ribbon alone is worn, the award of a bar is indicated by this circular emblem. All decorations and bars were issued named to the recipient and stamped with the serial number, rank and name.
Comments: *The award is granted to: (a) members of the South African Police or reserve police force who, in the discharge of their duties, have rendered services of a particularly meritorious or exemplary nature; (b) a member who has completed thirty years service (not necessarily continuous), and who has displayed an irreproachable character and exemplary conduct. The medal is also awarded to other persons (civilians) who have rendered services of a particularly meritorious nature to the South African Police. This medal is awarded for long service and good conduct as well as being a decoration for particularly exemplary or meritorious service (gallantry). The majority of awards to members of the police or reserve police were for acts of gallantry.*

VALUE: Named £70–90 Award for gallantry £375–475 *Miniature* £25–40

SA44. MEDAL FOR FAITHFUL SERVICE

Instituted: 1963.
Ribbon: 32mm, royal blue with 3mm old gold centre stripe.
Metal: Bronze.
Description: (Obverse): the coat of arms of the Republic of South Africa surrounded by a laurel. (Reverse): the official badge of the South African Police with the words TROUE DIENS and FAITHFUL SERVICE in embossed capital letters around.
Comments: *This medal replaced the Police Good Service Medal and was awarded to members of the South African Police who had displayed an irreproachable character and exemplary conduct and served for a qualifying period. A bronze bar embossed with the letters TDFS (Troue Diens/Faithful Service) in ornamental script was awarded for subsequent qualifying periods.*

VALUE	Named	£25–35	Unnamed	£10–25	*Miniature*	£15

SA45. STAR FOR FAITHFUL SERVICE

Instituted: 1979.
Ribbon: 36mm, divided into 11 parts: yellow 2mm, green 3mm, yellow 4mm, blue 2mm, yellow 4mm, green 6mm, repeated in reverse.
Metal: Silver.
Description: A circular medal with (obverse): an eight-pointed star, charged in the centre with a medallion, with four aloes in cross, each with three racemes, all in natural colours. (Reverse): the official badge of the South African Police with the words TROUE DIENS and FAITHFUL SERVICE around.
Comments: *This medal was an award to complement the two long service and good conduct awards already in existence.The qualifying period changed over the years and a gold bar bearing the letters TDFS in ornamental script was awarded for further periods of service. Medals were now awarded for 10 years service (Medal for Faithful Service), 20 years service (Star for Faithful Service), 30 years service (Star for Merit) and 40 years service (Bar to Star for Faithful Service).*

VALUE:	Named	£25–40	Unnamed	£20–30	*Miniature*	£15

SA46. MEDAL FOR COMBATING TERRORISM

Instituted: 1974.
Ribbon: 31.75mm red, with three wide and two narrow silver stripes.
Metal: Silver.
Description: (Obverse): A six-pointed star, with three long and three short points. Attached to the ribbon by means of a V-shaped silver clevis, which is in turn attached to the medal by means of a rimmed shield depicting a candlestick aloe with four leaves and three candles. (Reverse): The words BEKAMPING VAN TERRORISME— COMBATING TERRORISM around the official badge of the South African Police. A silver bar was authorised to denote a subsequent award. This plain bar bears, in the centre, a silver clasp corresponding to the design on the shield. A maximum of two bars only can be awarded, irrespective of any further qualification period. All medals were issued named to the recipient with the serial number, rank and name stamped on the reverse of the V shaped clevis.
Comments: *Awarded to a member of the South African Police or others who, in support of the police, on or at any time after 26 August 1966 (a) had been involved in combat with terrorists, or in the course of the performance of duties in connection with the prevention and combating of terrorism, sustained injuries arising from terrorist activities; or who, in the execution of such duties, displayed exceptional zeal, ingenuity, skills or leadership; (b) had performed counter insurgency duties for at least six months, which may be cumulative, in an area (operational area) fixed by the Minister; (c) had rendered exceptional and outstanding service to the South African Police in connection with the combating of terrorism. The original qualifying period of six months was later changed to sixty days. Any member of the South African Police who was stationed permanently for a continuous period of at least twelve months in an operational area and behaved in an exemplary manner also qualified for the award of the medal.*

VALUE: Named   £80–120   Unnamed   £60–85   *Miniature*   £15

SA47. 75th ANNIVERSARY MEDAL

Instituted: 1988.
Ribbon: Royal blue 32mm edged with light blue and old gold stripes.
Metal: Bronze.
Description: (Obverse): The figures "75", surmounted with an aloe with three racemes and the police motto "SERVAMUS ET SERVIMUS" above and the dates "1913-1988" below. (Reverse): The badge of the South African Police.
Comments: *Instituted to commemorate the 75th anniversary of the founding the South African Police on 1 April 1988. Awarded to permanent and temporary members of the Police Force and Reserve Police Force on 1 April 1988, or people who had rendered service of a particularly meritorious nature to the South African Police. A bar, bearing the figures "75" surmounted by an aloe and three racemes, is to be awarded to those still serving in the Force on 1 April 2013. All awards were issued named and were engraved on the reverse with the serial number, rank and name of the recipient.*

VALUE: Named   £15–20   Unnamed   £10–15   *Miniature*   £18

SA47A. RECONCILIATION AND AMALGAMATION MEDAL

Instituted: 2005.
Ribbon: 32mm, stripes as follows: 4mm blue, 2mm yellow, 5mm green, 3mm white with central 4mm red stripe then the first four stripes are repeated in reverse.
Metal: Lightly sprayed matt brass.
Description: (Obverse): A flowering aloe (the central motif of the SAPS cap badge) surrounded by a laurel wreath. (Reverse): Centrally placed embellished coat of Arms (1910–2003) of the Republic of South Africa, below which is the date 15 October 1995, around the perimeter of the reverse is the full title of the medal.
Comments: *Instituted to commemorate the foundation of the South African Police Service which incorporated the South African Police and police forces of the various homeland states. It was awarded to all members of the SAPS (permanent and temporary members) who were serving on 15 October 1995. All awards were issued named with the serial number, rank and name of the recipient, on the reverse*

VALUE: Named   £15–25   Unnamed   £10–15   *Miniature*   £8

SA47B. TEN YEAR COMMEMORATION MEDAL

Instituted: 2005.
Ribbon: 32mm, stripes as follows: 5mm blue, 2mm white, 4mm red, 3mm yellow, 4mm green, then the first four stripes are repeated in reverse.
Metal: Lightly sprayed matt brass.
Description: (Obverse): Crossed flags of the Republic of South Africa and SAPS. Above: the new post 2003 Arms of the Republic of South Africa. Below: the dates 1995–2005. (Reverse): Around the perimeter is the name of the medal, a centrally placed SAPS badge below which is an oblong panel with serial number of the medal. The number would correspond with the policeman's service number and name in an issue register/computer print out: a sad departure from the previous practice of naming medals to members of the SAPS.
Comments: *Instituted to commemorate the 10th anniversary of a Democratic South Africa and was awarded to permanent and temporary members of the Police Force and Reserve Police Force who were serving on 27 April 2005.*

VALUE: With certificate £15–25   without certificate £10–15   *Miniature* £8

SOUTH AFRICAN PRISONS AWARDS
(Later Department of Correctional Services)

An award system was set up in 1968 but was largely superseded in 1980 when
a new set of insignia was introduced—the medals included here are those most often
encountered by collectors.
All the following medals have the words "SOUTH AFRICAN PRISONS SERVICE" in their
correct title

SA48. DECORATION FOR VALOUR

Instituted: 1968.
Ribbon: Red with green edges divided by thin yellow lines..
Metal: Gold.
Description: A cross in the form of the Castle of Good Hope surmounted
on a star with suspender in form of a lifebuoy. Obverse: DEPARTMENT
VAN GEVANGENISSE / PRISONS DEPARTMENT at edge of medal
with a latin cross with scales of justice above and a lifebuoy on the
lower limb. Reverse: FOR VALOUR (top) and VIR DAPPERHEID
(below) together with the deed engraved below.
Comments: *Awarded to members of the SAPS who had displayed exceptional
bravery or courage in the performance of their duty. A bar with the medal's
obverse was awarded for subsequent acts of valour. Only six awards without
bars were made. Replaced in 1980 by the South African Prisons Service Cross
for Valour (Diamond and Ruby classes).*

VALUE: £850–1200   *Miniature*   £65

SA48A. MEDAL FOR MERIT

Instituted: 1968.
Ribbon: 35mm in width divided into seven parts: blue 6mm; white 5mm;
orange 6mm; white 1mm; then repeated in reverse.
Metal: Silver.
Description: Suspender in form of a lifebuoy. Obverse: DEPARTMENT
VAN GEVANGENISSE / PRISONS DEPARTMENT at edge of medal
with embellished South African coat of arms. Reverse: FOR MERIT
(top) and VIR VERDIENSTELIKHEID (below).
Comments: *Awarded to members of the SAPS who had rendered particularly
meritorious or exemplary service or distinguished himself by his ingenuity,
proficiency or perseverance for a period of not less than 35 years, displaying
irreproachable character and exemplary conduct. Impressed naming on reverse.
A plain bar of silver with the coat of arms of SA embossed in the centre was
awarded for subsequent acts of distinction. Replaced by SA51 (NCOs) in 1979.*

VALUE:
Named with bar	£85–120
Named	£45–60
Unnamed	£25–45
Miniature	£18

SA49. STAR FOR MERIT

Instituted: 1980
Ribbon: 32mm Green with two vertical white stripes each 2mm wide and 12mm from the side.
Metal: Silver.
Description: A 10-point cross with protea flowers in the angles and a plain ring for suspension from a straight bar.
Comments: *Awarded to Commissioned officers for outstanding services rendered on the grounds of ability, efficiency, perseverance or devotion in the discharge of duties. Post nominal title: SPM (Stella Pro Merito). 496 were issued.*

VALUE:
Named with certificate	£75–110
Named	£55–80
Unnamed	£25–40
Miniature (silver)	£25–35

SA50. CROSS FOR MERIT

Instituted: 1980.
Ribbon: 32mm green with three vertical white stripes each 2mm wide and 2mm from each other with the outer white stripes 11mm from each side.
Metal: Silver with gold plated border to cross.
Description: A cross pattée very similar to the German Iron Cross in appearance, but without any detail on the front. Fitted with a plain ring for suspension from a straight bar.
Comments: *No clasps granted for additional awards. Award conditions as for South Africa Prisons Service Star for Merit (SA49) but awarded to non-commissioned officers. Post nominal title: CPM (Crux Pro Merito). 2655 were issued.*

VALUE:
Named	£75–110
Unnamed	£35–50
Miniature	£25–30

SA51. MEDAL FOR MERIT

Instituted: 1980.
Ribbon: For Commissioned Officers: 32mm divided into seven parts—white 4mm; green 8mm; white 2mm; green 4mm and then repeated in reverse. **For NCOs:** 32mm, divided into nine parts; white 4mm; green 8mm; white 2mm; green 4mm white 2mm and then repeated in reverse.
Metal: Silver.
Description: A radiate star with an open protea floriate centre and an inverted V and ring for suspension from a straight bar.
Comments: *Same conditions of award as SA49 and SA50 except the word "outstanding" is replaced by "special". For the Officer's Medal the eight single rays are gold plated and the eight pairs of narrow rays are silver. The open protea flower in the centre is gold plated. The NCOs Medal is plain silver. 1,248 issued to officers and 5,059 issued to NCO's.*

VALUE:
Officer named	£50–65
NCO named	£50–65
Unnamed	£25–35
Miniature	£12–18

SA52. FAITHFUL SERVICE MEDAL

Instituted: 1965.
Ribbon: 31mm, divided into five parts: green 6mm; white 5mm; blue 9mm; and then repeated in reverse.
Metal: Silver.
Description: Obverse: coat of arms of the Republic of South Africa with the words DEPARTMENT VAN GEVANGENISSE—PRISONS DEPARTMENT. Reverse: VOOR TROUE DIENS—FOR FAITHFUL SERVICE.
Comments: *Awarded (1) for 18 years service (not necessarily continuous) that displayed exemplary conduct and unimpeachable character or (2) had displayed devotion to duty in a distinguished or gallant manner. This medal superseded No. 291. A bar with the words: VERDIENSTELIK/MERITORIOUS was granted for gallant or distinguished conduct.*

VALUE:

If awarded for (1)	£30–50
If awarded for (2)	£60–80
With bar	£75–90
Unnamed	£25–40
Miniature	£10–12

SA53. MEDAL FOR FAITHFUL SERVICE

Instituted: 1968.
Ribbon: 35mm divided into five parts: blue 6mm; white 5mm; green 13mm and then repeated in reverse.
Metal: Bronze.
Description: Obverse: In the form of the official badge of the Prisons Department with the circumscription DEPARTMENT VAN GEVANGINISSE (top) and PRISONS DEPARTMENT (bottom). Reverse: FOR FAITHFUL SERVICE (above) and VIR TROUE DIENS (below). In the central area the space received the engraved name, etc., and date of the award of the recipient.
Comments: *Awarded For: (1) as for (1) in SA52. (2) If the recipient had received SA52 for condition 2 of SA52 then he would receive this medal on completion of 18 years service, etc. (3) If the recipient was in possession of SA52 after 18 years service he could receive this medal after completion of a further 12 years. A bar of bronze with the Prisons Department badge in the centre denoted a further 15 years service following the award of the medal.*

VALUE:

Named	£25–40
Unnamed	£15–30
Miniature	£12–18

SA54. MEDAL FOR FAITHFUL SERVICE

Instituted: 1980.
Ribbon: 32mm yellow with two sets of three green stripes each 2mm wide and 2mm apart, the outer stripe set being 2mm from each edge (Gold); two sets of two green stripes each 2mm wide and 2mm apart, the outer stripe set being 2mm from each edge (Silver); or two green stripes each 2mm wide and 2mm from each edge (Bronze).
Metal: Silver-gilt, silver or bronze to denote 30, 20 or 10 years service.
Description: A circular medal with the arms of the Republic in the centre and a garland of protea blossom round the circumference.
Comments: *This replaced SA53. A silver-gilt bar for the gold medal was authorised, embossed with a central circle in the form of the obverse of the medal to indicate a further 10 years service.*

VALUE:

	Named	Unnamed	*Miniature*
Gold (1,130)	£50–70	£15–25	£10–12
With Bar to Gold	£55–80	£30–50	£12–15
Silver (5,594)	£25–40	£15–25	£10–12
Bronze (13,350)	£15–25	£10–20	£10–12

Gold ribbon.

LIFESAVING MEDAL RIBBONS
(Not all shown to scale, see reference number for actual sizes)

L1. Royal Humane Society (1921)

L1. Stanhope Gold Medal

L3. Hundred of Salford Humane Society Medals

L4. RNLI Medal

L4B. Port of Plymouth Swimming Assc. and Humane Society Medal

L5. Medals of the Society for the Protection of Life from Fire

L6. Lloyd's Medal for Saving Life at sea

L7. Liverpool S&H Society's Marine Medals

L8. SF&MRB Society Medal

L9. Tayleur Fund Medal

L10A. Jersey Humane Society Medal

L12. Lifesaving Medal of the Order of St John (Original)

L12. Lifesaving Medal of the Order of St John (1888 on)

L12. Lifesaving Medal of the Order of St John (1950–1953)

L12. Lifesaving Medal of the Order of St John (1954 on)

L13. Shropshire Society Life Saving Medal

L14. Liverpool Shipwreck and Humane Society's Fire Medal

L15. Liverpool Shipwreck and Humane Society's Swimming Medal

L15A. Ally Sloper's Medal

L16. Answers Medal for Heroism

L17. Lloyd's Medal for Meritorious Service

L18. Liverpool Shipwreck and Humane Society's General Medal

L19. Today Gallantry Fund Medal

L20. Imperial Merchant Service Guild Medal

L21. Pluck Medal for Heroism

L22. Tynemouth Medal

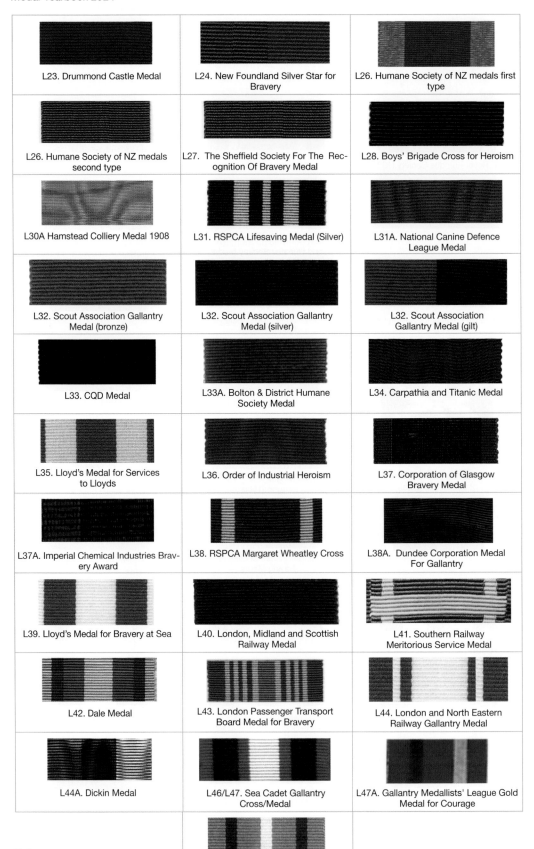

L23. Drummond Castle Medal

L24. New Foundland Silver Star for Bravery

L26. Humane Society of NZ medals first type

L26. Humane Society of NZ medals second type

L27. The Sheffield Society For The Recognition Of Bravery Medal

L28. Boys' Brigade Cross for Heroism

L30A Hamstead Colliery Medal 1908

L31. RSPCA Lifesaving Medal (Silver)

L31A. National Canine Defence League Medal

L32. Scout Association Gallantry Medal (bronze)

L32. Scout Association Gallantry Medal (silver)

L32. Scout Association Gallantry Medal (gilt)

L33. CQD Medal

L33A. Bolton & District Humane Society Medal

L34. Carpathia and Titanic Medal

L35. Lloyd's Medal for Services to Lloyds

L36. Order of Industrial Heroism

L37. Corporation of Glasgow Bravery Medal

L37A. Imperial Chemical Industries Bravery Award

L38. RSPCA Margaret Wheatley Cross

L38A. Dundee Corporation Medal For Gallantry

L39. Lloyd's Medal for Bravery at Sea

L40. London, Midland and Scottish Railway Medal

L41. Southern Railway Meritorious Service Medal

L42. Dale Medal

L43. London Passenger Transport Board Medal for Bravery

L44. London and North Eastern Railway Gallantry Medal

L44A. Dickin Medal

L46/L47. Sea Cadet Gallantry Cross/Medal

L47A. Gallantry Medallists' League Gold Medal for Courage

L49A. Royal Life Saving Proficiency Medals

L51. Tyne & Wear Fire and Civil Defence Authority Medal for Bravery

L53. Castleford Explosion Devotion To Duty Medal

L54. St Andrews Amublance association life saving MEDAL

IRISH REPUBLIC (EIRE) MEDAL RIBBONS
(Not all shown to scale, see reference number for actual sizes)

E1. 1916 Medal

E2. Military Medal for Gallantry

E2. Military Medal for Gallantry

E2. Military Medal for Gallantry

E3. Distinguished Service Medal

E4. Civil Medal for Bravery

E5. General Service Medal 1917-21

E6. The Emergency Service Medal 1939–46

E7. Merchant Service Medal 1939–46

E8. Permanent Defence Forces Service Medal

E10. St John Ambulance Brigade of Ireland Service Medal.

E11. The United National Peacekeepers Medal

E12. 1916–66 "Survivors" Medal

E13. 1921–71 "Survivors" Medal

E14. Reserve Defence Forces Long Service Medal

E14. Reserve Defence Forces Long Service Medal

E15. Scott Medal for Valor

E16. Garda Siochana Forces Long Service Medal

E17. Garda Siochana Golden Jubilee Service Medal

E18. Garda Siochana Millennium Medal

E19. Garda United Nations Services Medal

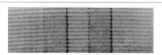

E20. Civil Defence Long Service Medal

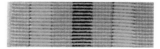

E21. Civil Defence Millennium Medal

E22. The Battle of Jadotville Medal

AUSTRALIAN
MEDAL RIBBONS
(Not all shown to scale, see reference number for actual sizes)

A1. Victoria Cross for Australia

A2. Cross of Valour

A3. Order of Australia (General)
A18. Medal of the Order of Australia (Gen.)

A3. Order of Australia (Military)
A18. Medal of the Order of Australia (Mil.)

A4. Star of Gallantry

A5. Star of Courage

A6. Distinguished Service Cross

A7. Member of the Order of Australia (A.M.) General Division

A7. Member of the Order of Australia (A.M.) Military Division

A8. Conspicuous Service Cross

A9. Nursing Service Cross

A10. Medal for Gallantry

A11. Bravery Medal

A12. Distinguished Service Medal

A13. Public Service Medal

A14. Australian Police Medal

A15. Australian Fire Service Medal

A16. Ambulance Service Medal

A17. Emergency Services Medal

A17A. Australian Corrections Medal

A17B. Australian Intelligence Medal

A18. Medal of the Order of Australia

A19. Conspicuous Service Medal

A20. Australian Antarctic Medal

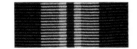
A24. Australian Active Service Medal 1945–1975

A25. Vietnam Medal

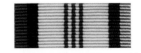
A26. Vietnam Logistic and Support Medal

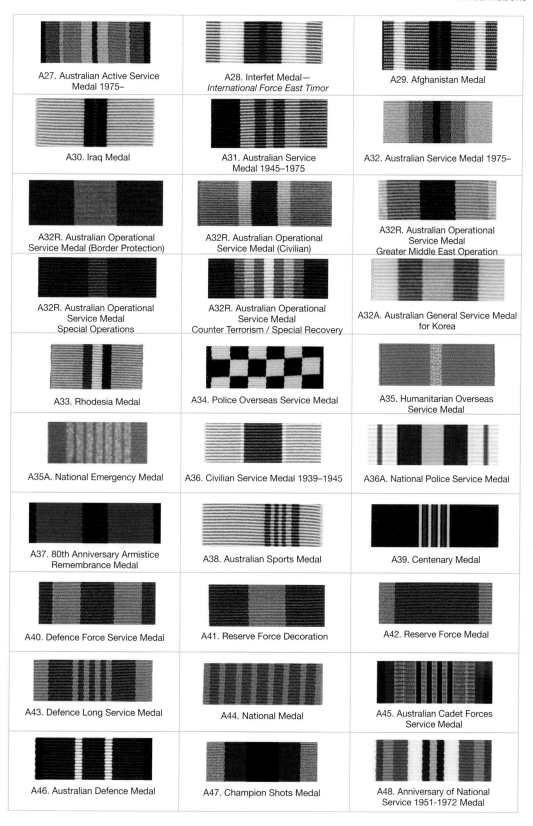

A27. Australian Active Service Medal 1975–

A28. Interfet Medal— *International Force East Timor*

A29. Afghanistan Medal

A30. Iraq Medal

A31. Australian Service Medal 1945–1975

A32. Australian Service Medal 1975–

A32R. Australian Operational Service Medal (Border Protection)

A32R. Australian Operational Service Medal (Civilian)

A32R. Australian Operational Service Medal Greater Middle East Operation

A32R. Australian Operational Service Medal Special Operations

A32R. Australian Operational Service Medal Counter Terrorism / Special Recovery

A32A. Australian General Service Medal for Korea

A33. Rhodesia Medal

A34. Police Overseas Service Medal

A35. Humanitarian Overseas Service Medal

A35A. National Emergency Medal

A36. Civilian Service Medal 1939–1945

A36A. National Police Service Medal

A37. 80th Anniversary Armistice Remembrance Medal

A38. Australian Sports Medal

A39. Centenary Medal

A40. Defence Force Service Medal

A41. Reserve Force Decoration

A42. Reserve Force Medal

A43. Defence Long Service Medal

A44. National Medal

A45. Australian Cadet Forces Service Medal

A46. Australian Defence Medal

A47. Champion Shots Medal

A48. Anniversary of National Service 1951-1972 Medal

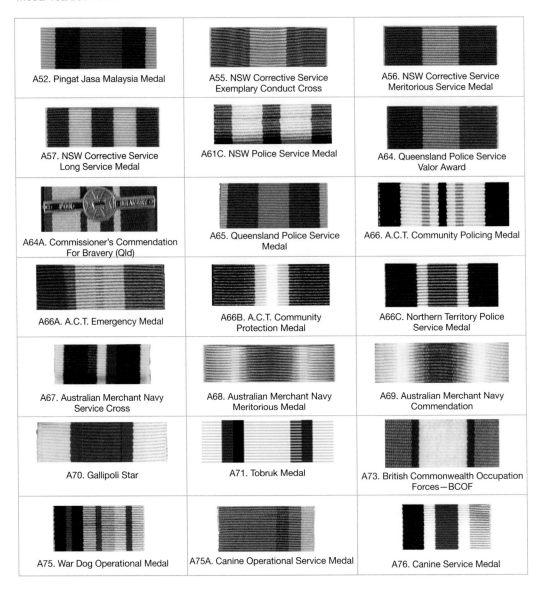

A52. Pingat Jasa Malaysia Medal	A55. NSW Corrective Service Exemplary Conduct Cross	A56. NSW Corrective Service Meritorious Service Medal
A57. NSW Corrective Service Long Service Medal	A61C. NSW Police Service Medal	A64. Queensland Police Service Valor Award
A64A. Commissioner's Commendation For Bravery (Qld)	A65. Queensland Police Service Medal	A66. A.C.T. Community Policing Medal
A66A. A.C.T. Emergency Medal	A66B. A.C.T. Community Protection Medal	A66C. Northern Territory Police Service Medal
A67. Australian Merchant Navy Service Cross	A68. Australian Merchant Navy Meritorious Medal	A69. Australian Merchant Navy Commendation
A70. Gallipoli Star	A71. Tobruk Medal	A73. British Commonwealth Occupation Forces—BCOF
A75. War Dog Operational Medal	A75A. Canine Operational Service Medal	A76. Canine Service Medal

CANADIAN NATIONAL MEDAL RIBBONS
(Not all shown to scale, see reference number for actual sizes)

C1. Victoria Cross for Canada

C2. Cross of Valour

C3. Order of Canada

C4. Order of Military Merit

C5. Order of Merit of the Police Forces

C6. L'Ordre National Du Québec

C7. Saskatchewan Order of Merit

C8. Order of Ontario

C9. Order of British Columbia

C10. Alberta Order of Excellence

C11. Order of Prince Edward Island

C12. Order of Manitoba

C12a. Order of New Brunswick

C12b. Order of Nova Scotia

C12c. Order of Newfoundland and Labrador

C13. Star of Military Valour

C14. Star of Courage

C15. Meritorious Service Cross (Military Division)

C15. Meritorious Service Cross (Civil Division)

C16. Medal of Military Valour

C17. Medal of Bravery

C18. Meritorious Service Medal (Military Division)

C18. Meritorious Service Medal (Civil Division)

C18A. Sacrifice Medal

C19. Canadian Volunteer Service Medal for Korea

C20. Gulf and Kuwait Medal

C21. Somalia Medal

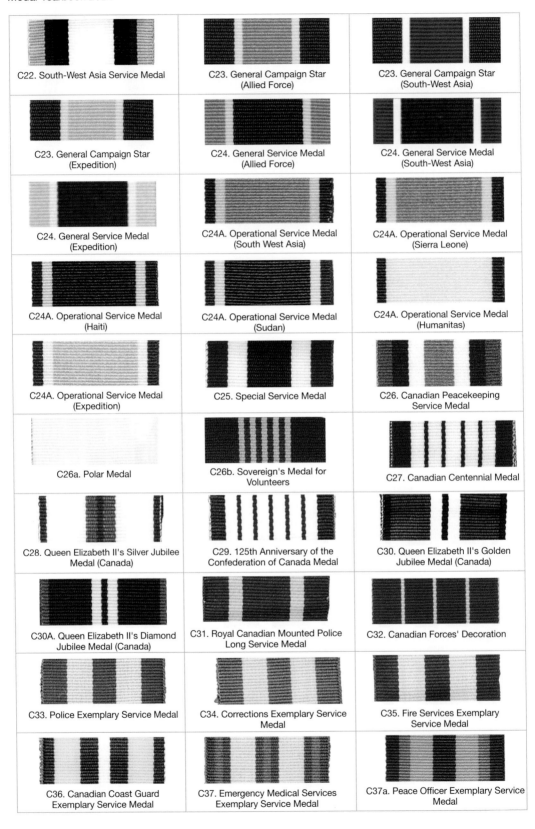

C22. South-West Asia Service Medal	C23. General Campaign Star (Allied Force)	C23. General Campaign Star (South-West Asia)
C23. General Campaign Star (Expedition)	C24. General Service Medal (Allied Force)	C24. General Service Medal (South-West Asia)
C24. General Service Medal (Expedition)	C24A. Operational Service Medal (South West Asia)	C24A. Operational Service Medal (Sierra Leone)
C24A. Operational Service Medal (Haiti)	C24A. Operational Service Medal (Sudan)	C24A. Operational Service Medal (Humanitas)
C24A. Operational Service Medal (Expedition)	C25. Special Service Medal	C26. Canadian Peacekeeping Service Medal
C26a. Polar Medal	C26b. Sovereign's Medal for Volunteers	C27. Canadian Centennial Medal
C28. Queen Elizabeth II's Silver Jubilee Medal (Canada)	C29. 125th Anniversary of the Confederation of Canada Medal	C30. Queen Elizabeth II's Golden Jubilee Medal (Canada)
C30A. Queen Elizabeth II's Diamond Jubilee Medal (Canada)	C31. Royal Canadian Mounted Police Long Service Medal	C32. Canadian Forces' Decoration
C33. Police Exemplary Service Medal	C34. Corrections Exemplary Service Medal	C35. Fire Services Exemplary Service Medal
C36. Canadian Coast Guard Exemplary Service Medal	C37. Emergency Medical Services Exemplary Service Medal	C37a. Peace Officer Exemplary Service Medal

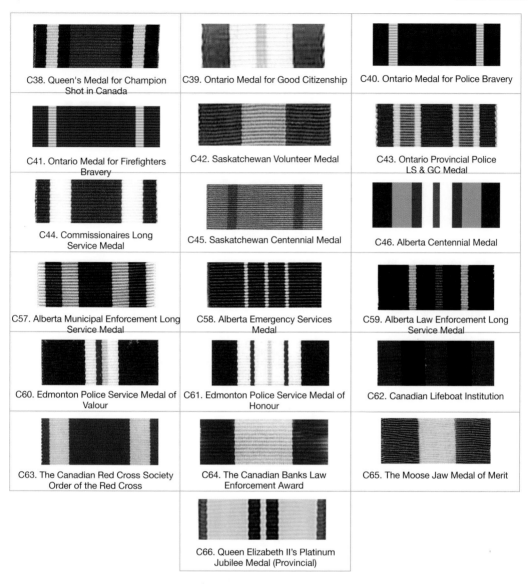

C38. Queen's Medal for Champion Shot in Canada

C39. Ontario Medal for Good Citizenship

C40. Ontario Medal for Police Bravery

C41. Ontario Medal for Firefighters Bravery

C42. Saskatchewan Volunteer Medal

C43. Ontario Provincial Police LS & GC Medal

C44. Commissionaires Long Service Medal

C45. Saskatchewan Centennial Medal

C46. Alberta Centennial Medal

C57. Alberta Municipal Enforcement Long Service Medal

C58. Alberta Emergency Services Medal

C59. Alberta Law Enforcement Long Service Medal

C60. Edmonton Police Service Medal of Valour

C61. Edmonton Police Service Medal of Honour

C62. Canadian Lifeboat Institution

C63. The Canadian Red Cross Society Order of the Red Cross

C64. The Canadian Banks Law Enforcement Award

C65. The Moose Jaw Medal of Merit

C66. Queen Elizabeth II's Platinum Jubilee Medal (Provincial)

NEW ZEALAND
MEDAL RIBBONS
(Not all shown to scale, see reference number for actual sizes)

NZ1. Victoria Cross for New Zealand

NZ2. New Zealand Cross with miniature emblem when worn alone

NZ3. Order of New Zealand

NZ4. NZ Order of Merit

NZ5. NZ Gallantry Star

NZ6. Queen's Service Order

NZ7. Gallantry Decoration

NZ8. Bravery Star

NZ9. Bravery Decoration

NZ10. Gallantry Medal

NZ11. Bravery Medal

NZ12. Queen's Service Medal

NZ12A. NZ Antarctic Medal

NZ12B. Distinguished Service Decoration

NZ12C. New Zealand Defence Meritorious Service Medal

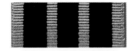

NZ12D. New Zealand Police Meritorious Service Medal

NZ13. Operational Service Medal

NZ14A. GSM 2002 (Solomon Islands)

NZ14B. GSM 2002 (Afghanistan) (primary)

NZ14B. GSM 2002 (Afghanistan) (secondary)

NZ14C. GSM 2002 (Iraq)

NZ14D. GSM 2002 (Timor-Leste)

NZ14E. GSM 2002 (Korea)

NZ15. NZ Service Medal 1946-49

NZ16. NZ General Service Medal (Warlike Operations)

NZ17. NZ General Service Medal (Non-Warlike Operations)

NZ18. East Timor Medal

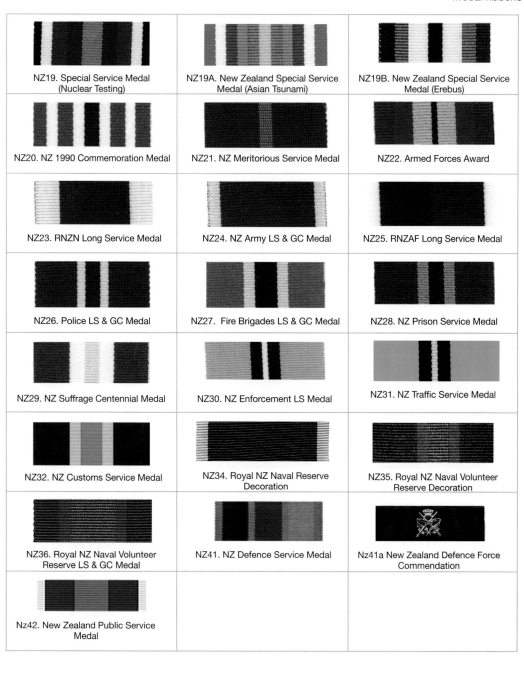

NZ19. Special Service Medal (Nuclear Testing)	NZ19A. New Zealand Special Service Medal (Asian Tsunami)	NZ19B. New Zealand Special Service Medal (Erebus)
NZ20. NZ 1990 Commemoration Medal	NZ21. NZ Meritorious Service Medal	NZ22. Armed Forces Award
NZ23. RNZN Long Service Medal	NZ24. NZ Army LS & GC Medal	NZ25. RNZAF Long Service Medal
NZ26. Police LS & GC Medal	NZ27. Fire Brigades LS & GC Medal	NZ28. NZ Prison Service Medal
NZ29. NZ Suffrage Centennial Medal	NZ30. NZ Enforcement LS Medal	NZ31. NZ Traffic Service Medal
NZ32. NZ Customs Service Medal	NZ34. Royal NZ Naval Reserve Decoration	NZ35. Royal NZ Naval Volunteer Reserve Decoration
NZ36. Royal NZ Naval Volunteer Reserve LS & GC Medal	NZ41. NZ Defence Service Medal	Nz41a New Zealand Defence Force Commendation
Nz42. New Zealand Public Service Medal		

SOUTH AFRICAN MEDAL RIBBONS
(Not all shown to scale, see reference number for actual sizes)

SA1. Star of South Africa

SA2. Order of the Star of South Africa (Military) First Class

SA2. Order of the Star of South Africa Silver (Military) Second Class - *Neck ribbon*

SA2. Order of the Star of South Africa Silver (Military) Second Class - *Breast ribbon*

SA3. Castle of Good Hope Decoration

SA4. Louw Wepener Decoration

SA5. Van Riebeeck Decoration

SA6. Van Riebeeck Medal

SA7. Honoris Crux 1952

SA8. Louw Wepener Medal

SA9. Honoris Crux Decoration (Diamond)

SA9. Honoris Crux Decoration (Gold)

SA9. Honoris Crux Decoration (Silver)

SA9. Honoris Crux Decoration

SA10. Pro Virtute Decoration

SA11. Pro Virtute Medal

SA12. Ad Astra Decoration

SA13. The S.A.D.F. Cross (Army)

SA13. The S.A.D.F. Cross (Air Force)

SA13. The S.A.D.F. Cross (Navy)

SA13. The S.A.D.F. Cross (SA Medical Services)

SA14. Southern Cross Medal 1952

SA15. Southern Cross Decoration

SA16. Southern Cross Medal

SA17. Pro Merito Medal (1967)

SA18. Pro Merito Decoration (1975)

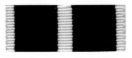
SA19. Pro Merito Medal (1975)

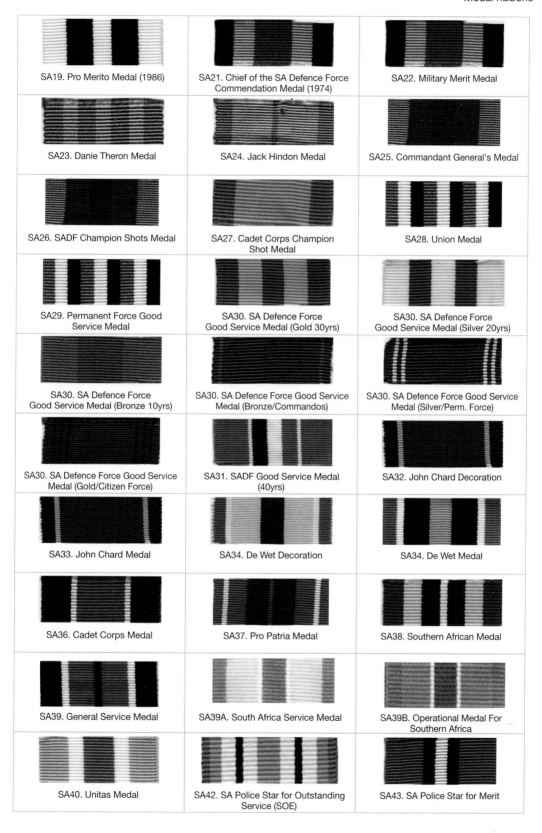

SA19. Pro Merito Medal (1986)	SA21. Chief of the SA Defence Force Commendation Medal (1974)	SA22. Military Merit Medal
SA23. Danie Theron Medal	SA24. Jack Hindon Medal	SA25. Commandant General's Medal
SA26. SADF Champion Shots Medal	SA27. Cadet Corps Champion Shot Medal	SA28. Union Medal
SA29. Permanent Force Good Service Medal	SA30. SA Defence Force Good Service Medal (Gold 30yrs)	SA30. SA Defence Force Good Service Medal (Silver 20yrs)
SA30. SA Defence Force Good Service Medal (Bronze 10yrs)	SA30. SA Defence Force Good Service Medal (Bronze/Commandos)	SA30. SA Defence Force Good Service Medal (Silver/Perm. Force)
SA30. SA Defence Force Good Service Medal (Gold/Citizen Force)	SA31. SADF Good Service Medal (40yrs)	SA32. John Chard Decoration
SA33. John Chard Medal	SA34. De Wet Decoration	SA34. De Wet Medal
SA36. Cadet Corps Medal	SA37. Pro Patria Medal	SA38. Southern African Medal
SA39. General Service Medal	SA39A. South Africa Service Medal	SA39B. Operational Medal For Southern Africa
SA40. Unitas Medal	SA42. SA Police Star for Outstanding Service (SOE)	SA43. SA Police Star for Merit

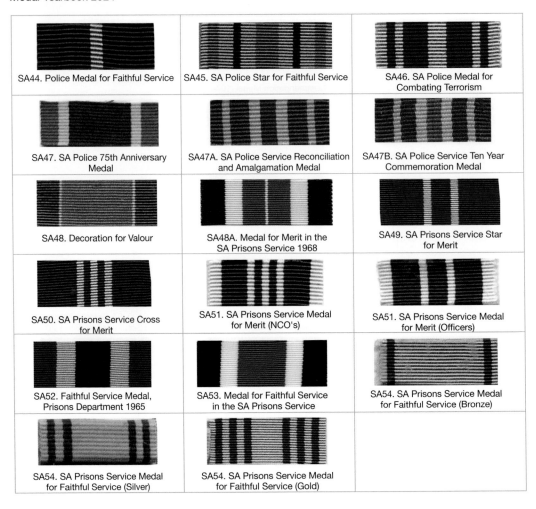

SA44. Police Medal for Faithful Service	SA45. SA Police Star for Faithful Service	SA46. SA Police Medal for Combating Terrorism
SA47. SA Police 75th Anniversary Medal	SA47A. SA Police Service Reconciliation and Amalgamation Medal	SA47B. SA Police Service Ten Year Commemoration Medal
SA48. Decoration for Valour	SA48A. Medal for Merit in the SA Prisons Service 1968	SA49. SA Prisons Service Star for Merit
SA50. SA Prisons Service Cross for Merit	SA51. SA Prisons Service Medal for Merit (NCO's)	SA51. SA Prisons Service Medal for Merit (Officers)
SA52. Faithful Service Medal, Prisons Department 1965	SA53. Medal for Faithful Service in the SA Prisons Service	SA54. SA Prisons Service Medal for Faithful Service (Bronze)
SA54. SA Prisons Service Medal for Faithful Service (Silver)	SA54. SA Prisons Service Medal for Faithful Service (Gold)	

APPENDICES
Current Regiments

As many British medals carry the names of regiments that no longer exist, we list here all of the regiments of the British Army as published in the current Army List, together with their predecessors, and the dates of amalgamations and redesignations The current regiment title is indicated in bold type with former names underneath in normal type. Old regimental numbers are included in brackets.

HOUSEHOLD CAVALRY REGIMENT

Life Guards

1st Life Guards
2nd Life Guards
The Life Guards (1st & 2nd)

Blues and Royals
(Royal Horse Guards and 1st Dragoons)

Royal Horse Guards (The Blues)
Royal Dragoons (1st Dragoons)

1st The Queen's Dragoon Guards

1st The King's Dragoon Guards
Queen's Bays (2nd Dragoon Guards)

Royal Scots Dragoon Guards
(Carabiniers and Greys)

3rd Dragoon Guards (Prince of Wales's)
Carabiniers (6th Dragoons)
3rd/6th Dragoon Guards
3rd Carabiniers (Prince of Wales's Dragoon Guards)
Royal Scots Greys (2nd Dragoons)

Royal Dragoon Guards

4th Royal Irish Dragoon Guards
7th Dragoon Guards (Princess Royal's)
4th/7th Dragoon Guards
4th/7th Royal Dragoon Guards
5th Dragoon Guards (Princess Charlotte of Wales's)
Inniskillings (6th Dragoon Guards)
5th/6th Dragoons
5th Inniskilling Dragoon Guards
5th Royal Inniskilling Dragoon Guards

Queen's Royal Hussars
(The Queen's Own & Royal Irish)

3rd The King's Own Hussars
7th The Queen's Own Hussars
Queen's Own Hussars
4th The Queen's Own Hussars
8th The King's Royal Irish Hussars
Queen's Royal Irish Hussars

King's Royal Hussars

10th Royal Hussars (Prince of Wales's Own)
11th Hussars (Prince Albert's Own)
Royal Hussars (Prince of Wales's Own)
14th King's Hussars
20th Hussars
14th/20th Hussars
14th/20th King's Hussars

Light Dragoons

13th Hussars
18th Royal Hussars (Queen Mary's Own)
13th/18th Hussars
13th/18th Royal Hussars (Queen Mary's Own)
15th The King's Hussars
19th Royal Hussars (Queen Alexandra's Own)
15th/19th Hussars
15th The King's Royal Hussars
15th/19th The King's Royal Hussars

Royal Lancers (Queen Elizabeths' Own)

9th/12th Royal Lancers (Prince of Wales's)
9th Queen's Royal Lancers
12th Royal Lancers (Prince of Wales's)
Queen's Royal Lancers
16th The Queen's Lancers
5th Royal Irish Lancers
16th/5th Lancers
16th/5th The Queen's Royal Lancers
17th (Duke of Cambridge's Own Lancers)
21st Lancers (Empress of India's)
17th/21st Lancers

Royal Tank Regiment

Heavy Branch Machine Gun Corps
Tank Corps
Royal Tank Corps

Royal Horse Artillery

Royal Regiment of Artillery

Royal Field Artillery
Royal Garrison Artillery
Royal Malta Artillery

Corps of Royal Engineers

Royal Corps of Signals

Grenadier Guards

Coldstream Guards

Scots Guards

Irish Guards

Welsh Guards

Royal Regiment of Scotland / 7 battalions

Royal Scots (The Royal Regiment)(1)
Royal Highland Fusiliers (Princess Margaret's Own Glasgow and Ayrshire Regiment)(21, 71 & 74)
Royal Scots Fusiliers (21)
Highland Light Infantry (City of Glasgow Regiment) (71 & 74)
King's Own Scottish Borderers (25)
Black Watch (Royal Highland Regiment)(42 & 73)
Highlanders (Seaforth, Gordons and Camerons)(72, 75, 78, 79 & 92)
Seaforth Highlanders (Ross-shire Buffs, Duke of Albany's)(72 & 78)
Queen's Own Cameron Highlanders (79)
Queen's Own Highlanders (Seaforth & Camerons) (72, 78 & 79)
Gordon Highlanders
Argyll & Sutherland Highlanders (Princess Louise's) (91 & 93)
52nd Lowland Regiment
51st Highland Regiment

Princess of Wales's Royal Regiment
(Queen's & Royal Hampshire)
(2, 3, 31, 35, 37, 50, 67, 70, 97 & 107)

Queen's Royal Regiment (West Surrey)(2)
East Surrey Regiment (31 & 70)
Queen's Royal Surrey Regiment
Buffs (Royal East Kent Regiment)(3)
Queen's Own Royal West Kent Regiment (50 & 97)
Queen's Own Buffs (The Royal Kent Regiment)
Royal Sussex Regiment (35 & 107)
Middlesex Regiment (Duke of Cambridge's Own) (57 & 77)
Queen's Regiment
Royal Hampshire Regiment (37 & 67)

Duke of Lancaster's Regiment
(King's, Lancashire and Border)
3 battalions

King's Own Royal Border Regiment (4, 34 & 55)
King's Own Royal Regiment (Lancaster)(4)
Queen's Lancashire Regiment (30, 40, 47, 59 81 & 82)
East Lancashire Regiment (30 & 59)
South Lancashire Regiment (The Prince of Wales's Volunteers)(40 & 82)
Lancashire Regiment (Prince of Wales's Volunteers)
Loyal Regiment (North Lancashire)(47 & 48)
Border Regiment (34 & 55)
King's Regiment (8, 63 & 96)

King's Regiment (Liverpool)(8)
Manchester Regiment (63 & 96)
King's Regiment (Manchester & Liverpool)(8, 63 & 96)

Royal Regiment of Fusiliers (5, 6, 7 & 20)

Royal Northumberland Fusiliers (5)
Royal Warwickshire Regiment (6)
Royal Warwickshire Fusiliers (6)
Royal Fusiliers (City of London Regiment) (7)
Lancashire Fusiliers (20)

Royal Anglian Regiment
(9, 10, 12, 16, 17, 44, 48, 56 & 58)

Bedfordshire & Hertfordshire Regiment (16)
Essex Regiment (44 & 56)
3rd East Anglian Regiment (16th/44th Foot)
Royal Norfolk Regiment (9)
Suffolk Regiment (12)
1st East Anglian Regiment (Royal Norfolk & Suffolk)
Royal Lincolnshire Regiment (10)
Northamptonshire Regiment (48 & 58)
2nd East Anglian Regiment (Duchess of Gloucester's Own Royal Lincolnshire & Northamptonshire)
Royal Leicestershire Regiment (17)

Yorkshire Regiment / 4 battalions

Prince of Wales's Own Regiment of Yorkshire (14 & 15)
West Yorkshire (Prince of Wales's Own) (14)
East Yorkshire Regiment (Duke of York's Own) (15)
Green Howards (Alexandra, Princess of Wales's Own Yorkshire Regiment) (19)
Duke of Wellington's Regiment (West Riding) (33 & 76)
Duke of Wellington's Regiment (33)
76th Regiment of Foot
Halifax Regiment

Mercian Regiment / 4 Battalions

Cheshire Regiment (22)
Worcestershire & Sherwood Foresters Regiment (29, 36, 45 & 95)
Worcester Regiment (29 & 36)
Sherwood Foresters (Nottingham & Derbyshire Regiment)(45 & 95)
Staffordshire Regiment (Prince of Wales's) (38, 64, 80 & 98)
South Staffordshire Regiment (38 & 80)
North Staffordshire Regiment (Prince of Wales's)(64 & 98)
The Mercian Regiment (Volunteers)

Royal Welsh / 2 battalions

Royal Welch Fusiliers (23)
Royal Regiment of Wales (24th/41st Foot)
South Wales Borderers (24)
Welch Regiment (41 & 69)
Monmouthshire Regiment TA
Royal Welsh Regiment TA

Royal Irish Regiment (27th (Inniskilling),
83rd, 87th, and Ulster Defence Regiment)

Royal Inniskilling Fusiliers (27 & 108)

Royal Ulster Rifles (83 & 86)
Royal Irish Rifles (83 & 86)
Royal Irish Fusiliers (Princess Victoria's) (87 & 89)
Ulster Defence Regiment
Royal Irish Rangers
4th/5th Battalion The Royal Irish Rangers
(Volunteers)

Parachute Regiment / 3 battalions

The Gurkha Brigade

The Royal Gurkha Rifles / 2 battalions

2nd King Edward VII's Own Gurkha Rifles (The
Sirmoor Rifles)
6th Queen Elizabeth's Own Gurkha Rifles
7th Duke of Edinburgh's Own Gurkha Rifles
10th Princess Mary's Own Gurkha Rifle

Queen's Gurkha Engineers

Queen's Gurkha Signals

Queen's Own Gurkha Logistic Regiment

22nd Special Air Service Regiment

The Rifles / 8 battalions

Devonshire & Dorset Light Infantry (11, 39, & 54)
Devonshire & Dorset Regiment (11, 39, & 54)
Devonshire Regiment (11)
Dorset Regiment (39 & 54)
Royal Gloucestershire, Wiltshire & Berkshire Light
Infantry (28, 49, 61, 62, 66 & 99)
Royal Gloucestershire, Wiltshire & Berkshire
Regiment (28, 49, 61, 62, 66 & 99)
Wiltshire Regiment (Duke of Edinburgh's) (62 & 99)
Royal Berkshire Regiment (Princess Charlotte of
Wales's) (49 & 66)
Duke of Edinburgh's Royal Regiment (Berkshire
and Wiltshire)
Gloucestershire Regiment (28 & 61)
Light Infantry (13, 32, 46, 51, 53, 68, 85, 105 & 106)
Somerset Light Infantry (Prince Albert's) (13)
Duke of Cornwall's Light Infantry (32 & 46)
Somerset & Cornwall Light Infantry (13, 32 & 46)
King's Own Yorkshire Light Infantry (51 & 105)
King's Shropshire Light Infantry (53 & 85)
Durham Light Infantry (68 & 106)
Royal Green Jackets (43rd & 52nd, King's Royal
Rifle Corps, Rifle Brigade)
Oxfordshire & Buckinghamshire Light Infantry (43 &
52)
1st Green Jackets (43 & 52)
King's Royal Rifle Corps (60)
2nd Green Jackets (The King's Royal Rifle
Corps) (60)
Rifle Brigade (Prince Consort's Own)
3rd Green Jackets (The Rifle Brigade)
Royal Rifle Volunteers
Rifle Volunteers
2nd (Volunteer) Battalion The Royal Gloucestershire,
Berkshire and Wiltshire Regiment
1st Battalion The Wessex Regiment (Rifle
Volunteers)
2nd Battalion The Wessex Regiment (Volunteers)

Army Air Corps

Glider Pilot Regiment
Air Observer Corps
Air Observation Post Squadrons, Royal Artillery

Special Reconnaissance Regiment

Royal Army Chaplains' Department

Royal Logistic Corps

Royal Army Service Corps
Royal Corps of Transport
Royal Army Ordnance Corps
Royal Pioneer Corps
Army Catering Corps
Royal Engineers—Postal and Courier Service

Royal Army Medical Corps

Corps of Royal Electrical & Mechanical Engineers

Adjutant General's Corps

Adjutant General's Corps
(Staff and Personnel Support Branch)

Royal Army Pay Corps
Women's Royal Army Corps (less those to
Regiments)
Royal Army Ordnance Corps Staff Clerks
Regimental Clerks

Adjutant General's Corps (Provost Branch)

Royal Military Police
Military Provost Staff Corps
Military Provost Guard Service

Adjutant General's Corps
(Education & Training Service Branch)

Royal Army Educational Corps

Adjutant General's Corps (Army Legal Branch)

Army Legal Services Staff List
Army Legal Corps

Royal Army Veterinary Corps

Small Arms School Corps

Royal Army Dental Corps

Intelligence Corps

Royal Army Physical Training Corps

Army Gymnastic Staff
Army Physical Training Corps

Queen Alexandra's Royal Army Nursing Corps

Queen Alexandra's Imperial Military Nursing
Service
Queen Alexandra's Military Families Nursing
Service

Corps of Army Music

Royal Military Academy Band Corps

ARMY RESERVE (formerly TERRITORIAL ARMY)

Royal Monmouth Royal Engineers (Militia)

Honourable Artillery Company

Royal Yeomanry

Westminster Dragoons
Sherwood Rangers Yeomanry
Staffordshire, Warwickshire, Worcestershire
  Yeomanry
Kent and Sharpshooters Yeomanry
Shropshire Yeomanry
Leicestershire and Derbyshire Yeomanry

Queen's Own Yeomanry

Yorkshire Yeomanry
Duke of Lancaster's Own Yeomanry
Cheshire Yeomanry
Northumberland Hussars

Scottish and North Irish Yeomanry

Lothian and Border Yeomanry
Ayrshire (Earl of Carrick's Own) Yeomanry
Fife and Forfar Yeomanry (Scottish Horse)
North Irish Horse

Royal Wessex Yeomanry

Royal Wiltshire Yeomanry (Prince of Wales's Own)
Royal Gloucestershire Hussars.
Royal Devon Yeomanry
Dorset Yeomanry

Royal Regiment of Artillery (Volunteers)

Corps of Royal Engineers (Volunteers)

Royal Corps of Signals (Volunteers)

Royal Regiment of Scotland

6th Battalion 52nd Lowland
7th Battalion 51st Highland

The London Regiment

3rd (Volunteer) Battalion The Princess of Wales's Royal Regiment (Queen's & Royal Hampshire)

4th Battalion the Duke of Lancaster's Regiment (King's, Lancashire and Border)

5th Battalion The Royal Regiment of Fusiliers

4th Battalion The Yorkshire Regiment

14/15, 19, 33/76 Foot)

4th Battalion The Mercian Regiment

3rd Battalion The Royal Welsh

The Welsh Volunteers
3rd Battalion Royal Welch Fusiliers
3rd Battalion Royal Regiment of Wales (24th/41st
  Foot)

4th Battalion Royal Regiment of Wales (24th/41st
  Foot)
The Royal Welsh Regiment

2nd Battalion The Royal Irish Regiment (27th Inniskilling), 83rd, 87th and Ulster Defence Regiment

4th Battalion The Parachute Regiment

6th Battalion The Rifles

7th Battalion The Rifles

21st Special Air Service (Artists)

23rd Special Air Service

6th Regiment Army Air Corps

Various Services/Corps as for the Regular Army with (Volunteers) in their titles)

Officer Training Corps

COLONIAL UNITS

Royal Gibraltar Regiment

The Bermuda Regiment

SOME FORMER TA INFANTRY REGIMENTS

East of England Regiment
Lancastrian and Cumberland Volunteers
Tyne-Tees Regiment
East & West Riding Reiment
West Midlands Regiment
King's and Cheshire Regiment

SOME DISBANDED REGIMENTS WITH NO LOGICAL SUCCESSOR

22nd Dragoons	25th Dragoons
23rd Hussars	26th Hussars
24th Lancers	27th Lancers

Reconnaissance Regiment
Highland Regiment
Lowland Regiment
Royal Irish Regiment (18)
Cameronians (Scottish Rifles)(26 & 90)
York and Lancaster Regiment (65)
Connaught Rangers (88 & 94)
Prince of Wales's Leinster Regiment (Royal Canadians)
  (100 & 109)
Royal Munster Fusiliers (101 & 104)
Royal Dublin Fusiliers (102 & 103)
Royal Guernsey Light Infantry
Royal Militia of the Island of Jersey
King's Own Malta Regiment of Militia
West India Regiment
Army Cyclist Corps
Machine Gun Corps
Army Remount Service
Cyprus Regiment
Royal Flying Corps
Royal Defence Corps
Queen' Mary's Army Auxiliary Corps
Auxiliary Territorial Service
Women's Royal Army Corps

SOCIETIES
For Medal Collectors

Listed here are some of the many societies around the world that cater for the medal collector or those interested in military history. The details given are mostly the private addresses or telephone numbers of the membership secretaries to whom all correspondence should be sent. We would appreciate any information from other Societies who would like their details included in the next YEARBOOK.

Aldershot Militaria Society Aldershot Military Museum, Queens Avenue, Aldershot Hampshirem, GU11 2LG. Tel: 01753 654763.

Association de Collectionneurs de Décorations et Médailles (MEDEC) Paasbloemstraat 81, B-2170 Merksem, Belgium.

Birmingham Medal Society Christopher Davies, Tel: 07984 625055, www.birminghammedalsociety.com.

Crewe & District Coin & Medal Society (CADCAMS) Stuart Hallworth. Tel: 07828 602611. email: stuart@hallworthresidential.com.

The Crimean War Research Society cwrs.russianwar.co.uk

Deutsche Gesellschaft fur Ordenskunde President, Daniel Krause, praesident@dgo-ev.de CEO Christian Bormann geschaeftsfuehrer@dgo-ev.de. Postfach 1108, 74257 Untereisesheim

Indian Military Historical Society A. N. McLenaghan, 33 High Street, Tilbrook, Huntingdon, Cambs PE28 0JP, email: membership@imhs.org.uk.

Life Saving Awards Research Society Kim Claxton, Waren Cottage, 14 Bedstone, Bucknell, Shropshire, SY7 0BE. tel: 01547 530611. email:kclaxton@btinternet.com.

London Medal Club Steve Law, 020 8482 1918

Medal Society of Ireland 1 The Hill, Stillorgan, Co. Dublin, Ireland, email: sales@msoi.eu.

Mid-Western Orders & Medals Society (MIDOMS) 5847 Gilbert Avenue, La Grange, IL 60525, USA.

Military Collector's Club of Canada (MCCofC) 1442 - 26A Street SW, Calgary, Alberta, Canada, T3C 1KA www.canadianmilitariaclub.org.

Orders & Medals Society of America (OMSA) PO Box 540, Claymont, DE 19703-0 540, USA. www.omsa.org.

Orders & Medals Research Society (OMRS) PO Box 12874, Sudbury, Suffolk, CO10 3EF. membershipsecretary@omrs.org.

ditto, Australia Branch (Sydney) Graeme Marfleet. Email: graemem@attachesoftware.com

ditto, Canada Branch (Ottawa) Mark Reid. Email: tapir@rogers.com.

ditto, Canada Branch (Toronto) Glenn Aiken, tel: 001 905 699 0807.

ditto, Cotswold Branch (Cheltenham) John Wright. Tel: 01242 519815, email: qcmilitaria@btconnect.com.

ditto, East Anglian Branch Dahlia Harrison. Email: redcrossrose@gmail.com

ditto, Hong Kong Branch Martin Heyes Tel: 852 9659 2410, email: secretary@omrs-hk.org.

ditto, Kent Branch Ian Hudson Tel: 07733251807, email: ianhudson2001@yahoo.co.uk.

ditto, London Branch Bob Barltrop. Tel: 01226 790723, email: robert.barltrop@btinternet.com.

ditto, Medal Ribbon Branch Graham Carter. Tel: 01202 304043, email: graham_carter@live.co.uk.

ditto, Miniature Medals Branch Mark Furniss-Roe, Branch Secretary, Email: miniaturemedalsbranch@gmail.com

ditto, New Zealand Branch (Wellington) Todd Skilton, email: tskilton@gmail.com.

ditto, Northern Branch (Manchester) Martyn Lovell. Tel/Fax: 01925 753039, email: martynlovell@btinternet.com.

ditto, Northumbrian Branch 41 Ashdown Avenue, Durham DH1 1DB.

ditto, Wessex (formerly Salisbury) Branch Kevin Asplin. email: kasplin@forces-war-records.co.uk.

ditto, Scottish Branch Gordon Taylor. Email: gort@btinternet.com

ditto, Sussex Branch Paul Turner. Email: paultur20@hotmail.com

ditto, Surrey Branch Graham Grist. Email: grahamila@googlemail.com.

ditto, Thames Valley Branch Peter Weedon. Email: peterweedon@btconnect.com.

Ordenshistorik Selskab Grønnevang 17, DK-2970 Hørsholm, Denmark. www.omsd.dk

Société Suisse de Phaleristique Mr J. C. Palthey, Avenue Victor Ruffy 9, 1012 Lausanne, Switzerland.

Stockport Militaria Collectors Society 10 Bradgate Place, Bradgate, Rotherham, South Yorkshire, S61 1LB. Tel: 01709 557622.

Studiekring Faleristiek Straatakker 2, 8700 Tielt, Belgium. www.skf-vzw.org.

Studiekring Ridderorden en Ondenscheidingen Bert Keers, Zamenhoflaan 23, 3706 VA, Zeist, Netherlands. www.vereniging-sro-nl.

Victorian Military Society 20 Priory Road, Newbury, Berks RG14 7QN. www.victorianmilitarysociety.org.uk.

West of England Medal Club (Exeter) 10 Drakes Avenue, Exmouth, EX8 4AB. Tel: 01395 264939.

Zimbabwe Medal Society (Harare) 14 Straker Ave, Gunhill, Harare, Zimbabwe, email: jreidrowland@hotmail.com

---

If your details listed above are incorrect, or if we have omitted to include your society in this listing, please advise us without delay. Details are included entirely free. Telephone: 01404 46972 or email: info@tokenpublishing.com
Thank you!

PROFESSIONAL
Directory

On the following pages are the names and addresses of auctioneers, dealers, booksellers and fair organisers, all of whom will be of assistance to the medal collector. Most are full time and many have retail shops and the collector is usually welcome during normal business hours. Some have extensive stocks of medals whilst others include medals in a more diverse inventory. A number of dealers are part time or work from small premises or from home and appointments are necessary as many keep their stock in the bank for security. Telephone numbers and email addresses have been included where known and it is always sensible to make contact before travelling any distance.

AUCTIONEERS

The following hold regular medal auctions or feature medals in general numismatic or militaria sales. The details were correct at the time of printing but it is always safest to check before travellng to any address.

Baldwin's
399 Strand, London, WC2R 0LX Tel: 02079 306879, www.baldwin.com. Regular auctions of coins and medals.

Nick Barber Auctions
154 Hamilton Road, Felixstowe. Tel: 01394 549084. www.nickbarberauctions.com
Medals, Vintage Collectables and Memorabilia.

Biddle & Webb
Icknield Square, Ladywood, Middleway, Birmingham. Tel: 0121 455 8042, www.biddleandwebb.com. Antiques and militaria.

Bosleys
Remnantz (The Old Military College), Marlow, Buckinghamshire, SL7 2BS. Tel: 01628 488188, www.bosleys.co.uk. Medals and militaria.

C&T Auctions
Unit 4, High House Business Park, Kenardington, Nr Ashford, Kent, TN26 2LF. Tel: 01233 510050, www.candtauctions.co.uk. Auctions of medals, badges, insignia, headdress and militaria items.

Charterhouse
The Long Street Salerooms, Sherbourne, Dorset, DT9 3BS. Tel: 01935 812277, www.charterhouse-auctions.co.uk. Medals and collectables.

Chilcotts
The Dolphin Salerooms, High Street, Honiton, Devon, EX14 1LS. Tel 01404 47783. www.chilcottsauctioneers.co.uk. General auctioneers.

City Coins
Tulbagh Square, Cape Town, South Africa. Tel: 0027 21 425 2639, fax: 0027 21 425 3939, email: auctions@citycoins.co.za, www.citycoins.com. Postal medal auctions.

Colonial Coins and Medals
218 Adelaide Street, Brisbane, Australia. Tel:+61 7 3221 8460, www.coinmedalshop.com.au. Auctions of medals and coins.

Corbitts
5 Mosley Street, Newcastle Upon Tyne, NE1 1YE. Tel: 0191 2327268, fax: 0191 2614130. Coins, medals, stamps and collectables.

Cotswold Auction Co.
Chapel Walk, Cheltenham, GL50 3DS. Tel: 01242 256363, www.cotswoldauction.co.uk. Auctioneers and valuers.

Diss Auction Rooms
Roydon Road, Diss, Norfok, IP22 4LN. Tel: 01379 650306, www.twgaze.com. Occasional auctions of medals and militaria.

Downie's
3 Redland Drive, Mitcham, Melbourne, Vic 3132, Australia. Tel:+61 (0)3 8456 8456, fax: +61 (0) 3 8456 8456), www.downies.com. Sales with emphasis on Australian and UK medals.

Dukes
Brewery Square, Dorchester, Dorset, DT1 1GA. Tel: 01305 265080, www.dukes-auctions.com. Regular auctions of coins, medals, militaria and ephemera.

eMedals
3245, Harvester Road, Unit 15, Burlington, Ontario, L7N 3T7, Canada, Tel: 001 905 634 3848, email: info@eMedals.com, www.eMedals.com. Orders, decorations, insignia.

Fellows
Augusta House, 19 Augusta Street, Birmingham, B18 6JA. Tel: 0121 212 2131, fax: 0121 212 1249, email: info@fellows.co.uk, www.fellows.co.uk. Medals and coins.

Fieldings
Mill Race Lane, Stourbridge, DY8 1JN. Tel: 01384 444140. www.fieldingsauctioneers.co.uk
Medals, Militaria, Coins and Collectables.

Gorringes
15 North Street, Lewes, East Sussex, BN7 2PD. Tel: 01273 472503, www.gorringes.co.uk. Sales of medals, militaria and fine art.

Halls
Halls Holdings House, Bowmen Way, Battlefield, Shrewsbury, SY4 3DR. Specialist Auctioneers.

Heritage Auctions
6 Shepherd St, London W1J 7JE (www.ha.com). Auctioneers of orders, decorations and medals. USA and world coins.

Hermann Historica
Linprunstr, 16, D–80335, Munich. Tel: +49 89 547 26490, email: contact@hermann-historica.com. Auctions of medals and militaria.

JB Military Antiques
2/135 Russell Street, Morley, WA, Australia, 6062. www.jbmilitaryantiques.com.au.

Alec Kaplan
115 Dunottar Street, Sydenham, Johannesburg, South Africa. Tel: 011 485 2195, email: medals@wirelessza.co.za. Regular sales of medals and militaria.

Künker
Nobbenburger Strasse 4a, 49076 Osnabrueck. Tel: 0049-541-962020, email: service@kuenker.de, www.kuenker.de. Coins and medals.

Laidlaw Auctioneers
Escott Business Park, Carlisle, CA2 5WD. Tel: 01228 90490, www.laidlawauctioneers.co.uk.

Lockdales
52 Barrack Square, Martlesham Heath, Ipswich, Suffolk, IP5 3RF. Tel: 01473 627110, www.lockdales.com. Medals, coins, collectables.

Mellors & Kirk
Gregory Street, Nottingham, NG7 2NL. Tel: 0115 979 0000, email: enquiries@mellorsandkirk.com, www.mellorsandkirk.com. Medals and collectables.

Morton & Eden
Nash House St George Street, London, W1S 2FQ. Tel: 020 7493 5344, fax: 020 7495 6325, www.mortonandeden.com. Advisory service and auctioneers of medals. Also coins and medallions.

Mowbray Collectables
247–253 Main Highway 1, Otaki 5581, New Zealand. Tel: +64 6 3648270, www.mowbraycollectables.co.nz. Auctioneers of Coins, medals and banknotes.

Noble Numismatics Pty Ltd
169 Macquarie Street, Sydney, 2000, Australia. Tel: +61 2 9223 45478, email: info@noble.net.au. British and Commonwealth medals.

Noonans
16 Bolton Street, Piccadilly, London, W1J 8BQ. Tel: 020 7016 1700, fax: 020 7016 1799, email: medals@dnw.co.uk, www.dnw.co.uk. Auctioneers and valuers. Regular auctions of medals. Also coin and banknote auctions.

Reeman Dansie
8 Wyncolls Road, Severalls Business Park, Colchester, Essex ,CO4 9HU. Tel: 01206 754754, www.reemandansie.com. Medals, militaria, coins.

Ryedale Auctioneers
Cooks Yard, New Road, Kirbymoorside, North Yorkshire, YO62 6DZ. Tel 01751 431544. www.ryedaleauctioneers.com. Militaria and collectables.

Smiths of Newent
The Old Chapel, Culver Street, Newent, GL18 1DB. Tel: 01531 821 776, www.smithsnewentauctions.co.uk. Coins and collectables.

Spink & Son Ltd
69 Southampton Row, Bloomsbury, London, WC1B 4ET. Tel: 020 7563 4000, fax: 020 7563 4085, email: info@spink.com, www.spink.com. Auctioneers and valuers. Regular sales of medals.

St James's Auctions
10 Charles II Street, London, SW1Y 4AA. Tel: 020 7930 7888, fax: 020 7930 824, email: info@stjauctions.com, www.stjauctions.com. Specialist auctioneers of coins and medals.

Stacey's
Essex Auction Rooms, 37 Websters Way, Rayleigh, Essex, SS6 8JQ. Tel: 01268 777122, www.staceyauction.com. Militaria and medals.

Stack's Bowers
123, West 57th Street, New York, NY 10019, USA. info@stacksBowers.com, www.stacksbowers.com. Auctioneers of world orders, decorations and medals. Also USA and world coins.

Tennants
The Auction Centre, Leyburn, North Yorkshire, DL8 5SG. Tel: 01969 623780, www.tennants.co.uk. Auctions of medals and coins.

Thomas Del Mar
25 Blythe Road, London, W14 0PD. Tel: 020 7602 4805, www.thomasdelmar.com. Antique arms, armour and militaria.

Thomson Roddick Auctioneers
The Auction Centre, Marconi Road, Carlisle, CA2 7NA. Tel: 01228 528 939, email: carlisle@thomsonroddick.com. Also at The Auction Centre, 118 Carnethie Street, Rosewell, Edinburgh, EH24 9AL. Tel: 0131 440 2448. Medals and militaria.

Wallis & Wallis
West Street Auction Galleries, Lewes, Sussex BN7 2NJ. Tel: 01273 480208, fax: 01273 476562, email: auctions@wallisandwallis.org, www.wallisandwallis.org. Militaria and medals.

Warwick & Warwick
Chalon House, Scar Bank, Millers Road, Warwick CV34 5DB. Tel: 01926 499031 fax: 01926 491906, www.warwickandwarwick.com. Medals and collectables.

Wellington Auctions
37 Rookery Lane, Great Totham, Maldon, Essex, CM9 8DF. Tel:07789 995782, www.wellingtonauctions.com. On-line auctions of orders, decorations and medals.

Whytes
38 Molesworth Street, Dublin 2, Ireland. Tel: +353 (0)1 676 2888 www.whytes.com. Irish Collectables. Bi-annual sales of coins and medals.

Dominic Winter Auctions
Mallard House, Broadway Lane, South Cerney, Nr Cirencester, GL7 5UQ. Tel: 01285 860006, fax: 01285 862461, email: henry@dominicwinter.co.uk, www.dominicwinter.co.uk. Medals, militaria, etc.

Richard Winterton Auctioneers
The Lichfield Auction Centre, Wood End Lane, Fradley Park, WS13 8NF. Tel: 01543 251081. Email: medals@richardwinterton.co.uk www.richardwinterton.co.uk. Medals and Collectables.

Woolley & Wallis
51–61 Castle Street, Salisbury, SP1 3SU. Tel: +44 (0)1722 424500 fax: 01722 424508. Medals, coins, collectables and specialist silver sales.

Information correct at the time of going to press. Please advise us if any details are incorrect or need updating.

DEALERS

Aberdeen Medals
PO Box 10524, Aberdeen, AB12 9DU. Tel: 07748 040021, www.aberdeenmedals.com. Specialists in medals to Scottish Regts, Indian Army & Colonial.

Ackley Unlimited
PO Box 82144, Portland, Oregon, USA, 97282-0144. Tel: 001 503 659 4681, email: ackleyunlimited@comcast.net. Orders, medals and decorations. Free quarterly lists on request.

Arctic Medals & Militaria
www.arcticmedals.com. Medals, Military badges and Insignia.

Michael Autengruber
Orders of the World, Schulthaissstrasse 10, D-78462 Konstanz, Germany. Tel: 0049 7531 284469, email: michael.autengruber@orden-der-welt.de. Orders, decorations & medals.

Award Productions Ltd
PO Box 300, Shrewsbury, Shropshire, SY5 6WP. Tel: 01952 510053, fax: 01952 510765, www.awardmedals.com. Suppliers of unofficial medals for veterans. Medallists to the Royal British Legion.

Louis Bannon
21 Royal Arcade, Cardiff, CF10 1AE. Tel: 02920 221528, www.bannon.co.uk. Medals and military antiques, medals to Welsh Regiments.

Bigbury Mint
Bigbury Mint, River Park, Ermington, Ivybridge, Devon, PL21 9NT. Tel: 01548 830717, email: info@bigburymint.com, www.bigburymint.com. Makers of fine medals and commemoratives.

Bostock Medals
"Pinewoods", 15 Waller Close, Leek Wootton, Nr Warwick, CV35 7QG. Tel: 01926 856381, Mob: 07815 615512, email: bostockmilitaria@aol.com, www.bostockmedals.co.uk. British orders, medals and decorations. Callers welcome by appointment.

British Medals (Rennie Alcock)
PO Box 14, Castletown, Isle of Man, IM99 5YY. Tel: 01624 827664, www.british-medals.co.uk. British orders, medals and decorations.

Gary Brown
PO Box 334, Gorleston-on-Sea, Great Yarmouth, Norfolk, NR30 9FF. Tel: 01493 651577, www.garybrownmedals.com. British orders & medals.

Cambridge Medal Mounting Services
3 Pepys Road, St Neots, PE19 2EN. Tel: 01480 395827, email: shelton946@aol.com.

Mark Carter
PO Box 470, Slough, Berkshire, SL3 6RR. Tel: 01753 534777, email: markgcarter6@gmail.com. Medal dealer and organiser of the Mark Carter Militaria & Medal Fairs in Stratford Upon Avon and Yate.

Cathedral Court Medals
First Floor Office, 30A Market Place, West Ripon, North Yorkshire, HG4 1BN. Tel: 01765 601 400. Coin and medal sales. Medal mounting/framing.

Chester Militaria
Shop B9, Chester Market, 6 Princess Street, Chester, CH1 2HH. Tel: 01244 376140, www.chestermedals.com. Medals, militaria and mounting service.

City Coins
Tulbagh Center, 9 Hans Strijdom Ave Lane, Cape Town. Tel 0027 21 425 2639, www.citycoins.com. Coins, banknotes, medals and accessories.

Coinote
74 Elwick Road, Hartlepool TS26 9AP. Tel: 01429 890894, www.coinote.co.uk. Medals, coins, banknotes and accessories. Regular stall holders at Stockton-on-Tees and Scorton (Nr Catrick) indoor market.

Norman W. Collett
56 Grierson Road, Honor Dale Park, London, SE23 1PE. Tel/fax: 020 8291 1435, www.medalsonline.co.uk. British medals, decorations, mainly groups.

Collectors World
190 Wollaton Road, Wollaton, Nottingham, NG8 1HJ. Tel: 01159 280347. Medals, coins, tokens, banknotes and accessories.

J. Collins Medals Limited
23 High Street, Shanklin, Isle of Wight, PO37 6JW Tel: 01983 853473 / 07711 963899, email: jonathan@jcollinsmedals.co.uk, www.jcollinsmedals.co.uk. Naval, Military, and Airforce Research Service.

Colonial Coins and Medals
Shop 1/218 Adelaide Street, Brisbane, QLD 4000, Australia. Tel: 61 7 3229 3949, email: coinshop@bigpond.net.au, www. coinmedalshop.com.au. British, Commonwealth orders and medals. Also coins and banknotes.

Constantius
Quality British Victorian campaign medals, WWI www.constantius.co.uk Tel: 015395 32452.

Peter R. Cotrel
7 Stanton Road, Bournemouth, Dorset BH10 5DS. Mail order—callers by appointment only please. Tel: 01202 388367. British, US, foreign medals and decorations. Medal albums. Regular email lists issued.

Cultman Collectables
27 Bowers Fold, Doncaster, South Yorkshire DN1 1HF. Tel: 07772 966375, or email: info@cultmancollectables.com, www.cultmancollectables.com. Militaria, medals, badges and police memorabilia.

DCM Medals
16 The Parade, St Mary's, Shrewsbury SY1 1DL Tel: 01743 600951, www.dcmmedals.com. British /Imperial orders, decorations & medals.

Dixon's Medals
1st Floor, 23 Prospect Street, Bridlington, East Yorkshire, YO15 2AE. Tel: 01262 603348, email: chris@dixonsmedals.co.uk, www.dixonsmedals.co.uk. British & world orders, medals and decorations. 4 lists a year £20 (UK), £25 USA, £30 (ROW) for 4 issues.

De Winters Medals
Tel: 07584 895918, email: dewintersmedals@hotmail.com, www.dewintersmedals.co.uk. Gurkha, Guards and RM campaign medals.

D.M.D. Services
P O Box 356, Reigate, Surrey, RH2 2AQ. Tel: 01737 216 246. Victorian campaign medals.

Frank Draskovic
PO Box 803, Monterey Park, CA 91754, USA. Tel: 001 626 281 9281, email: fdraskovic@hotmail.com. UK and worldwide orders and medals.

E.L.M.
57 Medal House, Yishun Industrial Estate, Park A, Singapore 768730. Tel: 0065 6487 7777. www.elm.com.sg. Manufacturer of medals. Medal mounting and restoration.

Fraser Medals
Telephone: Canada 001 905 982 0387. www.frasermedals.com. British and Commonwealth medals.

Bill Friar Medals
44 Knowsley Drive, Leigh, Lancs, WN7 3LY. Tel: 01942 671 980, email: sales@billfriarmedals.co.uk, www.billfriarmedals.co.uk. British medals and decorations.

Frontier Medals
8 Tai Hang Chung Sum Wai, Tai Hang, Tai Po, New Territories, Hong Kong. Tel: 00 852 94651496, www.frontiermedals.com. Medals.

Andy Garrett
Unit 9, Brackley Antique Cellar, Draymans Walk, Brackley, Northants NN13 6BE. British and foreign medals, groups, badges and militaria.

Gladman & Norman
51–53 Tenby St North, Birmingham B1 3EG. Tel: 0121 236 5752, www.gladman-norman.co.uk. Manufacturer of orders and medals.

Gradia Militaria
Woodpeckers, How Green Lane, Hever, Kent, TN8 7PS. Tel: 01732 700103, email: caroline@gradiamilitaria.com, www.gradiamilitaria.com. British, Commonwealth, cap badges, medals.

Great War Medals
PO Box 1914, Lymington, SO41 1FQ.
Tel: 020 8482 1918/ 07880 503188, email: info@greatwarmedals.com, www.greatwarmedals.com. Established 1985. Specialising in WWI British & Allied medals, plus badges & ephemera.

Louis E. Grimshaw
612 Fay Street, R.R. 1 Kingston, Ontario, Canada, K7L 4VI. Tel: 001 613 549 2500. Military antiques and collectables, including medals.

A. D. Hamilton & Co
7 St Vincent Place, Glasgow, G1 2DW. Tel: 0141 2215423, email: jefffineman@hotmail.com, www.adhamilton.co.uk. Medals, militaria, coins and banknotes. Retail shop open Monday–Friday, 10am–4.00pm (Saturday 10am–12.30pm).

Harland Military Antiques
Tel: 01429 232782/07904 349727. www.harlandmilitaryantiques.com. British Medals.

Intramark Limited
Windsor Lodge, 56 Windsor Street, Burbage, Leic, LE10 2EF. Tel: 01455 612400, email: intramark@btclick.com. Manufacturers of medals, etc.

Jager Medals & Militaria
Tel: 0141 840 2622, email: enquiries@jagermedals.com, www.jagermedals.com. British campaign medals bought and sold.

JB Military Antiques
2/135 Russell Street, Morley, WA, Australia, 6062. Tel: +61 (08) 9276 5113, www.jbmilitaryantiques.com.au.

Alec Kaplan & Son CC
115 Dunottar Street, Sydenham, 2192, Johannesburg, South Africa. Tel: 0027 11 485 2195, fax: 0027 11 640 3427, email: medals@wirelessza.co.za, www.aleckaplan.co.za. Contact for free catalogue.

Ian Laidler
No-Where, 17 Wavell Grove, Wakefield, WF2 6JW. Tel: 0781 548 4641, email: ian@ianlaidler.orangehome.co.uk. Medals and militaria.

Liverpool Medals
1 The Causeway, Altrincham, Cheshire, WA14 1DE, Tel: 0161 928 3272, email: sales@liverpoolmedals.com, www.liverpoolmedals.com. British & world orders, medals, decorations.

The London Medal Company
13 Cecil Court, London, WC2N 4AN. Tel: 020 7836 8877, email: shop@london-medals.co.uk, www.london-medals.co.uk. British and World orders, decorations and medals. Retail shop.

Ma–Shops
Lankernerstr. 42, 46395 Bocholt, Germany. Tel +49 2871 2180 383, www.ma-shops.com.

John Manning
18 Fengate, Heacham, nr. Kings Lynn, Norfolk, PE31 7BG. Tel: 01485 570153.

Medalbook.com
www.medalbook.com. Free, online database of world orders, decorations and medals. Makers identifaction registry, community forums.

The Medal Centre
10B Hencotes, Hexham, Northumberland, NE46 2EJ. Tel: 01434 609794 or 07950421704 www.themedalcentre.co.uk.

Medal Masters
PO Box 7204, Bundaberg North, Queensland, Australia, 4670. Tel: 0061 403 250170, email: info@medalmasters.com.au, www.medalmasters.com.au. Replica medals and specialist framers.

Medals, Mementos & More
3 Acacia Court, Strathalbyn, South Australia, 5255. Tel/fax: 0061 08 8536 8089. www.medalsmementos.com. Medal mounting/framing, replicas.

Medals of England
PO Box 258, Lingfield, Surrey, RH7 9AH. Tel: 01342 870926. www.medalsofengland.com. Medals and military items.

The Mess Dress Ltd
88 Stewart Road, Bournemouth, BH8 8NU. Tel: 01202 302846. www.messdress.com.

Military Memorabilia
PO Box 21-022, Henderson, Auckland, 0650, New Zealand. Tel: 0064 9 837 6150, +64 21 271 5141. email: medals@ihug.co.nz. Medal mounting & researcher.

Peter Morris

1 Station Concourse, Bromley North BR Station, Kent / PO Box 223, Bromley, Kent BR1 4EQ. . Tel: 020 8313 3410, email: info@petermorris.co.uk, www.petermorris.co.uk. Medals, decorations, militaria, coins & banknotes.

MSM Awards

8 Price Tce, Matamata, 3400, New Zealand. Tel: (NZ) 0064 7 888 9064, email: mikes@kol.co.nz, www.honours.homestead.com/home.html. Medal remounter for the serving military or Veteran.

Nordheide-Versand

Nordheid-Versand Kai Winkler, Schulstrasse 11a, 21220 Seevetal (Maschen). Tel: +0049 4105 665 832, www.nordheideversand.de. Medals, awards, award-documents, miniatures, pins, uniforms etc.

Officers Colours

Tel: 07867 805032, Email: paulread1944@gmail.com, www.officerscolours.com. Dealers in British and Commonwealth medals and militaria.

Poppy Militaria

4 Beatrice Street, Oswestry. Tel: 01691 670 079, www.poppymilitaria.co.uk, www.poppymedalframing.co.uk. Medal framing, medals and militaria for sale.

Q & C Militaria

22 Suffolk Road, Cheltenham, Gloucestershire, GL50 2AQ. Tel/fax: 01242 519815, www.qcmilitaria.com. British and Commonwealth orders, medals, decorations and miltaria.

RBJ Militaria

Parade Antiques Market, 27b New Street, Barbican, Plymouth, Devon, PL1 2NB. Tel: 07714 544777, www.rbjmilitaria.com.

Barbara Radman

Westfield House, 2G Westfield Road, Witney, Oxon, OX28 1JG. Tel: 01993 772705. British and Foreign orders, medals & decorations especially Russian.

RS Medal Mounting Service

PO Box 760, Taunton, TA1 9BA. Tel: 01823 259675, cmail: colin.hole15@gmail.com. Medal mounting.

ScotMint

68, Sandgate, Ayr, Scotland, KA7 1BX. Tel: 01292 268244 or 07939 345407, www.scotmint.com. British & worldwide medals groups, badges and militaria. Also coins and banknotes. Retail premises.

E. C. Snaith

Building 333, RAF College Cranwell, Lincolnshire NG34 8HB. Tel: 01400 266874. Regimental medals.

South African Militaria

Email: andrew@rolynengineering.co.za. www.southafricanmilitaria.com. Medals and militaria of SA interest.

Spink & Son Ltd

69 Southampton Row, Bloomsbury, London WC1B 4ET. Tel: 020 7563 4000, fax: 020 7563 4085, email: info@spink.com, www.spink.com. Tel: 01904 654769. Medal dealers and auctioneers.

Strachan Militaria

Tel : 0044 1543 490932, www.ismilitaria.co.uk. 20th Century German, British, US and militaria.

Sunset Militaria

Castle End Cottage, Lea, Ross on Wye, Herefordshire, HR9 7JY. Tel: 01989 750470, mobile: 07583 669571. Medals, Ribbons, Badges, Buttons, Militaria, Brooch Bars & Mini Medals.

Jeremy Tenniswood

2 Temple Road, Colchester, Essex, CO2 9JN. Tel: 01206 368787, fax: 01206 367836, www.militaria.co.uk. Medals, decorations, militaria and books.

Toye, Kenning & Spencer Ltd

Regalia House, Newtown Road, Bedworth, Warks, CV12 8QR. Tel: 024 7684 8800. Manufacturers of medals, badges, etc.

Treasure Bunker Militaria Shop

21 King Street, Merchant City, Glasgow, G1 5QZ. Tel/fax: 0141 552 8164, www.treasurebunker.com. Medals, badges, uniforms etc.

Ulric of England

PO Box 55, Church Stretton, Shropshire, SY6 6WR. Tel: 01694 781354, fax: 01694 781372, www.britishmilitarymedals.com. British medals.

Tanya Ursual

PO Box 788, Kemptville, Ontario, Canada, K0G 1J0. Tel: 001 613 258 5999, email: tanya@medalsofwar.com, www.medalsofwar.com. Medals, orders, decorations and militaria. Canadian and US distributor of the Medal Yearbook.

War & Son

14, Drapers Lane, Leominster, Herefordshire, HR6 8ND. Tel: 01568 616 414, or 07714 631313. www.warandson.co.uk. Specialists in British and world medals. Military Antiques. Retail outlet—see website for opening hours etc.

Stephen Wheeler

20 Cecil Court, Leicester Square, London, WC2N 4HE. Covent Garden Market, Stand 111, (Mondays). Tel: 02072406827 or 07778 848555. www.buymilitarymedals.com. British & Foreign medals. Retail shop.

Worcestershire Medal Service Ltd

56 Broad Street, Sidemoor, Bromsgrove, B61 8LL. Tel: 01527 835375, fax: 01527 576798. email: wms@worcmedals.com, www.worcmedals.com. Medals and medal mounting, storage and display cases, miniature medals, blazer badges and replacement medals. Ministry of Defence, official provider of UK MOD medals.

Worldwide Militaria

Jeffery Stone, 2000 Bloomingdale Road, Suite 200, Glendale Heights, IL 60139, USA. Tel 001 630 571 8340.

I. S. Wright

262 Castlereagh Street, Sydney, NSW, Australia. Tel: 0061 02 9264 7555, email: sydney@iswright.com.au. A wide range of military collectables.

Carsten Zeige

Eilenau 2, 22089, Hamburg, Germany. Tel:0049 40 3571 3636, email: info@zeige.com. www.zeige.com. German and Foreign medals.

IMPORTANT ORGANISATIONS

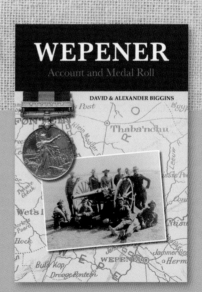

BOOKSELLERS/DEALERS

In addition to the names listed below, it should be noted that a number of the medal dealers listed above regularly or occasionally include books on their medal lists.

Peter Barnes
www.barnesbooks.co.uk. Pre-owned, out-of-print, rare, old and collectors editions of military, naval and aviation book.

Andrew Burroughs
34 High Street, St Martins, Stamford, Lincs, PE90 2LJ. Tel: 01780 765140. Military and naval.

Chelifer Books
Todd Close, Curthwaite, Wigton, Cumbria, CA7 8BE. Military history, including units. Lists available.

Empire Books
61 Broad Lane, Rochdale, Lancs, OL16 4PL. Tel: 01706 666678. Military, naval and aviation. Special interest Australian forces, Vietnam and Colonial wars.

Falconwood Transport and Military Bookshop.
5 Falconwood Parade, The Green, Welling, Kent, DA16 2PL. Tel: 020 8303 8291. Military, naval and aviation history.

Steven J. Hopkins
Court Farm, Kington, Flyford Flavell, Worcs, WR7 4DQ. Tel: 01386 793427, email: tokyngton@aol.com. Military books and prints.

John Lewcock
6 Chewells Lane, Haddenham, Ely, Cambs, CB6 3SS. Tel: 01353 741152. Naval history.

Liverpool Medal Company Ltd
1 The Causeway, Altrincham, Cheshire, WA14 1DE. Tel: 0161 9283272, fax: 0161 8202522. www.liverpoolmedals.com. Medal dealers, also an occasional separate book catalogue.

Ian Lynn
258 Upper Fant Road, Maidstone, Kent, ME16 8BX. Tel: 01622 728525. Military history.

McLaren Books
Tel: 07720223780, wwwmclarensbooks.com. Naval history.

Military Bookman at Chartwell Booksellers
55 East 52nd Street, New York, NY 10055, USA. www.militarybookman.com. Large stock of military history relating to all services worldwide and all periods.

Military History Bookshop
PO Box 590, Folkestone, Kent, CT20 2WX. Tel: 01303 246500. www.militaryhistorybooks.com. Military book specialists.

Military Medals and Books
20 Deep Spinney, Biddenham,Bedford, MK40 4QH Tel: 01234 224491. www.militarymedalsandbooks.com. Specialised books, antique military medals and more.

Pen & Sword Books Ltd.
47 Church Street, Barnsley, S. Yorks, S70 2AS. Tel: 01226 734222, fax: 01226 734438, www.pen-and-sword.co.uk. Military titles.

Anthony J. Simmonds
66 Royal Hill, Greenwich, London, SE10 8RT. Tel: 020 8692 1794, www.navalandmaritimebooks.com. Naval and maritime history. Occasional catalogues.

Spink & Son Ltd
69 Southampton Row, Bloomsbury, London, WC1B 4ET. Tel: 020 7563 4000, fax: 020 7563 4066, www.spink.com. Specialist Book Department. Publications produced on coins, medals, stamps etc.

Jeremy Tenniswood
2 Temple Road, Colchester, essex CO2 9JN. Tel: 01206 368787. Military books.

Token Publishing Ltd.
8 Oaktree Place, Manaton Close, Matford Business Park, Exeter EX2 8WA. Tel: 01404 46972, email: info@tokenpublishing.com, www.tokenpublishing.com. Publishers of MEDAL NEWS and COIN NEWS. Extensive range of medal, coin and banknote titles.

Turner Donovan Military Books
Flat 1, 22 Florence Road, Brighton, BN1 6DJ. www.turnerdonovan.com. Printed works and manuscript material relating to the British Military Services.

> **If your details listed above are incorrect, or if we have omitted to include you in this listing, please do let us know.**
> **Details are included free of charge.**

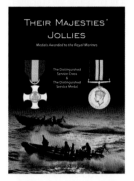

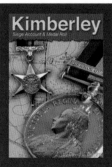

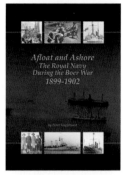
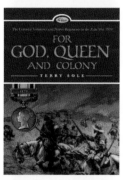
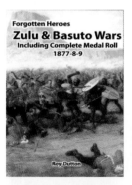
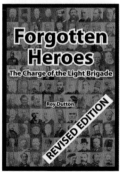

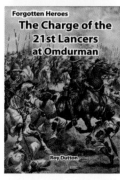

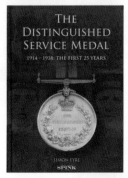

FAIRS

Many fairs are held regularly and organised by professionals and societies (Victorian Military Society, Aldershot Militaria Society, etc.). The dates are usually well advertised in MEDAL NEWS and other publications, however, times and venues are liable to change so it is advisable to telephone the organisers beforehand. Listed below are the major fair organisers and the events known to us.

Abergavenny Militaria and Medal Fair
Market Hall, Cross Street, Abergavenny. Tel: 01873 735811.

Cardiff Fair
City Hall, Cardiff. M.J. Promotions. Tel: 01792 415293.

Mark Carter Militaria & Medal Fairs
Britannia—Carisbrooke Hall, Victory Services Club, 63-79 Seymour Street, Marble Arch, London, W2 2HF. Organised by Mark Carter for Noonans.
Stratford upon Avon—Stratford Leisure Centre, Bridgefoot, CV37 6YY.
Yate (Bristol)—Yate Leisure Centre, Kennedy Way, BS37 4DQ. Mark Carter Tel: 01753 534777

Cheltenham Fair
Civil Service Sports and Social Club
Tewkesbury Road.
Cheltenham GL51 9LS
Jim Lightstone 01242 528587.

Dublin Coin & Medal Fair
Serpentine Hall, RDS, Ballsbridge, Dublin 4, Ireland. Mike Kelly Tel: 00353 8687 14 880.

The Medal Centre Medal and Militaria Fairs
Bowburn—Community Centre, Bowburn Village, County Durham, DH6 5AT.
Wakefield—Outwood Memorial Hall, Outwood, W. Yorks WF1 2NE.
Andrew Dukes Tel: 01434 609794

Medal and Militaria Fairs
Civic Centre, Kentish Way, Bromley, Kent, BR1 3UH
Hampton Sports and Leisure, Tydemans, Chelmsford, Essex, CM2 9FH.
The Historic Dockyard, Chatham, Kent, ME4 4TZ
James Aslett. Tel: 07595511981.

Northern Arms Fairs
Darlington—Scotch Corner Holiday Inn, DL10 6NR
Leeds—Pudsey Civic Hall, Dawsons Corner, Stanningley, Pudsey, LS28 5TA.
Liverpool—The Village Hotel, Whiston, L35 1RZ.
Newark—Cedric Ford Pavillion, Showground, Winthorpe Road, NG24 2NY.
Tel: 01423 780759.

OMRS Annual Convention
Venue to be confirmed.Contact: OMRS Membership Secretary, PO Box 248, Snettisham, King's Lynn, Norfolk PE31 7TA.

Preston Arms and Militaria Fair
Lancastrian Suite, Park Hall Hotel, Charnock Richard (Via Charnock Richard Services M6), Chorley, Lancashire, PR7 5LP. Tel: 01254 263260

Stockport Antique Arms, Medals & Militaria Fair
Stockport Masonic Guildhall, 69-171 Wellington Rd S, Stockport SK1 3UAY

York Coin & Medal Fair
The Grandstand, York Racecourse, York, YO23 1EX. Tel: 01793 513431 or 020 8946 4489.

Yorkshire Coin & Medal Fair
Cedar Court Hotel, Lindley Moor Road, Ainley Top, Huddersfield, HD3 3RH.
Neil Smith Tel: 01522 522772.

> The information included in this directory is correct at the time of going to press. Please check with fair organisers before setting off on a long journey.

Two of the stalwarts of the medal collecting fraternity—Andrew Jukes (left) and Mark Carter, organisers of important medal and militaria fairs across the country. Caught on camera at Mark Carter's hugely popular fair held in Stratford-upon-Avon. MEDAL NEWS Deputy Editor, Louise Bray-Mussell, looks on from behind the Token Publishing stand.

MUSEUMS

And Collections

The majority of the museums listed below are the regimental museums of the British Army, Militia, Yeomanry and Territorials, but we have included other museums pertaining to the Royal Navy, the Royal Marines and the Royal Air Force where medals form a significant part of the collections. So, too, the museums of the police forces, fire brigades, Red Cross, Royal National Lifeboat Institution and similar bodies have been included where relevant. Readers should also bear in mind that many general museums in our towns and cities boast fine collections of military medals pertaining to their local regiments. We have included those of which we are aware. The date of foundation is shown in brackets after the name.

Some service museums have been undergoing refits, relocations and amalgamations. We would welcome further information from readers about these changes and about other general museums in their areas with a good coverage of medals to local regiments.

Space prevents us from going into details regarding the scope of individual museum holdings. We give the postal address, telephone number wherever possible. Please contact the museums directly for opening times and admission prices. It is always sensible, particularly before travelling long distances to visit a museum or collection, to telephone and check that the published details are still correct.

Some museums may have libraries holding archival material; this should be checked out and the conditions for use ascertained as such holdings will not have the resources to answer detailed research enquiries.

Where museums are devoted to one particular regimental/service/unit or whatever, they are listed by title in alphabetical order. This may not always accord with the exact official name of the museum which is given on the address line. The well-known national museums are listed alphabetically by name. More general museums which include medal collections are listed by the name of the town. If you cannot see the name of the museum you require at first glance, it may be worth searching through the full list, as some museums escape neat classification and would require extensive cross-referencing to do them full justice.

Aberdeen Maritime Museum (1984)
Shiprow, Aberdeen, AB11 5BY. Tel: 0300 020 0293, www.aagm.co.uk/Venues/AberdeenMaritimeMuseum

Airborne Assault, Museum of the Parachute Regiment and Airborne Forces
Building 213, North Base, Imperial War Museum, Duxford, Cambridge, CB22 4QR. Tel: 01223 839 909, email: curator@paradata.org.uk www.paradata.org.uk.

Aldershot Military Museum
Queen's Avenue, Aldershot, Hants, GU11 2LG. Tel: 01252 314598, www.hampshireculture.org.uk/aldershot-military-museum

Argyll and Sutherland Highlanders Regimental Museum
The Castle, Stirling, FK8 1EH. Tel: 01786 448041 www.argylls.co.uk/museum.

Army Medical Services Museum
Keogh Barracks, Ash Vale, Aldershot, GU12 5RQ. Tel: 01252 523176, email: armymedicalmuseum@btinternet.com. www.museumofmilitarymedicine.org.

Army Flying Museum
Middle Wallop, Hampshire, SO20 8DY. Tel: 01264 781086, email: info@armyflying.com, www.armyflying.com

Royal Army Physical Training Corps Museum (1949)
Fox Lines, Queen's Avenue, Aldershot, Hampshire, GU11 2LB. Tel: 01252 787852 www.raptcmuseum.co.uk.

Arundel Toy and Military Museum (1978)
Dolls House, 23 High Street, Arundel, West Sussex, BN18 9AD. Tel: 01903 507446/882908.

Ayrshire Yeomanry Museum
Rozelle House, Monument Road, Alloway by Ayr, KA7 4NQ. Tel: 01292 445447.

Battle of Britain Museum (1969)
Aerodrome Road, Hawkinge, Nr Folkestone, Kent, CT18 7AG. Tel: 0130 389 3140, www.kbobm.org.

Bedfordshire and Hertfordshire Regimental Museum
Wardown Park Museum, Old Bedford Road, Luton, LU2 7HA. Tel: 01582 546722, www.culturetrust.com

HMS Belfast (1978)
The Queen's Walk, London, SE1 2JH. Tel: 020 7940 6300, www.iwm.org.uk/visits/hms-belfast.

Berkshire Yeomanry Museum
TA Centre, 86 Bolton Road, Windsor SL4 3JG. Tel: 01753 860600, www.berkshireyeomanrymuseum.co.uk.

Black Watch Museum (1924)
Balhousie Castle, Hay Street, Perth, PH1 5HR. Tel: 01738 638152, www.theblackwatch.co.uk.

100th Bomb Group Memorial Museum (1978)
Common Road, Dickleburgh, Diss, Norfolk, IP21 4PH. Tel: 01379 740708, www.100bgmus.org.uk. Medals and memorabilia.

British in India Museum (1972)

Hendon Mill, Hallam Road, Nelson, BB9 8AD. Tel: 01282 613129.

British Red Cross Museum and Archives (1984)

UK Office, 44 Moorfields, London, EC2Y 9AL. Tel: 0344 871 11 11, email: enquiry@redcross.org.uk, www. medicalmuseums.org.

Bygones

Fore Street, St Marychurch, Torquay, Devon, TQ1 4PR. Tel: 01803 326108, email: info@bygones.co.uk, www.bygones.co.uk.

Caernarfon Airworld Aviation Museum

Caernarfon Airport, Dinas Dinlle, Caernarfon, Gwynedd, LL54 5TP. Tel: 01286 832154, email: info @ airworldmuseum.co.uk. www.airworldmuseum.com.

Castle and Regimental Museum, Monmouth

The Castle, Monmouth, NP25 3BS. Tel: 01600 772175, email: moncasmus"icloud.com, www. monmouthcastlemuseum.org.uk.

Cheshire Military Museum (1972)

The Castle, Chester, CH1 2DN. Tel: 01244 327617, www.cheshiremilitarymuseum.org.uk

Churchill Museum and Cabinet War Rooms (1984)

Clive Steps, King Charles Street, London, SW1A 2AQ. 020 7416 5000, www.iwm.org.uk/visits/churchill-war-rooms.

Coldstream Museum

12 Market Square, Coldstream, TD12 4BD. Tel: 01890 882630, www.liveborders.org.uk/culture/museums/our-museums/coldstream-museum/

Dingwall Museum Trust (1975)

Town House, High Street, Dingwall, Ross-shire, IV15 9RY. Tel: 01349 865366, www.dingwallmuseum.info. Medals and militaria of the Seaforth Highlanders, and items pertaining to Major General Sir Hector Macdonald .

Duke of Cornwall's Light Infantry Regimental Museum (1925)

The Keep, Victoria Barracks, Bodmin, PL31 1EG. Tel: 01208 72810. www.cornwalls-regimental museum. org.

Duke of Wellington's Regiment Museum (1960)

Regimental Museum, Bankfield Museum, Boothtown Road, Halifax, HX3 6HG. Tel: 01422 352334, email: museums@calderdale.gov.uk, http://www.dwr.org.uk/museum

Essex Regiment Museum (1938)

Oaklands Park, Moulsham Street, Chelmsford, Essex, CM2 9AQ. Tel: 01245 605700, www.chelmsford.gov.uk/museums.

Firing Line, Cardiff Museum of the Welsh Soldier

The Interpretation Centre, Cardiff Castle, Cardiff, CF103RB. Tel: 02920 873623, www.cardiffcastlemuseum.org.uk.

Fleet Air Arm Museum (1964)

RNAS Yeovilton, Ilchester, Somerset, BA22 8HT. Tel: 023 9283 9766, www.fleetairarm.com.

Fusilier Museum London (1962)

HM Tower of London, EC3N 4AB. Tel: 0203 166 6912, www.fusiliermuseumlondon.org.

Fusiliers Museum of Northumberland

The Abbot's Tower, Alnwick Castle, Alnwick, NE66 1NG. Tel: 01665 602152, www.northumberlandfusiliers.org.uk.

Glasgow Museums (1854)

Glasgow Museums Resource Center, 200 Woodhead Road, Glasgow, G53 7NN. Tel: 0141 276 9300. Medals of the Glasgow Yeomanry, Highland Light Infantry and regiments associated with the city.

Gordon Highlanders' Museum (1961)

St Lukes, Viewfield Road, Aberdeen, AB15 7XH. Tel: 01224 311200. www.gordonhighlanders.com

Green Howards Regimental Museum

Trinity Church Square, Richmond, Yorkshire, DL10 4QN. Tel: 01748 826561. www.greenhowards.org.uk

Guards Museum (1988)

Wellington Barracks, Birdcage Walk, London, SW1E 6HQ. Tel: 0207 414 3428, www.theguardsmuseum. com.

Gurkha Museum (1974)

Peninsular Barracks, Romsey Road, Winchester, Hants, SO23 8TS. Tel: 01962 842832, www.thegurkhamuseum.co.uk.

Herefordshire Light Infantry Museum (1967)

Suvla Barracks, Harold Street, Hereford, HR1 2QX. Tel: 07726 566602, email: hfdlimuseum@gmail.com, www.herefordshirelightinfantrymuseum.com. By appointment

Hertfordshire Regiment Museum

At the Hertford Museum at 18 Bull Plain, Hertford, SG14 1DT. Tel: 01992 582 686.

www.hertfordmuseum.org.

Honourable Artillery Company Museum

Armoury House, City Road, London, EC1Y 2BQ. General enquiries Tel: 02073821537, www.hac.org.uk.

Hornsea Folk Museum (1978)

11-17 Newbegin, Hornsea, East Riding of Yorkshire, HU18 1AB. Tel: 01964 533443, email: info@hornseamuseum.co.uk, www.hornseamuseum.co.uk.

Household Cavalry Museum

Household Cavalry Museum, Horse Guards, Whitehall, London, SW1A 2AX. Tel: 020 7930 3070, email: museum@householdcavalry.co.uk.

www.householdcavalrymuseum.co.uk./museum

Household Cavalry Museum

Combermere Barracks, St Leonards Road, Windsor, Berkshire, SL4 3DN. Tel: 01753 755112.

Imperial War Museum (1917)

Lambeth Road, London, SE1 6HZ. Tel: 020 7416 5000, www.iwm.org.uk.

Imperial War Museum Duxford (1976)

Duxford, Cambridgeshire, CB22 4QR. Tel: 020 7091 30637.

Imperial War Museum North (2002)

The Quays, Trafford Wharf Road, Trafford Park, Manchester M17 1TZ. Tel: 0161 836 4000, www.iwm.org.uk.

Inns of Court and City Yeomanry Museum (1947)

10 Stone Buildings, Lincoln's Inn, London, WC2A 3TG. Tel: 020 7405 8112. www.iccy.org.uk

Jersey Militia Museum Collection

La Grande Route Des Mielles, St Ouen, Jersey, JE3 2FN. Tel: 07797 732072.

The Keep Military Museum

Barrack Road, Dorchester, DT1 1RN. Tel: 07586 161872, email: info@keepmilitarymuseum.org, www.keepmilitarymuseum.org.

Kent and Sharpshooters Yeomanry Museum (1966(
Hever Castle, Tonbridge, Kent, TN8 7NG.
www.ksymuseum.org.uk.

King's Own Royal Border Regiment Museum (1932)
Cumbria's Museum of Military Life, Alma Block,
The Castle, Carlisle, Cumbria, CA3 8UR. Tel: 01228
532774,
www.cumbriamuseumofmilitarylife.org.

King's Own Royal Regiment Museum (Lancaster)
Lancaster City Museum, Market Sq., Lancaster LA1
1HT. Tel: 01524 64637, www.kingsownmuseum.com.

King's Own Scottish Borderers Regimental Museum
(1954)
The Barracks Parade, Berwick-upon-Tweed, TD15
1DG. Tel: 01289 307426. www.kosb.co.uk.

King's Own Yorkshire Light Infantry Museum (1932)
Museum and Art Gallery, Chequer Road, Doncaster,
South Yorks, DN1 2AE. Tel: 01302 734293.

King's Regiment Museum (1930)
Museum of Liverpool, Pier Head, Liverpool L3 1DG.
Tel: 0151 478 4545, www.liverpoolmuseums.org.uk/
mol/visit/galleries/soldiers.

15th/19th King's Royal Hussars (Light Dragoons)
Discovery Museum, Blandford Square, Newcastle-
upon-Tyne, NE1 4JA. Tel : 0191 232 6789,
www.lightdragoons.org.uk.

Kohima Museum (1991)
Imphal Barracks, Fulford Road, York, YO10 4HD.
01904 665 806, www.kohimamuseum.co.uk.

HorsePower: The Museum of The King's Royal Hussars
Museum (1980)
Peninsula Barracks, Romsey Road, Winchester, SO23
8TS. Tel: 01962 828541, www.horsepowermuseum.
co.uk.

Lancashire Infantry Museum (1929)
Incorporating East Lancashire Regiment, South
Lancashire Regiment (Prince of Wales's Volunteers),
Queen's Lancashire, Loyal Reg.(North Lancashire)
Lancashire Regiment. Fulwood Barracks, Watling
Street Road, Preston, Lancs, PR2 8AA. Tel: 01772
260584.

Light Infantry Museum (1990)
Collection and archive at Bodmin Keep, The Keep,
Bodmin, Cornwall, PL31 1EG. Tel: 01208 72810,
email: info@bodminkeep.org, www.bodminkeep.org.
uk

Liverpool Scottish Regimental Museum
Archive Office: Artists Club, 5 Eberle Street, Liverpool
L2 2AG. Appointment only. Tel: 0151 645 5717.

London Fire Brigade Museum (1967)
Currently running as a virtual museum. www.london-
fire.gov.uk

The London Scottish Regimental Museum
Regimental Headquarters, 95 Horseferry Road,
London, SW1P 2DX. Tel: 020 7630 1639.

Military Intelligence Museum
Building 200 Chicksands, Shefford, Beds, SG17 5PR.
Tel: 01462 81463 email: mi-enquiries@outlook.com,
www.intelligencemuseum.org.

National Army Museum (1960)
Royal Hospital Road, Chelsea, London, SW3 4HT. 020
7730 0717, email: info@nam.ac.uk. www.nam.ac.uk.

National Maritime Museum (1934)
Park Row, Greenwich, London, SE10 9NF. Tel: 020
8858 4422, email: RMGenquiries@rmg.co.uk, www.
rmg.co.uk.

National Museum of Ireland—Decorative Arts and
History (1877)
Collins Barracks, Benburb Street, Dublin DO7 XKV4.
Tel +00353 16777 444, www.museum.ie.

The National Museum of the Royal Navy (1911)
HM Naval Base, Portsmouth PO1 3NH.
Tel 02392 839 766, www.nmrn.ORG.UK/
portsmouthhistoricdockyard.

National War Museum
The Castle, Edinburgh, EH1 2NG. Tel: 0300 123 6789,
email: info@nms.ac.uk enquiries, www.nms.ac.uk.

Newark (Notts & Lincs) Air Museum Ltd (1968)
Drove Lane, Newark,Nottinghamshire, NG24 2NY. Tel:
01636 707170, www.newarkairmuseum.org.

Northamptonshire Regimental Museum
Abington Park Museum, Park Avenue South,
Northampton, NN1 5LW. Tel: 01604 838110, www.
northampton.gov.uk./museums.

Order of St. John of Jerusalem Museum
St. John's Gate, St. John's Lane, Clerkenwell, London,
EC1M 4DA. Tel: 020 7324 4005. www.museumstjohn.
org.uk

Soldiers of Oxfordshire Museum
Park Street, Woodstock , OX20 1SN. Tel 01993
810211, www.sofo.org.uk.

Polish Institute and Sikorski Museum
20 Princes Gate, London, SW7 1PT. Tel: 020 7589
9249, www.pism.co.uk.

Prince of Wales's Own 9th /12th Lancers Regimental
Museum (1972)
Derby Museum and Art Gallery, The Strand, Derby,
DE1 1BS. Tel: 01322 641901, www.derbymuseums.
org/collection/the-soldiersstory.

Prince of Wales's Own Regiment of Yorkshire Museum
3 Tower Street, York YO1 9SB. Tel: 01904 461010,
www.yorkarmymuseum.co.uk.

Princess of Wales's Royal Regiment and Queen's
Regiment Museum (1987)
Dover Castle, Kent, CT16 1HU. Tel: 01304 240121,
www.armytigers.com

1st The Queen's Dragoon Guards Regimental Museum
Cardiff Castle, Cardiff, South Glamorgan, CF10 2RB.
Tel: 02920 873623, www.qdg.org.uk

Queen's Own Royal West Kent Regimental Museum
(1961)
Maidstone Museums, St Faith's Street, Maidstone,
Kent, ME14 1LH. Tel: 01622 602838, www.museum.
maidstone.gov.uk/our-museums/queens-own.

Queen's Royal Hussars Museum - Churchills Own
Trinity Mews, Priory Road, Warwick, CV34 4NA. www.
qrhmuseum.uk/home or Tel: 0207 756 2273.

Regimental Museum of the Royal Welsh (Brecon)
(1934)
Temporarily closed, Tel: 01874 613310, email: hello@
royalwelshmuseum.wales. The Rifles (Berkshire and
Wiltshire) Museum
The Wardrobe, 58 The Close, Salisbury, SP1 2EX. Tel
01722 419419, Royal Berkshire, www.thewardrobe.
org.uk.

Royal Air Force Museum (1963)

Grahame Park Way, London, NW9 5LL. Tel: 020 8205 2266, email: london@rafmuseum.org, www.rafmuseum.org.uk/london.

Royal Armoured Corps Museum (1939), The Tank Museum (1923)

Bovington, Wareham, Dorset, BH20 6JG. Tel: 01929 405096, www.tankmuseum.org.

Royal Armouries Museum (1996)

Armouries Drive, Leeds, LS10 1LT. Tel : 0113 220 1999, www.royalarmouries.org/leeds.

Royal Army Chaplains' Museum (1949)

Faringdon Road, Shrivenham, Oxfordshire, SN6 8EU. Tel: 07917 790916, royalarmychaplainsmuseum. business.site.

Royal Devon Yeomanry (1845)

Museum of Barnstaple and North Devon, The Square, Barnstaple, Devon, EX32 8LN. Tel: 01271 346747, www.barnstaplemuseum.org.uk

Royal Dragoon Guards Museum

The Regimental Museum of the Royal Dragoon Guards, 3 Tower Street, York, YO1 9SB. Tel: 01904 848026, email: info@rdgassociation.co.uk, www. rdgmuseum.org.uk

Royal East Kent Regiment, Third Foot (The Buffs) Museum

National Army Museum, Royal Hospital Road, London, SW3 4HT. Tel: 0207 730 0717, www.nam.ac.uk.

Royal Electrical and Mechanical Engineers Museum of Technology. (1958)

Prince Phillip Barracks, MoD Lyneham, Chippenham, SN15 4XX. Tel: 01249 894 869, email: enquiries@ rememuseum.org.uk, www.rememuseum.org.uk.

Royal Engineers Museum

Prince Arthur Road, Gillingham, Kent, ME7 1UR. Tel: 01634 822839, www.re-museum.co.uk.

Royal Green Jackets Museum

Peninsula Barracks, Romsey Road, Winchester, SO23 8TS. Tel: 01962 828549. www.rgjmuseum.co.uk

Royal Hampshire Regimental Museum (1933)

Serle's House, Southgate Street, Winchester, Hants SO23 9EG. Tel: 01962 863658, www. royalhampshireregiment.org.

Royal Highland Fusiliers Regimental Museum (1960)

518 Sauchiehall Street, Glasgow, G2 3LW. Tel: 0141 332 5639, www.rhf.org.uk

Royal Hospital Chelsea

Royal Hospital Road, Chelsea, London, SW3 4SR. Tel: 020 7881 5200, www.chelsea-pensioners.co.uk.

13th/18th Royal Hussars (Queen Mary's Own) Regiment (1957) and The Light Dragoons

Discovery Museum, Blanford Square, Newcastle Upon Tyne, NE1 4JA Tel: 0191 232 6789, www.lightdragoons.org.uk.

Royal Inniskilling Fusiliers Regimental Musuem

The Castle, Enniskillen, Co. Fermanagh, N. Ireland, BT74 7HL. Tel: 028 6632 3142, www. inniskillingsmuseum.com.

Royal Irish Fusiliers Museum

Sovereign's House, The Mall, Armagh, BT61 9DL. Tel: 028 37 522911, www.royal-irish.com.

Royal Irish Regiment Museum (1993)

Currently closed pending relocation. www.royal-irish. com/museums/royal-irish-regiment-museum

The Royal Lancers (Queen Elizabeths' Own), Nottingham Yeomanry Museum & South Nottinghamshire Hussars Museum

Thoresby Park, Ollerton, Newark, Nottinghamshire, NG22 9EP. Tel 01623 824222.

Royal Leicestershire Regiment Museum (1969)

Newarke Houses Museum, Leicester, LE2 7BY. Tel: 0116 225 4980, www.royalleicestershireregiment.org. uk/the-regimental-museum.

Royal Lincolnshire Regimental Museum (1985)

The Old Barracks, Burton Road, Lincoln, LN1 3LY. Tel: 01522 782040, www.thelincolnshireregiment.org/ museum.shtml.

Royal Logistic Corps Museum (1995)

Worthy Down, Nr Winchester SO21 2RG. Tel: 01962 887793, www.royallogisticcorps.co.uk/museum

Royal Marines Museum

Scheduled to relocate. www.nmrn.org.uk/royal-marines-museum/new-museum

Royal Military Police Museum (1979)

Southwick Park (Postal Point 38), Nr. Fareham, PO17 6EJ. Tel: 02392 284 372, email: museum@rhqrmp. org, www.rhqrmp.org. By appointment.

Royal National Lifeboat Institution Museums (1937)

Bamburgh NE69 7AE. Tel: 01668 214910

Cromer NR27 9HE. Tel 01263 511294

Chatham ME4 4TZ. Tel: 01634 823800

Eastbourne, BN21 4BY. Tel: 01323 730717

Salcombe TQ8 8BZ. Tel: 01548 844386

Whitby YO21 3PU. Tel 01947 602001

www.rnli.org/find-my-nearest-museums

Royal Navy Submarine Museum

Haslar Jetty Road, Gosport, Hampshire, PO12 2AS. Tel: 023 9283 9766, www.submarine-museum.co.uk.

Royal Norfolk Regimental Museum (1945)

Norwich Castle Museum and Art Gallery, Castle Hill, Norwich, NR1 3JU. Tel: 01603 493625, www.rnrm.org.uk.

Royal Observer Corps' Museum

C/o Solent Sky Museum, Albert Road S, Southampton, SO14 3FR. Tel: 023 8069 3823, www.therocmuseum.org.

The Royal Regiment of Fusiliers Museum (Royal Warwickshire)

St John's House, Warwick, CV34 4NF. Tel: 01926 491653, www.fusiliermuseumwarwick.com

The Royal Scots and The Royal Regiment of Scotland Museum (1951)

Edinburgh Castle, Edinburgh, EH1 2YT. Tel: 0131 310 5015, email: museum@theroyalscots.co.uk, www.theroyalscots.co.uk.

Royal Signals Museum

Blandford Camp, Blandford Forum, Dorset DT11 8RH. Tel: 01258 482248, email: info@ royalsignalsmuseum.com, www.royalsignalsmuseum. co.uk.

Police Museum of Northern Ireland (1983)

Brooklyn, 65 Knock Road, Belfast, BT5 6LE. Tel: 028 9070 0116, www.psni.police.uk/about-us/our-histroy/police-museum.

Royal Ulster Rifles Museum (1963)

2nd Floor, 28 Bedford Street, Belfast, BT7 2FE. Tel: 02890 232086, www.royal-irish.com/museums/royal-ulster-rifles-museum.

Royal Welch Fusiliers Museum (1955)

Caernarfon Castle, Gwynedd, LL55 2AY. 01286 673362, www.rwfmuseum.org.uk.

The Sandhurst Collection, RMAS

Royal Military Academy, Sandhurst, Camberley, Surrey, GU15 4PQ. www.sandhurstcollection.co.uk.

School of Infantry and Small Arms School Corps Weapons Collection (1953)

SASC, HQ Infantry, Land Warfare Centre, Warminster BA12 0DJ. Tel: 01985 222487, www.nam.ac.uk/explore/small-arms-school-corps

Scott Polar Research Institute Museum

University of Cambridge, Lensfield Road, Cambridge, CB2 1ER. Tel: 01223 336540, www.spri.cam.ac.uk/museum.

Sherwood Foresters Regimental Museum (1923)

Castle Museum, Nottingham, NG1 6EL. Tel: 0115 946 5415.

Shropshire Regimental Museum (1985)

The Castle, Shrewsbury, SY1 2AT. Tel: 01743 358516, Closed Thursdays and some Sundays, check website: www.soldiersofshropshire.co.uk

Soldiers of Gloucestershire Museum

Custom House, Gloucester Docks, Gloucester, GL1 2HE. Tel: 01452 522682, www.soldiersofglos.com. Medals of the Gloucestershire Regiment Royal Gloucestershire Hussars.

Somerset Military Museum (1974)

The Museum of Somerset, Taunton Castle, Taunton, Somerset, TA1 4AA. Tel: 01823 255088, www.somerset.gov.uk/museums.

Staffordshire Regiment Museum (1962)

DMS Whittington, Lichfield, Staffs WS14 9PY. Tel: 01543 434394, www.staffordshireregimentmuseum.com.

Storiel (Formerly Gwynedd Museum & Art Gallery, Bangor)

Ffordd Gwynedd, Bangor, Gwynedd, LL57 1DT. Tel: 01248 353368.Medals, militaria of Welsh regiments.

Suffolk Regiment Museum (1967)

The Keep, Out Risbygate, Bury St Edmunds, Suffolk IP33 3RN. Tel: 01284 749317, www.suffolkregimentmuseum.co.uk

Surrey Infantry Museum (1979)

The Surrey History Centre will now be dealing with research enquiries relating to The Queen's Royal, East Surrey and Queen's Royal Surrey Regiments (2nd, 31st and 70th Foot). Contact: Surrey History Centre, 130 Goldsworth Road, Woking, Surrey GU21 6ND. Tel: 01483 518737, www.surreycc.gov.uk/surreyhistoryservice.

Sussex & Surrey Yeomanry Collection (1993)

Newhaven Fort, Fort Road, Newhaven, East Sussex, BN9 9DS. Tel: 01273 517622.

Tangmere, Military Aviation Museum (1992)

Tangmere, near Chichester, West Sussex, PO20 2ES. Tel: 01243 790090, www.tangmere-museum.org.uk.

The 11 (Fighter) Group Operations Room

The Battle of Britain Bunker, Wren Avenue, Uxbridge, UB10 0GG Tel: 01895 238154, www.battleofbritainbunker.co.uk

The Fusilier Museum (1933)

Moss Street, Bury, Lancs, BL9 0DF. Tel: 0161 763 8950, www.fusiliermuseum.com.

The Highlanders Museum

Fort George, Ardersier, Inverness, IV2 7TD. Tel: 0131 310 8702, www.thehighlandersmuseum.com.

The Tank Museum (1923), Royal Armoured Corps Museum (1939)

Bovington, Wareham, Dorset, BH20 6JG. Tel: 01929 405096, email: archive@tankmuseum.org, (collections), or, visit@tankmuseum.org (visitors). www.tankmuseum.org. Towneley Hall Art Gallery and Museum (1902)

Towneley Holmes, Burnley, Lancs, BB11 3RQ. Tel: 01282 477130, www.townley.org.uk. Small collection including two VCs.

Warwickshire Yeomanry Museum (1981)

The Court House, Jury Street, Warwick, CV34 4EW. Tel: 01926 492212, www.warwickshire-yeomanry-museum.co.uk.

Wellington Museum

Apsley House, 149 Piccadilly, Hyde Park Corner, London, W1J 7NT. Tel: 0207 499 5676, www.wellingtoncollection.co.uk

West Midlands Police Museum (1991)

The Lock Up, Steelhouse Lane, Birmingham, B4 6NW, Tel: 0121 6091700, email: museum@west-midlands.pnn.police.uk, www.wmpeelers.com

Woodbridge, 390th Bomb Group Memorial Air Museum (1981)

Parham Airfield Museum, Parham, Framlingham, Suffolk IP13 9AF. Tel: 01728 621373, www.parhamairfieldmuseum.co.uk.

Mercian Regiment Museum (Worcestershire) (1925)

City Museum and Art Gallery, Foregate Street, Worcester. WR1 1DT. Tel: 01905 721982, www.worcestershireand mercianregimentmuseum.org

York and Lancaster Regimental Museum (1947)

Clifton Park and Museum, Clifton Lane, Rotherham, S65 2AA. Tel: 01709 336633.

Yorkshire Air Museum and Allied Air Forces Memorial

Halifax Way, Elvington, York, YO41 4AU. Tel: 01904 608595, www.yorkshireairmuseum.org.

The information included in this Directory is correct at the time of going to press. Please advise us on 01404 46972 or email: info@tokenpublishing.com should any of the above details be incorrect.

INDEX TO MEDAL NEWS

The following is the Cumulative Subject Index to the **MEDAL YEARBOOK**'s parent magazine **MEDAL NEWS**, commencing with the March 1989 issue, when it split from **COIN & MEDAL NEWS** to become a separate publication, and running to the summer of 2023—the index is updated in this **YEARBOOK** every year,

MEDAL NEWS was born in 1981 from the amalgamation of *Medals International* and *Coins & Medals*, into the popular title *Coin & Medal News*. However, the success of this magazine and the continuing growth of both the coin and the medal collecting hobbies prompted the separation of the two sections in March 1989. Since then both *Coin News* and **MEDAL NEWS** have grown from strength to strength and today are the hobby's leading publications, not only in the UK but **MEDAL NEWS** is the only independent magazine in the world devoted to the collecting and study of medals, battles and the history of heroes.

Many issues of **MEDAL NEWS** are still available for purchase at £5 per issue inclusive of postage—some of the earlier magazines may not be available to buy in their entirety but we may be able to provide photocopies of articles for readers. Please enquire whether we have the issue you are interested in before placing an order. Subscribers to **MEDAL NEWS** are able to access digital copies (from September 2007) of the magazine on-line for free, as long as their subscription is active. Simply log on to your account and find them all under "digital magazines" (earlier issues are pdf only, later ones give an option of downloadable pdf or reading them on-line as a "flip book"). .

NOTES

References are indicated **year, month, page**, for example 0404.18 means April 2004 issue, page 18; 0606.24 means June/July 2006 issue, page 24; 1101.12-14 means December 2010/January 2011 issue, pages 12 through 14. As a rule the early pages (06-08) shown are "news" pages which will only carry a small piece on the relevant subject. Later pages e.g. 20-23/33-36 etc. will indicate an article where the subject indexed is mentioned a number of times or where it/they are the main subject of the article. Please note that it has not been possible to index every medal group or recipient highlighted in the "Market Scene" section, however, medal groups/recipients of importance (Victoria Crosses, George Crosses, medals for famous actions etc.) that appear in the news section will be indexed.

Each year runs from December/January to November. For example the year 2012 includes the December 2011/January 2012 issue which is indexed thus 1201/xx (n.b. there are 10 issues per annum). The June/July issue is normally indexed as 06 with August as 08 (number 07 is therefore omitted) however, there was initial confusion over this with the original third-party indexer (the task is now done in house) so once again please check before ordering an issue.

Names of ships are indicated in italics.

Names of people have been included where they appear to be the major subject of an article or where more than trivial information is included.

Abbreviations used:
(cr)   Indicates the inclusion of a full or partial casualty list.
(mr)   Indicates the inclusion of a medal roll.
(nr)   Indicates nominal roll.
(i)   Indicates that the reference gives information rather than the object itself. For example it tells you where to find a medal roll rather than reproducing the roll itself.
(p)   Indicates that the reference is to a picture of a person or object where little or no other information is given.
(mp)   Same as (p) except that the picture is of medals.
(br)   Indicates Book Review.
(obit)   Indicates an obituary or death notice with reasonable detail.

The index is not exhaustive but it has been compiled with a view to aid research; however, despite our best efforts there will be errors and omissions, and items indexed that readers feel were not worthy of such, and for those we apologise in advance.

To order back issues contact us (Token Publishing Ltd) at the address on page 1.

7th Hussars 1202.21-23
12th Lancers 1510.24-26
13 Stationary Hospital Pinetown Bridge 0310.31-32
Col. Reginald Applin DSO OBE Lancashire Fusiliers 1311.19-21
    1401.27-29 & 1402.25-27
Baker, family heirlooms of Armr. Sgt. Alf 0205.26
Battle of Diamond Hill (nr) 0109.24-26
Bearcroft, Captain 0811.26-28
Belmont, battle of (cr) 9911.18-21
Bingley, Shoeing-Smith Arthur 0106.28-29
Border Scouts 0606.17-19
Boyd, John, Gordon Highlanders 0206.41-42
Buller's back road into Ladysmith (cr) 0002.18-21
Burne Lt at Colenso 0811.26-28
Cape Government Railways, 0803.17-19
Captain (later Major General Sir) Neville Howse VC , NSW Army
    Medical Corps 1706.24-27
"Clasp-less" medals to Conductors (mr) 0901.24-26
Colbeck, Lt C.E.B. RN 0903.20-23
Colenso, Saving the guns at 0608.28-31
Coulson, Lt Gustavus Hamilton Blenkinsop, VC 0303.25-26
Defence of Kimberley 1208.21-24 & 2105.17-20
Devonshire Regiment, Lt Walker and the charge at Wagon Hill (cr)
    0506.18-19
Devonshire Regiment, Pte John Manning 0509.23-25
Disaster at Helvetia. (cr) 1204.31-33
Double Issue of QSA to Trooper W.B. Wood S. Rhodesia Volunteers
    & Kitchener's F.S 1905.21-22
Erasmus, J.L.P., Commandant, 0106.28-29
Fairbrother, Cpl B., RFA, QSA to, 0205.18-19
Gordon Highlanders 0801.24-26
Gunner Isaac Lodge VC. 1702.19-20
Haig, Lt Douglas 7th Hussars 1202.21-23
HMS Hermes 2107.21-22
HMS Terpsichore 2107.21-22
Holland, Lt. H. H., 0811.26-28
Imperial Hospital Corps 9906.20-21
Imperial Light Horse 0903.20-23
James MacLellan Bett, Northumberland Fusiliers 1111.21-23 &
    1201.17-19
Jones, Captain E. P., 0811.26-28
Kimberley, siege of and 'Long Cecil' 9908.24-26
Kraaipan Train Incident (nr) 2109.28-30
Kroomen in the 0306.26-27
Leicestershire Imperial Yeomanry (pic) 1202.21-23
Livery Companies of the City of London in 0305.32
Manchester Regt at Caesar's Camp (cr) 0010.26-27
Medals, Medal Rolls and casualty lists 0502.15-16
Military Memorabilia of 0302.22
National Fire Brigades Union Ambulance Department 0206.24 & 60
Naval activity 9108.19-22
New Zealand Mounted Rifles 0304.30-33
    1st New Zealand Mounted Rifles (mr) 0301.14-17
Nicholson's Nek (cr) 0201.26-27
Northumberland Fusiliers 1111.21-23 & 1201.17-19
Nursing during 0310.31-32
One man's account Pte Edward Hammett 0103.18-19
Okiep (1902) 9108.21-22
O'Reilly, Bill 0001.20-21
Project Bibiography (i) 9403.05
Prothero, Captain 0811.26-28
Provisional Transvaal Constabulary (nr) 0906.19-20
QSAs to Lord Strathconas's Horse (mr) 0206.19-20
Railway Pioneer Regt. 0711.31-32
Raised date QSAs (mr) 1906.25-29
RAMC at Siege of Kimberley 1502.28-30
Royal Garrison Artillery Volunteers 0408.29
Royal Horse Artillery 1105.19-21
Royal Marines (cr) 0201.22-25
Royal Marines in, update 0304.29
Royal Navy 0811.26-28 & 1911.27-30
Sanna's Post, Saving the guns at 0208.25-26
Schofield, diary extracts of Frederick William 0009.28-29
Somerset Light Infantry 0108.18-20
South Australia connections 1511.22-24
South Lancashire Regt. 0208.33-34
Star (proposed) 9502.20
Talana, battle of (1899) (mr) 9909.24-26 & 9910.23-26
Town Guards in 0309.20-21
Volunteer Company 1st Battn. Leicestershire Regt. (nr) 0810.28-29
Volunteer Service Companies 9104.15-17
William Croucher "Kilimanjaro" West, Prince of Wales' Light Horse
    1906.21-23
Yorkshire Regiment DCMs (mr) 1106.26-29
Yorkshire Regiment Wittebergen Clasp (mr) 1106.26-29
Young, Sgt Maj A., VC 0106.28-29
Boer War, First,: Private J Bedford 2/21 Foot (Royal Scots Fusiliers) at
    Potchefstroom, 0501.44-46
Boffey, Colour-Sergeant Thomas RMLI Northern Patrol, 10th Cruiser
    Squadron 0901.35-37 and 0902.32-34
Bogdan Khemelnitsky, Order of (USSR) 9409.17-19
Boisleaux St Marc, 1st Battalion Grenadier Guards and 4th Machine

Gun Guards at, 1918 (cr) 1804.23-26
Boisragon, Lt VC Hunza-Nagar Campaign 1610.15-18
Bolshevik Alliance with Germany, 1918. Captain William Francis
    Richardson, 2101.39-40
Bolton, Ernest: served Four different countries (1891-1919) 9511.15
Bomb Disposal: Germany (1946) 9412.19
Bomb disposal: Northern Ireland 0102.25-27
'Bomb Disposal and the British Casualties of WWII' Chris Ransted (br)
    0601.49
Bomb disposal, World War II 0706.39-40
'Bombardment: The Day the East Was Bled' Mark Marsay (br) 0010.35
03/ Bombay Light Cavalry: Persian Gulf (1856-57) 9502.13-14
    Lt John Grant Malcolmson VC. 1802.40
18/ Bombay Native Infantry: Abyssinia (1868) 9502.14
Bombay Grenadiers: Somaliland (1903-04) 9006.15
Bombay Pioneers: Somaliland (1903-04) 9006.15
Bomber Command
    1944 0110.24-25
    aircraft loss reports (nr) 9410.15-17
    Sqdn Ldr Robert Anthony Maurice Palmer VC, DFC* AE. RAFVR
        1901.43-45
    WWII 9208.14-15
Bomber Command Clasp announced 1302.06
Bomber Command Clasp Controversy 1604.07
Bomber Command Clasp Criteria 1304.06
Bomber Command Medal designs. 2301.33
Bomber Command Memorial unveiled 1208.07 Bomber Command,
    Herbert Henry Sandford OBE, DFM 0501.47-48
Bomber Command Medal: overseas entitlement 9112.28
Bomber Command Memorial 0901.07 and 1106.07
Bond, Brian (edit) 'War Memoirs of Earl Stanhope 1914-1918' (br)
    0711.41
Bond James, Canadian Navy 0105.26-27
Bond, Walter, Canadian Navy 0105.26-27
Bonner, Ralph 1906.34-37 Bonner, Robert 'Great Gable to Gallipoli'
    (br) 0506.51
Bonnett , Chris & Mike Wilson 'The Great War Heroes of Bridlington'
    (br) 1302.47
Bonnici, Paolo AM 0905.18
Bonnievale Mine, Western Australia 0106.44-45
Booker, Col. G.E.N. CBE 0808.24-26
Booth, Colour Sgt Booth VC Effects sold 1410.08
Booth, Henry, Col. Sgt. 80th Foot: Ntombe River (1879) 8906.16-18
Booth, Lt-Col Henry at Gate Pa (NZ) 0610.36-38
Booth, Sgt Roy Cedric 2203.37-40 11/Border Regiment. Frankfort
    Trench. 1916 2102.23-26 (nr)
Border Mounted Rifles: Wagon Hill (1900) (cr) 9306.14-18
Border Regt
    at Gallipoli 1915' (br) 0306.51
    badges
    Cap badges 9711.26-27
    Frankfort Trench. 1916 2102.23-26 (nr) & 1916 2102.23-26 (nr)
    Lonsdale Battn WWI 9012.22
    Musician 9403.24
    Officer's 9710.30-31, 9711.26-27
    Roll of Honour, Kendal 1305.19
    Territorial Battn 9108.25-26
    Volunteer Bttn. 9710.30-31, 9711.26-27
Border scouts, South Africa, Boer War 0606.17-19
Borneo,1965 Australian National Servicemen 0001.16-17
Borneo, Japanese Invasion 1709.31-34
Borneo and Malay Peninsula to GSM 1962 clasps and Malaya and
    Brunei clasps to GSM 0510.37-38
Boronia Rail crossing 0908.36-37
Borton, Richard E. , Capt SS Vyner Brooke: MBE (1942) 9504.12
Boscawen, HMS 2107.37-39
Bosely, J., Pte 19/Hussars: DCM (1884) 8906.19
Bosnia, duty in 0202.23-25 Bosnia Medal: debate re eligibility
    9612.13-14
Bostock, Andrew, Look Who's Talking 1901.10
Boucher, Albert Boucher 16th Welsh 1209.31-32
Boulton: Trafalgar Medal 9705.20-21 (entitlement)
Bounton, Lt Charles RN Gallipoli 1109.17-20
Bounty, HMS. Capt William Bligh, medals sold 1109.06
Bouque, Simone: SOE French Sect 9303.20-21
Bourbon, Isle of 1603.40
Bourlon Woods. World War I Victoria Cross action. 2008.32-35
Bourne, Henry, Lt RN: NGS (p) 9512.06
Bourne, Pte Frederick 2/DCLI 2005.27-29
Boustead, Hugh 0206.34-35
Bovington Tank Museum 0105.22-23
Bowden, Asst. Surgeon A.G 1509.27-29
Bowder, Asst. Surgn. Arthur George, IMD 2211.24-26
Bowen, Robert; a 'Colonial' Soldier in World War I 0204.20
Bower, Tom 'Heroes of World War II' 9508.19
Bowie, Fl Off. John Graham 2203.37-40
Bowler, Captain Thomas. Royal Flying Corps late Dorsetshire
    Regiment. 1802.26-27
Bowman, J.A. 'Pickelhaube Vol 2' (br) 9208.26
Bowman, Major James 1/Gurkha Rifles 1104.06
Bowman, Martin 'The Immortal Few' (br) 1101.51
Bowman, Pte. 3rd Cavalry Brigade at Ypres, 21202.28-30 (cr)

Broom, Mrs Albert. Photographic collection 0903.09
Brotherhood of Locomotive Firemen and Enginemen – Bronze Tribute
 award (nr) 0011.20
Brothers, Air Commodore Peter Malam DSO DFC* Medals at Auction
 2103.08 & 2108.08
'Brothers in Arms' James Holland, (br) 2204.44
Brown, Able Seaman Richard Albert 1608.27-29
Brown, Captain Eric "Winkle"CBE, DFC Medals for Sale 1611.06
Brown, Captain Eric "Winkle" (obit) 1604.08 & Medals for sale 1611.06
Brown, Captain Roy, 3 Squadron AFC & the Red Baron 1901.30-32
Brown, Colin 'Scum of the Earth – What Happened to the Real British
 Heroes of Waterloo?' (br) 1510.44
Brown, F.C., AB Beryl: MID WWII 9609.23
Brown, Paul and Edwin Herbert 'The Secrets of Q Central' (br) 1506.49
Brown, Sq Ldr Ken CGM (obit) 0304.06
Brown, Malcolm 'The Imperial war Museum Book of the Somme' (br)
 9706.24
Brown, P., Gnr RMR: killed Ohio (1942) 9602.25
Brown Pte Stephen Ernest, KRRC 0608.24-25
Browne, General Sir Sam VC 1602.40
Browne, Harold RN. 2203.33-36
Browne, Major Francis Frye Army Gold Medal for Guadaloupe, 1501.34
Browne, Sidney, Dame QAIMNS (p) 9609.09
Browning-Smith, Sgn-Captain Sydney CMG Chitral Campaign
 1611.21-24
Bruce, Apothecary Samuel Barwick, Military General Service Medal
 1306.25-27
Bruce, Captain Charles RFA 2010.15-16
Bruce, Lt-Col. E; Inkerman 0704.15-16
Bruce, Lt M.N Yorkshire Regt. Suvla 1915 (p) 1508.23-25
Brudenell, Lt-Col James Thomas. 7th Earl of Cardigan 2201.21-23
Brunei General Service Miniature Medals 1502.42
Brunei General Service Miniature Medals 1502.42 Brunei: operationsin,
 1962 9804.13
Brunei General Service Miniature Medals 1502.42 BSAC Medal Sgt
 G.R. Tapp, Matabeleland Defence Force 1205.21-23
Brunei and Malaya clasps to GSM and GSM 1962 clasps Borneo and
 Malay Peninsula 0510.37-38
Brunei: scuttled (1942) 9504.13
Brunei, Sultanate of. Miniature Medals 2008.41 BSAC Natal 1906
 0711.15-17
Buchanan, Private A MM Singapore 1943 0501.32-34
Buckland, "Sir Anthony 1604.06
Buckingham, William F. 'Verdun 1916: Deadliest Battle of the First
 World War' (br) 1609.44
Buckman, Richard 'The Royal Sussex Regiment Military Honours
 and Awards 1864-1920' (br) 0205.35
Buchanan, Capt G.H.L KSLI 2206.17-18
Buchanan, Cecil Douglas, Polar Medal George VI 8904.11-13
Buck, Frederick and Captain Henry Percy, Royal Fusiliers 1308.16-18
 & 1309.17-19
Buckingham Palace Co: badge 9105.25
Buckinghamshire Yeomanry (Royal Buckinghamshire Hussars): Badges
 9712.28
Bucknall, Sgnmn Robert P RN 2006.37-38
Budd, Cpl Bryan VC 0702.03 and 06
Budgen, Marcus 1706.17-18, 1806.06 & 1809.06
Buffetaut, Yves 'The Battle of Verdun' (br) 0801.47
Buffs The,
 at Albuera 2310.16-17
 badges 1308.40-42
 on Melville Island, Northern Australia 1824 1704.17-19
 tropical helmet badge 9405.22
Buie, Gunner Robert & the Red Baron 1901.30-32
Bujak, Philip 'The Bravest Man in the British Army' (br) 1901.52
Bulge, Battle of; Britain's part in 0709.35-37
Bulkeley, John D., Lt US Navy Torpedo boats WWII 9112.13
Bull, Stephen 'The Old Frontline: The Centenary of the Western Front in
 Pictures' (be) 1704.44
Bullecourt, Australians at 2204.31-34
Bullen Farm, Battle of the Marne 0304.21-23
Buller, General sir Redvers at Colenso 0608.28-31
Buller, Redvers 0804.19-21
Buller, Redvers; back road into Ladysmith (cr) 0002.18-21
Buller, Sir Redvers VC (Statue) 2102.05, 2104.06 & 2105.38
Bullock, Jim. Medal to be sold at Dominic Winter 2111.08
Bullock, Jim, Romsey medals (p) 9505.06
 retirement 1810.
 (obit) 1906.08
Bulwark, Aden 1960s 0902.27-28
Bulwark, HMS. 2305.30-31
Bulwark sinking (1914) (cr) 9109.15-17
Bumstead Pte Benjamin 73rd Regt. Waterloo 1503.28-30
Bunce Don, CGM Fleet Air Arm and the Bismarck, Scharnhorst and
 Gneisenau 0011.15-16
Bunton, Edward George 2109.25-27
Bunton, J., Pte: medal group (mp) 9610.09
'Bunyan Meeting History: Padre W.J Coates- Letters from the Front'
 Nicola A.Serhod and Neil E. Allison (br) 1605.44
Burant, Alec B., Capt SS Kinta: MBE (1942)
 9504.12-13

Burgess, George KSLI & RN 0705.31-33
Burgess, Wat RN 0705.31-33
Burgess, William "Bill" 0705.31-33
Burgon, Robert, Berwick on Tweed Lifeboat (p) (mp) 9411.07
Burke, John William 1411.20-21
Burke, Joseph. General. US Civil War 1501.43-47
Burke, Lt Bernard Hamilton 68th Light Infantry (DLI) 1411.20-21
Burke, T, Sgt 550 Squad (1944) 9410.15-16
Burke, Thomas Hamilton 1411.20-21
'Burkes Peerage and Gentry: World Orders of Knighthood and Merit'
 Guy Stair Sainty and Rafal Heydel-Mankoo (br) 0709.41
Burma Campaign WWII 1101.44-46
Burma Campaign WWII II 2/Welch Regt 1602.28-31
Burma Hills, a pioneer in and the IGS 1854 0005.23-25
Burma
 (1890) KRRC (mr) 9312.15-18
 Kangaw WWII (nr) 0609.37-39
 WWII 9004.11-12, 9008.20
Burma Gallantry Medal 9202.26
Burma Railway POW: Pte. Stanley Evans, 2103.28-33-35
Burma-Siam Railway 0711.38
Burma Star Association. 1901.35-37 & & 1902.33-35
Burma Star: ribbon 8908.26
Burman, Phil (obit) 1702.06
Burne, Lt. at Colenso 0811.26-28
Burnell, Tom 'The Carlow War Dead' (br) 1110.43
Burnet, George Peninsular War 0104.16-17
Burnet, Sister Amy TFNS 1504.28-30
Burney, Christopher SOE 2201.44-46
Burns, David, Lt Col: OBE citation 9509.12
Burns, Robert J., Lt Cmdr Melbourne: George Medal 9404.18
Burridge, Quartermaster George 1904.33-34
Burrows, Brig. Gen. G.R.S. Girishk 1880 1511.17-20
Burslem, John Godolphin New Zealand War 2107.24-27
Burslem, Nathaniel Godolphin VC 2107.24-27
Burton, Captain William Adolphus. Charge of the Heavy Brigade
 0910.19-21
Burton, Elizabeth J.: sons & Indian Mutiny 9205.21-22
Burton, Percy Charles MM 0109.22
Burton, Richard F.: Nile explorations 9312.21-22
Burton, Richard DSC, RM. 9902.20-21 (mr)
Busaco, battle of (1810) 8906.11
Busby Capt. R.L. 2/8th Lancashire Fusiliers 1202.35-38
Bush End, Herts, War Memorial (nr) 1505.28-31
Bush, George J. RN: Zeebrugge (1918) 9104.19-20
Bush, Ivor (obit) 1408.08
Bush, Pte.William; Grenadier Guards, Court Martial.0710.19-20
Bush, WPS Ethel GM 1701.44-45
Bushire (Persian Gulf) (1856): 3rd Bombay Light Cavalry 9502.13
Bushranger's Medal 1104.18-21
Butcher, RSM Frederick Charles, 7/Dragoon Guards, Tel-El-Kebir (pic)
 1108.21-23
Butler, Captain John Fitzhardinge VC 0908.21-22
Butler, Detective Chief Superintendent Tommy MBE. Criminal Intel-
 ligence Department, New Scotland Yard 2107.46-47
Butler, Pte W.A.J Hereford R/KSLI. 2204.35-36
Butler, Roy (obit) 2301.09
Butler, Simon 'The War Horse: The Tragic Fate of A Million Horses
 Sacrificed in the First World War' (br) 1109.43
Butson, George GC (obit) 1505.07
Butt, Sir Alfred; Medallion to VC recipients 0110.22
Buttery, David 'Waterloo: Battlefield Guide' (br) 1410.43
Buttery, David 'Wellington Against Junot: The First Invasion of Portugal
 1807-1808' (br) 1201.51
Button, Sjt Joseph. 9th Foot. Peninsular War. Military General Service
 Medal 1501.21-23
Buxton, D. ' Honour to the Airborne, Pt I 1939-48' (br) 9504.22
Buying Medals. Caveat Emptor 0903.16-17
Byers, Senior Chief Edward US Navy Seal Medal of Honor 1603.07
Byford, CSjt Frederick MSM 1509.23-25
Bygones, Torquay 2309.17-18
Byng, J.H.G, Field Marsh. (p) 9511.07
Byrd Antarctic Expedition 0909.39-40
Byrne, Sera. London Marathon 1904.06
Byrne, Thomas, Pte, 21st Lancers: VC (p) 9602.08
Byrne, Pte T VC 21st Lancers. Medals sold 1508.08
Bythesea, Rear Admiral John VC; VC Sold 0706.06
Bywater, Richard Arthur Samuel GC (obit) 0506.22

- C -

Cabul Medal (1842): naming 9003.22
Cabrit, NATO Operation 2301.06
Cadet Forces Medal (1950): ribbon 8909.26
Cadet Norfolk Artillery Service Medal. Jack Motts 1406.32-33
Caen, 1944 0808.31-33
Caernarvon Castle: battle with Thor WWII 8906.22
Caesar's Camp (1900) (cr) 9306.14-18
Caffyn, Frederick, Capt Dunera: OBE WWII 9504.19
Caine, William 17th Foot 0311.14-16
Cairns, Sgt Hugh DCM– Canadian Expeditionary Force 0511.29

Lashly, William, ldg Stoker: Antarctic Expeditions 9402.17-19
Lassen, Anders VC 0109.29-30
Lassen, Anders, VC MC and two bars 0708.27-28
Lassen, Brigadier Peter DSO (obit) 0408.07
Latham, Captain Matthew 1/3rd (the East Kent) Regiment of Foot, 1408.37
Latham, Lt Matthew, The Buffs at Albuera 2310.16-17
Latvia, Russian soldiers reburied 1205.17
Lauder, Pte David Ross VC 1/4th Royal Scots 2107.28-30
Lavery, B. 'Nelson's Navy' (br) 9010.20
Law, Gerald. RAF 1703.41
Lawrence. 2/Lt Frank Helier 1/Gloucestershires 1108.37-38
Lawrence, Captain James War of 1812 1211.21-22
Lawrence, T.E.: as AC Shaw 9111.21
Lawrence, T.E., brother of 1108.37-38
Lawrenson, E., SPR RE 9208.13
Lawson, Lt Charles Indian Volunteers 1310.28-30
Lawson, Major General Richard, Congo 1962 0609.28
Lawson Pte Claude and the Anzac Artillery at Gallipoli, 0401.27-30
Lawson, Richard G., Royal Tank Regt: Congo DSO 9408.10-11
Lawyers at War 2110.17-19
Lay, Lt. Tudor 15th Bengal Native Inf. 2110.17-19
LCI see Landing Craft, Infantry
Le Cateau; Saving the Guns 0401.24-25
le Chene, Evelyn 'Silent Heroes: Bravery & Devotion of Animals in War 9503.20
Le Geyt, Alice Bell: RNLI Medal 8905.21
Le Marchant, Major Thomas. Charge of the Heavy Brigade 0910.19-21
Leach, Edgar, 2nd lt 2/Manchester 9309.26
Leach, Gnr Robert RA 1203.31-33
Leach, Pte E. Derbyshire Yeomanry 1208.26-28
League of Mercy, the Badge of the, miniature medals 1705.45
Leakey, L/Cpl Joshua VC 2101.17-19
Leander: Albania (1946) 9008.16-17
Leander, HMNZ 1909.33-36
Leasowe Castle, HMT Ned 2205.27-30
Lee, Christopher, Medals sold 1801.06
Lee, Fireman George 1506.21-24
Lee Flt Lt H.A. Battle of Britain 0009.16-19
Lee, General Robert E. 2101.48-50, 2102.30-31 & 2103.40-42
Lee, Harriet; Grenadier Guards 0605.18-19
Lee, James "Scotty"; 61 Tunnelling Company South African Engineers 0711.34-36
Lee, Joseph, Surgeon (mp) 9402.09
Lee, Major Clifford Harry RAMC 2302.25-27
Lee, Pte Thomas 20th Hussars 1406.29-31 Leech, Henry James AM, R101 Airship Disaster. Medals sold 1205.06
Leek, Alan 'Frederick Whirpool VC: The Hidden Victoria Cross' (br) 1911.44
Lees, Jonnie GM (obit) 0304.07
Leeds Pals: badge WWI 9012.22
Leefe-Robinson, William Lt RFC, VC. 9801.16-17
Legg, Captain Andrew SAS. Medals for sale 1804.08
Legget, William Richard 1910.23-24
Legion of Frontiersmen, medals to 0004.24-25
Legion d'honneur. D-Day veterans 1509.40-41
Legion of Honour (France): Napoleon's Legacy 9702.24-25
    award to surviving British veterans of WWI 9901.06
Legion of Honour Star (France) (p) 9512.07
Legion of Merit (USA): Australian awards (Vietnam) 9602.13
Legion Wallonie (German Army WWII) 9502.16-17
Leibbrandt, Meyder Johannes 2211.27-28
Leibbrandt, Sidney Robey 2211.27-28
Leicestershire Regt., 1st Battn Volunteer Company in the Boer War (nr) 0810.28-29
    badges 1208.40-42 & 1209.40-42 ,1208.40-42 & 1209.40-42
    Light infantry 0809.23-24
    Musician badges 9403.24
Leicestershire Yeomanry (Prince Albert's Own): badges 9804.26-27
Leicestershire and Derbyshire Yeomanry (Prince Albert's Own): badges 9804.26-27
Leicestershire and Derbyshire Yeomanry Badges.1701.47-49
Leigh, Chandos Maj: 2nd Battalion KOSB, Mons 9708.20-21
Leignes, John Charles Royal Humane Society Medal 2108.41-43
Leinster Regiment badges 1303.38-40
Leitch, Mr W. 2310.45
Leitch, W.: Britannia 8906.21-22, 8909.25
Leleu, Jean-Luc 'The Canadians at Falaise' (br) 0801.47
Leming, Airman Reis GM 1206.45-48
Lemon, Lt Thomas Trafalgar Clasp NGS for sale 2107.07
Lenin, Order of (USSR) 9409.15-16
Leningrad Blockade 0605.27
Lennox, Driver J P Colenso 0608.28-31
Leonard, Able Seaman. HMS Pandora 1503.18-23
Leopard, HMS War of 1812 1211.21-22
Leros, invasion of 1610.37-39
Leros Island WWII 9109.24-25
Leslie, Clr Sgt George. 71st Highland Light Infantry 1711.15-17
Lester, Frank VC to be sold 0203.07
Letham, Robert: Merchant Navy 0705.34-35

'Letters from the Forest' Peter Grant (br) 1705.44
'Letters from the Trenches: A Soldier of the Great War' (br) Bill Letts, Pte Charles. Singapore Volunteers World War II 1201.43-45
Leuk, Belgian Malinois, Dickin Medal 2107.06
Level III Gallantry awards, reassessment of 0103.15
Level 4 Gallantry emblems. Changes to. 1508.19-20
Lewes, Price Vaughan, service in Candia, Crete 0001.24-25
Lewis, Abraham World War II fireman 0505.33-34
Lewis, George Gordon 0009.24-25
Lewis, H.W., Pte Welch Regt: VC group (mp) 9402.08
Lewis Roatley HMT 1603.30-31
Lewis, Sgt David Lancashire Fusiliers, World War I 1203.18-21
Lewis, Surgeon Charles W. at Jutland, 2205.22-24
Leyland, Alfred 2309.25-27
Lhasa 1904 1701.27-29
Lhasa, Williamson mission to, 1935 0704.25-28
Li Wo, HMS 2104.38-41
Liberation of France Medal (France) 9011.23
Liberation of Norway Certificate 0602.32
Libya NATO Medal 1209.06 & 1211.08
Lichtenstein A1 Radar, RAF involvement 0504.33-34
Liddle, P.H. '1916 Battle of the Somme: a reappraisal' (br) 9303.22
Liddon, Matthew, Cmdr (c1819) (p) 9203.10
Lieut. Cdr H.D. Barlow (HMS Ladybird) Sino-Japanese Incident 1937-41 2101.44-47
'Lieutenant Colonel R.G.B. Jeffrey's Collected Letters 1916-18' Connor and Liam Dodd (eds) (br) 0806.48-49
Life Guards
    badges
    harness 9406.22-23
    tropical helmet 9405.22-23
Life Saving Medallion to E.F Openshaw 0004.28
Life Saving Awards Research Society (i) 9103.05, 9403.19
Life Saving Awards Research Society 0503.34
Life Saving Medal (US) (mp) 9509.09
Lifford, A.H.A: WWI & Police medals 9604.25
Light Brigade, Troop-Sergeant William Bentley at Balaclava 0101.27-28
Light Cavalry: badges 9410.23
11th Light Dragoons in India 2201.21-23
11th Light Dragoons in the Peninsular 2202.19-20
23rd Light Dragoons, Waterloo 0709.25-26
Light Dragoons
    at Waterloo 0401.33-35
    arm 9004.24
    badges 9305.25, 9306.22
    KGL 2002.17-18
Light Horse Regiment (AIF) 0802.21-23
Light Infantry
    85th 8910.20
    Albert Shako plates 9103.11-12
    Brigade badges 9709.27-28
Li Wo: WWII 8910.23, 9308.12-13, 9309.26
'Like Wolves on the Fold: The Defence of Rorke's Drift' M. Snook (br) 0608.41
Lillis, PO Ernest W. S. RN 0706.35-37 and 0708.21-23
Lily, Cross of the (France): miniature (mp) 9509.09
Limb, Sue & Cordingley, P. 'Captain Oates - Soldier and Explorer' (br) 9512.18
Limbu, Rambahadur, VC (obit) 2308,06
Lincoln, Lt-Cmdr. 30 Assault Unit 1810.35-37
Lincoln, Nurse Georgina June 2003.37-38
Lincolnshire Regiment: badges 9909.35-36
Lincolnshire Yeomanry: badges 9804.26-27
Lindall, H., Gnr, I Troop RHA (mp) 9602.08
Lindfield, William RN 0910.28-30
Lindi, World War I 1101.31-33
Lindop, Lt 80/Foot: Ntombe River (1879) 8906.15-17
59/ Line Infantry Regiment (France)
    Crimea 9508.15
    Italian Campaign 9508.16-17
Lindsay, Captain J.G MC 1708.31-33
Lindsay, Captain Lionel Arthur 0005.30-31
Lindsey, Dr Alton A 0909.39-40
Lindsay, Lt (later Lt Col).W.F. MC ED 1708.31-33
Linsdell, Act L/S D.H. RN 2104.34-36
Lion, HMS 0709.27-29 &1302.31-35
Liprandi: Balaclava (Crimea) 8908.15-18
Lisbon Maru Memorial 2103.06 & 2109.08
Lisbon Maru Memorial Unveiled 2111.06
Lisbon Maru, POWs on 1808.43, 1901.35-37 & & 1902.33-35
Lise Villameur SOE 0501.14
Lister, Frederick G., Capt 26 BNI: N.E. Frontier 9405.10-12
Lister Lt-Gen. George at Barasat 0603.30-31
Lister, Maurice AM Merchant Navy 2109.18-19
Litherland, A 'Standard Catalogue of Brit Orders Deorations & Medals' (br) 9104.25
Littleboy, Lt Wilfred Evelyn 1711.31-33
Littlewood Peter R 'Gallantry Awards to the Gloucestershire Regiment' (br) 0606.48

Queen Elizabeth, HMS Gallipoli 1109.17-20
Queen Elizabeth, The 1505.37-38
Queen Mary, HMS 1302.31-35
Queen Mary's Army Auxiliary Corps
  badge 9212.25
  OBE WWI (mr) 9302.15-17
Queen Victoria's Diamond Jubilee. Natal Native Horse, 1404.17-19
Queen Victoria's Visit to Ireland 1900 Miniature. 1304.41
4th Queen's Own Hussars at Vendelles 2205.25
133/ Queen's Own Light Cavalry: badge 9410.22
Queen's Ambulance Service Medal 1108.08
Queen's Commendation for Valuable Service in the Air: development
  9402.13
Queen's Commendation for Valuable Services 9410.20-21
Queen's Diamond Jubilee Medal 1108.06
Queen's Dragoon Guards
  badges 9309.23 & 1309.39-41 & 1310.39-41
  Campaign Service Medal (1962) 9009.27
Queen's Gallantry Medal to Gurkhas 1410.06
Queen's Gallantry Medal
  development 9402.14-15
  Inspector Dan Tanner 0909.36
  Miniature 1201.49
  recommendations for, concerning the Otranto Barrage (mr) 9811.20-22
  Register (i) 9004.05
  Sgt. Anthony Haw 2101.10-11
Queen's Golden Jubilee miniatures. 1206.31-33
Queen's Lancashire Regt: badges 9612.28
Queen's Long Service Medal for Ambulancemen: Thomas, Barrie
  9608.05
Queen's Messenger Badge 1002.17-18
Queen's Messenger badges and insignia 0804.37-38
Queen's Own Cameron Highlanders: tropical helmet badge 9405.23
Queen's Own Cameron Highlanders of Canada: badge 9106.27
Queen's Own Corps of Guides: badge 9410.22
Queen's Own Highlanders: piper's badge 9003.24
Queen's Own Hussars: badge 9306.23
Queen's Own Lowland Yeomanry
  badge 9210.25
  piper's badge 9003.25
Queen's Own Oxfordshire Hussars: badges 9807.25-26
Queen's Own Royal Glasgow Yeomanry: badge 9210.24-25
Queen's Own Royal West Kent Regt
  Kent County Battn badge WWI 9012.22
  Musician badge 9403.25
  Yeomanry badges 9803.26-27
Queen's Own Warwickshire and Worcestershire Yeomanry: badges
  9809.27-28
Queen's Own Royal Worcesteshire Yeomanry: badges 9809.27-28
Queen's Own Yeomanry: badges 9807.25-26
Queen's Own Yorkshire Yeomanry Badges1002.38-40
Queen's Police Medal, Special Constable Peter Smith 1402.06
Queen's Regt: badge 9412.23
Queen's Royal Irish Hussars: badge 9306.23
  9th Queens Royal Lancers, badges of 0609.31-32
Queen's Royal Irish Hussars: (mri) 9406.26
Queen's Royal Rifles: badges 9604.20-21
Queen's Royal Surrey Regt. museum 9810.22-23
Queen's Silver Jubilee Medal (1977): ribbon 8909.26
Queen's South Africa Medal 8904.08-09
  clasps 9502.20
  Double issue 1703.23-24
  ghost dates 9012.24, 9211.27, 9212.27
  Irish Hospital (mr QSA) 9405.16-17
  and KSA 8905.05
  naming 8904.09, 9002.18, 9004.18
  Pelorus (mr) 9111.15-18
  with raised dates (mp) 9612.10
  Rifle Brigade (mr) 8904.15-18
  Spion Kop (1900) 9408.14-17
  Volunteer Co (mr) 9104.15-17
Queen's Victoria Rifles: badges 9604.20-21
Queen's Volunteer Reserves (mr) 2003.39
Queen's Volunteer Reserves Medal Miniature. 2301.50
Queen's Volunteer Service medal: First Awarded 0002.07
Queen's Westminter & Civil Service Rifles: badges 9604.20-21
Queensland Museum VC Exhibition 1003.25-26
Quetta Earthquake (1883): Joynt, Christopher 9502.14
Quetta Earthquake (1935) (mr) 9305.11-13
Quick, Asst. Surgn. Christopher Francis Henry, IMD 2211.24-26
Quick. C.F.H. 1509.27-29
Quigg, Sgt Robert VC. Statue unveiled 1608.08
Quill, Col. Humphrey 30 Assault Unit 1811.39-40
Quinn, Betty – St John's Ambulance Brigade's first George Medal
  0310.26
Quiver Medal for Heroic Conduct in the saving of life (mp) 9409.08

- R -

R101 airship 9005.08-09
R101 Airship Disaster, Captain Herbert Carmichael Irwin. Medals sold
  1205.06

R101 Airship Disaster, Henry James Leech AM. Medals sold
  1205.06
115/ Railway Company (RE): WWI 9606.14
RAAF, peacetime awards to 0111.19-20
RAC, 1914 Stars to (mr) 0408.31
Rackstraw, AB E.W. RN 2208.32-36
Racoon HMS 1604.17-18
Radcliffe, Major Derwent George St John, Green Howards
  1410.33-34
Radcliffe, Richard. Lancashire Fusiliers 1406.29-31
Radley, James 2105.33-35
Radley-Moorhouse monoplane 2105.33-35 & 2107.32-34
RAF 100 Centenary Trophy: 1808.10-11
RAF 100: Bomber Command heroism. Sqdn Ldr Robert Anthony
  Maurice Palmer VC, DFC* AE.
RAF100 1804.05 & 1806.07
RAF (Bomber Command) Herbert Henry Sandford OBE, DFM
  0501.47-48
RAF bomber pilot, Derrick Bourchier Bailey, 0209.31-32
RAF LS&GC Miniatures 1202.30
RAF Museum Hendon 0206.31-33
Rafferty, Pte Patrick MGC 1906.34-37
RAFVR 1901.43-45
Raglan, Field Marshal Lord, Medals for sale 1408.08
Rahman, Seaman Motiur 0708.18-19
Railway Operating Division (RE) 9606.14
Railway Police Bravery 1711.26-28
Railway VCs 1703.31-33
Railwaymen: served in WWI 9606.14-17, 9608.24
Railways, Cape Government. Boer War 0803.17-19
Raised date QSAs (mr) 1906.25-29
Raj, Agansing VC (obit) 0008.09
Raj, Major Harkasing 6/Gurkhas 0810.24-25
Raj, personalities of 1109.26-27, 1111.32-33 & 1201.29-31
Raj Singh, Merchant Navy: Ord of Red Star (USSR) 9409.16
Raj, soldiers of the. (NAM exhibit) 9710.25
Rajputana HMS 1003.31-32
Raleigh, HMS 1711.23-25
  Boer War (pic) 0903.20-23
  at Zeebrugge 0804.26-27
Ralph, Gunner George RA St Jean d'Acre Medal 1605.40
Ram, Capt Bhandari VC (obit) 0208.08
Ram, Commander HMS Heroic 1711.18-20
Ram, Havildar Bhagrat. MM. Charmar Regt. 1702.4
Ramb I 1909.33-36
RAMC 89th Field Ambulance at Gallipoli 0106.30-31
  and the Third China War (mr) 0103.32-33
  at Siege of Kimberley 1502.28-30
  Surgical Consultants in WWI. 1904.25-27
Ramillies, HMS 1608.27-29
Ramsay, Bertram, Adm Sir: Diary (br) 9406.25
Ramsey, John, Sgt Maj RFC MC 9005.21
Ramsden, Lt. Edward. 5th Lancers (p) 1509.31-32
Ramsland, John 'The Legacy of Douglas Grant: A notable
  Aborigine in War and Peace' (br) 2004.45
Ramilles, Madagascar 1942 0901.40-43
Ranchi HMS 1003.31-32
Randall, Peter RAVC: award of George Medal 9804.22-23
'Random Shots from a Rifleman' Kincade, John Capt: (br) 9807.29
Ranjuhosho (Japan) 9002.26
Ranpura HMS 1003.31-32
Ransted, Chris 'Bomb Disposal and the British Casualties of
  WWII' (br) 0601.49
Rapid, HMS. Royal Naval Recipients of East and West Africa
  Medal (1887-8). (mr) 1808.21-24
Rapson, Victor, Ch/Sted Madura: MBE WWII 9504.19
Ratcliffe, Lt Leonard RNVR 1210.28-29
Rattey, Cpl Reginald Roy VC 0304.34-35
Rattray, David (obit) 0703.08
Ravenhill, Keith Richard 1904.37-39
Ravenhill, Pte George 0608.28-31
Raw, David 'Theodore Bayley Hardy VC, DSO, MC' (br) 1905.43
Rawnsey C.F. and Wright R. 'Night Fighter'(br) 9908.37
Ravenor, Pte Percy Villers-Cotterets September 1 1914 (cr)
  0810.35-39
Rawalpindi HMS 1003.31-32
Raweng, Awang anak GC (obit) 2011.07
Rawson, Andrew 'The Peninsular War: A Battlefield Guide' (br)
  1001.51
Rayner, Lt. Maurice Edward. 66th (Berkshire) Regt. at Maiwand
  1880 (p) 1601.26-28
Raysbrook, Robert D, Sgt 1/7 US Marines: CGM Guadalcanal
  9209.19-22, 28
Razeby, Captain E.I 1511.31-33
Read, LAC Samuel William, bomb disposal 0706.39-40
Read, Thomas, Master Mariner NGS 0701.35-37
Reay, Sarah 'The Half Shilling Curate' (br) 1806.51
Reckless, "Sergeant". Dickin Medal 1610.06
Reconnaissance Corps (mr) 9106.19-21, 9110.24
Reconnaissance Regiment, Sgt Charles Boyce DCM 0506.20-21
Recruiting in the 19th Century 9902.23-25

Sanders, 2/Lt W.J. Middx Regt. 1209.34
Sanders, Edgar "Sandy" MM LRDG 0905.32-35
Sanderson, G.E., Lt: Australian Camel Corps WWI (p) 9302.08
Sandford , Herbert Henry OBE, DFM Bomber Command 0501.47-48
Sandford, Lt R.D VC RN 0705.27-29
Sandpiper, HMS, China 1938 1101.34-37
Sandpiper, HMS Sino-Japanese Incident 1937-41 2101.44-47
Sandstette, Heinrich Operation Kondor 1210.39-41
Sanger, Sgt William, Shooting medal. 1810.19-20
Sanna's Post (1900): Q Battery RHA 8904.09
Sansom Major A.W. Field Security Service Operation Kondor 1210.39-
41
Sanson (nee Brailly, then Churchill, later Hallowes) Odette GC SOE
1409.35-36
Santa Fe. SAS on South Georgia 1903.14-15
Santo-Olalla, David, Lt Col 1/ Duke of Wellington's Regt: DSO citaion
9509.11
Sappho: Ostend (1918) 9009.27
'Sapper VCs, The': Gerald Napier (br) 9807.29
Sarah Ann: rescue (1875) 9403.18-19
Sargent, John Singer "Gassed" 1906.31-33
Sari Bair (1915)
Wellington Regt 9206.28, 9208.19-20
(cr) 9202.15-18
Sarker, Dilap 'Battle of Britain: the photographic Kaleidoscope' (br)
0003.36
Sarker Dilip 'Guards VC: Blitzkrieg 1940' (br) 9911.36
SAS; Lt Col. Robert Blair "Paddy" Mayne, DSO and three Bars 0704.37-
39
'SAS Rhodesia: Rhodesians in the Special Air Service' Jonathon
Pittaway and Craig Fourie (br) 0409.34
SAS on South Georgia 1903.14-15
Sasha, Dickin Medal for 1406.06
Sasson, Siegfried, MC withdrawn from sale 0709.07
Satellite (1894) 9310.18
Saumarez: Albania (1946) (cr) 9008.16-17
Saunders, Nicholas J and Mark R J Dennis 'Craft and Conflict:
Masonic Trench art and Military Memorabilia' (br) 0310.33
Saunders, Nicolas J. 'Trench Art: A brief history.' (br) 0203.34
Saunders, Pte William. Lancashire Fusiliers 1908.19-22
Savage, Major Frederick 68th Regiment. 1804.18-20
Savage, Pte Edward. Rorke's Drift 1108.06
Savage, W.A., AB (p) 9005.23
'Saved from the Flames: A History of the Society For The Protection of
Life From Fire' Roger Willoughby and John Wilson (br) 1301.51
Savill, Bernard Sgt: 9805.24-25
Saving Life at Sea Medal (Germany) 8903.09
Saving the Guns; Sanna's Post 0208.25-26
Saving the Guns; Maiwand, Afghanistan 1880 0209.14-15
Sawbridgeworth 0809.38-39
Sawyer, Miss. Tenterden Volunteers 1906.17-18
Scales, George; Croix de Guerre 0802.07
Scales, PRP Peter PRAW 0802.25-28
Scapa Flow, Scuttling of German Fleet 1910.27-29 & 1911.32-34
Scapa Flow: Sinking of the Royal Oak 1701.31-34
Scarab HMS, China 1938 1101.34-37
Scarab: Support at Wanhsien (1926) 9709.18-19
Scarf, Sq Ldr A.S.K "Pongo" VC. Cross Sold 2206.06
Scarf, Sq. Ldr. Arthur "Pongo" VC, export issues and appeal 2302.08,
2303.09, 2304.08 & 2306.06
Scarlett, Hon. James Charge of the Heavy Brigade 0910.19-21
Scarlett, R.J. 'The Sea Gallantry Medal' (br) 1106.49
Scharnhorst 1511.39-41 & 1806.45-47
Scharnhorst 1601.35-38 & 1602.31-33
Scharnhorst and the Fleet Air Arm 0011.15-16
Scharnhorst (1941) 9304.16-17
Scheldt River (1944) 8912.24-25
Shiers, Sgt. Wally AFM 0809.40-41
Schiess, Cpl Frederich VC Natal Native Contingent in the Zulu War.
1901.18-20
Schellenburg, Walter 1405.28-31
Schnorrer, Lt Karl "Quax" Luftwaffe 1406.35-36
Schoeman, Michael & Mac Eoin Bisset. 'The Register of Southern
African Airmen of the Great War 1914-1918' (br) 1811.44
Schofield, Capt (General) Harry Norton 0608.28-31
Schofield, Frederick William Yorkshire Regt (diary extracts) 0009.28-29
Schofield, Joe W., Pte Wellington Regt 9206.28
Schofield, Walter Philip: Medal of the Order of the Bristish Empire
9911.32
Scholefield, Edward R.C., RFC: DCM 9005.21
School of Musketry 1865 (nr) 0105.20
Schwarzkopf, Norman, Gen: Gulf War medals 9210.11-12
Scinde Campaign 0406.17-18
35/ Scinde Horse: badge 9410.22
Scinde Horse: badge 9410.23
Scinde Medal (1843): naming 9003.22
Scone, Heroes of:
part I 0409.21-22
part II 0410.19-20
part III 0411.30-31
part IV 0501.17-18

Scoones, Col: Quetta Earthquake 9305.12
Scorpion, HMS 2009.33-35
Scots Fusiliers of Canada: badge 9106.27
Scots Guards, badges 1302.47-49
cap 9706.25-26
foriegn service helmet 9706.25-26
officers 9706.25-26
officers 9706.25-26
Musician 9402.25
Piper's 9003.24, 9706.25-26
pouch & valise 9411.23
tropical helmet 9405.22
Scott, C.W., Act/Capt Labour Corps 9209.13
Scott, Captain Robert Falcon, medals 1302.06
Scott, DS Laurence GM 1803.35-36
Scott, Gunner Charles Herbert RN 1609.30-32
Scott, HMS. Loss of (cr) 2203.23-26
Scott, Jamie G. (CGD Rhodesia) (p) 8905.08
Scott, M. 'Ypres Salient' (br) 9303.22-23
Scott, PO Charles Herbert RN 1604.31-34
Scott, PO W.C. RN 1304.23-25
Scott, Pte John Argyll and Sutherland Highlanders (fraudulent
enlistment) 1705.40
Scott, Pte Manchester Regt: Wagon Hill (1900) 9306.14-15
Scott, Pte Thomas Arthur 2/ Border Regiment 2208.25-26 Scott, Sgt
J.P RCAF 1806.45-47
Scott-Amundson Centenary Race 1204.14-15
Scott's Antarctic Expedition: Harry Pennall RN. 0705.37-39
Scottish Division; Battle for Ghent, September 1944 0602.17-20
Scottish Division; Normandy, August 1944 0506.34-36 and 0511.34-
36
Scottish General Hospital, 2nd: Piper's badge 9003.25
Scottish Horse: badge 9210.24-25
Scottish Rifles
badge 9511.22-23
Scotty's Little Soldiers 2308.09
Spion Kop (1900) (cr) 9408.14-17
Scottish Yeomanry Regts: badges 9209.24-25, 9210.24-25
Scott's Antarctic Expedition: Harry Pennall RN. 0705.37-39
Scout, HMS. Sudan Medals to the Royal Navy 1904.18-19
Scout Memorial, Nelson, Lancashire 1303.21-22
Scouts: Edward George Mortiboy 0908.36-37
'Scum of the Earth – What Happened to the Real British Heroes of
Waterloo?' Colin Brown (br) 1510.44
Scurfield, Commader B. G.. DSO, OBE, RN Spain 1936-39 2303.34-
37
Scuttling of German Fleet 1910.27-29 & 1911.32-34
Scuttling of German Fleet June 1919 2111.47-49.
Scrope, Major Conyers Green Howards 1410.33-34
Seaborne Observers WWII 8904.26
Seaforth Highlanders (I Btn) Spottiswoode, Lt A.A. 0008.22-23
Seaforth Highlanders
1st 8903.12-13
(mr DCM/MSM) (i) 8903.13
badges 9506.22-23
Territorial Battn 9108.25-26
tropical helmet 9405.23
Indonesia (1945-46) 9005.17
Seaforth Highlanders of Canada: badge 9106.27
Sea Gallantry Medal 2204.18-20
naming 9002.18
to soldiers 9406.25
Seagar, Edward, Lt Gen (p) 9311.09
Sea-Gladiators, Malta WWII 9008.18-19
Norway WWII 9402.20
Seagrim, Cyril, RE WWII 9406.20
Seagrim, Derek A., Lt Col 7/Green Howards: VC 9406.20-21
Seagrim, Hugh P., Maj 19/Hyderabad Regt 9406.20-21
Seagrim, Jack, 2/Punjab Regt 9406.20
Seaman, Robert John: Award of GM 9807.06
Sear, Pte. Henry; Grenadier Guards, Court Martial.0710.19-20
Sebastiano Vero, loss of (nr) 0303.32-34
Second Balkan War 1801.44-45
'Secret Letters from the Railway' Brian Best (br) 0509.43
Secret Service Bureau (SSB) 1106.23-24
Secunderbagh, Storming of 2301.28-32 & 2304.16-19
Seedie rating titles RN 9106.17
'Seedie's List of awards to the Merchant Navy for World War II' (br)
Chatterton, Bill 9711.30
Seely, Ord. Sea. James HMS Pandora 1503.18-23
Seeley, Ordinary Seaman William VC 0610.31-32
Seigne, Louis J.L., R. West Kent/10 Fus 9004.15-17
Seiss, Kapitanleutnant Gustave U-73 1711.18-20
Seligman, Adrian, Lt Cmdr RNVR (WWII) 8908.25
Sell, Ethel Elemer. London Fire Brigade, WWI. (mr) (cr) 1806.31-35
Sell, Frederick Charles. London Fire Brigade, WWI. (mr) (cr) 1806.31-
35
Sell, Harold Sydney. Durham Light Infantry, World War II 1201.37-38
Sell, Winifred. London Fire Brigade, WWI. (mr) (cr) 1806.31-35
Sells, Lt Clement Perronet MC RAMC 1704.28-29
Sellwood, Henry, Boatswain Beryl: DSC WWII 9608.16-17, 9609.23

Serbia, 1915 British Naval Mission in (nr) 0306.41-43
Serbia, British Naval Mission to 1915 (nr) 0706.29-31
Serbian Gold Medal for Zeal. 1810.38
Serhod, Nicola A. and Neil E. Allison 'Bunyan Meeting History: Padre W.J Coates- Letters from the Front' (br) 1605.44
Seringapatam Medal 1799 0603.33-35 & 1301.30
    and the Tiger of Mysore 0101.14-15
Service Badges World War I 0802.34-35
Service Battalions WWI: badges 9012.21-22
Service Medal of the Order of St John, Miniatures. 1406.47
Service Medal - Regular Defence Force (Ireland) 9208.28
Service numbers in World War I, researching 0608.33-35
Service records: fakes 9102.18-19
'Services Rendered: Nominal Roll for the Silver War Badge Volume I' (br) Alan Stuart 0910.40
Settle, Pte Abner 1/Lancashire Fusiliers. Boer War 1301.22-23
Seven Years War: medals for 9608.23, 9610.26
Severn: Konigsberg (1914-15) (mr) 9205.19
Seymour, Gen. Sir Francis. 1805.14-16
Seymour, George (obit) 0501.08
Seymour, Lt. C.M. 59th Foot 2104.24-25
Seymour, Lt. Sir Albert. Lancashire Fusiliers & Middlesex Regiment 1805.14-16 & 1806.21-23
Shackleton. Sir Ernest. Medals to be sold 1510.06 & 1511.06
Shakespear, Major H.A. 5th Bengal Cavalry Afghanistan 1880 2202.22-24
Shako plates 9103.11-12
    Infantry 9208.24-25
    militia 9211.24-25
Shanghai and Hong Kong in World War II 2102.36-37
Shanghai Municipal Council Emergency Medal 1404.23-26
Shanghai Volunteer Corps Long Service Medal 9304.28, 9305.27
Shankland, Robert VC 43rd Canadian Infantry. Valour Road 1302.42-43
Shanks, Arthur Hutton 0008.28-29
Shannon: Indian Mutiny 9302.12-13
    HMS War of 1812 1301.15-17
Shannon, Major William 1811.18-20
Shannon, Major William Boyd Yorkshire Regt. Suvla 1915 1508.23-25
'Sharks among Minnows' Norman Franks (br) 0203.34
Sharpe, phil ' To Be a Chindit' (br) 9509.07
Sharrad's Stone, update 1702.07 & 1710.06
Shaw, Murray (obit) 1904.08
Shea, Pte 28th foot. Retreat to Corunna 1409.38
Shebbeare, Brevet Captain Robert VC 2301.24-26 & 2304.25-27
Shearer, Susan J., Sgt: QGM Northern Ireland 9611.03
Sheehan, John. 'Harrogate Terriers: The 1/5th Territorial Battalion West Yorkshire Regiment in the Great War.' (br) 1809.44
Sheehan, L/Cpl Albert Frederick MM 16/Rifle Brigade 1606.30-32
Sheean, Ord. Seaman Teddy RAN Victoria Cross award 2009.06
Sheffield, HMS 1606.35-38
Sheffield Pals: badge WWI 9012.22
Sheldon, Harry, 8/Gurkha Rifles WWII 9304.18-19
Sheldon, Capt H. Harry, war artist (obit) 0205.07
Shenandoah, CSS 1401.31-33
Shepherd, Brig-Gen Gordon DSO, MC, RFC, RAF 0006.32-33
Shepherd, Peter, Surgeon Major: Isandlwana 9102.13-14
Shepherd Memorial Medal for Surgery 9102.13
Shepherd, Lt Samuel John RM. George Cross 1501.06
Shepherd, Ruth 'Extraordinary Heroes' (br) 1110.43
Sheppard, S.H., Capt RE: Gyantse Fort (1904) 9404.21
Sheppard, Tony Durham Light Infantry in Korea (mr) 1606.41-43
Shepstone's Native horse: Isandhlwana (1879) 9008.11-13
Sherbrooke, Captain R. St V. VC RN (p) 1606.35-38
Sheridan, Colour-Sergeant (later RSM) John. 19th Regiment of Foot 2201.25-26
'Sherman Tank: A Pocket History' John Christopher (br) 1209.43
Sherwood Foresters at Neuve Chapelle 1801.32-35
Sherwood Foresters Territorial Battn: badge 9108.25-26
Sherwood Rangers at Scimitar Hill August 1915 0603.24-26
Shiers, Walter H., Act Sgt Australian Flying Corps: London to Australia flight (1919-20) 9509.16-17, 22
Shimell, Gunner Reginald Bertie RFA 1710.31-33
Shimoneski, Japan storming of 0610.31-32
Shipley Memorial. 2/Lt. Edgar Marsden Kermode DSO, MC* DCM. 1806.28-29
Shipp, Pte. 3rd Cavalry Brigade at Ypres, 21202.28-30 (cr)
Ships Badges various 0106.47
Shipwrecked Fishermen and Mariners Royal Benevolent Society Gold Medal sold. Captain William Morris 1404.07
Shipwrecked Fishermen and Mariners Royal Benevolent Society (SFMRBS) Silver Medal 1205.25-27
Shires, Private Harry 42nd Royal Highlanders. 1903.18
Sinclair, Air Vice Marshall Laurence (obit) 0208.08
Shields Corporal Robert, retrospective award of VC 0510.42
Shipster, John 'Mist on the Rice Fields' (br) 0203.35
Shooting medals, Volunteer Force 1810.19-20
Shores, C 'Above the Trenches' (br) 9111.23
Shore. George 28th Foot 1510.17-19
Shorland, Surgeon George, Memorial All Saints Church, Westbury, Wilts 1605.24-25
Shorto, Harry George. 1904.28-30

Shot at Dawn: 2nd Lt Eric Poole. Execution of 2011.31-32
Shot at Dawn. Alfred Thomas Ansted 4/Royal Fusiliers Memorial Plaque 2202.06 & 2203.06
'Shots from the Front: The British Soldier 1914-1918 (br) Richard Holmes 0908.41
Shoulder-belt plates see badges
Shout, Alfred VC – World record sale 0609.06
Shout, Captain Alfred John VC MC at Gallipoli 0501.41-43
Shout, Captain Alfred VC MC . History 0610.25-28
Shropshire Royal Horse Artillery Volunteers 8910.20-21
Shropshire Yeomanry 8910.20-21
    badges 9808.27-28
Siam (Thailand) Victory Medal 1509.19-21
Siberia, Royal Marines in, WWI 1103.26-27
Sibley, Pte. 3rd Cavalry Brigade at Ypres, 21202.28-30 (cr)
Sicily (1943): glider operations 9204.13
    Invasion of, No 3 Commando 1206.40-41
    Invasion of (1943) 9710.23-24
Sidmouth, RAF base 2309.39 &2310.06
Siege of Badajoz. Royal Regiment of Artillery at 1604.21-23
Siege of Lucknow, Storming of Secunderbagh 2301.28-32 & 2304.16-19
Siege of Singapore 1942 1603.25-27
Siege warfare in Victorian times 9908.28-29
Sierra Leone, Royal Navy in 1710.19-21
Signal Co. R.E.: gallantry awards WWI 9302.20
Signals Intelligence WWI 9208.13
2/ Sikhs: Somaliland (1903-04) 9006.15
Silchar Track (Burma) 9103.26
Silk, Owen
    24/Foot 9109.21
    88/Foot 9109.21
Silver Gallantry Medal for Montevideo 1103.15-18
Silver, L.R. 'Heroes of Rimau' (br) 9202.23
Silver Medal for War Merit (Germany) 8912.14
Silver Sea Gallantry Medal, Coastguardsman Robert Treadwell, 1104.08
Silver Star, USA 1706.37-39
    awarded to Major the Viscount Weymouth 0602.42
    Australian awards (Vietnam) 9602.13
    Perry, AC., SBLT, Royal Australian Navy 9602.12-13
Silver War Badge 0310.34, 0604.13 & 2003.28-30
    Joseph Humpheys, RAMC. 2102.21
    Mercantile Marine (mr) 9103.16-19
    (Newfoundland) (nr) 0805.34-36
    research tips 1201.26-27 & 13.01.38-39
Silwood, Sgt Harry 5th (Royal Irish) Lancers. Bourlon Woods. 2008.32-35
Simmonds, Henry RN World War I 1301.24-27
Simmons, A.F.T, Palestine 0808.28-29
Simmons, Mark 'Agent Cicero: Hitler's Most Successful Spy' (br) 1504.43
Simmons, Mark 'Alistair McLean's War: How the Royal Navy Shaped His Best Sellers' (br) 2211.52
Simmons, Mark 'Ian Fleming and Operation Goldeneye: Keeping Spain out of World War II' (br) 1903.41
Simmons, Mark 'The Battle of Matapan 1941: The Trafalgar of the Mediterranean' (br) 1109.43
Simmons, Mark 'The British and Cyprus: An Outpost of Empire to Sovereign Bases 1878-1974' (br) 1602.44
Simmons, Tommy HMS Eagle 2001.43-45
Simmons, V.G., Revd: Jewish Chaplain WWI 9312.12-14
Simmons W. J Lt (SLI) in Iraq 1920 9910.20-21
Simon, Ship's cat of the Amethyst 0411.28-29
Simons McDonald J. Lancer & Lighhorseman 9902.17-19
Simpkin, Sergeant Albert MM 1606.28-29
Simpson, A, Cpl R.E. Malta T.F.: BEM WWII 9008.19
Simpson, Eng A.M Merchant Navy World War II 0705.35
Simpson, Geoff 'A History of the Battle of Britain Fighter Association: Commemorating the few' (br) 1604.44
Simpson, John (Jack) award of Posthumous Australian VC (news) 0102.08
Simpson, John retrospective awards 1104.07
Simpson, Myrtle. Polar Medal 1706.06
Simpson, Pte John AIF 1402.22-23
Sims, A., Lt RN HM Coastguard: NGS/Shipwreck Medals (mp) 9511.08
Sims, E.C., Sqd Ldr 11 Squad RAAF 9409.11
Sinai: clasp to Australia Service Medal (1975) 9403.11
Sinclair, Captain J.L. DSO, RD, RNR HMS Kedah 2104.38-41
Sinclair, Constable George Alexander, Metropolitan Police 2308.40-42
Singapore 1943 POWs in 0501.32-33
Singapore, Fall of 1603.25-27
Singapore and Malaya. World War II. 2103.36-38 & 2104.38-41
Singh, Beant, L/Naik Punjab Regt/SOE: MM Borneo 9104.21
Singh, Havildar Hari, Bombay Engineers 1311.35-38
Singh, Hon. Capt Umaro VC (obit) 0602.06
Singh, Kabul: Quetta Earthquake 9305.12
Singh, Lance-Naik Maieya 2010.15-16
Singh, Surjan 'They Died for All Free Men' (br) 0411.32
Sink, Pte Joseph Purple Heart 1602.16-18
Sino-Japanese Incident 1937-41 2101.44-47

Thoroton, Lt-Col Charles Julian RM 1902.25-27 Thrussell, PC Thomas, Metropolitan Police 0201.46-47
'Three "Cats", a Pigeon and 27 Brave Men of Coastal Command' Jim Carlo (br) 1911.44
Thurlby (Lincolnshire)
  Bromhead family 8908.22
  Swinderby cemetery (cr) 8908.22-23
Thrush HMS 1604.17-18
Thurston, Alfred William RN 1409.21-24
Tibet Campaign 1701.27-29
Tibet, Frederick Williamson 0704.25-27
Tibet VC, Lt (later Col) J. D. Grant 8/Gurkha Rifles, Medal at auction 1405.06. Result 1408.06
Tiger, HMS 1302.31-35
'Tigers at Dunkirk: the Leicestershire Regiment and the fall of France' Matthew Richardson (br) 1101.51
Tigress: Goeben/Breslau WWI 9302.19
Tillard, Lt Cmdr Stephen HMS Barham 2004.15-17
Time Flies Gala 1901.12-13
Timberly, Harry and the Cerberus 0405.24-25
Timbers, Brig. Ken (editor) 'The Royal Artillery Woolwich: A celebration' (br) 0905.41
Titania, HMS World War I 2103.17-21
Titterton, Pte. Francis 92nd Regiment at Majuba Hill 2310.18-20
Tobruk 1942 Royal Marines (nr) 0906.32-34
Toti, Enrico. Italian Submarine WWII 1106.42-43
Towers, Private James VC 2/Cameronians Cross for sale 2105.08
Treo, Dickin Medal 1003.06
Timor, Australians in 0505.37-40
Tinson, Lt Col Ashley (obit) 1503.08
Tinson Lt-Col Ashley 'Medals will be Worn' (br) 9910.36
Tippoo Sultan, the end of 0101.14-15
Tipu Sultan 0603.33-35
Tirah campaign: soldiers later serving WWI 9304.13
Tirol. Defenders of 1915-18 0601.34-36
Tirot Singh (Khasi Chief): N.E. Frontier (1829-32) 9405.11-12
Tirpitz 1605.33-36 & 1606.35-38
Tisdall, Major Charles Arthur (pic) 0811.30-33
Titanic: Herbert Pitman's medals to be auctioned 9808.06
  delay of launch 9805.18-19, 9810.28 see also Gracie Fields
  Medal to Carpathia 0506.24-25
18/ Tiwana Lancers: badge 9409.23
'To the Victor the spoils', Sean Longden (br) 0506.51
Tobruk, Siege of 1905.26-29
Tofler, Lt A.J MC 1708.31-33
Togoland and the Cameroons 1914-1916: KAR & WAFF 9901.15-16
Tokar, 2310.28-29
Token Publishing Ltd 25th Anniversary 0804.40
Token Publishing Ltd. 40th Anniversary timeline 2304.28-29
Tollerton, Pte Ross VC 1/Queen's Own Cameron Highlanders 1610.28-31
Tomaseli, Phil 'Givenchy in the Great War: A village on the Front Line 1914-18' (br) 1808.44
Tombs, H., Brig Gen: Dewangiri 8910.15-16
Tombs, Major (Sir) Harry VC Bengal Horse Artillery. Medals sold 1801.08
Tomlinson, Peter, Sqd Ldr RAF (WWII) (Bomber Harris' Adjutant) 9506.15
Toms, L/Cpl N.G Grenadier Guards 1401.44-46
Tongans in World War II 0209.23-24
Tongue, Private Joshua 23rd Light Dragoons 1903.16
Tonkin, John, Maj (Antarctic) 9003.12-13
Toogood, W.G., 209 Squadron WWII 9310.17
Topaze, HMS 0708.18-19
Topley, John, Pte Coldstream Guards: Inkerman 9608.18-19, 9609.16-17
Toronto Scottish: badge 9106.27
Torbay, HM Submarine 1908.25-26
Torpedo Boats WWII 9112.13
Totman, L/Cpl Cubitt MM 5th (Royal Irish) Lancers. Bourlon Woods. 2008.32-35
Toulouse: 15/Hussars 9003.16
Tovey, Lt George 1611.16-18
Town Guards in the Boer War 0309.19-21
Townsend, G.E.A., Lt Devonshire Regt: MC (1945) (p) 9606.07
Townsend, George. Gardener at Walmer Castle 1802.23-25
Towers, Alfred, Norwich City Mounted Police Branch 9903.17-18
Toynton, Eric, R. Ulter Rifles: Normandy (1944) 9205.14
Towers, James 2/Cameronians. Medals sold 1505.13-14
Towers, Pte James VC 2/Cameronians. Medals for sale 1503.06
Tracey, Colour Sgt E F Zeebrugge Raid 0609.17-18
'Tracing your Army Ancestors; A Guide For Family Historians' Simon Fowler (br) 0703.41 ,1804.44
'Tracing your Servicemen Ancestors: A Guide for Family Historians' Mary Ingham (br) 1302.47
Trafalgar: account of the battle of 0510.18-20-
  Anniversary celebrations 0510. various
  battle of 0604.15-17
  Royal Marines at (mr) 0509.17-20
  Hardy's Medal for sale 0510.06
  Medal (1805) 9004.13-14, 9705.20-21 (entitlement)
  Remembering Lord Collingwood 0510.15-16

Sirius at (nr) 0605.14-17
Windsor Castle at (nr) 0605.14-17
Traill-Burroughs, Captain Sir Frederick, 93rd Highlanders. Storming of Secunderbagh 2301.28-32
Trans-Siberian Railway. Captain William Francis Richardson, 2101.39-40
Transport Column, 123(Scottish): piper's badge 9003.25
Transport Medal Miniature 1911.40
Transport Ships in World War I Awards to (mr) 2205.27-30
Transylvania, HMT S World War I. 1909.20-21
Travers, Susan French Foreign Legion 0603.18
Treadwell, Coastguardsman Robert Silver Sea Gallantry Medal 1104.08
Treadwell, Terry C. and Wood, Alan C 'German Knights of the Air 1914-1918' (br) 9711.31
Trebble, Marine Ray. Madagascar 1942 0901.40-43
'Trench Art: A brief history.' Nicolas J. Saunders (br) 0203.34
Treviglas Academy, Cornwall 2008.07
Trevor, W.S., Capt Bengal Eng: Dewangiri 8910.17-18
Tribal Horse: Somaliland (1903-04) 9006.15
Tribal Police (Kenya) 8906.24
Trickett, Private John, Northamptonshire Regt. 1905.24-25
Triguerios, Antonio M. 'A Viagem das Insignias. Valor e Lealdade' (br) 1803.08
Trinder, Lew. Legion d'Honneur 1608.06
Trinder, Lewis Legion d'Hon RN (obit) 2208.09
Trinder, PO Lewis RN 1601.06
Troops' Decoration of Honour (Germany) 8909.12-13
Tropical helmet badges 9404.22-23, 9405.22-23
Trotobas, Captain Michael SOE 2102.15-16
Trotobas, Michael, Sgt Middlesex Regt: SOE French Sect 9303.20-21, 9612.15-16
Trotman, Felicity 'The Writer's War' (br) 1611.40
Troubridge, Rear Admiral Sir Ernest, Serbia 0706.29-31
Trowbridge, Maurice, F/Sgt RAF att RCAF 9003.17-18, 9009.11
Trowell, F.R., Sgt Devonshire Regt (p) 9204.23
Trucial Oman Scouts Loyal Service Medal, Miniature. 1808.42
Truesdale, David & Doherty, Richard 'Irish Winners of the Victoria Cross' (br) 0008.35
Trveor-Roper, Flt Lt Richard. DFC/DFM Medals for sale 1502.06
Tsingtao (1914) 9703.15
Tubb, Derick E., PO RN: MID [i]Beryl[i] WWII 9608.16-17
Tucker, 2AM W.M RNAS 1302.25-27
Tucker, AB T H A RNVR 2310.37-39
Tucker, AC1 Kenneth Manley, RAF 2310.37-39
Tucker, A/Cpl (Sgt) Alfred Queen's Own (Royal West Kent Regiment) 1409.31-33
Tucker, Alfred. RN Ashantee Campaign 0904.19-22
Tucker, Capt Alfred, KOYLI 1409.31-33
Tucker, Capt W.T RFA 0802.21-23
Tucker, Charles, Maj 80/Foot: Ntombe River (1879) 8906.15-18
Tucker, Cpl E. DEOVRC 2108.27-28
Tucker, CSM John RGA 2305.36-37
Tucker, District Officer Caradog. 2304.41-43
Tucker, Dvr B. J. 0808.35-36
Tucker, Frederick John Gordon Highlanders 0801.24-26
Tucker, Gunner John at Dunkirk 2302.21-23
Tucker, Jacob RN Long Service Group 0511.31-32
Tucker, John Robert 2103.28-30
Tucker, L Stoker Joseph RFR 1911.36-37
Tucker, L. F AB, RN 0908.31-34
Tucker, Lt-Gen Sir Charles 1204.25-27
Tucker, Marine Joseph on HMS Rodney 0510.27-28
Tucker, Nick OMRS winner (pic) 1910.06
Tucker, Ordinary Seaman Clifford A.E. RN 2111.36-38
Tucker, Ord Smn George RN 2004.15-17
Tucker, Pte Alfred DCLI 1409.31-33
Tucker, Pte Arthur Rifle Brigade WWI 1103.39-41
Tucker, Pte E.P. R. Sussex Regt 1210.21-22
Tucker, Pte F 8/Royal Berkshire Regt at Loos 1403.19-20
Tucker, Pte F Worcester Regt. Dunster Force, Baku South Russia 1401.37-39
Tucker, Pte F.E.T DCLI 1201.26-27
Tucker, Pte F.L 15/ London Regt (Civil Service Rifles) World War I 1309.30-31
Tucker, Pte Frank Oliver 0909.23-25
Tucker, Pte H Cameron Highlanders/RFC/SAHA 1101.25-28
Tucker, Pte. R. 2/Welch Regt 1602.28-31
Tucker, Pte Joseph RM. 1503.18-21
Tucker, Pte L.S. 9/LHR AIF 1301.31-34
Tucker, Pte N. Northumberland Fusiliers 0711.19-21
Tucker, Pte R.C. 5/London Regt. World War I 0805.25-26
Tucker, Pte T 57th Foot Zulu War 0710.15-17
Tucker, Pte W 57th Foot Zulu War 0710.15-17
Tucker, Pte W. H. Somerset Light Infantry on the Northwest Frontier 1919 1609.35-37
Tucker, Pte W.T. AIF 0802.21-23
Tucker, Pte William James Royal Fusiliers 0603.20-22
Tucker, Pte/A.Sjt J.W. ASC 1st Cavalry Division 1914 1306.29-30
Tucker, Rifleman Leonard 4/3 New Zealand Brigade. 2003.31-33
Tucker, Spr Frank RE 1208.30-31
Tucker, Stk 1st Cl. Richard Henry, RN 2301.34-36

Villers-Cotterets September 1 1914 (cr) 0810.35-39 and 0811.30-33
Vimy, HMS 1906.40-42
Vimy Ridge 1711.31-33
Vindictive, HMS at Zeebrugge 0804.26-27
Vindictive: Zeebruge/Ostend (1918) 9005.13-14, 9009.27
Vine, 2/Lt Wilfred Harold MC 2/Yorks and Lancs 1903.22-25
Vinke-Tuke L/Cpl Patrick Ulster Defence Force 1708.40
Vinney, William Sampson RAMC 1909.20-22
Vintry Ward Volunteers 1505.40
Virginia Regt. William Reith 1910.18-20
Virtuti Militari, Order of. British and Commonwealth Recipients World
    War II (mr) 1306.42-44
Visit to Canada 1860 medal to Rev. P.C. Pratt RN 1710.15-17
Vittoria 8906.11, 13
    15/Hussars 9003.16
    battle of 0701.17-19
Vittoria, Royal Regiment of Artillery at 1604.21-23
Vittorio Veneto Italian Fleet1603.35-38
Vivian, Sgt: MM WWII 940221
'Vivid Courage: Victoria Crosses . Antecedent & Allied regiments of the
    Staffordshire Regiment' Robert Hope (br) 1703.45
Vogel, Trooper Frank Leon, Salisbury Horse. British South Africa
    Company medal to 0611.31-32
Volage: Albania (1946) (cr) 9008.16-17
Voltaire: sunk (1941) 8906.22
Voluntary Aid Detachment (VADs): memorial plaques 8905.11
Voluntary Medical Service miniature medal 2010.42 and 2011.44
Voluntary War Assistance Cross (Germany) (WWI) 8908.09
Volunteer Company 1st Battn. Leicestershire Regt. in the Boer War (nr)
    0810.28-29
Volunteer Engineers: badge 9312.24-25
Volunteer Force
    (1914-18) badges 8912.21-22
    shoulder-belt plates 9109.26-27
    1914 Badges of Part I 0606.23-24
    1914 Badges of Part II 0608.37-39
    shooting medals, 1810.19-20
Volunteer Long Service Medal: County of Devon (mr) 9311.13
Volunteer Militia Medals (mp) 9509.08
Volunteer Reserve Service Medal. Miniatures 2102.44
Volunteer Reserves, new medals 9906.15
Volunteer Service Company: Boer War (mr QSA) 9104.15-17
Volunteer Training Corps (1914-18): badges 8912.21-22
Von Brunner, Beatrice 1902.25-27
Von Luckner, Count Felix. The Sea Devil 1702.27-30
von Prondzynski, Oberleutnant-sur-See, Stephan 2101.20-21
Von Richtoffen , Manfred (the Red Baron) 2111.27-28
von Sallach, Alexander 'Die Orden Und Ehrenzeichen Unserer
    Republik' (br) 0404.33
Voorham, John A., PO (RAN): CSM Iraq (1991) 9608.14-15
Voyage (HMAS): loss 1964 (cr) (mr) 9404.16-17
Vyner Brooke, SS 2104.38-41
Vyner Brooke: sunk Feb (1942) 9504.12-13

- W -

Waddell, L.A., Lt Col: Gyantse Fort (1904) 9404.21
Waddell, Pte John Brough MM Seaforth Highlanders/Tank Corps
    1102.23-25
Wadsworth, Henry AM SS City of Cairo 9908.27
Wagon Hill (1900) (cr) 9306.14-18
Wagon Hill, charge of the Devonshire Regiment (cr) 0506.18-19
Wake, Nancy: George Medal sold 9406.04
Wake, Nancy 'The White Mouse' honoured 0405.06
Wake, Nancy. "The White Mouse" SOE 1110.32-33
Wakefield, Dr Arthur British Everest Expedition 1208.18-19
Wakeford, Ralph Leonard at Maktau 0109.32-35
Wakenshaw, Adam VC – memorial window 0411.07
Wakenshaw, Adam Herbert 9/DLI WWII 0606.35
Walker, Captain (Bvt Major) Mark VC 1711.40
Walker, Captain William VC 2010.15-16
Walker, Cpl K.W.J 11/South Staffs 1604.28-29
Walker, Carl GC (obit) 2301.06
Walker, D.N.R., Pte Glos Regt (p) 9010.09
Walker, Jonathon 'Aden Insurgency' (br) 0509.43
Walker, Jonathon 'The Blood Tub: General Gough and the Battle of
    Bullecourt 1917' (br) 9904.29
Walker, Joseph, 82/Foot 9109.21
Walker, Lt C E M with the Devonshire Regiment at the charge at Wagon
    Hill (cr) 0506.18-19
Walker, Paymaster Reginald Phelps, HMS Warrior at Jutland 0506.42-44
Walker, Pte Alfred. London Regiment 0306.29-30
Walker, Sgt C.D.N., MM. Hong Kong Defence Force. 2301.17-18
Wallace, Leslie B., Flt Sgt RNZAF: CGM(F) WWII 9609.14
Wallace, Mrs: RNLI Medal 8905.20-21
Wallace, Paul, Ed Paquette, Chris Enslen 'The Meritorious Service
    Medal to Canadians' (br) 0911.07
Wallace, Sapper Alexander. Royal Sappers and Miners. Baltic Medal
    1511.43
Walland, Beryl: obituary 9005.06
Walland, Fred (obit) 1306.07
Wallaroo, HMS. Royal Naval Recipients of East and West Africa Medal
    (1887-8). (mr) 1808.21-24

Waller, Captain Craig HMS Barham 2004.15-17
Waller D.D. Africa General Service Medal 1902-56 (mr) 0009.26-27
Wallflower, HMS. 2111.36-38
Wallingham HMS 0910.34-35
Wallis, Brigadier Royal Scots, Hong Kong 1941 0801.28-30
Walmer Castle 1802.23-25
Walsh, Tayleur Fund Medal 9403.19
Walsh, R.S., Capt.: Tank Corps DSO 9012.09
Walters, Boy Smn Stephen RN 1710.19-21 & 1711.23-35
Walters, Electrical Artificer Horace MiD 1903.31-33
Walters, Sgt George VC, 49th (Herfordshire) Regt. headstone
    dedication 0003.14-15
Walton, Eric W.K.: Albert Medal 9103.20
Walton, Eric William Kevin GC DSC 0803.32
Walton, Kevin: AM Antarctic 9003.12
Walton, Kevin GC, DSC (obit) 0905.06
Wanderer: and Lusitania 9006.10-12
Wanderer (p) 9003.11-13
Wandsworth Battalion: badge WWI 9012.22
Wanhsien. (cr, mr)9709.15-16
1812, War of 1211.21-22, 1301.15-17 & 1305.29-31
Wanhsien Incident (mr) Royal Navy in China between the Wars
    2209.35-39
Wanliu, Steamer. Royal Navy in China between the Wars 2209.35-39
Wantung, Steamer Royal Navy in China between the Wars 2209.35-39
War & Son 1708.08
    History Hunters 2004.08
    new shop 2208.08
War Aid Cross of Merit (Germany) (WWI) 8908.09
War Badge 0310.34
War Badges, World War I 0802.34-35
War Decoration of Honour (Germany) 8909.12
War Commemorative Cross (Germany) 8911.21
War Cross of Honour for Heroic Deeds (Germany) 8909.13
War Dog 'Jim'0806.36-37
War Dog 'Rob' Dickin Medal World Record 2211.06
'War in the Wilderness – the Chindits in Burma 1943-1944' Tony
    Redding (br) 1205.43 and 1602.44
War of Jenkins' Ear 1303.31
War Medal (1939-45): ribbon 8908.26
'War Memoirs of Earl Stanhope 1914-1918' Brian Bond (edit) (br)
    0711.41
War Memorial: Arkesden 1003.16-17
War Memorial: Thaxted 1003.16-17
War Memorials as a Resource 9105.20-21
War Merit Cross (Germany) 8909.13, 8911.20
War Merit Medal (German Empire) 8908.09
War Pensions, World War I 1908.19-22
War Service Badge 0601.24-25
War Welfare Work, Decoration of Honour for (Germany) 8909.12
Ward, Andrew 'Our Bones are Scattered' (br) 9706.24
Ward, Charles VC 2104.08
Ward, Cpl Mark MC Mercian Regt 1706.50
Ward, Henry Whitsted London Fire Brigade 0405.22
Ward, K. 'Courage Remembered' (br) 8912.06
Ward, Walter Pte: at the Alma: 9709 20-22
Wardle, Captain Thomas Erskine RN 2109.33-35
Wardrope, Pte Tom 1603.25-27
Warburton-Lee, Captain VC 0709.31-33
Warden, Arthur, Lt Cdr: Albert Medal(WWI) 9602.06
Warden, Driver James Colenso 0608.28-31
Warspite, HMS. World War II 2107.41-44
Warwick -Wright 0802.31-33
Warwickshire Regt, Royal. Badges 0703.34-36
Wark, Sarah Jane, L/Cpl: MM Northern Ireland 9611.03
Wark, Major Blair Anderson VC Queensland Museum Exhibition
    1003.25-26
Warner, Carl MC (obit) 0301.08
Warrant Officers class III WWII 9112.23
Warren, Col. D.S 2/14th Regiment Afghanistan 1880 2202.22-24
Warren Hastings: Pte Savage and the wreck of, 9904.14-15
Warrior HMS at Jutland 0506.42-44
Warrior, HMS WWI 1811.31-33
Warrior, Vanguard and Iron Duke 0402.18-19
Warsaw raid: 205 group RAF 9212.18-20
Warspite, HMS 1604.31-34 & 1609.30-32
Warspite, HMS, Battle of Crete, World War II 1705.31-33
Warwick & Warwick workforce buyout 2303.07
Warwickshire Regt: tropical helmet badge 9405.22
Warwickshire Yeomanry and the Birmingham Fire 1838 (nr) 0006.22-23
Warwickshire Yeomanry: badges 9809.27-28
Washington-Lafayette Medal, at auction 0802.09
Wasi, Platoon Commander Insua KAR 2010.15-16
Waterhouse, Darren, L/Sgt Coldstream Grds MC (1994) 9502.11
Waterloo (1815) 8906.11, 13, 9006.06
    '2/73rd at Waterloo: Including a Roll of all Ranks Present, with
        Biographical notes' Lagden, Alan and Sly, John (br) 9808.25-26
    15/Hussars at 9003.16
    23rd Light Dragoons at 0709.25-26
    95th Surgeons at 2002.25-26
    Battlefield Guide' David Buttery (br) 1410.43
    battle of 0701.17-19